Libraries and Information Services in the United Kingdom and the Republic of Ireland 2003

Published by Facet Publishing
7 Ridgmount Street
London
WC1E 7AE

Facet Publishing (formerly Library Association Publishing) is wholly owned by CILIP: the Chartered Institute of Library and Information Professionals.

First edition private circulation
Second edition 1960
Third edition 1966
Fourth edition 1969
Fourth edition (revised) 1971
Fifth edition 1974
Sixth edition 1975
Seventh edition 1977
Eighth edition 1979
Ninth edition 1981
Tenth edition 1983
Eleventh edition 1985
Reprinted 1985
Twelfth edition 1985
Thirteenth edition 1986
Fourteenth edition 1988
Fifteenth edition 1989
Sixteenth edition 1990
Reprinted 1990
Seventeenth edition 1991
Eighteenth edition 1991
Nineteenth edition 1992
Twentieth edition 1993
Twenty-first edition 1994
Twenty-second edition 1995
Twenty-third edition 1996
Reprinted 1997
Twenty-fourth edition 1997
Twenty-fifth edition 1999
Twenty-sixth edition 1999
Twenty-seventh edition 2000
Twenty-eighth edition 2001
Twenty-ninth edition 2002
(All previous editions published as *Libraries in the United Kingdom and the Republic of Ireland*)

ISBN 1-85604-450-5
ISSN 1369-9687

This twenty-ninth edition has been compiled by Lin Franklin and June York.

Typeset in 8/10pt Humanist 521 by Facet Publishing.
Printed and bound in Great Britain by MPG Books Ltd, Bodmin, Cornwall.

CONTENTS

PREFACE

How this book is organized

Libraries and Information Services in the United Kingdom and the Republic of Ireland is published annually, and is a listing of libraries falling into the four categories below.

1 *Public library authorities*

- All public library authorities in the UK and the Republic of Ireland, arranged under home countries
  - Public Libraries in England, Northern Ireland, Scotland, Wales and Crown Dependencies
  - Public Libraries in the Republic of Ireland

  It is clearly impossible to list here all branch libraries, mobile bases and so on, so each entry includes headquarters/central library details, together with major branches and area/regional/group libraries in that authority. Libraries in this section are arranged by name of authority.
- Children's, Youth and Schools Library Services

  This section gives you more specific information about what services for children and young people are available within the public library authorities, and how you can contact them.

This edition features a listing of the nine Government regions in England, indicating which public library authorities fall in their areas (see page 471).

2 *Academic libraries (arranged by name of institution)*

- University libraries in the UK and the Republic of Ireland, together with major department and site/campus libraries
- College libraries at the universities of Oxford, Cambridge and London

  Please note: potential users of the Oxford and Cambridge libraries should be aware that their use is restricted to members of the college, and to bona fide scholars on application to the Librarian; any additional information about their use is given with each entry.
- Scottish central institutions
- The university-equivalent colleges in the Republic of Ireland
- Other degree-awarding institutions in the UK

  All colleges of higher education funded by HEFCE, SHEFC and HEFCW are included.

3 Selected government, national and special libraries in the UK and the Republic of Ireland

- Entries for government departments include at least the main library for the department, together with any specialist libraries. For example, the entry for the Health and Safety Executive includes the Nuclear Safety Division.
- Special libraries are included if they are one of the main libraries or organizations in their subject field. For example, the Royal Photographic Society is included for photography, the Institution of Civil Engineers for civil engineering.

  Many of the libraries in this section require a prior appointment to be made before visiting.

4 Schools and departments of information and library studies

- Each academic institution offering courses in information and library studies, with full contact details of the departments concerned.

5 Key library agencies and other relevant organizations

- This edition continues to build on the new section incorporating the **key national and regional agencies, professional organizations and other relevant bodies**. This provides contact details for each body together with a short description of its function within the library profession.

Indexes

Again this year we have produced separate name and subject indexes to the book. We hope this will further assist you in finding the information you are looking for.

Updating *Libraries and Information Services in the UK*

The directory is compiled by mailing questionnaires or entries for updating to libraries already listed in this book, and to others that have been suggested for inclusion. We would like to thank them all for taking the time to reply to yet another mailing. With their assistance we received a 100% return rate. This means that every entry has been approved by the institution concerned.

We are dependent upon libraries to keep us informed of changes throughout the year. In this way we shall be able to ensure that our mailing label service is as current as possible. Libraries will, of course, be contacted afresh for the preparation of the next edition.

Mailing labels

The *Directory* is also available in the form of continually updated laser-quality mailing labels, with the option of either the named Chief Librarian or the Acquisitions Librarian as addressee. They are available in the following sets from Bookpoint Ltd, 130 Milton Park, Abingdon, Oxon OX14 4SB. (Tel: 01235 400400. Fax: 01235 400454):

Full set

Named Chief Librarian	ISBN 1 85604 026 7
Acquisitions Librarian	ISBN 1 85604 198 0

Public libraries (main headquarters)

Named Chief Librarian	ISBN 0 85365 587 1
Acquisitions Librarian	ISBN 1 85604 199 9

Public libraries (main headquarters and branches)

Named Chief Librarian	ISBN 1 85604 025 9

Academic and special libraries

Named Chief Librarian	ISBN 0 85365 959 1
Acquisitions Librarian	ISBN 1 85604 201 4

Children's, youth and schools library services

Named Children's/Schools Officer	ISBN 1 85604 247 2

Key library agencies

Named Chief Officer	ISBN 1 85604 447 5

Please help us to improve this directory

Any comments about additions or other changes to *Libraries and Information Services in the United Kingdom and the Republic of Ireland* will be welcomed. Please address them to:

The Editor, Libraries and Information Services in the UK, Facet Publishing,
7 Ridgmount Street, London WC1E 7AE

Tel: 020 7255 0590
e-mail: info@facetpublishing.co.uk

Public Libraries in the United Kingdom, the Channel Islands and the Isle of Man

England
Northern Ireland
Scotland
Wales
Crown Dependencies

ENGLAND

BARKING AND DAGENHAM

Authority London Borough of Barking and Dagenham
HQ Central Library, Barking, Essex IG11 7NB
☎020 8227 3608 (enquiries); 020 8227 3616 (administration)
Fax 020 8227 3699
e-mail: libraries@barking-dagenham.gov.uk
url: http://www.barking-dagenham.gov.uk/4-libraries/libraries-menu.html
Head of Library Services T R Brown MCLIP (e-mail: tbrown@barking-dagenham.gov.uk)
Principal Librarian (Learning & Development) Mrs S Leighton MA MCLIP (e-mail: sleighton@barking-dagenham.gov.uk)
Principal Librarian (Information & Resources) A Clifford BA MCLIP (e-mail: tclifford@barking-dagenham.gov.uk)
Principal Librarian (Customer & Professional Services) Ms S Currie BA MCLIP (e-mail: scurrie@barking-dagenham.gov.uk)
Principal Librarian (Quality & Standards) D W Bailey BSc MCLIP (e-mail: dbailey@barking-dagenham.gov.uk)

Community libraries

- Marks Gate Library, Rose Lane, Chadwell Heath, Essex RM6 5NJ
  ☎020 8270 4165
- Markyate Library, Markyate Road, Dagenham, Essex RM8 2LD
  ☎020 8270 4137
- Rush Green Library, Dagenham Road, Rush Green, Essex RM7 0TL
  ☎020 8270 4304
- Thames View Library, 2A Farr Avenue, Barking, Essex IG11 0NZ
  ☎020 8270 4164
- Valence Library, Becontree Avenue, Dagenham, Essex RM8 3HS
  ☎020 8227 5292
- Wantz Library, Rainham Road North, Dagenham, Essex RM10 7DX
  ☎020 8270 4169
- Whalebone Library, High Road, Chadwell Heath, Essex RM6 6AS
  ☎020 8270 4305
- Woodward Library, Woodward Road, Dagenham, Essex RM9 4SP
  ☎020 8270 4166
- Fanshawe Library, Fanshawe Community Centre, Barnmead Road, Dagenham, Essex RM9 5DX
  ☎020 8270 4244
- Rectory Library, Rectory Road, Dagenham, Essex RM9 5DX
  ☎020 8270 6233

BARNET

Authority London Borough of Barnet
HQ Cultural Services, The Old Town Hall, Friern Barnet Lane, London N11 3DL

☎020 8359 3164 (enquiries)
Fax 020 8359 3171
url: http://www.earl.org.uk/partners/barnet/index.html
Head of Cultural Services Ms P Usher BA(Hons) DMS MCLIP (e-mail: pam.usher@barnet.gov.uk)
Service Manager (Operations and Development) Ms T Little BA MCLIP (e-mail: tricia.little@barnet.gov.uk)
Service Manager (Quality and Support) Ms M Ross BA(Hons) MCLIP (e-mail: mary.ross@barnet.gov.uk)
Research and Development Manager B Hellen MCLIP (e-mail: bob.hellen@barnet.gov.uk)

Area libraries

- Chipping Barnet Library, 3 Stapylton Road, Barnet, Herts EN5 4QT
  ☎020 8359 4040
  e-mail: chipping.barnet.library@barnet.gov.uk
  Area Manager J Dixon BA MCLIP (e-mail: john.dixon@barnet.gov.uk)
- Church End Library, 24 Hendon Lane, Finchley, London N3 1TR
  ☎020 8346 5711
  e-mail: church.end.library@barnet.gov.uk
  Area Manager Ms V Padwick BA MCLIP (e-mail: veronica.padwick@barnet.gov.uk)
- Hendon Library, The Burroughs, London NW4 4BQ
  ☎020 8359 2628
  e-mail: hendon.library@barnet.gov.uk
  Area Manager Ms T Juric BLS MCLIP (e-mail: tracey.juric@barnet.gov.uk)

BARNSLEY

Authority Barnsley Metropolitan Borough Council
HQ Central Library, Shambles Street, Barnsley, South Yorkshire S70 2JF
☎(01226) 773911/12/30 (enquiries), (01226) 773913 (administration)
Fax (01226) 773955
e-mail: librarian@barnsley.ac.uk
url: http://www.barnsley.gov.uk/service/libraries/index.asp
Chief Libraries Officer S F Bashforth BA MCLIP

Central/largest library

Central Library, Shambles Street, Barnsley, South Yorkshire S70 2JF
☎(01226) 773940 (enquiries), (01226) 773927 (administration)
Fax (01226) 773955
e-mail: librarian@barnsley.ac.uk
Lending Services Officer Mrs K Green BA MCLIP

Group headquarters

- Goldthorpe Branch Library, Barnsley Road, Goldthorpe, Rotherham, South Yorkshire S63 9NE
  ☎(01709) 893278
  Fax (01709) 893278

Dearne Group Librarian J Coldwell BA MCLIP

- Royston Branch Library, Midland Road, Royston, Barnsley, South Yorkshire S71 4QP
  ☎(01226) 722870
  Royston Group Librarian R Wilson BSc(Econ) MCLIP
- Penistone Branch Library, High Street, Penistone, Sheffield S30 6BR
  ☎(01226) 762313
  Penistone Group Librarian Ms J Craven MCLIP
- Priory Information & Resource Centre, Pontefract Road, Lundwood, Barnsley, South Yorkshire S71 4QP
  ☎(01226) 770616
  Fax (01226) 771425
  Priory Information and Resource Officer Mrs S Gray BA CertEd MCLIP

BATH AND NORTH EAST SOMERSET

Authority Bath and North East Somerset Council
HQ Libraries and Information, Third Floor, 16a Broad Street, Bath, Somerset BA1 5LJ
☎(01225) 396404
Fax (01225) 396457
Head of Customer Service, Libraries and Information Mrs J Fieldhouse
Library Operations Manager Mrs J Brassington MCLIP

Central/largest library

Bath Central Library, The Podium, Northgate Street, Bath BA1 5AN
☎(01225) 787400 (enquiries), (01225) 787421 (administration)
Fax (01225) 787426
e-mail: bathlibraries@bathnes.gov.uk
Group Librarian Ms J Burton BLib MCLIP

Group libraries

- Midsomer Norton Library, High Street, Midsomer Norton, Somerset BA3 2DA
  ☎(01761) 412024
  Fax (01761) 417838
  e-mail: midsomernortonlibraries@bathnes.gov.uk
  Group Librarian Mrs H Moxham BA MCLIP
- Keynsham Library, The Centre, Keynsham, Bristol BS31 1ED
  ☎(01225) 394191
  Fax (01225) 394195
  e-mail: keynshamlibraries@bathnes.gov.uk
  Acting Group Librarian Ms S Holmes

BEDFORDSHIRE

Authority Bedfordshire County Council
HQ Libraries, County Hall, Cauldwell Street, Bedford MK42 9AP
☎(01234) 228752
Fax (01234) 213006
url: http://www.bedfordshire.gov.uk

Head of Libraries B S George MCLIP (01234 228752; e-mail: georgeb@deal.bedfordshire.gov.uk)
Library Services Manager Ms J Poad BA DMS MCLIP (01234 350931)
Library Resources Manager A Baker MCLIP (01234 228785)

Central/largest library

Bedford Central Library, Harpur Street, Bedford MK40 1PG
☎(01234) 350931 (enquiries/administration)
Fax (01234) 342163
e-mail: bedford-library@bedfordshire.gov.uk
Central Library Manager Ms R Gubbins

Gateway libraries

- Dunstable Library, Vernon Place, Dunstable, Bedfordshire LU5 4HA
  ☎(01582) 608441
  Fax (01582) 471290
  e-mail: dunstable-library@bedfordshire.gov.uk
  Library Manager Ms R Lambert
- Leighton Buzzard Library, Lake Street, Leighton Buzzard, Bedfordshire LU7 1RX
  ☎(01525) 371788
  Fax (01525) 815368
  e-mail: lbuzzard-library@bedfordshire.gov.uk
  Library Manager Ms H Kerr

Area libraries

- Biggleswade Library, Chestnut Avenue, Biggleswade, Bedfordshire SG18 0LL
  ☎(01767) 312324
  Fax (01767) 601802
  e-mail: biggleswade-library@bedfordshire.gov.uk
  Library Manager Ms S Townsend
- Flitwick Library, Conniston Road, Flitwick, Bedfordshire MK45 1QJ
  ☎(01525) 715268
  Fax (01525) 713897
  e-mail: flitwick-library@bedfordshire.gov.uk
  Library Manager J Booth
- Shefford Library, High Street, Shefford, Bedfordshire SG17 5DD
  ☎(01462) 639070
  Fax (01462) 639071
  e-mail: shefford-library@bedfordshire.gov.uk
  Library Manager G Tink

Neighbourhood libraries

- Houghton Regis Library, Bedford Square, Houghton Regis, Bedfordshire LU5 5ES
  ☎(01582) 865473
  Fax (01582) 868466
  e-mail: houghton-regis-library@bedfordshire.gov.uk
  Library Manager Ms J Pateman

- Kempston Library, Halsey Road, Kempston, Bedfordshire MK42 8AU
  ☎(01234) 853092
  Fax (01234) 841476
  e-mail: kempston-library@bedfordshire.gov.uk
  Library Manager Vacant
- Putnoe Library, Library Walk, Putnoe, Bedford MK41 8HQ
  ☎(01234) 353422
  Fax (01234) 272833
  e-mail: putnoe-library@bedfordshire.gov.uk
  Library Manager Ms R Willis

BEXLEY

Authority London Borough of Bexley
HQ Directorate of Education and Leisure Services, Libraries and Cultural Services, Thamesmead Centre, Yarnton Way, Thamesmead, Kent DA18 4DR
☎020 8320 0574
Fax 020 8320 4050
e-mail: libraries.els@bexley.gov.uk
url: http://www.bexley.gov.uk
Head of Libraries and Cultural Services F V Johnson LLB DMS MCLIP MILAM (020 8320 4131; e-mail: fred.johnson@bexley.gov.uk)
Library Development Manager H C M Paton BA DipLib MCLIP (020 8320 4134)
Principal Librarians G H Boulton BA MCLIP (020 8320 4052), Mrs L Sawbridge BA MCLIP (020 8320 4055)
Technical Services Librarian Mrs J A Peacock MCLIP (020 8320 4075)

Central/largest library

Central Library, Townley Road, Bexleyheath, Kent DA6 7HJ
☎020 8301 1066 (reception), 020 8301 5151 (information line)
Fax 020 8303 7872

BIRMINGHAM

Authority Birmingham City Council
HQ Central Library, Chamberlain Square, Birmingham B3 3HQ
☎0121 303 4511 (enquiries), 0121 303 2454 (management)
Fax 0121 303 4458 (enquiries), 0121 233 9702 (management)
Director, Leisure and Culture A Kerr
Assistant Director, Library and Information Services J Dolan OBE BA DipLib MCLIP (e-mail: john.dolan@birmingham.gov.uk)
Head of Community Library Services G Mills MSc BA DipLib MCLIP (e-mail: geoff.mills@birmingham.gov.uk)
Head of Children, Youth and Education Services Mrs P Heap BA MCLIP (e-mail: patsy.heap@birmingham.gov.uk)
Head of Best Value Mrs L Butler BA MCLIP (e-mail: linda.butler@birmingham.gov.uk)
Acting Head of Central Library B Gambles (e-mail: brian.gambles@birmingham.gov.uk)

BLACKBURN WITH DARWEN

Authority Blackburn with Darwen Borough Council
HQ Central Library, Town Hall Street, Blackburn, Lancs BB2 1AG
☎(01254) 661221 (enquiries), (01254) 587902 (administration)
Fax (01254) 690539
url: http://library.blackburnworld.com
Head of Library and Information Services Mrs S Law MCLIP (01254 587906; e-mail: susan.law@blackburn.gov.uk)
Information and Development Manager I Sutton MCLIP (01254 587901; e-mail: ian.sutton@blackburn.gov.uk)
Lending Services Manager Mrs K Sutton MCLIP (01254 587907; e-mail: kath.sutton@blackburn.gov.uk)
Reader Development Manager Vacant

BLACKPOOL

Authority Blackpool Borough Council
HQ Education, Leisure and Cultural Services, Lifelong Learning and Cultural Services Division, Progress House, Clifton Road, Blackpool, Lancs FY4 4GB
☎(01253) 478111 (enquiries), (01253) 478105 (administration)
Fax (01253) 478071
Assistant Director, Lifelong Learning and Cultural Services Mrs P Hansell MBA BA MCLIP (e-mail: pat.hansell@blackpool.gov.uk)
Principal Librarian, Support Services R Baker BA MCLIP DMS
Principal Librarian, Customer Services Ms A Toase BA MCLIP DMS
Arts Development Officer Ms L Fade MA

Central/largest library

Central Library, Queen Street, Blackpool, Lancs FY1 1PX
☎(01253) 478111
Fax (01253) 478082
Central Library Manager Mrs E Midgley BA(Hons) DMS PGCM MCLIP MCMI MInstLM

BOLTON

Authority Bolton Metropolitan Borough Council
HQ Central Library, Le Mans Crescent, Bolton, Lancs BL1 1SE
☎(01204) 332169 (administration), (01204) 333173 (enquiries)
Fax (01204) 332225
e-mail: central.library@bolton.gov.uk
Assistant Director, Heritage, Information and Arts Mrs K C Ryan BA MBA FCLIP
Chief Librarian Mrs Y Gill-Martin BA DMS MCLIP
Area Librarian, Central K F Bell BA MCLIP

Branch libraries HQ

Harwood Library, Gate Fold, Harwood, Bolton, Lancs BL2 3HN
☎(01204) 332340

Fax (01204) 332343
Area Librarian K A Beevers BA MCLIP

BOURNEMOUTH

Authority Bournemouth Borough Council
HQ Bournemouth Libraries, The Bournemouth Library, 22 The Triangle, Bournemouth BH2 5RQ
☎(01202) 454614 (administration and general enquiries)
Fax (01202) 454830
Head of Arts, Library and Museum Services Ms S Levett BA(Hons) CertEd MCLIP (based at Town Hall, Bourne Avenue, Bournemouth BH2 6DY; 01202 454615)
Principal Area Services Manager Mrs C Date GradIPD MCLIP (01202 454826)
Principal Development and Support Services Manager Mrs E Arthur BA(Hons) MCLIP DMS (01202 454825)

Central/largest library

The Bournemouth Library, 22 The Triangle, Bournemouth BH2 5RQ
☎(01202) 454848

BRACKNELL FOREST

Authority Bracknell Forest Borough Council
HQ Leisure Services, Town Square, Market Street, Bracknell, Berks RG12 1BH
☎(01344) 354103 (enquiries), (01344) 424642 (administration)
Fax (01344) 354100
e-mail: bracknell.library@bracknell-forest.gov.uk
Head of Libraries, Arts and Information Ms R Burgess BLib MCLIP (e-mail: ruth.burgess@bracknell-forest.gov.uk)

Central/largest library

Bracknell Library, Town Square, Bracknell, Berks RG12 1BH
☎(01344) 352400
Fax (01344) 352420
e-mail: bracknell.library@bracknell-forest.gov.uk
Library and Information Manager Ms K Chambers BA MCLIP

BRADFORD

Authority City of Bradford Metropolitan District Council
HQ Central Library, Prince's Way, Bradford, West Yorkshire BD1 1NN
☎(01274) 753600
Fax (01274) 395108
e-mail: public.libraries@bradford.gov.uk
Director, Arts, Heritage and Leisure Ms J Glaister BA FMA PGDipLib (01274 752647; e-mail: jane.glaister@bradford.gov.uk)
Head of Libraries, Archives and Information Service I Watson BA MCLIP (01274 753640; e-mail: ian.watson@bradford.gov.uk)

Area libraries

- Bradford East Area, c/o Eccleshill Library, Bolton Road, Eccleshill, Bradford, West Yorkshire BD2 4SR
  ☎(01274) 751544
  Fax (01274) 626667
  e-mail: eccleshill.library@bradford.gov.uk
  Area Librarian Mrs M Rogerson BA MCLIP (e-mail: marilyn.rogerson@bradford.gov.uk)
- Bradford West/Shipley Area, c/o Shipley Library, 2 Wellcroft, Shipley, West Yorkshire BD18 3QH
  ☎(01274) 757150
  Fax (01274) 530247
  e-mail: shipley.library@bradford.gov.uk
  Area Librarian Mrs J Kitwood BA DipLib MCLIP (e-mail: jackie.kitwood@bradford.gov.uk)
- Keighley & West Area, c/o Keighley Library, North Street, Keighley, West Yorkshire BD21 3SE
  ☎(01535) 618212
  Fax (01535) 618214
  e-mail: keighley.library@bradford.gov.uk
  Area Librarian Mrs J Triffitt BA MCLIP (e-mail: judi.triffitt@bradford.gov.uk)

BRENT

Authority London Borough of Brent
HQ Education, Arts and Libraries, 4th Floor, Chesterfield House, 9 Park Lane, Wembley, Middlesex HA9 7RW
☎020 8937 3144
Fax 020 8937 3023
url: http://www.brent.gov.uk
Assistant Director, Libraries and Lifelong Learning Ms K Tyerman BA(Hons) DipLib MCLIP (020 8937 3146; e-mail: karen.tyerman@brent.gov.uk)
Head of Library Service Ms M Locke BA MCLIP (020 8937 3149; e-mail: marianne.locke@brent.gov.uk)

Area libraries

- Barham Park Library, Harrow Road, Sudbury, Middlesex HA0 2HB
  ☎020 8937 3550
  Fax 020 8937 3553
  Principal Librarian, North K Batchelor MCLIP
- Ealing Road Library, Coronet Parade, Wembley, Middlesex HA0 4BR
  ☎020 8937 3560
  Fax 020 8795 3425
- Kingsbury Library, Stag Lane, Kingsbury, London NW9 9AE
  ☎020 8937 3520
  Fax 020 8905 0264
- Preston Library, Carlton Avenue East, Wembley, Middlesex HA9 8PL
  ☎020 8937 3510
  Fax 020 8908 6220

- Tokyngton Library, Monks Park, Wembley, Middlesex HA9 6JE
  ☎020 8937 3590
  Fax 020 8795 3440
- Town Hall Library, Brent Town Hall, Forty Lane, Wembley, Middlesex HA9 9HV
  ☎020 8937 3500
  Fax 020 8937 3504
- Cricklewood Library, 152 Olive Road, Cricklewood, London NW2 6UY
  ☎020 8937 3540
  Fax 020 8450 5211
  Principal Librarian, South M Perry BA(Hons) DMS
- Harlesden Library, Craven Park Road, Harlesden, London NW10 8SE
  ☎020 8965 7132
  Fax 020 8838 2199
- Kensal Rise Library, Bathurst Gardens, Harlesden, London NW10 5JA
  ☎020 8969 0942
  Fax 020 8960 8399
- Kilburn Library, Salusbury Road, Kilburn, London NW6 6NN
  ☎020 8937 3530
  Fax 020 7625 6387
- Outreach Library Service, 2-12 Grange Road, Willesden, London NW10 2QY
  ☎020 8937 3460
  Fax 020 8937 3460
- Neasden Library, 277 Neasden Lane, London NW10 1QJ
  ☎020 8937 3580
  Fax 020 8208 3909
- Willesden Green Library, 95 High Road, Willesden, London NW10 2ST
  ☎020 8937 3400
  Fax 020 8937 3401
  Principal Librarian, Willesden Green J Verstraete MLIS DLIS BA(Hons)

BRIGHTON AND HOVE

Authority Brighton and Hove Council
HQ Royal Pavilion, Libraries and Museums, 4-5 Pavilion Buildings, Brighton BN1 1EE
☎(01273) 292872/296930 (administration)
Fax (01273) 292871/296976 (administration)
url: http://www.citylibraries.info
Head of Libraries and ICT Ms S McMahon BA DipLib MCLIP (01273 296963)
Operational Resources Manager Ms J Hugall BA DipLib MCLIP (01273 296933)
Professional and Collections Manager N Imi BA DipLib MCLIP (01273 296953)
Community and Development Manager A Issler BA MCLIP (01273 296948)

Central libraries

- Brighton Library, Vantage Point, New England Street, Brighton BN1 2GW
  ☎(01273) 290800 (minicom)
  e-mail: brightonlibrary@brighton-hove.gov.uk
- Hove Library, 182-186 Church Road, Hove, East Sussex BN3 2EG
  ☎(01273) 290700 (minicom)

BRISTOL

Authority Bristol City Council
HQ Central Library, College Green, Bristol BS1 5TL
☎0117 903 7200 (all enquiries)
Fax 0117 922 1081
e-mail: bristol_library_service@bristol-city.gov.uk
url: http://www.bristol-city.gov.uk
Head of Libraries Ms K Davenport MA MCLIP DMS (e-mail: kate_davenport@bristol_city.gov.uk)
Community Services Manager (North and Central) Ms A Casey BA MCLIP
Community Services Manager (South and East) Ms J York BA MCLIP
Business Systems Manager Ms K Cole BA MCLIP
Central Library Manager Vacant

BROMLEY

Authority London Borough of Bromley
HQ Central Library, High Street, Bromley, Kent BR1 1EX
☎020 8460 9955 (enquiries & administration)
Fax 020 8313 9975
e-mail: reference.library@bromley.gov.uk
url: http://www.bromley.gov.uk
Chief Librarian B Walkinshaw BA MCLIP (e-mail: barry.walkinshaw@bromley.gov.uk)
Library Operations Manager L F Favret BA MIMgt DipMgt MCLIP (e-mail: leo.favret@bromley.gov.uk)
Library Development Manager D Brockhurst BA MCLIP (e-mail: david.brockhurst@bromley.gov.uk)

Central/largest library

Central Library, High Street, Bromley, Kent BR1 1EX
☎Tel/Fax etc. as HQ
Group Manager J Wilkins BSc MCLIP (e-mail: john.wilkins@bromley.gov.uk)

District libraries

- Beckenham Library, Beckenham Road, Beckenham, Kent BR3 4PE
  ☎020 8650 7292/3
  Area Manager Miss C Alabaster BA MCLIP (e-mail: tina.alabaster@bromley.gov.uk)
- Orpington Library, The Priory, Church Hill, Orpington, Kent BR6 0HH
  ☎(01689) 831551
  Area Manager T Woolgar MCLIP (e-mail: tim.woolgar@bromley.gov.uk)

BUCKINGHAMSHIRE

Authority Buckinghamshire County Council
HQ County Library, County Hall, Walton Street, Aylesbury, Bucks HP20 1UU
☎(01296) 383206
Fax (01296) 382405

Head of Libraries and Heritage R Strong BA DipLib MCLIP (01296 382251; fax 01296 382259; e-mail: rstrong@buckscc.gov.uk)
Libraries Manager Ms J Varney MCLIP (01296 382258; fax 01296 382259; e-mail: jmvarney@buckscc.gov.uk)
Community Development Librarian P Mussett MCLIP (01296 382254; fax 01296 382259; e-mail: pmussett@buckscc.gov.uk)
Learning Development Librarian M Ryan BA MCLIP (01296 382253; fax 01296 382259; e-mail: mryan@buckscc.gov.uk)
Resources Development Librarian M Bryant BA DipLib MCLIP (01296 382252; fax 01296 382259; e-mail: mbryant@buckscc.gov.uk)

Main group libraries

- Aylesbury Central Library, Walton Street, Aylesbury, Bucks HP20 1UU
  ☎(01296) 382248
  Fax (01296) 382405
  Group Librarian Vacant
- Beaconsfield Library, Reynolds Road, Beaconsfield, Bucks HP9 2NJ
  ☎(01494) 672295
  Fax (01494) 678772
  Group Librarians Mrs G Griffin MCLIP, Mrs T Cuthbert MCLIP
- Buckingham Library, Verney Close, Buckingham, Bucks MK18 1JP
  ☎(01280) 813229
  Fax (01280) 823597
  Group Librarian S Grant BA MCLIP
- Chesham Library, Elgiva Lane, Chesham, Bucks HP5 2JD
  ☎(01494) 772322
  Fax (01494) 773074
  Group Librarian Ms H Goreham BLib MCLIP

BURY

Authority Bury Metropolitan Borough Council
HQ Cultural Services, Athenaeum House, Market Street, Bury, Lancashire BL9 0BN
☎0161 253 5863 (administration)
Fax 0161 253 5915
e-mail: information@bury.gov.uk
url: http://www.bury.gov.uk/culture.htm
Principal Librarian Mrs D Sorrigan BA MCLIP (0161 253 6077; e-mail: d.sorrigan@bury.gov.uk)
Assistant Principal Librarian Mrs L Kelly BA MA DipLib DipMan MCLIP (0161 253 7579; e-mail: s.l.kelly@bury.gov.uk)
Assistant Principal Librarian T Jowett BA MA DipMan MCLIP (0161 253 5876; e-mail: t.jowett@bury.gov.uk)

Central/largest library

Central Library, Manchester Road, Bury, Lancashire BL9 0DG
☎0161 253 5873
Fax 0161 253 5857

e-mail: information@bury.gov.uk
Principal Librarian Mrs D Sorrigan BA MCLIP

Branch libraries

- Prestwich Library, Longfield Centre, Prestwich, Manchester M25 1AY
  ☎0161 253 7214
  Fax 0161 253 5372
  e-mail: prestwich.lib@bury.gov.uk
  Library Supervisors Ms J Watkiss BA DipLib, D Galloway (0161 253 7219)
- Radcliffe Library, Stand Lane, Radcliffe, Manchester M26 9WR
  ☎0161 253 7161
  Fax 0161 253 7165
  e-mail: radcliffe.lib@bury.gov.uk
  Library Supervisors Ms B Walker NEBS, J Smillie NEBS (0161 253 7160)
- Ramsbottom Library, Carr Street, Ramsbottom, Bury, Lancashire BL0 9AE
  ☎(01706) 822484
  Fax (01706) 824638
  e-mail: ramsbottom.lib@bury.gov.uk
  Library Supervisor Miss D Smith
- Tottington Library, Market Street, Tottington, Bury, Lancashire BL8 3LN
  ☎(01204) 882839
  e-mail: tottington.lib@bury.gov.uk
  Library Supervisors Mrs L Snape, Mrs S Lamb
- Unsworth Library, Sunnybank Road, Unsworth, Bury, Lancashire BL9 8EB
  ☎0161 253 7560
  e-mail: unsworth.lib@bury.gov.uk
  Library Supervisor Mrs L Guilboyle
- Whitefield Library, Pinfold Lane, Whitefield, Manchester M45 7NY
  ☎0161 253 7510
  e-mail: whitefield.lib@bury.gov.uk
  Library Supervisor Mrs W Rhodes

Outreach libraries

- Ainsworth Library, Church Street, Ainsworth, Lancashire BL2 5RT
  ☎(01204) 523841
  e-mail: ainsworth.lib@bury.gov.uk
- Topping Fold Library, Topping Fold Road, Bury, Lancashire BL9 7NG
  ☎0161 253 6361
  e-mail: topping.lib@bury.gov.uk
- New Kershaw Centre, Deal Street, Bury, Lancashire BL9 7PZ
  ☎0161 253 6400
  e-mail: kershaw.lib@bury.gov.uk
- Moorside Community Library, St John's Church Hall, Parkinson Street, Bury, Lancashire BL9 6NY
  ☎0161 253 5885
  e-mail: moorside.lib@bury.gov.uk

CALDERDALE

Authority Calderdale Metropolitan Borough
HQ Central Library, Northgate, Halifax, West Yorkshire HX1 1UN
☎(01422) 392605
Fax (01422) 392615
e-mail: libraries@calderdale.gov.uk
url: http://www.calderdale.gov.uk
Assistant Chief Leisure Services Officer (Libraries) Vacant

Central/largest library

Central Library, Northgate, Halifax, West Yorkshire HX1 1UN
☎(01422) 392630
Head of Central and Support Services D Duffy BA MCLIP

District and community libraries

c/o Central Library, Northgate, Halifax, West Yorkshire HX1 1UN
☎(01422) 392623
Head of Community Libraries J R Jebson MCLIP

CAMBRIDGESHIRE

Authority Cambridgeshire County Council
HQ Cambridgeshire Libraries and Information Services, Castle Court, Shire Hall, Cambridge CB3 0AP
☎(01223) 717023 (management)
Fax (01223) 717079
e-mail: libraries@cambridgeshire.gov.uk
Head of Libraries and Information Services M G Hosking MIMgt MCLIP (01223 717063; e-mail: mike.hosking@cambridgeshire.gov.uk)
Assistant Head of Service (Public Services) Mrs L Noblett MA MCLIP (01223 717292; e-mail: lesley.noblett@cambridgeshire.gov.uk)
Assistant Head of Service (Resources) C Heaton MA MCLIP (01223 717061; e-mail: chris.heaton@cambridgeshire.gov.uk)
Development and Marketing Manager Ms L Charlton (01480 375895; e-mail: leonore.charlton@cambridgeshire.gov.uk)
Partnership and Development Manager Ms L Martin MCLIP DMS MIMgt (01480 375194; e-mail: lynda.martin@cambridgeshire.gov.uk)

Budget and Administration Team, Libraries and Information Service, Roger Ascham Site, Ascham Road, Cambridge CB4 2BD
☎(01223) 718364
Fax (01223) 718380
Budget and Administration Manager J L Clifford (e-mail: jim.clifford@cambridgeshire.gov.uk)

Central/largest library

Central Library, 7 Lion Yard, Cambridge CB2 3QD

☎(01223) 712000
Fax (01223) 712018
e-mail: cambridge.central.library@cambridgeshire.gov.uk
Service Manager City M Wyatt BA MCLIP MIMgt (01223 712001; e-mail: michael.wyatt@cambridgeshire.gov.uk)

District libraries

- Ely Library, 6 The Cloisters, Ely, Cambs CB7 4ZH
  ☎(01353) 662350
  Fax (01353) 666623
- Huntingdon Library, Princes Street, Huntingdon, Cambs PE29 3PH
  ☎(01480) 375800
  Fax (01480) 459563
  Service Manager, Districts D Allanach MLS MCLIP (01480 375825; e-mail: david.allanach@cambridgeshire.gov.uk)
- March Library, City Road, March, Cambs PE15 9LT
  ☎(01354) 754754
  Fax (01354) 754760
- St Ives Library, Station Road, St Ives, Huntingdon, Cambs PE27 5BW
  ☎(01480) 398004
  Fax (01480) 386604
- St Neots Library, Priory Lane, St Neots, Huntingdon, Cambs PE19 2BH
  ☎(01480) 398006
  Fax (01480) 396006
- Wisbech Library, 1 Ely Place, Wisbech, Cambs PE13 1EU
  ☎(01945) 464009
  Fax (01945) 582784

CAMDEN

Authority London Borough of Camden
HQ Leisure and Community Services Department, The Crowndale Centre, 218 Eversholt Street, London NW1 1BD
☎020 7974 1593
Fax 020 7974 1587
Head of Libraries and Information Services D Jones BA(Hons) DipLib (020 7974 4058)

Leisure/departmental library

Central Library, Swiss Cottage Library, 88 Avenue Road, London NW3 3HA
☎020 7974 6522 (switchboard), 020 7974 6527 (general enquiries), 020 7974 6525 (library management)
Fax 020 7974 6532
Library Manager M Osterfield (020 7974 6509)

Main libraries

- Holborn Library, 32-38 Theobalds Road, London WC1X 8PA
  ☎020 7974 6345/6, 020 7974 6342 (Local studies)
  Fax 020 7974 6356

Library Manager R G P Gryspeerdt BA MCLIP (020 7974 6353)

- St Pancras Library, Town Hall Extension, Argyle Street, London WC1H 8NN
  ☎020 7974 5833
  Fax 020 7860 5963
  Library Manager Ms G Keys (020 7974 5865)
- Kentish Town Library, 262-266 Kentish Town Road, London NW5 2AA
  ☎020 7974 6253
  Fax 020 7842 5650
  Library Manager D B E Chase MCLIP (020 7974 6261/6253)
- West Hampstead Library, Dennington Park Road, London NW6 1AU
  ☎020 7974 6610
  Fax 020 7974 6539
  Library Manager Ms K Egbunike (020 7974 6620)
- Queen's Crescent Library, 165 Queen's Crescent, London NW5 4HH
  ☎020 7974 6243
  Fax 020 7485 6252
  Library Manager R Cioccari (020 7974 6243)
- Camden Town Library, Crowndale Centre, 218 Eversholt Street, London NW1 1BD
  ☎020 7974 1563
  Fax 020 7974 1582
  Library Manager Ms S Jacobs (020 7974 1563/1531)

Neighbourhood libraries

- Belsize Library, Antrim Road, London NW3 4XN
  ☎020 7974 6518
  Fax 020 7974 6508
- Heath Library, Keats' Grove, London NW3 2RR
  ☎020 7974 6520
  Fax 020 7974 6520
- Regent's Park Library, Compton Close, Robert Street, London NW1 3QT
  ☎020 7974 1530
  Fax 020 7974 1531
- Kilburn Library, Cotleigh Road, London NW6 2NP
  ☎020 7974 1965
  Fax 020 7974 6524
- Highgate Library, Chester Road, London N19 5DH
  ☎020 7974 5752, 020 7281 2546 (home library service)
  Fax 020 7974 5555
- Chalk Farm Library, Sharpleshall Street, London NW1 8YN
  ☎020 7974 6526
  Fax 020 7974 6502

CHESHIRE

Authority Cheshire County Council
HQ Community Development Department, Libraries and Culture Service, County Hall, Chester CH1 1SF
☎(01244) 602424 (County Hall switchboard)

Fax (01244) 602767
url: http://www.cheshire.gov.uk
County Librarian F I Dunn BA DAA FSA (01244 606034; e-mail: dunni@cheshire.gov.uk)
Manager of Public Library Operations A W Bell MCLIP (01244 605280; e-mail: bellaw@cheshire.gov.uk)
Resources and Development Manager E H Skinner DipEdTech MCLIP (01244 606023; e-mail: skinnereh@cheshire.gov.uk)

Group HQs

- Chester Library, Northgate Street, Chester CH1 2EF
  ☎(01244) 312935
  Fax (01244) 315534
  e-mail: ipchester@cheshire.gov.uk
  Group Librarian A Madders MCLIP (e-mail: maddersab@cheshire.gov.uk)
- Congleton Library, Market Square, Congleton, Cheshire CW12 1BU
  ☎(01260) 271141
  Fax (01260) 298774
  e-mail: ipcongleton@cheshire.gov.uk
  Group Librarian Miss S M Kane MCLIP (e-mail: kanesm@cheshire.gov.uk)
- Crewe Library, Prince Albert Street, Crewe, Cheshire CW1 2DH
  ☎(01270) 211123
  Fax (01270) 256952
  e-mail: ipcrewe@cheshire.gov.uk
  Group Librarian Mrs J Norton BA MCLIP, Mrs C Balabil BA MA MCLIP (e-mail: nortonrowland@cheshire.gov.uk)
- Ellesmere Port Library, Civic Way, Ellesmere Port, Cheshire L65 0BG
  ☎0151 357 4684
  Fax 0151 355 6849
  e-mail: ipeport@cheshire.gov.uk
  Group Librarian R D Booth BSc DipLib MCLIP (e-mail: boothrd@cheshire.gov.uk)
- Macclesfield Library, 2 Jordangate, Macclesfield, Cheshire SK10 1EE
  ☎(01625) 422512
  Fax (01625) 612818
  e-mail: ipmacclesfield@cheshire.gov.uk
  Group Librarian Miss P M Owen BA MCLIP (e-mail: owenpm@cheshire.gov.uk)
- Northwich Library, Witton Street, Northwich, Cheshire CW9 5DR
  ☎(01606) 44221
  Fax (01606) 48396
  e-mail: ipnorthwich@cheshire.gov.uk
  Group Librarian Mrs S Scragg BA MCLIP (e-mail: scraggs@cheshire.gov.uk)
- Wilmslow Library, South Drive, Wilmslow, Cheshire SK9 1NW
  ☎(01625) 415037
  Fax (01625) 548401
  Group Librarian B M West MCLIP (e-mail: westbm@cheshire.gov.uk)
- Cheshire Information Service, Ellesmere Port Library, Civic Way, Ellesmere Port, Cheshire CH65 0BG
  ☎0151 357 4689
  Fax 0151 357 4698

CORNWALL

Authority Cornwall County Council
HQ Education, Arts and Libraries, Unit 17, Threemilestone Industrial Estate, Threemilestone, Truro, Cornwall TR4 9LD
☎(01872) 324316 (enquiries)
Fax (01872) 223509
e-mail: library@cornwall.gov.uk
url: http://www.cornwall.gov.uk
Assistant Director, Education. Arts and Libraries C Ramsey BSc(Hons) MA AdvDipBFM(CIPFA)

Additional libraries

- Falmouth Library, The Moor, Falmouth, Cornwall TR11 3QA
  ☎(01326) 314901
  Fax (01326) 315385
- Redruth Library, Clinton Road, Redruth, Cornwall TR15 2QE
  ☎(01209) 219111
  Fax (01209) 314763
- St Austell Library, 2 Carlyon Road, St Austell, Cornwall PL25 4LD
  ☎(01726) 73348
  Fax (01726) 71214
- Truro Library, Union Place, Truro, Cornwall TR1 1EP
  ☎(01872) 279205
  Fax (01872) 263494
- Penzance Library, Morrab Road, Penzance, Cornwall TR18 4EY
  ☎(01736) 363954
  Fax (01736) 330644

COVENTRY

Authority Coventry Metropolitan District Council
HQ Central Library, Smithford Way, Coventry CV1 1FY
☎024 7683 2314 (enquiries); 024 7683 2321 (administration)
Fax 024 7683 2315
e-mail: library.office@coventry.gov.uk
url: http://www.coventry.org.uk
Strategic Director (Lifelong Learning) Ms C Goodwin
City Librarian A Green BA MSc DipLib MCLIP

CROYDON

Authority London Borough of Croydon
HQ Central Library, Katharine Street, Croydon CR9 1ET
☎020 8760 5400
Fax 020 8253 1004
url: http://www.croydon.gov.uk
Assistant Director, Libraries Ms A Scott BA MCLIP (020 8253 1001; e-mail: adie_scott@croydon.gov.uk)

CUMBRIA

Authority Cumbria County Council
HQ Community, Economy and Environment, Arroyo Block, The Castle, Carlisle, Cumbria CA3 8UR
☎(01228) 607300 (enquiries); (01228) 607296 (management)
Fax (01228) 607299
url: http://www.cumbria.gov.uk/libraries/
Acting Director of Community, Economy and Environment (Community Services) R Howard
Library Services Manager A J Welton BA MCLIP (01228 607307; e-mail: alan.welton@cumbriacc.gov.uk)
Principal Admin Officer P T Graham (01228 607294; e-mail: paul.graham@cumbriacc.gov.uk)

Group libraries

- Carlisle Library, 11 Globe Lane, Carlisle, Cumbria CA3 8NX
  ☎(01228) 607320
  Fax (01228) 607333
  e-mail: carlisle.library@cumbriacc.gov.uk
  Area Library Manager J Foster
- Penrith Library, St Andrews Churchyard, Penrith, Cumbria CA11 7YA
  ☎(01768) 242100
  Fax (01768) 242101
  e-mail: penrith.library@cumbriacc.gov.uk
  Area Library Manager Mrs E Bowe MCLIP
- Kendal Library, Stricklandgate, Kendal, Cumbria LA9 4PY
  ☎(01539) 773520
  Fax (01539) 773544
  e-mail: kendal.library@cumbriacc.gov.uk
  Area Library Manager Ms S Rochell BA MCLIP
- Barrow-in-Furness Library, Ramsden Square, Barrow-in-Furness, Cumbria LA14 1LL
  ☎(01229) 894370
  Fax (01229) 894371
  e-mail: barrow.library@cumbriacc.gov.uk
  Area Library Manager Ms C Mellor BA MCLIP
- Daniel Hay Library, Lowther Street, Whitehaven, Cumbria CA28 7QZ
  ☎(01946) 852900
  Fax (01946) 852911
  e-mail: whitehaven.library@cumbriacc.gov.uk
  Area Library Manager Mrs L Wood MCLIP
- Workington Library, Vulcans Lane, Workington, Cumbria CA14 2ND
  ☎(01900) 325170
  Fax (01900) 325181
  e-mail: workington.library@cumbriacc.gov.uk
  Area Library Manager O T Jones

DARLINGTON

Authority Darlington Borough Council
HQ Central Library, Crown Street, Darlington, Durham DL1 1ND
☎(01325) 462034 (enquiries), 349601 (administration)
Fax (01325) 381556
e-mail: crown.street.library@darlington.gov.uk
Libraries Manager P White MCLIP

Branch library

Cockerton Library, Cockerton Green, Darlington, Durham DL3 9AA
☎(01325) 461320
Assistant in Charge Mrs M Wood

DERBY

Authority Derby City Council
HQ Derby City Libraries, Department of Development and Cultural Services, Celtic House, Heritage Gate, Derby, Derbyshire DE1 1QX
☎(01332) 716607
Fax (01332) 715549
e-mail: libraries@derby.city.council.gov.uk
City Librarian R Rippingale MA MCLIP
Assistant City Librarian (Operations) D Potton MA DipLib MCLIP (01332 716610)
Assistant City Librarian (Planning and Development) M Elliott (01332 716609)

Central/largest library

Central Library, The Wardwick, Derby, Derbyshire DE1 1HS
☎(01332) 255398/9 (enquiries), 255389 (administration)
Fax (01332) 369570
Assistant City Librarian (Central Services) B Haigh MLS MCLIP

DERBYSHIRE

Authority Derbyshire County Council
HQ Libraries and Heritage Department, County Hall, Matlock, Derbyshire DE4 3AG
☎(01629) 580000 ext 6591 (enquiries), ext 6590 (administration)
Fax (01629) 585363
e-mail: derbyshire.libraries@derbyshire.gov.uk
Director of Libraries and Heritage M J Molloy BA DipLib MCLIP (e-mail: martin.molloy@derbyshire.gov.uk)
Deputy Director of Libraries and Heritage Miss J A Brumwell MCLIP (e-mail: jaci.brumwell@derbyshire.gov.uk)
Assistant Director of Libraries and Heritage R P Gent BA DMS MIMgt MCLIP (e-mail: robert.gent@derbyshire.gov.uk)
Assistant Director of Libraries and Heritage D W Gibbs BA MCLIP (e-mail: don.gibbs@derbyshire.gov.uk)

Central/largest library

Chesterfield Library, New Beetwell Street, Chesterfield, Derbyshire S40 1QN
☎(01246) 209292
Fax (01246) 209304
District Librarian Mrs A Ainsworth BA MCLIP (e-mail: ann.ainsworth@derbyshire.gov.uk)

Other main libraries

Amber Valley District
Alfreton Library, Severn Square, Alfreton, Derbyshire DE55 7BQ
☎(01773) 833199
Fax (01773) 521020
District Librarian Mrs J Potton BA MCLIP (e-mail: julie.potton@derbyshire.gov.uk)

Bolsover District
Bolsover Library, Church Street, Bolsover, Derbyshire S44 6HB
☎(01246) 823179
Fax (01246) 827237
District Librarian Ms H Doherty BA MCLIP (e-mail: hilary.doherty@derbyshire.gov.uk)

Derbyshire Dales District
Matlock Library, Steep Turnpike, Matlock, Derbyshire DE4 3DP
☎(01629) 582480
Fax (01629) 760749
District Librarian Ms T Hill BA DipLib MCLIP (e-mail: trisha.hill@derbyshire.gov.uk)

Erewash District
Ilkeston Library, Market Place, Ilkeston, Derbyshire DE7 5RN
☎0115 930 1104
Fax 0115 944 1226
District Librarian Mrs J Colombo BSc MCLIP (e-mail: jan.colombo@derbyshire.gov.uk)

High Peak District
Buxton Library, Kents Bank Road, Buxton, Derbyshire SK17 9HJ
☎(01298) 25331
Fax (01298) 73744
District Librarian Ms T Cozens BA MCLIP (e-mail: tessa.cozens@derbyshire.gov.uk)

North East Derbyshire District
Dronfield Library, Manor House, Dronfield, Derbyshire S18 6PY
☎(01246) 414001
Fax (01246) 291489
District Librarian Mrs S Crabb MLS MCLIP (e-mail: sue.crabb@derbyshire.gov.uk)

South Derbyshire District
Swadlincote Library, Civic Way, Swadlincote, Derbyshire DE11 0AD
☎(01283) 217701
Fax (01283) 216352
District Librarian Mrs P Jemison MCLIP (e-mail: polly.jemison@derbyshire.gov.uk)

DEVON

Authority Devon County Council
HQ Devon Library and Information Services, Barley House, Isleworth Road, Exeter, Devon EX4 1RQ
☎(01392) 384315
Fax (01392) 384316
e-mail: devlibs@devon.gov.uk
url: http://www.devon.gov.uk/library
Head of Library and Information Services Mrs L M Osborne BA MCLIP (e-mail: losborne@devon.gov.uk)

Group libraries

- South and East Devon. Central Library, Castle Street, Exeter, Devon EX4 3PQ
  ☎(01392) 384222
  Fax (01392) 384228
  Group Librarian M L G Maguire MCLIP (e-mail: mmaguire@devon.gov.uk)
- North and West Devon. North Devon Library and Record Office, Tuly Street, Barnstaple, Devon EX31 1EL
  ☎(01271) 388619 (Tel/fax)
  Group Librarian I P Tansley MCLIP (e-mail: itansley@devon.gov.uk)

Larger libraries

- Barnstaple Library, Tuly Street, Barnstaple, Devon EX31 1EL
  ☎(01271) 388619 (tel/fax)
  Library Manager G King
- Bideford Library, New Road, Bideford, Devon EX39 2HR
  ☎(01237) 476075 (tel/fax)
  Librarian i/c Mrs R Wiseman
- Exeter Central Library, Castle Street, Exeter, Devon EX4 3PQ
  ☎(01392) 384222
  Fax (01392) 384228
  Library Manager A Davey BSc MCLIP
- Exmouth Library, 40 Exeter Road, Exmouth, Devon EX8 1PR
  ☎(01395) 272677
  Fax (01395) 271426
  Public Services Librarian K Crook MCLIP
- Honiton Library, 48 New Street, Honiton, Devon EX14 1BS
  ☎(01404) 42818
  Fax (01404) 45326
  Librarian i/c Miss J Wood
- Kingsbridge Library, Ilbert Road, Kingsbridge, Devon TQ7 1EB
  ☎(01548) 852315
  Librarian i/c Mrs W Read
- Newton Abbot Library and Education Centre, Market Street, Newton Abbot, Devon TQ12 2RJ
  ☎(01626) 206420
  Librarian i/c Miss C Chilcott BA MCLIP

- Sidmouth Library, Blackmore Drive, Sidmouth, Devon EX10 8LA
  ☎(01395) 512192
  Librarian i/c Mrs G Spence
- St Thomas Library, Cowick Street, Exeter, Devon EX4 1AF
  ☎(01392) 252783
  Librarian i/c Mrs J Hughes
- Tavistock Library, The Quay, Plymouth Road, Tavistock, Devon PL19 8AB
  ☎(01822) 612218
  Fax (01822) 610690
  Librarian i/c Mrs M Andrews
- Teignmouth Library, Fore Street, Teignmouth, Devon TQ14 8DY
  ☎(01626) 774646
  Librarian i/c Mrs P Anderson MCLIP
- Tiverton Library, Angel Hill, Tiverton, Devon EX16 6PE
  ☎(01884) 252937
  Librarian i/c Mrs H Skinner

(Note: These do not represent the full list of branch libraries)

DONCASTER

Authority Doncaster Metropolitan Borough Council
HQ Central Library, Waterdale, Doncaster, South Yorkshire DN1 3JE
☎(01302) 734305 (general enquiries), (01302) 734298 (Principal Librarians' Office)
Fax (01302) 369749
e-mail: reference.library@doncaster.gov.uk
Head of Library and Information Services Ms G Johnson MA MCLIP

Area libraries

- Bibliographical Services HQ, Skellow Road, Carcroft, Doncaster, South Yorkshire DN6 8HF
  ☎(01302) 722327
  Fax (01302) 727293
  Senior Librarian Mrs M Lowndes MCLIP
- Mexborough Library, Area 1 HQ, John Street, Mexborough, South Yorkshire S64 9HS
  ☎(01709) 582037
  Area Manager D Butler BA MCLIP
- Bentley Library, Area 2 HQ, Cooke Street, Bentley, Doncaster, South Yorkshire DN5 0DP
  ☎(01302) 873456
  Area Manager Mrs J Whale MCLIP

DORSET

Authority Dorset County Council
HQ County Library HQ, Colliton Park, Dorchester, Dorset DT1 1XJ
☎(01305) 224455 (enquiries), (01305) 224450 (administration)
Fax (01305) 224344
e-mail: libraryhq@dorset-cc.gov.uk

url: http://www.dorset-cc.gov.uk/libraries
Head of Libraries & Arts Service I J Lewis BA MCLIP
Support Services Manager Mrs A Crockett MIPD
Senior Manager, Special Client Services Mrs V Chapman MCLIP

Divisional libraries

- Central Division. Dorchester Library, Colliton Park, Dorchester, Dorset DT1 1XJ
  ☎(01305) 224652 (Lending Library), (01305) 224448 (Reference Library)
  Fax (01305) 225160 (Lending Library), (01305) 266120 (Reference Library)
  Senior Manager, South Division N L Shirley MCLIP (01305 224458)
  Librarian i/c Miss A Davison BA(Hons) MCLIP
- East Division. Ferndown Library, Penny's Walk, Ferndown, Dorset BH22 9TH
  ☎(01202) 874534
  Fax (01202) 897097
  Senior Manager, East Division R J Dale MCLIP (01202 896545)
  Librarian i/c Miss R Irwin BLib MCLIP
- West Division. Weymouth Library, Great George Street, Weymouth, Dorset DT4 8NN
  ☎(01305) 762410 (lending), (01305) 762418 (reference)
  Fax (01305) 780316
  Senior Manager, West Division Mrs T Long BA MCLIP (01305 762401)
  Librarian i/c Mrs L Shirley MCLIP

Selected branch libraries

- Blandford Library, The Tabernacle, Blandford Forum, Dorset DT11 7DW
  ☎(01258) 452075
  Fax (01258) 459795
  Librarian i/c Vacant
- Bridport Library, South Street, Bridport, Dorset DT8 3EF
  ☎(01308) 422778
  Fax (01308) 421039
  Librarian i/c Mrs J E Read BA MCLIP
- Christchurch Library, Druitt Buildings, High Street, Christchurch, Dorset BH21 1AW
  ☎(01202) 485938
  Fax (01202) 490204
  Librarian i/c Mrs J Taylor MCLIP
- Gillingham Library, Chantry Fields, Gillingham, Dorset SP8 4UA
  ☎(01747) 822180
  Fax (01747) 826237
  Librarian i/c Mrs L C Antell BA(Hons) MCLIP
- Highcliffe Library, Gordon Road, Highcliffe, Dorset BH23 5HN
  ☎(01425) 272202
  Fax (01425) 279093
  Librarian i/c Vacant
- Lyme Regis Library, Silver Street, Lyme Regis, Dorset DT7 3HR
  ☎(01297) 443151
  Fax (01297) 444268
  Assistant i/c Mrs B A Preston

- Shaftesbury Library, Bell Street, Shaftesbury, Dorset SP7 8AE
  ☎(01747) 852256
  Fax (01747) 850154
  Assistant i/c Mrs J Heckford
- Sherborne Library, Digby Hall, Hound Street, Sherborne, Dorset DT9 3AA
  ☎(01935) 812683
  Fax (01935) 817623
  Librarian i/c Miss S J Everington BLS MCLIP
- Swanage Library, High Street, Swanage, Dorset BH19 2NU
  ☎(01929) 423485
  Fax (01929) 475876
  Librarian i/c Mrs R M Dreher BA(Hons) MCLIP
- Wareham Library, South Street, Wareham, Dorset BH20 4LR
  ☎(01929) 556146
  Fax (01929) 550672
  Librarian i/c Mrs R M Dreher BA(Hons) MCLIP
- Wimborne Library, Crown Mead, Rear of 55-57 High Street, Wimborne, Dorset BH21 1HH
  ☎(01202) 882770
  Fax (01202) 880392
  Librarian i/c A Fisher MCLIP

DUDLEY

Authority Dudley Metropolitan Borough Council
HQ Dudley Library, St James's Road, Dudley, West Midlands DY1 1HR
☎(01384) 815568 (administration)
Fax (01384) 815543
e-mail: dudlib.pls@mbc.dudley.gov.uk
url: http://www.dudley.gov.uk
Assistant Director of Education - Head of Libraries C A Wrigley BA MCLIP (01384 814746/814387; e-mail: chris.wrigley@dudley.gov.uk)
Assistant Head of Libraries (North) Mrs E J Woodcock BA (01384 815551; e-mail: elizabeth.woodcock@dudley.gov.uk)
Assistant Head of Libraries (South) Mrs K J Millin BLib MCLIP (01384 814745; e-mail: kate.millin@dudley.gov.uk)
Management Support Officer Miss S V Helm BA MCLIP DipMS (01384 815572; e-mail: s.helm@dudley.gov.uk)

Town libraries

- Brierley Hill Library, High Street, Brierley Hill, West Midlands DY5 3ET
  ☎(01384) 812865
  Fax (01384) 812866
  e-mail: brierlib.pls@mbc.dudley.gov.uk)
  Town Librarian S R Masters MCLIP
- Dudley Library, St James's Road, Dudley, West Midlands DY1 1HR
  ☎(01384) 815560
  Fax (01384) 815543

e-mail: dudlib.pls@mbc.dudley.gov.uk
Town Librarian Mrs J A Bright BA, Mrs H Riley BA MCLIP (job-share)

- Halesowen Library, Queensway Mall, The Cornbow, Halesowen, West Midlands B63 4AJ
  ☎(01384) 812980
  Fax (01384) 812981
  e-mail: hallib.pls@mbc.dudley.gov.uk
  Town Librarian Mrs A D Horton MCLIP
- Stourbridge Library, Crown Centre, Crown Lane, Stourbridge, West Midlands DY8 1YE
  ☎(01384) 812945
  Fax (01384) 812946
  e-mail: stourlib.pls@dudley.gov.uk)
  Town Librarian D C Hickman MSc MCLIP

Group Libraries Headquarters (North)

Sedgley Library, Ladies Walk Centre, Ladies Walk, Sedgley, West Midlands DY3 3UA
☎(01384) 812790
e-mail: sedglib.pls@mbc.dudley.gov.uk
Group Librarian Mrs H Birt MCLIP, Mrs L Watts BA (job-share)

Group Libraries Headquarters (South)

Kingswinford Library, Market Street, Kingswinford, West Midlands DY6 9LG
☎(01384) 812740
e-mail: kfordlib.pls@mbc.dudley.gov.uk
Group Librarian Mrs S Whitehouse BA

Archives and Local History Service

Mount Pleasant Street, Coseley, Dudley, West Midlands WV14 9JR
☎(01384) 812770 (tel/fax)
e-mail: archives.pls@mbc.dudley.gov.uk
Borough Archivist Mrs K H Atkins BA DipArchAd

DURHAM

Authority Durham County Council
HQ Arts, Libraries and Museums Department, County Hall, Durham DH1 5TY
☎0191 383 3595 (enquiries), 0191 383 3713 (administration)
Fax 0191 384 1336
e-mail: alm@durham.gov.uk
url: http://www.durham.gov.uk
Director, Arts, Libraries and Museums P Conway BA FRSA MCLIP MIMgt MILAM
Assistant Director, Collections and Strategy J Orr BA AMA
Assistant Director, Local Delivery and Support N S Canaway MBA MCLIP

Divisional libraries

- Northern Division. Durham City Library, South Street, Durham City DH1 4QS
  ☎0191 386 4003
  Fax 0191 386 0379
  Divisional Manager D English MCLIP

- Eastern Division. Peterlee Library, Burnhope Way, Peterlee, Co Durham SR8 1NT
  ☎0191 586 2279
  Fax 0191 586 6664
  Divisional Manager Ms S Owens BA MCLIP
- Western Division. Crook Library, Market Place, Crook, Co Durham DL15 8QH
  ☎(01388) 762269
  Fax (01388) 766170
  Divisional Manager J S Mallam MCLIP

EALING

Authority London Borough of Ealing
HQ Library Administrative Office, 3rd Floor, Perceval House, 14 Uxbridge Road, London W5 2HL
☎020 8825 5000
Fax 020 8579 5280
e-mail: libuser@ealing.gov.uk
url: http://www.ealing.gov.uk/libraries/index.htm
Head of Service Ms J E Battye BA MCLIP

Central/largest library

Central Library, 103 Ealing Broadway Centre, London W5 5JY
☎020 8567 3670 (enquiries), 020 8567 3656 (reference)
Fax 020 8840 2351
Library Manager L Bowen MCLIP

Main libraries

- Acton Library, High Street, London W3 6NA
  ☎020 8752 0999
  Fax 020 8992 6086
- Greenford Library, Oldfield Lane South, Greenford, Middlesex UB6 9LG
  ☎020 8578 1466
  Fax 020 8575 7800
- Southall Library, Osterley Park Road, Southall, Middlesex UB2 4BL
  ☎020 8574 3412
  Fax 020 8571 7629
- West Ealing Library, Melbourne Avenue, London W13 9BT
  ☎020 8567 2812
  Fax 020 8567 1736

EAST RIDING OF YORKSHIRE

Authority East Riding of Yorkshire Council
HQ Library and Information Services, Council Offices, Main Road, Skirlaugh, East Riding of Yorkshire HU11 5HN
☎(01482) 392702 (administration)
Fax (01482) 392710
Libraries, Museums and Archives Manager A Moir (e-mail: alan.moir@eastriding.gov.uk)

Library Operations Manager Ms M Slattery BA DMS (01482 392740; e-mail: margaret.slattery@eastriding.gov.uk)
Central Services Manager Ms E Herbert (01482 392715; e-mail: libby.herbert@eastriding.gov.uk)

EAST SUSSEX

Authority East Sussex County Council
HQ Libraries, Information and Arts, F-Floor, County Hall, St Anne's Crescent, Lewes, East Sussex BN7 1UE
☎(01273) 481870 (enquiries), (01273) 481538 (administration)
Fax (01273) 481716
Acting Head of Libraries and Information P Leivers BA MBA MCLIP (01273 481534; e-mail: paul.leivers@eastsussexcc.gov.uk)
Head of Lifelong Learning Vacant
Head of Information Management P Leivers BA MBA MCLIP (01273 481882; e-mail: paul.leivers@eastsussexcc.gov.uk)/Ms M Palmer BA MCLIP (01273 481882; e-mail: mary.palmer@eastsussexcc.gov.uk)
Customer Services Manager Mrs H Sykes MCLIP (01273 481872; e-mail: helena.sykes@eastsussexcc.gov.uk)

Central/largest library

Hastings Group Office, Hastings Library, Brassey Institute, 13 Claremont, Hastings, East Sussex TN34 1HE
☎(01424) 420501 (enquiries), (01424) 461955 (administration)
Fax (01424) 430261
Group Manager C Desmond MCLIP

Group area offices

- Eastbourne Library, Grove Road, Eastbourne, East Sussex BN21 4TL
  ☎(01323) 434206
  Fax (01323) 649174
  Group Manager M Bacon (01323 434203)
- Lewes Library, Albion Street, Lewes, East Sussex BN7 2ND
  ☎(01273) 474232
  Fax (01273) 477881
  Group Manager B Forster MCLIP (01273 479729)
- Uckfield Library (Wealden), High Street, Uckfield, East Sussex TN22 1AR
  ☎(01825) 763254
  Fax (01825) 769762
  Group Manager Mrs J Makin MCLIP (01825 769761)
- Bexhill Library (Rother), Western Road, Bexhill on Sea, East Sussex TN40 1DY
  ☎(01424) 212546
  Fax (01424) 819138
  Group Manager Ms N Finn (01424 819138)

ENFIELD

Authority London Borough of Enfield
HQ Leisure Services Group, PO Box 58, Civic Centre, Enfield, Middlesex EN1 3XJ
☎020 8366 2244 (enquiries), 020 8379 3752 (administration)
Fax 020 8379 3753
Assistant Director (Libraries and Culture) Ms C Lewis BA MSc MCLIP (e-mail: claire.lewis@enfield.gov.uk)
Library Resources and Development Manager Ms J Gibson MA MCLIP (e-mail: julie.gibson@enfield.gov.uk)

Central/largest library

Central Library, Cecil Road, Enfield, Middlesex EN2 6TW
☎020 8366 2244
Fax 020 8379 8400
Library Network Manager S Deakin MCLIP (e-mail: simon.deakin@enfield.gov.uk)
Area Library Manager Mrs S Barford MCLIP (020 8379 8301)

Area libraries

- Palmers Green Library, Broomfield Lane, London N13 4EY
  ☎020 8886 3728
  Fax 020 8379 2712
  Area Library Manager Ms P Tuttiett BA MCLIP (020 8379 2694)
- Edmonton Green Library, 36/44 South Mall, London N9 0NX
  ☎020 8807 3618
  Fax 020 8379 2615
  Area Library Manager P Brown BA MCLIP (020 8379 2605)

ESSEX

Authority Essex County Council
HQ County Library HQ, Goldlay Gardens, Chelmsford, Essex CM2 0EW
☎(01245) 284981
Fax (01245) 492780 (general), (01245) 436769 (Management Team)
e-mail: essexlib@essexcc.gov.uk
url: http://www.essexcc.gov.uk/libraries
Head of Library, Information, Heritage and Cultural Services Dr M Keeling PhD MA BA(Hons) MCLIP (01245 436080; e-mail: margaret.keeling@essexcc.gov.uk) (Based at Learning Services, PO Box 47, Chelmsford CM2 6WN)
Strategic Manager: Field Services Ms J Glayzer MCLIP (01245 436767; e-mail: jenny.glayzer@essexcc.gov.uk)
Strategic Manager: Policy and Development G Elgar DipLib BA(Hons) MCLIP (01245 436766)

Central/largest library

Chelmsford Library, PO Box 882, Market Road, Chelmsford, Essex CM1 1LH
☎(01245) 492758
Fax (01245) 492536 (enquiries), (01245) 436769 (administration)
e-mail: cfdlib@essexcc.gov.uk

District Headquarters

- Basildon, Brentwood and Castle Point District HQ, Basildon Central Library, St Martin's Square, Basildon, Essex SS14 1EE
  ☎(01268) 288533
  Fax (01268) 286326
  District Manager Ms E Adams BA MCLIP DMS (e-mail: elaine.adams@essexcc.gov.uk)
- Braintree and Uttlesford District HQ, Braintree Library, Fairfield Road, Braintree, Essex CM7 3YL
  ☎(01376) 320752
  Fax (01376) 553316
  Acting District Manager P Connell
- Colchester and Tendring District HQ, Colchester Library, Trinity Square, Colchester, Essex CO1 1JB
  ☎(01206) 245900
  Fax (01206) 245901
  e-mail: colchester.library@essexcc.gov.uk
  District Manager Ms N Baker BA MCLIP (e-mail: nicola.baker@essexcc.gov.uk)
- Harlow and Epping Forest District HQ, Harlow Library, The High, Harlow, Essex CM20 1HA
  ☎(01279) 413772
  Fax (01279) 424612
  District Manager G Bannister MA MCLIP (e-mail: graham.bannister@essexcc.gov.uk)
- Chelmsford, Maldon and Rochford District HQ, Chelmsford Library, PO Pox 882, Market Road, Chelmsford, Essex CM1 1LH
  ☎(01245) 492758
  Fax (01245) 492536
  e-mail: cfdlib@essexcc.gov.uk
  District Manager Ms M Shipley MCLIP (01245 436536; e-mail: marion.shipley@essexcc.gov.uk)

GATESHEAD

Authority Gateshead Metropolitan Borough Council
HQ Libraries, Arts and Information Services, Central Library, Prince Consort Road, Gateshead, Tyne and Wear NE8 4LN
☎0191 477 3478
Fax 0191 477 7454
e-mail: enquiries@gateshead.gov.uk
Head of Cultural Development W J Macnaught MA DipLib MCLIP e-mail: bill.macnaught@gateshead.gov.uk (located at Regent Street address)
Assistant Director, Lending Ms A Borthwick BA MCLIP
Assistant Director, Support Services M Watson BA MCLIP
Assistant Director, Information S Walters BSc MCLIP
Arts Development Manager Mrs E Wilson BA

Libraries, Arts and Information Services, Civic Centre, Regent Street, Gateshead, Tyne and Wear NE8 1HH
☎0191 433 2710

Fax 0191 478 3875
Head of Cultural Development W J Macnaught MA DipLib MCLIP e-mail: bill.macnaught@gateshead.gov.uk

Area libraries

- East Area. Birtley Library, Durham Road, Birtley, County Durham DH3 1LE
  ☎0191 410 5364
  Fax 0191 410 5855
  Area Manager Ms A Parker MCLIP (e-mail: a.parker@gateshead.gov.uk)
- West Area. Whickham Library, St Mary's Green, Whickham, Newcastle upon Tyne NE16 4DN
  ☎0191 488 1262
  Fax 0191 488 3926
  Area Manager Ms D Cameron MCLIP (e-mail: d.cameron@gateshead.gov.uk)

GLOUCESTERSHIRE

Authority Gloucestershire County Council
HQ County Library, Arts and Museums Service, Quayside House, Shire Hall, Gloucester GL1 2HY
☎(01452) 425020 (general enquiries), (01452) 425048 (management)
Fax (01452) 425042
e-mail: clams@gloscc.gov.uk
url: http://www.gloscc.gov.uk/libraries
Head of Library Services C Campbell MBA MCLIP (e-mail: ccampbel@gloscc.gov.uk)
Assistant County Librarian, Development and Client Services Ms E Dubber BA MCLIP (e-mail: edubber@gloscc.gov.uk)
Assistant County Librarian, Field Services J A Holland BA DipLib MCLIP (e-mail: jholland@gloscc.gov.uk)
Principal Librarian (Information) P Gaw BA MCLIP (e-mail: pgaw@gloscc.gov.uk)
Principal Librarian (Learning and Literacy) Ms H Briggs BA DMS MIMgt MCLIP (e-mail: hbriggs@gloscc.gov.uk)
Principal Librarian (Reader Services) Ms G Barker BA DipLib MCLIP, Ms E Haldon BA MCLIP (e-mail: plread@gloscc.gov.uk)

Central/largest libraries

- Gloucester Library, Brunswick Road, Gloucester GL1 1HT
  ☎(01452) 426973
  Fax (01452) 521468
  Library Manager Ms J Potter
- Cheltenham Library, Clarence Street, Cheltenham, Gloucestershire GL50 3JT
  ☎(01242) 532688
  Fax (01242) 510373
  Library Manager Mrs B French

Group libraries

- North. Based at, Cheltenham Library, Clarence Street, Cheltenham, Gloucestershire GL50 3JT

☎(01242) 532678
Fax (01242) 532673
Group Librarian G R Hiatt BA MCLIP (e-mail: ghiatt@gloscc.gov.uk)

- South. Based at Stroud Library, Lansdown, Stroud, Gloucestershire GL5 1BB
  ☎(01453) 756842
  Fax (01453) 757829
  Group Librarian Mrs M E Tucker BA MLib MCLIP (e-mail: mtucker@gloscc.gov.uk)
- West. Based at Gloucester Library, Brunswick Road, Gloucester GL1 1HT
  ☎(01452) 426976
  Fax (01452) 521468
  Group Librarian J Hughes BA MCLIP (e-mail: jhughes@gloscc.gov.uk)

Selected branch libraries

- Chipping Campden Library, High Street, Chipping Campden, Gloucestershire GL55 6AT
  ☎(01386) 840692
  Fax (01386) 841439
  Library Manager Ms B Armour
- Cirencester Bingham Library, The Waterloo, Cirencester, Gloucestershire GL7 2PZ
  ☎(01285) 659813
  Fax (01285) 640449
  Library Manager Ms C Summerell
- Fairford Library, London Road, Fairford, Gloucestershire GL7 4AQ
  ☎(01285) 712599
  Fax (01285) 711342
  Library Manager Ms J Abouyannis
- Lechlade Library, Market Place, Lechlade, Gloucestershire GL7 3AB
  ☎(01367) 252631
  Fax (01367) 250073
  Library Manager Ms A Watkins
- Painswick Library, Stroud Road, Painswick, Gloucestershire GL6 6UT
  ☎(01452) 812569
  Fax (01452) 814693
  Library Manager Ms R Davie
- Stow on the Wold Library, St Edwards Hall, The Square, Stow on the Wold, Gloucestershire GL54 1AF
  ☎(01451) 830352
  Fax (01451) 870150
  Library Manager Ms L Lal
- Tetbury Library, Close Gardens, Tetbury, Gloucestershire GL8 8DU
  ☎(01666) 502258
  Fax (01666) 504449
  Library Manager Ms S King
- Tewkesbury Library, Sun Street, Tewkesbury, Gloucestershire GL20 5NX
  ☎(01684) 293086
  Fax (01684) 290125
  Library Manager Ms J Thomson

- Winchcombe Library, Back Lane, Winchcombe, Gloucestershire GL54 5PZ
  ☎(01242) 602772
  Fax (01242) 603043
  Library Manager Ms B Herrod

GREENWICH

Authority London Borough of Greenwich
HQ Public Services, 13th Floor, Riverside House, Woolwich High Street, London SE18 6DN
☎020 8317 4466
Fax 020 8317 4868
e-mail: libraries@greenwich.gov.uk
url: http://www.greenwich.gov.uk
Head of Community Services Ms M Snook

District libraries

- Woolwich Library, Calderwood Street, London SE18 6QZ
  ☎020 8921 5750
  Fax 020 8316 1645
- Eltham Library, Eltham High Street, London SE9 1TS
  ☎020 8850 2268
  Fax 020 8850 1368
- Blackheath Library, 17-23 Old Dover Road, London SE3 7BT
  ☎020 8858 1131
  Fax 020 8853 3615

HACKNEY

Authority London Borough of Hackney
HQ Senior Management Team, Homerton Library, Homerton High Street, London E9 6AS
☎020 8356 1697
Fax 020 8356 1692
Head of Library Service Ms J Middleton MCLIP (e-mail: jmiddleton@gw.hackney.gov.uk) (based at Ground Floor, Maurice Bishop House, 17 Reading Lane, London E8 1HH; 020 8356 2560; fax 020 8356 7595)
Community Services Manager Vacant
Support Services Manager Vacant
Lifelong Learning Manager Vacant

Central/largest library

Hackney Central Library, 1 Reading Lane, London E8 1GQ
☎020 8356 2542
Library Manager Ms A Kane
Information Manager Vacant

Town centre libraries

- Clapton Library, Northwold Road, London E5 8RA
  ☎020 8356 2570

Fax 020 8806 7849
Library Manager Vacant

- C L R James Library, 24-30 Dalston Lane, London E8 3AZ
☎020 8356 1665
Fax 020 7254 4655
Library Manager Vacant
- Homerton Library, Homerton High Street, London E9 6AS
☎020 8356 1690
Fax 020 8525 7945
Library Manager Vacant
- Shoreditch Library, 80 Hoxton Street, London N1 6LP
☎020 8356 4350
Library Manager J Holland
- Stamford Hill Library, Portland Avenue, London N16 6SB
☎020 8356 2573
Fax 020 8809 5986
Library Manager Ms S Comitti
- Stoke Newington Library, Church Street, London N16 0JS
☎020 8356 5230
Fax 020 8356 5233
Library Manager Ms J Obeney
- Community Action Team, Stoke Newington Library, Church Street, London N16 0JS
☎020 8356 5238
Community Services Manager Ms J Middleton MCLIP

HALTON

Authority Halton Borough Council
HQ Halton Lea Library, Halton Lea, Runcorn, Cheshire WA7 2PF
☎(01928) 715351
Fax (01928) 790221
Library Services Manager Mrs P Reilly-Cooper BSc DipLib MCLIP (0151 424 2061 ext 4096; based at Runcorn Town Hall, Heath Road, Runcorn WA7 5TD; e-mail: paula.reilly-cooper@halton-borough.gov.uk)
Specialist Services Manager Mrs J Potter BA(Hons) MCLIP
Stock Specialist Officer Miss T Burr BA(Hons) MCLIP
Reference and Information Officer Mrs J Bradburn MCLIP
Young Persons Officer Mrs A Watt BA(Hons) MCLIP
Systems Officer P Cooke BA(Hons) MA (e-mail: philip.cooke@halton-borough.gov.uk)
Bibliographical Services Officer Mrs G Kane BA(Hons) MCLIP

Central/largest library

Halton Lea Library, Halton Lea, Runcorn, Cheshire WA7 2PF
☎Tel/Fax etc. as HQ
Senior Librarian Miss S Kirk BA(Hons) MCLIP

Area libraries

- Ditton Library, Queens Avenue, Ditton, Widnes, Cheshire WA8 8HR

☎0151 424 2459
Senior Librarian Mrs K Marshall BA MCLIP (0151 423 4818)

- Runcorn Library, Egerton Street, Runcorn, Cheshire WA7 1JL
  ☎(01928) 574495
  Senior Librarian Miss S Kirk BA(Hons) MCLIP (01928 715351)
- Widnes Library, Victoria Square, Widnes, Cheshire WA8 7QY
  ☎0151 423 4818
  Fax 0151 420 5108
  Senior Librarian Mrs K Marshall BA MCLIP (0151 423 4818)

HAMMERSMITH AND FULHAM

Authority London Borough of Hammersmith and Fulham
HQ Hammersmith Library, Shepherds Bush Road, London W6 7AT
☎020 8753 2400 (24-hr information phoneline), 020 8753 3823 (enquiries), 020 8753 3813 (administration)
Fax 020 8753 3815
e-mail: info@haflibs.org.uk
url: http://www.lbhf.gov.uk
Head of Libraries D Herbert BA MLS MCLIP (020 8753 3810; e-mail: d.herbert@libs.lbhf.gov.uk)
Support Services Manager J B Aquilina MCLIP (020 8753 3818; e-mail: j.aquilina@libs.lbhf.gov.uk)
Borough Archivist and Local History Manager Ms J Kimber BA(Hons) DAA MSc (020 8741 5159; e-mail: j.kimber@libs.lbhf.gov.uk)
Library Development Manager Ms A Stirrup BA MCLIP (020 8753 3811; e-mail: amandastirrup@hotmail.com)

Central/largest library

Hammersmith Library, Shepherds Bush Road, London W6 7AT
☎Tel/Fax etc. as HQ
Senior Librarian Ms G Lynch MCLIP, Ms L Hardman MSc MCLIP (job-share)

Area libraries

- Askew Road Library, 87/91 Askew Road, London W12 9AS
  ☎020 8753 3863
- Barons Court Library, North End Crescent, London W14 8TG
  ☎020 8753 3888
- Fulham Library, 598 Fulham Road, London SW6 5NX
  ☎020 8753 3879
  Senior Librarian Ms J Samuels MCLIP
- Sands End Library, The Community Centre, 59-61 Broughton Road, London SW6 2LA
  ☎020 8753 3885
- Shepherds Bush Library, 7 Uxbridge Road, London W12 8LJ
  ☎020 8753 3842
  Fax 020 8740 1712
- Mobile Library Service and Housebound Readers Service
  020 7610 4251

HAMPSHIRE

Authority Hampshire County Council
HQ County Library HQ, 81 North Walls, Winchester, Hampshire SO23 8BY
☎(01962) 846059 (enquiries), (01962) 846102 (administration)
Fax (01962) 856615
url: http://www.hants.gov.uk/library
Acting Head of Libraries J F Dunne BA MCLIP (01962 846100; e-mail: john.dunne@hants.gov.uk)
Assistant County Librarian, Information Services N R Fox BA FCLIP FRSA (01962 846077; e-mail: nick.fox@hants.gov.uk)
Assistant County Librarian, Bibliographic and Adult Lending Services B Kempthorne MA MCLIP (01962 846083; e-mail: barrie.kempthorne@hants.gov.uk)
Assistant County Librarian, Resource Planning J Haylock BA MCLIP (01962 846089; e-mail: john.haylock@hants.gov.uk)

Divisional libraries

- Central Division HQ, Lending Library, Jewry Street, Winchester, Hampshire SO23 8RX
  ☎(01962) 862748
  Fax (01962) 841489
  Divisional Librarian P A Dix BA MCLIP (01962 841499; e-mail: paul.dix@hants.gov.uk)
- North Division HQ, Basingstoke Library, 19/20 Westminster House, Potters Walk, Basingstoke, Hampshire RG21 7LS
  ☎(01256) 473901
  Fax (01256) 470666
  Divisional Librarian Miss S Greenfield BA MIMgt MCLIP (01256 363793; e-mail: sue.greenfield@hants.gov.uk)
- South Division HQ, Fareham Library, Osborn Road, Fareham, Hampshire PO16 7EN
  ☎(01329) 282715
  Fax (01329) 221551
  Divisional Librarian Mrs M Davies MCLIP (01329 221424; e-mail: marija.davies@hants.gov.uk)
- West Division HQ, The Old School, Cannon Street, Lymington, Hampshire SO41 9BR
  ☎(01590) 673050
  Fax (01590) 672561
  Divisional Librarian Miss M Franklin BA MCLIP (01590 675767; e-mail: mary.franklin@hants.gov.uk)

HARINGEY

Authority London Borough of Haringey
HQ Haringey Library Services, Central Library, High Road, Wood Green, London N22 6XD
☎020 8489 2700 (enquiries & administration)
Fax 020 8489 2722
Interim Manager Ms D Edmonds BA DipLib FCLIP

Central/largest library

Wood Green Central Library, High Road, Wood Green, London N22 6XD

☎020 8489 2700
Fax 020 8489 2722
Principal Librarian Ms G Harvey MCLIP

Area libraries

- Marcus Garvey Library, Tottenham Green, London N15 4JA
  ☎020 8489 5309
  Principal Librarian M Bott LLB
- Hornsey Library, Haringey Park, London N8 9JA
  ☎020 8489 1427
  Principal Librarian Ms M Stephanou

HARROW

Authority London Borough of Harrow
HQ Civic Centre Library, PO Box 4, Civic Centre, Station Road, Harrow, Middlesex HA1 2UU
☎020 8424 1055/6 (enquiries), 020 8424 1059/1970 (administration)
Fax 020 8424 1971
e-mail: library@harrow.gov.uk
Library Services Manager R J R Mills BSc MCLIP DMS (e-mail: bob.mills@harrow.gov.uk)

Central/largest library

Central Library, Gayton Road, Harrow, Middlesex HA1 2HL
☎020 8427 6012/8986
Principal Librarian (Lending Services) J E Pennells MCLIP DMS (e-mail: john.pennells@harrow.gov.uk)

HARTLEPOOL

Authority Hartlepool Borough Council
HQ Central Library, 124 York Road, Hartlepool, Cleveland TS26 9DE
☎(01429) 272905
Fax (01429) 275685
e-mail: reflib@hartlepool.gov.uk
Borough Librarian Mrs S Atkinson BA MCLIP DipRSA
Central Services Manager Vacant
Area Manager, South Ms K Tranter BA(Hons)
Area Manager, North Ms A Russell MCLIP

Bibliographical services

Bibliographical Services Section, 2 Cromwell Street, Hartlepool, Cleveland TS24 7LR
☎(01429) 523644
e-mail: bibservices@hartlepool.gov.uk
Bibliographical Services Officer Vacant

HAVERING

Authority London Borough of Havering
HQ Central Library, St Edwards Way, Romford, Essex RM1 3AR

☎(01708) 432389 (enquiries), (01708) 432379 (administration)
Fax (01708) 432391
e-mail: romfordlib2@rmplc.co.uk
Borough Librarian R K Worcester MA DipLib MCLIP

HEREFORDSHIRE

Authority Herefordshire Council
HQ Administration Section, Shirehall, Hereford HR1 2HY
☎(01432) 359830
Fax (01432) 260744
url: http://www.libraries.herefordshire.gov.uk
Acting Libraries and Information Services Manager M Warren BA(Hons) MA MILAM (01432 260617; e-mail: mjwarren@herefordshire.gov.uk)
Acquisitions Manager Mrs C Huckfield BA MCLIP (01432 261570; e-mail: chuckfield@herefordshire.gov.uk)
Information Services Development Manager Mrs L Davies DCA LLB (e-mail: ldavies@herefordshire.gov.uk)

Central/largest libraries

- Hereford Library, Broad Street, Hereford, Herefordshire HR4 9AU
  ☎(01432) 272456
  Fax (01432) 359668
  Hereford Group Librarian Revd N Spencer BA MCLIP DipAppTheol
- Leominster Library, 8 Buttercross, Leominster, Herefordshire HR6 8BN
  ☎(01568) 612384
  Fax (01568) 616025
  Leominster Group Librarian P Holliday BA DipEd MCLIP

Selected branch libraries

- Ledbury Library, The Homend, Ledbury, Herefordshire HR8 1BT
  ☎(01531) 632133
  Librarian i/c Mrs S Chedgzoy BA DipLib MCLIP
- Ross-on-Wye Library, Cantilupe Road, Ross-on-Wye, Herefordshire HR9 7AN
  ☎(01989) 567937
  Librarian i/c Miss E Teiser BLib MCLIP

HERTFORDSHIRE

Authority Hertfordshire County Council
HQ Community Information: Libraries, New Barnfield, Travellers Lane, Hatfield, Herts AL10 8XG
☎(01438) 737333 (enquiries & administration)
Fax (01707) 281589
e-mail: firstname.lastname@hertscc.gov.uk
url: http://www.hertsdirect.org
Director of Community Information A Robertson (01992 555609; Fax 01992 555614)

Head of Library Services Ms G Wood BA DipLib MCLIP (01992 555610; e-mail: glenda.wood@hertscc.gov.uk)
Stock Manager Ms S Valentine MA(Hons) (01707 281584; e-mail: sue.valentine@hertscc.gov.uk)
Library Information Services Manager A Bignell BA DipLib MCLIP (01707 281584; e-mail: andrew.bignell@hertscc.gov.uk)

Central/largest library

Central Resources Library, New Barnfield, Travellers Lane, Hatfield, Herts AL10 8XG
☎(01438) 737333
Fax (01707) 281514
Central Resources Librarian Vacant

District libraries

- Bishop's Stortford Library, The Causeway, Bishop's Stortford, Herts CM23 2EJ
  ☎(01438) 737333
  Fax (01279) 307471
  e-mail: bishopsstortford.library@hertscc.gov.uk
  District Librarian Ms J Holmes BA MCLIP
- Borehamwood Library, Elstree Way, Borehamwood, Herts WD6 1JX
  ☎(01923) 471333
  Fax (01923) 338414
  e-mail: borehamwood.library@hertscc.gov.uk
  District Librarian Ms R Bilton
- Hemel Hempstead Library, Central Library, Combe Street, Hemel Hempstead, Herts HP1 1HJ
  ☎(01438) 737333
  Fax (01442) 404660
  e-mail: hemelhempstead.library@hertscc.gov.uk
  District Librarian D Knight MCLIP
- Hitchin Library, Paynes Park, Hitchin, Herts SG5 1EW
  ☎(01438) 737333
  Fax (01462) 640529
  e-mail: hitchin.library@hertscc.gov.uk
  District Librarian Ms I Oakey BA DipLib MCLIP
- Hoddesdon Library, 98a High Street, Hoddesdon, Herts EN11 8HD
  ☎(01438) 737333
  Fax (01992) 411039
  e-mail: hoddesdon.library@hertscc.gov.uk
  District Librarian Ms C Hill BA MCLIP
- Rickmansworth Library, High Street, Rickmansworth, Herts WD3 1EH
  ☎(01923) 471333
  Fax (01923) 710384
  District Librarian Ms M Staunton BA DipLib MCLIP
- St Albans Library, The Maltings, St Albans, Herts AL1 3JQ
  ☎(01438) 737333
  Fax (01727) 848613

e-mail: stalbans.library@hertscc.gov.uk
District Librarian R Barrow BA(Hons) MCLIP

- Stevenage Library, Southgate, Stevenage, Herts SG1 1HD
  ☎(01438) 737333
  Fax (01438) 219026
  e-mail: stevenage.library@hertscc.gov.uk
  District Librarian Ms I Oakey BA DipLib MCLIP
- Watford Library, Hempstead Road, Watford, Herts WD1 3EU
  ☎(01923) 471333
  Fax (01923) 334688
  e-mail: watford.library@hertscc.gov.uk
  District Librarian Ms M Campbell MA MCLIP
- Welwyn Garden City Library, Campus West, Welwyn Garden City, Herts AL8 6AJ
  ☎(01438) 737333
  Fax (01707) 897595
  e-mail: wgc.library@hertscc.gov.uk
  District Librarian J Macrae MA MCLIP

HILLINGDON

Authority London Borough of Hillingdon
HQ Central Library, 14-15 High Street, Uxbridge, Middlesex UB8 1HD
☎(01895) 250600 (enquiries), (01895) 250700 (administration)
Fax (01895) 811164 (administration)
e-mail: clibrary@hillingdon.gov.uk
Head of Service Mrs T Grimshaw (01895 250700; fax 01895 811164; e-mail: tgrimshaw@hillingdon.gov.uk)
Head of Public Service Mrs J Mitchell MCLIP (01895 250716; e-mail: jmitchell@hillingdon.gov.uk)

Area libraries

- Central Library, 14-15 High Street, Uxbridge, Middlesex UB8 1HD
  ☎(01895) 250714
  Fax (01895) 811164
  e-mail: clibrary@hillingdon.gov.uk
  Central Services Manager Ms S Lake MCLIP (01895 277798; e-mail: slake@hillingdon.gov.uk)
- Hayes Library, Golden Crescent, Hayes, Middlesex UB3 1AQ
  ☎020 8848 0269
- Manor Farm Library, Bury Street, Ruislip, Middlesex HA4 7SU
  ☎(01895) 633651

HOUNSLOW

Authority London Borough of Hounslow
HQ Hounslow Library Network (CIP), Centrespace, Treaty Centre, High Street, Hounslow, Middlesex TW3 1ES
☎0845 456 2800 (enquiries), 0845 456 2921 (administration)
Fax 0845 456 2880

url: http://www.cip.org.uk
Director of Culture and Heritage/Borough Librarian Ms L Simpson BA MCLIP (e-mail: linda-simpson@cip.org.uk)
Principal Librarian Ms F Stanbury MCLIP (e-mail: frances-stanbury@cip.org.uk)
Strategic Library Managers (IT and Electronic Resources) Ms S Vass BA(Hons) MSc; (Project Development) R Kitchen; (Staff and Learning Development) Ms J Harrison MCLIP; (Stock and Reader Development) Ms E Lee BA MCLIP; Team Leaders (Adult Library Services) M Clift BA; (Bibliographical Services) Ms E Cutts MCLIP/Ms R Jones (020 8894 2550); (Community Services) Ms G Iqbal BA DipLib MCLIP; (Customer Services) Ms A Greene BA(Lib); (Systems Team) M Fahey (0845 456 2964)

Central/largest library

Hounslow Library, Treaty Centre, High Street, Hounslow, Middlesex TW3 1ES
☎0845 456 2800
Fax 0845 456 2880
Principal Librarian Ms F Stanbury MCLIP

Branch libraries

- Beavers Library, 103 Salisbury Road, Hounslow, Middlesex TW4 7NW
  ☎020 8572 6995
- Bedfont Library, Staines Road, Bedfont, Middlesex TW14 8DB
  ☎020 8890 6173
- Brentford Library, Boston Manor Road, Brentford, Middlesex TW8 8DW
  ☎020 8560 8801
- Chiswick Library, Duke's Avenue, Chiswick, London W4 2AB
  ☎020 8994 1008
- Cranford Library, Bath Road, Cranford, Middlesex TW5 9TL
  ☎020 8759 0641
- Feltham Library, 210 The Centre, High Street, Feltham, Middlesex TW13 4BX
  ☎020 8890 3506
- Hanworth Library, 2-12 Hampton Road West, Hanworth, Middlesex TW13 6AW
  ☎020 8898 0256
- Heston Library, New Heston Road, Heston, Middlesex TW5 0LW
  ☎020 8570 1028
- Isleworth Library, Twickenham Road, Isleworth, Middlesex TW7 7EU
  ☎020 8560 2934
- Osterley Library, St Mary's Crescent, Osterley, Middlesex TW7 4NB
  ☎020 8560 4295

ISLE OF WIGHT

Authority Isle of Wight Council
HQ Library Headquarters, Parkhurst Road, Newport, Isle of Wight PO30 5TX
☎(01983) 825717 (enquiries & administration)
Fax (01983) 528047
url: http://www.iwight.com/thelibrary
Head of Libraries T Blackmore MCLIP (e-mail: tblackmore@iwight.gov.uk)
Library Operational Manager M Lister BA MCLIP (01983 825717)

Community Services Librarian B Hawkins BA MCLIP (01983 825717)
Support Services Librarian A Walker BA MCLIP (01983 825717)
Stock Manager J English BLib DMS MCLIP (01983 825717)

Central/largest library

Lord Louis Library, Orchard Street, Newport, Isle of Wight PO30 1LL
☎(01983) 527655 (enquiries & administration)
Fax (01983) 825972

Area libraries

- Ryde Library, George Street, Ryde, Isle of Wight PO33 2JE
  ☎(01983) 562170
  Fax (01983) 615644
- Sandown Library, High Street, Sandown, Isle of Wight PO36 8AF
  ☎(01983) 402748
  Fax (01983) 402748
- Shanklin Library, Victoria Avenue, Shanklin, Isle of Wight PO37 6PG
  ☎(01983) 863126
  Fax (01983) 863126
- Ventnor Library, High Street, Ventnor, Isle of Wight PO38 1LZ
  ☎(01983) 852039
  Fax (01983) 852039
- Freshwater Library, School Green Road, Freshwater, Isle of Wight PO35 5NA
  ☎(01983) 752377
  Fax (01983) 752377
- Cowes Library, Beckford Road, Cowes, Isle of Wight PO31 7SG
  ☎(01983) 293341
  Fax (01983) 293341
- Bembridge Library, Church Road, Bembridge, Isle of Wight PO35 5NA
  ☎(01983) 873102
  Fax (01983) 873102
- Niton Library, High Street, Niton, Isle of Wight PO38 2AZ
  ☎(01983) 730863
  Fax (01983) 730863
- Brighstone, New Road, Brighstone, Newport, Isle of Wight PO30 4BB
  ☎(01983) 740150
  Fax (01983) 740150
- East Cowes Library, The York Centre, 11 York Avenue, East Cowes, Isle of Wight PO32 6QY
  ☎(01983) 293019
  Fax (01983) 293019

ISLINGTON

Authority London Borough of Islington
HQ Library and Information Service, Central Library, 2 Fieldway Crescent, London N5 1PF
☎020 7527 6900 (enquiries), 020 7527 6905 (administration)
Fax 020 7527 6906

e-mail: library.informationunit@islington.gov.uk
url: http://www.islington.gov.uk
Head of Library and Information Service Ms E Roberts MSc DMS MCLIP (020 7527 6903; e-mail: liz.roberts@islington.gov.uk)
Principal Librarian Ms V Dawson MCLIP BA(Lib) (020 7527 6907; e-mail: val.dawson@islington.gov.uk)
Principal Librarian B Redmond MCLIP (020 7527 6909; e-mail: brendan.redmond@islington.gov.uk)

Central/largest library

Central Library, 2 Fieldway Crescent, London N5 1PF
☎020 7527 6900 (enquiries), 020 7527 6905 (administration)
Fax 020 7527 6902
Principal Customer Services Manager Ms M Gibson MCLIP (020 7527 6915; e-mail: marilyn.gibson@islington.gov.uk)

Other libraries

- Archway Library, Hamlyn House, Highgate Hill, London N19 5PH
  ☎020 7527 7820
  Fax 020 7527 7833
- Arthur Simpson Library, Hanley Road, London N4 3DL
  ☎020 7527 7800
  Fax 020 7527 7808
- Finsbury Library, 245 St John Street, London EC1V 4NB
  ☎020 7527 7960
  Fax 020 7527 7998
- John Barnes Library, 275 Camden Road, London N7 0JN
  ☎020 7527 7900
  Fax 020 7527 7907
- Mildmay Library, 21-23 Mildmay Park, London N1 4NA
  ☎020 7527 7880
  Fax 020 7527 7898
- North Library, Manor Gardens, London N7 6JX
  ☎020 7527 7840
  Fax 020 7527 7854
- South Library, 115-117 Essex Road, London N1 2SL
  ☎020 7527 7860
  Fax 020 7527 7854
- West Library, Bridgeman Road, London N1 1BD
  ☎020 7527 7920
  Fax 020 7527 7929
- Lewis Carroll Library, 180 Copenhagen Street, London N1 0ST
  ☎020 7527 7936
  Fax 020 7527 7935

KENSINGTON AND CHELSEA

Authority Royal Borough of Kensington and Chelsea
HQ Central Library, Phillimore Walk, London W8 7RX

☎020 7937 2542 (general enquiries), 020 7361 3058 (management)
Fax 020 7361 2976
e-mail: christine.powell@rbkc.gov.uk
Head of Libraries and Arts J McEachen BSc MCLIP
Library Operations Manager Mrs I Pilkington MCLIP
Library Strategy Manager Ms I Lackajis BA MCLIP
Head of Bibliographical and Technical Services J Swindells MCLIP

Main libraries

- Central Library, Hornton Street, London W8 7RX
  ☎020 7937 2542
  Fax 020 7361 2976
- Chelsea Library, The Old Town Hall, Kings Road, London SW3 5EZ
  ☎020 7352 6056
- North Kensington Library, 108 Ladbroke Grove, London W11 1PZ
  ☎020 7727 6583
- Brompton Library, 210 Old Brompton Road, London SW5 0BS
  ☎020 7373 3111

KENT

Authority Kent County Council
HQ Arts and Libraries, Springfield, Maidstone, Kent ME14 2LH
☎(01622) 696517
Fax (01622) 690897
url: http://www.kent.gov.uk
Head of Arts and Libraries R Ward MLib MCLIP
Specialist Services Manager Vacant
Bibliographic Services Manager K Jarvis
Area Services Manager (East Kent) Ms P Tempest BA MCLIP/Ms J Bowie BA MCLIP
Area Services Manager (Mid Kent) Ms G Bromley MCLIP
Area Services Manager (West Kent) Ms S Sparks MCLIP

Central/largest library

County Central Library, Springfield, Maidstone, Kent ME14 2LH
☎(01622) 696511
Fax (01622) 753338
Information Services Manager Ms J Johnson MA DipLib
Principal Librarian Ms S Wheeler BA DipLib MCLIP
Public Services Supervisor Ms C Bristow

Main town centre libraries

- Ashford Library, Church Street, Ashford, Kent TN23 1QX
  ☎(01233) 620649
  Fax (01233) 620295
  Library Supervisor Ms L Jones
- Canterbury Library, High Street, Canterbury, Kent CT1 2JF
  ☎(01227) 463608

Fax (01227) 768338
Library Supervisor Ms L Catt

- Dartford Library, Central Park, Dartford, Kent DA1 1EU
  ☎(01322) 221133
  Fax (01322) 278271
  Library Supervisor Ms H Blackaby
- Dover Library, Maison Dieu House, Biggin Street, Dover, Kent CT16 1DW
  ☎(01304) 204241
  Fax (01304) 225914
  Library Supervisor Ms M Beatty
- Gravesend Library, Windmill Street, Gravesend, Kent DA12 1BE
  ☎(01474) 352758
  Fax (01474) 320284
  Library Supervisor Ms F Dutton
- Maidstone Library, St Faith's Street, Maidstone, Kent ME14 1LH
  ☎(01622) 752344
  Fax (01622) 754980
  Library Supervisor Ms M Griffiths
- Sevenoaks Library, Buckhurst Lane, Sevenoaks, Kent TN13 1LQ
  ☎(01732) 453118
  Fax (01732) 742682
  Library Supervisor Ms P Olive
- Shepway - Folkestone Library, 2 Grace Hill, Folkestone, Kent CT20 1HD
  ☎(01303) 850123
  Fax (01303) 242907
  Library Supervisor Ms C Cox
- Sittingbourne Library, Central Avenue, Sittingbourne, Kent ME10 4AH
  ☎(01795) 476545
  Fax (01795) 428376
  Library Supervisor Ms S Rees
- Thanet - Margate Library, Cecil Square, Margate, Kent CT9 1RE
  ☎(01843) 223626
  Fax (01843) 293015
  Library Supervisor Ms S Hannaford
- Tonbridge Library, Avebury Avenue, Tonbridge, Kent TN9 1TG
  ☎(01732) 352754
  Fax (01732) 358300
  Library Supervisor Ms A Bonny
- Tunbridge Wells Library, Mount Pleasant Road, Tunbridge Wells, Kent TN1 1NS
  ☎(01892) 522352
  Fax (01892) 514657
  Library Supervisor Ms J Taylor-Smith

Other town libraries

- Broadstairs Library, The Broadway, Broadstairs, Kent CT10 2BS
  ☎(01843) 862994

- Cranbrook Library, Carriers Road, Cranbrook, Kent TN17 3JT
  ☎(01580) 712463
- Deal Library, Broad Street, Deal, Kent CT14 6ER
  ☎(01304) 374726
- Faversham Library, Newton Road, Faversham, Kent ME13 8DY
  ☎(01795) 532448
- Herne Bay Library, 124 High Street, Herne Bay, Kent CT6 5JY
  ☎(01227) 374896
- Hythe Library, 1 Stade Street, Hythe, Kent CT21 6BQ
  ☎(01303) 267111
- Ramsgate Library, Guildford Lawn, Ramsgate, Kent CT11 9AY
  ☎(01843) 593532
- Sandwich Library, 13 Market Street, Sandwich, Kent CT13 9DA
  ☎(01304) 613819
- Sheerness Library, Russell Street, Sheerness, Kent ME12 1PL
  ☎(01795) 566100
- Swanley Library, London Road, Swanley, Kent BR8 7AE
  ☎(01322) 662570
- Tenterden Library, 55 High Street, Tenterden, Kent TN30 6BD
  ☎(01580) 762558
- Whitstable Library, 31-33 Oxford Street, Whitstable, Kent CT5 1DB
  ☎(01227) 273309

(Note: these do not represent the full list of branch libraries)

KINGSTON UPON HULL

Authority Kingston upon Hull City Council
HQ Central Library, Albion Street, Kingston upon Hull HU1 3TF
☎(01482) 210000 (enquiries), (01482) 616822 (administration)
Fax (01482) 616827
url: http://www.hullcc.gov.uk
Principal Libraries Officer Mrs J Edge BA DipLib (01482 616832; e-mail: jo.edge@hullcc.gov.uk)

Area libraries

- Anlaby Park Library, The Greenway, Anlaby High Road, Kingston upon Hull HU4 6TX
  ☎(01482) 505506
- Avenues Library, 76 Chanterlands Avenue, Kingston upon Hull HU5 3TS
  ☎(01482) 445912
  Fax (01482) 443764
- Bransholme Library, District Centre, Goodhart Road, Bransholme, Kingston upon Hull HU7 4EF
  ☎(01482) 826585
- Carnegie Library, Anlaby Road, Kingston upon Hull HU3 6JA
  ☎(01482) 352203
- Fred Moore Library, Wold Road, Derringham Bank, Kingston upon Hull HU5 5UN
  ☎(01482) 354765

- Garden Village Library, Shopping Centre, Garden Village, Kingston upon Hull HU8 8QE
  ☎(01482) 781723
- Gipsyville Library, 728-730 Hessle High Road, Kingston upon Hull HU4 6JA
  ☎(01482) 616973
- Greenwood Avenue Library, Greenwood Avenue, Kingston upon Hull HU6 9RU
  ☎(01482) 851180
- Harry Lewis Library, Annandale Road, Kingston upon Hull HU9 5HD
  ☎(01482) 784044
- Ings Library, Savoy Road, Kingston upon Hull HU8 0TX
  ☎(01482) 796201
- James Reckitt Library, Holderness Road, Kingston upon Hull HU9 1EA
  ☎(01482) 320015
- Kingswood Community Library, Wawne Road, Kingston upon Hull HU7 4WR
  ☎(01482) 878932
  Fax (01482) 878937
- Longhill Library, Shannon Road, Longhill Estate, Kingston upon Hull HU8 9RW
  ☎(01482) 815612
- Northern Library, Beverley Road, Kingston upon Hull HU3 1UP
  ☎(01482) 328397
- Preston Road Library, Preston Road, Kingston upon Hull HU9 5UZ
  ☎(01482) 376266
- Western Library, The Boulevard, Hessle Road, Kingston upon Hull HU3 3ED
  ☎(01482) 320399

KINGSTON UPON THAMES

Authority Royal Borough of Kingston upon Thames
HQ Kingston Library, Fairfield Road, Kingston upon Thames, Surrey KT1 2PS
☎020 8547 6413 (administration)
Fax 020 8547 6426
Assistant Director, Lifelong Leisure and Learning S Herbertson BA MA MCLIP (020 8547 5267; e-mail: scott.herbertson@rbk.kingston.gov.uk)
Head of Library Service Ms B Lee BA MCLIP (020 8547 6423; e-mail: barbara.lee@rbk.kingston.gov.uk)
ICT Development Manager M O'Brien (020 8547 6420; e-mail: mike.obrien@rbk.kingston.gov.uk)
Senior Team Librarian (Adult Services) Mrs E Ryder MCLIP (020 8547 6409)
Senior Team Librarian (Children's and Schools Library Service) M Treacy (020 8408 9100)
Lifelong Learning Manager Dr A Rizzo BA MA (020 8547 6421)

Branch libraries

- Kingston Library, Fairfield Road, Kingston upon Thames, Surrey KT1 2PS
  ☎020 8547 6400
  Fax 020 8547 6401
  Library Manager Ms S Gibson
- Hook and Chessington Library, Hook Road, Chessington, Surrey KT9 1EJ
  ☎020 8397 4931

Fax 020 8391 4410
Library Manager Ms R Fryer

- New Malden Library, Kingston Road, New Malden, Surrey KT3 3LY
  ☎020 8547 6540
  Fax 020 8547 6545
  Library Manager A Gale
- Old Malden Library, Church Road, Worcester Park, Surrey KT4 7RD
  ☎020 8337 6344
  Fax 020 8330 3118
  Library Manager Ms M Newman
- Surbiton Library, Ewell Road, Surbiton, Surrey KT6 6AG
  ☎020 8399 2331
  Fax 020 8339 9805
  Senior Library Manager Mrs J Allum
- Tolworth Community Library and IT Learning Centre, The Broadway, Tolworth, Surbiton, Surrey KT6 7DJ
  ☎020 8339 6950
  Fax 020 8339 6955
  e-mail: tolworth.library@rbk.kingston.gov.uk
  Library Manager Ms C Roberts
- Tudor Drive Library, Tudor Drive, Kingston upon Thames, Surrey KT2 5QH
  ☎020 8546 1198
  Fax 020 8547 2295
  Library Manager Ms S Montague
- Home and Mobile Library Service, Surbiton Library Annexe, Ewell Road, Surbiton, Surrey KT6 6AG
  ☎020 8339 7900
  Fax 020 8339 9805
  Library Manager Mrs I Abrahams

KIRKLEES

Authority Kirklees Metropolitan District Council
HQ Kirklees Cultural Services, Cultural Services HQ, Red Doles Lane, Huddersfield, West Yorkshire HD2 1YF
☎(01484) 226300
Fax (01484) 226342
e-mail: cultural-hq@geo2.poptel.org.uk
url: http://www.kirkleesmc.gov.uk
Head of Cultural Services J Drake MA AMA MILAM(Dip) FRGS MIFA (e-mail: jonathan.drake@kirkleesmc.gov.uk)
Assistant Head of Cultural Services (Libraries and Information) R Warburton BA MCLIP (e-mail: rob.warburton@kirkleesmc.gov.uk)

Central/largest library

Central Library, Princess Alexandra Walk, Huddersfield, West Yorkshire HD1 2SU
☎(01484) 226300

Fax (01484) 221952
Librarian i/c Ms C Morris BA DLIS MCLIP DMS

Area libraries

- Batley/Cleckheaton Area. Batley Library, Market Place, Batley, West Yorkshire WF17 5DA
  ☎(01924) 326305
  Librarian i/c Ms A Blakeley BA MCLIP DMS (e-mail: ann.blakeley@kirkleesmc.gov.uk)
- Dewsbury/Mirfield Area. Dewsbury Library, Railway Street, Dewsbury, West Yorkshire WF12 8EB
  ☎(01924) 325085
  Librarian i/c T Hobson BA MCLIP (e-mail: ted.hobson@kirkleesmc.gov.uk)
- West Kirklees Branches, Holmfirth Library, 47 Huddersfield Road, Holmfirth, West Yorkshire HD9 3JH
  ☎(01484) 222432
  Librarian i/c D Hatcher BSc DipLib MCLIP DMS (e-mail: david.hatcher@kirkleesmc.gov.uk)
- Mobiles and Home Service, Cultural Services HQ, Red Doles Lane, Huddersfield, West Yorkshire HD2 1YF
  ☎(01484) 226350
  Acting Librarian i/c A Peaden BA MCLIP (e-mail: alison.peaden@kirkleesmc.gov.uk)

KNOWSLEY

Authority Knowsley Metropolitan Borough Council
HQ Municipal Buildings, Archway Road, Huyton, Merseyside L36 9YX
☎0151 443 3680
Fax 0151 443 3492
url: www.knowsley.gov.uk
Head of Libraries P Marchant BH(Hons) DipLib DM MCLIP (e-mail: peter.marchant.dlcs@knowsley.gov.uk)

Central/largest library

Huyton Library, Civic Way, Huyton, Merseyside L36 9UN
☎0151 443 3738
Fax 0151 443 3739
Area Library Manager Mrs P Taylor BSc MCLIP

Branch libraries

- Kirkby Library, Newtown Gardens, Kirkby, Merseyside L32 8RR
  ☎0151 443 4289
  Fax 0151 546 1453
  Area Library Manager Miss G Hunter BA(Hons)
- Prescot Library, High Street, Prescot, Merseyside L34 3LD
  ☎0151 426 6449
  Fax 0151 430 7548
  Area Library Manager Miss S Stone BA MCLIP

- Halewood Library, Leathers Lane, Halewood, Merseyside L26 0TS
  ☎0151 486 4442
  Fax 0151 486 8101
  Area Library Manager Miss S Stone BA MCLIP
- Page Moss Library, Stockbridge Lane, Huyton, Merseyside L36 3SA
  ☎0151 489 9814
  Fax 0151 482 1309
  Area Library Manager Mrs P Taylor BSc MCLIP
- Stockbridge Village Library, The Withens, Stockbridge Village, Merseyside L28 1SU
  ☎0151 480 3925
  Fax 0151 480 3925
  Area Library Manager Mrs P Taylor BSc MCLIP
- Whiston Library, Dragon Lane, Whiston, Merseyside L3 3QW
  ☎0151 426 4757
  Fax 0151 493 0191
  Area Library Manager Miss S Stone BA MCLIP
- Stock Purchasing Unit, 599 Princess Drive, Huyton, Merseyside L14 9ND
  ☎0151 482 1302
  Fax 0151 482 1309

LAMBETH

Authority London Borough of Lambeth
HQ Lambeth Libraries and Archives, 3rd Floor, International House, Canterbury Crescent, London SW9 7QE
☎020 7926 0750 (enquiries)
Fax 020 7926 0751
Head of Libraries, Archives and Arts J Readman BA MA MCLIP

Area libraries

- Tate Library Brixton, Brixton Oval, London SW2 1JQ
  ☎020 7926 1056
  Fax 020 7926 1070
  Library Manager Ms M Bogle Mayne (e-mail: mboglemayne@lambeth.gov.uk)
- Vauxhall Group. Durning Library, 167 Kennington Lane, London SE11 4HF
  ☎020 7926 8682
  Fax 020 7926 8685
  Library Manager Ms S Winifred (e-mail: swinifred@lambeth.gov.uk)
- Streatham Group. Tate Library Streatham, 63 Streatham High Road, London SW16 1PL
  ☎020 7926 6768
  Fax 020 7926 5804
  Library Manager M Merson (e-mail: mmerson@lambeth.gov.uk)
- Clapham Library, 1 Northside, Clapham Common, London SW4 0QW
  ☎020 7926 0717 (tel/fax)
  Library Manager M Merson (e-mail: mmerson@lambeth.gov.uk)
- West Norwood Group. West Norwood Library, Norwood High Street, London SE27 9JX
  ☎020 7926 8092
  Fax 020 7926 8032

Library Manager Ms M Eaton BA(Hons), Ms C Tomlin BA MCLIP (e-mail: meaton@lambeth.gov.uk; ctomlin@lambeth.gov.uk)

Archives and Local History

Minet Archives and Library, 52 Knatchbull Road, London SE5 9QY
☎020 7926 6076
Fax 020 7926 6080
Archives and Library Manager Ms S McKenzie BA DAA, J Newman MA DAA (e-mail: smckenzie@lambeth.gov.uk; jnewman@lambeth.gov.uk)

Community Services Unit

(Mobile Libraries, Home Visit Service, Library Outreach Service), 3rd Floor, International House, Canterbury Crescent, London SW9 7QE
☎020 7926 0518
Fax 020 7926 0751
Development Manager, Social Inclusion Ms S Doyle MCLIP

Information Services Section

Lending and Reference Library, Tate Library Brixton, Brixton Oval, London SW2 1JQ
☎020 7926 1067
Fax 020 7926 1070
Principal Librarian, Reference Library D Kennedy
Manager, Lending and Reference Library Ms M Bogle Mayne

Support and Operations Unit

(Administration, Bibliographic Services, Library Computer Systems)
Lambeth Libraries and Archives, 4th Floor, Blue Star House, 234-244 Stockwell Road, London SW9 9SP
☎020 7926 6062/020 7926 0514
Fax 020 7926 0751
Support and Operations Manager Ms S Goodwin (e-mail: sgoodwin@lambeth.gov.uk)

Bibliographic Services Section

Carnegie Library, 188 Herne Hill Road, London SE24 0AG
☎020 7926 6068
Fax 020 7926 6072
Principal Librarian, Bibliographic Services Ms C Stockbridge-Bland BA MCLIP (e-mail: cstockbridgebland@lambeth.gov.uk)
Systems Manager Ms M Thomas BSc (e-mail: mthomas3@lambeth.gov.uk)

LANCASHIRE

Authority Lancashire County Council
HQ Education and Cultural Services Directorate, County Library Service, County Hall, PO Box 61, Preston, Lancs PR1 8RJ
☎(01772) 254868
Fax (01772) 264880
e-mail: library@lcl.lancscc.gov.uk

County Library Manager D G Lightfoot MA DMS MCLIP (01772 264010; e-mail: david.lightfoot@lcl.lancscc.gov.uk)
Bibliographic Services Manager D Blackett (based at Lancashire County Library, Bowran Street, Preston PR1 2UX; 01772 264091; fax 01722 264200; e-mail: david.blackett@lcl.lancscc.gov.uk)

Divisional libraries

- North Lancashire Division. Divisional Library, Market Square, Lancaster, Lancs LA1 1HY
  ☎(01524) 580700
  Fax (01524) 580706
  Divisional Librarian S J Eccles MCLIP
- Central Lancashire Division. Harris Library, Market Square, Preston, Lancs PR1 2PP
  ☎(01772) 404000
  Fax (01772) 404011
  Divisional Librarian Mrs L M Farnworth BA DMA MCLIP
- South Lancashire Division. Divisional Library, Union Street, Chorley, Lancs PR7 1EB
  ☎(01257) 277222
  Fax (01257) 231730
  Divisional Librarian D Whitham BSc MCLIP
- South East Lancashire Division. Divisional Library, St James' Street, Accrington, Lancs BB5 1NQ
  ☎(01254) 872385
  Fax (01254) 301066
  Acting Divisional Librarian P McKay BA DMS MCLIP
- East Lancashire Division. Divisional Library, Grimshaw Street, Burnley, Lancs BB11 2BD
  ☎(01282) 437115
  Fax (01282) 831682
  Divisional Librarian J D Hodgkinson BA MCLIP

LEEDS

Authority Leeds City Council
HQ Department of Leisure Services, The Town Hall, The Headrow, Leeds LS1 3AD
☎0113 247 8330 (management enquiries)
Fax 0113 247 8331
Head of Library and Information Services Ms C Blanshard BA MCLIP (e-mail: catherine.blanshard@leeds.gov.uk)

Library headquarters

Library Headquarters, 32 York Road, Leeds LS9 8TD
☎0113 214 3300 (general enquiries)
Fax 0113 214 3312
Head of Development Ms P Carroll BA MCLIP (e-mail: patricia.carroll@leeds.gov.uk)

Central/largest library

Central Library, Municipal Buildings, Calverley Street, Leeds LS1 3AB
☎0113 247 8274
Fax 0113 247 8268

url: http://www.leeds.gov.uk
Head of Service Provision Ms B Rice BA (e-mail: bev.rice@leeds.gov.uk)

LEICESTER

Authority Leicester City Council
HQ Education Department, Block A, New Walk Centre, Welford Place, Leicester LE1 6ZG
☎0116 252 6762 (administration)
Fax 0116 255 6048
e-mail: libraries@leicester.gov.uk
Head of Libraries and Information Services Ms P Flynn BA(Hons)
Libraries Manager A Wills BA DMS MCLIP (0116 252 7327; e-mail: willa002@leicester.gov.uk)
Network Quality & Development Manager Ms N Morgan BA MCLIP (0116 252 7337; e-mail: morgn001@leicester.gov.uk)
Inclusion and Diversity Manager Ms P Leahy BA(Hons) MCLIP (0116 252 7336)

Central/largest library

Central Lending Library, 54 Belvoir Street, Leicester LE1 6QL
☎0116 299 5402 (enquiries)
Fax 0116 299 5434
e-mail: central.lending@leicester.gov.uk
Central Libraries Manager M Maxwell BA DMS MCLIP

LEICESTERSHIRE

Authority Leicestershire County Council
HQ Libraries and Information Service HQ, County Hall, Glenfield, Leicester LE3 8SS
☎0116 265 7372 (enquiries), 0116 265 7380 (administration)
Fax 0116 265 7370
Chief Librarian P Oldroyd BA DipLib MCLIP DMS (poldroyd@leics.gov.uk)
Assistant Chief Librarian Ms M Bellamy MCLIP DMS MBA (e-mail: mbellamy@leics.gov.uk)
Support Services Manager P Love (e-mail: plove@leics.gov.uk)

District library HQs

- Hinckley Library, Lancaster Road, Hinckley, Leics LE10 0AT
  ☎(01455) 635106
  Fax (01455) 251385
  District Librarian N Thomas BLib(Hons) MCLIP
- Loughborough Library, Granby Street, Loughborough, Leics LE11 3DZ
  ☎(01509) 212985/266436
  Fax (01509) 610594
  District Librarian S Kettle BA DipLib DipMan MCLIP
- Wigston Library, Bull Head Street, Wigston, Leicester LE18 1PA
  ☎0116 288 7381/257 1891
  Fax 0116 281 2985
  District Librarian A Cooke BA MCLIP DMS

Market town libraries

- Coalville Library, High Street, Coalville, Leics LE67 3EA
  ☎(01530) 835951
  Fax (01530) 832019
  Senior Group Librarian Mrs J R StC Flint MLS MCLIP
- Melton Mowbray Library, Wilton Road, Melton Mowbray, Leics LE13 0UJ
  ☎(01664) 560161
  Fax (01664) 410199
  Senior Group Librarian Ms R J Pointer BA MCLIP
- Pen Lloyd Library, Adam & Eve Street, Market Harborough, Leics LE16 7LT
  ☎(01858) 821272
  Fax (01858) 821265
  Senior Group Librarian P Richardson MCLIP

LEWISHAM

Authority London Borough of Lewisham
HQ Education and Culture, 1st Floor, Town Hall Chambers, Catford, London SE6 4RU
☎020 8314 8024 (enquiries)
Fax 020 8314 3229
Head of Libraries and Information Ms J M Newton MCLIP (e-mail: julia.newton@lewisham.gov.uk)

Central/largest library

Lewisham Library, 199-201 Lewisham High Street, London SE13 6LG
☎020 8297 9677
Fax 020 8297 1169
Central Librarian Vacant

Neighbourhood library

Catford Library, Laurence House, Catford, London SE6 4RU
☎020 8314 6399
Fax 020 8314 1110
Neighbourhood Librarian M M Yarde

District library

Wavelengths Library, Giffin Street, Deptford, London SE8 4RJ
☎020 8694 2535
Fax 020 8694 9652
District Librarian G Englert

LINCOLNSHIRE

Authority Lincolnshire County Council
HQ Education and Cultural Services Directorate, County Offices, Newland, Lincoln, Lincs LN1 1YL
☎(01522) 553207
Fax (01522) 552811
Head of Libraries and Sport Ms L M Jubb BA (e-mail: lorraine.jubb@lincolnshire.gov.uk)

Central/largest library

Lincoln Central Library, Free School Lane, Lincoln, Lincs LN2 1EZ
☎(01522) 510800 (general enquiries), (01522) 579200 (management)
Fax (01522) 575011
e-mail: lincoln.library@dial.pipex.com
Service Manager Ms J E Adams BA DipLib MCLIP AMITD

Library Support Services, Brayford House, Lucy Tower Street, Lincoln, Lincs LN1 1XN
☎(01522) 552866
Fax (01522) 552858
Operations Manager R McInroy BA MCLIP (e-mail: mcinroyr@lincolnshire.gov.uk)

Special Services (Schools and Library Services to Centres), Brayford House, Lucy Tower Street, Lincoln, Lincs LN1 1XN
☎(01522) 552804
Fax (01522) 552858
Special Services Manager Ms V Wellington BA(Hons) DipLib MCLIP DMS MIM (e-mail: veronica.wellington@lincolnshire.gov.uk)

Area libraries

- North (Louth). Louth Library, Northgate, Louth, Lincs LN11 0LY
  ☎(01507) 602218
  Fax (01507) 608261
  Community Services Manager Ms G Fraser MA MCLIP (e-mail: fraserg@lincolnshire.gov.uk)
- Mid-Lincolnshire (Sleaford). Sleaford Library, Market Place, Sleaford, Lincs NG34 7SD
  ☎(01529) 414770
  Fax (01529) 415329
  Information Services Manager G Porter (e-mail: gary.porter@lincolnshire.gov.uk)

LIVERPOOL

Authority Liverpool City Council
HQ Liverpool Libraries and Information Services, 3rd Floor, Millennium House, 60 Victoria Street, Liverpool L1 6JH
☎0151 233 6346
Fax 0151 233 6399
Head of Libraries and Information Services Ms J H Little BA MBA MCLIP (e-mail: joyce.little@liverpool.gov.uk)
Manager (Central Library) Ms K Johnson (0151 233 5879; e-mail: kathy.johnson@liverpool.gov.uk)
Manager (Library Support Services) A Metcalf BSc DipLib MCLIP (0151 233 5808; e-mail: alan.metcalf@liverpool.gov.uk)
Manager (Community Libraries) R Travis (0151 233 5847; e-mail: ron.travis@liverpool.gov.uk)

Central/largest library

Central Library, William Brown Street, Liverpool L3 8EW

☎0151 233 5835 (enquiries), 0151 233 5851 (administration)
Fax 0151 233 5886 (enquiries), 0151 233 5824 (administration)
e-mail: refbt.central.library@liverpool.gov.uk
Manager Ms K Johnson

Other large libraries

- Allerton Library, Liverpool L18 6HG
  ☎0151 724 2987
  e-mail: allerton.library@liverpool.gov.uk
  Senior Community Librarian P Wallace
- Childwall Fiveways Library, Liverpool L15 6QR
  ☎0151 722 3214
  e-mail: childwall.library@liverpool.gov.uk
  Senior Community Librarian L Straughan BA DipLib MCLIP
- Norris Green Library, Townsend Avenue, Liverpool L11 5AF
  ☎0151 226 1714
  e-mail: norrisgreen.library@liverpool.gov.uk
  Senior Community Librarian A Johnson

LONDON, City of

Authority Corporation of London
HQ Guildhall Library, Aldermanbury, London EC2P 2EJ
☎020 7332 1852
Fax 020 7600 3384
Director D Bradbury MA MCLIP (e-mail: david.bradbury@corpoflondon.gov.uk)
Assistant Director (Libraries and Archives) Ms L Blundell BA MCLIP (e-mail: lesley.blundell@corpoflondon.gov.uk)
Assistant Director (Art Galleries and Support Services) B Cropper MA DipLib MCLIP MIMgt (e-mail: barry.cropper@corpoflondon.gov.uk)

Central/largest libraries

- Guildhall Library, Aldermanbury, London EC2P 2EJ
  ☎020 7332 1868
  Fax 020 7600 3384
  Librarian i/c Ms I F Gilchrist BD DipLib (e-mail: irene.gilchrist@corpoflondon.gov.uk)
- Barbican Library, Barbican Centre, Silk Street, London EC2Y 8DS
  ☎020 7638 0569
  Fax 020 7638 2249
  Librarian i/c J Lake BA MCLIP (e-mail: john.lake@corpoflondon.gov.uk)

Regional/district libraries

- Camomile Street Library, 12-20 Camomile Street, London EC3A 7EX
  ☎020 7247 8895
  Fax 020 7377 2972
  Librarian i/c M Key BA MCLIP (e-mail: malcolm.key@corpoflondon.gov.uk)
- City Business Library, 1 Brewers' Hall Garden, London EC2V 5BX
  ☎020 7332 1812
  Fax 020 7332 1847

Librarian i/c G P Humphreys MCLIP FRSA (e-mail: garry.humphreys@corpoflondon.gov.uk)

- St Bride Printing Library, Bride Lane, London EC4Y 8EE
  ☎020 7353 4660
  Fax 020 7583 7073
  Librarian i/c N Roche MA (e-mail: nigel.roche@corpoflondon.gov.uk)
- Shoe Lane Library, Hill House, Little New Street, London EC4A 3JR
  ☎020 7583 7178
  Fax 020 7353 0884
  Librarian i/c L King BA MCLIP (e-mail: leslie.king@corpoflondon.gov.uk)

LUTON

Authority Luton Borough Council
HQ Libraries Service, Central Library, St George's Square, Luton, Bedfordshire LU1 2NG
☎(01582) 547418/9 (enquiries), (01582) 547404 (administration)
Fax (01582) 547461
url: http://www.luton.gov.uk/library
Libraries Manager Ms J George BA DMS MCLIP (01582 547422; e-mail: georgej@luton.gov.uk)
Principal Librarian, Adult Services and Reader Development Ms F Marriott BA MCLIP (01582 547417; e-mail: marriottf@luton.gov.uk)
Principal Librarian, Luton Central R Evans BA MCLIP (01582 547424; e-mail: evansr@luton.gov.uk)
Principal Librarian, Information Services and Electronic Delivery Mrs L Cross BLib MCLIP (01582 547432)

Central/largest library

Central Library, St George's Square, Luton, Bedfordshire LU1 2NG
☎Tel/Fax etc. as HQ
Principal Librarian R Evans BA MCLIP (01582 547424; e-mail: evansr@luton.gov.uk)

Branch libraries

- Leagrave Library, Marsh Road, Luton, Bedfordshire LU3 2NL
  ☎(01582) 597851
  Library Manager Mrs D Boother
- Lewsey Library, Landrace Road, Luton, Bedfordshire LU4 0SW
  ☎(01582) 696094
  Library Manager Mrs S Saad
- Marsh Farm Library and Housebound Unit, Purley Centre, Luton, Bedfordshire LU3 3SR
  ☎(01582) 574803
  Library Manager Mrs L Lindars
- Stopsley Library, Hitchin Road, Luton, Bedfordshire LU2 7UG
  ☎(01582) 722791
  Library Manager Mrs M Woollison
- Sundon Park Library, Hill Rise, Luton, Bedfordshire LU3 3EE
  ☎(01582) 574573
  Library Manager Mrs A Soan

- Wigmore Library, Wigmore Lane, Luton, Bedfordshire LU3 8DJ
  ☎(01582) 455228
  Library Manager Mrs J Wigley

MANCHESTER

Authority Manchester City Council
HQ Central Library, St Peter's Square, Manchester M2 5PD
☎0161 234 1900
Fax 0161 234 1963
e-mail: mclib@libraries.manchester.gov.uk
Director of Libraries and Theatres Ms L Phelan BA MCLIP (e-mail: lisp@libraries.manchester.gov.uk)
Central Library Manager A Gallimore BSc MCLIP (e-mail: alecg@libraries.manchester.gov.uk)
District Libraries Manager Ms N Parker BA(Hons) MCLIP (e-mail: nicolap@libraries.manchester.gov.uk)

District libraries

- Central District HQ, Longsight Library, 519 Stockport Road, Manchester M12 4NE
  ☎0161 224 1411
  Fax 0161 225 2119
  Principal Officer Ms W Broadbent BA MCLIP (e-mail: wendyb@libraries.manchester.gov.uk)
- North District HQ, Crumpsall Library, Abraham Moss Centre, Manchester M8 5UF
  ☎0161 908 1900
  Fax 0161 908 1912
  Principal Officer Ms H Blagborough BSc DipLib MCLIP, Ms J Sharp BA DipLib MCLIP (e-mail: helenb@libraries.manchester.gov.uk; jsharp@libraries.manchester.gov.uk) (job-share)
- South District HQ, Wythenshawe Library, The Forum, Manchester M22 5RT
  ☎0161 935 4000
  Fax 0161 935 4039
  Principal Officer S Willis BA DipLib MCLIP (e-mail: stevew@libraries.manchester.gov.uk)
- Mobile Services, Hammerstone Road Depot, Gorton, Manchester M18 8EQ
  ☎0161 957 5900
  Fax 0161 957 5901
  Mobile Services Manager P Thompson (e-mail: pault@libraries.manchester.gov.uk)

MEDWAY

Authority Medway Council
HQ Education and Leisure Directorate, Civic Centre, Strood, Rochester, Kent ME2 4AU
☎(01634) 306000 (administration)
url: http://www.medway.gov.uk
Assistant Director, Leisure Mrs N Jones (01634 331013)
Libraries, Information and Museum Services Manager Ms G C Butler BA DipLib MCLIP

Adult Lending Services Manager Mrs K Woollacott MCLIP (01634 718161)
Reference, Archives and Local Studies Manager Mrs L Rainbow BA(Hons) MCLIP (01634 332714)

Central/largest libraries

- Chatham Library, Riverside, Chatham, Kent ME4 4SN
  ☎(01634) 843589
  Fax (01634) 827976
- Gillingham Library, High Street, Gillingham, Kent ME7 1BG
  ☎(01634) 281066
  Fax (01634) 855814

Town centre libraries

- Rainham Library, Birling Avenue, Rainham, Gillingham, Kent ME8 7LR
  ☎(01634) 231745
  Fax (01634) 263415
- Rochester Library, Northgate, Rochester, Kent ME1 1LU
  ☎(01634) 842415
  Fax (01634) 843837
- Strood Library, Bryant Road, Strood, Rochester, Kent ME2 3EP
  ☎(01634) 718161
  Fax (01634) 297919
- Medway Archives and Local Studies Centre, Civic Centre, Strood, Rochester, Kent ME2 4AU
  ☎(01634) 332714
  Fax (01634) 297060

MERTON

Authority London Borough of Merton
HQ Libraries and Heritage Services, Civic Centre, London Road, Morden, Surrey SM4 5DX
☎020 8545 3770
Fax 020 8545 3237
Head of Libraries and Heritage Services J Pateman BA DipLib MBA FCLIP (e-mail: john.pateman@merton.gov.uk)
Strategy and Commissioning Officers G Brewin MCLIP (020 8545 3773; e-mail: gordon.brewin@merton.gov.uk), S Durrani BA PGDip (020 8545 4061; e-mail: shiraz.durrani@merton.gov.uk)

Main libraries

- Mitcham Library, London Road, Mitcham, Surrey CR4 7YR
  ☎020 8648 4070
  Fax 020 8646 6360
  e-mail: mitcham.library@merton.gov.uk
  Library and Service Manager Mrs R Ahmad
- Morden Library, Civic Centre, London Road, Morden, Surrey SM4 5DX
  ☎020 8545 4040
  Fax 020 8545 4037

e-mail: morden.library@merton.gov.uk
Library and Service Manager Ms A Williams

- Wimbledon Library, Wimbledon Hill Road, London SW19 7NB
☎020 8946 7432/7979 (Reference and Information)
Fax 020 8944 6804
e-mail: wimbledon.library@merton.gov.uk
Library and Service Manager Ms P Rew BA DipLib MCLIP

MIDDLESBROUGH

Authority Middlesbrough Council
HQ Libraries and Information, Central Library, Victoria Square, Middlesbrough TS1 2AY
☎(01642) 263372 (administration)
Fax (01642) 263354
Head of Libraries and Information Miss C Mellor BSc(Econ) DipLib MCLIP (based at PO Box 134, 1st Floor, Civic Centre, Middlesbrough TS12YB; tel: 01642 262060; fax: 01642 263354; e-mail: chrys_mellor@middlesbrough.gov.uk)

Central/largest library

Central Library, Victoria Square, Middlesbrough TS1 2AY
☎(01642) 263397 (enquiries), (01642) 263372 (administration)
Fax (01642) 263354
Principal Librarian (Operations) Mrs J M Brittain BA (e-mail: jen_brittain@middlesbrough.gov.uk)
Principal Librarian (Resources) J Alder BA MCLIP (e-mail: jeremy_alder@middlesbrough.gov.uk)

MILTON KEYNES

Authority Milton Keynes Council
HQ Library Service, Central Library, 555 Silbury Boulevard, Saxon Gate East, Central Milton Keynes MK9 3HL
☎(01908) 254050
Fax (01908) 254089
url: http://www.mkweb.co.uk/library_services
Librarian Mrs T Carroll MCLIP (e-mail: teresa.carroll@milton-keynes.gov.uk)

Branch libraries HQ

Bletchley Library, Westfield Road, Bletchley, Milton Keynes MK2 2RA
☎(01908) 372797
Fax (01908) 645562
Librarian Mrs B Merrifield BA DipLib MCLIP

NEWCASTLE UPON TYNE

Authority Newcastle upon Tyne City Council
HQ City Library, Princess Square, Newcastle upon Tyne NE99 1DX
☎0191 277 4100
Fax 0191 277 4137

Head of Libraries and Information A J Durcan (e-mail: tony.durcan@newcastle.gov.uk)
Library and Information Manager (Citywide Services) A Wraight BA MCLIP DMS (e-mail: allan.wraight@newcastle.gov.uk)

Area libraries

- Gosforth Library (Central Group), Regent Farm Road, Gosforth, Newcastle upon Tyne NE3 1JN
  ☎0191 285 4244
  Area Library and Information Manager A Fletcher BA MCLIP (e-mail: andrew.fletcher@newcastle.gov.uk)
- Denton Park Library (Outer West Group), West Denton Way, West Denton, Newcastle upon Tyne NE5 2LF
  ☎0191 267 7922
  Area Library and Information Manager Ms E Burt MCLIP (e-mail: eileen.burt@newcastle.gov.uk)
- Fenham Library (Inner West Group), Fenham Hall Drive, Fenham, Newcastle upon Tyne NE4 9XD
  ☎0191 274 5837
  Area Library and Information Manager Ms E Michael MCLIP (e-mail: liz.michael@newcastle.gov.uk)
- Walker Library (East Group), Welbeck Road, Walker, Newcastle upon Tyne NE6 2PA
  ☎0191 265 7420
  Area Library and Information Manager Ms J Biggins BA MCLIP (e-mail: june.biggins@newcastle.gov.uk)

NEWHAM

Authority London Borough of Newham
HQ Library Management, Leisure Services Department, 292 Barking Road, East Ham, London E6 3BA
☎020 8430 2000 (switchboard), 020 8430 3994 (general enquiries)
Fax 020 8430 3921
Divisional Director, Leisure Services T Brill
Head of Library Service A Whittle BA(Hons) MCLIP (020 8430 2476; e-mail: adrian.whittle@newham.gov.uk)

Largest library

Stratford Library, 3 The Grove, Stratford, London E15 1EL
☎020 8430 6890
Library Manager M Blair

Branch libraries

- East Ham Library, High Street South, London E6 3EL
  ☎020 8430 3647
  Library Manager Ms A Scott
- Beckton Globe Library, 1 Kingsford Way, London E6 5JQ
  ☎020 8430 4063
  Library Manager Ms J Lee

NORFOLK

Authority Norfolk County Council
HQ Library and Information Service, County Hall, Martineau Lane, Norwich NR1 2UA
☎(01603) 222049
Fax (01603) 222422
e-mail: libraries@norfolk.gov.uk
url: http://www.library.norfolk.gov.uk
Director of Cultural Services T Turner BA DipLib (01603 223000; e-mail: terry.turner.lib@norfolk.gov.uk)
Head of Libraries Mrs J Holland BA(Hons) MCLIP (01603 222272; e-mail: jennifer.holland.lib@norfolk.gov.uk)
Head of Policy and Planning Miss S M Boden BA(Hons) MCLIP (01603 222271; e-mail: sue.boden.lib@norfolk.gov.uk)
Head of Finance and Administration J Perrott DMF (01603 222054; e-mail: john.perrott.lib@norfolk.gov.uk)
County Arts Officer Ms M Martin (01603 222269; e-mail: mari.martin.lib@norfolk.gov.uk)

Central/largest libraries

- Norfolk and Norwich Millennium Library, The Forum, Millennium Plain, Norwich NR2 1AW
  ☎(01603) 774774
  Fax (01603) 774705
  e-mail: millennium.lib@norfolk.gov.uk
  Area Librarian Ms J Holden BA DipLib MA
- Great Yarmouth Library, Tolhouse Street, Great Yarmouth, Norfolk NR30 2SH
  ☎(01493) 844551
  Fax (01493) 857628
  e-mail: yarmouth.lib@norfolk.gov.uk
  Area Librarian N Buxton MCLIP
- Gorleston Library, Lowestoft Road, Gorleston, Norfolk NR31 6SG
  ☎(01493) 662156
  Fax (01493) 446010
  e-mail: gorleston.lib@norfolk.gov.uk
  Area Librarian N Buxton MCLIP
- Thetford Library, Raymond Street, Thetford, Norfolk IP24 2EA
  ☎(01842) 752048
  Fax (01842) 750125
  e-mail: thetford.lib@norfolk.gov.uk
  Area Librarian Ms S Hassan BA(Hons) MA MCLIP
- King's Lynn Library, London Road, King's Lynn, Norfolk PE30 5EZ
  ☎(01553) 772568
  Fax (01553) 769832
  e-mail: kings.lynn.lib@norfolk.gov.uk
  Area Librarian D Stoney BA(Hons) DipLib MCLIP
- Dereham Library, Church Street, Dereham, Norfolk NR19 1DN
  ☎(01362) 693184

Fax (01362) 691891
e-mail: dereham.lib@norfolk.gov.uk
Area Librarian Ms S Hassan BA(Hons) MA MCLIP

Area library HQs

- Norwich Area, Norfolk and Norwich Millennium Library, The Forum, Millennium Plain, Norwich NR2 1AW
  ☎(01603) 774774
  Fax (01603) 774705
  e-mail: millennium.lib@norfolk.gov.uk
  Area Librarian Ms J Holden BA DipLib MA
- Great Yarmouth and Broadland Area, Wroxham Library, Norwich Road, Wroxham, Norfolk NR12 8RX
  ☎(01603) 782560
  Fax (01603) 783412
  e-mail: wroxham.lib@norfolk.gov.uk
  Area Librarian N Buxton MCLIP
- South Norfolk and Breckland Area, Attleborough Library, 31 Connaught Road, Attleborough, Norfolk NR17 2BW
  ☎(01953) 452319
  Fax (01953) 455196
  e-mail: attleborough.lib@norfolk.gov.uk
  Area Librarian Ms S Hassan BA(Hons) MA MCLIP
- King's Lynn and North Norfolk Area, Dersingham Library, Chapel Road, Dersingham, Norfolk PE31 6PN
  ☎(01485) 540181
  e-mail: dersingham.lib@norfolk.gov.uk
  Area Librarian D Stoney BA(Hons) DipLib MCLIP

NORTH EAST LINCOLNSHIRE

Authority North East Lincolnshire Council
HQ Central Library, Town Hall Square, Grimsby, North East Lincs DN31 1HG
☎(01472) 323600 (enquiries), (01472) 323617 (administration)
Fax (01472) 323618
url: http://www.nelincs.gov.uk
Head of Libraries A S Hipkins BA(Hons) MA DipLib MCLIP (01472 323611; e-mail: steve.hipkins@nelincs.gov.uk)
Strategy and Support Manager D A H Bell MCLIP (01472 323612; e-mail: david.bell@nelincs.gov.uk)
Principal Librarian (Customer Services) Mrs J Sargent BA DipLib (01472 323614; e-mail: joan.sargent@nelincs.gov.uk)
Resources Manager G Nugent BA(Hons) DipILM MCLIP (01472 323625; e-mail: gary.nugent@nelincs.gov.uk)
Finance and Administration Manager Mrs I Blow (01472 323616; e-mail: isola.blow@nelincs.gov.uk)

Branch libraries

- Cleethorpes Library, Alexandra Road, Cleethorpes, North East Lincs DN35 8LG
  ☎(01472) 323650
  Fax (01472) 323652
  Senior Library Supervisor Mrs S Staves
- Grant Thorold Library, Durban Road, Grimsby, North East Lincs DN32 8BX
  ☎(01472) 323631
  Library Supervisor Mrs L Wells
- Humberston Library, Church Lane, Humberston, North East Lincs DN36 4HZ
  ☎(01472) 323682
  Library Supervisor Mrs S Lawrence
- Immingham Library, Civic Centre, Pelham Road, Immingham, North East Lincs DN40 1QF
  ☎(01469) 516050
  Library Supervisor Mrs S Stokes
- Laceby Library, The Stanford Centre, Cooper Lane, Laceby, North East Lincs DN37 7AX
  ☎(01472) 323684
  Library Supervisor Mrs S Staves
- Nunsthorpe Library, Sutcliffe Avenue, Grimsby, North East Lincs DN33 1HA
  ☎(01472) 323636
  Library Supervisor J Radcliffe
- Scartho Library, St Giles Avenue, Grimsby, North East Lincs DN33 2HB
  ☎(01472) 323638
  Library Supervisor Mrs W Stark
- Waltham Library, High Street, Waltham, North East Lincs DN37 0LL
  ☎(01472) 323656
  Library Supervisor Mrs V Brunson
- Willows Library, Binbrook Way, Grimsby, North East Lincs DN37 9AS
  ☎(01472) 323679
  Library Supervisor Mrs S Owen
- Yarborough Library, Cromwell Road, Grimsby, North East Lincs DN31 2BX
  ☎(01472) 323658
  Library Supervisor Mrs P Turner

NORTH LINCOLNSHIRE

Authority North Lincolnshire Council
HQ Scunthorpe Central Library, Carlton Street, Scunthorpe, North Lincs DN15 6TX
☎(01724) 860161
Fax (01724) 860161
e-mail: ref.library@northlincs.gov.uk
url: http://www.northlincs.gov.uk/library/
Principal Librarian Mrs M Carr BA MCLIP (e-mail: margaret.carr@northlincs.gov.uk)

NORTH SOMERSET

Authority North Somerset Council
HQ Library and Information Service, Marketing and Leisure Department, PO Box 146, Town Hall, Weston-super-Mare, Somerset BS23 1LH

☎(01934) 634820
Fax (01934) 612006
url: http://www.foursite.somerset.gov.uk (online catalogue)
Libraries and Museum Manager Mrs J Petherbridge MCLIP DMS MIMgt (e-mail: jackie.petherbridge@n-somerset.gov.uk)

Area libraries

- Weston Library, The Boulevard, Weston-super-Mare, Somerset BS23 1PL
  ☎(01934) 636638 (enquiries), (01934) 620373 (administration)
  Fax (01934) 413046
  e-mail: weston.library@n-somerset.gov.uk
  South Area Library Manager N Kelly BA MCLIP DMS MIMgt (e-mail: nigel.kelly@n-somerset.gov.uk)
- Clevedon Library, 37 Old Church Road, Clevedon, Somerset BS21 6NN
  ☎(01275) 873498/874858
  Fax (01275) 343630
  e-mail: clevedon.library@n-somerset.gov.uk
  North Area Library Manager A Brisley BA MCLIP (e-mail: andy.brisley@n-somerset.gov.uk)

NORTH TYNESIDE

Authority North Tyneside Council
HQ Central Library, Northumberland Square, North Shields, Tyne and Wear NE30 1QU
☎0191 200 5424
Fax 0191 200 6118
e-mail: central.library@northtyneside.gov.uk
url: http://www.northtyneside.gov.uk/libraries/index
Libraries and Information Manager Mrs J Stafford BA MCLIP
East Area Libraries Manager P Bream BA MCLIP
West Area Libraries Manager Miss E Wiltshire BA MCLIP
Children and Young People Manager Mrs J Clements MBE BA MCLIP
Resources and Finance Manager Mrs L Bird

Main libraries

- Whitley Bay Library, Park Road, Whitley Bay, Tyne and Wear NE26 1EJ
  ☎0191 200 8500
  Fax 0191 200 8536
  e-mail: whitleybay.library@northtyneside.gov.uk
- Wallsend Library, Ferndale Avenue, Wallsend, Tyne and Wear NE28 7NB
  ☎0191 200 6968
  Fax 0191 200 6967
  e-mail: wallsend.library@northtyneside.gov.uk

NORTH YORKSHIRE

Authority North Yorkshire County Council
HQ County Library HQ, 21 Grammar School Lane, Northallerton, North Yorkshire DL6 1DF
☎(01609) 767800 (enquiries & administration)

Fax (01609) 780793
e-mail: libraries@northyorks.gov.uk
url: http://www.northyorks.gov.uk/libraries
Head of Libraries and Arts Ms J Blaisdale BA(Hons) MCLIP (e-mail: julie.blaisdale@northyorks.gov.uk)
Public Services Librarian M K Gibson BA MCLIP (e-mail: mike.gibson@northyorks.gov.uk)
Support Services Manager C Riley DMA ACIS MIPD (e-mail: chris.riley@northyorks.gov.uk)

Group headquarters

- Northallerton Group Library HQ, 1 Thirsk Road, Northallerton, North Yorkshire DL6 1PT
  ☎(01609) 767832
  Fax (01609) 780793
  e-mail: northallerton.libraryhq@northyorks.gov.uk
  Group Librarian Mrs R A Bullimore MCLIP
  Senior Library Assistant Ms J Stikans
- Scarborough Group Library HQ, Vernon Road, Scarborough, North Yorkshire YO11 2NN
  ☎(01723) 383400
  Fax (01723) 353893
  e-mail: scarborough.libraryhq@northyorks.gov.uk
  Group Librarian D Fay BA MCLIP
  Senior Library Assistants Ms C McGrath, Ms J Reed
- Harrogate Group Library HQ, Victoria Avenue, Harrogate, North Yorkshire HG1 1EG
  ☎(01423) 720320
  Fax (01423) 523158
  e-mail: harrogate.libraryhq@northyorks.gov.uk
  Group Librarian Ms I M Maynard MCLIP
  Senior Library Assistants Ms S Barker, Ms C Thompson
- Malton Group Library HQ, St Michael Street, Malton, North Yorkshire YO17 0LJ
  ☎(01653) 692714
  Fax (01653) 691200
  e-mail: malton.libraryhq@northyorks.gov.uk
  Group Librarian Miss B M Poole BA MCLIP
  Senior Library Assistant Ms N Stubbs
- Skipton Group Library HQ, High Street, Skipton, North Yorkshire BD23 1JX
  ☎(01756) 792926
  Fax (01756) 798056
  e-mail: skipton.libraryhq@northyorks.gov.uk
  Group Librarian Vacant
  Senior Library Assistant Ms J Crossley
- Sherburn Group Library HQ, Finkle Hill, Sherburn-in-Elmet, Leeds LS25 6EA
  ☎(01977) 681903
  Fax (01977) 685308
  e-mail: sherburn.libraryhq@northyorks.gov.uk
  Group Librarian D A Tanner BA MCLIP
  Senior Library Assistant Ms C Wright

Larger libraries

- Filey Library, Station Avenue, Filey, North Yorkshire YO14 9AE
  ☎(01723) 512328
  Fax (01723) 515786
  e-mail: filey.library@northyorks.gov.uk
  Senior Library Assistant Ms C Robinson
- Knaresborough Library, Market Place, Knaresborough, North Yorkshire HG5 8AG
  ☎(01423) 863054
  Fax (01423) 861539
  e-mail: knaresborough.library@northyorks.gov.uk
  Senior Library Assistant Ms L Barton
- Pickering Library, The Ropery, Pickering, North Yorkshire YO18 6DY
  ☎(01751) 472185
  Fax (01751) 476775
  e-mail: pickering.library@northyorks.gov.uk
  Senior Library Assistant Ms L Midgley
- Richmond Library, Queen's Road, Richmond, North Yorkshire DL10 4AE
  ☎(01748) 823120
  Fax (01748) 826977
  e-mail: richmond.library@northyorks.gov.uk
  Senior Library Assistant Ms P Todd
- Ripon Library, The Arcade, Ripon, North Yorkshire HG4 1AG
  ☎(01765) 604799
  Fax (01765) 608511
  e-mail: ripon.library@northyorks.gov.uk
  Senior Library Assistant Ms P Rumbold
- Selby Library, 52 Micklegate, Selby, North Yorkshire YO8 4EQ
  ☎(01757) 702020
  Fax (01757) 705396
  e-mail: selby.library@northyorks.gov.uk
  Senior Library Assistant Ms J Newton
- Stokesley Library, Manor House, Manor Close, Stokesley, Middlesbrough, North Yorkshire TS9 5AG
  ☎(01642) 711592
  e-mail: stokesley.library@northyorks.gov.uk
  Senior Library Assistant Ms L Smith
- Thirsk Library, Finkle Street, Thirsk, North Yorkshire YO7 1DA
  ☎(01845) 522268
  e-mail: thirsk.library@northyorks.gov.uk
  Senior Library Assistant Ms V Jacobs
- Whitby Library, Windsor Terrace, Whitby, North Yorkshire YO21 1ET
  ☎(01947) 602554
  Fax (01947) 820288
  e-mail: whitby.library@northyorks.gov.uk
  Senior Library Assistant Ms B Upton

(Note: These do not represent the full list of branch libraries. Please see our website for more details)

NORTHAMPTONSHIRE

Authority Northamptonshire County Council
HQ Libraries and Information Service, PO Box 216, John Dryden House, 8-10 The Lakes, Northampton NN4 7DD
☎(01604) 236236
Fax (01604) 237937
e-mail: nlis@northamptonshire.gov.uk
url: http://www.northamptonshire.gov.uk
County Libraries and Information Officer E W Wright MA BSocSci BPhil MCLIP (e-mail: ewright@northamptonshire.gov.uk)
Principal Libraries and Information Officer (Service Delivery) N L Matthews BA MCLIP DMS (e-mail: nmatthews@northamptonshire.gov.uk)
Principal Libraries and Information Officer (Service Development) Ms E L Jarvis BA MA DipLib DMS MCLIP (e-mail: ejarvis@northamptonshire.gov.uk)

Central/largest library

Central Library, Abington Street, Northampton, Northants NN1 2BA
☎(01604) 462040
Fax (01604) 462055
Central Library Manager Ms J Cox BLib MCLIP (e-mail: jcox@northamptonshire.gov.uk)

Area libraries

- Daventry Library, North Street, Daventry, Northants NN11 5PN
  ☎(01327) 703130
  Fax (01327) 300501
  Principal Librarian I J Clarke BA BSc MCLIP
- Kettering Library, Sheep Street, Kettering, Northants NN16 0AY
  ☎(01536) 512315
  Fax (01536) 411349
  Principal Librarian Ms A I Mercer BLS MCLIP
- Wellingborough Library, Pebble Lane, Wellingborough, Northants NN8 1AS
  ☎(01933) 225365
  Fax (01933) 442060
  Principal Librarian Mrs J M Sonpal BSc DipLIS MCLIP
- Weston Favell Library, Weston Favell Centre, Northampton, Northants NN3 8JZ
  ☎(01604) 403100
  Fax (01604) 403112
  Principal Librarian Mrs H Ward BA(Hons) MCLIP

NORTHUMBERLAND

Authority Northumberland County Council
HQ County Library HQ, The Willows, Morpeth, Northumberland NE61 1TA
☎(01670) 534501
Fax (01670) 534521 (administration)
url: http://www.northumberland.gov.uk
Divisional Director, Libraries, Arts and Heritage D E Bonser BA MCLIP

Central/largest library

County Library HQ, The Willows, Morpeth, Northumberland NE61 1TA
☎(01670) 534518 (lending); (01670) 534514 (reference)
Fax (01670) 534513
e-mail: amenities@northumberland.gov.uk

NOTTINGHAM

Authority City of Nottingham Council
HQ Department of Leisure and Community Services, Libraries, Information and Museums Services Division, 14 Hounds Gate, Nottingham NG1 7BD
☎0115 915 5555
Fax 0115 915 7200
e-mail: community_libraries.admin@nottinghamcity.gov.uk
Assistant Director, Libraries, Information and Museums Services B Ashley BA DipLib MCLIP (0115 915 7205)
Service Manager, Children's and Community Libraries Ms C Dyer BA MCLIP (0115 915 7240)

Central/largest library

Nottingham City Library, Angel Row, Nottingham NG1 6HP
☎0115 915 2828
Fax 0115 915 2850
e-mail: central_admin.library@nottinghamcity.gov.uk
Service Manager J P Turner BA MCLIP

NOTTINGHAMSHIRE

Authority Nottinghamshire County Council
HQ Community Services/Libraries, Archives and Information, 4th Floor, County Hall, West Bridgford, Nottingham NG2 7QP
☎0115 977 4401
Fax 0115 977 2428
Assistant Director (Libraries, Archives and Information) D Lathrope BSc DMS MCLIP (0115 977 4201; e-mail: david.lathrope@nottscc.gov.uk)
Principal Libraries Officer (Public Services, Operations and Quality) A J Cook BA MCLIP ALCM (0115 977 4437; e-mail: tony.cook@nottscc.gov.uk)
Principal Libraries Officer (Resources and Commissioning) A P Marshall BA MCLIP (0115 985 4201; e-mail: philip.marshall@nottscc.gov.uk)

Central/largest library

County Library, Four Seasons Centre, Westgate, Mansfield, Notts NG18 1NH
☎(01623) 627591 (enquiries), (01623) 653551 (administration)
Fax (01623) 629276
e-mail: mansfield.library@nottscc.gov.uk
Principal Librarian Mrs K Owen BA MCLIP

Group libraries

- North Nottinghamshire Group. County Library, Churchgate, Retford, Notts DN22 6PE

☎(01777) 708724
Fax (01777) 710020
e-mail: retford.library@nottscc.gov.uk
Principal Librarian Mrs L Turner BA MCLIP

- East Nottinghamshire Group. County Library, Beaumond Gardens, Baldertongate, Newark-on-Trent, Notts NG24 1UW
☎(01636) 703966
Fax (01636) 610045
e-mail: newark.library@nottscc.gov.uk
Principal Librarian R A J Vinnicombe MCLIP DMA
- West Nottinghamshire Group. County Library, Four Seasons Centre, Westgate, Mansfield, Notts NG18 1NH
☎(01623) 627591
Fax (01623) 629276
e-mail: mansfield.library@nottscc.gov.uk
Principal Librarian Mrs K Owen BA MCLIP
- Central Nottinghamshire Group. County Library, Front Street, Arnold, Nottingham NG5 7EE
☎0115 920 2247
Fax 0115 967 3378
e-mail: arnold.library@nottscc.gov.uk
Principal Librarian R S Jones BA MCLIP
- South Nottinghamshire Group. County Library, Foster Avenue, Beeston, Nottingham NG9 1AE
☎0115 925 5168/925 5084
Fax 0115 922 0841
e-mail: beeston.library@nottscc.gov.uk
Principal Librarian S I Robertson BA MCLIP

Other services

Support Services, Units 4-6, Glaisdale Parkway, Bilborough, Nottingham NG8 4GP
☎0115 985 4242
Fax 0115 928 6400
Principal Bibliographical Officer, Support Services Ms A Corin BA MCLIP (0115 985 4208; e-mail: anne.corin@nottscc.gov.uk)
Principal Systems Officer, Support Services N London MCLIP (0115 985 5172; e-mail: nick.london@nottscc.gov.uk)

OLDHAM

Authority Oldham Metropolitan Borough Council
HQ Oldham Library, Union Street, Oldham, Lancs OL1 1DN
☎0161 911 4645 (general enquiries)
Fax 0161 911 4630
e-mail: ecs.reference.lib@oldham.gov.uk
url: http://www.oldham.gov.uk
Head of Libraries, Information and Archives R J Lambert BA MA MCLIP (0161 911 4632; fax 0161 911 3222; e-mail: ecs.richard.lambert@oldham.gov.uk)

OXFORDSHIRE

Authority Oxfordshire County Council
HQ Cultural Services, Central Library, Westgate, Oxford OX1 1DJ
☎(01865) 810191
Fax (01865) 810187
Director D R Munro BA DipLib MCLIP (e-mail: richard.munro@oxfordshire.gov.uk)
County Librarian A Coggins MA MA(Lib) MCLIP (Based at Cultural Services, Holton, Oxford OX33 1QQ; 01865 810212; fax 01865 810205; e-mail: andrew.coggins@oxfordshire.gov.uk)

Central/largest library

Central Library, Westgate, Oxford OX1 1DJ
☎(01865) 815549
Fax (01865) 721694
e-mail: centlib.occdla@dial.pipex.com

Additional services

Performance and Development

Cultural Services, Holton, Oxford OX33 1QQ
☎(01865) 810234
Fax (01865) 810207
Assistant County Librarian R Harris MA DipLib MCLIP (e-mail: rex.harris@oxfordshire.gov.uk)

Operations

Cultural Services, Holton, Oxon OX33 1QQ
☎(01865) 810247
Fax (01865) 810205
Assistant County Librarian Mrs Y McDonald BA DMS DipLib MCLIP (e-mail: yvonne.mcdonald@oxfordshire.gov.uk)

Information Services and Lifelong Learning

Cultural Services, Holton, Oxford OX33 1QQ
☎(01865) 810221
Fax (01865) 810205
Assistant County Librarian C Pettit MA MA(Lib) MCLIP (e-mail: charles.pettit@oxfordshire.gov.uk)

PETERBOROUGH

Authority Peterborough City Council
HQ Community Services: Libraries, Central Library, Broadway, Peterborough PE1 1RX
☎(01733) 742700
Fax (01733) 319140
e-mail: libraries@peterborough.gov.uk
url: http://www.peterborough.gov.uk

Library Service Manager Mrs E Jewell BA MCLIP (01733 742700; e-mail: elaine.jewell@peterborough.gov.uk)
Customer Services Manager R Hemmings BA MCLIP DMS MIMgt DipM MCIM (e-mail: richard.hemmings@peterborough.gov.uk)
Outreach Services Manager Miss B D Lofthouse MCLIP (e-mail: barbara.lofthouse@peterborough.gov.uk)
Reader Services Manager Ms H Walton (e-mail: heather.walton@peterborough.gov.uk)
Enquiry Services Manager Vacant

District libraries

- Werrington Library, Staniland Way, Werrington, Peterborough PE4 6JT
  ☎(01733) 576666
  Manager Mrs S Rampal
- Bretton Library, Bretton Centre, Bretton, Peterborough PE3 8DS
  ☎(01733) 265519
  Manager Mrs V Hindocha
- Orton Library, Orton Centre, Orton, Peterborough PE2 0RQ
  ☎(01733) 234448
  Manager M Norman

PLYMOUTH

Authority Plymouth City Council
HQ Library and Information Services, Central Library, Drake Circus, Plymouth PL4 8AL
☎(01752) 305923 (enquiries and administration)
Fax (01752) 305929
e-mail: library@plymouth.gov.uk
url: http://www.plymouthlibraries.info; www.plymouth.gov.uk/star/library.htm; www.webopac.plymouth.gov.uk
City Librarian A MacNaughtan BA MCLIP DMS MIMgt (01752 305901)
Support and Development Librarian F Lowry MCLIP (01752 305911)
Resources and Information Manager C Goddard BMus DipLib MCLIP (01752 305900)
Public Services Librarian B Holgate MCLIP (01752 306790)
Coordinator of Library Services to Young People Ms S Walsh BA MCLIP, Ms A Gerrard BA MCLIP (01752 306798, job-share)

POOLE

Authority Borough of Poole
HQ Cultural Services, Central Library, Dolphin Centre, Poole BH15 1QE
☎(01202) 262437
Fax (01202) 262431
Head of Cultural Services Ms C Chidley BA MA MBA (e-mail: c.chidley@poole.gov.uk)

Central/largest library

Central Library, Dolphin Centre, Poole BH15 1QE
☎(01202) 262437
e-mail: poolelibrary@poole.gov.uk

Healthpoint (health information centre also serving Dorset)
e-mail: healthpoint@poole.gov.uk
Librarian Mrs V Grier BA ALA (01202 262436)

PORTSMOUTH

Authority Portsmouth City Council
HQ Library Service, Central Library, Guildhall Square, Portsmouth PO1 2DX
☎023 9281 9311
Fax 023 9283 9855
e-mail: library.admin@portsmouthcc.gov.uk
Library Service Manager C Brown MCLIP

Group libraries

- North Group. Cosham Library, Spur Road, Portsmouth PO6 3EB
  ☎023 9237 6023
  Fax 023 9266 8151
  e-mail: cosham.library@portsmouthcc.gov.uk
- South Group. North End Library, Gladys Avenue, North End, Portsmouth PO2 9AX
  ☎023 9266 2651
  Fax 023 9237 1877
  e-mail: northend.library@portsmouthcc.gov.uk

READING

Authority Reading Borough Council
HQ Reading Central Library, Abbey Square, Reading, Berks RG1 3BQ
☎0118 901 5950
Fax 0118 901 5954
e-mail: info@readinglibraries.org.uk
Head of Libraries A Kennedy BA(Hons) DMS MCLIP (0118 901 5964)
Library Services Manager R Thomas BA DipLib MCLIP (0118 901 5940)
Stock and System Manager Ms A England BA(Hons) DipLib MCLIP (0118 901 5962)
Senior Reference Librarian D Cliffe BA MCLIP (0118 901 3315)
Senior Lending Librarian Mrs E Delaney MCLIP (0118 901 3307)
Senior Branch Manager: Reading Libraries B Holder (0118 901 5947)

Branch libraries

- Battle Library, 420 Oxford Road, Reading, Berks RG3 1EE
  ☎0118 901 5100
  Branch Manager Mrs M McClure
- Caversham Library, Church Street, Caversham, Reading, Berks RG4 8AU
  ☎0118 901 5103
  Branch Manager Mrs J Jones
- Palmer Park Library, St Bartholomew's Road, Reading, Berks RG1 3QB
  ☎0118 901 5106
  Branch Manager Miss C Gosling
- Southcote Library, Southcote Lane, Reading, Berks RG3 3BA

☎0118 901 5109
Branch Manager Mrs E Long

- Tilehurst Library, School Road, Tilehurst, Reading, Berks RG3 5AS
☎0118 901 5112
Branch Manager Mrs J Brant
- Whitley Library, Northumberland Avenue, Reading, Berks RG2 7PX
☎0118 901 5115
Branch Manager Mrs C Kelly
- Mobile Library Services, c/o Tilehurst Library, School Road, Tilehurst, Reading, Berks RG3 5AS
☎0118 901 5118
Services Manager Mrs A Clift

REDBRIDGE

Authority London Borough of Redbridge
HQ Central Library, Clements Road, Ilford, Essex IG1 1EA
☎020 8478 7145
Fax 020 8553 3299
Chief Librarian M Timms BA MCLIP (020 8708 2436; e-mail: martin.timms@redbridge.gov.uk)
Central Library Manager P Ledger MCLIP (020 8708 2438; e-mail: peter.ledger@redbridge.gov.uk)
Development Officer Mrs M Barratt BA MCLIP DipLaw (020 8708 2425; e-mail: madeline.barratt@redbridge.gov.uk); Mrs C Clarke BA MCLIP (020 8708 2425; e-mail: carol.clarke@redbridge.gov.uk)

Community library

Aldersbrook Library, 2a Park Road, London E12 5HQ
☎020 8989 9319
Branch Librarian Ms L Hubbard BA DipLib MCLIP (020 8989 9462; e-mail: linda.hubbard@redbridge.gov.uk)

Branch libraries

- Fullwell Cross Library, 140 High Street, Barkingside, Ilford, Essex IG6 2EA
☎020 8550 4457
Branch Librarian Mrs M Barratt BA MCLIP DipLaw, Ms C Clarke BA MCLIP (e-mail: madeline.barratt@redbridge.gov.uk; carol.clarke@redbridge.gov.uk)
- Gants Hill Library, 490 Cranbrook Road, Gants Hill, Ilford, Essex IG2 6LA
☎020 8554 5211
Branch Librarian J Weeks MCLIP (e-mail: john.weeks@redbridge.gov.uk)
- Goodmayes Library, 76 Goodmayes Lane, Goodmayes, Ilford, Essex IG3 9QB
☎020 8590 8362
Branch Librarian Mrs A Brolly BA MCLIP (e-mail: anne.brolly@redbridge.gov.uk)
- Hainault Library, 100 Manford Way, Chigwell, Essex IG7 4DD
☎020 8500 1204
Branch Librarian Mrs E Reid BA MCLIP (e-mail: evelyn.reid@redbridge.gov.uk)
- South Woodford Library, 116 High Road, London E18 2QS

☎020 8504 1407
Branch Librarian Mrs G Pote BA MA MCLIP (e-mail: geraldine.pote@redbridge.gov.uk)

- Wanstead Library, Spratt Hall Road, London E11 2RQ
☎020 8989 9462
Branch Librarian Ms L Hubbard BA DipLib MCLIP (e-mail: e-mail: linda.hubbard@redbridge.gov.uk)
- Woodford Green Library, Snakes Lane, Woodford Green, Essex IG8 0DX
☎020 8504 4642
Branch Librarian A Black LLB DipLib MCLIP (e-mail: archie.black@redbridge.gov.uk)

REDCAR AND CLEVELAND

Authority Redcar and Cleveland Borough Council
HQ Department of Neighbourhood Services, Redcar and Cleveland House, PO Box 86, Kirkleatham Street, Redcar, Cleveland TS10 1XX
☎(01642) 444000
Fax (01642) 444341
Assistant Director, Advice and Information Mrs C Barnes BA DipLib (01642 444357)
Resource Services Officer Mrs C Zellweger BA MCLIP (01642 444321)
Stock Management Officer Mrs J Allinson (01642 444263)

Central/largest library

Central Library, Coatham Road, Redcar, Cleveland TS10 1RP
☎(01642) 472162
Fax (01642) 492253
Lending Services Officer I L Wilson BA MCLIP (01642 489163)

RICHMOND UPON THAMES

Authority London Borough of Richmond upon Thames
HQ Department of Education, Arts and Leisure, First Floor, Regal House, London Road, Twickenham, Middlesex TW1 3QB
☎020 8831 6136
Fax 020 8891 7904
e-mail: libraries@richmond.gov.uk
url: http://www.richmond.gov.uk/libraries
Chief Libraries and Arts Officer Ms C Taylor
Assistant Chief Librarian (Information Services) Vacant
Assistant Chief Librarian (Lending Services and Promotions) Ms S Harden BA MCLIP (e-mail: s.harden@richmond.gov.uk)

Central/largest library

Richmond Lending Library, Little Green, Richmond, Surrey TW9 1QL
☎020 8940 0981/6857
Fax 020 8940 7516
e-mail: richmond.library@richmond.gov.uk
Customer Services Manager L Cranfield MCLIP (e-mail: l.cranfield@richmond.gov.uk)

Branch libraries

- Twickenham Library, Garfield Road, Twickenham, Middlesex TW1 3JT
  ☎020 8892 8091
  e-mail: twickenham.library@richmond.gov.uk
- Teddington Library, Waldegrave Road, Teddington, Middlesex TW11 8LG
  ☎020 8977 1284
  e-mail: teddington.library@richmond.gov.uk
- East Sheen Library, Sheen Lane, London SW14 8LP
  ☎020 8876 8801
  e-mail: eastsheen.library@richmond.gov.uk
- Central Reference Library, Old Town Hall, Whitaker Avenue, Richmond, Surrey TW9 1TP
  ☎020 8940 5529/9125
  Fax 020 8940 6899
  e-mail: reference.services@richmond.gov.uk
  Central Reference Librarian Ms J Hall BA DipLib MCLIP DMS

ROCHDALE

Authority Rochdale Metropolitan Borough Council
HQ Wheatsheaf Library, Wheatsheaf Shopping Centre, Baillie Street, Rochdale, Greater Manchester OL16 1JZ
☎(01706) 864900 (enquiries), (01706) 864911 (administration)
Fax (01706) 864992
Principal Librarian Mrs S M Sfrijan MCLIP (01706) 864929
Bibliographical and Special Services Librarian Mrs F Fletcher MCLIP (01706 864964)
Reference and Information Development Librarians Mrs H M Haynes MCLIP, D L Martin MIPD MCLIP (01706 864989) (job-share)
Area Librarian (Rochdale) (based at Wheatsheaf Library) Vacant (01706 864976)

Main libraries

- Heywood Library, Church Street, Heywood, Greater Manchester OL10 1LL
  ☎(01706) 360947
  Fax (01706) 368683
  Area Librarian A Boughey
- Middleton Library, Long Street, Middleton, Greater Manchester M24 6DU
  ☎0161 643 5228
  Fax 0161 654 0745
  Area Librarian A Boughey

ROTHERHAM

Authority Rotherham Metropolitan Borough Council
HQ Central Library, Walker Place, Rotherham, South Yorkshire S65 1JH
☎(01709) 823611 (enquiries), (01709) 823623 (management)
Fax (01709) 823650 (enquiries), (01709) 823653 (management)
e-mail: central.library@rotherham.gov.uk
Libraries, Museums and Arts Manager G Kilminster BA(Hons) FMA (e-mail: guy.kilminster@rotherham.gov.uk)
Manager, Library and Information Service K Robinson MCLIP (01709 823699)

RUTLAND

Authority Rutland County Council
HQ Rutland County Library, Catmose Street, Oakham, Rutland LE15 6HW
☎(01572) 722918 (enquiries), (01572) 758434 (administration)
Fax (01572) 724906 (enquiries), (01572) 758403 (administration)
url: http://www.rutnet.co.uk/libraries
Head of Cultural Services R Knight BA MCLIP (e-mail: rknight@rutland.gov.uk)

Community libraries

- Uppingham Library, Queen Street, Uppingham, Rutland LE15 9QR
  ☎(01572) 823218
- Ketton Library, High Street, Ketton, Stamford, Lincs PE9 3TE
  ☎(01780) 720586
- Ryhall Library, Coppice Road, Ryhall, Stamford, Lincs PE9 4HY
  ☎(01780) 751726

ST HELENS

Authority Metropolitan Borough of St Helens
HQ Community Education and Leisure Services Department, The Rivington Centre, Rivington Road, St Helens, Merseyside WA10 4ND
☎(01744) 456989 (enquiries & administration)
Fax (01744) 20836
e-mail: criv@sthelens.gov.uk
Assistant Director (Community Education and Leisure Services) Mrs D A Bradley BSc(Hons) MCLIP DMS (01744 455300; fax 01744 455497; e-mail: dorothybradley@sthelens.gov.uk)

Central/largest library

Central Library, The Gamble Building, Victoria Square, St Helens, Merseyside WA10 1DY
☎(01744) 456950
Fax (01744) 20836
e-mail: criv@sthelens.gov.uk
Central Library Manager S Pindard (01744 456955)

SALFORD

Authority Salford City Council
HQ Education and Leisure Directorate, Minerva House, Pendlebury Road, Swinton, Salford M27 4EQ
☎0161 778 0141
Fax 0161 728 6234
url: http://www.salford.gov.uk/library
Libraries and Information Service Manager Ms S Spence BA(Hons) MCLIP (0161 793 3571; fax 0161 727 7071; e-mail: sarah.spence@salford.gov.uk)

Main libraries

- Swinton Library, Chorley Road, Swinton, Salford M27 4AE

☎0161 793 3560
Fax 0161 727 7071
Divisional Librarian C Farey BA(Hons) DipLIS DBA MCLIP (e-mail: chris.farey@salford.gov.uk)

- Eccles Library, Church Street, Eccles, Salford M30 0EP
  ☎0161 789 1430
  Fax 0161 787 8430
  Divisional Librarian Ms R Farnworth DBA MCLIP (e-mail: rosemary.farnworth@salford.gov.uk)
- Walkden Library, Memorial Road, Walkden, Salford M28 3AQ
  ☎0161 790 4579
  Fax 0161 703 8971
  Senior Librarian C Carson BA DMS MCLIP (e-mail: chris.carson@salford.gov.uk)
- Broadwalk Library, Broadwalk, Salford M6 5FX
  ☎0161 737 5802
  Fax 0161 745 9157
  Senior Librarian Mrs J Stonebanks BA(Hons) DMS (e-mail: julie.stonebanks@salford.gov.uk)

SANDWELL

Authority Sandwell Metropolitan Borough Council
HQ Education and Lifelong Learning, Shaftesbury House, PO Box 41, 402 HIgh Street, West Bromwich, West Midlands B70 9LT
☎0121 569 2200
Fax 0121 525 4648
e-mail: library.service@sandwell.gov.uk
url: http://www.kea.sandwell.gov.uk/libraries
Chief Librarian K W Heyes BA MBA MCLIP

Central/largest library

Central Library, High Street, West Bromwich, West Midlands B70 8DZ
☎0121 569 4904
Fax 0121 525 9465
Principal Libraries Officer (Information Services) Ms H Vickerman (0121 569 4906)

Additional services

- Community History and Archives Service, Smethwick Library, High Street, Smethwick, West Midlands B66 1AB
  ☎0121 558 2561
  Fax 0121 555 6064
- Special Needs Library Service, 63 Crosswells Road, Oldbury, West Midlands B68 8HH
  ☎0121 552 4136
  Fax 0121 569 9465
  Principal Libraries Officer (Specialist Services) Ms P Fouracres BA(Hons) MA MCLIP
- Library Support Services, Town Hall, High Street, West Bromwich, West Midlands B70 8DX

☎0121 569 4909
Fax 0121 569 4907
e-mail: dm025@viscount.org.uk
Principal Libraries Officer (Library Support Services) B Clark BLib MCLIP

- Community Libraries, c/o Central Library, High Street, West Bromwich, West Midlands B70 8DZ
☎0121 569 4922
Fax 0121 525 9465
Principal Libraries Officer (Community Libraries) A Piorowski MCLIP (0121 569 4922)

SEFTON

Authority Sefton Metropolitan Borough Council
HQ Leisure Services Department, Pavilion Buildings, 99-105 Lord Street, Southport PR8 1RH
☎0151 934 2381
Fax 0151 934 2370
e-mail: library.service@leisure.sefton.gov.uk
Head of Library and Information Services J Hilton MCLIP
Principal Library Services Officer (North) Mrs J E Stanistreet MA MCLIP
Principal Library Services Officer (South) Ms M Wall BA DMS MCLIP

Central/largest libraries

- Southport Library, Lord Street, Southport PR8 1DJ
☎0151 934 2118
Fax 0151 934 2115
Librarian Mrs V Owen BA MCLIP
- Crosby Library, Crosby Road North, Waterloo, Liverpool L22 0LQ
☎0151 257 6400
Fax 0151 330 5770
Librarian Miss L Roberts BA MCLIP

SHEFFIELD

Authority Sheffield City Council
HQ Sheffield Libraries, Archives and Information Services, Central Library, Surrey Street, Sheffield S1 1XZ
☎0114 273 4711/2 (enquiries), 0114 273 5052 (library management)
Fax 0114 273 5009
e-mail: sheffield.libraries@dial.pipex.com
City Librarian Ms J Maskort BA(Hons) MCLIP DMS (e-mail: janice.maskort@sheffield.gov.uk)
Group Manager, Central Circulation Services Ms J Adam MA DipLib MCLIP (0114 273 6645)
Group Manager, Archives and Local Studies Services Vacant (0224 273 4753)
Group Manager, Community Information and Bibliographic Services H Matthew BA MA MCLIP (0114 273 4254)
Group Manager, Central Information Services J Murphy BSc(Hons) MA (0114 273 6645)

Group Manager, North Ms A Jobey BA MCLIP (0114 203 7121)
Group Manager, South P Barr BA (0114 203 7700)
Policy and Development Manager M Dutch BA(Hons) DipLib (0114 203 7202)
Group Manager, Mobile Services Ms R Telfer BA(Hons) DipLib MCLIP (0114 273 4277)
Lifelong Learning Manager D Isaac BA(Hons) DipLib DMS

District libraries

- Broomhill Library, Taptonville Road, Sheffield S10 5BR
  ☎0114 273 4276
- Chapeltown Library, Nether Ley Avenue, Sheffield S35 1AE
  ☎0114 203 7000/1
- Darnall Library, Britannia Road, Sheffield S9 5JG
  ☎0114 203 7429
- Firth Park Library, 443 Firth Park Road, Sheffield S5 6QQ
  ☎0114 203 7433
- Hillsborough Library, Middlewood Road, Sheffield S6 4HD
  ☎0114 203 9529
- Manor Library, Ridgeway Road, Sheffield S12 2SS
  ☎0114 203 7805
- Crystal Peaks Library, 3 Peak Square, Crystal Peaks Complex, Waterthorpe, Sheffield S20 7PH
  ☎0114 248 1127
- Woodseats Library, Chesterfield Road, Sheffield S8 0SH
  ☎0114 274 9149
- Mobile Services, 443 Handsworth Road, Sheffield S13 9DD
  ☎0114 273 4277
- Highfield Library, London Road, Sheffield S2 4NF
  ☎0114 203 7204
- Stocksbridge Library, Manchester Road, Stocksbridge, Sheffield S36 1DH
  ☎0114 273 4205
- Totley Library, 205 Baslow Road, Sheffield S17 4DT
  ☎0114 236 3067

SHROPSHIRE

Authority Shropshire County Council
HQ Library and Information Services, Community and Environment Directorate, The Shirehall, Abbey Foregate, Shrewsbury, Shropshire SY2 6ND
☎(01743) 255000
Fax (01743) 255001
e-mail: libraries@shropshire-cc.gov.uk
url: http://www.shropshire-cc.gov.uk/library.nsf
Head of Library and Information Services J Roads BA MCLIP (e-mail: jim.roads@shropshire-cc.gov.uk)
Principal Librarian – Development and Support D Yuile BA MCLIP (e-mail: don.yuile@shropshire-cc.gov.uk)
Principal Librarian – Young People and Access G Dickins BA MCLIP (e-mail: gordon.dickins@shropshire-cc.gov.uk)

Central/largest library

- Castle Gates Library, Shrewsbury, Shropshire SY1 2AS
  ☎(01743) 255300
  Fax (01743) 255309
  Principal Librarian – Shrewsbury Ms E Moss MCLIP (e-mail: elaine.moss@shropshire-cc.gov.uk)
- Reference and Information Service, 1a Castle Gates, Shrewsbury, Shropshire SY1 2AQ
  ☎(01743) 255380
  Fax (01743) 255383
  Principal Librarian – Shrewsbury Ms E Moss MCLIP (e-mail: elaine.moss@shropshire-cc.gov.uk)

Area libraries

- North Area. Oswestry Library, Arthur Street, Oswestry, Shropshire SY11 1JN
  ☎(01691) 653211
  Fax (01691) 656994
  Principal Librarian – North Ms C Cartlidge MCLIP (e-mail: claire.cartlidge@shropshire-cc.gov.uk)
- South Area. Bridgnorth Library, Listley Street, Bridgnorth, Shropshire WV16 4AW
  ☎(01746) 763257
  Fax (01746) 766625
  Principal Librarian – South A Williams BA MCLIP (e-mail: adrian.williams@shropshire-cc.gov.uk)

SLOUGH

Authority Slough Borough Council
HQ Libraries, Arts, Heritage and Information, Learning and Cultural Services, Town Hall, Bath Road, Slough SL1 3UQ
☎(01753) 875578
Fax (01753) 875419
Head of Libraries, Arts, Heritage and Information Mrs Y M Cope MIMgt MCLIP (e-mail: yvonne.cope@slough.gov.uk)
Library Services Manager, Strategy & Improvement Mrs D Flood BA(Hons) DMS MCLIP (01753 875425; e-mail: diane.flood@slough.gov.uk)

Central/largest library

Slough Library, High Street, Slough SL1 1EA
☎(01753) 535166
Fax (01753) 825050
Library Services Manager, Operations Mrs J Menniss BA(Hons) DipIM MCLIP (01753 787506; e-mail: jackie.menniss@slough.gov.uk)
Library IT Manager D Guy (e-mail: damon.guy@slough.gov.uk)

SOLIHULL

Authority Solihull Metropolitan Borough Council
HQ Central Library, Homer Road, Solihull, West Midlands B91 3RG
☎0121 704 6965 (public enquiries), 0121 704 6971 (administration)

Fax 0121 704 6991
url: http://www.solihull.gov.uk
Head of Libraries and Arts N Ward BA MA DMS MCLIP (0121 704 6945; e-mail: nward@solihull.gov.uk)
Support Services Manager Ms H Halliday BA MCLIP (0121 704 8227; e-mail: hhalliday@solihull.gov.uk)

Main area libraries

- Central Library, Homer Road, Solihull, West Midlands B91 3RG
  ☎0121 704 6965
  Fax 0121 704 6991
  Central Area Manager Vacant
- Chelmsley Wood Library, Stephenson Drive, Chelmsley Wood, Solihull, West Midlands B37 5TA
  ☎0121 788 4380
  Fax 0121 788 4391
  North Area Manager Ms J Hand BA(Hons) DipLib MCLIP (e-mail: jhand@solgrid.org.uk)
- Knowle Library, Chester House, 1667-9 High Street, Knowle, Solihull, West Midlands B93 0LL
  ☎(01564) 775840
  Fax (01564) 770953
  South Area Manager Ms Y Negus BA MCLIP MISM (01564 776331; e-mail: ynegus@solgrid.org.uk)

SOMERSET

Authority Somerset County Council
HQ Libraries, Arts and Information Service, Library Administration Centre, Mount Street, Bridgwater, Somerset TA6 3ES
☎(01278) 451201
Fax (01278) 452787
e-mail: klbidgood@somerset.gov.uk
url: http://www.somerset.gov.uk/libraries
County Librarian R N Froud BLib DMS MIMgt FCLIP (e-mail: rnfroud@somerset.gov.uk)
Principal Assistant County Librarian: Information and Support Services Ms C Eastell BA(Hons) MA MCLIP (e-mail: ceastell@somerset.gov.uk)
Assistant County Librarian: (Operations) P Nichols BA MCLIP (located at Yeovil Library; 01935 429614, e-mail: penichols@somerset.gov.uk)
Assistant County Librarian: Policy and Development Miss R Boyd BA MCLIP (e-mail: rboyd@somerset.gov.uk)
Finance and Personnel Manager S G May (e-mail: sgmay@somerset.gov.uk)
County Arts Officer Ms S Isherwood BA (e-mail: sisherwood@somerset.gov.uk)
Manager, Foursite Bibliographic Services Section Miss C Gold (e-mail: cgold2@somerset.gov.uk)
Manager, Enquiry Centre Mrs J Gill BA MCLIP (e-mail: jgill@somerset.gov.uk)
Research, Projects and Marketing Officer P Smith BA(Hons) DipLib DMS MCLIP (e-mail: psmith@somerset.gov.uk)

Group libraries

- Mendip & Sedgemoor Group, Bridgwater Library, Binford Place, Bridgwater, Somerset TA6 3LF
  ☎(01278) 458373
  Fax (01278) 451027
  Group Librarian Mrs S Crowley BA MCLIP (e-mail: sacrowley@somerset.gov.uk)
- South Somerset Group, Yeovil Library, King George Street, Yeovil, Somerset BA20 1PY
  ☎(01935) 423144
  Fax (01935) 431847
  Group Librarian N J Humphrey BLib MA (e-mail: nhumphrey@somerset.gov.uk)
- Taunton Deane & West Somerset Group, Taunton Library, Paul Street, Taunton, Somerset TA1 3XZ
  ☎(01823) 336334
  Fax (01823) 340302
  Group Librarian D J Cawthorne BA MCLIP (e-mail: dcawthorne@somerset.gov.uk)

SOUTH GLOUCESTERSHIRE

Authority South Gloucestershire Council
HQ Library Service, Civic Centre, High Street, Kingswood, South Gloucestershire BS15 9TR
☎(01454) 865782
Fax (01454) 868535
url: http://www.southglos.gov.uk/libs.htm
Head of Library and Information Service M Burton BA MCLIP (e-mail: martin_burton@southglos.gov.uk)
Team Manager (North) Ms A Hartridge MCLIP (01454 865664)
Team Manager (South) M Duffy MCLIP (01454 868450)

Central/largest library

Yate Library, 44 West Walk, Yate, South Gloucestershire BS37 4AX
☎(01454) 865661
Fax (01454) 865665
Group Librarian N Weston BA MCLIP

Group libraries

- Downend Library, Buckingham Gardens, Downend, South Gloucestershire BS16 5TW
  ☎(01454) 865666
  Librarian Mrs H Egarr MCLIP
- Kingswood Library, High Street, Kingswood, South Gloucestershire BS15 4AR
  ☎(01454) 865650
  Librarians G Clayton BA MCLIP, A Rennie MCLIP
- Thornbury Library, St Mary Street, Thornbury, South Gloucestershire BS35 2AA
  ☎(01454) 865655
  Librarian R Filer BA MCLIP

SOUTH TYNESIDE

Authority South Tyneside Metropolitan Borough Council
HQ South Tyneside Libraries, Central Library, Prince Georg Square, South Shields, Tyne and Wear NE33 2PE
☎0191 427 1818
Fax 0191 455 8085
e-mail: reference.library@s-tyneside-mbc.gov.uk
Libraries Manager M C E Freeman BA MCLIP (e-mail: mark.freeman@s-tyneside-mbc.gov.uk)

SOUTHAMPTON

Authority Southampton City Council
HQ City Library, Archives and Information Service, Central Library, Civic Centre, Southampton SO14 7LW
☎023 8083 2459 (administration)
Fax 023 8033 6305
City Librarian H A Richards BA MCLIP (e-mail: t.richards@southampton.gov.uk)
Principal Bibliographic Services Librarian M Ceresa

Central/largest library

Central Library, Civic Centre, Southampton SO14 7LW
☎023 8083 2597 (Lending Library renewals), 023 8083 2664 (enquiry desk), 023 8083 2462 (Reference Library)
Principal Lending Librarian R Ashman
Principal Reference Librarian M Illingworth

Branch libraries

- Burgess Road Library, Burgess Road, Southampton SO16 3HF
  ☎023 8067 8873
  Librarian Ms M Tilbury
- Cobbett Road Library, Cobbett Road, Southampton SO18 1HL
  ☎023 8022 5565
  Supervisor Ms N Belbin
- Eastern Library, Bitterne Road East, Southampton SO18 5EG
  ☎023 8044 9909
  Librarian Mrs G Webb
- Lord's Hill Library, Lord's Hill District Centre, Southampton SO16 8HY
  ☎023 8044 9909
  Librarian Mrs P Hallett
- Millbrook Library, 67 Cumbrian Way, Southampton SO16 4AT
  ☎023 8044 9909
  Supervisor Mrs A Zabiela
- Portswood Library, Portswood Road, Southampton SO17 2NG
  ☎023 8055 4634
  Librarian M Pavey

- Shirley Library, Redcar Street, Southampton SO15 5LL
  ☎023 8077 2136
  Librarian Mrs J Moore
- Thornhill Library, 380 Hinkler Road, Southampton SO19 6DF
  ☎023 8044 7245
  Supervisor J Poucher
- Weston Library, 6 Wallace Road, Weston, Southampton SO19 9GX
  ☎023 8044 4363
  Supervisor Mrs C Taplin
- Woolston Library, Portsmouth Road, Southampton SO19 9AF
  ☎023 8044 8481
  Librarian Miss K Eaves

SOUTHEND ON SEA

Authority Southend on Sea Borough Council
HQ Education and Library Services, PO Box 6, The Civic Centre, Southend on Sea, Essex SS2 6EX
☎(01702) 215972
Fax (01702) 351090
url: http://www.southend.gov.uk
Director of Education and Libraries Vacant
Assistant Director: Libraries and Lifelong Learning H Gordon BA MCLIP

Central/largest library

Southend Library, Victoria Avenue, Southend on Sea, Essex SS2 6EX
☎(01702) 612621
Fax (01702) 469241
url: http://www.southendlibrary.com
Library Services Manager S May BSc MSc MCLIP
Head of Information and Resources C Hayes BA DipLib MCLIP

SOUTHWARK

Authority London Borough of Southwark
HQ Southwark Education and Culture, 15 Spa Road, London SE16 3QW
☎020 7525 1993
Fax 020 7525 1505
e-mail: southwark.libraries@southwark.gov.uk
Head of Libraries and Information A Olsen BA MCLIP (020 7525 1577; e-mail: adrian.olsen@southwark.gov.uk)
Library Operations Manager Ms C Brown BA MCLIP (020 7703 3324; e-mail: christine.brown@southwark.gov.uk)
Library Development and Support Manager S Woollard MCLIP (020 7525 1578; e-mail: stuart.woollard@southwark.gov.uk)

Branch libraries

- Blue Anchor Library, Market Place, Southwark Park Road, London SE16 3UQ
  ☎020 7231 0475

Fax 020 7232 1842

- Brandon Library, Maddock Way, Cooks Road, London SE17 3NH
  ☎020 7735 3430 (Tel/Fax)
  Librarian Ms P Jakeman
- Camberwell Library, 17-21 Camberwell Church Street, London SE5 8TR
  ☎020 7703 3763
  Fax 020 7708 4597
- Dulwich Library, 368 Lordship Lane, London SE22 8NB
  ☎020 8693 5171
  Fax 020 8693 5135
- East Street/Old Kent Road Library, 168-170 Old Kent Road, London SE1 5TY
  ☎020 7703 0395
  Fax 020 7703 2224
- Grove Vale Library, 25-27 Grove Vale, London SE22 8EQ
  ☎020 8693 5734 (Tel/Fax)
- John Harvard Library, 211 Borough High Street, London SE1 1JA
  ☎020 7407 0807 (Tel/Fax)
- Kingswood Library, Seeley Drive, London SE21 8QR
  ☎020 8670 4803
  Fax 020 8671 5125
- Local Studies Library, 211 Borough High Street, London SE1 1JA
  ☎020 7403 3507
  Fax 020 7403 8633
- Newington Library, 155-7 Walworth Road, London SE17 1RS
  ☎020 7703 3324
  Fax 020 7252 6115
- Newington Reference Library, 155-7 Walworth Road, London SE17 1RS
  ☎020 7708 0516
  Fax 020 7252 6115
- Nunhead Library, Gordon Road, London SE15 3RW
  ☎020 7639 0264
  Fax 020 7277 5721
- Peckham Library, 122 Peckham Hill Street, London SE15 5JR
  ☎020 7525 0200
- Rotherhithe Library, Albion Street, London SE16 1JA
  ☎020 7237 2010
  Fax 020 7394 0672
- Special Library Services, Rotherhithe Library, Albion Street, London SE16 1JA
  ☎020 7237 1487
  Fax 020 7237 8417
- Education Library Service, Southwark Education Resource Centre, Cator Street, London SE15 6AA
  ☎020 7525 2830
  Fax 020 7525 2837

STAFFORDSHIRE

Authority Staffordshire County Council
HQ Library and Information Services, Cultural and Property Services Department, 16 Martin Street, Stafford ST16 2LG
☎(01785) 278311
Fax (01785) 278319
County Librarian Mrs O Spencer MCLIP (01785 278422; e-mail: olivia.spencer@staffordshire.gov.uk)
Head of Library Support Services Mrs M Williams MA(Hons) DipLib MCLIP (e-mail: morna.williams@staffordshire.gov.uk)
Head of Operational Services West Mrs J Goodson MCLIP (01785 278320; e-mail: judy.goodson@staffordshire.gov.uk)
Head of Operational Services East Mrs E Rees-Jones BA(Hons) MCLIP (01785 278344; e-mail: elizabeth.rees-jones@staffordshire.gov.uk)
Lead Officer Best Value Implementation Mrs H Jackson BLib MCLIP (01785 278591; e-mail: hilary.jackson@staffordshire.gov.uk)

Portal clusters

- Cannock Library, Manor Avenue, Cannock, Staffs WS11 1AA
  ☎(01543) 510365
  Fax (01543) 510373
  e-mail: cannock.library@staffordshire.gov.uk
  Portal Librarian Miss S Parker BA(Hons) MCLIP (01543 510366; e-mail: sue.parker@staffordshire.gov.uk)
- Burton Library, Riverside, High Street, Burton-on-Trent, Staffs DE14 1AH
  ☎(01283) 239556
  Fax (01283) 239571
  e-mail: burton.library@staffordshire.gov.uk
  Portal Librarian Mrs P Phelps MCLIP (01283 239559; e-mail: pat.phelps@staffordshire.gov.uk)
- Tamworth Library, Corporation Street, Tamworth, Staffs B79 7DN
  ☎(01827) 475645
  Fax (01827) 475658
  e-mail: tamworth.library@staffordshire.gov.uk
  Portal Librarian A Medway BLib MCLIP (01827 475652; e-mail: alan.medway@staffordshire.gov.uk)
- Newcastle Library, Ironmarket, Newcastle, Staffs ST5 1AT
  ☎(01782) 297300
  Fax (01782) 297323
  e-mail: newcastle.library@staffordshire.gov.uk
  Portal Librarian K Reynolds MCLIP (01782 297305; e-mail: kevin.reynolds@staffordshire.gov.uk)
- Shire Hall Library, Market Street, Stafford ST16 2LQ
  ☎(01785) 278585
  Fax (01785) 278309
  e-mail: stafford.library@staffordshire.gov.uk

Portal Librarian Mrs A Reynolds BA(Hons) MA MCLIP (01785 278573; e-mail: alison.reynolds@staffordshire.gov.uk)

STOCKPORT

Authority Stockport Metropolitan Borough Council
HQ Community Services, Stopford House, Piccadilly, Stockport, Cheshire SK1 3XE
☎0161 474 4447 (enquiries & administration)
Fax 0161 429 0335
Acting Head of Library and Information Services J Condon (e-mail: john.condon@stockport.gov.uk)

Central/largest library

Central Library, Wellington Road South, Stockport, Cheshire SK1 3RS
☎0161 474 4540 (lending), 4524 (information library), 4530 (local heritage library)
Fax 0161 474 7750
e-mail: central.library@stockport.gov.uk
Librarian Ms J Lynch BA(Hons) DipLib MCLIP (e-mail: judith.lynch@stockport.gov.uk)

Bibliographical Services Unit, Phoenix House, Bird Hall Lane, Stockport, Cheshire SK3 0RA
☎0161 474 5605
Fax 0161 491 6516

STOCKTON-ON-TEES

Authority Stockton-on-Tees Borough Council
HQ Education, Leisure and Cultural Services, Stockton Borough Libraries, Municipal Buildings, Church Road, Stockton-on-Tees TS18 1XE
☎(01642) 393939
Fax (01642) 393479
url: http://www.stockton.gov.uk
Head of Cultural Services Mrs A Barker MCLIP (01642 415376; e-mail: andrea.barker@stockton.gov.uk)
Manager, Libraries and Information Services Mrs L A King BA(Hons) (01642 393995; e-mail: lesley.king@stockton.gov.uk)
Community Libraries Officer Ms E Shields MSc (01642 393996; e-mail: emma.shields@stockton.gov.uk)
Priority Services Officer Mrs P Wilson MCLIP (01642 397597; e-mail: pam.wilson@stockton.gov.uk)

Central/largest library

Stockton Central Library, Church Road, Stockton-on-Tees TS18 1TU
☎(01642) 393999
Fax (01642) 393929
Librarian Mrs P Slee
Open Technology Centre Manager Mrs C Durnion (01642 393997; e-mail: christine.durnion@stockton.gov.uk)
Reference and Information Services Officer Mrs M Murphy (01642 393994; e-mail: mary.murphy@stockton.gov.uk)

Branch libraries

- Billingham Branch Library, Bedale Avenue, Billingham, Stockton-on-Tees TS23 1AJ
☎(01642) 397595
Branch Librarian J Hannah BA MCLIP
- Egglescliffe Branch Library, Butterfield Drive, Orchard Estate, Egglescliffe, Stockton-on-Tees TS16 0EL
☎(01642) 391840
Branch Librarian Miss M Chapman MA(Lib)
- Fairfield Branch Library, Fairfield Road, Stockton-on-Tees TS19 7AJ
☎(01642) 391750
Branch Librarian R Lacey MCLIP
- Norton Branch Library, 87 High Street, Norton, Stockton-on-Tees TS20 1AE
☎(01642) 397592
Branch Librarian Mrs C Maddison BSc DipLib
- Roseberry Billingham Branch Library, The Causeway, Billingham, Stockton-on-Tees TS23 2LB
☎(01642) 397600
Branch Librarian Miss B Sandles MCLIP
- Roseworth Branch Library, Redhill Road, Stockton-on-Tees TS19 9BX
☎(01642) 397604
Branch Librarian Mrs C Pratt BA MCLIP
- Thornaby Westbury Street Branch Library, Westbury Street, Thornaby, Stockton-on-Tees TS17 6PG
☎(01642) 393987
Branch Librarian J Hannah BA MCLIP
- Thornaby Central Branch Library, The Pavillion, New Town Centre, Thornaby, Stockton-on-Tees TS17 9EW
☎(01642) 391610
Branch Librarian Mrs S Freeman MCLIP
- Yarm Branch Library, 41 High Street, Yarm, Stockton-on-Tees TS15 9BH
☎(01642) 391843
Branch Librarian Mrs W Sandham BA MCLIP

STOKE-ON-TRENT

Authority Stoke-on-Trent City Council
HQ Libraries, Information and Archives, Swift House, Glebe Street, Stoke-on-Trent ST4 1HP
☎(01782) 238455 (enquiries), (01782) 236923 (administration)
Fax (01782) 232872
e-mail: stoke.libraries@stoke.gov.uk
url: http://www.stoke.gov.uk/council/libraries
Head of Library Services Ms M Green BA MLS MCLIP (e-mail: margaret.green@stoke.gov.uk)
Principal Operations Manager Mrs J Simpson BA MCLIP (e-mail: janet.simpson@stoke.gov.uk)
Strategy and Service Development Manager I Van Arkadie BA DMS MIMgt MCLIP (e-mail: ian.vanarkadie@stoke.gov.uk)

Central Library

Hanley Library, Bethesda Street, Hanley, Stoke-on-Trent ST1 3RS
☎(01782) 238455
Fax (01782) 238499
Principal Librarian: Central and Support Services Ms J Thursfield BA MCLIP

Group Library

Longton Library, Sutherland Institute, Lightwood Road, Longton, Stoke-on-Trent ST13 4HY
☎(01782) 238424
Fax (01782) 238429
Principal Librarian: Community Libraries Ms H Jones BA MCLIP

SUFFOLK

Authority Suffolk County Council
HQ Libraries and Heritage, St Andrew House, County Hall, Ipswich, Suffolk IP4 1LJ
☎(01473) 584564 (enquiries & administration)
Fax (01473) 584549
url: http://www.suffolkcc.gov.uk/libraries_and_heritage)
Assistant Director (Libraries and Heritage) Ms G J Pachent BA DLIS MCLIP MILAM (01473 584558; e-mail: guenever.pachent@libher.suffolkcc.gov.uk)
County Manager R McMaster BA MA MCLIP (e-mail: roger.mcmaster@libher.suffolkcc.gov.uk)

Central/largest library

County Library, Northgate Street, Ipswich, Suffolk IP1 3DE
☎(01473) 583702/3 (enquiries & administration)
Fax (01473) 583700
Ipswich Locality Manager Ms A Hewitt (e-mail: amanda.hewitt@libher.suffolkcc.gov.uk)

Area libraries

- Central Library, Sergeant's Walk, Off St Andrew's Street North, Bury St Edmunds, Suffolk IP33 1TZ
  ☎(01284) 352542
  Fax (01284) 352566
  St Edmundsbury Locality Manager B King (e-mail: brandon.king@libher.suffolkcc.gov.uk)
- Central Library, Clapham Road South, Lowestoft, Suffolk NR32 1DR
  ☎(01502) 405342
  Fax (01502) 405350
  Waveney Locality Manager Ms G Jenkins (e-mail: gill.jenkins@libher.suffolkcc.gov.uk)

Selected branch libraries

- Beccles Library, Blyburgate, Beccles, Suffolk NR34 9TB
  ☎(01502) 714073/716471
  Fax (01502) 714073
  Library Manager Ms M Storey

- Felixstowe Library, Crescent Road, Felixstowe, Suffolk IP11 7BY
  ☎(01394) 625766
  Fax (01394) 625770
  Library Manager Mrs L Gibbs
- Haverhill Library, Camps Road, Haverhill, Suffolk CB9 8HB
  ☎(01440) 702638
  Library Manager Ms M Tuck
- Newmarket Library, 1a The Rookery, Newmarket, Suffolk CB8 8EQ
  ☎(01638) 661216
  Library Manager Mrs G Myers-Crump
- Stowmarket Library, Milton Road North, Stowmarket, Suffolk IP14 1EX
  ☎(01449) 613143
  Fax (01449) 672629
  Library Manager Ms F Law
- Sudbury Library, Market Hill, Sudbury, Suffolk CO10 2EN
  ☎(01787) 296000
  Fax (01787) 296004
  Library Manager Ms S Curtis
- Woodbridge Library, New Street, Woodbridge, Suffolk IP12 1DT
  ☎(01394) 625095
  Fax (01394) 625091
  Library Manager Ms L Firth
- Hadleigh Library, 29 High Street, Hadleigh, Ipswich, Suffolk IP7 5AG
  ☎(01473) 823778
  Fax (01473) 822557
  Library Manager G Ross BA
- Mildenhall Library, Chestnut Close, Mildenhall, Bury St Edmunds, Suffolk IP28 7HL
  ☎(01638) 713558
  Fax (01638) 510108
  Library Manager Ms T Stewart

SUNDERLAND

Authority City of Sunderland Metropolitan District Council
HQ City Library and Arts Centre, Fawcett Street, Sunderland, Tyne and Wear SR1 1RE
☎0191 514 1235 (enquiries & administration)
Fax 0191 514 8444
e-mail: user@edcom.sunderland.gov.uk
Head of Libraries, Arts and Information Ms J F Hall BA(Hons) MCLIP
Assistant Chief Librarian Ms V Craggs MCLIP
Manager, City Library and Arts Centre Ms V Foster BA
Senior Librarian, Reader Development Ms J Parkinson BA(Hons)
Principal Officer, ICT and Systems Management Ms J McCann BA(Hons) MCLIP
Principal Officer, Library Projects Ms J Graham
Principal Officer, Community Libraries and Lifelong Learning Ms A Scott MCLIP

Area library

Washington Town Centre Library, Independence Square, Washington, Tyne and Wear NE38 7RZ
☎0191 219 3440

SURREY

Authority Surrey County Council
HQ Community Services, Room 176, County Hall, Kingston upon Thames, Surrey KT1 2DN
☎020 8541 9071
Fax 020 8541 9003
url: http://www.surreycc.gov.uk/libraries
Head of Libraries C Norris BA MPhil MBA (e-mail: chris.norris@surreycc.gov.uk)

Area management teams

- East Area Office, St Davids, 70 Wray Park Road, Reigate, Surrey RH2 0EJ
  ☎(01737) 226136
  Fax (01737) 226135
  Library Service Manager Mrs H Ely MA MCLIP (020 8541 7060)
  Largest library: Redhill Library, Warwick Quadrant, Redhill, Surrey RH1 1NN
  ☎(01737) 763332
  Library Manager Mrs M Saberi
- South West Area Office, AO3 London Square, Cross Lanes, Guildford, Surrey GU1 1FA
  ☎(01483) 517402
  Fax (01483) 517401
  Library Service Manager I Milton BA DipLib MCLIP (01483 517407)
  Largest library: Guildford Library, 77 North Street, Guildford, Surrey GU1 4AL
  ☎(01483) 568496
  Library Manager Mrs S Bray
- Mid-Surrey Area Office, Opus 2, Bay Tree Avenue, Kingston Road, Leatherhead, Surrey KT22 7SY
  ☎(01372) 363920
  Fax (01372) 360169
  Library Service Manager Miss S Parker BA MCLIP (01372 363920)
  Largest library: Epsom Library, 6 The Derby Square, Epsom, Surrey KT19 8AG
  ☎(01372) 721707
  Library Manager Mrs P Fella
- North West Area Office, Runnymede Centre, Chertsey Road, Addlestone, Surrey KT15 2EP
  ☎(01932) 582700
  Fax (01932) 582727
  Library Service Manager Mrs R Wilson BA(Hons) (01932 582700; e-mail: r.wilson@surreycc.gov.uk)
  Largest library: Woking Library, Gloucester Walk, Woking, Surrey GU21 1EP
  ☎(01483) 770591
  Library Manager Ms C Simmons

Selected branch libraries

- Camberley Library, Knoll Road, Camberley, Surrey GU15 3SY
  ☎(01276) 63184; (01276) 27718 (administration)
  Fax (01276) 65701
  Library Manager Ms P D'Dornan (01276 683626)
- Caterham Hill Library, Westway, Caterham, Surrey CR3 5TP
  ☎(01883) 342008
  Fax (01883) 340885
  Library Manager Mrs J Campbell
- Caterham Valley Library, Stafford Road, Caterham, Surrey CR3 6JG
  ☎(01883) 343580
  Fax (01883) 330872
  Library Manager Mrs J Campbell
- Chertsey Library, Guildford Street, Chertsey, Surrey KT16 9BE
  ☎(01932) 564101
  Library Manager Mrs S Cundy
- Dorking Library, Pippbrook House, Regiate Road, Dorking, Surrey RH4 1SL
  ☎(01306) 882948
  Fax (01306) 875006
  Library Manager D Bailey
- Farnham Library, Vernon House, 28 West Street, Farnham, Surrey GU9 7DR
  ☎(01252) 716021
  Fax (01252) 717377
  Library Manager Miss P Brewster
- Godalming Library, Bridge Street, Godalming, Surrey GU7 1HT
  ☎(01483) 422743
  Fax (01483) 425480
  Learning Centre Administrator Mrs M Collings
- Haslemere Library, 91 Wey Hill, Haslemere, Surrey GU27 1HP
  ☎(01428) 642907
  Fax (01428) 641258
  Library Manager Ms J Allison
- Staines Library, Friends Walk, Staines, Middlesex TW18 4PG
  ☎(01784) 454430; (01784) 463279 (administration)
  Fax (01784) 461780
  Library Manager Miss W Broadfoot

SUTTON

Authority London Borough of Sutton
HQ Sutton Central Library, St Nicholas Way, Sutton, Surrey SM1 1EA
☎020 8770 4700 (enquiries), 020 8770 4602 (administration)
Fax 020 8770 4777
e-mail: sutton.library@sutton.gov.uk
url: www.sutton.gov.uk
Executive Head of Library, Heritage and Registration Services T Knight MLib FCLIP
Principal Librarian Mrs C McDonough BSc MCLIP DipLib/Mrs Angela Fletcher BA(Hons) PGCE (job-share)

Library Manager, Sutton J Ward
Quality Services Manager D Bundy BA MCLIP

Main libraries

- Carshalton Library, The Square, Carshalton, Surrey SM5 3BN
  ☎020 8647 1151
- Cheam Library, Church Road, Cheam, Surrey SM3 8QH
  ☎020 8644 9377
- Wallington Library, Shotfield, Wallington, Surrey SM6 0HY
  ☎020 8770 4900
- Worcester Park Library, Windsor Road, Worcester Park, Surrey KT4 8ES
  ☎020 8337 1609

SWINDON

Authority Swindon Borough Council
HQ Education and Community, Premier House, Station Road, Swindon, Wilts SN1 1TZ
☎(01793) 466036
Fax (01793) 466484
Library Services Manager D M Allen MCLIP (e-mail: dallen@swindon.gov.uk)

Central/largest library

Swindon Central Library, Regent Circus, Swindon, Wilts SN1 1QG
☎(01793) 463238
Fax (01793) 541319
e-mail: reference.library@mail.tameside.gov.uk

Group libraries

- Coate Group. Central Library, Regent Circus, Swindon, Wilts SN1 1QG
  ☎(01793) 463238
  Fax (01793) 541319
  Group Library Manager M Jones MCLIP (01793 463232)
- Lydiard Group. West Swindon Library, Link Centre, Whitehill Way, Swindon, Wilts SN5 7DL
  ☎(01793) 465555
  Fax (01793) 465557
  Group Library Manager S Smith MCLIP (01793 465552)
- Acquisitions Group. Library Support Unit, Liden Library, Barrington Close, Liden, Swindon, Wilts SN3 6HF
  ☎(01793) 463510
  Fax (01793) 463508
  Stock Manager Miss J Hayes MCLIP (01793 463512)

TAMESIDE

Authority Tameside Metropolitan District Council
HQ Education and Culture, Learning and Information, Council Offices, Wellington Road, Ashton-under-Lyne, Tameside OL6 6DL
☎0161 342 3673

Fax 0161 342 3260
url: http://www.tameside.gov.uk/libraries
Borough Librarian Mrs C Simensky MCLIP (0161 342 3673)
Service Delivery and Inclusion Manager Ms J Hall BLib MCLIP
Operations Manager Ms D Lockyer FCLIP
Service Development Manager B Delve MCLIP

Central/largest library

Tameside Central Library, Old Street, Ashton-under-Lyne, Tameside OL6 7SG
☎0161 342 2029 (lending/enquiries), 0161 342 2029 (administration), 0161 342 2035 (bibliographical services), 0161 342 2031 (reference)
Fax 0161 330 4762
e-mail: reference.library@mail.tameside.gov.uk
Senior Community Librarian Ms J Hall BA MCLIP
Reference and Information Librarian P F Jones BA MCLIP

Other large library

Hyde Library, Union Street, Hyde, Cheshire SK14 1ND
☎0161 368 2447
Fax 0161 368 0205
e-mail: hyde.library@mail.tameside.gov.uk

TELFORD AND WREKIN

Authority Telford and Wrekin Council
HQ Leisure, Culture and Community Learning, PO Box 440, Civic Offices, Telford, Shropshire TF3 4LA
☎(01952) 202747
Libraries and Heritage Manager Mrs P Davis MCLIP (e-mail: pat.davis@wrekin.gov.uk)
Acquisitions Manager Mrs M Criddle MCLIP (01952 210077)
Senior Librarian, Information Services Mrs H Nahal BLib MCLIP

Central/largest library

Telford Library, St Quentin Gate, Telford, Shropshire TF3 4JG
☎(01952) 292151 (enquiries), (01952) 292135 (administration)
Fax (01952) 292078
Assistant Libraries and Heritage Manager Mrs S Smith BA MCLIP

THURROCK

Authority Thurrock Council
HQ Libraries and Cultural Services Department, Grays Library, Orsett Road, Grays, Essex RM17 5DX
☎(01375) 383611 (enquiries), (01375) 382555 ext 221 (administration)
Fax (01375) 385504
Head of Libraries and Cultural Services S Black
Chief Librarian Mrs A Halliday BA(Hons) DipLIS MCLIP (01375 383611 ext 32; e-mail: ahalliday@thurrock.gov.uk)

Information Manager Ms A Cairns BA(Hons) DipLib MCLIP (01375 383611 ext 34; e-mail: acairns@thurrock.gov.uk (enquiries))

Central/largest library

Grays Library, Orsett Road, Grays, Essex RM17 5DX
☎(01375) 383611 (enquiries), (01375) 383611 ext 29 (administration)
Fax (01375) 370806
Group Manager Ms A Prince BA(Hons) DMS (01375 383611 ext 37)

TORBAY

Authority Torbay Council
HQ Torquay Library, Lymington Road, Torquay, Devon TQ1 3DT
☎(01803) 208300 (enquiries), (01803) 208310 (administration)
Fax (01803) 208311
url: http://www.torbay.gov.uk/
Head of Library Services P J Bottrill BA MCLIP (01803 208310; e-mail: peter.bottrill@torbay.gov.uk)
Professional Services Librarian G M Langridge MA MLS MCLIP (01803 208286; e-mail: geoff.langridge@torbay.gov.uk)
Resources and Technical Services Librarian Miss E G Kent BSc MCLIP (01803 208287; e-mail: liz.kent@torbay.gov.uk)
Operational Services Librarian N G Niles BA DipLib (01803 208288; e-mail: nick.niles@torbay.gov.uk)

Branch libraries

- Paignton Library, Courtland Road, Paignton, Devon TQ3 2AB
  ☎(01803) 208321
  Branch Librarian Miss C M Weeks MCLIP
- Brixham Library, Market Street, Brixham, Devon TQ5 8EU
  ☎(01803) 853870
  Branch Librarian Mrs G M Downes
- Churston Library, Broadsands Road, Paignton, Devon TQ4 6LL
  ☎(01803) 843757
  Branch Librarian Mrs R J Corby BA MCLIP

TOWER HAMLETS

Authority London Borough of Tower Hamlets
HQ Bancroft Library, 277 Bancroft Road, London E1 4DQ
☎020 8980 4366
Fax 020 8981 9965
Minicom 020 8983 4114
Head of Libraries Ms A Cunningham
Library Manager (Development) Ms K Pitman, Ms S Bridgwater BA MPhil MCLIP
Library Manager (Customer Services) S Clarke BA MCLIP (020 8980 4366)
Library Manager (Operations) J Hagerty (020 7364 2527)

Central/largest library

Bancroft Library, 277 Bancroft Road, London E1 4DQ
☎020 8980 4366
Fax 020 8983 4510
Minicom 020 8983 4114
Community Librarian S Avery

Divisional libraries

- West Division. Bethnal Green Reference Library, Cambridge Heath Road, London E2 0HL
  ☎020 8980 3902
  Fax 020 8981 6129
  Minicom 020 8980 3902
  Principal Information Librarian J Jasinski MCLIP (e-mail: 100633.624@compuserve.com)
  Community Librarian Ms S Brown BA
- West Division. Bancroft Library, 277 Bancroft Road, London E1 4DQ
  ☎020 8980 4366
  Fax 020 8983 4510
  Minicom 020 8983 4114
  Local History Librarian C Lloyd BLib MCLIP
  Borough Archivist M Barr-Hamilton BA DAS
  Principal Librarian, Outreach Services G Pollard
- Mid Division. Bow Idea Store, 1 Gladstone Place, Roman Road, London E3 5ES
  ☎020 7364 4332
  Idea Store Manager S Doguani
- Mid Division. Dorset Library, Ravenscroft Street, London E2 7QX
  ☎020 7739 9489
  Fax 020 7729 2548
  Minicom 020 7739 9489
  Community Librarian Ms S Brown BA (020 8980 3902)
- Mid Division. Stepney Library, Lindley Street, London E1 3AX
  ☎020 7790 5616
  Fax 020 7264 9873
  Minicom 020 7790 5616
  Community Librarian S Avery (020 8980 4366)
- Mid Division. Watney Market Library, 30-32 Watney Market, London E1 2PR
  ☎020 7790 4039
  Fax 020 7265 9401
  Minicom 020 7790 4039
  Community Librarian Mrs L Harris MCLIP, Ms S Paxton
- Mid Division. Whitechapel Library, 77 Whitechapel High Street, London E1 7QX
  ☎020 7247 5272
  Fax 020 7377 0396
  Minicom 020 7247 0265
  Community Librarian Ms C Algar BA DipLib MCLIP
- East Division. Lansbury Library, 23-27 Market Way, London E14 6AH
  ☎020 7987 3573
  Fax 020 7538 5520

Minicom 020 7537 4064
Community Librarian Ms B Stretch

- East Division. Cubitt Town Library, Strattondale Street, London E14 3HG
  ☎020 7987 3152
  Fax 020 7538 2795
  Minicom 020 7987 3152
  Community Librarian Ms S Murray BA MCLIP DMS
- East Division. Limehouse Library, 638 Commercial Road, London E14 7HS
  ☎020 7364 2527
  Fax 020 7364 2502
  Minicom 020 7364 2552
  Community Librarian Ms S Murray BA MCLIP DMS
- East Division. Library Resources Department, Limehouse Library, 638 Commercial Road, London E14 7HS
  ☎020 7364 2527
  Fax 020 7364 2502
  Minicom 020 7364 2552
  Library Resources Coordinator D Hancock (020 7364 2537)

TRAFFORD

Authority Trafford Metropolitan Borough Council
HQ Community Rights, Learning and Libraries, Trafford Town Hall, Talbot Road, Stretford, Manchester M32 0EL
☎0161 912 4044 (enquiries & administration)
Fax 0161 912 1267
Head of Service (Community Rights, Learning and Libraries) R G Luccock BA MCLIP

Regional/district libraries

- Altrincham Library, 20 Stamford New Road, Altrincham, Cheshire WA14 1EJ
  ☎0161 912 5920
  Fax 0161 912 5926
- Sale Library, Tatton Road, Sale, Cheshire M33 1YS
  ☎0161 912 3008
  Fax 0161 912 3019
- Stretford Library, Kingsway, Stretford, Greater Manchester M32 8AP
  ☎0161 912 5150
  Fax 0161 865 3835
- Urmston Library, Crofts Bank Road, Urmston, Cheshire M41 0TZ
  ☎0161 912 2727
  Fax 0161 912 2947
- Bibliographical Services, Davyhulme Site, Hayeswater Road, Davyhulme, Manchester M41 7BL
  ☎0161 912 2882
  Fax 0161 912 2895

UPPER NORWOOD JOINT LIBRARY

HQ Upper Norwood Joint Library, Westow Hill, London SE19 1TJ
☎020 8670 2551
Fax 020 8670 5468
e-mail: unjl@unisonfree.net
Chief Librarian B J Millington MCLIP

WAKEFIELD

Authority Wakefield Metropolitan District Council
HQ Library Headquarters, Balne Lane, Wakefield, West Yorkshire WF2 0DQ
☎(01924) 302210 (enquiries & administration)
Fax (01924) 302245
Libraries & Information Services Manager C J MacDonald BA MBA DipLib MCLIP
Principal Librarian (Community Services) Ms C Threapleton MCLIP DMS
Principal Librarian (Information Services) Mrs A Farrington BA(Hons) MCLIP
Principal Librarian (Resource Services) N Scarlett DMA

Major libraries

- Castleford Library, Carlton Street, Castleford, West Yorkshire WF10 1BB
  ☎(01977) 722085
  Senior Librarian Ms W Mitchell BA(Hons) DipLib PGCE
- Ossett Library, Station Road, Ossett, West Yorkshire WF5 8AB
  ☎(01924) 303040
  Senior Librarian Ms C Wadsworth MCLIP
- Pontefract Library, Shoemarket, Pontefract, West Yorkshire WF8 1BD
  ☎(01977) 727692
  Senior Librarian Ms W Mitchell BA(Hons) DipLib PGCE
- Drury Lane Library, Drury Lane, Wakefield, West Yorkshire WF1 2TD
  ☎(01924) 305376
  Senior Librarian Ms K Harrison BA(Hons) DipLib MCLIP
- Balne Lane Reference and Information Library, Balne Lane, Wakefield, West Yorkshire WF2 0DQ
  ☎(01924) 302230
  Senior Librarian Ms K Harrison BA(Hons) DipLib MCLIP
- Featherstone Library and Community Centre, Victoria Street, Featherstone, West Yorkshire WF7 5BB
  ☎(01977) 722745
  Senior Librarian A Wraight BMus(Hons) DipLib
- Stanley Library and Community Centre, Lake Lock Road, West Yorkshire WF3 4HU
  ☎(01924) 303130
  Senior Librarian P Winterbottom BA(Hons) MCLIP DMS
- Normanton Library and Community Centre, Market Street, Normanton, West Yorkshire WF6 2AR
  ☎(01924) 302525
  Senior Librarian Mrs J Britton BA(Hons) DipLib MCLIP

WALSALL

Authority Walsall Metropolitan District Council
HQ Leisure and Community Services Division, PO Box 42, Civic Centre, Darwall Street, Walsall, West Midlands WS1 1TZ
☎(01922) 653130
Fax (01922) 722687
e-mail: thelibrarian@walsall.gov.uk
url: http://www.walsall.gov.uk/libraries
Group Co-ordinator – Libraries and Heritage S Grainger MCLIP (e-mail: graingers@walsall.gov.uk)

Central/largest library

Central Library, Lichfield Street, Walsall, West Midlands WS1 1TR
☎(01922) 653121 (lending), (01922) 653110 (reference)
Fax (01922) 722687 (lending), (01922) 654013 (reference)
e-mail: librarycentref@walsall.gov.uk
Central Library Manager Vacant
Information Services Manager Ms R Kennedy

Area libraries

- Aldridge Library, Rookery Lane, Aldridge, Walsall, West Midlands WS9 8LZ
  ☎(01922) 743601
- Beechdale Library, Stephenson Square, Beechdale Estate, Walsall, West Midlands WS2 7DX
  ☎(01922) 721431
- Bentley Library, Queen Elizabeth Avenue, Bentley, Walsall, West Midlands WS2 0HP
  ☎(01922) 721392
- Bloxwich Library, Elmore Row, Bloxwich, Walsall, West Midlands WS3 2HR
  ☎(01922) 710059
- Brownhills Library, Brickiln Street, Brownhills, Walsall, West Midlands WS8 6AU
  ☎(01543) 452017
  Fax (01543) 371832
- Coalpool Library, Coalpool Lane, Walsall, West Midlands WS3 1RF
  ☎(01922) 721325
- Darlaston Library, 1 King Street, Darlaston, Walsall, West Midlands WS10 8DD
  ☎0121 526 4530
  Fax 0121 526 2298
- Forest Gate Library, New Invention, Willenhall, Walsall, West Midlands WV12 5LF
  ☎(01922) 710208
- Furzebank Library, Furzebank Way, Willenhall, Walsall, West Midlands WV12 4BD
  ☎(01902) 630530
- Pelsall Library, High Street, Pelsall, Walsall, West Midlands WS3 4LX
  ☎(01922) 682212
- Pheasey Library, Collingwood Drive, Pheasey, Birmingham B43 7NY
  ☎0121 366 6503
- Pleck Library, Darlaston Road, Pleck, Walsall, West Midlands WS2 9RE
  ☎(01922) 721307

- Rushall Library, Pelsall Lane, Walsall, West Midlands WS4 1NL
  ☎(01922) 721310
- Shelfield Library, Birch Lane, Shelfield, Walsall, West Midlands WS4 1AS
  ☎(01922) 682760
- Sneyd Community Library, Sneyd School, Sneyd Lane, Bloxwich, Walsall, West Midlands WS3 2PA
  ☎(01922) 710728
- South Walsall Library, West Bromwich Road, Walsall, West Midlands WS5 4NW
  ☎(01922) 721347
- Streetly Library, Blackwood Road, Streetly, Birmingham B74 3PL
  ☎0121 353 4230
- Walsall Wood Library, Lichfield Road, Walsall Wood, Walsall, West Midlands WS9 9NT
  ☎(01543) 452517 (tel/fax)
- Willenhall Library, Walsall Street, Willenhall, Walsall, West Midlands WV13 2EX
  ☎(01902) 366513
- Local History Centre, Essex Street, Walsall, West Midlands WS2 7AS
  ☎(01922) 721305
  Fax (01922) 634954
- Home Library Service and Public Mobile Library, Mobile Library Depot, Willenhall Lane, Bloxwich, Walsall, West Midlands WS3 2XN
  ☎(01922) 710625

WALTHAM FOREST

Authority London Borough of Waltham Forest
HQ Administrative Office, Central Library, High Street, London E17 7JN
☎020 8520 5822 (enquiries & administration)
Fax 020 8509 9539
Head of Libraries and Cultural Services C Richardson MCLIP

Central/largest library

Central Library, High Street, London E17 7JN
☎020 8520 3031/4733; 020 8520 3017 (information services)
Fax 020 8509 0649; 020 8509 9654 (information services)
Customer Services Manager C Prince BA
Information Services Manager Vacant
Group Manager (Libraries) C Fardon BA DMS MCLIP

WANDSWORTH

Authority Wandsworth Council
HQ Leisure and Amenity Services Department, Wandsworth High Street, London SW18 2PU
☎020 8871 6364 (enquiries & administration)
Fax 020 8871 7630
e-mail: libraries@wandsworth.gov.uk
Head of Libraries, Museum and Arts Ms J Allen BA(Hons) DMS DipLib MCLIP
Assistant Head of Libraries Ms M Jones MCLIP

Largest libraries

- Balham Library, Ramsden Road, London SW12 8QY
  ☎020 8871 7195
  Fax 020 8675 4015
- Battersea Library, Lavender Hill, London SW11 1JB
  ☎020 8871 7466
  Fax 020 7978 4376
- Putney Library, Disraeli Road, London SW15 2DR
  ☎020 8871 7090
  Fax 020 8789 6175
- Tooting Library, Mitcham Road, London SW17 9PD
  ☎020 8871 7175
  Fax 020 8672 3099

WARRINGTON

Authority Warrington Borough Council
HQ Warrington Library, Museum Street, Warrington, Cheshire WA1 1JB
☎(01925) 442889 (enquiries), (01925) 442733 (administration)
Fax (01925) 411395
e-mail: library@warrington.gov.uk
url: http://www.warrington.gov.uk
Library and Information Services Manager M Gaw BA DipLib MCLIP
Resources Manager Vacant
Field Operations Managers Ms F Barry BA MCLIP (01925 442892)

Branch libraries

- Birchwood Library, Brock Road, Warrington, Cheshire WA3 7PT
  ☎(01925) 827491 (Tel/Fax)
- Burtonwood Library, Chapel Lane, Burtonwood, Warrington, Cheshire WA5 4PS
  ☎(01925) 226563 (Tel/Fax)
- Culcheth Library, Warrington Road, Culcheth, Warrington, Cheshire WA3 5SL
  ☎(01925) 763293 (Tel/Fax)
- Grappenhall Library, Victoria Avenue, Grappenhall, Warrington, Cheshire WA4 2PE
  ☎(01925) 262861 (Tel/Fax)
- Great Sankey Library, Marina Avenue, Great Sankey, Warrington, Cheshire WA5 1JH
  ☎(01925) 231451 (Tel/Fax)
- Lymm Library, Davies Way, Off Brookfield Road, Lymm, Warrington, Cheshire WA13 0QW
  ☎(01925) 754367 (Tel/Fax)
- Orford Library, Poplars Avenue, Orford, Warrington, Cheshire WA2 9LW
  ☎(01925) 812821 (Tel/Fax)
- Padgate Library, Insall Road, Padgate, Warrington, Cheshire WA2 0HD
  ☎(01925) 818096 (Tel/Fax)
- Penketh Library, Honiton Way, Penketh, Warrington, Cheshire WA5 2EY
  ☎(01925) 723730
  Fax (01925) 791264

- Stockton Heath Library, Alexandra Park, Stockton Heath, Warrington, Cheshire WA4 2AN
  ☎(01925) 261148
  Fax (01925) 267787
- Westbrook Library, Westbrook Centre, Westbrook Crescent, Warrington, Cheshire WA5 5UG
  ☎(01925) 416561
  Fax (01925) 230462
- Winwick Library, Myddleton Lane, Winwick, Warrington, Cheshire WA2 8LQ
  ☎(01925) 417678
- Woolston Library, Holes Lane, Woolston, Warrington, Cheshire WA1 3UJ
  ☎(01925) 816146 (Tel/Fax)

WARWICKSHIRE

Authority Warwickshire County Council
HQ Department of Libraries, Heritage and Trading Standards, Barrack Street, Warwick, Warwickshire CV34 4TH
☎(01926) 412550 (enquiries and administration)
Fax (01926) 412471/412165
e-mail: librariesandheritage@warwickshire.gov.uk
url: http://www.warwickshire.gov.uk
Director N C Hunter FITSA FRSA (01926 412166)
Head of Library and Information Service Ms K Birla LLB(Hons) DTS MBA (01926 412862)
Core Services, Quality and Operations Manager Mrs L Kay BA MCLIP DMS (01926 418154)

Divisional libraries

- Central Warwickshire Division. Leamington Library (Central Divisional Library), Royal Pump Rooms, The Parade, Leamington Spa, Warwickshire CV32 4AA
  ☎(01926) 742721/742722
  Fax (01926) 742749
  e-mail: leamingtonlibrary@warwickshire.gov.uk
  Divisional Librarian P MacDermott BA DipLib MCLIP
  Area Manager, Central Warwickshire J Crossling BSc AMA
- North Warwickshire Division. Atherstone Library (North Divisional Library), Long Street, Atherstone, Warwickshire CV9 1AX
  ☎(01827) 712395/712034
  Fax (01827) 720285
  e-mail: atherstonelibrary@warwickshire.gov.uk
  Divisional Librarian A Button BA MCLIP
  Area Manager, North Warwickshire A Litvinoff MA FRSA
- Nuneaton and Bedworth Division. Nuneaton Library, Church Street, Nuneaton, Warwickshire CV11 4DR
  ☎024 7638 4027/024 7634 7006
  Fax 024 7635 0125
  e-mail: nuneatonlibrary@warwickshire.gov.uk

Divisional Librarian D Reed MB MCLIP

- South/East Division. Rugby Library (South Divisional Library), Little Elborow Street, Rugby, Warwickshire CV21 3BZ
  ☎(01788) 542687/571813/535348
  Fax (01788) 533252
  e-mail: rugbylibrary@warwickshire.gov.uk
  Divisional Librarian Ms C Barnsley MCLIP
  Area Manager, South Warwickshire Ms J Wilkinson MA PGDipLib MCLIP
- Stratford Library, Henley Street, Stratford-upon-Avon, Warwickshire CV37 6PZ
  ☎(01789) 292209/296904
  Fax (01789) 268554
  e-mail: stratfordlibrary@warwickshire.gov.uk
  Divisional Librarian Mrs B Evans MCLIP

WEST BERKSHIRE

Authority West Berkshire Council
HQ Library, Information and Communication Service, Council Offices, Market Street, Newbury, Berkshire RG14 5LD
☎(01635) 519813
Fax (01635) 519392
url: http://www.westberks.gov.uk
Libraries and Information Manager K Richardson BA(Hons) DipLib MCLIP (01635 519813; e-mail: krichardson@westberks.gov.uk)
Technical Services Manager Mrs J Jones BA MCLIP (01635 519817; e-mail: jjones@westberks.gov.uk)
Central Services Manager Mrs C Owen BA(Hons) MCLIP (01635 40972; e-mail: newbury_library@westberks.gov.uk)
Community Services Manager M Brook BA(Hons) DipLib MCLIP (01635 519820; e-mail: mbrook@westberks.gov.uk)

Central/largest library

Newbury Central Library, The Wharf, Newbury, Berkshire RG14 5AU
☎(01635) 519900

WEST SUSSEX

Authority West Sussex County Council
HQ Library Service Administration Centre, Tower Street, Chichester, West Sussex PO19 1QJ
☎(01243) 756700
Fax (01243) 756714
BT Gold 74: SKK125
url: http://www.westsussex.gov.uk
County Librarian Mrs S I Houghton BA(Hons) MCLIP (e-mail: susan.houghton@westsussex.gov.uk)
(For management enquiries contact headquarters; for services contact one of the principal libraries)

Principal libraries

- Worthing Library, Richmond Road, Worthing, West Sussex BN11 1HD
  ☎(01903) 206961
  Fax (01903) 821902
  Group Librarian: Worthing Miss R Edser BA MCLIP (e-mail: robina.edser@westsussex.gov.uk)
- Crawley Library, Northgate Avenue, Crawley, West Sussex RH10 1XG
  ☎(01293) 895130
  Fax (01293) 895141
  Group Librarian: Crawley Mrs R M A Lucas MCLIP (e-mail: rlucas@westsussex.gov.uk)

WESTMINSTER

Authority Westminster City Council
HQ Department of Education, 13th Floor, Westminster City Hall, 64 Victoria Street, London SW1E 6QP
☎020 7641 2496
Fax 020 7641 3404/6
url: http://www.westminster.gov.uk/libraries/gateway
Assistant Director (Lifetime Learning) D Ruse MCLIP MILAM (e-mail: druse@westminster.gov.uk)
Head of Cultural Services Ms L Goode (020 7641 8741; e-mail: lgood01@westminster.gov.uk)
Business Unit Manager A Stevens BA MCLIP (020 7641 6573; e-mail: astevens@dial.pipex.com)
Customer Services Manager Ms I Cairns MCLIP (020 7641 6567; e-mail: ionacairns@dial.pipex.com)
Lifelong Learning Manager Ms S Wilkie BLib MCLIP (020 7641 6571; e-mail: swilkie@dial.pipex.com)

Largest libraries

- Westminster Reference Library, 35 St Martin's Street, London WC2H 7HP
  ☎020 7641 4636
  Fax 020 7641 4606
  Manager Mrs T Arathoon (e-mail: tarathoon@dial.pipex.com)
- Marylebone Library, 109-117 Marylebone Road, London NW1 5PS
  ☎020 7641 1037 (lending), 020 7641 1039 (Marylebone Information Service)
  Manager Ms L Tobey, Ms H Rogers (e-mail: ltobey@dial.pipex.com; hrogers@dial.pipex.com)
- Charing Cross Library, 4 Charing Cross Road, London WC2H 0HG
  ☎020 7641 4623 (Chinese service enquiries)
  Manager M Knowles (e-mail: mknowles@dial.pipex.com)
- Victoria Library, 160 Buckingham Palace Road, London SW1W 9UD
  ☎020 7641 4287 (lending), 020 7641 4292 (Westminster Music Library)
  Manager Ms C Jones, Ms R Rogers (e-mail: chrissjones@dial.pipex.com; rrogers@dial.pipex.com)
- Paddington Library, Porchester Road, London W2 5DU

☎020 7641 4475
Manager Ms S Barnes (e-mail: susannabarnes@dial.pipex.com)

Other services

- Outreach Services, Church Street Library, Church Street, London NW8 8EU
  ☎020 7641 4806
  Manager M Parmiter (e-mail: mark.parmiter@dial.pipex.com)
- City of Westminster Archives Centre, 10 St Ann's Street, London SW1P 2DE
  ☎020 7641 5180
  Fax 020 7641 5179
  City Archivist Ms S Rayner MA (e-mail: srayner2@westminster.gov.uk)

WIGAN

Authority Wigan Council
HQ Leisure and Cultural Services Department, The Indoor Sports Complex, Loire Drive, Robin Park, Wigan, Lancs WN5 0UL
☎(01942) 828153 (enquiries & administration)
Fax (01942) 828156
e-mail: infounit@wiganmbc.gov.uk
Head of Libraries and Lifelong Learning Ms K Buddle BA(Hons) MCLIP
Libraries Management Team
Operational Services Manager Ms R Patterson MCLIP
Information Services and Learning Support Manager Ms S M Underwood BA
Service Development Manager S Ruffley BA(Hons) MCLIP DMS

Central libraries

- Wigan Library, College Avenue, Wigan, Lancs WN1 1DQ
  ☎(01942) 827621 (lending), (01942) 827619 (information)
  Fax (01942) 827640
- Leigh Library, Turnpike Centre, Civic Square, Leigh, Lancs WN7 1EB
  ☎(01942) 404556 (lending), (01942) 404557 (information)
  Fax (01942) 404567

WILTSHIRE

Authority Wiltshire County Council
HQ Libraries and Heritage, Bythesea Road, Trowbridge, Wilts BA14 8BS
☎(01225) 713700 (enquiries), (01225) 713727 (information)
Fax (01225) 713993
e-mail: libraryenquiries@wiltshire.gov.uk
Head of Libraries and Heritage Ms P Dyer MCLIP DMS MIMgt (e-mail: paulinedyer@wiltshire.gov.uk)
Principal Librarian B M Little MPhil FCLIP (e-mail: montelittle@wiltshire.gov.uk)
Heritage Manager T Craig MA BA (e-mail: tomcraig@wiltshire.gov.uk)
Stock Manager D Green BA MCLIP (e-mail: davidgreen@wiltshire.gov.uk)
Information Services Manager C Wildridge BA MCLIP (e-mail: christopherwildridge@wiltshire.gov.uk)

District libraries

- Salisbury District: Salisbury Library, Market Place, Salisbury, Wilts SP1 1BL
  ☎(01722) 324145
  Fax (01722) 413214
  District Librarian C S Harling BA(Hons) MCLIP (01722 330606; e-mail: chrisharling@wiltshire.gov.uk)
- Kennet District: Devizes Library, Sheep Street, Devizes, Wilts SN10 1DL
  ☎(01380) 726878/9
  Fax (01380) 722161
  District Librarian M A Chandler MCLIP (01380 724099; e-mail: mauricechandler@wiltshire.gov.uk)
- West Wilts District: Trowbridge Library, Mortimer Street, Cradle Bridge, Trowbridge, Wilts BA14 8BB
  ☎(01225) 761171
  Fax (01225) 769447
  District Librarian Mrs M Liddle BA MCLIP (01225 713706; e-mail: maryliddle@wiltshire.gov.uk)
- North Wilts District: Chippenham Library, Timber Street, Chippenham, Wilts SN15 3EJ
  ☎(01249) 650536
  Fax (01249) 443793
  District Librarian Ms J Davis BALib MCLIP (01249 445005; e-mail: joandavis@wiltshire.gov.uk)

Selected branch libraries

- Bradford on Avon Library, Bridge Street, Bradford on Avon, Wilts BA15 1BY
  ☎(01225) 863280/868127
  Fax (01225) 868647
  Community Librarian Mrs P England MCLIP (e-mail: pennyengland@wiltshire.gov.uk)
- Corsham Library, Pickwick Road, Corsham, Wilts SN13 9BJ
  ☎(01249) 713159
  Fax (01249) 714076
  Community Librarian Mrs J Dunmow BA(Hons) MCLIP (e-mail: janedunmow@wiltshire.gov.uk)
- Malmesbury Library, Cross Hayes, Malmesbury, Wilts SN16 9BG
  ☎(01666) 823611
  Fax (01666) 824953
  Librarian Ms C Kennedy BA(Hons) MCLIP (e-mail: carolynkennedy@wiltshire.gov.uk)
- Marlborough Library, 91 High Street, Marlborough, Wilts SN8 1HD
  ☎(01672) 512663
  Fax (01672) 515896
  Librarian Ms S Edwards BA MLS MCLIP (e-mail: sabinaedwards@wiltshire.gov.uk)
- Wilton Library, South Street, Wilton, Wilts SP2 0JS
  ☎(01722) 743230
  Fax (01722) 743804
  Community Librarian Ms H Glyde MCLIP (e-mail: hilaryglyde@wiltshire.gov.uk)

WINDSOR AND MAIDENHEAD

Authority Royal Borough of Windsor and Maidenhead
HQ Library and Information Services, Maidenhead Library, St Ives Road, Maidenhead, Berks SL6 1QU
☎(01628) 796969
Fax (01628) 796971
e-mail: maidenhead.library@rbwm.gov.uk
url: http://www.rbwm.gov.uk
Library and Information Services Manager M Taylor (01628 796989; fax: 01628 796971; e-mail: mark.taylor@rbwm.gov.uk)
Service Development Manager Ms S Hudson BA DipLib MCLIP (01628 796742)
Web Manager Ms M Harper BSc DipLib MCLIP (01628 796741)

Central/largest library

Maidenhead Library, St Ives Road, Maidenhead, Berks SL6 1QU
☎(01628) 796968 (reference), 796969 (issue desk), 796985 (administration)
Fax (01628) 796971
e-mail: maidenhead.library@rbwm.gov.uk
Assistant Library and Information Services Manager B Marpole MCLIP (01628 796976; e-mail: brian.marpole@rbwm.gov.uk)
Senior Librarian, Adult Ms P Curtis MCLIP (01628 796979)
Senior Librarian, Young People Ms P Dobby MCLIP (01628 796999)
Stock Services Officer, Stock Services Section P Douch BA MCLIP (01628 796987)
Administration Officer Vacant (01628 796985)
Library Supervisor, Branches Mrs M Simpson (07747 757919)

Other libraries

- Windsor Library, Bachelors Acre, Windsor, Berks SL4 1ER
  ☎(01753) 743940
- Ascot Library, Winkfield Road, Ascot, Berks SL5 7EX
  ☎(01344) 620653
- Cookham Library, High Road, Cookham Rise, Maidenhead, Berks SL6 9JF
  ☎(01626) 526147
- Datchet Library, Village Hall, Horton Road, Datchet, Berks SL3 9HR
  ☎(01753) 545310
- Dedworth Library, Dedworth County School, Smith's Lane, Windsor, Berks SL4 5PE
  ☎(01753) 868733
- Eton Library, 136 High Street, Eton, Berks SL4 6LT
  ☎(01753) 860506
- Eton Wick Library, Village Hall, Eton Wick, Berks SL4 6LT
  ☎(01753) 857933
- Old Windsor Library, Memorial Hall, Straight Road, Windsor, Berks SL4 2JL
  ☎(01753) 852098
- Sunninghill Library, Reading Room, School Road, Sunninghill, Berks SL5 7AD
  ☎(01344) 621493

Container Library operating at four sites:
- Cox Green (01628 673942)
- Holyport (01628 673931)
- Sunningdale (01344 626720)
- Wraysbury (01784 482431)

WIRRAL

Authority Metropolitan Borough of Wirral
HQ Education and Cultural Services Department, Hamilton Building, Conway Street, Birkenhead, Wirral CH41 4FD
☎0151 666 2121
Fax 0151 666 4207
url: http://www.wirral-libraries.net
Head of Libraries, Museums and Arts O D R Roberts DMS MCLIP (e-mail: owenroberts@wirral.gov.uk)

Central/largest library

Birkenhead Central Library, Borough Road, Birkenhead, Wirral CH41 2XB
☎0151 652 6106 (enquiries), 0151 653 4700 (administration)
Fax 0151 653 7320
e-mail: birkenhead.library@merseymail.com
Area Librarian J C Baxter BA DipLib MCLIP (e-mail: johnbaxter@merseymail.com)

Regional/district libraries

- Bebington Central Library, Civic Way, Bebington, Wirral CH63 7PN
  ☎0151 643 7219
  Fax 0151 643 7231
  e-mail: beb@library.wirral.gov.uk
  Area Librarian Ms S Powell BA MCLIP (e-mail: sue.powell@merseymail.com)
- Wallasey Central Library, Earlston Road, Wallasey, Wirral CH45 5DY
  ☎0151 639 2334
  Fax 0151 691 2040
  e-mail: wallasey.central.lib@merseymail.com
  Area Librarian P Irons BA MCLIP (e-mail: paul.i@merseymail.com)
- West Kirby Library, The Concourse, West Kirby, Wirral CH48 4HX
  ☎0151 625 6381
  Fax 0151 625 2558
  e-mail: westkirby.library@merseymail.com
  Team Librarians Mrs J Mann BA MCLIP, Mrs J Barkway BA DipLib MCLIP

WOKINGHAM

Authority Wokingham District Council
HQ Libraries and Lifelong Learning, Education and Cultural Services Dept, Shute End, Wokingham, Berks RG40 1WN
☎0118 974 6000
Head of Libraries and Lifelong Learning C J Hamilton MCLIP (0118 974 6261; e-mail: chris.hamilton@wokingham.gov.uk)

Central/largest library

Wokingham Library, Denmark Street, Wokingham, Berks RG40 2BB
☎0118 978 1368
Fax 0118 989 1214

WOLVERHAMPTON

Authority Wolverhampton City Council
HQ Lifelong Learning – Leisure Services Department, Cultural Services Division, Libraries and Information Services, Central Library, Snow Hill, Wolverhampton WV1 3AX
☎(01902) 552025 (enquiries & administration)
Fax (01902) 552024
e-mail: wolverhampton.libraries@dial.pipex.com
City Librarian Mrs K Lees BA MCLIP (01902 552010)
Assistant City Librarian G Kent BA DipLib (01902 552011)
Assistant City Librarian A Scragg DipHE LLB(Hons) MCLIP (01902 552012)

Branch libraries

Group One
Branch Group Librarian Mrs K Fletcher MCLIP (01902 556293)

- Ashmore Park Library, Griffiths Drive, Wednesfield, Wolverhampton WV11 2JW
  ☎(01902) 556296
- Low Hill Library, Showell Circus, Low Hill, Wolverhampton WV10 9JJ
  ☎(01902) 556293
- Mary Pointon Community Library, Ettingshall Road, Wood Cross, Wolverhampton WV14 9UG
  ☎(01902) 556263
- Pendeford Library, Whitburn Close, Pendeford, Wolverhampton WV9 5NJ
  ☎(01902) 556250
- Penn Library, Coalway Avenue, Penn, Wolverhampton WV3 7LT
  ☎(01902) 556281
- Whitmore Reans Library, Bargate Drive, Evans Street, Whitmore Reans, Wolverhampton WV4 4PT
  ☎(01902) 556269
- Collingwood Community Library, 24 The Broadway, Bushbury, Wolverhampton WV10 8EB
  ☎(01902) 556302

Group Two
Branch Group Librarian K Hudson BA (01902 556257)

- Bilston Library, Mount Pleasant, Bilston, Wolverhampton WV14 7LU
  ☎(01902) 556253
- Daisy Bank Community Library, Ash Street, Bradley, Bilston, Wolverhampton WV14 8UP
  ☎(01902) 556305
- Eastfield Library, Hurstbourne Crescent, Eastfield, Wolverhampton WV1 2EE
  ☎(01902) 556257
- Finchfield Library, White Oak Drive, Finchfield, Wolverhampton WV3 9AF
  ☎(01902) 556260

- Heath Town Community Library, Tudor Road, Heath Town, Wolverhampton WV10 0LT
  ☎(01902) 556266
- Oxley Library, Probert Road, Oxley, Wolverhampton WV10 6UF
  ☎(01902) 556287
- Tettenhall Library, Upper Street, Tettenhall, Wolverhampton WV6 8QF
  ☎(01902) 556308

Group Three
Branch Group Librarian Mrs D Jones BA (01902 556284)

- Bradmore Community Library, Bantock House, Bradmore Road, Wolverhampton WV3 9BH
  ☎(01902) 556299
- Long Knowle Library, Wood End Road, Wednesfield, Wolverhampton WV11 1YG
  ☎(01902) 556290
- Scotlands Community Library, Masefield Road, Wolverhampton WV10 8SA
  ☎(01902) 552199
- Spring Vale Library, Bevan Avenue, Wolverhampton WV4 6SG
  ☎(01902) 556284
- Warstones Library, Pinfold Grove, Penn, Wolverhampton WV4 9PT
  ☎(01902) 556275
- Wednesfield Library, Church Street, Wednesfield, Wolverhampton WV11 1SR
  ☎(01902) 556278

WORCESTERSHIRE

Authority Worcestershire County Council
HQ Cultural Services Division (Libraries and Information Service), County Hall, Spetchley Road, Worcester WR5 2NP
☎(01905) 766231
Fax (01905) 766244
url: http://www.worcestershire.gov.uk/libraries
Library Services Manager Mrs C Evans MCLIP (01905 766232; e-mail: cevans@worcestershire.gov.uk)
Strategic Library Manager, North and Services to Young People Mrs C Reed BA MCLIP (01905 766233; e-mail: creed@worcestershire.gov.uk)
Strategic Library Manager, South and Special Services N Preedy BSc MCLIP (01905 766239; e-mail: npreedy@worcestershire.gov.uk)
Strategic Library Manager, Information Services D Drewitt BA MCLIP (01905 766240; e-mail: ddrewitt@worcestershire.gov.uk)

Main libraries

- Bromsgrove Library, Stratford Road, Bromsgrove, Worcestershire B60 1AP
  ☎(01527) 575855 (575856 outside office hours)
  Fax (01905) 575855
  e-mail: bromsgrovelib@worcestershire.gov.uk
  Bromsgrove Librarian G T C Marshall BA MCLIP
- Droitwich Library, Victoria Square, Droitwich, Worcestershire WR9 8DQ
  ☎(01905) 773292

Fax (01905) 797401
e-mail: droitwichlib@worcestershire.gov.uk
Droitwich Librarian Miss V Booler MCLIP

- Evesham Library, Oat Street, Evesham, Worcestershire WR11 4JP
☎(01386) 442291/41348
Fax (01386) 765855
e-mail: eveshamlib@worcestershire.gov.uk
Evesham Librarian Mrs L Downes MCLIP
- Kidderminster Library, Market Street, Kidderminster, Worcestershire DY10 1PE
☎(01562) 824500
Fax (01562) 512907
e-mail: kidderminsterlib@worcestershire.gov.uk
Kidderminster Librarian R Hoggarth MA MCLIP
- Malvern Library, Graham Road, Malvern, Worcestershire WR14 2HU
☎(01902) 552199
Fax (01684) 892999
e-mail: malvernlib@worcestershire.gov.uk
Malvern Librarian K E Barber BA MCLIP
- Redditch Library, 15 Market Place, Redditch, Worcestershire B98 8AR
☎(01527) 63291
Fax (01527) 68571
e-mail: redditchlib@worcestershire.gov.uk
Redditch Librarian Vacant
- Worcester Library, Foregate Street, Worcester WR1 1DT
☎(01905) 765314
Fax (01905) 726664
e-mail: worcesterlib@worcestershire.gov.uk
Worcester Librarian J Stafford BA MCLIP
- Countywide Information Service (Intranet and Website), Information and Business Systems Division, County Hall, Spetchley Road, Worcester WR5 2NP
☎(01497) 847987
url: http://www.worcestershire.gov.uk
Web Manager P Taylor (e-mail: ptaylor@worcestershire.gov.uk)

YORK

Authority City of York Council
HQ York Library, Museum Street, York, North Yorkshire YO1 7DS
☎(01904) 655631
Fax (01904) 611025
url: http://library.york.gov.uk
Head of Library Service Ms A Mauger MCLIP

NORTHERN IRELAND

BELFAST EDUCATION AND LIBRARY BOARD

Authority Belfast Education and Library Board
HQ Belfast Public Libraries, Central Library, Royal Avenue, Belfast, Northern Ireland BT1 1EA
☎028 9050 9150
Fax 028 9033 2819
e-mail: info@libraries.belfast-elb.gov.uk
Chief Librarian Ms L Houston BLS MCLIP MBA (e-mail: l.houston@libraries.belfast-elb.gov.uk)

NORTH EASTERN EDUCATION AND LIBRARY BOARD

Authority North Eastern Education and Library Board
HQ Area Library HQ, Demesne Avenue, Ballymena, Co Antrim, Northern Ireland BT43 7BG
☎028 2566 4100
Fax 028 2563 2038
e-mail: library.enquiries@neelb.org.uk
url: http://www.neelb.org.uk
Chief Librarian Mrs P Valentine BA(Hons) FCLIP (028 2566 4101)
Acting Chief Librarian M McFaul MBA(Hons) DipM MCLIP (028 2566 4103)
Assistant Chief Librarian (Youth and Training) Ms N McNee BA MCLIP (028 2566 4139)
Assistant Chief Librarian (Information and Support) Ms A Peoples BA MCLIP DMS (028 2566 4102)
Assistant Chief Librarian (Public Services) Ms A Bryson BA MCLIP (028 2566 4104)

Group libraries

- Antrim Group Library, Ballycraigy School, Antrim, Co Antrim, Northern Ireland BT41 1PU
  ☎028 9446 8125
  Acting Group Librarian Ms E J Clarke BSc MCLIP
- Ballymena Group Library, Demesne Avenue, Ballymena, Co Antrim, Northern Ireland BT43 7BG
  ☎028 2566 4133
  Group Librarian Mrs J Stafford PGDipLib MCLIP MBA
- Carrickfergus Group Library, Joymount Court, Carrickfergus, Northern Ireland BT38 7DQ
  ☎028 9336 2261
  Group Librarian Mrs J Y Austin BA MCLIP
- Coleraine Group Library, County Hall, Castlerock Road, Coleraine, Northern Ireland BT1 3HP
  ☎028 7032 0201
  Group Librarian Mrs E Cooper MA PGDipLib BA(Hons)

- Magherafelt Group Library, The Bridewell Centre, 6 Church Street, Magherafelt, Northern Ireland BT45 6AN
  ☎028 7963 4887
  Group Librarian B Porter BSc MCLIP

SOUTH EASTERN EDUCATION AND LIBRARY BOARD

Authority South Eastern Education and Library Board
HQ Library Headquarters, Windmill Hill, Ballynahinch, Co Down, Northern Ireland BT24 8DH
☎028 9756 6400
Fax 028 9756 5072
e-mail: libraries@seelb.org.uk
url: http://www.seelb.org.uk
Chief Librarian Mrs B Porter BA(Hons) DipLibStud MCLIP (028 9756 6402)
Assistant Chief Librarians Mrs L Plummer BA(Hons) DipLibStud MCLIP (028 9756 6406), Ms A Adair BA(Hons) MPhil DipLibStud MCLIP (028 9756 6408)

Area libraries

- Dairy Farm Library, Dairy Farm Centre, Unit 17, Stewartstown Road, Dunmurry, Belfast, Co Antrim, Northern Ireland BT17 0AW
  ☎028 9043 1266
  Fax 028 9043 1278
  e-mail: dfarmlib@hotmail.com
  Group Library Manager Mrs M Bell BLS MCLIP
- Downpatrick Library, Market Street, Downpatrick, Co Down, Northern Ireland BT30 6LZ
  ☎028 4461 2895
  Fax 028 4461 9039
  e-mail: dpatricklib@hotmail.com
  Group Library Manager Mrs P Cooper BLS PGDipA&LS MCLIP
- Holywood Library, Sullivan Building, 86-88 High Street, Holywood, Co Down, Northern Ireland BT18 9AE
  ☎028 9042 4232
  Fax 028 9042 4194
  e-mail: hwoodlib@hotmail.com
  Group Library Manager Mrs N Millar BA(Hons) DipLibStud MCLIP
- Tullycarnet Library, Kinross Avenue, Kings Road, Belfast, Co Antrim, Northern Ireland BT5 7GF
  ☎028 9048 5079
  Fax 028 9048 2342
  e-mail: tullycarnetlib@hotmail.com
  Group Library Managers Mrs A McVey BA DipLibStud MCLIP

SOUTHERN EDUCATION AND LIBRARY BOARD

Authority Southern Education and Library Board
HQ Library Headquarters, 1 Markethill Road, Armagh, Co Armagh, Northern Ireland BT60 1NR
☎028 3752 5353
Fax 028 3752 6879
url: http://www.selb.org
Chief Librarian Vacant
Assistant Chief Librarians R Dougan (028 3752 0703), P Reid (028 3752 0707)
Coordinator: Education Services Mrs M Pender FLAI (028 3752 0740)
Coordinator: Promotion and Marketing G Burns BA (028 3752 0754)
Coordinator: Public Services Miss J Blair MCLIP (028 3752 0715)
Coordinator: Stock Services P Pender MCLIP (028 3752 0760)

Group library headquarters

- Lurgan Group Library HQ, Carnegie Street, Lurgan, Co Armagh, Northern Ireland BT66 6AS
  ☎028 3832 3912
  Group Librarian B McGeown BA(Hons) MBA
- Newry Group Library Headquarters, 79 Hill Street, Newry, Co Down, Northern Ireland BT34 1DG
  ☎028 3066 1652
  Group Librarian M Doran MSc MCLIP
- Irish and Local Studies Service, 39c Abbey Street, Armagh, Co Armagh, Northern Ireland BT61 7EB
  ☎028 3752 7851
  Irish and Local Studies Librarian Ms M McVeigh BA MSSc(Irish Studies) DipLib
- Local Government Information Service, 24-26 Church Street, Portadown, Co Armagh, Northern Ireland BT62 3LQ
  ☎028 3833 6122
  Librarian Mrs S Young BA MCLIP

WESTERN EDUCATION AND LIBRARY BOARD

Authority Western Education and Library Board
HQ Library Headquarters, 1 Spillars Place, Omagh, Co Tyrone, Northern Ireland BT78 1HL
☎028 8224 4821
Fax 028 8224 6716
e-mail: librarian@omalib.demon.co.uk
url: http://www.welbni.org
Head of Libraries and Information Ms H Osborn MLib MCLIP
Assistant Chief Librarians Mrs R A Adams BA MCLIP, L P Crossey BA MCLIP

Central/largest library

Central Library, Foyle Street, Londonderry, Northern Ireland BT48 1AL
☎028 7127 2310
Fax 028 7126 9084
Divisional Librarian Mrs P Ward BA MCLIP

Divisional library headquarters

- North West Divisional HQ, Central Library, Foyle Street, Londonderry, Northern Ireland BT48 1AL
  ☎028 7127 2315
  Fax 028 7126 1374
  Divisional Librarian Mrs P Ward BA MCLIP
- South West Divisional HQ, Hall's Lane, Enniskillen, Co Fermanagh, Northern Ireland BT74 7DR
  ☎028 6632 2886
  Fax 028 6632 4685
  Divisional Librarian D Preston BA MCLIP
- Omagh Library, 1 Spillars Place, Omagh, Co Tyrone, Northern Ireland BT78 1HL
  ☎028 8224 4821
  Fax 028 8224 6772
  Librarian Ms G McSorley BA MCLIP
- Enniskillen Library, Halls Lane, Enniskillen, Co Fermanagh, Northern Ireland BT74 7DR
  ☎028 6632 2886
  Fax 028 6632 4685
  Librarian S Bleakley BA(Hons) DLS
- Strabane Library, Butcher Street, Strabane, Co Tyrone, Northern Ireland BT82 8BJ
  ☎028 7138 3686
  Fax 028 7138 2745
  Librarian Mrs A Harron BA MCLIP
- Limavady Library, 5 Connell Street, Limavady, Londonderry, Northern Ireland BT47 0EA
  ☎028 7776 2540
  Fax 028 7772 2006
  Librarian Mrs L Brown BA MCLIP

ABERDEEN

Authority Aberdeen City Council
HQ Arts and Recreation Dept, Library and Information Services, Central Library, Rosemount Viaduct, Aberdeen AB25 1GW
☎(01224) 652500 (enquiries & administration)
Fax (01224) 641985
e-mail: centlib@arts-rec.aberdeen.net.uk
url: http://www.aberdeencity.gov.uk
Principal Officer, Library and Information Services N M Bruce MA DipLib LLM MCLIP (01224 652536; e-mail: neilbr@arts-rec.aberdeen.net.uk)
Public Services Librarian (Lending) J D Grant BA MCLIP (01224 652549; e-mail: jgrant@arts-rec.aberdeen.net.uk)
Public Services Librarian (Information) J A Pratt MCLIP (01224 652534; e-mail: jpratt@arts-rec.aberdeen.net.uk)
Network Development Librarian A Rennie MCLIP (01224 652522; e-mail: arennie@arts-rec.aberdeen.net.uk)

ABERDEENSHIRE

Authority Aberdeenshire Council
HQ Library and Information Service, Meldrum Meg Way, Oldmeldrum, Aberdeenshire AB51 0GN
☎(01651) 872707 (enquiries & administration)
Fax (01651) 872142
e-mail: alis@aberdeenshire.gov.uk
url: http://www.aberdeenshire.gov.uk/alis
Principal Librarian G Moore BA MCLIP (01651 871202; e-mail: gerald.moore@aberdeeenshire.gov.uk)
Media Resources Manager Mrs L A Addison BA MCLIP (01651 871203; e-mail: lynne.addison@aberdeenshire.gov.uk; fax: as above)
Central Support Services Manager Mrs A A M Harrison MCLIP (01651 871210; e-mail: anne.harrison@aberdeenshire.gov.uk; fax: as above)
Client Services Librarians Mrs H W Dewar MA MCLIP (01358 729208; e-mail: helen.dewar@aberdeenshire.gov.uk; fax: 01358 722864), R A de Silva BA MBA MCLIP Med (01330 823784; e-mail: rufus.de.silva@aberdeenshire.gov.uk; fax: 01330 824516)

ANGUS

Authority Angus Council
HQ County Buildings, Market Street, Forfar, Angus DD8 3WF
☎(01307) 461460
Fax (01307) 462590
Head of Cultural Services N K Atkinson DipEd AMA FMA
Libraries Manager J Doherty BSc MCLIP
Cultural Resources Manager C Dakers BA MCLI

Central/largest library

Library Support Services, 50 West High Street, Forfar, Angus DD8 1BA
☎(01307) 466966
Fax (01307) 468451
e-mail: central.services@angus.gov.uk
Support Services Librarian J Fraser BA DipLib MCLIP

Area libraries

- Arbroath Library, Hill Terrace, Arbroath, Angus DD11 1AH
  ☎(01241) 872248
  Fax (01241) 434396
  e-mail: arbroath.library@angus.gov.uk
  Librarian Ms T Roby MCLIP
- Brechin Library, 10 St Ninian's Square, Brechin, Angus DD9 7AA
  ☎(01356) 622687
  Fax (01356) 624271
  e-mail: brechin.library@angus.gov.uk
  Librarian G Hunter MCLIP
- Carnoustie Library, 21 High Street, Carnoustie, Angus DD7 6AN
  ☎(01241) 859620
  e-mail: carnoustie.library@angus.gov.uk
  Librarian A Sutherland BA MCLIP
- Forfar Library, 50-56 West High Street, Forfar, Angus DD8 1BA
  ☎(01307) 466071
  Fax (01307) 468451
  e-mail: forfar.library@angus.gov.uk
  Librarian I K Neil MA MCLIP
- Kirriemuir Library, Town Hall, 28/30 Reform Street, Kirriemuir, Angus DD8 4BS
  ☎(01575) 572357
  Librarian Ms C Sharp BA MCLIP
- Monifieth Library, High Street, Monifieth, Angus DD5 4AE
  ☎(01382) 533819
  e-mail: monifieth.library@angus.gov.uk
  Librarian Ms D Milne MCLIP
- Montrose Library, 214 High Street, Montrose, Angus DD10 8PH
  ☎(01674) 673256
  Fax (01674) 671810
  e-mail: montrose.library@angus.gov.uk
  Librarian Ms E Brown BA MCLIP

ARGYLL AND BUTE

Authority Argyll and Bute Council
HQ Library and Information Service HQ, Highland Avenue, Sandbank, Dunoon, Argyll PA23 8PB
☎(01369) 703214/703735
Fax (01369) 705797

Principal Library and Information Services Officer A I Ewan MCLIP
(e-mail: andy.ewan@argyll-bute.gov.uk)

Area libraries

- Campbeltown Library, Hall Street, Campbeltown, Argyll PA28 6BS
  ☎(01586) 552366 ext 2237
  Fax (01586) 552938
  Area Librarian Ms S Fortune MCLIP
- Dunoon Library, 248 Argyll Street, Dunoon, Argyll PA23 7LT
  ☎(01369) 703735 ext 7522
  Fax (01369) 701323
  Area Librarian Ms P Flynn BA MCLIP
- Helensburgh Library, West King Street, Helensburgh, Dunbartonshire G84 8EB
  ☎(01436) 674626
  Fax (01436) 679567
  Area Librarian/IT Systems Development Manager P McCann BA MCLIP
- Oban Library, Corran Halls, Oban, Argyll PA34 5AB
  ☎(01631) 571444
  Fax (01631) 571372
  Area Librarian K Baker BA DipLib MCLIP
- Rothesay Library, Moat Centre, Stuart Street, Rothesay, Bute PA20 0EP
  ☎(01700) 503266
  Fax (01700) 500511
  Branch Librarian E Monaghan MCLIP

CLACKMANNANSHIRE

Authority Clackmannanshire Council
HQ Clackmannanshire Libraries, Alloa Library, 26-28 Drysdale Street, Alloa, Clackmannanshire FK10 1JL
☎(01259) 722262
Fax (01259) 219469
e-mail: libraries@clacks.gov.uk
Library Services Manager D A Hynd MCLIP
Team Leader, Community Library Service J A Blake BSc DipLib MCLIP DipEdTech
Training and Stock Circulation Librarian Ms H Finlayson MA DipLib MCLIP
Information Librarian and Archivist I D Murray MA DipLib MCLIP DAA
Mobile Librarian A Flanagan

Branches within community access points

- Alva Community Access Point, 153 West Stirling Street, Alva, Clackmannanshire
  ☎(01259) 760652
  Fax (01259) 760354
  Senior Community Access Officer Ms N Foster
- Clackmannan Community Access Point, Main Street, Clackmannan, Clackmannanshire
  ☎(01259) 721579
  Fax (01259) 212493
  Senior Community Access Officer Ms J Laird

- Dollar Community Access Point, Dollar Civic Centre, Park Place, Dollar, Clackmannanshire
  ☎(01259) 743253
  Fax (01259) 743328
  Senior Community Access Officer Ms K Waddell
- Menstrie Community Access Point, The Dumyat Leisure Centre, Main Street East, Menstrie, Clackmannanshire
  ☎(01259) 769439
  Fax (01259) 762941
  Senior Community Access Officer W Huggan
- Sauchie Community Access Point, 42-48 Main Street, Sauchie, Clackmannanshire
  ☎(01259) 721679
  Fax (01259) 218750
  Senior Community Access Officer Ms M Hunter
- Tillicoultry Branch Library, 99 High Street, Tillicoultry, Clackmannanshire
  ☎(01259) 751685 (Tel/Fax)
  Branch Library Coordinator Ms L Paterson
- Tullibody Library, Leisure Centre, Abercromby Place, Tullibody, Clackmannanshire
  ☎(01259) 218725
  Branch Library Coordinator Ms I Dykes

COMHAIRLE NAN EILEAN SIAR (formerly Western Isles)

Authority Comhairle nan Eilean Siar
HQ Public Library, 19 Cromwell Street, Stornoway, Isle of Lewis HS1 2DA
☎(01851) 708631
Fax (01851) 708677
e-mail: stornoway-library@cne-siar.gov.uk
Chief Librarian R M Eaves BA DipEd MCLIP (e-mail: bobeaves@cne-siar.gov.uk)
Senior Librarian, Adult Services D J Fowler MCLIP (e-mail: dfowler@cne-siar.gov.uk)
Senior Librarian, Youth Services Mrs M Ferguson MA MCLIP (e-mail: mary-ferguson@cne-siar.gov.uk)

Area libraries

- Community Library, Sgoil Lionacleit, Liniclate, Isle of Benbecula HS7 5PJ
  ☎(01870) 602211
  Fax (01870) 602817
  e-mail: sgoil-lionacleit-library@cne-siar.gov.uk
  Community Librarian Mrs J F Bramwell BA MCLIP
- Community Library, Castlebay Community School, Castlebay, Isle of Barra HS9 5XD
  ☎(01871) 810471
  Fax (01871) 810650
  e-mail: castlebaylibrary@eileansiar.biblio.net
  Senior Library Assistant Mrs L Mackinnon
- Community Library, Sgoil Shiaboist, Shawbost, Isle of Lewis HS2 9PQ
  ☎(01851) 710213
  e-mail: shawlib@eileansiar.biblio.net
  Library Assistant Mrs C A Campbell

- Community Library, Sir E Scott School, Tarbert, Isle of Harris HS3 3BG
  ☎(01859) 502000
  e-mail: sir-e-scott-library@cne-siar.gov.uk
  Library Assistant Mrs F Morrison MA
- Community Library, Daliburgh School, Daliburgh, Isle of South Uist HS8 5SS
  ☎(01878) 700673
  e-mail: daliburgh-library@cne-siar.gov.uk
  Library Assistant M Walker

DUMFRIES AND GALLOWAY

Authority Dumfries and Galloway Council
HQ Libraries, Information and Archives, Central Support Unit, Catherine Street, Dumfries DG1 1JB
☎(01387) 253820 (enquiries), (01387) 252070 (administration)
Fax (01387) 260294
e-mail: libs&i@dumgal.gov.uk
Libraries, Information and Archives Manager A R Johnston BA MCLIP FSA(Scot)

District libraries

- Annan Library, Charles Street, Annan, DG12 5AG
  ☎(01461) 202809
  Fax (01461) 202809
- Archive Centre, 33 Burns Street, Dumfries DG1 2PS
  ☎(01387) 269254
  Fax (01387) 264126
- Castle Douglas Library, Market Hill, King Street, Castle Douglas, DG7 1AE
  ☎(01556) 502643
  Fax (01556) 502643
- Dalbeattie Library, 23 High Street, Dalbeattie, DG5 4AD
  ☎(01556) 610898
  Fax (01556) 610898
- Dalry Library, Main Street, Dalry, Castle Douglas, DG7 3UP
  ☎(01644) 430234
  Fax (01644) 430234
- Eastriggs Library, Eastriggs Community School, Eastriggs, Annan, DG12 6PZ
  ☎(01461) 40844
  Fax (01461) 40844
- Ewart Library, Catherine Street, Dumfries DG1 1JB
  ☎(01387) 253820/252070/260000
  Fax (01387) 260294
- Gatehouse Library, 63 High Street, Gatehouse of Fleet, DG7 2HS
  ☎(01557) 814646
  Fax (01557) 814646
- Georgetown Library, Gillbrae Road, Georgetown, Dumfries DG1 4EJ
  ☎(01387) 256059
  Fax (01387) 256059
- Gretna Library, The Richard Greenhow Centre, Central Avenue, Gretna, DG16 5AQ

☎(01461) 338000
Fax (01461) 338000

- Kirkconnel Library, Greystone Avenue, Kelloholm, DG4 6RA
☎(01659) 67191
Fax (01659) 67191
- Kirkcudbright Library, Sheriff Court House, High Street, Kirkcudbright, DG6 4JW
☎(01557) 331240
Fax (01557) 331240
- Langholm Library, Charles Street, Old Langholm, DG13 0AA
☎(013873) 80040
Fax (013873) 80040
- Lochmaben Library, Masonic Hall, High Street, Lochmaben, Lockerbie DG11 1NQ
☎(01387) 811865
Fax (01387) 811865
- Lochside Library, Lochside Road, Dumfries DG2 0LW
☎(01387) 268751
Fax (01387) 268751
- Lochthorn Library, Lochthorn, Dumfries DG1 1UF
☎(01387) 265780
Fax (01387) 266424
- Lockerbie Library, 31-33 High Street, Lockerbie, DG11 2JL
☎(01576) 203380
Fax (01576) 203380
- Moffat Library, Town Hall, High Street, Moffat, DG10 9HF
☎(01683) 220952
Fax (01683) 220952
- Newton Stewart Library, Church Street, Newton Stewart, DG8 6ER
☎(01671) 403450
Fax (01671) 403450
- Port William Library, Church Street, Port William, Newton Stewart, DG8 9QJ
☎(01988) 700406
Fax (01988) 700406
- Sanquhar Library, 106 High Street, Sanquhar, DG4 6DZ
☎(01659) 50626
Fax (01659) 50626
- Stranraer Library, North Strand Street, Stranraer, DG9 7LD
☎(01776) 707400/707440
Fax (01776) 703565
- Thornhill Library, Townhead Street, Thornhill, DG3 5NW
☎(01848) 330654
Fax (01848) 330654
- Whithorn Library, St John's Street, Whithorn, DG8 8PF
☎(01988) 500406
Fax (01988) 500406
- Wigtown Library, Duncan Park, Wigtown, DG8 9JD
☎(01988) 403329
Fax (01988) 403329

DUNDEE

Authority Dundee City Council
HQ Neighbourhood Resources and Development Department, Floor 1, Podium Block, Tayside House, Crichton Street, Dundee DD1 3RZ
☎(01382) 433283
Fax (01382) 433871
Director, Neighbourhood Resources and Development F Patrick BA DipYCW (e-mail: fraser.patrick@dundeecity.gov.uk)
Neighbourhood Resources Manager Mrs M Methven MCLIP (e-mail: moira.methven@dundeecity.gov.uk)

Development and Quality Assurance Team, Arthurstone Neighbourhood Library, Arthurstone Terrace, Dundee DD4 6RT
Unit Leader R Hardie (01382 433461)
Senior Adult Library and Information Worker Ms F Macpherson MA DipLib MCLIP (01382 438893)
Senior Youth Library and Information Worker Ms L Moy BA MCLIP (01382 438889)
Senior Library and Information Worker (Development) Ms J Gair (01382 438893)
Unit Leader Library and Information Ms F Foster MCLIP (01382 435803)

Central/largest library

Central Library, The Wellgate, Dundee DD1 1DB
☎(01382) 434318 (enquiries), (01382) 434323 (administration)
Fax (01382) 434642
url: www.dundeecity.gov.uk/dcchtml/nrd/centlib/welcome.htm
Section Leader Mrs J Dobbie (01382 434323; e-mail: judy.dobbie@dundeecity.gov.uk)
Unit Leader Ms C Ferguson MA MCLIP (01382 434376; e-mail: christine.ferguson@dundeecity.gov.uk)
Community Information Team Leader Mrs F Robertson MA MCLIP (01382 434336; e-mail: frances.robertson@dundeecity.gov.uk)

Neighbourhood libraries

- Ardler Neighbourhood Library, Ardler Complex, Turnberry Avenue, Ardler, Dundee DD2 3TP
  ☎(01382) 432863
  Fax (01382) 432862
  Neighbourhood Library and Information Worker Miss B Cook BA MCLIP
- Arthurstone Neighbourhood Library, Arthurstone Terrace, Dundee DD4 6RT
  ☎(01382) 438881
  Fax (01382) 438881
  Senior Neighbourhood Library and Information Assistant Mrs S Westgate
- Blackness Neighbourhood Library, 225 Perth Road, Dundee DD2 1EJ
  ☎(01382) 435843
  Fax (01382) 435942
  Neighbourhood Library and Information Worker Mrs E Young
- Broughty Ferry Neighbourhood Library, Queen Street, Broughty Ferry, Dundee DD5 2HN

☎(01382) 436919
Fax (01382) 436913
Neighbourhood Library and Information Worker I Cranmer MCLIP

- Charleston Neighbourhood Library, 60 Craigowan Road, Dundee DD2 4NL
☎(01382) 436723
Fax (01382) 436643
Senior Neighbourhood Library and Information Assistant Ms E Darling
- Coldside Neighbourhood Library, 150 Strathmartine Road, Dundee DD3 7SE
☎(01382) 432849
Fax (01382) 432850
Neighbourhood Library and Information Worker Mrs S Wood
- Douglas Community and Library Centre, Balmoral Place, Douglas, Dundee DD4 8SH
☎(01382) 436864
Fax (01382) 436922
Senior Neighbourhood Library and Information Assistant Mrs R McDowall
- Fintry Neighbourhood Library, Finmill Centre, Findcastle Street, Dundee DD4 9EW
☎(01382) 432560
Fax (01382) 432559
Senior Neighbourhood Library and Information Assistant Ms L Smales
- The Hub Neighbourhood Centre and Library, Pitkerro Road, Dundee DD4 8ES
☎(01382) 438626
Fax (01382) 438627
Senior Neighbourhood Library and Information Assistant Mrs L Kell
- Kirkton Neighbourhood Library, Derwent Avenue, Dundee DD3 0BW
☎(01382) 432851
Fax (01382) 432852
Senior Neighbourhood Library and Information Assistant Mrs A Smith
- Lochee Neighbourhood Library, High Street, Lochee, Dundee DD2 3AU
☎(01382) 432675
Fax (01382) 432677
Senior Neighbourhood Library and Information Assistant Mrs J Rodger
- Menzieshill Neighbourhood Centre and Library, Orleans Place, Menzieshill, Dundee DD2 4BN
☎(01382) 435965
Fax (01382) 435992
Senior Neighbourhood Library and Information Assistant Miss L Andrews
- Whitfield Library and Learning Centre, Whitfield Drive, Dundee DD4 0DX
☎(01382) 432569
Fax (01382) 432562
Neighbourhood Library and Information Worker S Robertson

EAST AYRSHIRE

Authority East Ayrshire Council
HQ Library, Registration and Information Services, Dick Institute, 14 Elmbank Avenue, Kilmarnock, Ayrshire KA1 3BU
☎(01563) 554300 (general enquiries)
Fax (01563) 554311

e-mail: libraries@east-ayrshire.gov.uk
url: http://www.east-ayrshire.gov.uk/comleilib/
Library, Registration and Information Services Manager G Cairns BA DipLib MCLIP DMS (e-mail: gerard.cairns@east-ayrshire.gov.uk)
Senior Librarian Mrs E Gray MA Dip Lib MCLIP (e-mail: elaine.gray@east-ayrshire.gov.uk)
Senior Librarian J Laurenson BSc MCLIP (e-mail: john.laurenson@east-ayrshire.gov.uk)
Support Services Librarian Mrs J A Harvey MA DipLib MCLIP (e-mail: julia.harvey@east-ayrshire.gov.uk)
Information Officer Ms D Vallance BA(Hons) DipLib MCLIP (e-mail: dawn.vallance@east-ayrshire.gov.uk)
Community Librarian (Staff Development) Mrs L J Mee BA MCLIP (e-mail: lynn.mee@east-ayrshire.gov.uk)
Community Librarian (Marketing) Mrs G Downie BA MCLIP (e-mail: geraldine.downie@east-ayrshire.gov.uk)
Community Librarian (Heritage Services) Mrs A Geddes MCLIP (e-mail: baird.institute@east-ayrshire.gov.uk)
Community Librarian (Operations) H MacLean MA DipLib MCLIP (e-mail: hugh.maclean@east-ayrshire.gov.uk)

EAST DUNBARTONSHIRE

Authority East Dunbartonshire Council
HQ Strategic Directorate: Community: Department of Social Inclusion and Community Development, William Patrick Library, 2 West High Street, Kirkintilloch, East Dunbartonshire G66 1AD
☎0141 776 5666
Fax 0141 776 0408
e-mail: libraries@eastdunbarton.gov.uk
url: http://www.eastdunbarton.gov.uk
Information and Learning Manager Ms E Brown MA MCLIP (e-mail: elizabeth.brown@eastdunbarton.gov.uk)
Assistant Manager, Adult Lending and Support Services D Kenvyn BA MCLIP (e-mail: david.kenvyn@eastdunbarton.gov.uk)
Support Services Librarian Ms A Hamilton BA MCLIP (e-mail: anne.hamilton@eastdunbarton.gov.uk)
Assistant Manager, Learning and Outreach Vacant
Assistant Manager, Information and Archives D Martin FCLIP (0141 776 8090; e-mail: don.martin@eastdunbarton.gov.uk)
Bibliographical Services Librarian Ms S Busby BA MCLIP (e-mail: sandra.busby@eastdunbarton.gov.uk)

Central/largest library

William Patrick Library, 2 West High Street, Kirkintilloch, East Dunbartonshire G66 1AD
☎0141 776 7484 (enquiries), 0141 776 5666 (administration)
Fax 0141 776 0408
Branch Librarian Mrs D Fergusson, Mrs E Morris BA (job-share)

Branch libraries

- Brookwood Library, 166 Drymen Road, Bearsden, East Dunbartonshire G61 3RJ
  ☎0141 942 6811
  Fax 0141 943 1119
  Branch Librarian J Rae BA MCLIP
- Bishopbriggs Library, 170 Kirkintilloch Road, Bishopbriggs, East Dunbartonshire G64 2LX
  ☎0141 772 4513
  Fax 0141 762 5363
  Branch Librarian Mrs E Clifford MCLIP, Mrs F Warner BA MCLIP (job-share)
- Craighead Library, Craighead Road, Milton of Campsie, East Dunbartonshire G65 8DL
  ☎(01360) 311925
  Assistant in Charge Mrs M Newton, Mrs S Vernon (job-share)
- Lennoxtown Library, Main Street, Lennoxtown, East Dunbartonshire G65 7DG
  ☎(01360) 311436
  Fax (01360) 311436
  Senior Library Supervisor Ms E Gordon
- Lenzie Library, 13 Alexandra Avenue, Lenzie, East Dunbartonshire G66 5BG
  ☎0141 776 3021
  Library Supervisor Ms L Finlayson
- Milngavie Library, Community Centre, Allander Way, Milngavie, East Dunbartonshire G62 8PN
  ☎0141 956 2776
  Fax 0141 570 0052
  Branch Librarian J Murray MCLIP
- Westerton Library, 82 Maxwell Avenue, Bearsden, East Dunbartonshire G61 1NZ
  ☎0141 943 0780
  Library Supervisor Mrs L Mann, Ms E Bushfield (job-share)

EAST LOTHIAN

Authority East Lothian Council
HQ Library and Museum Headquarters, Dunbar Road, Haddington, East Lothian EH41 3PJ
☎(01620) 828205 (enquiries), (01620) 828200 (administration)
Fax (01620) 828201
e-mail: jstevenson@eastlothian.gov.uk (for general enquiries)
Principal Libraries Officer D Moody MCLIP

Largest library

Musselburgh Library, 10 Bridge Street, Musselburgh, East Lothian EH21 6AG
☎0131 665 2183
e-mail: musselburgh.library@eastlothian.gov.uk
Branch Librarian Ms J Paterson BA DipLib

Branch libraries

- Dunbar Library, Castellau, Belhaven Road, Dunbar, East Lothian EH42 1DA
  ☎(01368) 863521
  e-mail: dunbar.libary@eastlothian.gov.uk
  Assistant i/c Ms R Barton

- Haddington Library, Newton Port, Haddington, East Lothian EH41 3NA
  ☎(01620) 822531
  Fax (01620) 822531
  e-mail: haddington.library@eastlothian.gov.uk
  Branch Librarian Ms T Gavan MCLIP, Ms M Daly MCLIP (job-share)
- North Berwick Library, The Old School, School Road, North Berwick, East Lothian EH39 4JU
  ☎(01620) 893470
  e-mail: northberwick.library@eastlothian.gov.uk
  Branch Librarian Ms S Butts MA DipLib
- Prestonpans Library, West Loan, Prestonpans, East Lothian EH32 9NX
  ☎(01875) 810788
  e-mail: prestonpans.library@eastlothian.gov.uk
  Branch Librarian Ms E Thomson BA MCLIP
- Tranent Library, 3 Civic Square, Tranent, East Lothian EH33 1LH
  ☎(01875) 610254
  e-mail: tranent.library@eastlothian.gov.uk
  Branch Librarian Ms D Elliott MA DipLib
- Ormiston Library, 5A Meadowbank, Ormiston, East Lothian EH35 5LQ
  ☎(01875) 616675
  Fax (01875) 612272
  e-mail: ormiston.library@eastlothian.gov.uk
  Assistant i/c W Wilson
- Port Seton Library, Community Centre, South Seton Park, Port Seton, East Lothian EH32 0BG
  ☎(01875) 811709
  Fax (01875) 815177
  e-mail: portseton.library@eastlothian.gov.uk
  Assistant i/c Mrs I Muir

Specialist library

Local History Centre, Newton Port, Haddington, East Lothian EH41 3NA
☎(01620) 823307
Local History Librarian Mrs V Wallace MCLIP (e-mail: vwallace@eastlothian.gov.uk)

EAST RENFREWSHIRE

Authority East Renfrewshire Council
HQ Cultural Services, Glen Street, Barrhead, East Renfrewshire G78 1QA
☎0141 577 3500 (enquiries)
Fax 0141 577 3501
url: http://www.eastrenfrewshire.gov.uk
Head of Cultural Services K McKinlay MA(Hons) PGDipLib MCLIP (0141 577 3103; e-mail: ken.mckinlay@eastrenfrewshire.gov.uk)
Cultural Services Manager: Performance Management and Quality E Fox MCLIP (0141 577 3512; e-mail: eric.fox@eastrenfrewshire.gov.uk)
Cultural Services Manager: Information & Learning Services Mrs E McGettigan BA MCLIP (0141 577 3503; e-mail: liz.mcgettigan@eastrenfrewshire.gov.uk)

Cultural Services Manager: Arts & Support Services M Wright MCLIP (0141 577 3502; e-mail: malcolm.wright@eastrenfrewshire.gov.uk)
Team Leader, Community Services Miss A Rowson BA(Hons) MA MCLIP (0141 577 3516; e-mail: amanda.rowson@eastrenfrewshire.gov.uk)
Systems Librarian S Simpson BA PGDipIT (0141 577 3509; e-mail: scott.simpson@eastrenfrewshire.gov.uk)

Community libraries

- Barrhead Community Library, Glen Street, Barrhead, East Renfrewshire G78 1QA
  ☎0141 577 3518
  e-mail: barrheadl@eastrenfrewshire.gov.uk
- Busby Community Library, Duff Memorial Hall, Main Street, Busby, East Renfrewshire G76 8DX
  ☎0141 577 4971
  e-mail: busbyl@eastrenfrewshire.gov.uk
- Clarkston Community Library, Clarkston Road, Clarkston, East Renfrewshire G76 8NE
  ☎0141 577 4972
  Fax 0141 577 4973
  e-mail: clarkstonl@eastrenfrewshire.gov.uk
- Eaglesham Community Library, Montgomerie Hall, Eaglesham, East Renfrewshire G76 0LH
  ☎(01355) 302649
  Fax (01355) 302649
  e-mail: eagleshaml@eastrenfrewshire.gov.uk
- Giffnock Community Library, Station Road, Giffnock, East Renfrewshire G46 6JF
  ☎0141 577 4976
  Fax 0141 577 4978
  e-mail: giffnockl@eastrenfrewshire.gov.uk
- Mearns Community Library, McKinley Place, Newton Mearns, East Renfrewshire G77 6EZ
  ☎0141 577 4979
  Fax 0141 577 4980
  e-mail: mearnsl@eastrenfrewshire.gov.uk
- Neilston Community Library, Main Street, Neilston, East Renfrewshire G78 3NN
  ☎0141 577 4981
  Fax 0141 577 4982
  e-mail: neilstonl@eastrenfrewshire.gov.uk
- Netherlee Library Centre, Netherlee Pavilion, Linn Park Avenue, East Renfrewshire G44 3PH
  ☎0141 637 1301
- Thornliebank Community Library, 1 Spiersbridge Road, Thornliebank, East Renfrewshire G46 7SJ
  ☎0141 577 4983
  Fax 0141 577 4816
  e-mail: thornliebankl@eastrenfrewshire.gov.uk
- Uplawmoor Library Centre, Mure Hall, Tannoch Road, Uplawmoor, East Renfrewshire G78 4AF
  ☎(01505) 850564

EDINBURGH

Authority City of Edinburgh Council
HQ Central Library, George IV Bridge, Edinburgh EH1 1EG
☎0131 242 8000
Fax 0131 242 8009
e-mail: eclis@edinburgh.gov.uk
Acting Head of Libraries and Information Services W Wallace MA MCLIP
Acting Central Library and Information Services Manager J Thompson BA DipLib MCLIP
Strategic Library Services Manager Ms M Corr BA DipLib MCLIP
Bibliographic and Support Services Manager M Hinds BA DipLib MCLIP
Community Library Services Manager Ms G McCaig DipLib MCLIP

Divisional libraries

- East Division. Newington Library, 17 Fountainhall Road, Edinburgh EH9 2LN
  ☎0131 529 5536
  Fax 0131 529 5491
  e-mail: newington.library@edinburgh.gov.uk
  Principal Library Officer M Spells
- North Division. Leith Library, 28 Ferry Road, Edinburgh EH6 5AE
  ☎0131 529 5517
  Fax 0131 554 2720
  e-mail: leith.library@edinburgh.gov.uk
  Principal Library Officer Ms M McChrystal BLib MCLIP
- South Division. Wester Hailes Library, 1 Westside Plaza, Wester Hailes, Edinburgh EH14 2FT
  ☎0131 529 5667
  Fax 0131 529 5671
  e-mail: westerhailes.library@edinburgh.gov.uk
  Principal Library Officer Ms L Spells BSc DipLib MCLIP
- West Division. Blackhall Library, 56 Hillhouse Road, Edinburgh EH4 5EG
  ☎0131 529 5595
  Fax 0131 336 5419
  e-mail: blackhall.library@edinburgh.gov.uk
  Principal Library Officer Ms E Kilmurry BA MCLIP

FALKIRK

Authority Falkirk Council
HQ Library, Victoria Buildings, Queen Street, Falkirk FK2 7AF
☎(01324) 506800
Fax (01324) 506801
url: http://www.falkirk.gov.uk
Libraries Manager Mrs S Allison MA MCLIP (e-mail: sue.allison@falkirk.gov.uk)

Central/largest library

Falkirk Library, Hope Street, Falkirk FK1 5AU

☎(01324) 503605
Fax (01324) 503606
e-mail: falkirk.library@falkirk.gov.uk
Principal Librarian Ms A Herron MA DipLib MCLIP

Other libraries

- Grangemouth Library, Bo'ness Road, Grangemouth, Falkirk FK3 8AG
  ☎(01324) 504690
  Fax (01324) 504691
  e-mail: grangemouth.library@falkirk.gov.uk
  Senior Librarians Mrs S Woodforde MCLIP, Mrs R Williams BSc(Hons) DipLib
- Larbert Library, Main Street, Stenhousemuir, Larbert, Falkirk FK5 3JX
  ☎(01324) 503590
  Fax (01324) 503592
  e-mail: larbert.library@falkirk.gov.uk
  Senior Librarians Mrs K Jaffray BA MCLIP, Miss T Milligan MA MCLIP
- Denny Library, 49 Church Walk, Denny, Falkirk FK6 6DF
  ☎(01324) 504242
  Fax (01324) 504240
  e-mail: denny.library@falkirk.gov.uk
  Librarians Mrs L Alexander BA MCLIP, Mrs S Hill BA MCLIP
- Bo'ness Library, Scotland's Close, Bo'ness, Falkirk EH51 0AH
  ☎(01506) 778520
  Fax (01506) 778521
  e-mail: bo'ness.library@falkirk.gov.uk
  Librarians R Murray MCLIP, Miss C Simm BA MCLIP
- Bonnybridge Library, Bridge Street, Bonnybridge, Falkirk FK4 1AD
  ☎(01324) 503295
  Fax (01324) 503296
  e-mail: bonnybridge.library@falkirk.gov.uk
  Librarian Vacant
- Slamannan Library, The Cross, Slamannan, Falkirk FK1 3EX
  ☎(01324) 851373
  Fax (01324) 851862
  e-mail: slamannan.library@falkirk.gov.uk
  Librarian Mrs I McIntyre MCLIP

FIFE

Authority Fife Council
HQ Arts, Libraries and Museums, Town House, Kirkcaldy, Fife KY1 1XW
☎(01592) 417388
Fax (01592) 417847
Service Manager, Arts, Libraries, Museums I Whitelaw

Area libraries

- Central Area Library HQ, East Fergus Place, Kirkcaldy, Fife KY1 1XT
  ☎(01592) 412930

Fax (01592) 412941
Libraries Cultural Services Coordinator D Spalding MCLIP
Libraries Systems and Support Coordinator D Burns

- East Area Library HQ, Area Library, County Buildings, St Catherine Street, Cupar, Fife KY15 4TA
☎(01334) 412736
Fax (01334) 412941
Libraries Information Services Coordinator Ms A McLachlan MA MCLIP
- West Area Library HQ, Central Library, Abbot Street, Dunfermline, Fife KY12 7NL
☎(01383) 312604
Fax (01383) 314314
Libraries Policy and Learning Services Coordinator Ms D Miller MBA MA MCLIP

Area/group libraries

- Central Library, War Memorial Gardens, Kirkcaldy, Fife KY1 1YG
☎(01592) 412878
Fax (01592) 412750
Customer Services Librarian Ms T Steedman MCLIP
- Glenwood Library, Glenwood Shopping Centre, Glenrothes, Fife KY6 1PA
☎(01592) 416840
Fax (01592) 416843
Library Supervisor Ms M Cook
- Methil Library, Wellesley Road, Methil, Fife KY8 3QR
☎(01333) 592470
Fax (01333) 592415
Library Supervisor Ms H Kirkwood
- Leven Library, Durie Street, Leven, Fife KY8 4HE
☎(01333) 592650
Fax (01333) 592655
Library Supervisor Ms L Cullis
- Rosyth Library, Parkgate Community Centre, Rosyth, Fife KY11 2JW
☎(01383) 416177
Fax (01383) 416777
Library Supervisor Ms D Hutton
- Dalgety Bay Library, Regents Way, Dalgety Bay, Fife KY11 5UY
☎(01383) 318981
Fax (01383) 318988
Library Supervisor Ms B Gilmour
- St Andrews Library, Church Square, St Andrews, Fife KY16 9NN
☎(01334) 412687
Fax (01334) 413029
Community Librarian D Castle-Smith
- Cupar Library, 33-35 Crossgate, Cupar, Fife KY15 5AS
☎(01334) 412285
Fax (01334) 412467
Community Librarian Ms L Cordiner MCLIP

GLASGOW

Authority Glasgow City Council
HQ Cultural and Leisure Services, Libraries, Information and Learning, The Mitchell Library, North Street, Glasgow G3 7DN
☎0141 287 2999 (enquiries), 0141 287 2870 (administration)
Fax 0141 287 2815
Head of Libraries, Information and Archives M Wade BA MLib MCLIP (located at 20 Trongate, Glasgow G1 5ES; 0141 287 5114; e-mail: martyn.wade@cls.glasgow.gov.uk)
Service Development Manager Ms K Cunningham MA DipLib MCLIP (0141 287 2881; e-mail: karen.cunningham@cls.glasgow.gov.uk)
Information Services Manager G Anderson BA MCLIP (0141 287 2949; e-mail: gordon.anderson@cls.glasgow.gov.uk)
Community Libraries Network Manager Ms P Tulloch MA MBA DipLib MCLIP (0141 287 2862; e-mail: pamela.tulloch@cls.glasgow.goc.uk)
Community Learning Manager Ms J Edgar DipYouth/Community Work (0141 287 2806; e-mail: jane.edgar@cls.glasgow.gov.uk)
Archivist K Magee (0141 287 2907, fax: 0141 226 8452; e-mail: archives@gcl.glasgow.gov.uk)

Community libraries

- Lending Services Department, The Mitchell Library, North Street, Glasgow G3 7DN
  ☎0141 287 2870 (enquiries)
  Fax 0141 287 2871
- Anderston Library, Berkeley Street, Glasgow G3 7DN
  ☎0141 287 2872 (tel./fax)
- Baillieston Library, 141 Main Street, Glasgow G69 6AA
  ☎0141 771 2433 (tel./fax)
- Barmulloch Library, 99 Rockfield Road, Glasgow G21 3DY
  ☎0141 558 6185 (tel.fax)
- Bridgeton Library, 23 Landressy Street, Glasgow G40 1BP
  ☎0141 554 0217 (tel.fax)
- Cardonald Library, 1113 Mosspark Drive, Glasgow G52 3BU
  ☎0141 882 1381
  Fax 0141 810 5490
- Castlemilk Library, 100 Castlemilk Drive, Glasgow G45 9TN
  ☎0141 634 2066 (tel./fax)
- Couper Institute Library, 84 Clarkston Road, Glasgow G44 3DA
  ☎0141 637 1544 (tel./fax)
- Dennistoun Library, 2a Craigpark, Glasgow G31 2NA
  ☎0141 554 0055
  Fax 0141 551 9971
- Drumchapel Library, 65 Hecla Avenue, Glasgow G15 8LX
  ☎0141 944 5698 (tel./fax)
- Easterhouse Library, 5 Shandwick Street, Glasgow G34 9DP
  ☎0141 771 5986
  Fax 0141 771 5643
- Elder Park Library, 228a Langlands Road, Glasgow G51 3TZ

☎0141 445 1047 (tel./fax)

- Govanhill Library, 170 Langside Road, Glasgow G42 7JU
  ☎0141 423 0335 (tel./fax)
- Hillhead Library, 348 Byres Road, Glasgow G12 8AP
  ☎0141 339 7223
  Fax 0141 337 2783
- Ibrox Library, 1 Midlock Street, Glasgow G51 1SL
  ☎0141 427 5831
  Fax 0141 427 1139
- Knightswood Library, 27 Dunterlie Avenue, Glasgow G13 3BB
  ☎0141 959 2041 (tel./fax)
- Langside Library, 2 Sinclair Drive, Glasgow G42 9QE
  ☎0141 632 0810
  Fax 0141 632 8982
- Maryhill Library, 1508 Maryhill Road, Glasgow G20 9AD
  ☎0141 946 2348 (tel./fax)
- Milton Library, 163 Ronaldsay Street, Glasgow G22 7AP
  ☎0141 772 1410 (tel./fax)
- Parkhead Library, 64 Tollcross Road, Glasgow G31 4XA
  ☎0141 554 0198 (tel.fax)
- Partick Library, 305 Dumbarton Road, Glasgow G11 6AB
  ☎0141 339 1303 (tel./fax)
- Pollok Library, Cowglen Road, Glasgow G53 6DW
  ☎0141 881 3540 (tel./fax)
- Pollokshaws Library, 50-60 Shawbridge Street, Glasgow G43 1RW
  ☎0141 632 3544 (tel./fax)
- Pollokshields Library, 30 Leslie Street, Glasgow G41 2LF
  ☎0141 423 1460 (tel./fax)
- Possilpark Library, 127 Allander Street, Glasgow G22 5JJ
  ☎0141 336 8110 (tel./fax)
- Riddrie Library, 1020 Cumbernauld Road, Glasgow G33 2QS
  ☎0141 770 4043 (tel./fax)
- Royston Library, 67 Royston Road, Glasgow G21 2QW
  ☎0141 552 1657 (tel./fax)
- Shettleston Library, 154 Wellshot Road, Glasgow G32 7AX
  ☎0141 778 1221
  Fax 0141 778 9004
- Springburn Library, 179 Ayr Street, Glasgow G21 4BW
  ☎0141 558 5559 (tel./fax)
- Stirling's Library, 62 Miller Street, Glasgow G1 1DT
  ☎0141 221 1876
  Fax 0141 226 2498
- Temple Library, 350 Netherton Road, Glasgow G13 1AX
  ☎0141 954 6265 (tel./fax)
- Whiteinch Library, 14 Victoria Park Drive South, Glasgow G14 9RL
  ☎0141 959 1376 (tel./fax)
- Woodside Library, 343 St George's Road, Glasgow G3 6JQ

☎0141 832 1808 (tel./fax)

- Sighthill Drop-in Centre, Sighthill Library, Fountainwell Square, Glasgow G21 1RF
  ☎0141 557 0710
  Fax 0141 558 9087

HIGHLAND

Authority The Highland Council
HQ Library Support Unit, 31A Harbour Road, Inverness IV1 1UA
☎(01463) 235713
Fax (01463) 236986
e-mail: libraries@highland.gov.uk
url: http://www.libraries@highland.gov.uk
Libraries, Information and Archives Manager Vacant
Library and Information Services Co-ordinator C Phillips BA DipLib MCLIP

Area libraries

Inverness

- Culloden Library, Keppoch Road, Culloden, Inverness IV1 2LL
  ☎(01463) 792531
  Fax (01463) 739162
  e-mail: culloden.library@highland.gov.uk
  Librarian Ms A Donald MCLIP
- Inverness Library, Farraline Park, Inverness IV1 1NH
  ☎(01463) 236463
  Fax (01463) 237001
  e-mail: inverness.library@highland.gov.uk
  Libraries Officer Ms C Goodfellow MA MCLIP

Lochaber

- Fort William Library, Airds Crossing, Fort William, Inverness-shire PH33 6BA
  ☎(01397) 703552
  Fax (01397) 703538
  e-mail: fortwilliam.library@highland.gov.uk
  Libraries Officer S J Moore BA(Hons) MA MLib MPhil MCLIP

Ross and Cromarty

- Dingwall Library, Old Academy Buildings, Tulloch Street, Dingwall, Ross-shire IV15 9JZ
  ☎(01349) 863163
  Fax (01349) 865239
  e-mail: dingwall.library@highland.gov.uk
  Librarian Ms S Paterson MCLIP
  Libraries Officer Ms A Nicol MA DipEd DipLib MCLI
- Invergordon Library, High Street, Invergordon, Ross-shire IV18 0DG
  ☎(01349) 852698 (tel/fax)
  e-mail: invergordon.library@highland.gov.uk
  Librarian Ms P Collett MCLIP
- Ullapool Library, Ullapool High School, Mill Street, Ullapool, Ross-shire IV26 2UN

☎(01854) 612543 (tel/fax)
e-mail: ullapool.library@highland.gov.uk
Librarian Ms C MacArthur MCLIP

Caithness

- Thurso Library, Davidson's Lane, Thurso, Caithness KW14 7AF
  ☎(01847) 893237
  Fax (01847) 896114
  e-mail: thurso.library@highland.gov.uk
  Libraries Officer Ms J Brown BA MCLIP
- Wick Library, Sinclair Terrace, Wick, Caithness KW1 5AB
  ☎(01955) 602864
  Fax (01955) 603000
  e-mail: wick.library@highland.gov.uk
  Librarian Ms A Robertson MCLIP

Skye and Lochalsh

- Portree Library, Bayfield Road, Portree, Isle of Skye, Inverness-shire IV51 9EL
  ☎(01478) 612697
  Fax (01478) 613314
  e-mail: portree.library@highland.gov.uk
  Libraries Officer D Linton MCLIP

Badenoch and Strathspey

- Nairn Library, 68 High Street, Nairn, Nairn-shire IV12 4AU
  ☎(01667) 458506
  Fax (01667) 458548
  e-mail: nairn.library@highland.gov.uk
  Libraries Officer Ms E Somerville BEd DipLib MCLIP

Sutherland

- Dornoch Library, Carnegie Building, High Street, Dornoch, Sutherland IV25 3SH
  ☎(01862) 811585
  Fax (01862) 811079
  e-mail: dornoch.library@highland.gov.uk
  Libraries Officer Ms A Forrest BA MCLIP

INVERCLYDE

Authority Inverclyde Council
HQ Central Library, Clyde Square, Greenock, Renfrewshire PA15 1NA
☎(01475) 712323
Fax (01475) 712339
Acting Libraries Manager Miss S MacDougall (e-mail: sandra.macdougall@inverclyde.gov.uk)

MIDLOTHIAN

Authority Midlothian Council
HQ Library HQ, 2 Clerk Street, Loanhead, Midlothian EH20 9DR
☎0131 271 3980
Fax 0131 440 4635
e-mail: library.hq@midlothian.gov.uk
url: http://www.midlothian.gov.uk/library/
Library Services Manager A Reid MA MCLIP

Central/largest library

Dalkeith Library, White Hart Street, Dalkeith, Midlothian EH22 1AE
☎0131 663 2083
Fax 0131 654 9029
e-mail: dalkeith.library@midlothian.gov.uk
Senior Librarian Ms J Fergus MCLIP

Branch libraries

- Bonnyrigg Library, Polton Street, Bonnyrigg, Midlothian EH19 3HB
  ☎0131 663 6762
  Fax 0131 654 9019
  e-mail: bonnyrigg.library@midlothian.gov.uk
  Senior Librarian D Stevenson BA MCLIP
- Danderhall Library, 1A Campview, Danderhall, Midlothian EH22 1QD
  ☎0131 663 9293
  e-mail: danderhall.library@midlothian.gov.uk
  Assistant i/c Ms J Brown
- Gorebridge Library, Hunterfield Road, Gorebridge, Midlothian EH23 4TT
  ☎(01875) 820630
  Fax (01875) 823657
  e-mail: gorebridge.library@midlothian.gov.uk
  Assistant i/c Ms J Hamilton
- Loanhead Library, George Avenue, Loanhead, Midlothian EH20 9HD
  ☎0131 440 0824
  e-mail: loanhead.library@midlothian.gov.uk
  Assistant i/c Ms G Renwick
- Mayfield Library, Stone Avenue, Mayfield, Dalkeith, Midlothian EH22 5PB
  ☎0131 663 2126
  e-mail: mayfield.library@midlothian.gov.uk
  Assistant i/c Ms I Allen
- Newtongrange Library, St Davids, Newtongrange, Midlothian EH22 4LG
  ☎0131 663 1816
  e-mail: newtongrange.library@midlothian.gov.uk
  Assistant i/c Ms J Elliot
- Penicuik Library, Bellmans Road, Penicuik, Midlothian EH26 0AB
  ☎(01968) 672340
  Fax (01968) 679968

e-mail: penicuik.library@midlothian.gov.uk
Assistant Librarian Ms F Bell BA MCLIP

- Roslin Library, 9 Main Street, Roslin, Midlothian EH25 9LD
  ☎0131 448 2781
  e-mail: roslin.library@midlothian.gov.uk
  Assistant i/c Vacant
- Woodburn Library, Dalkeith Leisure Centre, 6 Woodburn Road, Dalkeith, Midlothian EH22 2AR
  ☎0131 663 3445
  e-mail: woodburn.library@midlothian.gov.uk
  Assistant i/c Ms I Allen/Ms J Brown
- Local Studies, 2 Clerk Street, Loanhead, Midlothian EH20 9DR
  ☎0131 271 3976
  Fax 0131 440 4635
  e-mail: local.studies@midlothian.gov.uk
  Local Studies Officer Ms S Millar

MORAY

Authority The Moray Council
HQ Educational Services Department, Council Office, High Street, Elgin, Moray IV30 1BX
☎(01343) 562600 (enquiries), (01343) 563398 (administration)
Fax (01343) 563410
Libraries and Museums Manager G A Campbell MA BCom MCLIP (e-mail: campbea@moray.gov.uk)

Central/largest library

Elgin Library, Cooper Park, Elgin, Moray IV30 1HS
☎(01343) 562600
Fax (01343) 562630
e-mail: elgin.library@moray.gov.uk
Principal Librarian (Central Services) Ms S Campbell MCLIP (e-mail: sheila.campbell@moray.gov.uk)

Area libraries

- Buckie Library, Cluny Place, Buckie, Banffshire AB56 1HB
  ☎(01542) 832121
  Fax (01542) 835237
  e-mail: buckie.library@moray.gov.uk
  Senior Librarian (Buckie) Vacant
- Forres Library, Forres House, High Street, Forres, Moray IV36 0BU
  ☎(01309) 672834
  Fax (01309) 675084
  e-mail: forres.library@moray.gov.uk
  Community Librarian (Forres) Ms E Parker
- Keith Library, Union Street, Keith, Banffshire AB55 5DP
  ☎(01542) 882223
  Fax (01542) 882177

e-mail: keith.library@moray.gov.uk
Senior Librarian (Keith) P Marland BA MCLIP

NORTH AYRSHIRE

Authority North Ayrshire Council
HQ Library, 39-41 Princes Street, Ardrossan, Ayrshire KA22 8BT
☎(01294) 469137
Fax (01294) 604236
e-mail: libraryhq@north-ayrshire.gov.uk
Principal Officer (Library Operations) Miss J Martin MA DipLib MCLIP
Area Officer (Three Towns and Arran) Mrs M Vint MCLIP (01294 469137; fax: 01294 604236)
Area Officer (Irvine/Kilwinning) Miss S Kerr MCLIP (01294 554699; fax: 01294 557628)
Area Officer (North Coast and Garnock Valley) P Cowan BEd DipLib MCLIP (01505 503613; fax 01505 503417)

Central/largest library

Irvine Library, Cunninghame House, Irvine, Ayrshire KA12 8EE
☎(01294) 324251
Fax (01294) 324252
Senior Librarian Miss M A Scott MCLIP

Area libraries

- Saltcoats Library, Springvale Place, Saltcoats, Ayrshire KA21 5LS
  ☎(01294) 469546
  Fax (01294) 469546
  Senior Librarian J Macaulay MCLIP DipLib
- Largs Library, Allanpark Street, Largs, Ayrshire KA30 9AS
  ☎(01475) 673309
  Fax (01475) 673309
  Senior Librarian J West BA DipLib MCLIP

NORTH LANARKSHIRE

Authority North Lanarkshire Council
HQ Dept of Community Services, Buchanan Tower, Buchanan Business Park, Cumbernauld Road, Stepps, Glasgow, North Lanarkshire G33 6HR
☎0141 304 1800
Fax 0141 304 1902
url: http://www.northlan.gov.uk
Libraries and Information Manager J Fox DMS MCLIP (e-mail: foxj@northlan.gov.uk)

Central/largest library

Motherwell Library, 35 Hamilton Road, Motherwell, North Lanarkshire ML1 3BZ
☎(01698) 332626
Fax (01698) 332625

Information Services Manager C Bennett BA MCLIP (e-mail: bennettc@northlan.gov.uk)
Lending Services Manager South Mrs C Wales BA MCLIP

Area libraries

- Cumbernauld Library, 8 Allander Walk, Cumbernauld, North Lanarkshire G67 6EE
  ☎(01236) 725664
  Fax (01236) 458350
  Lending Services Manager North Mrs W Bennett BA MCLIP (e-mail: bennettw@northlan.gov.uk)
- Coatbridge Library, 25 Academy Street, Coatbridge, North Lanarkshire ML5 3AW
  ☎(01236) 424150
  Fax (01236) 437997
  Lending Services Manager Central D McGuinness MCLIP (e-mail: mcguinnessd@northlan.gov.uk)

ORKNEY

Authority Orkney Islands Council
HQ Council Offices, School Place, Kirkwall, Orkney KW15 1NW
☎(01856) 873166 (enquiries & administration)
Fax (01856) 875260
e-mail: orkney.library@orkney.gov.uk
Chief Librarian R K Leslie MCLIP (e-mail: robert.leslie@orkney.gov.uk)

Central/largest library

The Orkney Library, Laing Street, Kirkwall, Orkney KW15 1NW
☎(01856) 873166 (enquiries & administration)
Fax (01856) 875260
Chief Librarian R K Leslie MCLIP
Depute Librarian Ms K I Walker BA (e-mail: karen.walker@orkney.gov.uk)

PERTH AND KINROSS

Authority Perth and Kinross Council
HQ The A K Bell Library, York Place, Perth, Perthshire PH2 8EP
☎(01738) 444949
Fax (01738) 477010
e-mail: library@pkc.gov.uk
url: http://www.pkc.gov.uk/library
Head of Libraries and Archives M C G Moir BA MCLIP (e-mail: mmoir@pkc.gov.uk)
Principal Librarian I MacRae BA MCLIP (e-mail: imr@pkc.gov.uk)

Area libraries

- Auchterarder Branch Library, Aytoun Hall, Chapel Wynd, Auchterarder, Perthshire PH3 1BL
  ☎(01764) 663850
  Fax (01764) 663917
  Branch Librarian Mrs K Mayall BA

- Blairgowrie Branch Library, 46 Leslie Street, Blairgowrie, Perthshire PH10 6AW
  ☎(01250) 872905
  Fax (01250) 872905
  Branch Librarian S McGowan MA
- Crieff Branch Library, 6 Comrie Street, Crieff, Perthshire PH7 4AX
  ☎(01764) 653418
  Fax (01764) 653418
  Branch Librarian Ms M Gordon BA
- Kinross Branch Library, 112-114 High Street, Kinross, Kinross-shire KY13 7DA
  ☎(01577) 864202
  Branch Library Assistant Ms M Garden
- Scone Branch Library, Sandy Road, Scone, Perth, Perthshire PH2 6LJ
  ☎(01738) 553029
  Fax (01738) 553029
  Branch Librarian Mrs E Wallace BA

RENFREWSHIRE

Authority Renfrewshire Council
HQ Library HQ, Abbey House, 8A Seedhill Road, Paisley, Renfrewshire PA1 1AJ
☎0141 840 3003
Fax 0141 840 3004
Principal Librarian Ms V Kerr BA MCLIP MSc MIM (0141 840 3001; e-mail: vivian.kerr@renfrewshire.gov.uk)

Central/largest library

Paisley Central Library, High Street, Paisley, Renfrewshire PA1 2BB
☎0141 887 3672, 0141 889 2360
Fax 0141 887 6468
e-mail: ce.els@renfrewshire.gov.uk (lending services); locstuds.els@renfrewshire.gov.uk (local studies); ref.els@renfrewshire.gov.uk (ref/info services)

Community libraries

- Renfrew Community Library, Paisley Road, Renfrew, Renfrewshire PA4 8LJ
  ☎0141 886 3433
  Fax 0141 886 1660
  e-mail: rw@renfrewshire.gov.uk
- Johnstone Community Library, Houston Court, Johnstone, Renfrewshire PA5 8DL
  ☎(01505) 329726
  Fax (01505) 336657
  e-mail: jo.els@renfrewshire.gov.uk

SCOTTISH BORDERS

Authority Borders Council
HQ Scottish Borders Library Service, St Mary's Mill, Selkirk, Selkirkshire TD7 5EW
☎(01750) 20842
Fax (01750) 22875

Head of Cultural and Interpretative Services A Hasson MA MBA DipLib MCLIP MIMgt
Library and Information Services Manager Ms M Menzies BA MLib MCLIP
Principal Librarian Youth Services Ms R Collins BA(Hons) MCLIP
Community and Operations Librarian Ms G McNay MA MCLIP DipLib
Information Systems Librarian Ms S Milne MA MCLIP DipLib

Area libraries

- Hawick Library, North Bridge Street, Hawick, Roxburghshire TD9 9QT
  ☎(01450) 372637
  Fax (01450) 370991
  e-mail: libhawick@scotborders.gov.uk
  Area Librarian J Beedle BA MCLIP
- Galashiels Library, Lawyer's Brae, Galashiels, Selkirkshire TD1 3JQ
  ☎(01896) 752512
  Fax (01896) 753575
  e-mail: libgalashiels@scotborders.gov.uk
  Area Librarian Miss C R Letton MA FSA(Scot) MCLIP DipLib
- Peebles Library, Chambers Institute, High Street, Peebles, Peeblesshire EH45 8AG
  ☎(01721) 720123
  Fax (01721) 724424
  e-mail: libpeebles@scotborders.gov.uk
  Area Librarian P Taylor BSc FSA MCLIP

Branch libraries

- Kelso Library, Bowmont Street, Kelso, Roxburghshire TD5 7JH
  ☎(01573) 223171
  Fax (01573) 226618
  e-mail: libkelso@scotborders.gov.uk
  Branch Librarian Mrs M Blake
- Selkirk Library, Ettrick Terrace, Selkirk, Selkirkshire TD7 4LE
  ☎(01750) 20267 (tel/fax)
  e-mail: libselkirk@scotborders.gov.uk
  Branch Librarian Mrs J Gammie BSc MCLIP
- Duns Library, 49 Newtown Street, Duns, Berwickshire TD11 3AU
  ☎(01361) 882622
  Fax (01361) 884104
  e-mail: libduns@scotborders.gov.uk
  Branch Librarian Vacant
- Coldstream Library, Gateway Centre, Coldstream TD12 4AE
  ☎(01890) 883314 (tel/fax)
  e-mail: libcoldstream@scotborders.gov.uk
  Branch Librarian I Hope
- Innerleithen Library, Buccleuch Street, Innerleithen EH44 6LA
  ☎(01896) 830789 (tel/fax)
  e-mail: libinnerleithen@scotborders.gov.uk
  Branch Librarian Mrs E Hogarth

- Jedburgh Library, Castlegate, Jedburgh TD8 6AS
  ☎(01835) 863592 (tel/fax)
  e-mail: libjedburgh@scotborders.gov.uk
  Branch Librarian Mrs C Chisholm
- Melrose Library, 18 Market Square, Melrose TD6 9PN
  ☎(01896) 823052 (tel/fax)
  e-mail: libmelrose@scotborders.gov.uk
  Branch Librarian Mrs M Wight
- Eyemouth Library, Manse Road, Eyemouth TD14 5JE
  ☎(01890) 750300
  Fax (01890) 751633
  e-mail: libeyemouth@scotborders.gov.uk
  Branch Librarian Mrs J Thomas
- Earlston Library, High School, Earlston TD4 6ED
  ☎(01896) 849282
  Fax (01896) 848918
  e-mail: libearlston@scotborders.gov.uk
  Branch Librarian Mrs A Tait
- Archive & Local History Centre, St Mary's Mill, Selkirk TD7 5EW
  ☎(01750) 20842
  Fax (01750) 22875
  e-mail: archives@scotborders.gov.uk
  Librarian Miss H Darling BA(Hons) MCLIP

SHETLAND ISLANDS

Authority Shetland Islands Council
HQ Shetland Library, Lower Hillhead, Lerwick, Shetland ZE1 0EL
☎(01595) 693868 (enquiries and administration)
Fax (01595) 694430
e-mail: info@shetland-library.gov.uk
Library and Information Services Manager Ms A Hunter (alison.hunter@sic.shetland.gov.uk)
Assistant Chief Librarian D Garden (e-mail: douglas.garden@sic.shetland.gov.uk)
Acting Assistant Chief Librarian Ms A Henry (e-mail: anna.henry@sic.shetland.gov.uk)
Secretary/Administration Assistant Mrs A J Anderson (e-mail: agnes.anderson@sic.shetland.gov.uk)
Administration Assistant Miss K Williamson (e-mail: katrina.williamson@sic.shetland.gov.uk)

SOUTH AYRSHIRE

Authority South Ayrshire Council
HQ Library HQ, 26 Green Street, Ayr KA8 8AD
☎(01292) 288820
Fax (01292) 619019
Libraries and Galleries Manager C Deas BA MCLIP (e-mail: charles.deas@south-ayrshire.gov.uk)

Central/largest library

Carnegie Library, 12 Main Street, Ayr KA8 8ED
☎(01292) 286385
Fax (01292) 611593
e-mail: carnegie@south-ayrshire.gov.uk

SOUTH LANARKSHIRE

Authority South Lanarkshire Council
HQ Libraries and Community Learning Service, Education Resources, Council Offices, Almada Street, Hamilton, South Lanarkshire ML3 0AA
☎(01698) 454545
Fax (01698) 454465
Libraries and Community Learning Service Manager Ms D Barr BA MCLIP MIMgt (01698 454412)

Central/largest library

East Kilbride Central Library, 40 The Olympia, East Kilbride, South Lanarkshire G74 1PG
☎(01355) 220046
Fax (01355) 229365
Libraries Co-ordinator D Leitch MCLIP

Divisional libraries

- Hamilton Central Library, 98 Cadzow Street, Hamilton, South Lanarkshire ML3 6HQ
  ☎(01698) 452406
  Fax (01698) 286334
  Libraries Co-ordinator Ms I Walker MCLIP
- Rutherglen Library, 163 Main Street, Rutherglen, Glasgow G73 2HB
  ☎0141 647 6453
  Fax 0141 647 5164
  Libraries Co-ordinator D Moncrieff MCLIP
- Lanark Library, Hope Street, Lanark, Lanarkshire ML11 7NH
  ☎(01555) 661144
  Fax (01555) 665884
  Libraries Co-ordinator Ms F Renfrew BA MCLIP

STIRLING

Authority Stirling Council
HQ Library HQ, Borrowmeadow Road, Springkerse, Stirling FK7 7TN
☎(01786) 432383 (enquiries/administration)
Fax (01786) 432395
Head of Service, Libraries, Heritage and Culture A Gillies MCLIP (Based at Stirling Council, Viewforth, Stirling FK8 2ET) (01786 443398)
Development Librarian S J Dolman BA(Hons) MCLIP (01786 432388)
Operations Librarian A Muirhead MA MLitt MCLIP (01786 432386)

Central/largest library

Central Library, Corn Exchange Road, Stirling FK8 2HX

☎(01786) 432106/7 (enquiries), (01786) 432108 (administration)
Fax (01786) 473094
Area Librarian Ms M McIntyre MA MCLIP

WEST DUNBARTONSHIRE

Authority West Dunbartonshire Council
HQ West Dunbartonshire Libraries, Levenford House, Helenslee Road, Dumbarton G82 4AH
☎(01389) 608046 (enquiries), (01389) 608039 (administration)
Fax (01389) 608044
Manager of Lifelong Learning Mrs S Carragher BA(Hons) MCLIP

Area libraries

- Clydebank Library, Dumbarton Road, Clydebank, Dumbarton G81 1XH
  ☎0141 952 1416 (enquiries), (01389) 738707 (administration)
  Fax 0141 951 8275
  Senior Officer (Libraries) Miss F MacDonald MA MCLIP
- Dumbarton Library, Strathleven Place, Dumbarton G82 1BD
  ☎(01389) 763129 (enquiries), (01389) 608038 (administration)
  Fax (01389) 607302
  Senior Officer (Libraries) I Baillie MCLIP

WEST LOTHIAN

Authority West Lothian Council
HQ Library HQ, Connolly House, Hopefield Road, Blackburn, West Lothian EH47 7HZ
☎(01506) 776336 (enquiries), (01506) 776342 (administration)
Fax (01506) 776345
e-mail: library.info@westlothian.gov.uk
Library Services Manager W S Walker BA MCLIP (01506 776780)
Support Services Manager Vacant (01506 776325)
Area Manager Mrs I Brough (01506 776327)
Area Manager Ms A Hunt MA DipLib MCLIP (01506 776326)
Area Manager Mrs B Main BA DipLib (01506 776327)

Central/largest library

Carmondean Library, Carmondean Centre, Livingston, West Lothian EH54 8PT
☎(01506) 777602 (enquiries)
Branch Manager S Harris MA MSc MCLIP

Branch libraries

- Linlithgow Branch Library, The Vennel, Linlithgow, West Lothian EH49 7EX
  ☎(01506) 775490
  Branch Manager Ms K Ali BA, Ms M Sheldon MCLIP
- East Calder Branch Library, Main Street, East Calder, West Lothian EH53 0EJ
  ☎(01506) 883633
  Branch Manager Ms G Downie BA MCLIP
- Armadale Branch Library, West Main Street, Armadale, West Lothian EH48 3JB

☎(01501) 778400
Branch Manager Ms E Hunter MCLIP

- Almondbank Branch Library, The Mall, Craigshill, Livingston, West Lothian EH54 5EJ
☎(01506) 777500
Branch Manager R Fisher BA MCLIP
- Fauldhouse Branch Library, Lanrigg Road, Fauldhouse, West Lothian EH47 9JA
☎(01501) 770358
Branch Manager Ms M James
- Bathgate Branch Library, 66 Hopetoun Street, Bathgate, West Lothian EH48 1TD
☎(01506) 776400
Branch Manager Mrs A Mackintosh BA MCLIP, Mrs M Armstrong MCLIP
- Lanthorn Branch Library, Lanthorn Centre, Kenilworth Rise, Dedridge, Livingston, West Lothian EH54 6NY
☎(01506) 777700
Branch Manager Ms G Downie BA MCLIP
- Broxburn Branch Library, West Main Street, Broxburn, West Lothian EH52 5RH
☎(01506) 775600
Branch Manager Ms L Reid BA MCLIP
- Whitburn Branch Library, Union Road, Whitburn, West Lothian EH47 0AR
☎(01506) 778050
Branch Manager Ms H Gibson
- West Calder Branch Library, Main Street, West Calder, West Lothian EH55 8BJ
☎(01506) 871371
Branch Manager Ms L Reid BA MCLIP
- Blackburn Branch Library, Ash Grove, Blackburn, West Lothian EH47 7LJ
☎(01506) 776500
Branch Manager Ms F Cranston
- Blackridge Branch Library, Craig Inn Centre, Blackridge, West Lothian EH48 3RJ
☎(01501) 752396
Branch Manager Ms M McCabe
- Pumpherston Branch Library, Pumpherston Primary School, 18 Uphall Station Road, Pumpherston, West Lothian EH53 0LP
☎(01506) 435837
Branch Manager Ms M Lamond

ANGLESEY, ISLE OF

Authority Isle of Anglesey County Council
HQ Department of Education and Leisure, Parc Mownt, Fford Glanhwfa, Llangefni, Ynys Môn LL77 7EY
☎(01248) 752092 (enquiries); (01248) 752908 (administration)
Fax (01248) 752999
url: http://www.ynysmon.gov.uk
Corporate Director: Education and Leisure R P Jones MA (01248 752900; e-mail: rpjed@ynysmon.gov.uk)
Head of Service: Lifelong Learning and Information J R Thomas BSc(Econ) DipLib MCLIP (01248 752908; e-mail: jrtlh@ynysmon.gov.uk)
Principal Librarian Vacant
Archivist Ms A Venables BA DipAA (01248 752080)

Central/largest library

Llangefni Central Library, Lôn-y-Felin, Llangefni, Ynys Môn LL77 7RT
☎(01248) 752092
Fax (01248) 750197
e-mail: dhelh@ynysmon.gov.uk

Branch libraries

- Holyhead Library, Newry Fields, Holyhead, Ynys Môn LL65 1LA
  ☎(01407) 762917
  Fax (01407) 769616
  e-mail: kpxlh@ynysmon.gov.uk
- Amlwch Library, Lôn Parys, Amlwch, Ynys Môn LL68 9EA
  ☎(01407) 830145
  Fax (01407) 830145
  e-mail: kbxlh@ynysmon.gov.uk
- Menai Bridge Library, Ffordd y Ffair, Menai Bridge, Ynys Môn LL59 5AS
  ☎(01248) 712706
  Fax (01248) 712706
  e-mail: dbxlh@ynysmon.gov.uk
- Record Office, Shirehall, Glanhwfa Street, Llangefni, Ynys Môn LL77 7TW
  ☎(01248) 752083
  Fax (01248) 751289

BLAENAU GWENT

Authority Blaenau Gwent County Borough Council
HQ Community Services, Municipal Offices, Civic Centre, Ebbw Vale, Blaenau Gwent NP23 6XB
☎(01495) 355318 (enquiries), (01495) 355319 (administration)
Fax (01495) 312357

e-mail: bg.libs@dial.pipex.com
County Borough Librarian Mrs M Jones MLib MCLIP (01495 355311; e-mail: mary.jones@blaenau-gwent.gov.uk)
Information Officer S Hardman (01495 355318; e-mail: steve.hardman@blaenau-gwent.gov.uk)

Central/largest library

Ebbw Vale Library, 21 Bethcar Street, Ebbw Vale, Blaenau Gwent NP23 6HS
☎(01495) 303069
Fax (01495) 350547
Library Manager Mrs S White MCLIP (01495 301122; e-mail: sue.white@blaenau-gwent.gov.uk)

Area libraries

- Abertillery Library, Station Hill, Abertillery, Blaenau Gwent NP13 1UJ
  ☎(01495) 212332/217640
  Fax (01495) 320995
  Library Manager J Leacy BA MCLIP
- Blaina Library, Reading Institute, High Street, Blaina, Blaenau Gwent NP13 3BN
  ☎(01495) 290312
  Fax (01495) 290312
  Librarian Miss J Davies BA MCLIP
- Tredegar Library, The Circle, Tredegar, Blaenau Gwent NP22 3PS
  ☎(01495) 722687
  Fax (01495) 717018
  Librarian Miss J C Karn BA MCLIP
- Brynmawr Library, Market Square, Brynmawr, Blaenau Gwent NP23 4AJ
  ☎(01495) 310045
  Fax (01495) 310045
  Librarian J Leacy BA MCLIP
- Cwm Library, Canning Street, Cwm, Blaenau Gwent NP23 7RW
  ☎(01495) 370454
  Fax (01495) 370454
  Librarian Miss J C Karn BA MCLIP
- Llanhilleth Library, Workmen's Institute, Llanhilleth, Blaenau Gwent NP13 2JH
  ☎(01495) 214485
  Fax (01495) 214485
  Librarian P Marley BA MCLIP
- Reaching Out Mobile, c/o Brynmawr Library, Market Square, Brynmawr, Blaenau Gwent NP23 4AJ
  ☎(01495) 722687
  Fax (01495) 717018
  Special Services Librarian Miss I J Corey BSc MCLIP
- Acquisitions Dept, c/o Abertillery Library, Station Hill, Abertillery, Blaenau Gwent NP13 1UJ
  ☎(01495) 217640
  Fax (01495) 320995
  Acquisitions Librarian J Leacy BA MCLIP

BRIDGEND

Authority Bridgend County Borough Council
HQ Library and Information Service, Coed Parc, Park Street, Bridgend CF31 4BA
☎(01656) 767451
Fax (01656) 645719
e-mail: blis@bridgendlib.gov.uk
url: http://www.bridgend.gov.uk/english/library
County Borough Librarian John C Woods BSc MCLIP (e-mail: woodsjc@bridgend.gov.uk)

Central/largest libraries

- Reference and Information Centre, Coed Parc, Park Street, Bridgend CF31 4BA
  ☎(01656) 661813
  Fax (01656) 645719
  e-mail: blis@bridgend.gov.uk
  Reference Librarian Mrs C Phillips MCLIP
- Bridgend Lending Library, Wyndham Street, Bridgend CF31 1EF
  ☎(01656) 653444
  Fax (01656) 667886
  e-mail: bridgendlib@bridgend.gov.uk
  Site Librarian J Robinson MA MCLIP
- Maesteg Library, North's Lane, Maesteg CF34 9AA
  ☎(01656) 733201
  Fax (01656) 731098
  e-mail: maestlib@bridgend.gov.uk
  Branch Librarian Ms H Pridham MCLIP
- Pencoed Library, Penybont Road, Pencoed CF35 5RA
  ☎(01656) 860358
  Fax (01656) 863042
  e-mail: penclib@bridgend.gov.uk
  Branch Librarian Ms A Uren BA MCLIP
- Porthcawl Library, Church Place, Porthcawl CF36 3AG
  ☎(01656) 782059
  Fax (01656) 722745
  e-mail: porthcawllib@bridgend.gov.uk
  Branch Librarian Mrs L A Milne BA MCLIP
- Pyle Library, Pyle Life Centre, Helig Fan, Pyle CF33 6BS
  ☎(01656) 740631
  Fax (01656) 744865
  e-mail: pylelib@bridgend.gov.uk
  Life Centre Manager Ms J Arbery

CAERPHILLY

Authority Caerphilly County Borough Council
HQ Lifelong Learning and Leisure, Unit 7, Woodfieldside Business Park, Penmaen Road, Pontllanfraith, Blackwood, Caerphilly NP12 2DG
☎(01495) 235587

Fax (01495) 235567
e-mail: libraries@caerphilly.gov.uk
Principal Officer: Libraries Ms M Palmer MLib MCLIP
Assistant Director P Gomer

Central/largest library

Caerphilly Library, Morgan Jones Park, Caerphilly CF8 1AP
☎(02920) 852543 (enquiries)
Fax (02920) 865585
Area Manager: South Ms Y Harris MCLIP

Group libraries

- Blackwood Library, 192 High Street, Blackwood, Caerphilly NP12 1AJ
  ☎(01495) 233000
  Fax (01495) 233002
  Area Manager: North Mrs D Madhaven MCLIP
- Risca Library, Park Place, Risca, Caerphilly NP11 6AS
  ☎(01633) 600920
  Fax (01633) 600922
  Area Manager: Central Ms M Davies MCLIP

CARDIFF

Authority Cardiff County Council
HQ Cardiff Libraries and Information Service, Central Library, St David's Link, Frederick Street, Cardiff CF10 2DU
☎029 2038 2116
Fax 029 2087 1599
e-mail: centrallibrary@cardiff.gov.uk
url: http://www.cardiff.gov.uk/libraries
Central Library Manager R Boddy BA MCLIP (e-mail: rboddy@cardiff.gov.uk)
Branch Library Manager Ms E Morris BA MCLIP (e-mail: emorris@cardiff.gov.uk)
Stock Manager Ms S Best (e-mail: sbest@cardiff.gov.uk)

CARMARTHENSHIRE

Authority Carmarthenshire County Council
HQ Temporary HQ address: Carmarthen Area Library, St Peter's Street, Carmarthen, Carmarthenshire SA31 1LN
☎(01267) 224830
Fax (01267) 221839
Area Librarian D P Thomas BA DipLib MCLIP

Area libraries

- Llanelli Area Library, Vaughan Street, Llanelli, Carmarthenshire SA15 3AS
  ☎(01554) 773538
  Fax (01554) 750125
  Area Librarian R H Davies BSc DipLib MCLIP

- Ammanford Area Library, Talbot Road, Ammanford, Carmarthenshire SA16 3BB
  ☎(01269) 592207
  Fax (01269) 592207
  Area Librarian W T Phillips BA DipLib MCLIP

CEREDIGION

Authority Ceredigion County Council
HQ Public Library, Corporation Street, Aberystwyth, Ceredigion SY23 2BU
☎(01970) 617464
Fax (01970) 625059
Assistant Director (Cultural Services) D Geraint Lewis MA MCLIP
County Libraries Officer W H Howells BA MLib MCLIP (e-mail: williamh@ceredigion.gov.uk)

Branch library

Branch Library, Canolfan Teifi, Pendre, Cardigan, Ceredigion SA43 1JL
☎(01239) 612578
Fax (01239) 612285
e-mail: teifillb@ceredigion.gov.uk
Branch Librarian D G Evans MCLIP

CONWY

Authority Conwy County Borough Council
HQ Library, Information and Archives Service, Bodlondeb, Conwy LL32 8DU
☎(01492) 576140
Fax (01492) 592061
e-mail: llyfr.lib.pencadlys.hq@conwy.gov.uk
url: http://www.conwy.gov.uk/library
County Librarian and Archivist Ms R Aldrich MLib MCLIP (e-mail: rona.aldrich@conwy.gov.uk)
Principal Librarian Ms Rh G Williams BA DipLib MCLIP (01492 576139; e-mail: rhian.williams@conwy.gov.uk)
Corporate Information Librarian D J Smith BA(Hons) DMS MCLIP MCMI (01492 576137; e-mail: david.smith@conwy.gov.uk)
Senior Archivist Mrs S Ellis BA DAA (01492 860882; e-mail: susan.ellis@conwy.gov.uk)

Regional/community libraries

- Colwyn Bay Library, Woodland Road West, Colwyn Bay, Conwy LL29 7DH
  ☎(01492) 532358
  Fax (01492) 534474
  e-mail: llyfr.lib.baecolwynbay@conwy.gov.uk
  Senior Community Librarian M Thomas BSc(Econ) DipLib MCLIP
- Abergele Library, Market Street, Abergele, Conwy LL22 7BP
  ☎(01745) 832638
  Fax (01745) 823376
  e-mail: llyfr.lib.abergele@conwy.gov.uk

Community Librarian Mrs C Williams BA MCLIP, Mrs C Hesketh BA DipLib MCLIP (job-share)

- Conwy Library, Civic Hall, Castle Street, Conwy LL32 6AY
  ☎(01492) 596242
  Fax (01492) 582359
  e-mail: llyfr.lib.conwy@conwy.gov.uk
  Community Librarian Mrs S Morgan BA(Hons) DipLIS MCLIP
- Llandudno Library, Mostyn Street, Llandudno, Conwy LL30 2RP
  ☎(01492) 574010/574020
  Fax (01492) 876826
  e-mail: llyfr.lib.llandudno@conwy.gov.uk
  Community Librarian Ms M L Jones BLib MCLIP
- Llanrwst Library, Plas yn Dre, Station Road, Llanrwst, Conwy LL26 0DF
  ☎(01492) 640043
  Fax (01492) 642316
  e-mail: llyfr.lib.llanrwst@conwy.gov.uk
  Community/County Children's Librarian Mrs T Jones BA(Hons) MCLIP

DENBIGHSHIRE

Authority Denbighshire County Council
HQ Library and Information Service, Directorate of Lifelong Learning, Yr Hen Garchar, Clwyd Street, Ruthin, Denbighshire LL15 1HP
☎(01824) 708205 (enquiries)
Fax (01824) 708202
Assistant Director, Culture and Leisure Ms A Gosse (01824 708200; e-mail: anne.gosse@denbighshire.gov.uk)
Principal Librarian R Arwyn Jones BMus MCLIP DipLib (01824 708203; e-mail: arwyn.jones@denbighshire.gov.uk)

Central/largest library

Rhyl Library, Museum and Arts Centre, Church Street, Rhyl, Denbighshire LL18 3AA
☎(01745) 353814
Fax (01745) 331438
e-mail: rhyl.library@denbighshire.gov.uk
Principal Community Librarian A Barber BSc DipLib MCLIP

FLINTSHIRE

Authority Flintshire County Council
HQ Library and Information Services, Library Headquarters, County Hall, Mold, Flintshire CH7 6NW
☎(01352) 704400 (management), (01352) 704406 (administration)
Fax (01352) 753662
e-mail: libraries@flintshire.gov.uk
Head of Libraries, Culture and Heritage L Rawsthorne MLib FCLIP MIMgt
Principal Librarian, Community and Arts Mrs S Kirby MCLIP (01352 704402)
Senior Information Librarian Mrs G Fraser BA MCLIP (01352 704416)

Group libraries

- Mold Library, Earl Road, Mold, Flintshire CH7 1AP
  ☎(01352) 754791
  Fax (01352) 754655
  Community Librarian Miss N W Jones BLib MCLIP
- Flint Library, Church Street, Flint, Flintshire CH6 5AP
  ☎(01352) 703737
  Fax (01352) 731010
  Community Librarian Mrs E A Martin BLib MCLIP
- Connah's Quay Library, Wepre Drive, Connah's Quay, Deeside, Flintshire CH5 4HA
  ☎(01244) 830485
  Fax (01244) 856672
  Community Librarian Mrs C A Guy BA MCLIP
- Buckley Library, The Precinct, Buckley, Flintshire CH7 2EF
  ☎(01244) 549210
  Fax (01244) 548850
  Community Librarian Mrs P Corbett MLib MCLIP
- Broughton Library, Broughton Hall Road, Broughton, Nr Chester, Flintshire CH4 0QQ
  ☎(01244) 533727
  Community Librarian Miss K Morris BA DipLib MCLIP
- Holywell Library, North Street, Holywell, Flintshire CH8 7TQ
  ☎(01352) 713157
  Fax (01352) 710744
  Community Librarian Mrs C E Barber MCLIP, Mrs M Wallbank MCLIP

GWYNEDD

Authority Gwynedd Council
HQ Caernarfon Library Centre, Pavilion Hill, Caernarfon, Gwynedd LL55 1AS
☎(01286) 679504
Fax (01286) 677347
e-mail: llyfrgell@gwynedd.gov.uk
Principal Librarian H James BA DipLib MCLIP

Central/largest library

Caernarfon Library, Pavilion Hill, Caernarfon, Gwynedd LL55 1AS
☎(01286) 679463
Fax (01286) 671137
e-mail: llyfrgellcaernarfon@gwynedd.gov.uk
Community Librarian Mrs E Thomas MCLIP

Community libraries

- Bangor Library, Ffordd Gwynedd, Bangor, Gwynedd LL57 1DT
  ☎(01248) 353479
  Fax (01248) 370149
  e-mail: llyfrgellbangor@gwynedd.gov.uk
  Community Librarian Vacant

- Porthmadog Library, Stryd Wesla, Porthmadog, Gwynedd LL49 9BT
  ☎(01766) 514091
  Fax (01766) 513821
  e-mail: llyfrgellporthmadog@gwynedd.gov.uk
  Community Librarian Mrs D Eckley BA DipLib MCLIP
- Dolgellau Library, Ffordd y Bala, Dolgellau, Gwynedd LL40 2YF
  ☎(01341) 422771
  Fax (01341) 423560
  e-mail: llyfrgelldolgellau@gwynedd.gov.uk
  Community Librarian E Evans MCLIP

MERTHYR TYDFIL

Authority Merthyr Tydfil County Borough Council
HQ Central Library, High Street, Merthyr Tydfil, South Wales CF47 8AF
☎(01685) 723057
Fax (01685) 370690
e-mail: library.services@merthyr.gov.uk
Head of Libraries G James BA MCLIP

Area libraries

- Dowlais Library, Church Street, Merthyr Tydfil, South Wales CF48 3HS
  ☎(01685) 723051
  Fax (01685) 723051
  Librarian North Mrs C Roberts
- Treharris Library, Perrott Street, Treharris, Merthyr Tydfil, South Wales CF46 5ET
  ☎(01443) 410517
  Fax (01443) 410517
  Librarian South Mrs V Mitchell

MONMOUTHSHIRE

Authority Monmouthshire County Council
HQ Libraries and Information Service, Lifelong Learning and Leisure Directorate, County Hall, Cwmbran NP44 2XH
☎(01291) 635731 (enquiries), (01291) 635649 (administration)
Fax (01633) 644545
url: http://www.monmouthshire.gov.uk/leisure/libraries
Libraries and Culture Manager K A Smith BA (e-mail: kevinsmith@monmouthshire.gov.uk)
Principal Librarian Mrs A Jones Mlib ALA (e-mail: annjones@monmouthshire.gov.uk)

Area libraries

- Bryn-a-Cwm, Abergavenny Library, Baker Street, Abergavenny, Monmouthshire NP7 5BD
  ☎(01873) 735980
  Fax (01873) 735985
  e-mail: abergavennylibrarymonmouthshire.gov.uk

Community Library Managers Mrs J Greenway MCLIP, Mrs A M Newsam BA DipLIS MCLIP

- Severnside, Caldicot Library, Woodstock Way, Caldicot, Monmouthshire NP26 4DB
  ☎(01291) 426425
  Fax (01291) 426426
  e-mail: caldicotlibrarymonmouthshire.gov.uk
  Community Library Managers Dr K Flatten BSc MSc PED MCLIP, R Skinner MCLIP
- Lower Wye, Chepstow Library, Manor Way, Chepstow, Monmouthshire NP16 5HZ
  ☎(01291) 635730
  Fax (01291) 635736
  e-mail: chepstowlibrarymonmouthshire.gov.uk
  Community Library Manager Mrs M Stimson
- Central Monmouthshire, Monmouth Library, Rolls Hall, Whitecross Street, Monmouth, Monmouthshire NP25 3BY
  ☎(01600) 775215
  Fax (01600) 775218
  e-mail: monmouthlibrarymonmouthshire.gov.uk
  Community Library Manager Mrs V Thomas BA BD MCLIP

NEATH PORT TALBOT

Authority Neath Port Talbot County Borough Council
HQ Library and Information Services, Reginald Street, Velindre, Port Talbot SA13 1YY
☎(01639) 899829
Fax (01639) 899152
e-mail: npt.libhq@neath-porttalbot.gov.uk
Cultural Services Co-ordinator J L Ellis BA MCLIP (e-mail: j.l.ellis@neath-porttalbot.gov.uk)

Central/largest libraries

- Neath Library, Victoria Gardens, Neath SA11 3BA
  ☎(01639) 644604/635017
  Fax (01639) 641912
  Team Leader, Neath A W John MCLIP (e-mail: w.john@neath-porttalbot.gov.uk)
- Port Talbot Library, Aberavon Shopping Centre (1st Floor), Port Talbot SA13 1PB
  ☎(01639) 763490/1
  Fax (01639) 763489
  e-mail: porttalbot.library@neath-porttalbot.gov.uk
  Team Leader, Port Talbot E G Williams MCLIP

NEWPORT

Authority Newport City Council
HQ Newport Library and Information Service, Central Library, John Frost Square, Newport NP20 1PA
☎(01633) 265539 (enquiries & administration)
Fax (01633) 222615
e-mail: central.library@newport.gov.uk

url: http://www.newport.gov.uk/libraries
Borough Librarian Mrs G John MBA MCLIP

PEMBROKESHIRE

Authority Pembrokeshire County Council
HQ County Library, Dew Street, Haverfordwest, Pembrokeshire SA61 1SU
☎(01437) 762070 (enquiries), (01437) 775241 (administration)
Fax (01437) 767092
e-mail: judy.mcquaker@pembrokeshire.gov.uk
Cultural Services Manager N Bennett BSc DMS MCLIP (01437 775240; e-mail: neil.bennett@pembrokeshire.gov.uk)
Group Librarian, Central Mrs S Matthews MCLIP (01437 775242; e-mail: sandra.matthews@pembrokeshire.gov.uk)
Group Librarian, Haven C Richards MCLIP (01646 692892; e-mail: clive.richards@pembrokeshire.gov.uk)
Group Librarian, North Mrs A Thomas MCLIP (01348 872694; e-mail: anita.thomas@pembrokeshire.gov.uk)
Group Librarian, East Mrs E Evans (01834 861781)

Community libraries

- Pembroke Dock Library, Water Street, Pembroke Dock, Pembrokeshire SA72 6DW
  ☎(01646) 686356
  Fax (01646) 687071
  Senior Library Assistant S Croxford
- Milford Haven Library, Hamilton Terrace, Milford Haven, Pembrokeshire SA73 3HP
  ☎(01646) 692892 (tel/fax)
  Community Librarian Vacant
- Fishguard Library, High Street, Fishguard, Pembrokeshire SA65 9AR
  ☎(01348) 872694 (tel/fax)
  Community Librarian Vacant
- Tenby Library, Green Hill Avenue, Tenby, Pembrokeshire SA70 7LB
  ☎(01834) 843934 (tel/fax)
  Senior Library Assistant Mrs J Sutcliffe
- Haverfordwest Library, Dew Street, Haverfordwest, Pembrokeshire SA61 1SU
  ☎(01437) 762070
  Senior Library Assistant Mrs A Haywood

POWYS

Authority Powys County Council
HQ County Library HQ, Cefnllys Road, Llandrindod Wells, Powys LD1 5LD
☎(01597) 826860 (general enquiries)
Fax (01597) 826872
County Librarian Miss T L Adams BA MCLIP

Management/Administrative Centre, Community, Leisure and Recreation Department, County Hall, Llandrindod Wells, Powys LD1 5LG

☎(01597) 826155
Fax (01597) 826243
Principal Librarian (Field Services) Mrs H Edwards BLib MCLIP
Principal Librarian (Support Services) Mrs M Mason BLib MCLIP
Principal Librarian (Education, Schools and Children) Mrs D Jones MCLIP

Main libraries

- Newtown Library, Park Lane, Newtown, Powys SY16 1EJ
  ☎(01686) 626934
  Fax (01686) 624935
  Branch Librarian Vacant
- Brecon Library, Ship Street, Brecon, Powys LD3 9AE
  ☎(01874) 623346
  Fax (01874) 622818
  Branch Librarian Mrs K Murray MCLIP

RHONDDA CYNON TAFF

Authority Rhondda Cynon Taff County Borough Council
HQ Education Centre, Grawen Street, Porth, Rhondda Cynon Taff CF39 0BU
☎(01443) 687666
Fax (01443) 680286
Head of Library and Museum Services Mrs J A Jones BA MCLIP (01443 680289; e-mail: julieajones@rhondda-cynon-taff.gov.uk)
Principal Librarian (Reader Services) Mrs N Jones MSc MCLIP (01685 885319)
Area Librarian (North) Mrs R Williams MSc MCLIP (01685 885316)
Area Librarian (South) Mrs L Morris BA MCLIP (01443 486850)

Largest library

Aberdare Library, Green Street, Aberdare, Rhondda Cynon Taff CF44 7AG
☎(01685) 885318
Fax (01685) 881188
Branch Librarian Ms C Langdon BA MCLIP

Regional libraries

- Pontypridd Library, Library Road, Pontypridd, Rhondda Cynon Taff CF37 2DY
  ☎(01443) 486850
  Fax (01443) 493258
  Branch Librarian Mrs C Morgan BA MCLIP
- Treorchy Library, Station Road, Treorchy, Rhondda Cynon Taff CF42 6NN
  ☎(01443) 773204
  Fax (01443) 777047
  Branch Librarian D Price BSc(Econ)

SWANSEA

Authority Swansea City and County Council
HQ County Library HQ, County Hall, Oystermouth Road, Swansea SA1 3SN

☎(01792) 636430
Fax (01792) 636235
e-mail: swansea.libraries@swansea.gov.uk
url: www.swansea.gov.uk/culture/Libraries/LibraryIntro.htm
County Librarian M Allen BA MSc MCLIP (e-mail: michael.allen@swansea.gov.uk)
Assistant County Librarian, Systems and Development Mrs P Morris MCLIP (01792 637132; e-mail: pauline.morris@swansea.gov.uk)
Assistant County Librarian, Lending and Information Services Mrs K A Rowe BLib MCLIP (01792 636628; e-mail: katharine.rowe@swansea.gov.uk)

Central/largest library

Swansea Library, Alexandra Road, Swansea SA1 5DX
☎(01792) 516750/516751
Fax (01792) 516759
e-mail: central.library@swansea.gov.uk
Librarian Miss E Rees BA DipLIS

Branch libraries

- Bonymaen Library, Bonymaen Community Centre, Bonymaen Road, Bonymaen, Swansea SA1 7AW
  ☎(01792) 469203
  Librarian Mrs J Woodward
- Brynhyfryd Library, Llangyfelach Road, Brynhyfryd, Swansea SA5 9LH
  ☎(01792) 650953
  Librarian Mrs C Skudra
- Brynmill Library, Bernard Street, Brynmill, Swansea SA2 0DT
  ☎(01792) 466072
  Librarian Mrs S Moon
- Clydach Library, High Street, Clydach, Swansea SA6 5LN
  ☎(01792) 843300
  Fax (01792) 844768
  e-mail: clydach.library@swansea.gov.uk
  Librarian Mrs S Varley
- Fforestfach Library, Kings Head Road, Gendros, Swansea SA5 8DA
  ☎(01792) 586978
  Librarian Mrs P Young
- Gorseinon Library, 15 West Street, Gorseinon, Swansea SA4 4AA
  ☎(01792) 516780
  Fax (01792) 516772
  e-mail: gorseinon.library@swansea.gov.uk
  Librarian Mrs I Redman
- Gowerton Library, Mansel Street, Gowerton, Swansea SA4 3BU
  ☎(01792) 873572
  e-mail: gowerton.library@swansea.gov.uk
  Librarian Mrs P Hill
- Killay Library, St Hilary's Church Hall, Gower Road, Killay, Swansea SA2 7DY
  ☎(01792) 203453

e-mail: killay.library@swansea.gov.uk
Librarian Mrs P McDonnell

- Llansamlet Library, 242 Peniel Green Road, Llansamlet, Swansea SA7 9BD
☎(01792) 771652
Librarian Mrs K Walters
- Morriston Library, Treharne Road, Morriston, Swansea SA6 7AA
☎(01792) 516770
Fax (01792) 516771
e-mail: morriston.library@swansea.gov.uk
Librarian Mrs J Clement BLib MCLIP
- Oystermouth Library, Dunns Lane, Mumbles, Swansea SA3 4AA
☎(01792) 368380
Fax (01792) 369143
e-mail: oystermouth.library@swansea.gov.uk
Librarian Mrs J James BA DipLib MCLIP
- Penlan Library, Heol Frank, Penlan, Swansea SA5 7AH
☎(01792) 584674
Librarian Mrs M Nash
- Pennard Library, Pennard Road, Southgate, Pennard, Swansea SA3 2AD
☎(01792) 233277
Librarian Mrs P Hopkins
- Pontarddulais Library, St Michael's Avenue, Pontarddulais, Swansea SA4 1TE
☎(01792) 882822
Librarian Mrs D Jenkins
- St Thomas Library, Miers Street, St Thomas, Swansea SA1 8BZ
☎(01792) 655570
Librarian Mrs B Price
- Sketty Library, Vivian Road, Sketty, Swansea SA2 0UN
☎(01792) 202024
e-mail: sketty.library@swansea.gov.uk
Librarian Mrs C Bonham
- Townhill Library, Phoenix Centre, Powys Avenue, Townhill, Swansea SA1 6PH
☎(01792) 512370
Fax (01792) 512371
Librarian Mrs S Millward

TORFAEN

Authority Torfaen County Borough Council
HQ Torfaen Libraries HQ, Civic Centre, Pontypool, Torfaen NP4 6YB
☎(01495) 766311
Fax (01495) 766317
Cultural Services Manager Ms S Johnson MCLIP (e-mail: sue.johnson@torfaen.gov.uk)

Central/largest library

Cwmbran Library, Gwent House, Cwmbran, Torfaen NP44 1XQ
☎(01633) 483240
Fax (01633) 838609

e-mail: gil48@dial.pipex.com
Principal Librarian Mrs C George BA DipLib MCLIP

Group library

Pontypool Library, Hanbury Road, Pontypool, Torfaen NP4 6JL
☎(01495) 762820
Fax (01495) 752530
e-mail: xcr12@dial.pipex.com
Senior Librarian M Tanner BA DipLib MCLIP

VALE OF GLAMORGAN

Authority Vale of Glamorgan Council
HQ Directorate of Learning and Development, Civic Offices, Holton Road, Barry, Vale of Glamorgan CF63 4RU
☎(01446) 709381
Chief Librarian Ms S E Jones BSc(Econ) MSc(Econ) MCLIP (e-mail: sjones@valeofglamorgan.gov.uk)
Principal Librarian C Edwards BA DipLib MCLIP (e-mail: cdedwards@valeofglamorgan.gov.uk)

Central/largest library

Barry Library, King Square, Barry, Vale of Glamorgan CF63 4RW
☎(01446) 735722
Senior Librarian Ms S Wildsmith MCLIP
Children's Librarian Ms M Holt
Information Librarian Ms K Owen MCLIP

Main libraries

- Penarth Library, Stanwell Road, Penarth, Vale of Glamorgan CF64 2YT
  ☎029 2070 8438
  Senior Librarian M Payne BA DipLib MCLIP
- Cowbridge Library, Old Hall, Cowbridge, Vale of Glamorgan CF7 7AH
  ☎(01446) 773941
  Community Librarian R Matthews BA MCLIP
- Dinas Powys Library, The Murch, Dinas Powys, Vale of Glamorgan CF64 4QU
  ☎029 2051 2556
  Community Librarian Ms M Weeks
- Llantwit Major Library, Boverton Road, Llantwit Major, Vale of Glamorgan CF61 9XZ
  ☎(01446) 792700
  Community Librarian Ms H Price MCLIP

WREXHAM

Authority Wrexham County Borough Council
HQ Education and Leisure Service, Tŷ Henblas, Queen's Square, Wrexham LL13 8AZ
☎(01978) 297430
Fax (01978) 297422

Chief Leisure, Libraries and Culture Officer A Watkin BA DipLib FCLIP MIM
Libraries Officer D Hughes BA DipLib MCLIP (01978 297442)

Central/largest library

Wrexham Library, Rhosddu Road, Wrexham LL11 1AU
☎(01978) 292090
Fax (01978) 292611
e-mail: reference.library@wrexham.gov.uk
Community Librarian Mrs M Thomas MCLIP (01978 292600)

Group/branch libraries

- Brynteg Library, Quarry Road, Brynteg, Wrexham LL11 6AB
  ☎(01978) 759523
  Community Librarian Vacant
- Rhosllanerchrugog Library, Princes Road, Rhos, Wrexham LL14 1AB
  ☎(01978) 840328
  Community Librarian Miss A L Hughes MA MCLIP

CROWN DEPENDENCIES

ALDERNEY

HQ Alderney Library, Island Hall, Royal Connaught Square, Alderney, Channel Islands GY9 3UE
☎(01481) 824178
Chairman, Alderney Library Committee Mrs E Mignot BA
(Alderney Library is a voluntary organization)

GUERNSEY

HQ Guille-Alles Library, Market Street, St Peter Port, Guernsey, Channel Islands GY1 1HB
☎(01481) 720392
Fax (01481) 712425
e-mail: ga@library.gg
url: http://www.library.gg
Chief Librarian Miss M J Falla BA MA MLib MCLIP

Priaulx Library, Candie Road, St Peter Port, Guernsey, Channel Islands GY1 1UG
☎(01481) 721998
Fax (01481) 713804
e-mail: priaulx.library@gov.gg
url: http://www.gov.gg/priaulx
Chief Librarian Mrs M E R Harris MCLIP CMS
(The Priaulx Library is a reference and lending library specializing in local history and family history research in the Channel Islands)

ISLE OF MAN

HQ Douglas Public Library, Ridgeway Street, Douglas, Isle of Man IM1 1EP
☎(01624) 623021
Fax (01624) 662792
Librarian J R Bowring BA MCLIP (e-mail: jbowring@douglas.org.im)

Onchan Library, Willow House, 61-69 Main Road, Onchan, Isle of Man IM3 1AJ
☎(01624) 621228
Fax (01624) 663482
e-mail: onchan.library@onchan.org.im
url: http://www.onchan.org.im/library.htm
Librarian Mrs P Hand

Ramsey Library, Town Hall, Parliament Square, Ramsey, Isle of Man IM8 1RT
☎(01624) 810146
e-mail: rtc@mcb.net
Librarian P Boulton BA

Castletown Library, Farrants Way, Castletown, Isle of Man IM9 1NR
☎(01624) 829355
e-mail: library@castletown.org.im
Librarian Mrs F Tasker

Ward Library, 38 Castle Street, Peel, Isle of Man IM5 1AL
☎(01624) 843533
e-mail: ward_library@hotmail.com
Librarian Mrs C Horton

George Herdman Library, Bridson Street, Port Erin, Isle of Man IM9 6AL
☎(01624) 832365
e-mail: gh_library@hotmail.com
Librarian Miss A Dryland BSc

Junior and Mobile Library, Nobles Hall, Westmoreland Road, Douglas, Isle of Man
☎(01624) 671043
Librarian Ms M Cousins

JERSEY

Authority Jersey Library Service
HQ Jersey Library, Halkett Place, St Helier, Jersey, Channel Islands JE2 4WH
☎(01534) 759991 (enquiries), (01534) 759992 (reference), (01534) 759993 (administration)
Fax (01534) 69444
e-mail: jsylib@itl.net
url: http://www.jsylib.gov.je
Chief Librarian Mrs M Corrigan MCLIP LLCM

Public Libraries in the Republic of Ireland

CARLOW COUNTY LIBRARY

HQ Carlow Central Library, Tullow Street, Carlow, Republic of Ireland
☎(00 353 503) 70094
Fax (00 353 503) 40548
County Librarian T King MA DipLib
Executive Librarian Ms D Cudron BComm DipLib
Assistant Librarian Ms C Flahavan BA(Open) DipLib
Assistant Librarian P Dolan BA DipLib

CAVAN COUNTY LIBRARY

HQ Cavan County Library, Farnham Street, Cavan, Republic of Ireland
☎(00 353 49) 433 1799
Fax (00 353 49) 437 1832
e-mail: cavancountylibrary@tinet.ie
County Librarian Ms J Brady BA DLIS
Executive Librarian T Sullivan DLIS
Assistant Librarians T Treacy BA DLIS, M Doherty

CLARE COUNTY LIBRARY

HQ Clare County Library HQ, Mill Road, Ennis, Co Clare, Republic of Ireland
☎(00 353 65) 684 2461/684 6350
Fax (00 353 65) 684 2462
e-mail: mailbox@clairelibrary.ie
url: http://www.clarelibrary.ie
County Librarian N Crowley FLAI

Central/largest library

De Valera Branch Library, Ennis, Co Clare, Republic of Ireland
☎(00 353 65) 682 1616/684 6353

Area libraries

- Sean Lemass Library, Town Centre, Shannon, Co Clare, Republic of Ireland
  ☎(00 353 61) 364266
- The Library, The Square, Ennistymon, Co Clare, Republic of Ireland
  ☎(00 353 65) 707 1245
- Kilrush Library, Kilrush, Co Clare, Republic of Ireland
  ☎(00 353 65) 905 1504
- The Library, Kilnasoolagh Park, Newmarket-on-Fergus, Co Clare, Republic of Ireland
  ☎(00 353 61) 368411
- Sweeney Memorial Library, O'Connell Street, Kilkee, Co Clare, Republic of Ireland
  ☎(00 353 65) 9056034
- The Library, The Lock House, Killaloe, Co Clare, Republic of Ireland
  ☎(00 353 61) 376062
- The Library, Ballard Road, Miltown Malbay, Co Clare, Republic of Ireland
  ☎(00 353 65) 708 4822

- Local Studies Centre, The Manse, Harmony Row, Ennis, Co Clare, Republic of Ireland
  ☎(00 353 65) 682 1616/684 6271
- Kilfinaghty Library, Church Street, Sixmile Bridge, Co Clare, Republic of Ireland
  ☎(00 353 61) 369678

CORK CITY LIBRARY

HQ Cork City Library, Grand Parade, Cork, Republic of Ireland
☎(00 353 21) 427 7110
Fax (00 353 21) 427 5684
e-mail: citylibrary@corkcity.ie
url: http://www.corkcitylibrary.ie
City Librarian Ms H O'Sullivan FLAI

Branch libraries

- Douglas Library, Village Shopping Centre, Douglas, Cork, Republic of Ireland
  ☎(00 353 21) 427 7110
  Fax (00 353 21) 427 5684
  e-mail: douglas_library@corkcity.ie
- Mayfield Library, Old Youghal Road, Cork, Republic of Ireland
  ☎(00 353 21) 427 7110
  Fax (00 353 21) 427 5684
  e-mail: mayfield_library@corkcity.ie
- St Mary's Road Library, Cork, Republic of Ireland
  ☎(00 353 21) 427 7110
  Fax (00 353 21) 427 5684
  e-mail: stmarys_library@corkcity.ie
- Tory Top Road Library, Ballyphehane, Cork, Republic of Ireland
  ☎(00 353 21) 427 7110
  Fax (00 353 21) 427 5684
  e-mail: torytop_library@corkcity.ie
- Hollyhill Library, Shopping Centre, Hollyhill, Cork, Republic of Ireland
  ☎(00 353 21) 439 2998
  Fax (00 353 21) 439 3032
  e-mail: hollyhill_library@corkcity.ie

CORK COUNTY LIBRARY

HQ Cork County Library, Farranlea Road, Cork, Republic of Ireland
☎(00 353 21) 454 6499
Fax (00 353 21) 434 3254
e-mail: corkcountylibrary@eircom.net
County Librarian Ms R Flanagan BA DipLib ALAI

DONEGAL COUNTY LIBRARY

HQ Donegal County Library Admin. Centre, Rosemount, Letterkenny, Co Donegal, Republic of Ireland
☎(00 353 74) 21968 (enquiries & administration)

Fax (00 353 74) 21740
e-mail: dglcolib@iol.ie
County Librarian L Ronayne BCL DipLib ALAI

Central/largest library

Central Library & Arts Centre, Oliver Plunkett Road, Letterkenny, Co Donegal, Republic of Ireland
☎(00 353 74) 24950
Fax (00 353 74) 24950
e-mail: dglcolib@iol.ie
Assistant Librarian G McHugh BA DipLib

DUBLIN CORPORATION PUBLIC LIBRARIES

HQ Dublin Public Libraries, Central Department, 2nd Floor, Cumberland House, Fenian Street, Dublin 2, Republic of Ireland
☎(00 353 1) 664 4800
Fax (00 353 1) 676 1628
e-mail: dublin.city.libs@iol.ie
City Librarian and Director Ms D Ellis-King BA DipLib ALAI MPhil
Deputy City Librarian Ms M Hayes BA DipLib HDipEd ALAI

Central/largest library

Central Public Library, ILAC Centre, Henry Street, Dublin 1, Republic of Ireland
☎(00 353 1) 873 4333
Fax (00 353 1) 872 1451
e-mail: dubcelib@iol.ie

DUN LAOGHAIRE/RATHDOWN COUNTY COUNCIL PUBLIC LIBRARY SERVICE

HQ Public Library Service, Duncairn House, 14 Carysfort Avenue (First Floor), Blackrock, Co Dublin, Republic of Ireland
☎(00 353 1) 278 1788
Fax (00 353 1) 278 1792
e-mail: libraries@dlrcoco.ie
url: http://www.dlrcoco.ie/library
County Librarian M Ó Raghaill BSc(Econ) MCLIP
Senior Librarian, Bibliographic Control Ms J A Lloyd BA DLT
Senior Librarian, Administration and Staff Ms O Gallagher BSocSc DLT
Senior Librarian (IT) Ms M Boyle
Senior Librarian (Cultural Librarian) Ms M Keyes BA MA DLIS
Librarian, Cataloguing Ms A Duffy BA HDip(Psych) DLT MA
Librarian, Staff and Interlibrary Loans Ms G McHugh MA DLIS ALAI
Librarian, Finance Ms E Prout
Librarian, Cataloguing (Store Project) N Curtin
Librarian, Young People and Schools Ms P Corish BA HDipEd DLIS

Branch libraries

- Blackrock Library, Main Street, Blackrock, Co Dublin, Republic of Ireland
  ☎(00 353 1) 288 8117
  Librarian D McNally
- Cabinteely Library, Old Bray Road, Cabinteely, Dublin 18, Republic of Ireland
  ☎(00 353 1) 285 5363
  Librarian Ms S Lynch
- Dalkey Library, Castle Street, Dalkey, Co Dublin, Republic of Ireland
  ☎(00 353 1) 285 5277
  Librarian Ms P Byrne
- Deansgrange Library, Clonkeen Drive, Deansgrange, Dublin 18, Republic of Ireland
  ☎(00 353 1) 285 0860
  Senior Librarian Ms K Guinan BA DLIS
  Librarian Ms O Brennan
- Dundrum Library, Upper Churchtown Road, Dublin 14, Republic of Ireland
  ☎(00 353 1) 298 5000
  Senior Librarian T Curran BA DLIS
  Librarian Ms A Millane
- Dun Laoghaire Library, Lower George's Street, Dun Laoghaire, Co Dublin, Republic of Ireland
  ☎(00 353 1) 280 1147
  Librarian P Walsh
- Sallynoggin Library, Senior College, Sallynoggin, Co Dublin, Republic of Ireland
  ☎(00 353 1) 285 0127
  Librarian Ms C Kelly
- Shankill Library, Library Road, Shankill, Co Dublin, Republic of Ireland
  ☎(00 353 1) 282 3081
  Librarian Ms D O'Connor
- Stillorgan Library, St Laurence's Park, Stillorgan, Co Dublin, Republic of Ireland
  ☎(00 353 1) 288 9655
  Senior Librarian D Griffin BA DLT
  Librarian Ms M Jennings

FINGAL COUNTY LIBRARIES

HQ Fingal County Libraries, County Hall, Main Street, Swords, Co Dublin, Republic of Ireland
☎(00 353 1) 890 5520 ext 5524 (enquiries), ext 5525 (administration)
Fax (00 353 1) 873 2021
e-mail: libraries@fingalcoco.ie
url: http://www.iol.ie/-fincolib/
County Librarian P Harris DLIS ALAI
Senior Librarian (Personnel & Finance) Ms A Finn
Senior Librarian (Circulations & Development) Ms R Mullet
Senior Librarian (Projects) R Farrell
Librarian (Development/PR) Ms Y Reilly (e-mail: yvonne.reilly@fingalcoco.ie)

Central/largest library

Blanchardstown Library, Civic Centre, Blanchardstown Centre, Dublin 15, Republic of Ireland
☎(00 353 1) 890 5563
Fax (00 353 1) 890 5569
e-mail: blanlib@fingalcoco.ie
Senior Librarians D Bregazzi (Adult Lending), Ms E Conway (Childrens), Ms B Fennell (Reference & Research)

Branch libraries

- Balbriggan Library, St George's Square, Balbriggan, Co Dublin, Republic of Ireland
  ☎(00 353 1) 841 1128
  Fax (00 353 1) 841 2101
  Senior Librarian J Walsh
- Malahide Library, Main Street, Malahide, Co Dublin, Republic of Ireland
  ☎(00 353 1) 845 2026
  Fax (00 353 1) 845 2199
  e-mail: malalib@eircom.net
  Senior Librarian Ms M Sliney
- Rathbeale Library, Swords Shopping Centre, Swords, Co Dublin, Republic of Ireland
  ☎(00 353 1) 840 4179
  Fax (00 353 1) 840 4417
  e-mail: rathbeale.lib@eircom.net
  Senior Librarian Ms C Keane
- Howth Library, Main Street, Howth, Co Dublin, Republic of Ireland
  ☎(00 353 1) 832 2130
  Fax (00 353 1) 832 2273
  Librarian Ms A O'Reilly
- Skerries Library, Strand Street, Skerries, Co Dublin, Republic of Ireland
  ☎(00 353 1) 849 1900
  Fax (00 353 1) 849 5142
  Librarian Ms G Bollard
- Mobile Library Services, Unit 34, Coolmine Industrial Estate, Coolmine, Dublin 15, Republic of Ireland
  ☎(00 353 1) 822 1564
  Fax (00 353 1) 822 1568
  Senior Librarian Ms M Coakley
- Schools' Library Services, Unit 34, Coolmine Industrial Estate, Coolmine, Dublin 15, Republic of Ireland
  ☎(00 353 1) 822 5056
  Fax (00 353 1) 822 1568
  e-mail: finsclib@indigo.ie
  Librarian Ms C McLoughlin
- Housebound Services, Unit 34, Coolmine Industrial Estate, Coolmine, Dublin 15, Republic of Ireland
  ☎(00 353 1) 822 1564
  Fax (00 353 1) 822 1568
  Librarian Ms J Knight

- Local Studies, 11 Parnell Square, Dublin 1, Republic of Ireland
  ☎(00 353 1) 878 6910
  Fax (00 353 1) 878 6919
  Librarian J Black

GALWAY COUNTY LIBRARIES

HQ Galway County Library HQ, Island House, Cathedral Square, Galway, Republic of Ireland
☎(00 353 91) 562471
Fax (00 353 91) 565039
e-mail: info@galwaylibrary.ie
url: http://www.galwaylibrary.ie
County Librarian P McMahon DipLib
Deputy Librarian Ms M Moran
Librarian, Branch System P Rabbitt
Librarian ICT J Fitzgibbon

Central/largest library

Galway City Library, Hynes Building, St Augustine Street, Galway, Republic of Ireland
☎(00 353 91) 561666
Executive Librarian, Galway City Services Mrs B Kelly BA DipLib
Assistant Librarian Mrs J Vahey

Branch libraries

- Public Library, Fairgreen, Ballinasloe, Co Galway, Republic of Ireland
  ☎(00 353 905) 43464
  Assistant Librarian Mrs M Dillon
- Public Library, Tuam, Co Galway, Republic of Ireland
  ☎(00 353 93) 24287
  Senior Library Assistant E O'Connor
- Public Library, Clifden, Co Galway, Republic of Ireland
  ☎(00 353 95) 21092
  Senior Library Assistant P Keogh
- Public Library, Portumna, Co Galway, Republic of Ireland
  ☎(00 353 509) 41261
  Library Assistant Ms T Tierney
- Public Library, Athenry, Co Galway, Republic of Ireland
  Branch Librarian Ms A Ridge
- Public Library, Gort, Co Galway, Republic of Ireland
  Branch Librarian Mrs J Hickey
- Public Library, Loughrea, Co Galway, Republic of Ireland
  Senior Library Assistant Ms A Callanan
- Public Library, Oranmore, Co Galway, Republic of Ireland
  Senior Library Assistant Vacant

KERRY COUNTY LIBRARY

HQ Kerry County Library, Moyderwell, Tralee, Co Kerry, Republic of Ireland
☎(00 353 66) 712 1200
Fax (00 353 66) 712 9202
e-mail: kerrycolibrary@eircom.net
url: http://www.kerrycountylibrary.com
Chief Librarian Mrs K Browne FLAI

Area libraries

- Killarney Branch Library, Killarney, Co Kerry, Republic of Ireland
  ☎(00 353 64) 32655
  Fax (00 353 64) 36065
  e-mail: killarneylibrary@eircom.net
- Ballybunion Branch Library, Ballybunion, Co Kerry, Republic of Ireland
  ☎(00 353 68) 27615
  e-mail: ballybunionlibrary@eircom.net
- Cahirciveen Branch Library, Cahirciveen, Co Kerry, Republic of Ireland
  ☎(00 353 66) 947 2287
  e-mail: caherciveenlibrary@eircom.net
- Castleisland Branch Library, Castleisland, Co Kerry, Republic of Ireland
  ☎(00 353 66) 714 1485
  e-mail: castleislandlibrary@eircom.net
- Dingle Branch Library, Dingle, Co Kerry, Republic of Ireland
  ☎(00 353 66) 915 1499
  e-mail: dinglelibrary@eircom.net
- Kenmare Branch Library, Kenmare, Co Kerry, Republic of Ireland
  ☎(00 353 64) 41416
  e-mail: kenmarelibrary@eircom.net
- Killorglin Branch Library, Killorglin, Co Kerry, Republic of Ireland
  ☎(00 353 66) 976 1272
  e-mail: killorglinlibrary@eircom.net
- Listowel Branch Library, Listowel, Co Kerry, Republic of Ireland
  ☎(00 353 68) 23044
  e-mail: listowellibrary@eircom.net

KILDARE COUNTY LIBRARY

HQ Kildare County Library Service, Riverbank Cultural Campus, Main Street, Newbridge, Co Kildare, Republic of Ireland
☎(00 353 45) 431109/431486 (enquiries)
Fax (00 353 45) 432490
e-mail: colibrary@kildarecoco.ie
url: http://www.kildare.ie
County Librarian Ms B Gleeson

Main branch libraries

- Community Library, Town Hall, Athy, Co Kildare, Republic of Ireland
  ☎(00 353 507) 31144

- Branch Library, Celbridge, Co Kildare, Republic of Ireland
  ☎(00 353 1) 627 2207
- Branch Library, Newtown House, Leixlip, Co Kildare, Republic of Ireland
  ☎(00 353 1) 624 4240
- Branch Library, Main Street, Maynooth, Co Kildare, Republic of Ireland
  ☎(00 353 1) 628 5530
- Branch Library, Canal Harbour, Naas, Co Kildare, Republic of Ireland
  ☎(00 353 45) 879111
- Branch Library, Athgarvan Road, Newbridge, Co Kildare, Republic of Ireland
  ☎(00 353 45) 436453

KILKENNY COUNTY LIBRARY

HQ Kilkenny County Library, 6 John's Quay, Kilkenny, Co Kilkenny, Republic of Ireland
☎(00 353 56) 22021 (enquiries), 22606 (administration)
Fax (00 353 56) 70233
e-mail: katlibs@iol.ie
County Librarian J Fogarty DLIS ALAI

Central/largest library

Kilkenny City Library, John's Quay, Kilkenny, Co Kilkenny, Republic of Ireland
☎(00 353 56) 22021 (enquiries), 22606 (administration)
Fax (00 353 56) 70233
e-mail: katlibs@iol.ie
Assistant Librarians D Macaulay BSc DLIS, D O'Reilly DLIS ALAI

Area libraries

- Graiguenamanagh Library, Convent Road, Graiguenamanagh, Co Kilkenny, Republic of Ireland
  ☎(00 353 503) 24224
  e-mail: graiglib@eircom.net
  Assistant Librarian Ms B Ward BA DLIS
- Urlingford Library, The Courthouse, Urlingford, Co Kilkenny, Republic of Ireland
  ☎(00 353 56) 31656
- Castlecomer Library, Kilkenny Street, Castlecomer, Co Kilkenny, Republic of Ireland
  ☎(00 353 56) 40055
  e-mail: comlibrary@eircom.net
  Assistant Librarian Ms M Morrissey

LAOIS COUNTY LIBRARY

HQ Laois County Library, Library HQ, Kea-Lew Business Park, Mountrath Road, Portlaoise, Co Laois, Republic of Ireland
☎(00 353 502) 72340/1
Fax (00 353 502) 64558
e-mail: library@laoiscoco.ie
County Librarian G Maher LLB(Hons) DLIS

Central/largest library

Portlaoise Branch Library, Dunamase House, Portlaoise, Co Laois, Republic of Ireland
☎(00 353 502) 22333
Assistant Librarian Mrs C Kavanagh

Branch libraries

- Abbeyleix Branch Library, Abbeyleix, Co Laois, Republic of Ireland
  ☎(00 353 502) 30020
  Branch Librarian Ms E Sutton
- Mountmellick Branch Library, Mountmellick, Co Laois, Republic of Ireland
  ☎(00 353 502) 24733
  Branch Librarian Ms E Broomfield
- Mountrath Branch Library, Mountrath, Co Laois, Republic of Ireland
  ☎(00 353 502) 56046
  Branch Librarian Ms J Phelan
- Portarlington Branch Library, Portarlington, Co Laois, Republic of Ireland
  ☎(00 353 502) 43751
  Branch Librarian Ms B Doris
- Rathdowney Branch Library, Rathdowney, Co Laois, Republic of Ireland
  ☎(00 353 505) 46852
  Branch Librarian Mrs C Fitzpatrick
- Stradballly Branch Library, Stradbally, Co Laois, Republic of Ireland
  ☎(00 353 505) 25005
  Branch Librarian Ms P Norton
- Clonaslee Branch Library, Clonaslee, Co Laois, Republic of Ireland
  ☎(00 353 505) 48397
  Branch Librarian Ms M Cusack
- Timahoe Branch Library, Timahoe, Co Laois, Republic of Ireland
  ☎(00 353 505) 27231
  Branch Librarian Ms M Scully

LEITRIM COUNTY LIBRARY (LEABHARLANN CHONTAE LIATROMA)

HQ Leitrim County Library, Ballinamore, Co Leitrim, Republic of Ireland
☎(00 353 78) 44012
Fax (00 353 78) 44425
e-mail: leitrimlibrary@eircom.net
County Librarian S O Suilleabhain DLT FLAI ALAI

LIMERICK CITY LIBRARY

HQ Limerick City Library, The Granary, Michael Street, Limerick, Republic of Ireland
☎(00 353 61) 415799 (general enquiries), 314668 (direct line)
Fax (00 353 61) 411506
City Librarian Ms D Doyle BA FLAI ALAI (e-mail: ddoyle@citylib.limerickcity.ie)

LIMERICK COUNTY LIBRARY

HQ Limerick County Library, 58 O'Connell Street, Limerick, Republic of Ireland

☎(00 353 61) 214452 (enquiries & administration)
Fax (00 353 61) 318570
e-mail: colibrar@limerickcoco.ie
County Librarian D Brady BA LAI DLIS
Executive Librarians Ms A Bennett BA DLIS, Ms H Walsh DLIS LAI

Central/largest library

Dooradoyle Branch Library, Crescent Shopping Centre, Dooradoyle Road, Limerick, Republic of Ireland
☎(00 353 61) 301101
Executive Librarian Ms N O'Neill

Branch libraries

- Adare Branch Library, Adare, Co Limerick, Republic of Ireland
  ☎(00 353 61) 396822
  Assistant Librarian Ms M O'Reilly BA DLIS
- Newcastlewest Branch Library, Newcastlewest, Co Limerick, Republic of Ireland
  ☎(00 353 69) 62273
  Executive Librarian Ms A Dillane BA DLIS
- Foynes Branch Library, Foynes, Co Limerick, Republic of Ireland
  ☎(00 353 69) 65365
  Assistant Librarian Ms S Prendiville DLIS
- Abbeyfeale Branch Library, Bridge Street, Abbeyfeale, Co Limerick, Republic of Ireland
  ☎(00 353 68) 32488
  Senior Library Assistant M McInerney

LOUTH COUNTY LIBRARY

HQ Louth County Library, Roden Place, Dundalk, Co Louth, Republic of Ireland
☎(00 353 42) 935 3190
Fax (00 353 42) 933 7635
url: www.louthcoco.ie
County Librarian Miss A Ward BA DLT (e-mail: ann.ward@louthcoco.ie)

MAYO COUNTY LIBRARY

HQ Mayo County Library, Library HQ, Mountain View, Castlebar, Co Mayo, Republic of Ireland
☎(00 353 94) 24444 (enquiries & administration)
Fax (00 353 94) 24774
url: http://www.mayolibrary.ie
County Librarian A Vaughan BA DLIS (e-mail: avaughan@mayococo.ie)

Central/largest library

Mayo Central Library, The Mall, Castlebar, Co Mayo, Republic of Ireland
☎(00 353 94) 24444
Fax (00 353 94) 26491
e-mail: avaughan@mayococo.ie

MEATH COUNTY LIBRARY

HQ Meath County Library, Railway Street, Navan, Co Meath, Republic of Ireland
☎(00 353 46) 21134/21451
e-mail: colibrar@meathcoco.ie
County Librarian C Mangan BA MLIS
Executive Librarian Ms G Donnelly DLIS

Branch libraries

- Ashbourne Library, Killegland, Ashbourne, Co Meath, Republic of Ireland
  Branch Librarian Ms P Synnott
- Athboy Library, Main Street, Athboy, Co Meath, Republic of Ireland
  ☎(00 353 46) 32539
  Branch Librarian Ms T Doherty
- Duleek Library, Main Street, Duleek, Co Meath, Republic of Ireland
  ☎(00 353 41) 988 0700
  Branch Librarian Ms M McGreal
- Dunboyne Library, Castleview, Dunboyne, Co Meath, Republic of Ireland
  ☎(00 353 1) 825 1248
  Branch Librarian Ms C Cunningham
- Dunshaughlin Library, Main Street, Dunshaughlin, Co Meath, Republic of Ireland
  ☎(00 353 1) 825 0504
  Branch Librarian Vacant
- Kells Library, Maudlin Street, Kells, Co Meath, Republic of Ireland
  ☎(00 353 46) 41592
  Branch Librarian Ms R Grimes
- Laytown Library, Laytown, Co Meath, Republic of Ireland
  Branch Librarian Ms I Cunningham
- Nobber Library, Nobber, Co Meath, Republic of Ireland
  ☎(00 353 46) 52732
  Branch Librarian Ms I Griffin
- Oldcastle Library, Millbrook Road, Oldcastle, Co Meath, Republic of Ireland
  Branch Librarian Ms K Nally
- Slane Library, Castle Hill, Slane, Co Meath, Republic of Ireland
  ☎(00 353 41) 982 4955
  Branch Librarian Ms K Carroll
- Trim Library, High Street, Trim, Co Meath, Republic of Ireland
  ☎(00 353 46) 36014
  Branch Librarian Ms H Smith

MONAGHAN COUNTY LIBRARY

HQ Monaghan County Library, The Diamond, Clones, Co Monaghan, Republic of Ireland
☎(00 353 47) 51143
Fax (00 353 47) 51863
e-mail: moncolib@eircom.net
County Librarian J McElvaney DLIS
Executive Librarian C Elliott BSocSc

Central/largest library

Monaghan Branch Library, North Road, Monaghan Town, Republic of Ireland
☎(00 353 47) 81830
e-mail: monaghan@eircom.net
Senior Library Assistant Ms J Ryan

Branch libraries

- Clones Branch Library, The Diamond, Clones, Co Monaghan, Republic of Ireland
  ☎(00 353 47) 51143
  Fax (00 353 47) 51863
  Senior Library Assistant Ms C Lennon
- Carrickmacross Branch Library, Market Square, Carrickmacross, Co Monaghan, Republic of Ireland
  ☎(00 353 42) 61148
  e-mail: cmxlibrary@eircom.net
  Senior Library Assistant Ms B Moore
- Castleblayney Branch Library, Unit 3, Castleblayney Enterprise Centre, Dublin Road, Castleblayney, Co Monaghan, Republic of Ireland
  ☎(00 353 42) 974 0281
  e-mail: castleblayneylibrary@eircom.net
  Branch Librarian B McDonald
- Ballybay Library, Main Street, Ballybay, Co Monaghan, Republic of Ireland
  ☎(00 353 42) 974 1256
  e-mail: ballybaylibrary@eircom.net
  Branch Librarian Mrs R McDonnell

OFFALY COUNTY LIBRARY

HQ Offaly County Library, O'Connor Square, Tullamore, Co Offaly, Republic of Ireland
☎(00 353 506) 46834
Fax (00 353 506) 52769
e-mail: colibrar@offalycoco.ie
url: http://www.offaly.ie
County Librarian Miss A M Coughlan DLT MCLIP

ROSCOMMON COUNTY LIBRARY

HQ Roscommon County Library, Abbey Street, Roscommon, Republic of Ireland
☎(00 353 903) 37272/37273 (enquiries & administration)
Fax (00 353 903) 37101
e-mail: roslib@eircom.net
County Librarian Mrs H Kilcline BA ALAI FLAI (00 353 903 37271)

Central/largest library

Roscommon Branch Library, Abbey Street, Roscommon, Republic of Ireland
☎(00 353 903) 37277
Fax (00 353 903) 37101
Assistant Librarian i/c E Bolger DLIS

Branch libraries

- Boyle Branch Library, The King House, Boyle, Co Roscommon, Republic of Ireland
  ☎(00 353 79) 68200
  e-mail: bbl@eircom.net
  Branch Librarian Ms M Costelloe
- Ballaghaderreen Branch Library, Barrack Street, Ballaghaderreen, Co Roscommon, Republic of Ireland
  ☎(00 353 907) 77044
  e-mail: dbl@eircom.net
  Branch Librarian Ms E McDermott
- Castlerea Branch Library, Main Street, Castelrea, Co Roscommon, Republic of Ireland
  ☎(00 353 907) 20745
  e-mail: cbl@eircom.net
  Branch Librarian Ms M Carroll
- Elphin Branch Library, Main Street, Elphin, Co Roscommon, Republic of Ireland
  ☎(00 353 78) 35775
  e-mail: ebl@eircom.net
  Branch Librarian Ms M Walsh
- Strokestown Branch Library, Elphin Street, Strokestown, Co Roscommon, Republic of Ireland
  ☎(00 353 78) 34027
  e-mail: sbl@eircom.net
  Branch Librarian Ms M Lane
- Ballyforan Branch Library, Ballyforan, Co Roscommon, Republic of Ireland
  Branch Librarian Ms M Kelly

SLIGO COUNTY LIBRARY

HQ Sligo County Library, The Westward Town Centre, Bridge Street, Sligo, Republic of Ireland
☎(00 353 71) 47190
Fax (00 353 71) 46798
e-mail: sligolib@sligococo.ie
County Librarian D Tinney BA DLIS ALAI
Executive Librarian Ms P Brennan DLIS
Assistant Librarian P Gannon BA DLIS
Senior Library Assistant Ms C Morgan DipLib

Central/largest library

Sligo City Library, Stephen Street, Sligo, Republic of Ireland
☎(00 353 71) 42212
Fax (00 353 71) 46798
Assistant Librarian F Hegarty FLAI
Senior Library Assistant Ms F Walsh

TIPPERARY JOINT LIBRARIES COMMITTEE

HQ Tipperary County Library, Castle Avenue, Thurles, Co Tipperary, Republic of Ireland
☎(00 353 504) 21555

Fax (00 353 504) 23442
e-mail: info@tipperarylibraries.ie
url: http://www.tipperarylibraries.ie
County Librarian M Maher

Branch libraries

- Borrisokane Library, Main Street, Borrisokane, Co Tipperary, Republic of Ireland
  ☎(00 353 67) 27199
  Branch Librarian Mrs F O'Carroll
- Cahir Library, The Square, Cahir, Co Tipperary, Republic of Ireland
  ☎(00 353 52) 42075
  Branch Librarian Mrs A Tuohy
- Carrick-on-Suir Library, Fair Green, Carrick-on-Suir, Co Tipperary, Republic of Ireland
  ☎(00 353 51) 640591 (tel/fax)
  Senior Library Assistant O Corbett
- Cashel Library, Friar Street, Cashel, Co Tipperary, Republic of Ireland
  ☎(00 353 62) 63825
  Fax (00 353 62) 63948
  Assistant Librarian Ms M Ryan
- Clonmel Library, Emmet Street, Clonmel, Co Tipperary, Republic of Ireland
  ☎(00 353 52) 24545
  Fax (00 353 52) 27336
  e-mail: clonmlib@iol.ie
  Assistant Librarian Mrs M Boland
- Cloughjordan Library, Main Street, Cloughjordan, Co Tipperary, Republic of Ireland
  ☎(00 353 505) 42425
  Branch Librarian Mrs M Brady
- Killenaule Library, Bailey Street, Killenaule, Co Tipperary, Republic of Ireland
  ☎(00 353 52) 56028
  Branch Librarian Mrs R Lahart
- Nenagh Library, O'Rahilly Street, Nenagh, Co Tipperary, Republic of Ireland
  ☎(00 353 67) 34404
  Fax (00 353 67) 34405
  e-mail: nenalib@iol.ie
  Assistant Librarian Ms B Hannon
- Roscrea Library, Birr Road, Roscrea, Co Tipperary, Republic of Ireland
  ☎(00 353 505) 22032 (tel/fax)
  Assistant Librarian Ms A Beausang
- Templemore Library, Town Hall, Templemore, Co Tipperary, Republic of Ireland
  ☎(00 353 504) 32421
  Branch Librarian Ms M Looby
- Thurles Library, Castle Avenue, Thurles, Co Tipperary, Republic of Ireland
  ☎(00 353 504) 21555
  Assistant Librarian Vacant
- Tipperary Library, Dan Breen House, Tipperary, Co Tipperary, Republic of Ireland
  ☎(00 353 62) 51761 (tel/fax)
  Branch Librarian Ms N Butler, Ms G Hughes

- Fethard Library, Main Street, Fethard, Co Tipperary, Republic of Ireland
  ☎(00 353 52) 31728
  Branch Librarian Vacant

WATERFORD CITY LIBRARY

HQ Waterford Cty Library, 35 The Mall, Waterford, Republic of Ireland
☎(00 353 51) 860839
Fax (00 353 51) 849704
e-mail: citylibrary@waterfordcity.ie
City Librarian Ms J Cantwell
Assistant Librarian Ms K Collins
Acting Assistant Librarian Ms M Cunningham

Branch libraries

- Ballybricken Library, 31 Ballybricken, Waterford, Republic of Ireland
  ☎(00 353 51) 309975
  Fax (00 353 51) 850031
  e-mail: library@waterfordcity.ie
  Assistant Librarian Ms K Moran
- Lisduggan Library, Paddy Brown's Road, Waterford, Republic of Ireland
  ☎(00 353 51) 860845
  e-mail: lisdugganlibrary@waterfordcity.ie
- Ardkeen Library, Ardkeen Shopping Centre, Dunmore Road, Waterford, Republic of Ireland

WATERFORD COUNTY LIBRARY

HQ Waterford County Library, West Main Street, Lismore, Co Waterford, Republic of Ireland
☎(00 353 58) 54128
Fax (00 353 58) 54877
e-mail: libraryhq@waterfordcoco.ie
url: http://www.waterford.coco.ie
County Librarian D Brady (e-mail: dbrady@waterfordcoco.ie)
Systems Administrator E Byrne (e-mail: ebyrne@waterfordcoco.ie)

Central/largest library

Dungarvan Branch Library, Davitt's Quay, Dungarvan, Co Waterford, Republic of Ireland
☎(00 353 58) 41231
e-mail: dungarvanlibrary@waterfordcoco.ie
Librarian Ms M O'Brien (mgtobrien@waterfordcoco.ie)

Area libraries

- Tramore Branch Library, Market Square, Waterford, Republic of Ireland
  ☎(00 353 51) 381479
  e-mail: tramorelibrary@waterfordcoco.ie
  Librarian Ms K Murphy (e-mail: kmurphy@waterfordcoco.ie)

- Cappoquin Branch Library, Cappoquin, Waterford, Republic of Ireland
  e-mail: cappoquinlibrary@waterfordcoco.ie
  Branch Librarian Mrs M Tobin
- Dunmore Branch Library, Dunmore East, Waterford, Republic of Ireland
  ☎(00 353 51) 383211
  e-mail: dunmorelibrary@waterfordcoco.ie
  Branch Librarian Ms C O Mullain
- Lismore Branch Library, Main Street, Lismore, Waterford, Republic of Ireland
  ☎(00 353 58) 54128
  e-mail: lismorelibrary@waterfordcoco.ie
  Branch Librarian Ms N Tobin
- Portlaw Branch Library, The Square, Portlaw, Waterford, Republic of Ireland
  ☎(00 353 51) 387402
  e-mail: portlawlibrary@waterfordcoco.ie
  Branch Librarian Ms L Kinsella
- Tallow Branch Library, Convent Street, Waterford, Republic of Ireland
  e-mail: tallowlibrary@waterfordcoco.ie

WESTMEATH COUNTY LIBRARY

HQ Westmeath County Library HQ, Dublin Road, Mullingar, Co Westmeath, Republic of Ireland
☎(00 353 44) 40781/2/3 (enquiries & administration)
Fax (00 353 44) 41322
County Librarian Miss M Farrell BA HDE DLIS ALAI (e-mail: mfarrell@westmeathcoco.ie
Executive Librarian M Stuart DLIS (e-mail: mstuart@westmeathcoco.ie)

Branch libraries

- Mullingar Library, Church Avenue, Mullingar, Co Westmeath, Republic of Ireland
  ☎(00 353 44) 48278
  Assistant Librarian C A Cox DLIS (e-mail: tcox@westmeathcoco.ie)
- Athlone Library, Father Matthew Hall, Athlone, Co Westmeath, Republic of Ireland
  ☎(00 353 902) 92166/94533
  Fax (00 353 902) 94900
  Executive Librarian G O'Brien DLIS FLAI (e-mail: gobrien@westmeathcoco.ie)
- Castlepollard Library, Town Hall, Castlepollard, Co Westmeath, Republic of Ireland
  ☎(00 353 44) 61646
  Branch Librarian Ms R Moran
- Kilbeggan Library, Tullamore Road, Co Westmeath, Republic of Ireland
  ☎(00 353 506) 32001
  Branch Librarian Mrs E Gorman (e-mail: lgorman@westmeathcoco.ie)
- Killucan Library, St Joseph's Hall, Killucan, Co Westmeath, Republic of Ireland
  ☎(00 353 44) 74260
  Branch Librarian Ms G Corroon
- Moate Library, The Courthouse, Main Street, Moate, Co Westmeath, Republic of Ireland
  ☎(00 353 902) 81888 (tel/fax)
  Branch Librarian Ms N Brennan-Gavin (e-mail: ngavin@westmeathcoco.ie)

WEXFORD COUNTY LIBRARY

HQ Library Management Services, The Kent Building, Ardcavan, Co Wexford, Republic of Ireland
☎(00 353 53) 24922/24928
Fax (00 353 53) 21097
e-mail: libraryhq@wexfordcoco.ie
url: http://www.wexford.ie
County Librarian Ms F Hanrahan BA DLIS MLIS MCLIP ALAI

Central/largest library

Wexford Town Library, Selskar House, McCauley's Carpark, off Redmond Square, Co Wexford, Republic of Ireland
☎(00 353 53) 21637
Fax (00 353 53) 21639
e-mail: wexfordlib@eircom.net
Librarian Ms H Percival BA DLIS

Area libraries

- New Ross Branch Library, Barrack Lane, New Ross, Co Wexford, Republic of Ireland
  ☎(00 353 51) 421877
  e-mail: newrosslib@eircom.net
  Senior Library Assistant Ms J Lambert
- Enniscorthy Branch Library, Lymington Road, Enniscorthy, Co Wexford, Republic of Ireland
  ☎(00 353 54) 36055
  e-mail: enniscorthylib@eircom.net
  Librarian Ms C Kelly BA DLIS

WICKLOW COUNTY LIBRARY

HQ Wicklow County Library, Library HQ, Boghall Road, Bray, Co Wicklow, Republic of Ireland
☎(00 353 1) 286 6566 (enquiries & administration)
Fax (00 353 1) 286 5811
e-mail: wcclhq@eircom.ie
County Librarian B Martin BA DLIS
Executive Librarians Ms C Moore DLIS (Administration), Ms N Ringwood BA DLIS (Schools and Outreach)
Assistant Librarians Ms M O'Driscoll BSocSc DLIS (IT), Ms M Ryan (Local Studies)

Largest library

Bray Public Library, Eglinton Road, Bray, Co Wicklow, Republic of Ireland
☎(00 353 1) 286 2600
Assistant Librarian T French BA DLIS

Area libraries

- Greystones Public Library, Church Road, Greystones, Co Wicklow, Republic of Ireland
  ☎(00 353 1) 287 3548
  Assistant Librarian Ms G Misstear BA MA
- Ballyweltrim Public Library, Boghall Road, Bray, Co Wicklow, Republic of Ireland
  ☎(00 353 1) 272 3205
  Assistant Librarian Ms M Ryan BA DipLib

Children's, Youth and Schools Library Services in the United Kingdom, the Channel Islands and the Isle of Man

England
Scotland
Wales
Crown Dependencies

For Northern Ireland please see entries under Northern Ireland Education and Library Boards in the Public Libraries section.

BARKING AND DAGENHAM

Authority London Borough of Barking and Dagenham
Central Library, Barking, Essex IG11 7NB
☎020 8227 3611 (School Library Service 020 8227 3614)
Fax 020 8227 3699
Principal Librarian, Learning and Development Ms S Leighton MA MCLIP (e-mail: sleighton@barking-dagenham.gov.uk)

BARNET

Authority London Borough of Barnet
Cultural Services, The Old Town Hall, 1 Friern Barnet Lane, London N11 3DL
☎020 8359 3164
Principal Librarian: Children and Youth Ms H Richens DipILM MCLIP (020 8359 2867)

School Library Resources Service, Grahame Park Library, The Concourse, Grahame Park, London NW9 5XL
☎020 8200 8948
Fax 020 8201 3018
e-mail: sls@barnet.gov.uk
Manager N Angrave BA MCLIP

BARNSLEY

Authority Barnsley Metropolitan Borough Council
Central Library, Shambles Street, Barnsley, South Yorkshire S70 2JF
☎(01226) 773952/773920
Fax (01226) 773955
e-mail: librarian@barnsley.ac.uk
url: http://bmbc-online/review/services/libraries/index.asp
Children's Services Officer Mrs J E Matthews BLib(Hons) MCLIP (e-mail: janematthews@barnsley.gov.uk)

BATH AND NORTH EAST SOMERSET

Authority Bath and North East Somerset Council
Central Library, The Podium, Northgate Street, Bath BA1 5AN
☎(01225) 787402
Fax (01225) 787426
Children's Librarians Mrs L S Hamer MCLIP, Mrs J E Ball BLib MCLIP

BEDFORDSHIRE

Authority Bedfordshire County Council
Bedfordshire County Council, Kempston Library, Halsey Road, Kempston, Beds MK42 8AU

☎(01234) 853092
Fax (01234) 841476
Principal Librarian, Youth Services Ms K O'Neil BA(Hons) MCLIP (e-mail: oneilk@bedfordshire.gov.uk)

Schools Library Service, Riverside Building, County Hall, Cauldwell Street, Bedford MK42 9AP
☎(01234) 228755
Fax (01234) 228666
Senior Librarian, Schools Library Service Ms S Arkle BA MCLIP (e-mail: arkles@bedfordshire.gov.uk)

Leighton Buzzard Library, Lake Street, Leighton Buzzard, Beds LU7 8RX
☎(01525) 371788
Fax (01525) 851368
Senior Librarian, Youth Services Ms V Fox MCLIP (e-mail: foxv@bedfordshire.gov.uk)

BEXLEY

Authority Bexley Council
Directorate of Education and Leisure, Thamesmead Centre, Yarnton Way, Erith, Kent DA18 4DR
☎020 8320 4138
Fax 020 8320 4050
e-mail: libraries.els@bexley.gov.uk
Youth Services Librarians Mrs F Mason BA MCLIP, Mrs R White BA MA MCLIP (job-share)

BIRMINGHAM

Authority Birmingham Metropolitan District Council
Central Library, Chamberlain Square, Birmingham B3 3HQ
☎0121 303 2418
Fax 0121 233 9702
Head of Children's, Youth and Education Services Mrs P Heap BA MCLIP (e-mail: patsy.heap@birmingham.gov.uk)

Schools Library Service, Ellen Street, Hockley, Birmingham B18 6QZ
☎0121 464 1900/0757
Fax 0121 464 1852
e-mail: sls@birmingham.gov.uk
Managers, Schools Library Service Mrs S Rogers BA MCLIP, Mrs S Needham MCLIP

BLACKBURN WITH DARWEN

Authority Blackburn with Darwen Borough Council
Children's and Schools' Services, Blackburn Central Library, Town Hall Street, Blackburn BB2 1AG
☎(01254) 587937

Fax (01254) 679565
Children's and Schools' Librarian Ms J Gabbatt BLib MCLIP (e-mail: jean.gabbatt@blackburn.gov.uk)

BLACKPOOL

Authority Blackpool Borough Council
Lifelong Learning and Cultural Services, Progress House, Clifton Road, Blackpool, Lancs FY4 4US
☎(01253) 478111 (enquiries), (01253) 478107 (administration)
Fax (01253) 478071
e-mail: cultural-services@blackpool.gov.uk
Senior Librarian, Youth and Community Services Mrs V Battison MCLIP (01253 478112)
Senior Librarian, Schools' Library Services Mrs L Cowap-French (01253 476627)

BOLTON

Authority Bolton Metropolitan Borough Council
Children's and Schools' Library Service, Castle Hill Centre, Castleton Street, Bolton BL2 2JW
☎(01204) 525372
Fax (01204) 385381
e-mail: childrens.library.services@bolton.gov.uk
url: http://www.library.bolton.gov.uk/library
Special Services Librarian Ms M Keane BA(Hons) DipLib MCLIP

BOURNEMOUTH

Authority Bournemouth Borough Council
Children and Learning, The Bournemouth Library, 22 The Triangle, Bournemouth, Dorset BH2 5RQ
☎(01202) 454827
Fax (01202) 454830
Libraries Officer, Children and Learning Ms H Young BA DipIM MCLIP (e-mail: heather.young@bournemouthlibraries.org.uk)
(Bournemouth has joint provision with Dorset for school library services: see Dorset)

BRACKNELL FOREST

Authority Bracknell Forest Borough Council
Bracknell Library, Town Square, Market Street, Bracknell, Berks RG12 1BH
☎(01344) 352400
Fax (01344) 352420
url: http://www.bracknell-forest.gov.uk/libraries
Library and Information Manager Ms K Chambers BA MCLIP

Education Library Resource Centre (Berkshire authorities), 2-4 Darwin Close, Reading, Berks RG2 0TB
☎0118 901 5989

Fax 0118 901 5988
Head of Centre J Saunders BA MCLIP (0118 901 5990)

BRADFORD

Authority City of Bradford Metropolitan Council
Central Library, Princes Way, Bradford BD1 1NN
☎(01274) 753643
Fax (01274) 395108
Librarian, Children's Services and Xchange Ms C Binns MCLIP (e-mail: chris.binns@bradford.gov.uk)

Education Library Service, 36 Spencer Road, Bradford BD7 2EU
☎(01274) 414600
Fax (01274) 414604
Principal Education Librarian R Wilkes BEd FCLIP (e-mail: bob.wilkes@bradford.gov.uk)

BRENT

Authority London Borough of Brent
Library Service, 4th Floor, Chesterfield House, 9 Park Lane, Wembley, Middlesex HA9 7RW
☎020 8937 3143
Fax 020 8937 3008
Development and Project Officer Ms T Dabiri (e-mail: tola.dabiri@brent.gov.uk)

BRIGHTON AND HOVE

Authority Brighton and Hove City Council
Brighton Library, Vantage Point, New England Street, Brighton, East Sussex BN1 2GW
☎(01273) 290800 (enquiries)
Fax (01273) 296951
Community and Development Manager A Issler BA MCLIP (01273 296948)
Professional and Collections Manager N Imi BA DipLib MCLIP (01273 296953)
(Brighton and Hove has joint provision with East Sussex for schools library services: see East Sussex)

BRISTOL

Authority Bristol City Council
Cheltenham Road Library, Cheltenham Road, Bristol BS6 5QX
☎0117 903 8565 (tel/fax)
Children's and Young People's Adviser Mrs J Randall MCLIP (e-mail: janet_randall@bristol-city.gov.uk)

Bristol School Library Service, Nelson Parade, Bedminster, Bristol BS3 4HY
☎0117 966 2471
Fax 0117 953 2751
Service Manager Mrs B Newman

BROMLEY

Authority London Borough of Bromley
Central Library, High Street, Bromley, Kent BR1 1EX
☎020 8460 9955 ext 7185
Fax 020 8313 9975
Stock and Service Manager (Children and Young People) Vacant

BUCKINGHAMSHIRE

Authority Buckinghamshire County Council
County Library Service, Walton Street, Aylesbury, Bucks HP20 1UU
☎(01296) 383161
Fax (01296) 382259
Chief Youth Services Librarian Ms S A Hyland BA MCLIP DPSE(EdTech) (01296 382273; e-mail: shyland@buckscc.gov.uk)

Library and Information Service for Schools (LISS)
Details as above
e-mail: liss@buckscc.gov.uk

BURY

Authority Bury Metropolitan Borough Council
Library Service, Bury Central Library, Manchester Road, Bury, Lancashire BL9 0DG
☎0161 253 5873
Fax 0161 253 5857
e-mail: information@bury.gov.uk
url: http://www.bury.gov.uk/culture.htm
Principal Librarian Mrs D Sorrigan BA MCLIP (0161 253 6077)

Schools Library Service, New Kershaw Centre, Deal Street, Bury, Lancashire BL9 7PZ
☎0161 253 6440
Schools Librarian Ms J E Hamer MCLIP

Learning Support Services, Unsworth Library, Sunnybank Road, Bury, Lancashire BL9 8EB
☎0161 253 7561
Fax 0161 253 7564
Learning Support Librarian Mrs C Almond (e-mail: c.almond@bury.gov.uk)

CALDERDALE

Authority Calderdale Metropolitan Borough
Children's and Schools' Library Service, Central Library, Northgate, Halifax HX1 1UN
☎(01422) 392618
Fax (01422) 392615
Principal Librarian, Children's Services Mrs H Cerroti BA MCLIP (e-mail: helen.cerroti@calderdale.gov.uk)

CAMBRIDGESHIRE

Authority Cambridgeshire County Council
Schools Library Service, Units 1-3, Springwater Business Park, Station Road, Whittlesey, Peterborough, Cambs PE7 2EU
☎(01733) 758010
Fax (01733) 758015
Head of Service Mrs M Smith MCLIP (e-mail: margaret.smith@cambridgeshire.gov.uk)

CAMDEN

Authority London Borough of Camden
Children's and Youth Service, Swiss Cottage Library, 88 Avenue Road, London NW3 3HA
☎020 7974 5438
Fax 020 7974 6532
Principal Librarian, Reader Development Ms F Page BA MCLIP (e-mail: felicity.page@camden.gov.uk)

Schools Library Service, Unit 5, James Cameron House, 12 Castlehaven Road, London NW1 8QW
☎020 7482 0891
Fax 020 7424 0777
e-mail: sls@camden.gov.uk
Schools Library Service Manager Ms J Andrew BA MCLIP (e-mail: janet.andrew@camden.gov.uk)

Reader Development Services, Holborn Library, 32-38 Theobalds Road, London WC1X 8PA
☎020 7974 6355
Fax 020 7974 6356
Principal Librarian, Reader Development Ms F Page BA MCLIP (e-mail: felicity.page@camden.gov.uk)

CHESHIRE

Authority Cheshire County Council
Libraries and Culture, County Hall, Chester CH1 1SF
☎(01244) 606023
Fax (01244) 602767
Resources and Development Manager E H Skinner DipEdTech MCLIP

Education Library Service, Browning Way, Woodford Park Industrial Estate, Winsford, Cheshire CW7 2JN
☎(01606) 557126
Fax (01606) 861412
Young People's Services Officer Ms S Maddocks BA MCLIP
Primary School Specialist Ms C Shaw
Secondary School Specialist Ms L Simons

Young People's Specialists Ms S Wilkinson/Ms C Maplesden (Ellesmere Port Library; 0151 357 4686), Ms C Ashbee (Winsford Library; 01606 552065), Ms J Roberts (Wilmslow Library; 01625 528977)

CORNWALL

Authority Cornwall County Council
Education Library Services, Unit 17, Threemilestone, Truro, Cornwall TR4 9LD
☎(01872) 324310
Fax (01872) 323819
e-mail: els@library.cornwall.gov.uk
Acting Head of Young Persons' Service Mrs V Morley BEd MA

COVENTRY

Authority Coventry City Council
School Library Service, Central Library, Smithford Way, Coventry CV1 1FY
☎024 7683 2338
Fax 024 7683 2338
e-mail: sls@coventry.gov.uk
Senior Schools Librarian Mrs J E Court BA(Hons) DipLib

CROYDON

Authority London Borough of Croydon
Central Library, Katharine Street, Croydon CR9 1ET
☎020 8760 5400 ext 1051
Fax 020 8253 1004
url: http://www.croydon.gov.uk
Children's Services Manager Ms M Fraser MA MCLIP, Ms G McElwee BA(Hons) DipLib MCLIP (e-mail: margaret_fraser@croydon.gov.uk; grace_mcelwee@croydon.gov.uk) (job-share)

Croydon Schools Library Service, Croydon QDI, Davidson Professional Centre, Davidson Road, Croydon CR0 6DD
☎020 8655 1299
Fax 020 8656 1544
Service Manager Mrs S Smith BA(Hons) PGDipLib (e-mail: sharon_smith@croydon.gov.uk)

CUMBRIA

Authority Cumbria County Council
Library Services for Schools HQ, Botchergate, Carlisle, Cumbria CA1 1RZ
☎(01228) 607277
Fax (01228) 607275
School Library Services Manager Mrs A Singleton MCLIP (e-mail: ann.singleton@cumbriacc.gov.uk)

Penrith Library, St Andrew's Churchyard, Penrith, Cumbria CA11 7YA
☎(01768) 242100
Fax (01768) 242101
e-mail: penrith.library@cumbriacc.gov.uk
Coordinator of Public Library Services for Young People in Cumbria Ms E Bowe

DARLINGTON

Authority Darlington Borough Council
Education Department, Darlington Library and Art Gallery, Crown Street, Darlington DL1 1ND
☎(01325) 462034
Fax (01325) 381556
e-mail: crown.street.library@darlington.gov.uk
Service Development Librarian Ms K Dickinson BA(Hons)
(Schools Library Service in partnership with Durham: see Durham)

DERBY

Authority Derby City Council
Department of Development and Cultural Services, Room 526, Celtic House, Friary Street, Derby DE1 1QX
☎(01332) 716604
Fax (01332) 715549
Senior Librarian, Children and Education Ms F Renwick MA MCLIP (e-mail: fran.renwick@derby.gov.uk)
(Derby has joint provision with Derbyshire for schools library services: see Derbyshire)

DERBYSHIRE

Authority Derbyshire County Council
County Library HQ, County Hall, Matlock, Derbyshire DE4 3AG
☎(01629) 580000 ext 6587
Fax (01629) 585363
Service Manager (Young People and Policy Development) Ms A Everall (e-mail: annie.everall@derbyshire.gov.uk)

Kedleston Road Centre, 184 Kedleston Road, Derby
☎(01332) 371921
School Library Service Manager Ms D Pritchard (01332 371921; fax 01332 371381)

DEVON

Authority Devon County Council
North Devon Library and Record Office, Tuly Street, Barnstaple, Devon EX31 1EL
☎(01271) 388622
Fax (01271) 388619
Group Librarian, North & West Devon (i/c Children's Services) I Tansley MCLIP (e-mail: itansley@devon.gov.uk)

Devon Library Services, Barley House, Isleworth Road, Exeter EX4 1RQ
☎(01392) 384304
Fax (01392) 384316
url: http://www.devon.gov.uk/eal/dsls
Head of Schools Library Service Ms L Medlock BEd MCLIP (e-mail: lmedlock@devon.gov.uk)

DONCASTER

Authority Doncaster Metropolitan District Council
Education and Young People's Service, Top Road, Barnby Dun, Doncaster, South Yorkshire DN3 1DB
☎(01302) 881787
Fax (01302) 881787
Manager T W Finch MCLIP (e-mail: trevor.finch@doncaster.gov.uk)

DORSET

Authority Dorset County Council
County Library HQ, Colliton Park, Dorchester, Dorset DT1 1XJ
☎(01305) 224455 (enquiries), (01305) 224450 (administration)
Fax (01305) 224344
Service Development Manager (Children) Miss S Holmes BA(Hons) MA MCLIP (e-mail: s.e.holmes@dorset-cc.gov.uk)
Senior Manager, Children's and Stock Ms V Chapman MCLIP

Education Resources Centre, College Road, Blandford Camp, Blandford, Dorset DT11 8BG
☎(01258) 451151
Fax (01258) 480076
School Library Service Manager Ms A Burgess BA DipLib MCLIP MLib (e-mail: a.f.burgess@dorset-cc.gov.uk)
(Dorset has joint provision with Bournemouth and Poole for schools library services)

DUDLEY

Authority Dudley Metropolitan Borough Council
Schools Library and Information Service, Unit 29, Wallowes Industrial Estate, Fens Pool Avenue, Brierley Hill DY5 1QA
☎(01384) 812850
Fax (01384) 812851
Principal Librarian Mrs D M Ward MCLIP
(Temporary premises following fire damage)

DURHAM

Authority Durham County Council
Cultural Services Department, County Hall, Durham DH1 5TY
☎0191 383 4459

Fax 0191 383 3858
url: http://www.durham.gov.uk/dlr
Youth Services Manager P Burns MCLIP (e-mail: peter.burns@durham.gov.uk)
(Includes responsibility for schools library services)

EALING

Authority London Borough of Ealing
Central Library, Ealing Broadway Centre, Ealing, London W5 5JY
☎020 8567 3670
Fax 020 8840 2351
url: http://www.ealing.gov.uk
Children's Librarian Ms C Downie BA (e-mail: downiec@ealing.gov.uk)

West Ealing Library, Melbourne Avenue, London W13 9BA
☎020 8758 8837
Fax 020 8567 1736
Schools Librarian Mrs P A Jefferies MCLIP DMS (e-mail: pjefferies@ealing.gov.uk)

EAST RIDING OF YORKSHIRE

Authority East Riding of Yorkshire Council
Library and Information Services, Council Offices, Main Road, Skirlaugh, East Riding of Yorkshire HU11 5HN
☎(01482) 392726 (office)
Fax (01482) 392710
Schools Library Service Manager A Kurvits BSc MPhil DipLib (01482 392725; e-mail: avo.kurvits@eastriding.gov.uk)

EAST SUSSEX

Authority East Sussex County Council
Libraries, Information and Arts, 44 St Anne's Crescent, Lewes, East Sussex BN7 1SQ
☎(01273) 481329
Fax (01273) 481716
Head of Lifelong Learning Mrs V Warren BA MCLIP (e-mail: viv.warren@eastsussexcc.gov.uk)

Schools Library Service, Hammonds Drive, Lottbridge Drove, Hampden Park, Eastbourne, East Sussex BN23 6PW
☎(01323) 416324
Fax (01323) 412806
Manager, Schools Library Service Ms R Drever MA(Hons) DipLib MCLIP (e-mail: rhona.drever@eastsussexcc.gov.uk)

ENFIELD

Authority London Borough of Enfield
PO Box 58, Civic Centre, Silver Street, Enfield EN1 3XJ

☎020 8379 3748
Fax 020 8379 3753
Principal Librarian, Children and Education Ms L Love BA(Hons) DipLib MCLIP (e-mail: lucy.love@enfield.gov.uk)

Library Resources Unit, Southgate Town Hall, Green Lanes, London N13 4XD
☎020 8379 2708
Fax 020 8379 2761
url: http://www.enfield.gov.uk
Schools Library Service Librarian Ms S Smith BSc MA MCLIP

ESSEX

Authority Essex County Council
Schools Library Service, Unit 3, Atholl Road, Dukes Park Industrial Estate, Chelmsford, Essex CM2 6TB
☎(01245) 542600
Fac (01245) 542601
e-mail: sls@essexcc.gov.uk
url: http://www.essexcc.gov.uk/libraries/
Children's and Learners Services Manager Mrs M Tarrant (e-mail: moira.tarrant@essexcc.gov.uk)
School Library Service Manager Ms C Hughes

GATESHEAD

Authority Gateshead Metropolitan Borough Council
Youth Services Team, Dryden PDC, Evistones Road, Low Fell, Gateshead NE9 5UR
☎0191 487 1895
Fax 0191 487 1895
Youth Services Manager Mrs B Wood BA MCLIP

GLOUCESTERSHIRE

Authority Gloucestershire County Council
County Library, Quayside House, Shire Hall, Gloucester GL1 2HY
☎(01452) 425020
Fax (01452) 425042
e-mail: clams@gloscc.gov.uk
Principal Librarian, Learning and Literacy Mrs H Briggs BA DMS MIMgt MCLIP (01452 425030; e-mail: hbriggs@gloscc.gov.uk)
Senior Librarian, Children and Learning Mrs R Armstrong BA MCLIP (01452 425033; e-mail: rarmstrg@gloscc.gov.uk), Mrs L Squires BLib MCLIP (01452 425033; e-mail: lsquires@gloscc.gov.uk) (job share)

School Library Service, Hucclecote Centre, Churchdown Lane, Gloucester GL3 3QL
☎(01452) 427240
Fax (01452) 427243
Senior Librarian Ms S Laurence BA DipLib MCLIP (e-mail: slaurence@gloscc.gov.uk)

GREENWICH

Authority London Borough of Greenwich
Children's and Young People's Service, Plumstead Library, Plumstead High Street, London SE18 1JL
☎020 8317 4466
Fax 020 8317 4868
Librarian with responsibility for library services to young people Ms S Saunders DMS BA(Hons) MCLIP (e-mail: sally.saunders@greenwich.gov.uk)
Education Librarian Ms K Croll BA(Hons) MSc MCLIP

Schools Library Service, West Greenwich Library, Greenwich High Road, Greenwich, London SE10 8NN
☎020 8853 1691
Fax 020 8858 3512

HACKNEY

Authority London Borough of Hackney
Lifelong Learning, Homerton Library, Homerton High Street, London E9 6AS
☎020 8356 1690
Fax 020 8356 1692
Lifelong Learning Manager Vacant
Head of Library Service Ms J Middleton (020 8356 2560)
Community Services Manager Vacant (020 8356 1696)

HALTON

Authority Halton Borough Council
Halton Lea Library, Halton Lea, Runcorn, Cheshire WA7 2PF
☎(01928) 715351
Fax (01928) 790221
Young Persons Officer Mrs A Watt BA(Hons) MCLIP (e-mail: allyson.watt@halton-borough.gov.uk)
(Schools library services provided by Education Library Service, Cheshire: see Cheshire)

HAMMERSMITH AND FULHAM

Authority London Borough of Hammersmith and Fulham
Children's Services, Hammersmith Library, Shepherds Bush Road, Hammersmith, London W6 7AT
☎020 8753 3811
Fax 020 8753 3815
Library Development Manager Ms A Stirrup BA MCLIP (e-mail: amandastirrup@hotmail.com)

Schools Library Service, c/o Hammersmith Library, Shepherds Bush Road, Hammersmith, Fulham, London W6 7AT

☎020 8753 3886
Fax 020 7381 4641
e-mail: schoolslibrary@hotmail.com

HAMPSHIRE

Authority Hampshire County Council
County Library, 81 North Walls, Winchester, Hants SO23 8BY
☎(01962) 846084
Fax (01962) 856615
url: http://www.hants.gov.uk/library/index.html
Acting Assistant County Librarian, Children's and Schools E A Marley BA MCLIP (e-mail: anne.marley@hants.gov.uk)

HARINGEY

Authority London Borough of Haringey
Hornsey Library, Haringey Park, Hornsey, London N8 9JA
☎020 8489 1427
Fax 020 8374 6942
Principal Librarian: Children's Services Ms M Stephanou
Senior Librarian: Children's Services Ms V Platt

Wood Green Central Library, High Road, Wood Green, London N22 6XD
☎020 8489 2700
Fax 020 8489 2722
Children's Librarian Ms C Garnsworthy

Marcus Garvey Library, Tottenham Green Centre, 1 Philip Lane, Tottenham, London N15 4JA
☎020 8489 5360
Fax 020 8489 5338
Senior Librarian: Children's Services Ms E Venner

Professional Development Centre, Downhills Park Road, London N17 6AR
☎020 8489 5043
Fax 020 8489 5004
School Services Librarian Ms C Collingborn

HARROW

Authority London Borough of Harrow
Young People's and School Library Services, Civic Centre Library, PO Box 4, Civic Centre, Harrow, Middlesex HA1 2UU
☎020 8424 1052
Fax 020 8424 1971
Principal Librarian, Young People's Services Mrs S Bussey BA MCLIP (e-mail: sue.bussey@harrow.gov.uk)

HARTLEPOOL

Authority Hartlepool Borough Council
Central Library, 124 York Road, Hartlepool TS26 9DE
☎(01429) 272905
Fax (01429) 275685
e-mail: childrens.services@hartlepool.gov.uk
Children's Services Officer Ms D Sparrowhawk BA(Hons) DipLib
Children's Librarian Ms P Richardson BA DipLib MCLIP
Schools Resources Service: see Redcar & Cleveland (cooperative service with Middlesbrough, Redcar & Cleveland and Stockton-on-Tees)

HAVERING

Authority London Borough of Havering
Central Library, St Edwards Way, Romford, Essex RM1 3AR
☎(01708) 432397
Fax (01708) 432391
Acting Principal Librarian, School Library Service Mrs K Doyle MCLIP

HEREFORDSHIRE

Authority Herefordshire Council
Young People's Library Service, Shirehall, Hereford HR1 2HY
☎(01432) 260661
e-mail: sls@herefordshire.gov.uk
Young People's Library Services Manager Mrs J Radburn BA PGCE DipLib MCLIP, Ms S Chedgzoy BA MCLIP DipLib (job-share)
Schools Library Service Librarian Mrs R Fleming BA MCLIP

HERTFORDSHIRE

Authority Hertfordshire County Council
Community Information Directorate: Libraries, New Barnfield, Travellers Lane, Hatfield, Herts AL10 8XG
☎(01438) 737333
Fax (01707) 281589
Young People's and Community Services Manager Ms C Hall BA MCLIP (01438 737333; e-mail: christine.hall@hertscc.gov.uk)
Head of Schools Library Service Ms S Jones MA MCLIP (01707 281630; fax 01707 281611; e-mail: sue.jones@herts-sls.org.uk)

HILLINGDON

Authority London Borough of Hillingdon
Central Library, 14-15 High Street, Uxbridge, Middlesex UB8 1HD
☎See below
Fax (01895) 811164/239794 (Hillingdon Libraries)
e-mail: clibrary@hillingdon.gov.uk
url: http://www.hillingdon.gov.uk

Children and Youth Services Manager Ms L McMillan MCLIP (01895 250703; e-mail: lmcmillan@hillingdon.gov.uk)
Children and Schools Manager Ms E Smyth MCLIP (01895 250715; e-mail: esmyth@hillingdon.gov.uk)

HOUNSLOW

Authority London Borough of Hounslow
Young People's Library Service, Centrespace, 24 Treaty Centre, High Street, Hounslow, Middlesex TW3 1ES
☎0845 456 2921
Fax 0845 456 2928
url: http://www.cip.com
Principal Librarian, Library Management Group Ms F Stanbury MCLIP (e-mail: frances-stanbury@cip.org.uk)

ISLE OF WIGHT

Authority Isle of Wight Council
Young People's Library Service, Thompson House, Sandy Lane, Newport, Isle of Wight PO30 3NA
☎(01983) 525731/529212
Fax (01983) 529463
e-mail: ypls@iow.gov.uk
Young People's Services Librarian R Jones BA MCLIP CertEd

ISLINGTON

Authority London Borough of Islington
Central Library, 2 Fieldway Crescent, London N5 1PF
☎020 7527 6997
Manager, Services to Children and Young People G A James BA(Hons) DipLib MCLIP (e-mail: geoff.james@islington.gov.uk)

Education Library Service, Block D, Barnsbury Complex, Barnsbury Park, London N1 1QG
☎020 7457 5827
Fax 020 7457 5564
e-mail: lb@iels.demon.co.uk
Head of Education Library Service Ms P Dix

KENSINGTON AND CHELSEA

Authority Royal Borough of Kensington and Chelsea
Kensington Central Library, Phillimore Walk, London W8 7RX
☎020 7361 3014
Fax 020 7361 2976
Service Development Manager - Young People and Family Learning Ms A T Cahill BSc DipLib MCLIP (e-mail: aileen.cahill@rbkc.gov.uk)

Schools Library Service, Isaac Newton Centre for Professional Development, 108A Lancaster Road, London W11 1QS
☎020 7598 4896
Fax 020 7243 1570
Schools' Librarian Ms S Riley MLS MCLIP (e-mail: sue.riley@rbkc.gov.uk)

KENT

Authority Kent County Council
Arts and Libraries, Gibson Drive, Kings Hill, West Malling, Kent ME19 4AL
☎(01622) 605213
Fax (01622) 605221
url: www.kent.gov.uk/e&l/artslib
Principal Young People's Librarian and Learning Resources Manager Mrs S V Sperling BA MA MCLIP, Ms L Prestage BA MA MCLIP DipMgt (01622 605211; e-mail: sharon.sperling@kent.gov.uk; lindsay.prestage@kent.gov.uk) (job-share)

KINGSTON UPON HULL

Authority Kingston upon Hull City Council
Hull Central Library, Albion Street, Kingston upon Hull HU1 3TF
☎(01482) 616846
Fax (01482) 616827
url: http://www.hullcc.gov.uk
Specialist Librarian – Children Ms C Bennett BA PGDipLib (e-mail: claire.bennett@hull.gov.uk)

Schools Library Service, James Reckitt Library, Holderness Road, Kingston upon Hull HU9 1EA
☎(01482) 225587
Fax (01482) 224509
Schools Librarian M Hardwick BA MCLIP

KINGSTON UPON THAMES

Authority Royal Borough of Kingston upon Thames
Kingston Library, Fairfield Road, Kingston, Surrey KT1 2PS
☎020 8408 9100
Fax 020 8547 6426
Senior Librarian Children's Services M Treacy (e-mail: michael.treacy@rbk.kingston.gov.uk)

Schools Library Service, Fairfield Centre, Fairfield East, Kingston upon Thames, Surrey KT1 2PT
☎020 8408 9100
Schools Library Service Manager M Treacy (e-mail: michael.treacy@rbk.kingston.gov.uk)

KIRKLEES

Authority Kirklees Metropolitan Council
Cultural Services HQ, Red Doles Lane, Huddersfield HD2 1YF
☎(01484) 226325 (direct), (01484) 226300
Fax (01484) 226342
Assistant Head of Cultural Services (Libraries and Information) R Warburton BA MCLIP (e-mail: rob.warburton@kirkleesmc.gov.uk)

KNOWSLEY

Authority Knowsley Metropolitan Borough Council
Page Moss Library, Stockbridge Lane, Huyton, Knowsley, Merseyside L36 3SA
☎0151 482 1304
Fax 0151 482 1307
Learning Resource Unit Manager Ms P Jones BA MCLIP (e-mail: pam.jones.dlcs@knowsley.gov.uk)

Kirkby Library, Newtown Gardens, Kirkby, Knowsley, Merseyside L32 8RR
☎0151 443 4285
Fax 0151 443 4283
School Library Service Manager G Williams BA (e-mail: gerry.williams.dlcs@knowsley.gov.uk)

LAMBETH

Authority London Borough of Lambeth
Lambeth Libraries, Arts and Archives, 3rd Floor, International House, Canterbury Crescent, London SW9 7QE
☎020 7926 0750
Fax 020 7926 0751
url: http://www.lambeth.gov.uk
Development Manager, Social Inclusion Ms S Doyle (020 7926 6060, fax 020 7926 0751; e-mail: sdoyle@lambeth.gov.uk)

LANCASHIRE

Authority Lancashire County Council
School Library Service, 218-222 North Road, Preston, Lancs PR1 1SY
☎(01772) 264041
Fax (01772) 263391
e-mail: preston.sls@lcl.lancscc.gov.uk
County Library Manager D G Lightfoot MA DMS MCLIP
Manager, Young People's Services Mrs J Wolstenholme DMS MCLIP (01772 264040)

LEEDS

Authority Leeds City Council
Library and Information Services HQ, 32 York Road, Leeds LS9 8TD
☎0113 214 3346

Fax 0113 214 3339
url: http://www.leeds.gov.uk
Young People's Services Manager Mrs S Kift BA MCLIP (e-mail: sarah.kift@leeds.gov.uk)

School Library Service, Foxcroft Close, Leeds LS6 3NT
☎0113 214 4531
Fax 0113 214 4532
e-mail: schoollibrariesleeds@talk21.com
School Library Service Manager Mrs M Drinkwater MA MCLIP

LEICESTER

Authority Leicester City Council
Libraries and Information Services, Fosse Library, Mantle Road, Leicester LE4 5HG
☎0116 225 4997
Fax 0116 225 4999
Community Library Manager (Children and Young People Services) P Gobey (0116 299 5460)
(Leicester has joint provision for schools library services with Leicestershire: see Leicestershire)

LEICESTERSHIRE

Authority Leicestershire County Council
Leicestershire Libraries and Information Service, County Hall, Glenfield, Leicester LE3 8SS
Contact: Mrs G Willars (see below)

Library Services for Education, Rothley Crossroads, 929-931 Loughborough Road, Rothley, Leicester LE7 7NH
☎0116 267 8000
Fax 0116 267 8039
Head of Library Services for Education Mrs G Willars MA MCLIP (e-mail: gwillars@leics.gov.uk)

LEWISHAM

Authority London Borough of Lewisham
Lewisham Education and Culture Library Service, 3rd Floor, Laurence House, 1 Catford Road, Catford, London SE6 4RU
☎020 8695 6000 ext 8027
Fax 020 8314 3039
Head of Libraries and Information Service Ms J Newton

Lewisham Libraries and Information Service, 1st Floor, Town Hall Chambers, Rushey Green, Catford, London SE6 4RU
☎020 8314 7131
Fax 020 8314 3229
Advisory Librarian (Children and Young People) Vacant

Lewisham Libraries and Information Service, 1st Floor, Town Hall Chambers, Rushey Green, Catford, London SE6 4RU
☎020 8314 6129
Fax 020 8314 3229
Early Years Librarian Ms E Day (e-mail: liz.day@lewisham.gov.uk)

LINCOLNSHIRE

Authority Lincolnshire County Council
Education and Cultural Services Directorate, Brayford House, Lucy Tower Street, Lincoln LN1 1XN
☎(01522) 552804
Fax (01522) 552858
Special Services Manager Ms V Wellington BA(Hons) DipLib DipIM MCLIP MCMI (e-mail: wellingv@lincolnshire.gov.uk)

LIVERPOOL

Authority Liverpool City Council
Central Library, William Brown Street, Liverpool L3 8EW
☎0151 233 5841
Fax 0151 233 5801
e-mail: css@liverpool.gov.uk
url: http://www.liverpool.gov.uk
Librarian, Children's Support Services Ms I Mandelkow BA MCLIP, Ms P Lee MCLIP

LONDON, City of

Authority Corporation of London
Barbican Library, Barbican Centre, London EC2Y 8DS
☎020 7628 9447
Fax 020 7638 2249
e-mail: barbicanlib@corpoflondon.gov.uk
Children's Librarian Mrs M-A Stevens BA MCLIP (e-mail: mary-ann.stevens@corpoflondon.gov.uk)

LUTON

Authority Luton Borough Council
Children & Young People's Service, Luton Central Library, St George's Square, Luton LU1 2NG
☎(01582) 547433
Fax (01582) 547461
Principal Librarian (Children, Young People and Schools Library Service) Mrs J Humm MCLIP (01582 574541; e-mail: hummj@luton.gov.uk)

Schools Library Service, Leagrave Library, Marsh Road, Luton LU3 2NL
☎(01582) 598065
Fax (01582) 847077

Senior Librarian, Schools Library Service R Luscombe BA MLS MCLIP (e-mail: luscomber@luton.gov.uk)

MANCHESTER

Authority Manchester City Council
North District Libraries, Crumpsall Library, Abraham Moss Centre, Crescent Road, Manchester M8 5UF
☎0161 908 1907/1909
Fax 0161 908 1912
e-mail: libbyt@libraries.manchester.gov.uk
Senior Librarian, Children's Services Ms L Tempest MA MCLIP

MEDWAY

Authority Medway Council
Children's and Young People's Services, Gillingham Library, High Street, Gillingham, Kent ME7 1BG
☎(01634) 281066
Fax (01634) 855814
Library Services Manager: Children and Young People D Mead BA MCLIP (e-mail: duncan.mead@medway.gov.uk)

Children's and Young People's Services, Strood Library, Bryant Road, Strood, Rochester, Kent ME2 3EP
☎(01634) 718161 (tel/fax)
Fax e-mail: strood.library@medway.gov.uk
Children's and Young People's Librarian Mrs G Paterson MA DipLib MCLIP
(Medway shares a learning resources service provided by Kent: see Kent)

MERTON

Authority London Borough of Merton
Libraries and Heritage Services, Merton Civic Centre, London Road, Morden, Surrey SM4 5DX
☎020 8545 3773
Fax 020 8545 3629
e-mail: tracie.gleeson@merton.gov.uk
Strategy and Commissioning Officer G Brewin MCLIP (e-mail: gordon.brewin@merton.gov.uk)
Library and Service Manager: Lifelong Learning Ms A Williams MCLIP (020 8545 3775; e-mail: ali.williams@merton.gov.uk)

MIDDLESBROUGH

Authority Middlesbrough Borough Council
Education Support Service, c/o Acklam Library, Acklam Road, Acklam, Middlesbrough TS5 7AB
☎(01642) 817810

Fax (01642) 270444
Librarian, Education Support Miss C Dack
(Schools Resources Service: see Redcar and Cleveland. Cooperative service with Hartlepool, Redcar & Cleveland, and Stockton-on-Tees)

MILTON KEYNES

Authority Milton Keynes Council
Central Library, 555 Silbury Boulevard, Central Milton Keynes MK9 3HL
☎(01908) 254050
Fax (01908) 254089
Children's Librarian Mrs E Carrick BA MCLIP, Mrs M Herriman BA DipLib MCLIP (job share) (01908 254081)
School Library Service, Bletchley Library, Westfield Road, Bletchley, Milton Keynes MK2 2RA
☎(01908) 647611 (tel/fax)
Schools Librarian Mrs E Brand BA MCLIP

NEWCASTLE UPON TYNE

Authority Newcastle upon Tyne City Council
Priority Services, Brinkburn Centre, Brinkburn Street, Newcastle upon Tyne NE6 2AR
☎0191 278 4200
Fax 0191 278 4202
Priority Services Manager Mrs J Hall MCLIP (e-mail: janice.hall@newcastle.gov.uk)

NEWHAM

Authority London Borough of Newham
Canning Town Library, Barking Road, London E16 4HQ
☎020 7476 2925
Fax 020 7511 8693
Children and Young People's Service Manager Ms J Appleteon
Resources Manager Ms J Francis

NORFOLK

Authority Norfolk County Council
Library and Information Service, County Hall, Martineau Lane, Norwich NR1 2UA
☎(01603) 222049
Fax (01603) 222422
url: http://www.library.norfolk.gov.uk
Head of Libraries Mrs J Holland BA MCLIP MIMgt (01603 222272; e-mail: jennifer.holland.lib@norfolk.gov.uk)
Development Officer Ms L Payne MA MCLIP (01603 222273; fax 01603 222422; e-mail: lorna.payne.lib@norfolk.gov.uk)
Senior Librarian, Young People's Services Dr D Fraser BA MCLIP (01603 222270; e-mail: dorne.fraser.lib@norfolk.gov.uk)

School Library Service, County Hall, Martineau Lane, Norwich NR1 2UA
☎(01603) 222266

Fax (01603) 222422
School Library Service Manager P Cocker (01603 222266; e-mail: philip.cocker.lib@norfolk.gov.uk)

NORTH EAST LINCOLNSHIRE

Authority North East Lincolnshire Council
Schools Library Service, Broadway, Grimsby, North East Lincolnshire DN34 5RS
☎(01472) 323654
Fax (01472) 323653
Principal Librarian (Customer Services) Mrs J M Sargent BA DipLib (01472 323614; e-mail: joan.sargent@nelincs.gov.uk)
Schools Service Librarian Mrs M Shaw BA PGCE MCLIP

NORTH LINCOLNSHIRE

Authority North Lincolnshire Council
Scunthorpe Central Library, Carlton Street, Scunthorpe, North Lincolnshire DN15 6TX
☎(01724) 860161
Fax (01724) 860161
Senior Librarian, Young People's Services C Brabazon BA DipLib MCLIP (e-mail: colin.brabazon@northlincs.gov.uk)

Young People's Services, Riddings Library, Willoughby Road, Scunthorpe, North Lincolnshire DN17 2NW
☎(01724) 865412
Librarian, Young People's Services Mrs R Scotting BLib MCLIP (e-mail: rosie.scotting@northlincs.gov.uk)

NORTH SOMERSET

Authority North Somerset Council
Service for Children and Young People, Weston Library, The Boulevard, Weston-super-Mare, Somerset BS23 1PL
☎(01934) 620373/636638
Fax (01934) 413046
e-mail: weston.library@n-somerset.gov.uk
Librarian for Services to Children and Young People (South Area) Mrs M M Coleman MCLIP (e-mail: maura.coleman@n-somerset.gov.uk)

NORTH TYNESIDE

Authority North Tyneside Metropolitan District Council
Children and Young People's Library Service, St Edmund's Building, Station Road, Backworth, Tyne and Wear NE27 0RU
☎0191 200 8223
Fax 0191 200 8231
e-mail: cypls@northtyneside.gov.uk

Libraries and Information Manager Mrs J Stafford BA MCLIP (e-mail: julia.stafford@northtyneside.gov.uk)
(Includes a support service to schools)

NORTH YORKSHIRE

Authority North Yorkshire County Council
County Library HQ, 21 Grammar School Lane, Northallerton, North Yorkshire DL6 1DF
☎(01609) 767800
Fax (01609) 780793
Special Services Adviser Mrs B J Scatchard MCLIP (e-mail: june.scatchard@northyorks.gov.uk)
Principal Librarian, School Library Service Mrs B Hooper BSc MCLIP (01609 767849; e-mail: brenda.hooper@northyorks.gov.uk)

NORTHAMPTONSHIRE

Authority Northamptonshire County Council
Libraries and Information Service, PO Box 216, John Dryden House, 8-10 The Lakes, Northampton NN4 7DD
☎(01604) 236236
Fax (01604) 237937
Principal Libraries and Information Officer (Service Development) Ms E L Jarvis BA MA DipLib MCLIP DMS (e-mail: ejarvis@northamptonshire.gov.uk)
Service Development Librarian, Children and Young People Ms L McMahon DipLib MCLIP (e-mail: lmcmahon@northamptonshire.gov.uk)

Learning Resources for Education, Northamptonshire Libraries and Information Service, Booth Meadow House, Museum Way, Riverside Park, Northampton NN3 9HW
☎(01604) 620262
Fax (01604) 626789
Principal Libraries and Information Officer (Service Delivery) N L Matthews BA MCLIP DMS (e-mail: nmatthews@northamptonshire.gov.uk)
Learning Resources Manager Ms P Adams BA MCLIP (e-mail: padams@northamptonshire.gov.uk)

NORTHUMBERLAND

Authority Northumberland County Council
Amenities Division, County Library HQ, The Willows, Morpeth, Northumberland NE61 1TA
☎(01670) 534507
Fax (01670) 534521
Principal Library and Archive Officer C Baker MCLIP (e-mail: cbaker@northumberland.gov.uk)

Schools Library Service, Hepscott Park, Stannington, Morpeth, Northumberland NE61 6NF
☎(01670) 534354
Fax (01670) 533591
Principal Library and Archive Officer C Baker MCLIP

NOTTINGHAM

Authority City of Nottingham Council
Libraries, Information and Museums Services, 14 Hounds Gate, Nottingham NG1 7BD
☎0115 915 7240
Service Manager Ms C Dyer BA MCLIP (e-mail: christina.dyer@nottinghamcity.gov.uk)
Children's Services Librarians Ms D Sheppard MCLIP, Ms E Dykes BA MCLIP (job share)
(Schools Library Service offered in partnership with Nottinghamshire County Council: see Nottinghamshire)

NOTTINGHAMSHIRE

Authority Nottinghamshire County Council
Education Library Service, Glaisdale Parkway, Nottingham NG8 4GP
☎0115 985 4200
Fax 0115 928 6400
e-mail: elsg@nottscc.gov.uk
Principal Libraries Officer (Resources and Commissioning) P Marshall BA DipLib MCLIP
Principal Librarian (Advisory) Mrs C Brittan MA MCLIP
Principal Librarian (Resources) Mrs J Huffer BA DipLib MCLIP

OLDHAM

Authority Oldham Metropolitan District Council
Children's Library Service, Oldham Library, Union Street, Oldham, Lancs OL1 1DN
☎0161 911 4641
Fax 0161 911 4630
Children's Services Librarian Ms B Fitzsimons (0161 911 4080; e-mail: ecs.beverley.fitzsimons@oldham.gov.uk)

Schools Library Service, Fitton Hill Library, Fir Tree Avenue, Fitton Hill, Oldham, Lancs OL8 2QP
☎0161 678 6539
Schools Librarian Ms R Radcliffe

OXFORDSHIRE

Authority Oxfordshire County Council
Cultural Services, Holton, Oxford OX33 1QQ
☎(01865) 810220
Fax (01865) 810207
County Children's Librarian Ms C Stitson BA DipLib MCLIP

PETERBOROUGH

Authority Peterborough City Council
Children's Library Services, Central Library, Broadway, Peterborough PE1 1RX
☎(01733) 742700
Fax (01733) 319140

e-mail: libraries@peterborough.gov.uk
url: http://www.peterborough.gov.uk
Reader Services Manager Ms H Walton BLS MCLIP (e-mail: heather.walton@peterborough.gov.uk)
(Schools Library Service shared with Cambridgeshire County Council: see Cambridgeshire)

PLYMOUTH

Authority Plymouth City Council
Schools Library Centre, Chaucer Way, Manadon, Plymouth PL5 3EJ
☎(01752) 780713
Fax (01752) 767623
e-mail: sls@plymouth.gov.uk
Coordinator of Library Services to Young People Mrs A Gerrard, Mrs S Walsh (e-mail: amanda.gerrard@plymouth.gov.uk; sally.walsh@plymouth.gov.uk)
Centre Manager Mrs A Smith (e-mail: smithae@plymouth.gov.uk)

POOLE

Authority Borough of Poole
Children's and Youth Services, Parkstone Library, Britannia Road, Parkstone, Poole BH14 8AZ
☎(01202) 261650
Fax (01202) 261651
Children's and Youth Services Librarian Mrs M C Dike MCLIP (e-mail: m.dike@poole.gov.uk)
(Schools library service provided by Dorset: see Dorset)

PORTSMOUTH

Authority Portsmouth City Council
Children's Library Service, Central Library, Guildhall Square, Portsmouth PO1 2DX
☎023 9281 9311
Fax 023 9283 9855
City Children's Librarian Mrs L Elliott BA MCLIP (e-mail: lelliott@portsmouthcc.gov.uk)

School Library Service, King Richard School, Allaway Avenue, Paulsgrove, Portsmouth PO6 4QP
☎023 9232 6612
Fax 023 9237 5245
City Schools Librarian P Bone BA MCLIP (e-mail: pbone@portsmouthcc.gov.uk)

READING

Authority Reading Borough Council
Central Library, Abbey Square, Reading, Berks RG1 3BQ
☎0118 901 5950
url: http://www.readinglibraries.org.uk
Senior Young Persons Librarian Ms S Davis BA MCLIP, Ms N Shepherd BA MCLIP
(Shared Education Library Resource Centre: see Bracknell Forest)

REDBRIDGE

Authority London Borough of Redbridge
Central Library, Clements Road, Ilford, Essex IG1 1EA
☎020 8708 2422
Fax 020 8553 4185
Senior Children's and Schools' Librarian Ms A Fowler BA MCLIP (020 8708 2422; e-mail: anne.fowler@redbridge.gov.uk)

REDCAR AND CLEVELAND

Authority Redcar and Cleveland Borough Council
Library Service, Redcar and Cleveland House, PO Box 86, Kirkleatham Street, Redcar TS10 1XX
☎(01642) 444319
Fax (01642) 444341
Children's and Special Services Officer Ms S Anderson BA(Lib) (01642 444319; e-mail: sue_anderson@redcar-cleveland.gov.uk)
Children's Services Officer Ms A Prunty BA(Hons) MCLIP (01642 444320; e-mail: alison_prunty@redcar-cleveland.gov.uk)

Schools Resources Service, The Cooper Centre, Beech Grove, South Bank, Middlesbrough TS6 6SU
☎(01642) 289199
Fax (01642) 287811
e-mail: resources_schools@redcar-cleveland.gov.uk
Schools Resources Officer Mrs C Rimmington MCLIP
(Cooperative service with Hartlepool, Middlesbrough and Stockton-on-Tees)

RICHMOND UPON THAMES

Authority London Borough of Richmond upon Thames
Young People's Services, The Cottage, Little Green, Richmond TW9 1QL
☎020 8940 0590
Fax 020 8940 8030
e-mail: yps@richmond.gov.uk
Assistant Chief Librarian, Young People's and Schools' Services Mrs S Kirkpatrick BLS MCLIP (based at Education, Arts and Leisure, Regal House, London Road, Twickenham TW1 3QB; 020 8831 6116; e-mail: s.kirkpatrick@richmond.gov.uk)

ROCHDALE

Authority Rochdale Metropolitan District Council
Wheatsheaf Library, Baillie Street, Rochdale, Greater Manchester OL16 1JZ
☎(01706) 864972
Fax (01706) 864992
Bibliographical and Special Services Librarian Mrs F Fletcher MCLIP (01706 864964)
Children's Services Librarian R Stearn BA MCLIP (01706 864972)

ROTHERHAM

Authority Rotherham Metropolitan Borough Council
Education and Young People's Services, Maltby Library HQ, High Street, Maltby, Rotherham, South Yorkshire S66 8LA
☎(01709) 813034
Fax (01709) 818051
e-mail: schools-library-service@rotherham.gov.uk
Principal Librarian, Education and Young People's Services S J Hird BA MCLIP

RUTLAND

Authority Rutland County Council
Children and Young People's Service, Oakham Library, Catmose Street, Oakham, Rutland LE15 6HW
☎(01572) 722918
Fax (01572) 724906
e-mail: oakhamlibrary@rutnet.co.uk
Children and Young People's Librarian Ms D Wright BA(Hons) MCLIP

ST HELENS

Authority Metropolitan Borough of St Helens
The Rivington Centre, Rivington Road, St Helens, Merseyside WA10 4ND
☎(01744) 455403
Fax (01744) 455413
e-mail: librarysservicesschools@sthelens.gov.uk
East District Manager, Libraries (Children's Services) Ms S Thomas BA DMS (e-mail: suethomas@sthelens.gov.uk)
Schools Library Service Manager Ms J Lilley BA(Hons) DipLib (01744 455412)

SALFORD

Authority Salford City Council
Swinton Library, Chorley Road, Swinton, Manchester M27 4AE
☎0161 793 3568
Fax 0161 727 7071
url: http://www.salford.gov.uk/library/Services/childservices.htm
Senior Librarian, Children and Young People Mrs P Manley BA MLS PGDipLib MA(Ed) (e-mail: pamela.manley@salford.gov.uk)

Schools' Library Service, c/o Tech Train, 122 Churchill Way, Salford M6 5DB
☎0161 736 3443 (tel/fax)
Senior Librarian, Children and Young People Mrs P Manley BA MLS PGDipLib MA(Ed) (e-mail: pamela.manley@salford.gov.uk)

SANDWELL

Authority Sandwell Metropolitan Borough Council
Training & Development Centre, Popes Lane, Oldbury, West Midlands B69 4PJ

☎0121 569 4412
Fax 0121 569 4481
url: http://www.lea.sandwell.gov.uk/libraries
Principal Libraries Officer (Special Library Services) Ms P Fouracres MA MCLIP (e-mail: trish.fouracres@sandwell.gov.uk)

SEFTON

Authority Sefton Council
Schools and Children's Library Services, Crosby Library, Crosby Road North, Waterloo, Merseyside L22 0LQ
☎0151 257 6403/0151 330 5771
Fax 0151 330 5778
Schools and Children's Officer Ms J H Briscoe JP MCLIP (e-mail: Judith.Briscoe@leisure.sefton.gov.uk)

SHEFFIELD

Authority Sheffield City Council
Learning and Young People's Unit, Bannerdale Education Centre, 125 Carter Knowle Road, Sheffield S7 2EX
☎0114 250 6840
Fax 0114 250 6841
e-mail: sheffsls@dial.pipex.com
Group Manager A Milroy BA DipLib (0114 250 6839)

SHROPSHIRE

Authority Shropshire County Council
The Annexe, Shirehall, Abbey Foregate, Shrewsbury SY2 6ND
☎(01743) 255030
Fax (01743) 255050
e-mail: libraries@shropshire-cc.gov.uk
url: http://www.shropshire-cc.gov.uk/library.nsf
Principal Librarian: Young People and Access G Dickins BA MCLIP (01743 255005)

SLOUGH

Authority Slough Borough Council
Slough Library, High Street, Slough SL1 1EA
☎(01753) 535166
Fax (01753) 825050
url: http://www.sloughlibrary.org.uk
Library Services Manager: Operations Ms J Menniss BA(Hons) DipIM MCLIP (01753 787506)
Principal Librarian: Children and Young People C Bray BLib MCLIP (01753 787530)
(Shared Education Library Resource Centre: see Bracknell Forest)

SOLIHULL

Authority Solihull Metropolitan Borough Council
Central Library, Homer Road, Solihull, West Midlands B91 3RG
☎0121 704 8401
Fax 0121 704 6991
Head of Children's and Schools Services Ms T Scragg MA BLS(Hons) MCLIP (e-mail: tscragg@solihull.gov.uk)
Schools Library Service, Central Library, Homer Road, Solihull, West Midlands B91 3RG
☎0121 704 6984
Fax 0121 704 6991
Schools Librarian Mrs C Crawford MCLIP DipPSPE (e-mail: ccrawford@solihull.gov.uk)

SOMERSET

Authority Somerset County Council
Libraries, Arts and Information Admin Centre, Mount Street, Bridgwater, Somerset TA6 3ES
☎(01278) 451201
Fax (01278) 452787
Assistant County Librarian, Policy and Development Miss R Boyd BA MCLIP (e-mail: rboyd@somerset.gov.uk)

Resources for Learning, The Library, Parkway, Bridgwater, Somerset TA6 4RL
☎(01935) 423144
Fax (01935) 429133
Head of Resources for Learning (Schools Library Service) C Jones BSc MCLIP (01278 421015; e-mail: cbjones@somerset.gov.uk)

SOUTH GLOUCESTERSHIRE

Authority South Gloucestershire Council
Downend Library, Buckingham Gardens, Downend, South Gloucestershire BS16 5TW
☎(01454) 868451
Children and Young People's Librarian Ms W Nicholls MCLIP (e-mail: wendy_nicholls@southglos.gov.uk)

SOUTH TYNESIDE

Authority South Tyneside Metropolitan Borough Council
Central Library, Prince George Square, South Shields, Tyne and Wear NE33 2PE
☎0191 424 7884
Fax 0191 455 8085
Young People's Services Co-ordinator Ms K Armstrong MA (e-mail: kathryn.armstrong@s-tyneside-mbc.gov.uk)

School Library Service, Chuter Ede Education Centre, Galsworthy Road, South Shields, Tyne and Wear NE34 9UG
☎0191 519 1909 ext 405
Fax 0191 519 0600
Schools Librarian Miss K Hall BA MCLIP

SOUTHAMPTON

Authority Southampton City Council
Central Children's Library, Civic Centre, Southampton SO14 7LW
☎023 8083 2598
Fax 023 8033 6305
e-mail: childrens.library@southampton.gov.uk
url: http://www.southampton.gov.uk/libraries/
Principal Children's Librarian C Barnes BA MCLIP (023 8083 2163; e-mail: c.barnes@southampton.gov.uk)

School Library Service Centre, Warren Crescent, Shirley Warren, Southampton SO16 6AY
☎023 8078 0507
Fax 023 8070 2783
Senior Schools Librarian Miss C Thomas MCLIP (e-mail: c.thomas@southampton.gov.uk)

SOUTHEND ON SEA

Authority Southend on Sea Borough Council
Southend Library, Victoria Avenue, Southend on Sea, Essex SS2 6EX
☎(01702) 612621
Fax (01702) 469241
Head of Children's and Access Services M Thres BA MCLIP (e-mail: markthres@southend.gov.uk)

SOUTHWARK

Authority London Borough of Southwark
Southwark Education and Culture, 15 Spa Road, London SE16 3QW
☎020 7525 3920
Fax 020 7525 1568
Library Operations Manager Ms C Brown BA MCLIP (e-mail: christine.brown@southwark.gov.uk)
Service Development Officer, Children and Young People Ms C Styles (e-mail: claire.styles@southwark.gov.uk)
Library Development and Support Manager S Woollard MCLIP (e-mail: stuart.woollard@southwark.gov.uk)

Peckham Library, 122 Peckham High Street, London SE15 5JR
☎020 7525 0200
Fax 020 7525 0202
Senior Librarian – Children and Young People Vacant

Education Library Service, Education Resource Centre, Cator Street, London SE15 6AA
☎020 7525 2830
Fax 020 7525 2837
Manager Ms E Brumant (e-mail: e.brumant@southwark.gov.uk)

STAFFORDSHIRE

Authority Staffordshire County Council
Childrens Library Service, Cannock Library, Manor Avenue, Cannock, Staffs WS11 1AA
Service Advisor: Children's Services Mrs B W Kettle MCLIP (01543 510375; e-mail: beryl.kettle@staffordshire.gov.uk)

STOCKPORT

Authority Stockport Metropolitan Borough Council
Dialstone Centre, Lisburne Lane, Stockport SK2 7LL
☎0161 474 2253
Fax 0161 474 2257
e-mail: sls@stockport.gov.uk
Head of Services to Children Ms A Ellison BA MA (e-mail: andrea.ellison@stockport.gov.uk)

STOCKTON-ON-TEES

Authority Stockton-on-Tees Borough Council
Children and Youth Services, East Precinct, Town Centre, Billingham, Stockton-on-Tees TS23 2JZ
☎(01642) 358544
Fax (01642) 358501
Libraries and Information Services Manager Mrs L King BA(Hons)
Children and Youth Services Officer T Quantrill BSc(Hons) MCLIP
Children's Librarian Mrs J Atkinson BA(Hons) PGDipILM
(Schools Resources Service: see Redcar & Cleveland. Cooperative service with Middlesbrough, Redcar & Cleveland and Hartlepool)

STOKE-ON-TRENT

Authority Stoke-on-Trent City Council
Children's and Youth Service, Floor F, Hanley Library, Bethesda Street, Hanley, Stoke-on-Trent ST1 3RS
☎(01782) 238496
url: http://www.stoke.gov.uk/council/libraries
Principal Children's and Young People's Librarian Mrs C Lovatt BA MCLIP, Mrs A Mackey BA MCLIP (e-mail: caroline.lovatt@stoke.gov.uk; anne.mackey@stoke.gov.uk)

Schools Library Service, Staffordshire Library and Information Service, Friars Terrace, Stafford ST17 4AY
☎(01785) 278340/1
Fax (01785) 278421
e-mail: sls@staffordshire.gov.uk
Service Advisor: Young People's Services Mrs B W Kettle MCLIP (01785 278346; e-mail: beryl.kettle@staffordshire.gov.uk)
(Shared service with Staffordshire)

SUFFOLK

Authority Suffolk County Council
Schools Library Service, 3 Holywells Close, Ipswich, Suffolk IP3 0AW
☎(01473) 583507
Fax (01473) 583509
url: http://www.suffolkcc.gov.uk/libraries_and_heritage/
Schools Library Service Manager Ms H Boothroyd BA MCLIP (e-mail: helen.boothroyd@libher.suffolkcc.gov.uk)

SUNDERLAND

Authority City of Sunderland Metropolitan District Council
City Library and Arts Centre, 30-32 Fawcett Street, Sunderland SR1 1RE
☎0191 514 1235
Fax 0191 514 8444
Principal Officer, Community Libraries, Young People and Special Services Mrs A Scott MCLIP (e-mail: Ann.Scott@edcom.sunderland.gov.uk)

Sandhill View Learning Centre, Grindon Lane, Sandhill View, Sunderland
Manager Miss A Straughan

SURREY

Authority Surrey County Council
Runnymede Centre, Chertsey Road, Addlestone, Surrey KT15 2EP
☎(01932) 582700
Fax (01932) 582727
e-mail: r.wilson@surreycc.gov.uk
Library Service Manager, North West Surrey Ms R Wilson (01932 582707)

SUTTON

Authority London Borough of Sutton
Central Library, St Nicholas Way, Sutton, Surrey SM1 1EA
☎020 8770 4766
Fax 020 8770 4777
Children's Services Manager Mrs P Deakin BA MCLIP, Mrs J Allen BA MCLIP (020 8770 4622; e-mail: pauline.deakin@sutton.gov.uk; jane.allen@sutton.gov.uk) (job-share)

Central Library, St Nicholas Way, Sutton, Surrey SM1 1EA
☎020 8770 4754
Fax 020 8770 4777
e-mail: schools.libraryservice@sutton.gov.uk
Schools Library Service Manager Mrs A McNally MCLIP (020 8770 4777)

SWINDON

Authority Swindon Borough Council
Premier House, Station Road, Swindon SN1 1TZ
☎(01793) 463230
Fax (01793) 466484
Library Services Manager D Allen (01793 463230; e-mail: dallen@swindon.gov.uk)

School Library Service, Wiltshire and Swindon Learning Resources, c/o Wiltshire County Council Libraries HQ, Bythesea Road, Trowbridge, Wilts BA14 8BS
☎(01225) 713744
Fax (01225) 350029
Head Mrs S McCulloch BA MCLIP (01225 713742; e-mail: susan.mcculloch@wiltshire.gov.uk)

TAMESIDE

Authority Tameside Metropolitan District Council
Young People's Services, Central Library, Old Street, Ashton-under-Lyne, Tameside OL6 7SG
☎0161 342 2032
Fax 0161 330 4762
Service Delivery and Inclusion Manager Ms J Hall BLib MCLIP (e-mail: judith.hall@mail.tameside.gov.uk)

Schools Library Services, Education Development Centre, Lakes Road, Dukinfield, Tameside SK16 4TR
☎0161 331 3155
Fax 0161 331 3133
e-mail: schoollibrary-service@mail.tameside.gov.uk
Education Services Librarian Ms L Craigs MCLIP (e-mail: lynne.craigs@mail.tameside.gov.uk)

TELFORD AND WREKIN

Authority Telford and Wrekin Council
Telford Library, St Quentin Gate, Town Centre, Telford, Shropshire TF3 4JG
☎(01952) 292151
Fax (01952) 292078
Lead Specialist, Children and Young People Mrs H Stokes (01952 292151; e-mail: helen_stokeslibrary@hotmail.com)
(Schools library service offered in partnership with Shropshire County Council: see Shropshire)

THURROCK

Authority Thurrock Borough Council
Libraries and Cultural Services Department, Grays Library, Orsett Road, Grays, Essex RM17 5DX

☎(01375) 383611 (enquiries), (01375) 382555 ext 221 (administration); Mobile 07788 423434
Fax (01375) 370806
url: http://www.thurrock.gov.uk/libraries
Children's Services Manager Miss R Jones BA(Hons) DipLib (e-mail: rjones@thurrock.gov.uk)

TORBAY

Authority Torbay Council
Young People's Services, Torquay Central Library, Lymington Road, Torquay, Devon TQ1 3DT
Fax (01803) 208311
Young People's Services Librarian Mrs T Dickinson (01803 208289; e-mail: tracey.dickinson@torbay.gov.uk)

Torquay Central Library, Lymington Road, Torquay, Devon TQ1 3DT
☎(01803) 208293
Fax (01803) 208311
e-mail: slssouth@devon.gov.uk
Centre Manager Miss M Granata
Senior Schools Librarian Mrs J Hyde
School Librarian Mrs C Kennett MA DipLib MCLIP
(School Library Service provided by Devon County Council)

TOWER HAMLETS

Authority London Borough of Tower Hamlets
Children's Library Service, Whitechapel Library, 77 Whitechapel High Street, London E1 7QX
☎020 7247 9510
Fax 020 7247 5731
Coordinator, Children's Library Service G Harrison BSc(Econ) MSc MCLIP GradCertEd

Tower Hamlets Professional Development Centre, English Street, London E3 4TA
☎020 7364 6428
Fax 020 7334 6422
Library Adviser Ms G Harris

TRAFFORD

Authority Trafford Metropolitan District Council
Davyhulme Library, Hayeswater Road, Davyhulme, Greater Manchester M41 7BL
☎0161 912 2981/2982/2983
Fax 0161 912 2895
e-mail: schlib@pop3.poptel.org.uk
Education Services Librarian Miss S Kift BA MCLIP
Assistant Education Services Librarian Mrs J Brooks BA(Hons)

WAKEFIELD

Authority Wakefield Metropolitan District Council
Library HQ, Balne Lane, Wakefield WF2 0DQ
☎(01924) 302238
Fax (01924) 302245
Senior Librarian, Schools Library Services Mrs K Smith BA MCLIP (e-mail: kasmith@wakefield.gov.uk)

Featherstone Library and Community Centre, Station Lane, Featherstone, Pontefract WF7 5BB
☎(01977) 722745
Fax (01924) 722749
e-mail: featherstonelibrary@yahoo.co.uk
Senior Librarian, Children's Services A Wright BMsc(Hons) DipLib

WALSALL

Authority Walsall Metropolitan Borough Council
Central Library, Lichfield Street, Walsall WS1 1TR
☎(01922) 653120
Fax (01922) 722687
url: http://www.walsall.gov.uk/libraries
Children's and School Library Services Manager P Thompson BA MCLIP (e-mail: pthompson@walsallgfl.org.uk)

Schools Library Support Services, Education Development Centre, Pelsall Lane, Rushall, Walsall WS4 1NG
☎(01922) 685812
Fax (01922) 685813
Children's and School Library Services Manager P Thompson BA MCLIP (e-mail: pthompson@walsallgfl.org.uk)

WALTHAM FOREST

Authority London Borough of Waltham Forest
Young People's Library Service, Central Library, High Street, Walthamstow, London E17 7JN
☎020 8520 3031
e-mail: ypls@a.l.lbwf.gov.uk
Young People's Library Services Manager Vacant
Lending Services Manager Ms L Mitchell

WANDSWORTH

Authority London Borough of Wandsworth
Children's Library Service, Battersea Library, Lavender Hill, London SW11 1JB
☎020 8871 7466
Fax 020 7978 4376

url: http://www.wandsworth.gov.uk
Library Service Development Manager, Children and Young People Miss H Manning BA(Hons) MA MCLIP (e-mail: hmanning@wandsworth.gov.uk)

WARRINGTON

Authority Warrington Borough Council
Warrington Library, Museum Street, Warrington, Cheshire WA1 1JB
☎(01925) 442889 (switchboard), (01925) 443232 (specialist services)
Fax (01925) 411395
url: http://www.libraryatwarrington.gov.uk
Managers of Young People's Services Mrs K Syder BA DipLib MCLIP, Mrs A Cowsill BA DipLib MCLIP
(Schools library services provided by Education Library Service, Cheshire: see Cheshire)

WARWICKSHIRE

Authority Warwickshire County Council
Schools Library Service, Unit 11b, Montague Road, Warwick CV34 5LT
☎(01926) 413461/2
Fax (01926) 413438
e-mail: schoolslibraryservice@warwickshire.gov.uk
Manager Mrs C Merriman BA MCLIP
Resource Manager Mrs K Jones BA MCLIP

WEST BERKSHIRE

Authority West Berkshire District Council
Newbury Library, The Wharf, Newbury RG14 5AU
☎(01635) 519900
Fax (01635) 519906
Children's Librarians Mrs B Magee BA MA MCLIP, Ms S Deering-Punshon BLib(Hons) MCLIP, Mrs R Preuss BA MCLIP
Community Librarian – Children's Specialist Mrs F Harrison BA(Hons) MPhil MCLIP (based at Thatcham Library; 01635 866049)
(Shared Education Library Resource Centre: see Bracknell Forest)

WEST SUSSEX

Authority West Sussex County Council
Library Service, Bibliographical Support Services, Willow Park, 4B Terminus Road, Chichester, West Sussex PO19 8EQ
☎(01243) 816753
Fax (01243) 816752
Head of Services to Children and Young People Ms L Sim BA MCLIP (e-mail: lesley.sim@westsussex.gov.uk)

School Library Services Administration Centre, Willow Park, 4B Terminus Road, Chichester, West Sussex PO19 8EQ

☎(01243) 816755
Fax (01243) 816752
Head of Schools Library Service Ms S A Heyes BA(Hons) CertEd MCLIP (e-mail: susan.heyes@westsussex.gov.uk)

WESTMINSTER

Authority Westminster City Council
Schools Library Service, 62 Shirland Road, London W9 2EH
☎020 7641 4321
Fax 020 7641 4322
e-mail: sls@dial.pipex.com
url: http://www.westminster.gov.uk/el/libarch
Schools Library Service Manager N Fuller BA(Hons) AgDipLib MCLIP (e-mail: nick.fuller@dial.pipex.com)

Children's Library Service, Victoria Library, 160 Buckingham Palace Road, London SW1W 9UD
☎020 7641 4253
Fax 020 7641 6551
Children's Lifelong Learning Co-ordinator Ms V Ross (e-mail: val.ross@dial.pipex.com)

WIGAN

Authority Wigan Council
Children and Young People's Library Service, Leigh Library, Turnpike Centre, Civic Square, Leigh WN7 1EB
☎(01942) 404874
Children and Young People's Co-ordinator Ms C Appleton

Schools Library Service, Shevington Library, Gathurst Lane, Shevington, Wigan WN6 8HA
☎(01257) 253269
Schools Library Service Manager Mrs T Stirrup

WILTSHIRE

Authority Wiltshire County Council
Libraries and Heritage HQ, Bythesea Road, Trowbridge, Wiltshire BA14 8BS
☎(01225) 713744
Fax (01225) 350029
Head, Wiltshire and Swindon Learning Resources Mrs S McCulloch BA MCLIP (01225 713742; e-mail: susan.mcculloch@wiltshire.gov.uk)

Children's Public Library Services, c/o Westbury Library, Edward Street, Westbury, Wiltshire BA13 3BD
☎(01373) 822294
Fax (01373) 859208
County Children's Librarian Miss S Hillier BA PGCE MCLIP (e-mail: sarahhillier@wiltshire.gov.uk)

WINDSOR AND MAIDENHEAD

Authority Royal Borough of Windsor and Maidenhead Council
Maidenhead Central Library, St Ives Road, Maidenhead, Berks SL6 1QU
☎(01628) 796969
Fax (01628) 796971
e-mail: maidenhead.library@rbwm.gov.uk
url: http://www.rbsm.gov.uk
Senior Librarian, Young People Mrs P Dobby MCLIP (e-mail: pauline.dobby@rbwm.gov.uk)
(Shared Education Library Resource Centre: see Bracknell Forest)

WIRRAL

Authority Metropolitan Borough of Wirral
Children's Library Services, Bebington Central Library, Civic Way, Bebington, Wirral CH63 7PN
☎0151 643 7222
Fax 0151 643 7231
Area Librarian South, Children and Schools Ms S Powell BA MCLIP (e-mail: suepowell@wirral-libraries.net)

Wirral Schools Library Service, Wirral Education Centre, Acre Lane, Bromborough, Wirral CH62 7BZ
☎0151 346 6502
Fax 0151 346 6739
e-mail: sls@wirral.gov.uk
Schools' Librarian Ms M Bryning BA DipLib (e-mail: marybryning@hotmail.com)

WOKINGHAM

Authority Wokingham District Council
Woodley Library, Headley Road, Woodley, Reading RG5 4JA
☎0118 969 9421
Principal Librarian: Stock Resources Mrs H Barnes BA MCLIP (e-mail: heather.barnes@wokingham.gov.uk)

WOLVERHAMPTON

Authority Wolverhampton Metropolitan Borough Council
Central Library, Snow Hill, Wolverhampton WV1 3AX
☎(01902) 552023
Fax (01902) 552024
Children and Young People's Service Manager Mrs M Cockin MCLIP (e-mail: marion.cockin@dial.pipex.com)

Education Library Service, Jennie Lee Professional Centre, Lichfield Road, Wednesfield, Wolverhampton WV11 3HT
☎(01902) 555906

Fax (01902) 555966
Senior Librarian, Children's and Young People's Services Mrs S Jenkins BA(Hons)

WORCESTERSHIRE

Authority Worcestershire County Council
Cultural Services, County Hall, Spetchley Road, Worcester WR5 2NP
☎(01905) 766233
Fax (01905) 766244
Principal Librarian, North and Services to Young People Ms C Reed BA MCLIP (e-mail: creed@worcestershire.gov.uk)

YORK

Authority City of York Council
Acomb Library, Front Street, Acomb, York YO24 3BZ
☎(01904) 791135/787511 (tel/fax)
Community Development Librarians Ms F Postlethwaite BA MCLIP, Ms A Masters BSc MCLIP (e-mail: frances.postlethwaite@york.gov.uk; ann.masters@york.gov.uk)

SCOTLAND

ABERDEEN

Authority Aberdeen City Council
Arts & Recreation Department (Libraries), Central Library, Rosemount Viaduct, Aberdeen AB25 1GW
☎(01224) 652500
Fax (01224) 641985
Children's Services Librarian Ms A Stephen BEd MCLIP (e-mail: astephen@arts-rec.aberdeen.net.uk)
Assistant Librarian, Central Children's Library Ms M Wands MA (e-mail: mwands@arts-rec.aberdeen.net.uk)

Curriculum Resources and Information Service, Summerhill Education Centre, Stronsay Drive, Aberdeen AB15 6JA
☎(01224) 346114
Fax (01224) 346116
e-mail: cris@education.aberdeen.net.uk
Principal Officer Mrs A Turriff BA MEd FCLIP (01224 346110; e-mail: a.turriff@education.aberdeen.net.uk)

ABERDEENSHIRE

Authority Aberdeenshire Council
Library & Information Service, Meldrum Meg Way, The Meadows Industrial Estate, Oldmeldrum, Aberdeenshire AB51 0GN
☎(01651) 872707
Fax (01651) 872142
Young People and Schools Resources Librarian Mrs F Gillies BA MCLIP (e-mail: fiona.gillies@aberdeenshire.gov.uk)
Primary School Librarian Mrs A Hogg BA (e-mail: angela.hogg@aberdeenshire.gov.uk)

ANGUS

Authority Angus Council
Cultural Services Department, County Buildings, Market Street, Forfar, Angus DD8 3WF
☎(01307) 461460
Fax (01307) 462590
e-mail: cultural@angus.gov.uk
Head of Cultural Services N K Atkinson DipEd AMA FMA

Educational Resource, Bruce House, Wellgate, Arbroath, Angus DD11 1TL
☎(01241) 435045
Educational Resources Librarian Ms M Hood BA MCLIP

ARGYLL AND BUTE

Authority Argyll and Bute Council
Library HQ, Highland Avenue, Sandbank, Dunoon, Argyll PA23 8PB
☎(01369) 703214
Fax (01369) 705797
Youth Services Librarian Ms D A McLennan MA(Hons) MCLIP (e-mail: dorothy.mclennan@argyll-bute.gov.uk)

CLACKMANNANSHIRE

Authority Clackmannanshire Council
Library Services, 26-28 Drysdale Street, Alloa FK10 1JL
☎(01259) 722262
Fax (01259) 219469
e-mail: libraries@clacks.gov.uk
Senior Librarian Vacant
Team Leader (Childrens Services) Ms A Fulton BSc DipLib MCLIP (ext 24)
Team Leader (Community Services) J Blake BSc DipLib DipEdTech MCLIP (ext 24)
Children's Librarian Ms R Bruce BA MCLIP (ext 25)

COMHAIRLE NAN EILEAN SIAR

Authority Comhairle Nan Eilean Siar
Public Library, Cromwell Street, Stornoway, Isle of Lewis HS1 2DA
☎(01851) 708631
Fax (01851) 708677
Senior Librarian, Youth Services Mrs M Ferguson MA MCLIP

Education Resource Centre, Kenneth Street, Stornoway, , Isle of Lewis HS1 2DA
☎(01851) 708646
Fax (01851) 708677
Senior Library Assistant Mrs K MacKinnon

DUMFRIES AND GALLOWAY

Authority Dumfries and Galloway Council
Central Support Unit, Catherine Street, Dumfries DG1 1JB
☎(01387) 253820
Fax (01387) 260294
e-mail: libs&i@dumgal.gov.uk
Section Librarian, Young People and Schools Ms G Swales BA MCLIP DipLib
Children's Librarian Mrs A Jardine BA MCLIP

DUNDEE

Authority Dundee City Council
Children's Department, Central Library, The Wellgate, Dundee DD1 1DB
☎(01382) 434328
Fax (01382) 434642

e-mail: central.childrens@dundeecity.gov.uk
Library and Information Worker Ms S Donaldson BSc

Neighbourhood Resources and Development Department, Development and QA Team, Arthurstone Neighbourhood Library, Arthurstone Terrace, Dundee DD4 6RT
☎(01382) 438888
Fax (01382) 436881
Senior Library and Information Worker Ms L Moy BA MCLIP (e-mail: lynn.moy@dundeecity.gov.uk)

School Library Service, Central Library, The Wellgate, Dundee DD1 1DB
☎(01382) 434335
Fax (01382) 434642
e-mail: schools.service@dundeecity.gov.uk
Senior Library and Information Worker S Syme BA MCLIP (01382 434373; e-mail: stuart.syme@dundeecity.gov.uk)

EAST AYRSHIRE

Authority East Ayrshire Council
Council Offices, Lugar, Cumnock KA18 3JQ
☎(01563) 555457
Fax (01563) 555400
Education Liaison Officer Miss P Standen BA MCLIP (01563 555451; e-mail: pat.standen@east-ayrshire.gov.uk)
Community Librarians (Young People) Mrs A McInnes BA DipLib MCLIP (e-mail: ailsa.mcinnes@east-ayrshire.gov.uk), Mrs M Patterson BA MCLIP (e-mail: margaret.patterson@east-ayrshire.gov.uk)

EAST DUNBARTONSHIRE

Authority East Dunbartonshire Council
Cultural Services HQ, 2 West High Street, Kirkintilloch G66 1AD
☎0141 776 5666
Fax 0141 776 0408
Young People's Resource Co-ordinator Ms F MacArthur MA MCLIP (e-mail: frances.macarthur@eastdunbarton.gov.uk)
Assistant Librarian, Young People's Services I Gibson BA MCLIP

Education Resource Service, Curriculum Support Unit, Brookwood Villa, 166 Drymen Road, Bearsden, Glasgow G61 3RJ
☎0141 570 2307
Fax 0141 570 1688
Education Resource Officers Ms L Owens, Ms L Farrar

EAST LOTHIAN

Authority East Lothian Council
Library and Museum HQ, Dunbar Road, Haddington, East Lothian EH41 3PJ

☎(01620) 828212 (Senior Librarian), (01620) 828213 (Librarian)
Fax (01620) 828201
Senior Librarian, Young People's Services Ms A Hunter BA DipLib MCLIP (e-mail: ahunter@eastlothian.gov.uk)
Librarian, Young People's Services Mrs L Nowell (e-mail: lnowell@eastlothian.gov.uk)

EAST RENFREWSHIRE

Authority East Renfrewshire Council
Cultural Services, Glen Street, Barrhead G78 1QA
☎0141 577 3513
Fax 0141 577 3501
url: http://www.eastfrenfrewshire.gov.uk
Library Development Officer, Children's and Young People's Services Ms J Weir BA MCLIP (0141 577 3515; e-mail: janice.weir@eastrenfrewshire.gov.uk)
Children's Librarian Mrs J Watt
Library Development Worker Ms M Curran
Education Resources Assistant Ms P Cairns

EDINBURGH

Authority City of Edinburgh Council
Central Library, George IV Bridge, Edinburgh EH1 1EG
☎0131 242 8120
Fax 0131 242 8127
e-mail: eclis@edinburgh.gov.uk
url: http://www.edinburgh.gov.uk
Principal Library Officer, Youth Services Ms B Rowan BA MCLIP (e-mail: brenda.rowan@edinburgh.gov.uk)

Education Resources, St Bernard's Education Centre, Dean Park Street, Edinburgh EH4 1JS
☎0131 311 5600
Fax 0131 332 3848
Principal Officer, Education Resources Ms C Jones MA MCLIP (e-mail: cleo.jones@educ.edin.gov.uk)

FALKIRK

Authority Falkirk Council
Library Services, Victoria Buildings, Queen Street, Falkirk FK2 7AF
☎(01324) 506800
Fax (01324) 506801
Convenor, Young People's Services Team Ms Y Manning MA DipLib MCLIP (e-mail: yvonne.manning@falkirk.gov.uk)

FIFE

Authority Fife Council
East Area Library Services, Library HQ, St Catherine Street, Cupar, Fife KY15 4TA

☎(01334) 412737
Fax (01334) 412941
Learning Services Librarian Ms M Nikolic (e-mail: margaret.nikolic@fife.gov.uk)

Central Area Library Services, Library HQ, East Fergus Place, Kirkcaldy, Fife KY1 1XT
☎(01592) 412930
Fax (01592) 412941
Community Librarian, Young People's Services Ms E Dickson (e-mail: ella.dickson@fife.gov.uk)

West Area Library Services, Carnegie Library, 1 Abbot Street, Dunfermline KY12 7NL
☎(01383) 312600
Fax (01383) 312608
Community Librarian, Young People's Services Ms F Craig (e-mail: frances.craig@fife.gov.uk)

Schools Library Service, Auchterderran Centre, Woodend Road, Cardenden, Fife KY5 0NE
☎(01592) 414612
Fax (01592) 414641
Young People's Services Librarian Mrs M Gray (e-mail: maggie.gray@fife.gov.uk)

GLASGOW

Authority Glasgow City Council
Libraries, Information and Learning, The Mitchell Library, North Street, Glasgow G3 7DN
☎0141 287 2867
Fax 0141 287 2815
Young People's Services Coordinator Ms P McClean BA MCLIP (e-mail: pamela.mcclean@clsglasgow.gov.uk)

Education Resource Service, St Teresa's Primary RC School, 97 Scone Street, Glasgow G21 1JF
☎0141 336 7407
Fax 0141 336 7412
e-mail: ersglasgow@easynet.co.uk
Principal Resources Development Officer Ms F Walker
Resource Centre Manager Ms M Ward
Educational Resource Librarians Ms E Galt, Ms L Hogg

HIGHLAND

Authority The Highland Council
Thurso Library, Davidson's Lane, Thurso, Caithness KW14 7AF
☎(01847) 893237
Fax (01847) 896114
Caithness Area Libraries Officer Ms J Brown BA MCLIP (e-mail: joyce.brown@highland.gov.uk)

Inverness Library, Farraline Park, Inverness IV1 1NH
☎(01463) 236463
Fax (01463) 237001
e-mail: inverness.library@highland.gov.uk
Inverness Area Libraries Officer Ms C Goodfellow MA MCLIP (e-mail: carol.goodfellow@highland.gov.uk)
Assistant Librarian S McDowell BA MCLIP MCIPD (e-mail: sam.mcdowell@highland.gov.uk)

Education, Culture and Sport Services, Mamore House, The Parade, Fort William, Inverness-shire PH33 6EU
☎(01397) 702102
Fax (01397) 707102
Lochaber Area Libraries Officer S J Moore BA(Hons) MA MLib MPhil MCLIP (e-mail: simeon.moore@highland.gov.uk)

Nairn Library, 68 High Street, Nairn IV12 4AU
☎(01667) 458506
Fax (01667) 458548
Nairn + Badenoch & Strathspey Area Libraries Officer Ms E Somerville BEd DipLib MCLIP (e-mail: eleanor.somerville@highland.gov.uk)
Nairn + Badenoch & Strathspey Area Assistant Librarian Mrs J Murdoch MCLIP BA (e-mail: jennifer.murdoch@highland.gov.uk)

Ross House, High Street, Dingwall, Ross-shire IV15 9QN
☎(01349) 868460
Fax (01349) 863107
Ross & Cromarty Area Libraries Officer Ms A Nicol MA MCLIP (e-mail: ann.nicol@highland.gov.uk)

Ullapool Community Library, Ullapool High School, Ullapool IV26 2XE
☎(01854) 612543 (tel/fax)
West Ross Librarian Mrs C E Macarthur BA(Hons) DipLib MCLIP (e-mail: charlotte.macarthur@highland.gov.uk)

Tigh-na-Sgire (Town Hall), Park Lane, Portree IV51 9GP
Skye & Lochalsh Area Libraries Officer D Linton MCLIP (01478 613861; fax: 01478 613751; e-mail: david.linton@highland.gov.uk)

Dornoch Library, Carnegie Building, High Street, Dornoch IV25 3SH
☎(01862) 811585
Fax (01862) 811585
Sutherland Area Libraries Officer Mrs A Forrest BA MCLIP (e-mail: alison.forrest@highland.gov.uk)

Library Support Unit, 31A Harbour Road, Inverness IV1 1UA
☎(01463) 235713

Fax (01463) 236986
Central Stock Coordinator Ms K Finlay MCSP DipLib (e-mail: kate.finlay@highland.gov.uk)

INVERCLYDE

Authority Inverclyde Council
Central Library, 1 Clyde Square, Greenock PA15 1NA
☎(01475) 712323
Fax (01475) 712334
Children's Services Librarian Mrs J Skimming MCLIP (e-mail: judith.skimming@inverclyde.gov.uk)

Education Services Department, 105 Dalrymple Street, Greenock, Renfrewshire PA15 1HT
☎(01475) 712333
Fax (01475) 712850
Education Resource Service Librarian Mrs I Gilchrist MA(Hons) DipLib MCLIP (e-mail: irene.gilchrist@inverclyde.gov.uk)

MIDLOTHIAN

Authority Midlothian Council
Library HQ, 2 Clerk Street, Loanhead, Midlothian EH20 9DR
☎0131 271 3980
Fax 0131 440 4635
e-mail: library.hq@midlothian.gov.uk
Senior Librarian, Young People's Services Vacant
Assistant Librarian, School Library Service Ms R Dryburgh MA DipLib MCLIP
Children's Mobile Librarian Mrs A M Smith BA(Hons) DipLib MCLIP

MORAY

Authority Moray Council
Department of Educational Services, Library and Information Services, Elgin Library, Cooper Park, Elgin IV30 1HS
☎(01343) 562611
Fax (01343) 562630
Principal Librarian, Young People's Services Ms H Adair BA(Hons) MCLIP (e-mail: helen.adair@moray.gov.uk)

NORTH AYRSHIRE

Authority North Ayrshire Council
Library HQ, 39-41 Princes Street, Ardrossan KA22 8BT
☎(01294) 469137
Fax (01294) 604236
e-mail: acquisitions@naclibhq.prestel.co.uk
Children's Resource Officer Mrs I Gilmour BA MCLIP

Education Resource Service, Greenwood Teachers' Centre, Dreghorn, Irvine KA11 4HJ
☎(01294) 212716
Fax (01294) 222509
e-mail: nacers@netcentral.co.uk
Information and Resource Manager Ms M McLarty MA MCLIP

NORTH LANARKSHIRE

Authority North Lanarkshire Council
Community Services Dept, Buchanan Tower, Buchanan Business Park, Cumbernauld Road, Stepps, Glasgow G33 6HR
☎0141 304 1843
Fax 0141 304 1902
Libraries and Information Manager J Fox DMS MCLIP (e-mail: foxj@northlan.gov.uk)
Young Persons Services Librarian Ms M Bell MCLIP

Education Resource Service, 8 Kildonan Street, Coatbridge ML5 3LP
☎(01236) 434377
Fax (01236) 436224
e-mail: nlaners@rmplc.co.uk
Principal Librarian Ms L Wilson MA(Hons) DipLib MCLIP
Senior Team Librarian R Brown BA(Hons) MCLIP

ORKNEY

Authority Orkney Islands Council
The Orkney Library, Laing Street, Kirkwall, Orkney KW15 1NW
☎(01856) 873166
Fax (01856) 875260
e-mail: orkney.library@orkney.gov.uk
Assistant Librarian Ms K Miller BSc(Econ) PGAG MCLIP (e-mail: karen.miller@orkney.gov.uk)

PERTH AND KINROSS

Authority Perth and Kinross Council
Leisure and Cultural Services, Libraries and Archives Division, A K Bell Library, York Place, Perth PH2 8EP
☎(01738) 477039
Fax (01738) 477046
Senior Librarian, Children's Services Ms M Kelly MA DipLib MCLIP
Librarian, Children's Services Ms A Pirie BSc(Hons) DipLib
Assistant Children's and Schools' Librarian Ms E Hallyburton MA(Hons) DipLib

SCOTTISH BORDERS

Authority Scottish Borders Council
Library HQ, St Mary's Mill, Selkirk TD7 5EW
☎(01750) 20842
Fax (01750) 22875

Principal Librarian, Youth Services Ms R D M Collin BA MCLIP (01750 724906; e-mail: rcollin@scotborders.gov.uk)
Alternative address: Melrose Education Centre (01896 823517; fax: 01896 823422)

SHETLAND ISLANDS

Authority Shetland Islands Council
Shetland Library, Lower Hillhead, Lerwick, Shetland ZE1 0EL
☎(01595) 693868
Fax (01595) 694430
e-mail: info@shetland-library.gov.uk
Library and Information Services Manager Ms A Hunter (e-mail: alison.hunter@sic.shetland.gov.uk)

SOUTH AYRSHIRE

Authority South Ayrshire Council
Carnegie Library, 12 Main Street, Ayr KA8 8EB
☎(01292) 286385
Fax (01292) 611593
e-mail: carnegie@south-ayrshire.gov.uk
url: http://www.south-ayrshire.gov.uk/libraries/index.htm
Children's Services Librarian Vacant

Library HQ, 26 Green Street, Ayr KA8 8AD
☎(01292) 2888820
Fax (01292) 619019
Libraries and Galleries Manager C Deas BA MCLIP

SOUTH LANARKSHIRE

Authority South Lanarkshire Council
East Kilbride Central Library, The Olympia, East Kilbride G74 1PG
☎(01355) 243652/220046
Fax (01355) 229365
Literacy Development Coordinator Ms M Cowan MCLIP

STIRLING

Authority Stirling Council
Educational Resources and Information Service, Resource Centre, Modan Road, Stirling FK7 9BS
☎(01786) 474974
Fax (01786) 474980
(e-mail: eris@stirling.gov.uk)
Principal Librarian Ms M Murray BA MCLIP

WEST DUNBARTONSHIRE

Authority West Dunbartonshire Council
West Dunbartonshire Libraries, Levenford House, Helenslee Road, Dumbarton G82 4AH
☎(01389) 608043
Fax (01389) 608044
Children's Librarian Ms M McLean MA (e-mail: mary.mclean@west-dunbarton.gov.uk)

Education Resource Service, Edinbarnet Campus, Craigpark Street, Faifley, Clydebank G81 5BS
☎(01389) 890011
Fax (01389) 891414
Librarian M O'Donnell BA DipLib

WEST LOTHIAN

Authority West Lothian Council
Library HQ, Connolly House, Hopefield Road, Blackburn, West Lothian EH47 7HZ
☎(01506) 776336
Fax (01506) 776345
url: http://www.westlothian.gov.uk/libraries
Library Services Manager B Walker BA MCLIP (e-mail: bill.walker@westlothian.gov.uk)
Area Managers (Children's Services) Mrs J Brough, Mrs A Hunt, Mrs B Main

ANGLESEY, ISLE OF

Authority Isle of Anglesey County Council
Llangefni Library, Lôn-y-Felin, Llangefni, Anglesey LL77 7RT
☎(01248) 752088
Fax (01248) 750197
url: http://www.ynysmon.gov.uk
Children and Young People's Librarian Mrs M Clarke BA (e-mail: mcxlh@ynysmon.gov.uk)

BLAENAU GWENT

Authority Blaenau Gwent County Borough Council
Ebbw Vale Library, 21 Bethcar Street, Ebbw Vale, Blaenau Gwent NP23 6HH
☎(01495) 303069
Fax (01495) 350547
Library Manager Ms S White MCLIP (01495 301122; e-mail: sue.white@blaenau-gwent.gov.uk)
Information Officer, Library Service S Hardman (e-mail: steve.hardmans@blaenau-gwent.gov.uk)
(Blaenau Gwent has joint provision with Caerphilly for schools library services: see Caerphilly)

BRIDGEND

Authority Bridgend County Borough Council
Bridgend Library and Information Service, Coed Parc, Park Street, Bridgend, South Wales CF31 4BA
☎(01656) 767451
Fax (01656) 645719
e-mail: blis@bridgendlib.gov.uk
url: http://www.bridgend.gov.uk/english/library
Children's/Promotions Librarian Mrs M A Griffiths BLib MCLIP (e-mail: griffma@bridgend.gov.uk)

CAERPHILLY

Authority Caerphilly County Borough Council
Youth and Schools, Library HQ, Unit 4, Woodfieldside Business Park, Penmaen Road, Pontllanfraith, Blackwood, Caerphilly NP12 2DG
☎(01495) 235565
Fax (01495) 235566
Schools Library Service Manager Ms C Selby MSc(Econ) MCLIP (01495 235563; e-mail: selbyc@caerphilly.gov.uk)
Children's and Youth Services Manager Ms L Case MCLIP (01495 235562; e-mail: casel@caerphilly.gov.uk)

CARDIFF

Authority Cardiff Council
Central Library, St David's Link, Frederick Street, Cardiff CF10 2DU
☎029 2038 2116
Fax 029 2087 1599
e-mail: centrallibrary@cardiff.gov.uk
url: http://www.cardiff.info.com/libraries
Operational Manager Lifelong Learning J Rickard (e-mail: jrickard@cardiff.gov.uk)
Childrens Services Manager Mrs H Noble (e-mail: hnoble@cardiff.gov.uk)

CARMARTHENSHIRE

Authority Carmarthenshire County Council
Area Library, St Peter's Street, Carmarthen SA31 1LN
☎(01267) 224832
Fax (01267) 221839
Children's/Schools Librarian K Bowen BA MCLIP

CEREDIGION

Authority Ceredigion County Council
Public Library, Corporation Street, Aberystwyth, Ceredigion SY23 2BU
☎(01970) 617464
Fax (01970) 625059
Assistant Librarian, Primary Schools J Leeding MCLIP

CONWY

Authority Conwy County Borough Council
Services to Children and Young People, Llanrwst Library and Offices, Plas yn Dre, Station Road, Llanrwst, Conwy LL26 0DF
☎(01492) 640043
Fax (01492) 642316
e-mail: llyfr.lib.llanrwst@conwy.gov.uk
url: http://www.conwy.gov.uk
Community Librarian, Services to Children and Young People Ms T Jones MCLIP BA(Hons) (e-mail: tanis.jones@conwy.gov.uk)
(Schools Library Service: see Flintshire. Cooperative service with Denbighshire, Flintshire and Wrexham)

DENBIGHSHIRE

Authority Denbighshire County Council
Library and Information Service, Yr Hen Garchar, 46 Clwyd Street, Ruthin LL15 1HP
☎(01824) 708207
Fax (01824) 708202
e-mail: library.services@denbighshire.gov.uk

Children and Young People and Welsh Services Library Adviser Ms B Hughes BA DipLib MCLIP (e-mail: bethan.hughes@denbighshire.gov.uk)
(Schools Library Service: see Flintshire. Cooperative service with Flintshire, Conwy and Wrexham)

FLINTSHIRE

Authority Flintshire County Council
Library HQ, County Hall, Mold, Flintshire CH7 6NW
☎(01352) 704405
Fax (01352) 753662
Lifelong Learning Librarian Ms L E Courtney MCLIP (e-mail: lesley_courtney@flintshire.gov.uk)

North East Wales Schools Library Service, c/o Library and Information HQ, County Hall, Mold, Flintshire CH7 6NW
☎(01352) 704441
Fax (01352) 753662
e-mail: newalessls@flintshire.gov.uk
Schools Library Service Manager D Barker BA MCLIP
(Cooperative service with Conwy, Denbighshire and Wrexham)

GWYNEDD

Authority Gwynedd Council
Caernarfon Library Centre, Pavilion Hill, Caernarfon, Gwynedd LL55 1AS
☎(01286) 679465
Fax (01286) 671137
e-mail: llyfrgell@gwynedd.gov.uk
Children and Young People's Librarian Ms N Gruffydd MLib MCLIP (e-mail: NiaGruffydd@gwynedd.gov.uk)

MERTHYR TYDFIL

Authority Merthyr Tydfil County Borough Council
Central Library, High Street, Merthyr Tydfil CF47 8AF
☎(01685) 723057
Fax (01685) 370690
e-mail: library@merthyrgov.bt.internet.com
Customer Services Librarian Ms K E Pugh BA(Hons) MCLIP

MONMOUTHSHIRE

Authority Monmouthshire County Council
Chepstow Library, Manor Way, Chepstow NP16 5HZ
☎(01291) 635730
Fax (01291) 635736
url: http://www.monmouthshire.gov.uk
Reading and Youth Manager Ms F Ashley BLib MCLIP (e-mail: fionaashley@monmouthshire.gov.uk)

Schools Library Service, County Hall, Cwmbran NP44 2XH
☎(01633) 644565
Fax (01633) 644564
Schools Library Service Manager Ms A Noble BA PGCE DipLib MCLIP (e-mail: angelanoble@monmouthshire.gov.uk)
Librarian, Schools Library Service Mrs K Cox BA DMS MCLIP
(Schools library service in partnership with Newport and Torfaen)

NEATH PORT TALBOT

Authority Neath Port Talbot County Borough Council
Library HQ, Reginald Street, Velindre, Port Talbot SA13 1YY
☎(01639) 899829
Fax (01639) 899152
e-mail: npt.libhq@neath-porttalbot.gov.uk
Senior Assistant Librarian (Children's Services) Ms J O'Brien

Education, Library and Resource Service, Glanafan Lower School, Reginald Street, Velindre, Port Talbot SA13 1YY
☎(01639) 899829
Fax (01639) 899152
Assistant County Librarian/Head of Education, Library and Resource Service
C Biscoe MCLIP
(Schools library service in partnership with Swansea)

NEWPORT

Authority Newport City Council
Central Library, John Frost Square, Newport, South Wales NP20 1PA
☎(01633) 265539
Fax (01633) 222615
Children & Young People's Services Manager Mrs L Watts BSc DipLib (e-mail: louise.watts@newport.gov.uk)
(Schools library service in partnership with Monmouthshire and Torfaen: see Monmouthshire)

PEMBROKESHIRE

Authority Pembrokeshire County Council
County Library, Dew Street, Haverfordwest, Pembrokeshire SA61 1SU
☎(01834) 861781
Fax (01437) 767092
Group Librarian, East Mrs E Evans

POWYS

Authority Powys County Council
Education, Schools' and Children's Services, County Library HQ, Cefnllys Road, Llandrindod Wells, Powys LD1 5LD

☎(01597) 826866
Fax (01597) 826872
Principal Librarian Mrs D Jones MCLIP (01597 826867; e-mail: diannej@powys.gov.uk)

RHONDDA CYNON TAFF

Authority Rhondda Cynon Taff County Borough Council
Mountain Ash Library, Knight Street, Mountain Ash, Rhondda Cynon Taff CF45 3EY
☎(01443) 478463
Fax (01443) 477270
Senior Librarian, Children's/Youth Services Ms C Roberts MCLIP DipEd

Mountain Ash Library, Knight Street, Mountain Ash, Rhondda Cynon Taff CF45 3EY
☎(01443) 478463
Fax (01443) 477270
Librarian, Schools and Related Services Ms M Lile MCLIP BA

SWANSEA

Authority Swansea City and County Council
Library HQ, County Hall, Oystermouth Road, Swansea SA1 3SN
☎(01792) 636430
Fax (01792) 636235
e-mail: swansealibraries@swansea.gov.uk
url: http://www.swansea.gov.uk
Children's Services Librarian Mrs R Rees MCLIP
(Schools library service in partnership with Neath Port Talbot: see Neath Port Talbot)

TORFAEN

Authority Torfaen County Borough Council
Pontypool Library, Hanbury Road, Pontypool, Torfaen NP4 6JL
☎(01495) 762820
Fax (01495) 752530
e-mail: pontypool.library@torfaen.gov.uk
Senior Librarian M Tanner BA(Hons) DipLib MCLIP (e-mail: mark.tanner@torfaen.gov.uk)
(Schools library service in partnership with Newport and Monmouthshire: see Monmouthshire)

VALE OF GLAMORGAN

Authority Vale of Glamorgan Council
Barry Library@the Leisure Centre, Greenwood Street, Barry, Vale of Glamorgan CF63 4RU
☎(01446) 735722
Fax (01446) 709377
e-mail: barrylibrary@thevaleofglamorgan.gov.uk
Children's Librarian Ms M Holt

WREXHAM

Authority Wrexham County Borough Council
Children's and Young People's Service, Wrexham Library, Rhosddu Road, Wrexham LL11 1AU
☎(01978) 292643
Fax (01978) 292611
Children's Librarian Ms S Kensall DipLib MCLIP
(Schools Library Service: see Flintshire. Cooperative service with Conway, Denbighshire and Flintshire)

CROWN DEPENDENCIES

GUERNSEY

Guille-Allès Library, Market Street, St Peter Port, Guernsey GY1 1HB
☎(01481) 720392
Fax (01481) 712425
e-mail: sls@library.gg
Head of Services to Education and Young People Mrs J Falla BA DipLib MCLIP

Schools' Library Service
☎(01481) 714098
Fax (01481) 714436
Other details as above

ISLE OF MAN

Authority IOM Government
Junior and Mobile Library, Nobles Hall, Westmoreland Road, Douglas, Isle of Man IM1 1RL
☎(01624) 673123
Fax (01624) 671043
Librarian – Mobile Library Mrs S Henderson MCLIP
Librarian – Junior Library Ms M Cousins
Assistant Librarian Mrs L Strickett

JERSEY

States of Jersey Library Service, Jersey Library, Halkett Place, St Helier, Jersey, Channel Islands JE2 4WH
☎(01534) 759991
Fax (01534) 769444
e-mail: jsylib@itl.net
Principal Librarian, Young People's Services Ms J Graham MCLIP (e-mail: j.graham03@jsylib.gov.je)
Younger Readers' Librarian Mrs J O'Grady BSc MCLIP (e-mail: j.o'grady03@jsylib.gov.je)

Children's, Youth and Schools Library Services in the Republic of Ireland

(listed under public library authority)

In the Republic of Ireland, local authority public library services generally provide a service to primary schools on an agency basis for the Department of Education (there is no similar service for second level schools). Within public libraries it is not usual for staff to be appointed with specific responsibility for children's or youth libraries. Please contact the appropriate library authority as listed in the Public Libraries in the Republic of Ireland Section for information. The exceptions that follow are Dublin, Dun Laoghaire, Fingal, Galway and Wexford.

DUBLIN

Children's and Schools' Section, Dublin Corporation Public Libraries, Kevin Street Library, Lower Kevin Street, Dublin 8, Republic of Ireland
☎(00 353 1) 475 8791
e-mail: schollib@iol.ie
Senior Librarian, Children's and Schools' Section Ms E Turley BA HDipEd DPLIS

DUN LAOGHAIRE/RATHDOWN

Duncairn House, 14 Carysfort Avenue, Blackrock, Co Dublin, Republic of Ireland
☎(00 353 1) 278 1788
Fax (00 353 1) 278 1792
e-mail: libraries@dlrcoco.ie
Librarian, Young People and Schools Ms P Corish

FINGAL

Schools Library Service, 2nd Floor, Unit 34, Coolmine Industrial Estate, Coolmine, Dublin 15, Republic of Ireland
☎(00 353 1) 822 5056
Fax (00 353 1) 822 1568
e-mail: finsclib@indigo.ie
Librarian Ms C McLoughlin BA HDipEd DipLIS

GALWAY

Galway County Library HQ, Island House, Cathedral Square, Galway, Republic of Ireland
☎(00 353 91) 562471
Fax (00 353 91) 565039
e-mail: info@galwaylibrary.ie
url: http://www.galwaylibrary.ie
Librarian, Schools Library Service M Keating

WEXFORD

Wexford County Library, Ardcavan, Co Wexford, Republic of Ireland
☎(00 353 53) 24922
Fax (00 353 53) 21097
e-mail: libraryhq@wexfordcoco.ie
url: http://www.wexford.ie/library
County Librarian Ms F Hanrahan BA DipLib MLIS MCLIP MCLIPI
Schools and Children's Librarian R Kennedy BA HDIT DLIS

Libraries in Academic Institutions in the United Kingdom

ABERDEEN UNIVERSITY

Directorate of Information Systems and Services: Historic Collections, Aberdeen University, King's College, Aberdeen AB24 3SW
☎(01224) 272598 (enquiries)
Fax (01224) 273891
e-mail: speclib@abdn.ac.uk
url: http://www.abdn.ac.uk/diss/historic
Manager, Historic Collections A G Knox BSc PhD

Special Libraries and Archives

Details as above

Directorate of Information Systems and Services: Library Services, Aberdeen University, Queen Mother Library, Meston Walk, Aberdeen AB24 3UE
☎(01224) 272579 (enquiries), (01224) 272573 (administration)
Fax (01224) 487048
e-mail: library@abdn.ac.uk
url: http://www.abdn.ac.uk/diss/infoserv
Librarian and Manager, Library Services C I Munro MA DipLib (01224 273321; e-mail: c.munro@abdn.ac.uk)

Site libraries

- Taylor Library and European Documentation Centre, Aberdeen University, Taylor Building, Aberdeen AB24 3UB
  ☎(01224) 272601 (enquiries & administration)
  Fax (01224) 273893
  e-mail: lawlib@abdn.ac.uk
  Site Services Manager J L Oates BA MA MCLIP
- Medical Library, Aberdeen University, Polwarth Building, Foresterhill, Aberdeen AB25 2ZD
  ☎(01224) 681818 ext 52488 (enquiries), ext 52740 (administration)
  Fax (01224) 685157
  e-mail: medlib@abdn.ac.uk
  Site Services Manager K H Nockels MA DipLib MCLIP
- Education Library, Aberdeen University, Hilton Place, Aberdeen AB24 4FA
  ☎(01224) 283571 (enquiries & administration)
  Fax (01224) 283655
  e-mail: edulib@abdn.ac.uk
  Site Services Manager K Corrall MA MCLIP

UNIVERSITY OF ABERTAY DUNDEE

Information Services, University of Abertay Dundee, Bell Street, Dundee DD1 1HG
☎(01382) 308899
Fax (01382) 308877
e-mail: infodesk@abertay.ac.uk
url: http://vlib.abertay.ac.uk/
Head of Information Services I G Lloyd BA DipLib MLib MCLIP (e-mail: i.lloyd@abertay.ac.uk)

ANGLIA POLYTECHNIC UNIVERSITY

Main libraries

- Cambridge Campus Library, Anglia Polytechnic University, East Road, Cambridge CB1 1PT
  ☎(01223) 363271 ext 2301
  Fax (01223) 352973
  url: http://libweb.apu.ac.uk
  Campus Library Manager R Shepherd BA DipLib MCLIP (e-mail: r.c.shepherd@apu.ac.uk)
- Rivermead Campus Library, Anglia Polytechnic University, Bishop Hall Lane, Chelmsford, Essex CM1 1SQ
  ☎(01245) 493131 ext 3757
  Fax (01245) 495920
  url: http://www/libweb.apu.ac.uk
  University Librarian Ms N Kershaw BA CertEd MCLIP (01245 493131 ext 3763; e-mail: n.j.kershaw@apu.ac.uk)
  Electronic Services and Systems Manager G Howorth BA MSc MCLIP (01245 493131 ext 3145; e-mail: g.howorth@apu.ac.uk)
  Campus Library Manager (Essex) Ms M March BA MA MCLIP (e-mail: m.march@apu.ac.uk)

THE ARTS INSTITUTE AT BOURNEMOUTH

AIB Library Ltd, The Arts Institute at Bournemouth, Wallis Down, Poole, Dorset BH12 5HH
☎(01202) 363257
Fax (01202) 537729
e-mail: library@arts-inst-bournemouth.ac.uk
http://www.aib.ac.uk
Librarian Ms J Waite

ASTON UNIVERSITY

Library & Information Services, Aston University, Aston Triangle, Birmingham B4 7ET
☎0121 359 3611 ext 4412 (enquiries), ext 4398 (administration)
Fax 0121 359 7358
e-mail: library@aston.ac.uk
url: http://www.aston.ac.uk/lis/
Acting Director of Library and Information Services Mrs J Brocklebank BA MIL DipLib MCLIP, Mrs H Whitehouse BSc DipInfSc
Acting Team Leader Mrs A Cawood BA DipLIS MCLIP
Team Leader and Head of Public Services Mrs J Lambert BSc DipLib MA MCLIP

UNIVERSITY OF BATH

Library and Learning Centre, University of Bath, Bath BA2 7AY
☎(01225) 826835 (enquiries), (01225) 826084 (administration)
Fax (01225) 826229
e-mail: library@bath.ac.uk

url: http://www.bath.ac.uk/library
University Librarian H D Nicholson MA MCLIP

BATH SPA UNIVERSITY COLLEGE

Library, Bath Spa University College, Newton Park, Newton St Loe, Bath BA2 9BN
☎(01225) 875490
Fax (01225) 875493
url: http://www.bathspa.ac.uk
Head of Library and Information Services Mrs J Parry MLib MCLIP (01225 875634; e-mail: j.parry@bathspa.ac.uk)
Head of Academic Services N Drew BA MLib MCLIP (01225 875477; e-mail: n.drew@bathspa.ac.uk)
Head of Library Systems Ms A Siswell BA DipLib MCLIP (01225 875678; e-mail: a.siswell@bathspa.ac.uk)
Information Managers Mrs B Molloy BA MCLIP (01225 875430; e-mail: b.molloy@bathspa.ac.uk), Mrs M Floyd MCLIP (01225 875476; e-mail: m.floyd@bathspa.ac.uk)

Campus library

Library, Bath Spa University College, 8 Somerset Place, Bath BA1 5SF
☎(01225) 875648
Fax (01225) 427080
Campus Librarians Ms H Rayner BA(Hons) DipInf (01225 875648; e-mail: h.rayner@bathspa.ac.uk); Ms C Tylee MA MCLIP (01225 875648; e-mail: c.tylee@bathspa.ac.uk)

BELL COLLEGE

Library, Bell College, Hamilton Campus, Almada Street, Hamilton, Lanarkshire ML3 0JB
☎(01698) 894424
Fax (01698) 286856
e-mail: library@bell.ac.uk
url: http://www.bell.ac.uk/llibrary.htm
College Librarian Ms B Catt BA MCLIP

Campus library

Library, Bell College, Crichton Hall, Crichton University Campus, Bankhead Road, Dumfries DG1 4ZN
☎(01387) 244305
Fax (01387) 702111
e-mail: library@bell.ac.uk
url: http://www.bell.ac.uk/library.htm
Campus Librarian Ms J Anderson MA MCLIP

UNIVERSITY OF BIRMINGHAM

Main Library, Information Services, University of Birmingham, Edgbaston, Birmingham B15 2TT

☎0121 414 5817 (enquiries), 0121 414 6572 (administration)
Fax 0121 471 4691
e-mail: library@bham.ac.uk
url: http://www.bham.ac.uk/is
Librarian and Director of Information Services C D Field MA DPhil

Site libraries

- Barber Fine Art Library, University of Birmingham, Edgbaston, Birmingham B15 2TT
  ☎0121 414 7334
  Librarian Vacant
- Barber Music Library, University of Birmingham, Edgbaston, Birmingham B15 2TT
  ☎0121 414 5852
  Librarian A Greig BA MSc
- Barnes Library (Medicine, Health Sciences, Life Sciences), University of Birmingham, Edgbaston, Birmingham B15 2TT
  ☎0121 414 3567
  Librarian J Scott BA DipLib MCLIP
- Baykov Library, Centre for Russian and East European Studies, University of Birmingham, Edgbaston, Birmingham B15 2TT
  ☎0121 414 3614
  Librarian G A Dix BA MA MCLIP
- Chemical Engineering Library, University of Birmingham, Edgbaston, Birmingham B15 2TT
  ☎0121 414 5321
  Librarian P A Beasley BA DipTEFL
- Ronald Cohen Dental Library, Birmingham Dental Hospital, University of Birmingham, St Chad's Queensway, Birmingham B4 6NN
  ☎0121 237 2859
  Librarian G R Price MCLIP
- Education Library, University of Birmingham, Edgbaston, Birmingham B15 2TT
  ☎0121 414 4869
  Librarian D Vuong BSocSc
- Electronic and Electrical Engineering Library, University of Birmingham, Edgbaston, Birmingham B15 2TT
  ☎0121 414 4321
  Librarian P A Beasley BA DipTEFL
- Harding Law Library, University of Birmingham, Edgbaston, Birmingham B15 2TT
  ☎0121 414 5865
  Librarian L Withecombe BA(Hons) MSc(Econ) MCLIP
- Shakespeare Institute Library, University of Birmingham, Shakespeare Institute, Mason Croft, Church Street, Stratford upon Avon, Warwicks CV37 6HP
  ☎(01789) 293384
  Librarian J Shaw BA MA MCLIP
- Learning and Media Resource Centre, University of Birmingham, Edgbaston, Birmingham B15 2TT
  ☎0121 414 5960
  Librarian L C Priestley BA MA MCLIP

- Orchard Learning Resources Centre, University of Birmingham, Hamilton Drive, Weoley Park Road, Selly Oak, Birmingham B29 6QW
  ☎0121 415 2255
  e-mail: olrc@bham.ac.uk
  url: http://www.is.bham.ac.uk/olrc/index.htm
  Manager Ms M Nielsen BA MLib MCLIP

BISHOP GROSSETESTE COLLEGE

Sibthorp Library, Bishop Grosseteste College, Newport, Lincoln LN1 3DY
☎(01522) 530771/527347
Librarian J C Child BA MCLIP (ext 312; e-mail: c.child@bgc.ac.uk)
Assistant Librarian K E McBride BA (ext 227; e-mail: k.e.mcbride@bgc.ac.uk)

BOLTON INSTITUTE

Eagle Learning Support Centre, Bolton Institute, Deane Road, Bolton, Greater Manchester BL3 5AB
☎(01204) 903092 (enquiries), (01204) 903160 (administration)
Fax (01204) 903166
url: http://www.bolton.ac.uk/learning/
Dean of Learning Support and Development Ms R Jenkinson MSc BA(Hons) DipLib MCLIP (01204 903160; e-mail: RMJ1@bolton.ac.uk)
Learning Support and Development Manager Mrs K Senior MA MCLIP MLib (01204 903160; e-mail: k.senior@bolton.ac.uk)

Chadwick Learning Support Centre, Bolton Institute, Chadwick Street, Bolton, Greater Manchester BL2 1JW
(01204) 903262
Senior library staff as above

BOURNEMOUTH UNIVERSITY

Dorset House Library, Bournemouth University, Talbot Campus, Fern Barrow, Poole, Dorset BH12 5BB
☎(01202) 595083 (enquiries), (01202) 595044 (administration)
Fax (01202) 595475
e-mail: jascott@bournemouth.ac.uk
url: http://www.bournemouth.ac.uk
Associate Head of Academic Services (University Librarian) D Ball MA(Oxon) DipLib MLitt FCLIP MIMgt

Site library

Bournemouth House Library, Bournemouth University, Bournemouth House, 19 Christchurch Road, Bournemouth, Dorset BH1 3LG
☎(01202) 504297 (site librarian), (01202) 504301 (enquiries)
Fax (01202) 504298
User Services Manager Ms R Geeson

UNIVERSITY OF BRADFORD

J B Priestley Library, University of Bradford Library, University of Bradford, Bradford, West Yorkshire BD7 1DP
☎(01274) 233400
Fax (01274) 233398
e-mail: library@bradford.ac.uk
url: http://www.brad.ac.uk/lss/library/
Director of Learning Support Services Dr S J Houghton (01274 233400; e-mail: s.j.houghton@bradford.ac.uk)
University Librarian (Academic Services) J J Horton MA MPhil MCLIP (01274 233375; e-mail: j.j.horton@bradford.ac.uk))
University Librarian (Resource Management) P M Ketley BA MA (01274 233366; e-mail: p.m.ketley@bradford.ac.uk)

UNIVERSITY OF BRIGHTON

Information Services, University of Brighton, Moulsecoomb, Brighton, Sussex BN2 4GJ
☎(01273) 600900
Fax (01273) 642988
url: http://www.bton.ac.uk
Director of Information Services M P Toole MA(Cantab)

Central/largest library

The Aldrich Library, Information Services, University of Brighton, Cockcroft Building, Lewes Road, Brighton, Sussex BN2 4GJ
☎(01273) 642760
Fax (01273) 642988
Librarian i/c Ms L Turpin MA MCLIP

Site libraries

- Information Services, University of Brighton, St Peter's House, 16-18 Richmond Place, Brighton, Sussex BN2 2NA
  ☎(01273) 643221
  Librarian i/c Mrs H L Tucker BA
- Information Services, University of Brighton, Falmer, Brighton, Sussex BN1 9PH
  ☎(01273) 643569
  Librarian i/c K Baxter BA
- Information Services, University of Brighton, Queenwood Library, Darley Road, Eastbourne, Sussex BN20 7UN
  ☎(01273) 643822
  Librarian i/c M J R Ainscough BA MCLIP

UNIVERSITY OF BRISTOL

Arts and Social Sciences Library, University of Bristol, Tyndall Avenue, Bristol BS8 1TJ
☎0117 928 9000 ext 8017, 0117 928 8004 (administration)
Fax 0117 925 5334
e-mail: library@bris.ac.uk

url: http://www.bris.ac.uk/is
Director of Information Services and University Librarian G Ford MSc MCLIP

Site libraries

- Biological Sciences Library, University of Bristol, Woodland Road, Bristol BS8 1UG
  ☎0117 928 7943
  Librarian
- Canynge Hall Library (Social Medicine), University of Bristol, Whiteladies Road, Bristol BS8 2PR
  ☎0117 928 7366
  Librarian
- Chemistry Library, University of Bristol, School of Chemistry, Cantocks Close, Bristol BS8 1TS
  ☎0117 928 7947
  Librarian
- Continuing Education Library, University of Bristol, 10 Berkeley Square, Bristol BS8 1HH
  ☎0117 928 7177
  Librarian
- Dental Library, University of Bristol, Lower Maudlin Street, Bristol BS1 2LY
  ☎0117 928 4419
  Librarian
- Education Library, University of Bristol, 35 Berkeley Square, Bristol BS8 1JA
  ☎0117 928 7062
  Librarian
- Geography Library, University of Bristol, University Road, Bristol BS8 1SS
  ☎0117 928 8116
  Librarian
- Medical Library, University of Bristol, Medical School, University Walk, Bristol BS8 1TD
  ☎0117 928 7945
  Librarian
- Physics Library, University of Bristol, H. H. Wills Physics Laboratory, Tyndall Avenue, Bristol BS8 1TL
  ☎0117 928 7960
  Librarian
- Queen's Library (Engineering, Mathematics, Computer Science), University of Bristol, Queen's Building, University Walk, Bristol BS8 1TR
  ☎0117 928 7628
  Librarian
- Veterinary Science Library, University of Bristol, School of Veterinary Science, Churchill Building, Langford, Bristol BS40 5DU
  ☎0117 928 9205
  Librarian
- Wills Memorial Library (Law, Earth Sciences, EDC), University of Bristol, Wills Memorial Building, Queen's Road, Bristol BS8 1RJ
  ☎0117 954 5398
  Librarian

BRUNEL UNIVERSITY

Library, Brunel University, Uxbridge, Middlesex UB8 3PH
☎(01895) 274000 ext 2787 (enquiries), (01895) 274000 ext 2782 (administration)
Fax (01895) 203263
e-mail: library@brunel.ac.uk
url: http://www.brunel.ac.uk/depts/lib
Director of Information Services Dr L C Y Lee BSc PhD MInstP CPhys FBCS FRSA
Head of Library Services N Bevan BSc MSc(Econ) DipLib MSc(InfSc) MCLIP
User Services Manager Ms C Pickaver MSc(Econ) BA MCLIP
Support Services Manager M Emmett BSc MCLIP

Campus libraries

- Osterley Campus Library, Brunel University, Borough Road, Isleworth, Middlesex TW7 5DU
  ☎020 8891 0121
  Fax 020 8891 8251
  Subject Liaison Librarian J Langridge (e-mail: james.langridge@brunel.ac.uk)
- Runnymede Campus Library, Brunel University, Coopers Hill, Englefield Green, Egham, Surrey TW20 0JZ
  ☎(01784) 431341
  Subject Liaison Librarian J Aanonson BSc MSc MCLIP (e-mail: john.aanonson@brunel.ac.uk)
- Twickenham Campus Library, Brunel University, 300 St Margaret's Road, Twickenham, Middlesex TW1 1PT
  ☎020 8891 0121
  Fax 020 8891 8240
  Subject Liaison Librarian J Langridge (e-mail: james.langridge@brunel.ac.uk)

UNIVERSITY OF BUCKINGHAM

University Library, University of Buckingham, Hunter Street, Buckingham MK18 1EG
☎(01280) 814080
Fax (01280) 820312
e-mail: library@buckingham.ac.uk
url: http://www.buckingham.ac.uk
Chief Librarian J L Holah BA Mlib

Site libraries

- Franciscan Library, University of Buckingham, London Road, Buckingham MK18 1EG
  ☎(01280) 814080
  Fax (01280) 828288
  Assistant Librarian L M Hammond BSc
- Hunter Street Library, University of Buckingham, Hunter Street, Buckingham MK18 1EG
  ☎(01280) 814080
  Fax (01280) 820312
  Assistant Librarians S H Newell BA DipLib LLB

BUCKINGHAMSHIRE CHILTERNS UNIVERSITY COLLEGE

Library, Buckinghamshire Chilterns University College, Queen Alexandra Road, High Wycombe, Bucks HP11 2JZ
☎(01494) 522141 ext 5107 (enquiries), ext 3270 (administration)
Fax (01494) 450774
e-mail: hwlib@bcuc.ac.uk
Resources Librarian Mrs A Badhams MCLIP (ext 3293; e-mail: a.badhams@bcuc.ac.uk)

Campus libraries

- Campus Library, Buckinghamshire Chilterns University College, Queen Alexandra Road, High Wycombe, Bucks HP11 2JZ
  ☎(01494) 522141 ext 3465
  Fax (01494) 450774
  Campus Librarian and Acting Head of Dept Mrs I Sims MCLIP (ext 3294; e-mail: i.sims@bcuc.ac.uk)
- Campus Library, Buckinghamshire Chilterns University College, Wellesbourne Campus, Kingshill Road, High Wycombe, Bucks HP13 5BB
  ☎(01494) 522141 ext 4055
  Fax (01494) 450774
  Faculty Librarian Mrs F Clements BA MA MCLIP (e-mail: fcleme01@bcuc.ac.uk)
- Campus Library, Buckinghamshire Chilterns University College, Chalfont Campus, Newland Park, Gorlands Road, Chalfont St Giles, Bucks HP8 4AD
  ☎(01494) 522141 ext 2333
  Fax (01494) 603082
  Campus Librarian Mrs S Woodbridge (ext 3081; e-mail: swoodb01@bcuc.ac.uk)

UNIVERSITY OF CAMBRIDGE

Cambridge University Library, University of Cambridge, West Road, Cambridge CB3 9DR
☎(01223) 333000
Fax (01223) 333160
e-mail: library@ula.cam.ac.uk
url: http://www.lib.cam.ac.uk
Librarian P K Fox MA AKC MCLIP
Deputy Librarians D J Hall MA FSA, A Murray MA

Site libraries

- Scientific Periodicals Library, University of Cambridge, Benet Street, Cambridge CB2 3PY
  ☎(01223) 334744
  Fax (01223) 334748
  Librarian M L Wilson MA
- Squire Law Library, University of Cambridge, 10 West Road, Cambridge CB3 9DZ
  ☎(01223) 330077
  Fax (01223) 330048
  Librarian D F Wills BA MCLIP

- University Medical Library, University of Cambridge, Addenbrooke's Hospital, Hills Road, Cambridge CB2 2SP
  ☎(01223) 336757
  Fax (01223) 331918
  Librarian P B Morgan MA MCLIP
- Betty and Gordon Moore Library, University of Cambridge, Wilberforce Road, Cambridge CB3 0WD
  ☎(01223) 765670
  Fax (01223) 765678
  e-mail: science@ula.cam.ac.uk
  Librarian M L Wilson MA

UNIVERSITY OF CAMBRIDGE

(College, Institute and Departmental)

Cambridge Union Society

Keynes Library, 9(A) Bridge Street, Cambridge CB2 1UB
☎(01223) 568439
Fax (01223) 566466
e-mail: cuslibrary@hotmail.com
url: http://www.cambridge-union.org
Senior Librarian Ms P Aske MA (01223 338121)
Assistant Librarian Vacant

Christ's College

Library, Christ's College, Cambridge CB2 3BU
☎(01223) 334950
Fax (01223) 334967
url: http://www.christs.cam.ac.uk
Librarian Ms V Cox PhD
Sub-Librarian Miss C J E Guite MA MCLIP LTCL (e-mail: cjeg2@cam.ac.uk)

Churchill College

Library, Churchill College, Storey's Way, Cambridge CB3 0DS
☎(01223) 336138
Fax (01223) 336160
url: http://www.chu.cam.ac.uk/members/library
Librarian Ms M Kendall MA MCLIP (e-mail: librarian@chu.cam.ac.uk)
(NB The Library is available to College Members only)

Clare College

Forbes Mellon Library, Clare College, Cambridge CB3 9AJ
☎(01223) 333202
Fax (01223) 765560
e-mail: clarelib@hermes.cam.ac.uk
url: http://www.clare.cam.ac.uk/academic/library.html
Librarian Ms A Hughes MA

Fellows' Library, Clare College, Cambridge CB2 1TL
☎(01223) 333202
Fax (01223) 765560
e-mail: clarelib@hermes.cam.ac.uk
url: http://www.clare.cam.ac.uk/academic/library.html
Fellows' Librarian Dr H Jahn

Corpus Christi College

Parker Library, Corpus Christi College, Cambridge CB2 1RH
☎(01223) 338025
Fax (01223) 338041
e-mail: parker-library@corpus.cam.ac.uk
url: http://www.corpus.cam.ac.uk
Librarian Dr C de Hamel
Sub-Librarian Mrs G C Cannell

Darwin College

Library, Darwin College, Silver Street, Cambridge CB3 9EU
☎(01223) 763547
Fax (01223) 335667
e-mail: librarian@dar.cam.ac.uk
url: http://www.dar.cam.ac.uk
Librarian Dr D J C MacKay MA PhD

Department of Land Economy

Department of Land Economy Library, Mill Lane Library, 8 Mill Lane, Cambridge CB2 1RX
☎(01223) 337110
Fax (01223) 337130
url: http://www.landecon.cam.ac.uk/library/library.htm
Librarian Ms W Thurley BA ALAA (e-mail: wt10000@cam.ac.uk)

Downing College

The Maitland Robinson Library, Downing College, Regent Street, Cambridge CB2 1DQ
☎(01223) 334829 (enquiries), (01223) 335352 (administration)
Fax (01223) 363852
Fellow Librarian Dr P Duffett-Smith MA PhD url: http://www.dow.cam.ac.uk
College Librarian Mrs H M Canning MA(Oxon) (e-mail: hmc24@cam.ac.uk)

Emmanuel College

Library, Emmanuel College, Cambridge CB2 3AP
☎(01223) 334233
Fax (01223) 334426
e-mail: library@emma.cam.ac.uk
College Librarian H C Carron BA MA MPhil PhD MCLIP
Assistant Librarian C E P Bonfield BA

Faculty of Education

Library and Information Service, Faculty of Education, 17 Brookside, Cambridge CB2 1JG
☎(01223) 336297
Fax (01223) 336255
e-mail: educ-library@lists.cam.ac.uk
Librarian Ms A Cutts BA DipLib MCLIP
Deputy Librarian Ms E J Batchelor BA DipILS MCLIP

Library and Information Service, Faculty of Education, Shaftesbury Road, Cambridge CB2 2BX
☎(01223) 369631
Fax (01223) 324421
url: http://www.educ.cam.ac.uk/library/index.html

Faculty of Oriental Studies

Faculty of Oriental Studies Library, Sidgwick Avenue, Cambridge CB3 9DA
☎(01223) 335112 (enquiries), (01223) 335111 (administration)
Fax (01223) 335110
e-mail: oriental-library@lists.cam.ac.uk
url: http://www.oriental.cam.ac.uk/guide1.html
Librarian Mrs C A Ansorge MA MCLIP (01223 335111)

Fitzwilliam College

Library, Fitzwilliam College, Cambridge CB3 0DG
☎(01223) 332042
Fax (01223) 464162
e-mail: library@fitz.cam.ac.uk
Librarian Miss M A MacLeod MA DipLib

Girton College

Library, Girton College, Cambridge CB3 0JG
☎(01223) 338970
Fax (01223) 339890
e-mail: library@girton.cam.ac.uk
url: http://www-lib.girton.cam.ac.uk
Fellow and Librarian Ms F Gandy MA BA MCLIP
Assistant Librarian Mrs J Blackhurst MA MA MCLIP
Archivist Mrs K Perry

Gonville and Caius College

Library, Gonville and Caius College, Cambridge CB2 1TA
☎(01223) 332419
Fax (01223) 332430
e-mail: library@cai.cam.ac.uk
url: http://www.cai.cam.ac.uk/caius/library/index.php
Librarian J H Prynne MA
Sub-Librarian M S Statham MA MCLIP

(Working library open to members of the College only. Old library open to scholars by appointment. All enquiries should be addressed to the Sub-Librarian)

Homerton College
The New Library, Homerton College, Hills Road, Cambridge CB2 2PH
☎(01223) 507259
College Librarian G Mizen (e-mail: gml0009@cam.ac.uk)

Institute of Criminology
Radzinowicz Library of Criminology, Institute of Criminology, 7 West Road, Cambridge CB3 9DT
☎(01223) 335375
Fax (01223) 335356
url: http://www.crim.cam.ac.uk/library/
Librarian Mrs H Krarup BA(Open) MSc (e-mail: hek10@cus.cam.ac.uk)
Senior Assistant Librarian Mrs M Gower MCLIP

Jesus College
Quincentenary Library, Jesus College, Cambridge CB5 8BL
☎(01223) 339451
Fax (01223) 324910
url: http://www.jesus.cam.ac.uk/library.index.html
Fellow Librarian Dr A Tooze
Quincentenary Librarian Ms R K Watson (e-mail: r.watson@jesus.cam.ac.uk)

The Old Library, Jesus College, Cambridge CB5 8BL
☎(01223) 339405
url: http://www.jesus.cam.ac.uk/library.index.html
Acting Keeper of the Old Library Dr S Heath
Assistant to the Keeper Dr F H Willmoth
(Apply in writing)

King's College
Library, King's College Cambridge, Cambridge CB2 1ST
☎(01223) 331232
Fax (01223) 331891
e-mail: library@kings.cam.ac.uk
url: http://www.kings.cam.ac.uk/library/
Librarian I A Fenton PhD

Lucy Cavendish College
Library, Lucy Cavendish College, Lady Margaret Road, Cambridge CB3 0BU
☎(01223) 332183
Fax (01223) 332178
e-mail: lcc-admin@lists.cam.ac.uk
Librarian Ms C A Reid BSc MSc MCLIP
Assistant Librarian J M Harris BA

(The Library is open only to the members of the College; it is essentially an undergraduate library)

Magdalene College
Libraries, Magdalene College, Cambridge CB3 0AG
☎(01223) 332100
e-mail: magd-lib@lists.cam.ac.uk
College Librarian N G Jones MA LLM PhD
Pepys Librarian R Luckett MA PhD
(College Library: available only to members of the College. The Old Library: readers by appointment in writing. The Pepys Library: readers by appointment in writing, and open to visitors during full term only in Oct–Mar 2.30–3.30; Apr-Aug 11.30–12.30 and 2.30–3.30; parties by appointment. Application for the Old and Pepys Libraries to R Luckett MA PhD (fax 01223 332187))

New Hall
Rosemary Murray Library, New Hall, Huntingdon Road, Cambridge CB3 0DF
☎(01223) 762202
Fax (01223) 763110
e-mail: library@newhall.cam.ac.uk
url: http://www.newhall.cam.ac.uk
Librarian Ms A Wilson BA MLitt MSc MCLIP
(Admittance to New Hall members only; for special collections, please write to the Librarian)

Newnham College
Library, Newnham College, Sidgwick Avenue, Cambridge CB3 9DF
☎(01223) 335740/335739
url: http://www.newn.cam.ac.uk/library/
Librarian Ms D Hodder MA MCLIP

Pembroke College
Library, Pembroke College, Cambridge CB2 1RF
☎(01223) 338100
Fax (01223) 338163
e-mail: lib@pem.cam.ac.uk
Librarian T R S Allan MA BCL(Oxon)
Assistant Librarian Mrs P Judd BA MA DipLib

Peterhouse
Ward and Perne Libraries, Peterhouse, Cambridge CB2 1RD
☎(01223) 338200
e-mail: lib@pet.cam.ac.uk
Ward Librarian M S Golding MA (ext 338218) (Members of Peterhouse only)
Assistant Librarian E A McDonald BA MCLIP (ext 338218)
Project Cataloguer Dr S Preston MA PhD DipLIS (ext 338218)
Perne Librarian Dr R W Lovatt MA DPhil FSA (ext 338233)
(Scholars' library: by appointment only)

Queens' College
Library, Queens' College, Cambridge CB3 9ET
☎(01223) 335549, (Porter's Lodge 01223 335511)
Fax (01223) 335522
e-mail: que1@ula.cam.ac.uk
url: http://www.quns.cam.ac.uk
Librarian M Williams BA (e-mail: jmw49@cam.ac.uk)
Fellow Librarian Dr I Patterson

Robinson College
Library, Robinson College, Cambridge CB3 9AN
☎(01223) 339124
College Librarian Miss L Read MA BA MCLIP

St Catharine's College
Library, St Catharine's College, Cambridge CB2 1RL
☎(01223) 338343
Fax (01223) 338340
url: http://www.caths.cam.ac.uk/library
Librarian J R Shakeshaft MA PhD
Assistant Librarian Mrs S N T Griffiths MA MCLIP (e-mail: sntg100@cam.ac.uk)

St Edmund's College
Library, St Edmund's College, Mount Pleasant, Cambridge CB3 0BN
☎(01223) 336250 (enquiries)
Fax (01223) 762822
url: http://www.st-edmunds.cam.ac.uk
Librarian Dr P Dunstan MA PhD
(Please write in with enquiries)

St John's College
Library, St John's College, Cambridge CB2 1TP
☎(01223) 338661 (administration), (01223) 338662 (enquiries)
Fax (01223) 337035
e-mail:library@joh.cam.ac.uk
url: http://www.joh.cam.ac.uk/library/
Librarian Dr M Nicholls MA PhD

Scott Polar Research Institute
Library, Scott Polar Research Institute, Lensfield Road, Cambridge CB2 1ER
☎(01223) 336552
Fax (01223) 336549
url: http://www.spri.cam.ac.uk
Librarian and Keeper W J Mills MA MCLIP CertEd (e-mail: wjm13@cam.ac.uk)

Selwyn College
Library, Selwyn College, Grange Road, Cambridge CB3 9DQ

☎(01223) 335880
Fax (01223) 335837
e-mail: lib@sel.cam.ac.uk
url: http:/www.sel.cam.ac.uk/current/libguide.shtml
College Librarian Vacant
Assistant Librarian M P Wilson BA(Hons) MA

Sidney Sussex College

Library, Sidney Sussex College, Cambridge CB2 3HU
☎(01223) 338800 (enquiries), (01223) 338852 (administration)
Fax (01223) 338884
e-mail: librarian@sid.cam.ac.uk
url: http://www.sid.cam.ac.uk/indepth/lib/library.html
Librarian Mrs H E Lane MA(Oxon) DipLib MCLIP (e-mail: hel20@cus.cam.ac.uk)

Section library

Archive and Muniment Room, Sidney Sussex College, Cambridge CB2 3HU
☎(01223) 338824
Fax (01223) 338884
e-mail: sid1@ula.cam.ac.uk/archivist@sid.cam.ac.uk
Research Assistant N J Rogers MA MLitt (01223 338824; e-mail: njr1002@cus.cam.ac.uk)

Trinity College

Library, Trinity College, Cambridge CB2 1TQ
☎(01223) 338488
Fax (01223) 338532
e-mail: jeb30@hermes.cam.ac.uk
Librarian Dr D J McKitterick FBA
(Undergraduate Library open to members of the College only. Wren Library: readers by appointment. Visitors: Mon–Fri 12–2pm; Sat 10.30–12.30, full term only)

Trinity Hall

Library, Trinity Hall, Trinity Lane, Cambridge CB2 1TJ
☎(01223) 332546
Fax (01223) 332537
Fellow Librarian Dr P Hutchinson
College Librarians Dr A C Lacey (e-mail: acl28@cam.ac.uk/); Mrs A M Hunt BA MCLIP (e-mail: amh55@cam.ac.uk)

University Music School

Pendlebury Library of Music, University Music School, West Road, Cambridge CB3 9DP
☎(01223) 335182
Fax (01223) 335183
url: http://www.mus.cam.ac.uk
Librarian A Bennett BA MLitt DipLib ARCO

Wolfson College
The Lee Library, Wolfson College, Barton Road, Cambridge CB3 9BB
☎(01223) 335965 (direct), (01223) 335900 (Porters' Lodge)
Fax (01223) 335937
e-mail: library@wolfson.cam.ac.uk
Librarian Ms H Pattison MA MA

CANTERBURY CHRIST CHURCH UNIVERSITY COLLEGE

Library, Canterbury Christ Church University College, North Holmes Road, Canterbury, Kent CT1 1QU
☎(01227) 782514 (enquiries), (01227) 782403 (administration)
Fax (01227) 767530
e-mail: lib1@cant.ac.uk
url: http://www.cant.ac.uk
Director of Library Services Dr A Conyers MA PhD MCLIP (01227 782232; e-mail: a.d.conyers@cant.ac.uk)

Site libraries

- Thanet Learning Centre, Canterbury Christ Church University College, Northwood Road, Broadstairs, Kent CT10 2WA
  ☎(01843) 609121
  Fax (01843) 609130
  e-mail: thanetlc@cant.ac.uk
  Learning Centre Manager Ms E Unter (e-mail: e.d.unter@cant.ac.uk)
- Salomons Mansion Library, Canterbury Christ Church University College, David Salomons Estate, Broomhill Road, Southborough, Tunbridge Wells, Kent TN3 0TG
  ☎(01892) 507717
  Fax (01892) 507719
  e-mail: salomons_library@cant.ac.uk
  Site Librarian Mrs K Chaney MCLIP (e-mail: k.v.chaney@cant.ac.uk)
- Salomons Hayloft Library, Canterbury Christ Church University College, David Salomons Estate, Broomhill Road, Southborough, Tunbridge Wells, Kent TN3 0TG
  ☎(01892) 507514
  Fax (01892) 507501
  e-mail: hayloftlibrary@cant.ac.uk
  Librarian Ms A Ford BA DipLib MCLIP (e-mail: a.ford@cant.ac.uk)

CARDIFF UNIVERSITY

Information Services, Cardiff University, PO Box 430, Cardiff CF10 3XT
☎029 2087 4876
e-mail: library@cardiff.ac.uk
url: http://www.cf.ac.uk/infos/
Director of Information Services P Martin

UNIVERSITY OF CENTRAL ENGLAND IN BIRMINGHAM

Library Services, University of Central England in Birmingham, Perry Barr, Birmingham B42 2SU
☎0121 331 5289 (enquiries), 0121 331 5300 (administration)
Fax 0121 356 2875
e-mail: kenrick.library.enquiry.desk@uce.ac.uk
url: http://www.uce.ac.uk/library/public/
Director of Library Services Ms J Andrews MA DipLib MCLIP (e-mail: judith.andrews@uce.ac.uk)

UNIVERSITY OF CENTRAL LANCASHIRE

Library and Learning Resource Services, University of Central Lancashire, Preston, Lancashire PR1 2HE
☎(01772) 892284 (enquiries), (01772) 892260 (administration)
Fax (01772) 892937
e-mail: l.library@uclan.ac.uk
url: http://www.ucan.ac.uk
Head of Library and Learning Resource Services K Ellard BA MA DMS MCLIP (01772 892261; e-mail: krellard@uclan.ac.uk)
Head of Information Services J Andrew BSc (01772 892264; e-mail: jsandrew@uclan.ac.uk)
Head of User Support Ms M L Weaver BA MSc MCLIP
Head of Circulation Services K Coulling (01772 892272; e-mail: krcoulling@uclan.ac.uk)
Head of Distributed Services Mrs J Hilton (01772 892106; e-mail: jahilton@uclan.ac.uk)
Head of Resource Services Mrs E Boaler (01772 892295; e-mail: eboaler@uclan.ac.uk)
Head of Systems Support D Miller-Crook (01772 892298; e-mail: dcrook@uclan.ac.uk)

Site libraries

- Cumbria Campus Library, University of Central Lancashire, Cumbria Campus, Newton Rigg, Penrith, Cumbria CA11 0AH
  ☎(01768) 863791
  Fax (01768) 867249
  Librarian/Resource Centre Manager D Singleton BSc MA DipLib MCLIP (01772 894201; e-mail: dsingleton@uclan.ac.uk)
- Blackpool Site, Education Centre, University of Central Lancashire, Victoria Hospital, Whinney Heys Road, Blackpool, Lancs FY3 8NR
  ☎(01253) 303831
  Fax (01253) 303566
- Ormskirk Site, Education Centre, University of Central Lancashire, Ormskirk and District General Hospital, Ormskirk, Merseyside L39 2AZ
  ☎(01695) 583790
  Fax (01695) 575359
- The Library, Wigan Site, University of Central Lancashire, Bernard Surgeon Suite, The Elms, Royal Albert Edward Infirmary, Wigan Lane, Wigan, Lancs WN1 2NN
  ☎(01942) 822162

Fax (01942) 822444

- The Library, Education Centre, University of Central Lancashire, Burnley General Hospital, Casterton Avenue, Burnley, Lancs BB10 2PQ
  ☎(01282) 474699
- Blackburn Site, Education Centre, University of Central Lancashire, Blackburn Royal Infirmary, Bolton Road, Blackburn, Lancs BB2 3LR
  ☎(01254) 294312
  Fax (01254) 294318
- Postgraduate Education Centre, University of Central Lancashire, Chorley and South Ribble NHS Trust, Chorley and District Hospital, Preston Road, Chorley, Lancashire PR7 1PP
  ☎(01257) 245607
  Fax (01257) 245623

CENTRAL SCHOOL OF SPEECH AND DRAMA

Learning and Information Services, Central School of Speech and Drama, Embassy Theatre, 64 Eton Avenue, London NW3 3HY
☎020 7559 3942 (enquiries)
Fax 020 7722 4132
e-mail: library@cssd.ac.uk
url: http://www.cssd.ac.uk

Head of Learning and Information Services J A Edwards BA MSc MCLIP (020 7559 3995; e-mail: a.edwards@cssd.ac.uk)
Library Services Manager P Collett BA PGDipLib MCLIP (020 7559 3995; e-mail: p.collett@cssd.ac.uk)
Systems Manager B Harry BSc (020 7559 3969; e-mail: b.harry@cssd.ac.uk)
Media Services Manager R West (020 7559 3934; e-mail: r.west@cssd.ac.uk)

CHELTENHAM AND GLOUCESTER COLLEGE OF HIGHER EDUCATION see UNIVERSITY OF GLOUCESTERSHIRE

CHESTER COLLEGE OF HIGHER EDUCATION

Library/Learning Resources, Chester College of Higher Education, Parkgate Road, Chester CH1 4BJ
☎(01244) 375444 ext 3301 (enquiries)
Fax (01244) 392811
url: http://www.chester.ac.uk/lr

Director of Learning Resources Mrs C Stockton BA MBA MCLIP (ext 3300; e-mail: c.stockton@chester.ac.uk)
Assistant Director (Academic and User Services) Mrs A Walsh BLib MA MCLIP (ext 3308; e-mail: a.walsh@chester.ac.uk)
Assistant Director (Teaching and Learning Support Services) Mrs C Thomas BA MA MCLIP (ext 3311; e-mail: c.thomas@chester.ac.uk)

Assistant Director (Quality Assurance) P F Williams BA MA MCLIP (ext 3305; e-mail: p.williams@chester.ac.uk)
Assistant Director (Nursing and Midwifery) Mrs W Fiander BSc MA MCLIP (ext 3307; e-mail: w.fiander@chester.ac.uk)

Nursing and midwifery site libraries

- Library, Chester College of Higher Education, Chester College School of Nursing and Midwifery, Arrowe Park Hospital, Upton, Wirral CH49 5PE
  ☎0151 604 7291
  Fax 0151 678 5322
  Librarian Mrs C Holly BSc (e-mail: c.holly@chester.ac.uk)
- Library, Chester College of Higher Education, Chester College School of Nursing and Midwifery, Countess of Chester Health Park, Liverpool Road, Chester CH2 1UL
  ☎(01244) 364664
  Librarian Mrs E Downey BA MCLIP (e-mail: e.downey@chester.ac.uk)
- JET (Joint Education and Training) Library, Chester College of Higher Education, Leighton Hospital, Middlewich Road, Crewe, Cheshire CW1 4QJ
  ☎(01270) 255141 ext 2538/2705
  Libarian Vacant

UNIVERSITY COLLEGE CHICHESTER

Library, University College Chichester, Bishop Otter Campus, College Lane, Chichester, West Sussex PO19 4PE
☎(01243) 816089 (enquiries), (01243) 816091 (administration)
Fax (01243) 816080
url: http://www.ucc.ac.uk
Director of Information Services T A Hanson BA DipLib (01243 816150; e-mail: t.hanson@ucc.ac.uk)
Head of Library Services S O Robertson MA MEd MCLIP (01243 816090; e-mail: s.robertson@ucc.ac.uk)

Campus library

Library, University College Chichester, Bognor Regis Campus, Upper Bognor Road, Bognor Regis, West Sussex PO21 1HR
☎(01243) 816099
Fax (01243) 816081
Campus Librarian Ms N Leigh BLib MA MCLIP (01243 816082; e-mail: n.leigh@ucc.ac.uk)

CITY UNIVERSITY

University Library, City University, Northampton Square, London EC1V 0HB
☎020 7040 4061 (enquiries)
Fax 020 7040 8194
e-mail: library@city.ac.uk
url: http://www.city.ac.uk/library
Director of Library and Information Services B M Casey BA DipLib
Head of Operations Ms E D Harris

Site libraries

- Learning Resource Centre, City University, Cass Business School, 106 Bunhill Row, London EC1Y 8TZ
  ☎020 7040 8787 (enquiries)
  Fax 020 7638 1080
  e-mail: cklib@city.ac.uk
  url: http://www.city.ac.uk/library/ckl
  Sub-Librarian L R Baldwin BA DipLib
- West Smithfield Site Library, City University, St Bartholomew's School of Nursing and Midwifery, 20 Bartholomew Close, London EC1A 7QN
  ☎020 7040 5759 (enquiries)
  url: http://www.city.ac.uk/library/sonm
  Acting Sub-Librarian Ms S O Leitch
- Whitechapel Site Library, City University, Alexandra Building, Philpot Street, London E1 2EA
  ☎020 7040 5859 (enquiries)
  url: http://www.city.ac.uk/library/sonm
  Acting Sub-Librarian Mrs D M Beckett
- Library and Information Services, City University, Inns of Court School of Law, 4 Gray's Inn Place, Gray's Inn, London WC1R 5DX
  ☎020 7400 3605 (enquiries)
  Fax 020 7831 4188
  e-mail: ltrc@icsl.ac.uk
  url: http://www.city.ac.uk/icsl/ltrc/
  Head of Library and Information Services Ms B Zolynski MCLIP DipECLaw

COVENTRY UNIVERSITY

Lanchester Library, Coventry University, Frederick Lanchester Building, Gosford Street, Coventry CV1 5DD
☎024 7688 7575
Fax 024 7688 7525
url: http://www.library.coventry.ac.uk
University Librarian P Noon BA MBA DipLib MCLIP

CRANFIELD UNIVERSITY

Kings Norton Library, Cranfield University, Cranfield, Bedford MK43 0AL
☎(01234) 754444 (general enquiries)
Fax (01234) 752391
url: http://www.cranfield.ac.uk/library/
University Librarian Dr H Woodward PhD BA MCLIP (e-mail: h.woodward@cranfield.ac.uk)
Deputy University Librarian J S Town MA DipLib FCLIP MIMgt

Other libraries

- Management Information Resource Centre, Cranfield University, Cranfield, Bedford MK43 0AL
  ☎(01234) 754440

Fax (01234) 751806
Head Ms L Edwards BA(Hons) DipLib MCLIP (e-mail: l.edwards@cranfield.ac.uk)

- Library, Cranfield University, Cranfield University at Silsoe, Silsoe, Bedford MK45 4DT
☎(01525) 863000 ext 3022
Fax (01525) 863001
Librarian C J Napper BA DipLib MCLIP (e-mail: c.napper@cranfield.ac.uk)
- Royal Military College of Science, Cranfield University, Library, Shrivenham, Swindon, Wiltshire SN6 8LA
☎(01793) 785484 (general enquiries)
Fax (01793) 785555
e-mail: library2@rmcs.cranfield.ac.uk
Director of Information Services J S Town MA DipLib FCLIP MIMgt (01793 785480; e-mail: stown@rmcs.cranfield.ac.uk)

CUMBRIA INSTITUTE OF THE ARTS
(formerly Cumbria College of Art and Design)

Library, Cumbria Institute of the Arts, Brampton Road, Carlisle CA3 9AY
((01228) 400312
Fax (01228) 514491
url: http://www.cumbria.ac.uk/library.php
College Librarian Ms C Daniel BA MA MCLIP (e-mail: cdaniel@cumbria.ac.uk)

DARTINGTON COLLEGE OF ARTS

Library, Dartington College of Arts, Totnes, Devon TQ9 6EJ
☎(01803) 861651 (enquiries), (01803) 862224 (administration)
Fax (01803) 861666
e-mail: library@dartington.ac.uk
url: http://www.dartington.ac.uk
Director of Academic Services Ms D Faulkner BA(Hons) DipLib MA MCLIP (01803 861652; e-mail: d.faulkner@dartington.ac.uk)
Deputy Librarian R Taylor BA PGDip MCLIP (e-mail: r.taylor@dartington.ac.uk)

DE MONTFORT UNIVERSITY

Kimberlin Library, De Montfort University, The Gateway, Leicester LE1 9BH
☎0116 255 7165
Fax 0116 257 7046
url: http://www.library.dmu.ac.uk
Head of Library Services K J Arnold BA DipLib MCLIP (e-mail: karnold@dmu.ac.uk)
Library Services Manager (Leics) E S Loveridge MAMgt BA DipLib MCLIP (e-mail: esl@dmu.ac.uk)
Quality and Staff Resources Manager M E Oldroyd BA(Hons) MLib MCLIP (e-mail: meo@dmu.ac.uk)
Electronic Services Development Manager Vacant

Campus libraries

- Information Centre, De Montfort University, Milton Keynes Campus, Hammerwood Gate, Kents Hill, Milton Keynes MK7 6HP
  ☎(01908) 834921
  Fax (01908) 834929
  Campus Librarian N Scantlebury BA DipLib PGCE (e-mail: nscantlb@dmu.ac.uk)
- Polhill Campus Library, De Montfort University, Polhill Avenue, Bedford MK41 9EA
  ☎(01234) 351671
  Fax (01234) 217738
  Library Services Manager (MK/Bedford) D Saulsbury BA MA PGDipLib CertEdFE (e-mail: ds@dmu.ac.uk)
- Scraptoft Campus Library, De Montfort University, Scraptoft Lane, Leicester LE7 9SU
  ☎0116 257 7867
  Fax 0116 257 7866
  Campus Librarian M O Reynard MLS MCLIP (e-mail: mor@dmu.ac.uk)
- Charles Frears Campus Library, De Montfort University, 266 London Road, Leicester LE2 1RQ
  ☎0116 270 0661
  Fax 0116 270 9722
  Campus Librarian Ms B Freeman BA MCLIP

UNIVERSITY OF DERBY

University Library, University of Derby, Kedleston Road, Derby DE22 1GB
☎(01332) 622222
Fax (01332) 597767
url: http://www.derby.ac.uk/library/homelib.html
Librarian J G Brewer BA MA MCLIP

DUNDEE UNIVERSITY

University Library, Dundee University, Small's Wynd, Dundee DD1 4HN
☎(01382) 344087 (enquiries), (01382) 344084 (administration)
Fax (01382) 229190
e-mail: library@dundee.ac.uk
url: http://www.dundee.ac.uk/Library
Librarian J M Bagnall MA DipLib MCLIP

Site libraries

- Conservation Unit, Dundee University, Dundee DD1 4HN
  ☎(01382) 344094
  Fax (01382) 345614
  e-mail: conservation@libnet.dundee.ac.uk
  Conservator Mrs Y M T Player-Dahnsjo MA AKC HND
- Law Library, Dundee University, Scrymgeour Building, Dundee DD1 4HN
  ☎(01382) 344100
  Fax (01382) 228669
  e-mail: lawlib@libnet.dundee.ac.uk
  Librarian D R Hart MA MCLIP

- Ninewells Medical Library, Dundee University, Ninewells Hospital and Medical School, Dundee DD1 9SY
  ☎(01382) 632519
  Fax (01382) 566179
  e-mail: medlib@libnet.dundee.ac.uk
  Librarian D A Orrock MA
- Nursing and Midwifery Library, Fife Campus, Dundee University, Fife School of Nursing and Midwifery, Forth Avenue, Kirkcaldy, Fife KY2 5YS
  ☎(01592) 268888 ext 5930
  Fax (01592) 642910
  e-mail: snmfifelib@libnet.dundee.ac.uk
  Librarian A Aiton MA DipLib MCLIP
- Duncan of Jordanstone Faculty of Art Library, Dundee University, Matthew Building, 13 Perth Road, Dundee DD1 4HT
  ☎(01382) 345255 (enquiries)
  Fax (01382) 229283
  e-mail: dojlib@libnet.dundee.ac.uk
  College Librarian Ms M C Simmons BA MCLIP
- Nursing and Midwifery Library, Dundee University, Tayside Campus, Tayside School of Nursing and Midwifery, Ninewells Hospital and Medical School, Dundee DD1 9SY
  ☎(01382) 632012
  e-mail: username@dundee.ac.uk
  Learning Resources Manager A Jackson BA(Hons) MCLIP
- Faculty of Education and Social Work Library, Dundee University, Gardyne Road Campus, Gardyne Road, Dundee DD5 1NY
  ☎(01382) 464267
  Fax (01382) 464255
  Librarian J McCaffery BA DipLib MCLIP

UNIVERSITY OF DURHAM

University Library, University of Durham, Stockton Road, Durham DH1 3LY
☎0191 374 3018
Fax 0191 374 7481
e-mail: main.library@durham.ac.uk
url: http://www.dur.ac.uk/Library
Chief Librarian J T D Hall BA PhD

Departmental libraries

- Library, Education Section, University of Durham, Leazes Road, Durham DH1 1TA
  ☎0191 374 7867
- Library, University of Durham, Palace Green Section (Law, Music, Archives & Special Collections), Palace Green, Durham DH1 3RN
  ☎0191 374 3032
  Librarian Mrs S M Hingley MA MCLIP
- Library, University of Durham, Stockton Campus Section, University Boulevard, Stockton-on-Tees, Durham TS17 6BH
  ☎(01642) 335340

Fax (01642) 335339
e-mail: stockton.library@durham.ac.uk
Librarian Mrs C W Purcell MA MTheol MCLIP

UNIVERSITY OF EAST ANGLIA

Library, University of East Anglia, Norwich, Norfolk NR4 7TJ
☎(01603) 592421 (enquiries), (01603) 592407 (administration)
Fax (01603) 259490
e-mail: library@uea.ac.uk
url: http://www.lib.uea.ac.uk
Director of Library and Learning Resources Mrs J C Steward BA MA MCLIP (01603 592424; e-mail: j.steward@uea.ac.uk)
Director of Library Resources Ms K Inglis (01603 592430; e-mail: k.inglis@uea.ac.uk)
Office Manager Mrs C Christopher BA(Hons) PGCE (01603 592407; e-mail: c.christopher@uea.ac.uk)
Subject Librarian (Arts and Humanities) A Noel-Tod MA DipLib (01603 592428; e-mail: a.noel-tod@uea.ac.uk)
Subject Librarian (Social Sciences) J Marsh BSc(Econ) MA DipLib (01603 592431; e-mail: j.marsh@uea.ac.uk)
Subject Librarian (Sciences) Ms E B Clarke BSc PhD (01603 592412; e-mail: e.clarke@uea.ac.uk)
Acquisitions Librarian Mrs A B Baker BA MCLIP (01603 592429; e-mail: a.b.baker@uea.ac.uk)
Circulation Librarian Mrs C Reeman (01603 592420; e-mail:c.reeman@uea.ac.uk)
Acting Director of User Technology I Reeman (01603 592423; e-mail: i.reeman@uea.ac.uk)
Electronic Resources Librarian N Lewis (01603 592382; e-mail: nicholas.lewis@uea.ac.uk)
Head of Services Mrs S McGregor BA(Hons) (01603 592382; e-mail: s.mcgregor@uea.ac.uk)

Nursing library

NAM Library, Peddars Centre, University of East Anglia, Hellesdon, Drayton High Road, Norwich, Norfolk NR6 5BE
☎(01603) 421527
e-mail: a.cook@uea.ac.uk
Head of Services Mrs S McGregor BA(Hons) (01603 421527; e-mail: s.mcgregor@uea.ac.uk)

UNIVERSITY OF EAST LONDON

Learning Support Services, University of East London, Longbridge Road, Dagenham, Essex RM8 2AS
☎020 8223 2614 (enquiries), 020 8223 2392 (administration)
Fax 020 8223 3612
e-mail: library@uel.ac.uk
University Librarian and Head of Learning Support Services Dr M Davies BA PhD DipLib MCLIP (020 8223 2620; e-mail: m.davies@uel.ac.uk)

Campus learning resource centres

- Barking LRC, University of East London, Longbridge Road, Dagenham, Essex RM8 2AS
  ☎020 8223 2614 (enquiries)
  Deputy Head of Learning Support Services Ms E Jolly BA(Hons) DipILS MCLIP
- Docklands LRC, University of East London, Docklands Campus, Royal Albert Way, London E16 2QJ
  ☎020 8223 3434
  Campus LRC Manager Ms J Preece BA MCLIP
- Stratford LRC, University of East London, Maryland House, Manbey Park Road, Stratford, London E15 1EY
  ☎020 8223 4224 (enquiries)
  Campus LRC Manager P Chopra MA PGDipLib MCLIP
- Duncan House LRC, University of East London, Duncan House, High Street, Stratford, London E15 2JA
  ☎020 8223 3363 (enquiries)
  Site Manager Vacant
- Holbrook LRC, University of East London, Holbrook, Holbrook Road, London E15 3EA
  ☎020 8223 3252 (enquiries)
  Site Manager S Lyes BA DipLIS PGDip

EDGE HILL COLLEGE OF HIGHER EDUCATION

Learning Resource Centre, Edge Hill College of Higher Education, St Helens Road, Ormskirk, Lancs L39 4QP
☎(01695) 584298 (enquiries), (01695) 584284 (administration)
Fax (01695) 584592
Head of Information and Media Services Ms S Roberts BA(Hons) DipLib MA (01695 584284; e-mail: robertss@edgehill.ac.uk)
Learning Services and Development Manager Vacant
User Services Manager Ms C Black BA(Hons) (01695 584334; e-mail: blackc@edghill.ac.uk)

Site libraries

- Learning Resource Centre, Edge Hill College of Higher Education, Woodlands Campus, Southport Road, Chorley, Lancs PR7 1QR
  ☎(01257) 239736
  Learning Resource Centre Manager Ms R Wilson BA DipLib MCLIP (01257 239737; e-mail: wilsonr@edgehill.ac.uk)
- The Library and Information Resource Centre, Edge Hill College of Higher Education, Clinical Sciences Centre, University Hospital Aintree, Longmoor Lane, Liverpool L9 7AL
  LIRC Manager Ms R Bury BA(Hons) MCLIP (0151 529 5857; e-mail: buryr@edgehill.ac.uk)

EDINBURGH COLLEGE OF ART

Site libraries

- Lauriston Library, Edinburgh College of Art, Lauriston Place, Edinburgh EH3 9DF
  ☎0131 221 6034
  Fax 0131 221 6033

url: http://www.lib.eca.ac.uk
Principal Librarian W Smith MA DipLib (e-mail: w.smith@eca.ac.uk)

- Grassmarket Library, Edinburgh College of Art, 79 Grassmarket, Edinburgh EH1 2HJ
  ☎0131 221 6180
  Fax 0131 221 6293
  url: http://www.lib.eca.ac.uk

UNIVERSITY OF EDINBURGH

Edinburgh University Library, University of Edinburgh, George Square, Edinburgh EH8 9LJ
☎0131 650 3384 (Administration); 0131 650 3409 (Access and Lending Services); 0131 650 3374 (Enquiry Desk); 0131 651 1825 (Online Information Services); 0131 650 8379 (Special Collections)
Fax 0131 667 9780/650 3380
e-mail: library@ed.ac.uk
url: Library Online: http://www.lib.ed.ac.uk/
Librarian I R M Mowat MA BPhil FCLIP FRSE (e-mail: ian.mowat@ed.ac.uk)
Deputy Librarian Mrs S E Cannell MA MCLIP (e-mail: s.cannell@ed.ac.uk)

Site libraries

- Erskine Medical Library, University of Edinburgh, Hugh Robson Building, George Square, Edinburgh EH8 9XE
  ☎0131 650 3684/5
  Fax 0131 650 6841
  Librarian Ms I McGowan BA MCLIP (e-mail: i.mcgowan@ed.ac.uk)
- Law & Europa Library, University of Edinburgh, Old College, South Bridge, Edinburgh EH8 9YL
  ☎0131 650 2044
  Fax 0131 650 6343
  Librarian Mrs E J Stevenson (e-mail: e.j.stevenson@ed.ac.uk)
- New College Library (Divinity), University of Edinburgh, Mound Place, Edinburgh EH1 2LU
  ☎0131 650 8957
  Fax 0131 650 6579
  Librarian Mrs E Dickson MA MCLIP (e-mail: eileen.dickson@ed.ac.uk)
- Reid Music Library, University of Edinburgh, Alison House, Nicolson Square, Edinburgh EH8 9DF
  ☎0131 650 2436
  Fax 0131 650 2425
  Site and Services Supervisor Ms T Jones (e-mail: teresa.jones@ed.ac.uk)
- Science Libraries, University of Edinburgh, West Mains Road, Edinburgh EH9 3JF
  ☎0131 650 5205
  Fax 0131 650 6702
  Librarian R Battersby BA DipLib MCLIP (e-mail: r.battersby@ed.ac.uk)
- Veterinary Library, University of Edinburgh, Summerhall, Edinburgh EH9 1QH
  ☎0131 650 6175
  Fax 0131 650 6593
  Liaison Librarian Mrs F Brown (e-mail: f.brown@ed.ac.uk)

- Moray House Library (Education), University of Edinburgh, Dalhousie Land, St John Street, Edinburgh EH8 8AQ
  ☎0131 651 6193
  Fax 0131 557 3458
  Librarian Mrs D Colledge BA MCLIP (e-mail: dennyc@mhie.ac.uk)

ESSEX UNIVERSITY

The Albert Sloman Library, Essex University, Wivenhoe Park, Colchester, Essex CO4 3SQ
☎(01206) 873188
Fax (01206) 872289
Librarian R Butler MSc

UNIVERSITY OF EXETER

University Library, University of Exeter, Stocker Road, Exeter EX4 4PT
☎(01392) 263873 (enquiries), (01392) 263869 (administration)
Fax (01392) 263871
e-mail: library@exeter.ac.uk
url: http://www.ex.ac.uk/library/
Librarian A T Paterson MA MCLIP

Departmental Libraries

- Law Library, University of Exeter, Amory Building, Rennes Drive, Exeter
  ☎(01392) 263356
  Librarian P V G Kershaw BA MA
- St Luke's Campus Library, University of Exeter, Exeter EX1 2LU
  ☎(01392) 264785
  Librarian R Davies BSc DipLib DipCompSci MCLIP
- Library, University of Exeter, Camborne School of Mines, Pool, Redruth, Cornwall TR15 3SE
  ☎(01209) 714866
  Fax (01209) 716977
  Librarian Ms J Foote BSc DipLib MCLIP

FALMOUTH COLLEGE OF ARTS

Library and Information Services, Falmouth College of Arts, Woodlane, Falmouth, Cornwall TR11 4RA
☎(01326) 213815
Fax (01326) 211205
e-mail: library@falmouth.ac.uk
Head of Library and Information Services R C Towe BA PGDipLib (01326 213817; e-mail: rogert@falmouth.ac.uk)
Cataloguing Librarian S Gibson BA (e-mail: stepheng@falmouth.ac.uk)
Visual Resources Librarian Ms R Ball BA(Hons) PGDipLib (e-mail: rebeccab@falmouth.ac.uk)
Library IT Officer S Pellow BA(Hons) PGCE (e-mail: steve@falmouth.ac.uk)

Campus library

Tremough Campus Library, Falmouth College of Arts, Treliever Road, Penryn, Cornwall TR10 9EZ
☎(01326) 370441
Fax (01326) 370437
e-mail: library@falmouth.ac.uk
Site Librarian Ms J Davey

UNIVERSITY OF GLAMORGAN

Learning Resources Centre, University of Glamorgan, Pontypridd CF37 1DL
☎(01443) 482625 (enquiries)
Fax (01443) 482629
e-mail: lrcenq@glam.ac.uk
url: http://www.glam.ac.uk/lrc
Head of Learning Resources Centre J Atkinson BSc MPhil DipLib MCLIP
Deputy Head of Learning Resources Centre S Morgan BA MEd MBA FCLIP

GLASGOW CALEDONIAN UNIVERSITY

City Campus, Glasgow Caledonian University, Caledonian Library and Information Centre, Cowcaddens Road, Glasgow G4 0BA
☎0141 331 3867 (enquiries), 0141 331 3859 (administration)
Fax 0141 331 3968
e-mail: library@gcal.ac.uk
url: http://www.lib.gcal.ac.uk
Acting Chief Librarian Mrs F Smith MA MCLIP (0141 331 3860)
Depute Librarian P Blount MA MLib MCLIP (0141 331 3863)

GLASGOW SCHOOL OF ART

Library, Glasgow School of Art, 167 Renfrew Street, Glasgow G3 6RQ
☎0141 353 4551
Fax 0141 353 4670
url: http://www.gsa.ac.uk/library/
Head of Information Services J McKay MA DipLib MCLIP (e-mail: j.mckay@gsa.ac.uk)

GLASGOW UNIVERSITY

University Library, Glasgow University, Hillhead Street, Glasgow G12 8QE
☎0141 330 6704/5 (enquiries), 0141 330 5634 (administration)
Fax 0141 330 4952
e-mail: library@lib.gla.ac.uk
url: http://www.lib.gla.ac.uk
Director of Library Services C Bailey MA DipLib MCLIP

Site/departmental libraries

- Adam Smith Library, Glasgow University, Adam Smith Building, Bute Gardens, Glasgow G12 8RT
  ☎0141 330 5648

e-mail: adamsmith@lib.gla.ac.uk
Librarian J J K Ross

- Chemistry Branch, Glasgow University, Joseph Black Building, Glasgow G12 8QQ
☎0141 330 5502
e-mail: library@lib.gla.ac.uk
Librarian Mrs D Currie
- James Ireland Memorial Library, Glasgow University, Dental School and Hospital, Sauchiehall Street, Glasgow G2 3JZ
☎0141 211 9705
e-mail: library@dental.gla.ac.uk
Librarian Ms B Rankin
- James Herriot Library, Glasgow University, Veterinary School, Garscube Estate, Bearsden, Glasgow G61 1QH
☎0141 330 5708
e-mail: vetlib@lib.gla.ac.uk
Librarian Mrs M McGovern

UNIVERSITY OF GLOUCESTERSHIRE
(formerly Cheltenham and Gloucester College of Higher Education)

Learning Centre, University of Gloucestershire, PO Box 220, The Park, Cheltenham, Gloucestershire GL50 2QF
☎(01242) 543458
Fax (01242) 543492
url: http://www.glos.ac.uk
Learning Centres Manager Ms A E Mathie BA MCLIP (01242 532944; e-mail: amathie@glos.ac.uk)

Site libraries

- Learning Centre, University of Gloucestershire, Francis Close Hall, Swindon Road, Cheltenham, Gloucestershire GL50 4AZ
☎(01242) 532913
User Services Team Manager T Smith (01242 532911; e-mail: tsmith@glos.ac.uk)
- Learning Centre, University of Gloucestershire, Pittville Campus, Albert Road, Cheltenham, Gloucestershire GL52 3JG
☎(01242) 532259
ICT Co-ordinator S Jordan (01242 543491; e-mail: sjordan@glos.ac.uk)
- Learning Centre, University of Gloucestershire, Oxstalls Campus, Oxstalls Lane, Gloucester GL2 9HW
☎(01452) 876602
Information Services Team Leader Mrs A Cummings (e-mail: acummings@glos.ac.uk)

UNIVERSITY OF GREENWICH

Library and Information Service, University of Greenwich, Riverside House, Beresford Street, London SE18 6BU
☎020 8331 8192 (administration)
Fax 020 8331 9084

url: http://www.gre.ac.uk/directory/library
University Librarian D A Heathcote MA MCLIP (e-mail: d.heathcote@greenwich.ac.uk)
Head of Information Services Ms A Murphy BA DipLib (020 8331 8196, e-mail: a.e.murphy@greenwich.ac.uk)

Campus libraries

- Avery Hill Campus Library, University of Greenwich, Bexley Road, London SE9 2PQ
  ☎020 8331 8484
  Fax 020 8331 9645
  Campus Librarian D Mitchell BSc MCLIP (e-mail: d.mitchell@greenwich.ac.uk)
- Dreadnought Library, University of Greenwich, Maritime Greenwich Campus, Old Royal Naval College, Park Row, Greenwich, London SE10 9LS
  ☎020 8331 7788
  Fax 020 8331 7775
  Campus Librarian Ms C Hogg BA MCLIP (e-mail: c.g.hogg@greenwich.ac.uk)
- Medway University Campus Library, University of Greenwich, Nelson Building, Chatham Maritime, Central Avenue, Chatham, Kent ME4 4TB
  ☎020 8331 9617
  Fax 020 8331 9837
  Campus Librarian/Librarian of NRI T Cullen BSc MSc MIBiol MCLIP (e-mail: t.cullen@greenwich.ac.uk)
- Library and Information Services Group, Natural Resources Institute, University of Greenwich, Chatham Maritime, Central Avenue, Chatham, Kent ME4 4TB
  ☎020 8331 7542 (enquiries)
  Fax 020 8331 9837
  e-mail: a.d.larkin@greenwich.ac.uk
  url: http://www.nri.org
  Head of Library and Information Services Group T Cullen MSc MCLIP MIBiol

HARPER ADAMS UNIVERSITY COLLEGE

Library, Harper Adams University College, Edgmond, Newport, Shropshire TF10 8NB
☎(01952) 820280
url: http://www.harper-adams.ac.uk
Librarian Ms K Greaves BLib(Hons) MCLIP

HERIOT-WATT UNIVERSITY

University Library, Heriot-Watt University, Edinburgh EH14 4AS
☎0131 451 3571
Fax 0131 451 3164
e-mail: library@hw.ac.uk
url: http://www.hw.ac.uk/library
Librarian M Breaks BA DipLib

UNIVERSITY OF HERTFORDSHIRE

Learning and Information Services, University of Hertfordshire, College Lane, Hatfield, Hertfordshire AL10 9AB

☎(01707) 284678 (enquiries), (01707) 284653 (administration)
Fax (01707) 284666
e-mail: lisadmin@herts.ac.uk
url: http://www.herts.ac.uk/lis
Director of Learning and Information Services Ms D Martin MA DipLib MCLIP CertEd MCIPD

Learning resources centres

- Hatfield Campus Learning Resources Centre, University of Hertfordshire, College Lane, Hatfield, Hertfordshire AL10 9AB
  ☎(01707) 284678
  Campus LIS Manager Mrs C Parr MA MCLIP
- Hertford Campus Learning Resources Centre, University of Hertfordshire, Balls Park, Mangrove Road, Hertford, Herts SG13 8QF
  ☎(01707) 284678
  Campus LIS Manager K Thompson BSc DipLib
- St Albans Campus Learning Resources Centre, University of Hertfordshire, 6 Hatfield Road, St Albans, Herts AL1 3RS
  ☎(01707) 284678
  Campus LIS Manager N Goodfellow MA MCLIP CertEd
- Watford Campus Learning Resources Centre, University of Hertfordshire, Aldenham, Watford, Herts WD2 8AT
  ☎(01707) 284678
  Campus LIS Manager K Thompson BSc DipLib

UNIVERSITY OF HUDDERSFIELD

Learning Centre, University of Huddersfield, Queensgate, Huddersfield, West Yorkshire HD1 3DH
☎(01484) 472040 (enquiries), (01484) 472039 (administration)
Fax (01484) 517987
e-mail: ills@hud.ac.uk
url: http://www.hud.ac.uk
Director of Computing and Library Services P Sykes BA DipLib MCLIP
Deputy Director of Computing and Library Services Ms S White BA DipLib MCLIP

UNIVERSITY OF HULL

The Brynmor Jones Library, Academic Services: Libraries, University of Hull, Cottingham Road Campus, Cottingham Road, Hull HU6 7RX
☎(01482) 466581
Fax (01482) 466205
e-mail: libhelp@hull.ac.uk
url: http://www.hull.ac.uk/lib/
Director of Academic Services and Librarian R G Heseltine BA DPhil DipLib
Library Manager Mrs S Geale BA MA (01482 466831; e-mail: s.e.geale@hull.ac.uk)

Campus library

Keith Donaldson Library, University of Hull, Scarborough Campus, Filey Road,

Scarborough, North Yorkshire YO11 3AZ
☎(01723) 357277
Fax (01723) 357328
Team Leader Mrs J Crowther (01723 357254; e-mail: j.crowther@hull.ac.uk)

ISLE OF MAN COLLEGE

Library, Isle of Man College, Homefield Road, Douglas, Isle of Man IM2 6RB
☎(01624) 648207
Fax (01624) 663675
e-mail: libiomc@enterprise.net
Senior Librarian Miss C I Graham BA MCLIP MSc (e-mail: Carole.Graham@college.doe.gov.im)
College Librarian T Kenyon BA MCLIP MA (e-mail: Tim.Kenyon@college.doe.gov.im)

KEELE UNIVERSITY

Department of Information Services, Keele University, Keele, Staffordshire ST5 5BG
☎(01782) 583535 (enquiries), (01782) 583232 (office)
Fax (01782) 711553
e-mail: kis@keele.ac.uk
url: http://www.keele.ac.uk/depts/li/lihome.html
Director of Information Services A Foster BA FCLIP (e-mail: a.j.foster@keele.ac.uk)
Assistant Director M J Phillips MA MCLIP (e-mail: m.j.phillips@keele.ac.uk)

Departmental library

Health Library, Keele University, City General Hospital, Newcastle Road, Stoke-on-Trent, Staffordshire ST4 6QG
☎(01782) 552949
Fax (01782) 712941
Health Faculty Librarian D Bird BA MA MA (e-mail: d.t.bird@keele.ac.uk)

KENT INSTITUTE OF ART AND DESIGN

Library, Kent Institute of Art and Design, Oakwood Park, Maidstone, Kent ME16 8AG
☎(01622) 757286
Fax (01622) 621100
e-mail: librarymaid@kiad.ac.uk
url: http://www.kiad.ac.uk
Head of Library and Learning Resources Ms V Crane BA MCLIP (e-mail: vcrane@kiad.ac.uk)
Librarian, Maidstone Mrs A McKie MA MCLIP (e-mail: amckie@kiad.ac.uk)

Campus libraries

- Library, Kent Institute of Art and Design, Canterbury Campus, New Dover Road, Canterbury, Kent CT1 3AN
  ☎(01227) 769371
  Fax (01227) 817500
  e-mail: librarycant@kiad.ac.uk

Librarian, Canterbury Mrs K Godfrey MA(Ed) MCLIP (e-mail: kgodfrey@kiad.ac.uk)

- Library, Kent Institute of Art and Design, Rochester Campus, Design Fort Pitt, Rochester, Kent ME1 1DZ
  ☎(01634) 830022
  Fax (01634) 820300
  e-mail: libraryroch@kiad.ac.uk
  Librarian, Rochester Mrs P Sowry BA MCLIP (e-mail: psowry@kiad.ac.uk)

UNIVERSITY OF KENT AT CANTERBURY

Templeman Library, University of Kent at Canterbury, Canterbury, Kent CT2 7NU
☎(01227) 823570 (enquiries), 823565 (administration)
Fax (01227) 823984
e-mail: library@ukc.ac.uk
url: http://www.ukc.ac.uk/library
Director of Information Services and Librarian M M Coutts MA(Glas) MA(Sheff) MCLIP

Site libraries

- Horsted Centre, University of Kent at Medway, Maidstone Road, Chatham, Kent ME5 9UQ
  ☎(01634) 830633 Ext 2315
  Information Officer S I Root
- Bridge Wardens' College, University of Kent at Canterbury, Clocktower Building, Chatham Historic Dockyard, Chatham, Kent ME4 4TF
  ☎(01634) 888999
  Information Assistant A Welsh
- University Centre Tonbridge, University of Kent at Canterbury, Avebury Avenue, Tonbridge, Kent TN9 1TG
  ☎(01732) 368449
  Library Supervisor D Straker

KING ALFRED'S COLLEGE, WINCHESTER

Library, King Alfred's College, Winchester, Sparkford Road, Winchester, Hants SO22 4NR
☎(01962) 827306
Fax (01962) 827443
url: http://www.lrc.wkac.ac.uk
Librarian D Farley BA(Hons) MCLIP (01962 827229; e-mail: d.farley@wkac.ac.uk)
Deputy Librarian Ms E Fletcher BA(Hons) MA (01962 827374; e-mail: e.a.fletcher@wkac.ac.uk)
School Resources Librarian Ms S Bunn BA MCLIP (e-mail: s.bunn@wkac.ac.uk)

KINGSTON UNIVERSITY

Department of Library and Media Services, Kingston University, Penrhyn Road, Kingston upon Thames, Surrey KT1 2EE
☎020 8547 7101 (enquiries), 020 8547 7105 (administration)
Fax 020 8547 7111

e-mail: library@kingston.ac.uk
url: http://www.kingston.ac.uk/library_media/
Head of Library and Media Services Vacant

Site libraries

- University Library, Kingston University, Kingston Hill, Kingston upon Thames, Surrey KT2 7LB
  ☎020 8547 7384
  Fax 020 8547 7312
  Librarian i/c Ms S O Robertson MCLIP (e-mail: s.robertson@kingston.ac.uk)
- University Library, Kingston University, Knights Park, Kingston upon Thames, Surrey KT1 2QJ
  ☎020 8547 8035
  Fax 020 8547 8039
  Librarian i/c Ms J Savidge MA MCLIP (e-mail: j.savidge@kingston.ac.uk)
- University Library, Kingston University, Penrhyn Road, Kingston upon Thames, Surrey KT1 2EE
  ☎020 8547 7101
  Fax 020 8547 8115
  Librarian i/c Mrs E Malone BA(Hons) DipLib MCLIP, Ms H Ward BA(Hons) DipLib (e-mail: e.malone@kingston.ac.uk; h.ward@kingston.ac.uk)
- University Library, Kingston University, Roehampton Vale, Friars Avenue, London SW15 3DW
  ☎020 8547 7903 (tel/fax)
  Librarian i/c W Downey BA MCLIP (e-mail: downey@kingston.ac.uk)

UNIVERSITY OF LANCASTER

University Library, University of Lancaster, Bailrigg, Lancaster LA1 4YH
☎(01524) 592517 (enquiries), (01524) 592537 (administration)
Fax (01524) 63806
url: http://www.libweb.lancs.ac.uk
University Librarian Ms J M Whiteside MA MCLIP FRSA (e-mail: j.whiteside@lancaster.ac.uk)

LEEDS METROPOLITAN UNIVERSITY

Learning and Information Services, Leeds Metropolitan University, Calverley Street, Leeds LS1 3HE
☎0113 283 7467 or 283 5968
Fax 0113 283 3123
url: http://www/lmu.ac.uk/lis/lss
Head of Learning Support Services P Payne BA MCLIP (0113 283 5966; e-mail: p.payne@lmu.ac.uk)
Electronic Services Development Manager Ms J Driver (0113 283 2600 ext 4733; e-mail: j.driver@lmu.ac.uk)

Campus libraries

- The Learning Centre, Leeds Metropolitan University, Leslie Silver Building, City Campus, Calverley Street, Leeds LS1 3HE
  ☎0113 283 3106 (counter), 0113 283 5450 (enquiries)
  Fax 0113 283 3123
  Learning Centre Manager Ms M Message BA MCLIP (0113 283 2600 ext 3975; e-mail: m.message@lmu.ac.uk)
- Beckett Park Learning Centre, Leeds Metropolitan University, Beckett Park, Leeds LS6 3QS
  ☎0113 283 3164 (counter), 0113 283 7467 (enquiries)
  Fax 0113 283 3211
  Learning Centre Manager Ms N Thompson MA(Lib) (0113 283 7468; e-mail: n.thompson@lmu.ac.uk)
- Harrogate College Learning Resource Centre, Leeds Metropolitan University, Hornbeam Park, Harrogate HG2 8QT
  ☎(01423) 878216/878213
  Learning Resources Manager A Sargeant MA BA(Hons) CertFE (01423 878282; e-mail: a.sargeant@lmu.ac.uk)

UNIVERSITY OF LEEDS

University Library, University of Leeds, Leeds LS2 9JT
☎0113 343 6388 (general enquiries), 0113 343 5507 (administration)
Fax 0113 343 5561
e-mail: library@library.leeds.ac.uk
url: http://www.leeds.ac.uk/library/library.html
The Librarian/Keeper of the Brotherton Collection Ms J Wilkinson BA DipLib DMS CNAA FCLIP FRSA (0113 343 5501)

UNIVERSITY OF LEICESTER

University Library, University of Leicester, PO Box 248, University Road, Leicester LE1 9QD
☎0116 252 2042 (general enquiries), 0116 252 2031 (Librarian's secretary)
Fax 0116 252 2066
e-mail: library@leicester.ac.uk
url: http://www.le.ac.uk/library/
Acting University Librarian Ms M Bettles

Site libraries

- Education Library, University of Leicester, 21 University Road, Leicester LE1 7RF
  ☎0116 252 3738
  Fax 0116 252 5798
  Librarian i/c R W Kirk BA MCLIP
- Clinical Sciences Library, University of Leicester, Clinical Sciences Building, Leicester Royal Infirmary, PO Box 65, Leicester LE2 7LX
  ☎0116 252 3104
  Fax 0116 252 3107
  Librarian i/c Ms L Jones MA DipLib MCLIP

UNIVERSITY OF LINCOLN
(formerly University of Lincolnshire and Humberside)

Learning Resources, University of Lincoln, Brayford Pool, Lincoln LN6 7TS
☎(01522) 886222 (general enquiries)
e-mail: phughes@lincoln.ac.uk
url: http://www.uln.ac.uk
Head of Learning Resources Ms M Anderson BA(Hons) MA

LIVERPOOL HOPE UNIVERSITY COLLEGE

Sheppard–Worlock Library, Liverpool Hope University College, PO Box 95, Hope Park, Liverpool L16 9JD
☎0151 291 2000 (issue desk), 0151 291 2001 (administration), 0151 291 2041 (enquiries), 0151 291 2038 (IT help desk)
Fax 0151 291 2037
url: http://www.hope.ac.uk/lib/lrd.htm
Director of Learning Resources Ms L J Taylor MEd BA MCLIP (0151 291 3528; e-mail: taylorl@hope.ac.uk)
Deputy Manager Learning Resources Ms S Murray MA BSc MCLIP (0151 291 2002; e-mail: murrays@hope.ac.uk)
Academic Services Managers Mrs A Duckworth BA MCLIP (0151 291 2008; e-mail: duckwoa@hope.ac.uk); Mrs R Keane MA BA BPhil DipLib MCLIP (0151 291 2008; e-mail: keaner@hope.ac.uk) (job-share)
Technical Services Manager Mrs C Hughes BA(Hons) MCLIP (0151 291 2016; e-mail: hughesc@hope.ac.uk)

LIVERPOOL INSTITUTE FOR PERFORMING ARTS

Learning Services, Liverpool Institute for Performing Arts, Mount Street, Liverpool L1 9HF
☎0151 330 3111
Fax 0151 330 3110
url: http://www.lipa.ac.uk
Director of Information Services and Technical Support K O'Donoghue BA MA DLIS CertEd (0151 330 3250; e-mail: k.odonoghue@lipa.ac.uk)
Learning Services Manager Ms C Holmes BA(Hons) PGDipLib (0151 332 3111; e-mail: c.holmes@lipa.ac.uk)

LIVERPOOL JOHN MOORES UNIVERSITY

Learning and Information Services, Liverpool John Moores University, Aldham Robarts Learning Resource Centre, Mount Pleasant, Liverpool L3 5UZ
☎0151 231 3544
Fax 0151 231 3113
Director of Learning and Information Services Ms M Melling BA PGDipLib MLib MCLIP (0151 231 3682; e-mail: m.melling@livjm.ac.uk)
User Services Manager G K L Chan MSc BSc MCLIP (0151 231 3178; e-mail: g.k.chan@livjm.ac.uk)

Site libraries

- Aldham Robarts Learning Resource Centre, Liverpool John Moores University, Mount Pleasant, Liverpool L3 5UZ
  ☎0151 231 3634/3701
  Fax 0151 707 1307
  Learning Resource Centre Manager K R Graham BA PGDipLib (0151 231 3436; e-mail: k.r.graham@livjm.ac.uk)
- I M Marsh Library, Liverpool John Moores University, Barkhill Road, Liverpool L17 6BD
  ☎0151 231 5216
  Learning Resource Centre Manager Mrs B J Badger BA DipLib MCLIP (0151 231 5300; e-mail: b.j.badger@livjm.ac.uk)
- Avril Robarts Learning Resource Centre, Liverpool John Moores University, Tithebarn Street, Liverpool L2 2ER
  ☎0151 231 4022
  Fax 0151 231 4479
  Learning Resource Centre Manager J W Ainsworth BA MCLIP (0151 231 4020; e-mail: j.w.ainsworth@livjm.ac.uk)

UNIVERSITY OF LIVERPOOL

University Library, University of Liverpool, Liverpool L69 3DA
☎0151 794 2679 (enquiries), 0151 794 2674 (administration)
Fax 0151 794 2681/5417
url: http://www.liv.ac.uk/library/libhomep.html
University Librarian Ms F M Thomson MA BLitt (e-mail: thomson@liverpool.ac.uk)

Site libraries

- Sydney Jones Library (Humanities, Social Sciences, Special Collections and Archives), University of Liverpool, Chatham Street, Liverpool L69 3DA
  ☎0151 794 2679
  Fax 0151 794 2681
  User Services Manager Ms C E Kay BA MA DipLib (e-mail: c.kay@liv.ac.uk)
- Harold Cohen Library (Science, Medicine, Engineering, Veterinary and Dental Science), University of Liverpool, Ashton Street, Liverpool L69 3DA
  ☎0151 794 5411
  Fax 0151 794 5417
  User Services Manager Mrs L F Oldham BA DipLib (e-mail: loldham@liv.ac.uk)
- Law Library, University of Liverpool, Chatham Street, Liverpool L69 3DA
  ☎0151 794 2832
  e-mail: qlis07@liv.ac.uk
  Law Librarian Mrs W Spalton BA DipLib MCLIP
- Education Library, University of Liverpool, 19 Abercromby Square, Liverpool L69 3DA
  ☎0151 794 2633
  Social and Environmental Studies Librarian Miss L Bryce BA MA (e-mail: lbryce@liv.ac.uk)
- Continuing Education Library, University of Liverpool, 126 Mount Pleasant, Liverpool L69 3DA

☎0151 794 3285
Liaison Services Librarian Vacant

LONDON GUILDHALL UNIVERSITY

London Guildhall University and the University of North London are merging on 1 August 2002, and will be known as London Metropolitan University from that date. London Guildhall buildings will become part of the London City Campus of London Metropolitan University and University of North London buildings will become part of the London North Campus. All telephone and e-mail addresses below will continue to operate for the next year. The new main phone number for the University is 020 7432 0000.

Library, London Guildhall University, Calcutta House, Old Castle Street, London E1 7NT
☎020 7320 1173 (administration), 020 7320 1185 (enquiries)
Fax 020 7320 1177
url: http://www.lgu.ac.uk/as/
Director of Academic Services Miss M E Castens BSc MA MCLIP DMS (e-mail: castens@lgu.ac.uk)
Head of Information Services and Learning Resources Ms A Constable BA DipLib MCLIP (e-mail: constabl@lgu.ac.uk)
Head of Information and Communication Technology Services J Robinson (e-mail: j.robinson@lgu.ac.uk)
Head of Corporate Information and User Services Ms C Saunders (e-mail: saun@lgu.ac.uk)

Site/departmental libraries

- Calcutta House Library, London Guildhall University, Old Castle Street, London E1 7NT
  ☎020 7320 1185
  Fax 020 7320 1182
  Learning Resources Manager Ms H Dalton BSc MCLIP
- Commercial Road Library, London Guildhall University, 41-71 Commercial Road, London E1 1LA
  ☎020 7320 1869
  Fax 020 7320 2831
  Learning Resources Manager Ms C Walsh
- Moorgate Library, London Guildhall University, 84 Moorgate, London EC2M 6SQ
  ☎020 7320 1567
  Fax 020 7320 1565
  Learning Resources Manager Ms D Pinfold

(See also The Women's Library in Selected Government, National and Special Libraries section)

THE LONDON INSTITUTE

Library, The London Institute, 65 Davies Street, London W1K 5DA
☎020 7514 6000
url: http://www.linst.ac.uk/library

Director of Library and Learning Resources Ms M J Auckland BSc MSc MCLIP (020 7514 8072; e-mail: m.auckland@linst.ac.uk)

College/site libraries

Camberwell College of Arts

Library, Camberwell College of Arts, The London Institute, 43-45 Peckham Road, London SE5 8UF
☎020 7514 6349
Fax 020 7514 6324
e-mail: pr-lib@linst.ac.uk
Head of Learning Resources Ms L Kerr BA PGDip (Photography) PGDip (Library & Archive Studies) MCLIP

Central Saint Martins College of Art and Design

- Library, Central Saint Martins College of Art and Design, The London Institute, Southampton Row, London WC1B 4AP
  ☎020 7514 7037
  Fax 020 7514 7033
  e-mail: sr-lib@linst.ac.uk
  Head of Learning Resources Ms P Christie BA MCLIP
- Library, Central Saint Martins College of Art and Design, The London Institute, 107 Charing Cross Road, London WC2H 0DU
  ☎020 7514 7190
  Fax 020 7514 7189
  e-mail: cx-lib@linst.ac.uk
  Site Librarian Ms A Huxstep BA(Hons) MA DipLib

London College of Fashion

Library, London College of Fashion, The London Institute, 20 John Princes Street, Oxford Circus, London W1M 0BJ
☎020 7514 7455/7543
Fax 020 7514 7580
Library Manager Ms D Mansbridge BA MA MCLIP (e-mail: d.mansbridge@lcf.linst.ac.uk)

Chelsea College of Art and Design

- Library, Chelsea College of Art and Design, The London Institute, Manresa Road, London SW3 6LS
  ☎020 7514 7773
  Fax 020 7514 7785
  e-mail: mr-lib@linst.ac.uk
  Acting Head of Learning Resources Ms E Ward BA MA MCLIP
- Library, Chelsea College of Art and Design, The London Institute, Hugon Road, London SW6 3ES
  ☎020 7514 7091
  e-mail: hr-lib@linst.ac.uk
  Site Manager Ms E O'Callaghan BA MCLIP

- Library, Chelsea College of Art and Design, The London Institute, Lime Grove, London W12 8EA
  ☎020 7514 7833
  e-mail: lg-lib@linst.ac.uk
  Site Manager Ms T Olsson MA MCLIP

London College of Printing

- London College of Printing, Library and Learning Resources, The London Institute, Elephant and Castle, London SE1 6SB
  ☎020 7514 6527 (enquiries), 020 7514 6581 (administration)
  Fax 020 7514 6597
  e-mail: ec-lib@linst.ac.uk
  Head of Learning Resources Ms E Davison BA MCLIP
- Library and Learning Resources, The London Institute, London College of Printing, Backhill, London EC1R 5LQ
  ☎020 7514 6882
  Fax 020 7514 6867
  e-mail: bh-lib@linst.ac.uk
  Site Manager P Mellinger MSc(Econ)

LONDON METROPOLITAN UNIVERSITY

See London Guildhall University and University of North London

London Guildhall University and the University of North London are merging on 1 August 2002, and will be known as London Metropolitan University from that date. London Guildhall buildings will become part of the London City Campus of London Metropolitan University and University of North London buildings will become part of the London North Campus. All telephone and e-mail addresses will continue to operate for the next year. The new main phone number for the University is 020 7432 0000.

UNIVERSITY OF LONDON

University Library, University of London, Senate House, Malet Street, London WC1E 7HU
☎020 7862 8500 (enquiries), 020 7862 8432 (administration)
Fax 020 7862 8480
e-mail: ull@ull.ac.uk
url: http://www.ull.ac.uk
University Librarian Mrs E-J Robinson BSc MCLIP FRSA (020 7862 8411; e-mail: erobinson@ull.ac.uk)
Senior Sub-Librarian, Academic Services P McLaughlin MA MCLIP (020 7862 8413; e-mail: pmclaughlin@ull.ac.uk)
Sub-Librarian, Administration, Planning and Resources Mrs G Duggett BA MA MSc FRSA (020 7862 8412; e-mail: gduggett@ull.ac.uk)
Sub-Librarian, Information Strategy S Clews MA DipLib (020 7862 8452; e-mail: sclews@ull.ac.uk)
Head of Historic Collections Services Mrs C Wise (020 7862 8471; e-mail: cwise@ull.ac.uk)

(Includes libraries of the Institute of United States Studies, the Institute for English Studies, the Institute of Romance Studies, and of the Australian and Canadian High Commissions)

Depository Library, University of London, Spring Rise, Egham, Surrey TW20 9PP
☎(01784) 434560 (tel/fax)
Depository Librarian T West BA MCLIP (e-mail: twest@ull.ac.uk/dpmail@ull.ac.uk)

UNIVERSITY OF LONDON

(College, Institute and Departmental)
Each College listed below is an independent self-governing institution funded, where applicable, by HEFCE, and awarding degrees of the University of London, of which each is a member.

Australian High Commission Library

See University of London, Senate House

Birkbeck College

Library, Birkbeck College, Malet Street, London WC1E 7HX
☎020 7631 6064 (administration), 020 7631 6063/6239 (enquiries)
Fax 020 7631 6066
e-mail: libhelp@bbk.ac.uk
url: http://www.bbk.ac.uk/lib/
Librarian Ms P Dolphin MA DipLib MCLIP (020 7631 6250; e-mail: p.dolphin@bbk.ac.uk)
Deputy Librarian Vacant

Site libraries

- Gresse Street Library, Birkbeck College, Gresse Street, London W1P 2LL
  ☎020 7631 6492/3
  Fax 020 7631 6435
  Librarian
- Faculty of Continuing Education Library, Birkbeck College, 39 Gordon Square, London WC1H 0PD
  ☎020 7631 6167
  Fax 020 7631 6163
  Librarian Ms E Charles MSc MCLIP
  (Postal address: 26 Russell Square, London WC1B 5DQ)

Canadian High Commission Library

See University of London, Senate House

Courtauld Institute of Art

Library, Courtauld Institute of Art, Somerset House, Strand, London WC2R 0RN
☎020 7848 2701 (enquiries), 020 7848 2645 (administration)
Fax 020 7848 2887
e-mail: booklib@courtauld.ac.uk
url: http://www.courtauld.ac.uk
Librarian Dr S M Price BSc MA MSc PhD MCLIP (020 7848 2705)

Goldsmiths College
Information Services Department, Goldsmiths College, New Cross, London SE14 6NW
☎020 7919 7150 (enquiries), 020 7919 7161 (administration)
Fax 020 7919 7165
e-mail: library@gold.ac.uk
url: http://www.goldsmiths.ac.uk/infos/lib/index.html
Director of Information Services Ms J G Pateman BSc

Heythrop College
Library, Heythrop College, University of London, Kensington Square, London W8 5HQ
☎020 7795 4250 (enquiries), 020 7795 4252 (administration)
Fax 020 7795 4253
e-mail: library@heythrop.ac.uk
url: http://www.heythrop.ac.uk
Librarian C J Pedley SJ BA(Econ) BA MTh ThM DipIM
Deputy Librarian M Morgan BA DipLib MCLIP

Imperial College of Science and Technology
Central Library, Imperial College of Science, Technology and Medicine, South Kensington, London SW7 2AZ
☎020 7594 8820 (enquiries), 020 7594 8816 (administration)
Fax 020 7594 8876
e-mail: library@ic.ac.uk
url: http://www.lib.ic.ac.uk
Director of Library Services Ms C Jenkins BA DipLib MCLIP (020 7594 8880; e-mail: c.jenkins@ic.ac.uk)
Assistant Director, e-Strategy, Information Resources and Systems Management (ESIRSM) Ms J Evans BA DipLib MCLIP (020 7594 8829; e-mail: janet.evans@ic.ac.uk)
Reader Services Sub-Librarian R Halls MA DipLib (020 7594 8823; e-mail: r.halls@ic.ac.uk)
Collections and Information Resources Sub-Librarian Ms J Yeadon BSc MSc MCLIP (020 7594 8840; e-mail: j.yeadon@ic.ac.uk)

Departmental libraries

- Aeronautics Library, Imperial College of Science, Technology and Medicine, London SW7 2BY
  ☎020 7594 5069
  Fax 020 7584 8120
  Librarian Ms E Corbett BA DipLib MCLIP (e-mail: e.corbett@ic.ac.uk)
- Chemical Engineering and Chemical Technology Library, Imperial College of Science, Technology and Medicine, London SW7 2BY
  ☎020 7594 5598
  Fax 020 7594 5604
  Librarian Ms E Corbett BA DipLib MCLIP (e-mail: e.corbett@ic.ac.uk)
- Chemistry Library, Imperial College of Science, Technology and Medicine, London SW7 2AY
  ☎020 7594 5736

Fax 020 7594 5804
Librarian Ms S Irwin MSc MCLIP (e-mail: s.irwin@ic.ac.uk)

- Civil Engineering Library, Imperial College of Science, Technology and Medicine, London SW7 2BU
☎020 7594 6007
Fax 020 7225 2716
Librarian Ms S Parry BLib MCLIP (e-mail: s.t.parry@ic.ac.uk)
- Electrical and Electronic Engineering Library, Imperial College of Science, Technology and Medicine, London SW7 2BT
☎020 7594 6182
Fax 020 7823 8125
Librarian Mrs E Haigh BA DipInfSci MCLIP (e-mail: e.haigh@ic.ac.uk)
- Materials Library, Imperial College of Science, Technology and Medicine, London SW7 2BP
☎020 7594 6751
Fax 020 7584 3194
Librarian Ms E Corbett BA DipLib MCLIP (e-mail: e.corbett@ic.ac.uk)
- Mathematics Library, Imperial College of Science, Technology and Medicine, London SW7 2BZ
☎020 7594 8542
Fax 020 7589 9463
Librarian A Clark BA DipLib (e-mail: a.clark@ic.ac.uk)
- Mechanical Engineering Library, Imperial College of Science, Technology and Medicine, London SW7 2BX
☎020 7594 7166
Fax 020 7594 8517
Librarian Ms A R Sage BA DipLib MCLIP (e-mail: a.sage@ic.ac.uk)
- Physics Library, Imperial College of Science, Technology and Medicine, London SW7 2BZ
☎020 7594 7871
Librarian Ms P Hatch BSc MA (e-mail: p.hatch@ic.ac.uk)

Medical libraries

- Library, Charing Cross Campus, Imperial College of Science, Technology and Medicine, Imperial College School of Medicine, The Reynolds Building, St Dunstan's Road, London W6 8RP
☎020 7594 0755
Fax 020 7594 0851
e-mail: librarycx@ic.ac.uk
Acting Campus Librarian P Morrell (e-mail: p.morrell@ic.ac.uk)
- The Library, Chelsea and Westminster Hospital, Imperial College of Science, Technology and Medicine, Imperial College School of Medicine, 369 Fulham Road, London SW10 9NH
☎020 8746 8107
Fax 020 8746 8215
e-mail: librarycw@ic.ac.uk
Librarian R Wentz DipLBibl (e-mail: r.wentz@ic.ac.uk)

- Wellcome Library, Hammersmith Campus, Imperial College of Science, Technology and Medicine, Imperial College School of Medicine, Du Cane Road, London W12 0NN
  ☎020 8383 3246
  Fax 020 8383 2195
  e-mail: libhamm@ic.ac.uk
  Acting Librarian Ms G Going (e-mail: g.going@ic.ac.uk)
- Library, National Heart and Lung Institute, Imperial College of Science, Technology and Medicine, Royal Brompton Campus, Imperial College School of Medicine, Dove House Street, London SW3 6LY
  ☎020 7351 8150
  Fax 020 7351 8117
  Librarian Miss R Shipton BA DipLib MCLIP (e-mail: r.shipton@ic.ac.uk)
- Library, St Mary's Campus, Imperial College of Science, Technology and Medicine, Imperial College School of Medicine, Norfolk Place, London W2 1PG
  ☎020 7594 3692
  Fax 020 7402 3971
  Librarian N Palmer BA MCLIP (e-mail: n.palmer@ic.ac.uk)
- The Michael Way Library, Imperial College of Science, Technology and Medicine, Silwood Park, Buckhurst Road, Ascot, Berkshire SL5 7TA
  ☎(01491) 829112
  Fax (01491) 829123
  e-mail: biosciencelibrary@cabi.org
  Senior Librarian Ms L Wheater (e-mail: l.wheater@ic.ac.uk)
- The Kempe Centre, Imperial College at Wye, Wye, Ashford, Kent TN25 5AH
  ☎020 7594 2915
  Fax 020 7594 2929
  Librarian Ms M Lucas (e-mail: m.lucas@ic.ac.uk)

Institute for English Studies

See University of London, Senate House

Institute of Advanced Legal Studies

Library, Institute of Advanced Legal Studies, University of London, School of Advanced Study, 17 Russell Square, London WC1B 5DR
☎020 7862 5800
Fax 020 7862 5770
e-mail: ials@sas.ac.uk
url: http://www.ials.sas.ac.uk
Librarian J R Winterton BA LLB MCLIP
Reader Services Manager D R Gee BA MA MCLIP
Head of Information Systems S J Whittle BA MA

Institute of Cancer Research

Library, Institute of Cancer Research, 237 Fulham Road, London SW3 6JB
☎020 7352 5946/8133 ext 5120
Fax 020 7352 6283
e-mail: fullib@icr.ac.uk

Librarian Vacant
Assistant Librarian Vacant

Site library
Library, Institute of Cancer Research, 15 Cotswold Road, Belmont, Sutton, Surrey SM2 5NG
☎020 7352 8133 ext 4230, 4430
Fax 020 8661 1823
e-mail: sutlib@icr.ac.uk
Assistant Librarian Mrs S Sugden MCLIP

Institute of Classical Studies

Institute of Classical Studies Library and Joint Library of the Hellenic and Roman Societies, Institute of Classical Studies, Senate House, Malet Street, London WC1E 7HU
☎020 7862 8709
Fax 020 7862 8724
url: http://www.sas.ac.uk/icls/
Librarian C H Annis MA MCLIP (e-mail: ch.annis@sas.ac.uk)

Institute of Commonwealth Studies

Library, Institute of Commonwealth Studies, School of Advanced Study, 28 Russell Square, London WC1B 5DS
☎020 7862 8842 (library enquiries)
Fax 020 7862 8820
e-mail: icommlib@sas.ac.uk
url: http://www.sas.ac.uk/commonwealthstudies/
Information Resources Manager Ms E Gwynnett BA DipLib (020 7862 8840; e-mail: erika.gwynnett@sas.ac.uk)
Deputy Information Resources Manager Vacant

Institute of Education

Information Services, Institute of Education, 20 Bedford Way, London WC1H 0AL
☎020 7612 6080 (enquiries)
Fax 020 7612 6093
e-mail: lib.enquiries@ioe.ac.uk
url: http://ioewebserver.ioe.ac.uk/ioe/index.html
Head of Information Services and Librarian Ms A Peters (020 7612 6052)

Institute of Germanic Studies

Library, Institute of Germanic Studies, 29 Russell Square, London WC1B 5DP
☎020 7862 8965 (administration), 020 7862 8967 (library)
Fax 020 7862 8970
e-mail: igslib@sas.ac.uk
url: http://www.sas.ac.uk/igs
Librarian W Abbey BA

Institute of Historical Research

Library, Institute of Historical Research, School of Advanced Study, Senate House, Malet Street, London WC1E 7HU

☎020 7862 8760
Fax 020 7862 8762
e-mail: IHR.Library@sas.ac.uk
url: http://www.history.ac.uk/ihrlibrary/
Librarian R Lyons BA DipLib

Institute of Latin American Studies
Library, Institute of Latin American Studies, School of Advanced Study, 31 Tavistock Square, London WC1H 9HA
☎020 7862 8501
Fax 020 7862 8971
e-mail: ilas.lib@sas.ac.uk
url: http://www.sas.ac.uk/ilas/
Latin American Bibliographer A Biggins BSc DipLib MCLIP (e-mail: alan.biggins@sas.ac.uk)
Information Resources Manager Ms E Gwynnett BA DipLib (020 7862 8840; e-mail: erika.gwynnett@sas.ac.uk)

Institute of Ophthalmology and Moorfields Eye Hospital
Joint Library, Institute of Ophthalmology and Moorfields Eye Hospital, 11-43 Bath Street, London EC1V 9EL
☎020 7608 6814
Fax 020 7608 6814
e-mail: ophthlib@ucl.ac.uk
url: http://www.ucl.ac.uk/ioo/library
Librarian Ms D Heatlie BA (020 7608 6815; e-mail: d.heatlie@ucl.ac.uk)
Assistant Librarian Mrs K Munro BA DipLib (020 7608 6814: e-mail: k.munro@ucl.ac.uk)

Institute of Psychiatry
Library, King's College Institute of Psychiatry, De Crespigny Park, London SE5 8AF
☎020 7848 0204
Fax 020 7703 4515
e-mail: spyllib@kcl.ac.uk
Librarian M Guha BA MCLIP
Deputy Librarian Ms C Martin BA MCLIP

Institute of Romance Studies
See University of London, Senate House

Institute of United States Studies
See University of London, Senate House

King's College London
King's College London, Strand, London WC2R 2LS
☎020 7848 2139/2140 (administration)
Fax 020 7848 1777

e-mail: libraryenquiry@kcl.ac.uk
url: http://www.kcl.ac.uk/iss
Director of Information Services and Systems A MacDougall MA PhD FRSA MCLIP
Director of Information Resources and Services Ms A Bell BA MA MCLIP
(There is no longer a library at this site. Library now located at Chancery Lane: see below)

For site information contact
Site Services Manager Mrs V Robertson BA MCLIP
☎020 7848 2424
Fax 020 7848 2277

Guy's Campus

- Information Services Centre, King's College London, New Hunt's House, London SE1 9RT
  ☎020 7848 6900
  Fax 020 7848 6743
- F S Warner Library and Information Centre, King's College London, Floor 18, Guy's Tower, Guy's Hospital, London SE1 9RT
  ☎020 7955 4238
  Fax 020 7955 4103

King's Denmark Hill Campus

- Library and Information Services Centre, King's College London, Weston Education Centre, Bessemer Road, London SE5 9PJ
  ☎020 7848 5541/5542
  Fax 020 7848 5550
- Maughan Library and Information Services Centre, King's College London, Chancery Lane, London WC2A 1LR
  ☎020 7848 2424
  Fax 020 7848 2277

St Thomas' Campus

- Medical Library, King's College London, Sherrington Building, St Thomas' Hospital, Lambeth Palace Road, London SE1 7EH
  ☎020 7928 9292 ext 2367
  Fax 020 7401 3932
- Calnan Library, King's College London, Institute of Dermatology, Block 7, St Thomas' Hospital, Lambeth Palace Road, London SE1 7EH
  ☎020 7928 9292 ext 1313
  Fax 020 7928 1428

Waterloo Campus

Information Services Centre, King's College London, Franklin-Wilkins Building, 150 Stamford Street, London SE1 9NN
☎020 7848 3000
Fax 020 7848 4290

London Business School

Library, London Business School, Sussex Place, Regent's Park, London NW1 4SA
☎020 7262 5050
Fax 020 7706 1897
e-mail: library@london.edu
LA-NET 79:LLA2027
url: http://www.london.edu/library/
Director, Information Systems R Altendorff
Head of Library Ms H Edwards BA MCLIP

Business Information Service, London Business School, Sussex Place, Regent's Park, London NW1 4SA
☎020 7723 3404
Fax 020 7706 1897
e-mail: infoserve@london.edu
url: http://www.bestofbiz.com/bis/
Manager Ms S Watt DipLib MCLIP

London School of Economics

British Library of Political and Economic Science, London School of Economics, 10 Portugal Street, London WC2A 2HD
☎020 7955 7229 (enquiries), 020 7955 7219 (administration)
Fax 020 7955 7454
e-mail: library.information.desk@lse.ac.uk
url: http://www.library.lse.ac.uk
Librarian and Director of Information Services Ms J M Sykes MA MLitt DipLib MCLIP (020 7955 7218; e-mail: j.sykes@lse.ac.uk)
Deputy Librarian Ms M P Wade BA DipLib MCLIP (020 7955 7224; e-mail: m.wade@lse.ac.uk)
Information Services Manager Ms K Sloss BA PGDip MCLIP (020 7955 7217; e-mail: k.sloss@lse.ac.uk)
Technical Services Manager G Price BA DipLib MCLIP (020 7995 6755; e-mail: g.price@lse.ac.uk)
User Services Manager Ms H Cocker BA MPhil (020 7955 6336; e-mail: h.cocker@lse.ac.uk)
Archivist Ms S Donnelly BA DipArchiveAdmin (020 7955 7223; e-mail: document@lse.ac.uk)
IT Support Manager T Green DipCompStud (020 7955 6140; e-mail: t.green@lse.ac.uk)

London School of Hygiene and Tropical Medicine Library

London School of Hygiene and Tropical Medicine, Keppel Street, London WC1E 7HT
☎020 7927 2276 (enquiries), 020 7927 2283 (administration)
Fax 020 7927 2273
e-mail: library@lshtm.ac.uk
url: http://www.lshtm.ac.uk/as/library/libintro.htm
Librarian and Director of Information Services R B Furner BA MSc MCLIP

London School of Jewish Studies

Library, London School of Jewish Studies, Schaller House, 44A Albert Road, London NW4 2SJ
☎020 8203 6427
Fax 020 8203 6420
e-mail: marilynk@lsjs.ac.uk
Head Librarian E Kahn JL
Assistant Librarians A Prys BA MPhil DipLib MCLIP, K Roberg BA, E Zimmels

Moorfields Eye Hospital

See University of London Institute of Ophthalmology and Moorfields Eye Hospital

Queen Mary

Library, Queen Mary University of London, Mile End Road, London E1 4NS
☎020 7882 3300 (enquiries), 020 7882 3302 (administration)
Fax 020 8981 0028
e-mail: library@qmul.ac.uk
url: http://www.library.qmul.ac.uk/
Director of Information Services B Murphy BA MCLIP (020 7882 5004; e-mail: b.murphy@qmul.ac.uk)
Main Library Manager N Entwistle BA MA MCLIP (020 7882 3304; e-mail: n.w.entwistle@qmul.ac.uk)
Medical Librarian P Hockney BSc MCLIP (020 7882 7114; e-mail: p.s.hockney@qmul.ac.uk)

Site libraries

- Medical and Dental Library (Whitechapel), Queen Mary University of London, Turner Street, London E1 2AD
  ☎020 7882 7115
  Fax 020 7882 7113
  e-mail: library@qmul.ac.uk
  Site Librarian Ms J Thomas BSc DipLib (020 7882 7116; e-mail: j.h.thomas@qmul.ac.uk)
- Medical Library (West Smithfield), Queen Mary University of London, West Smithfield, London EC1A 7BA
  ☎020 7601 7849
  Fax 020 7601 7853
  Site Librarian Ms M Montague BEd MCLIP (e-mail: m.b.montague@qmul.ac.uk)
- Medical Library (Charterhouse Square), Queen Mary University of London, Charterhouse Square, London EC1M 6BY
  ☎020 7882 6019
  Fax 020 7882 6053
  Site Librarian Ms F Moussavi BA MA DipLib (e-mail: f.moussavi@qmul.ac.uk)

Royal Holloway

Library, Royal Holloway, Egham, Surrey TW20 0EX
☎(01784) 443823 (enquiries), 443334 (administration)

Fax (01784) 477670
url: http://www.rhul.ac.uk (College); http://www.lb.rhul.ac.uk (Library)
Librarian and Deputy Director of Information Services Ms S E Gerrard BA DipLib MCLIP (01784 443330; e-mail: s.gerrard@rhul.ac.uk)
Academic Services Manager D Ward BA DipLib (01784 443123; e-mail: d.ward@rhul.ac.uk)
Services Manager (Operations) Dr C Grogan BMus PhD DipLIS (01784 414066; e-mail: c.grogan@rhul.ac.uk)

Music Library, Royal Holloway, Egham, Surrey TW20 0EX
☎(01784) 443560
Fax (01784) 477670
e-mail: library@rhbnc.ac.uk
Music Librarian Dr C Grogan BMus PhD DipLIS (01784 414066; e-mail: c.grogan@rhul.ac.uk)

Royal Veterinary College

Library, Royal Veterinary College, Royal College Street, London NW1 0TU
☎020 7468 5162
Fax 020 7468 5162
url: http://www.rvc.ac.uk
Deputy College Librarian D Walker BSc(Hons) DipLIS MCLIP (e-mail: dwalker@rvc.ac.uk)

Campus library

Hawkshead Campus Library, Royal Veterinary College, Hawkshead House, Hawkshead Lane, North Mimms, Hatfield, Herts AL9 7TA
☎(01707) 666214 (tel/fax)
College Librarian S Jackson MA MCLIP (e-mail: sjackson@rvc.ac.uk)

St George's Hospital Medical School

St George's Library, St George's Hospital Medical School, Hunter Wing, Cranmer Terrace, London SW17 0RE
☎020 8725 5466 (direct line)
Fax 020 8767 4696
url: http://www.sghms.ac.uk/depts/is/
Librarian and Director of Information Services Mrs S Gove BSc DipLib FLS FZS (e-mail: s.gove@sghms.ac.uk)

School of Oriental and African Studies Library

School of Oriental and African Studies, Thornhaugh Street, Russell Square, London WC1H 0XG
☎020 7898 4163 (enquiries), 020 7898 4160 (library office)
Fax 020 7898 4159
url: http://www.libenquiry@soas.ac.uk
Librarian and Director of Information Services K Webster BSc Mlib MCLIP HonFCLIP (e-mail: kw@soas.ac.uk)

Library Manager Ms K A McIlwaine BA(Oxon) MA MPhil (020 7898 4161; e-mail: am90@soas.ac.uk)

School of Pharmacy

Library, School of Pharmacy, 29-39 Brunswick Square, London WC1N 1AX
☎020 7753 5833
Fax 020 7753 5947
e-mail: library@ulsop.ac.uk
Head of Library and Information Services Mrs L Lisgarten BA MCLIP

University College London

Library Services, University College London, Gower Street, London WC1E 6BT
☎020 7679 7700 (enquiries), 020 7679 7051 (administration)
Fax 020 7679 7373
e-mail: library@ucl.ac.uk
url: http://www.ucl.ac.uk/library
Director of Library Services P Ayris MA PhD MCLIP
Group Manager, Planning and Resources Mrs J Percival (020 7679 7791; e-mail: j.percival@ucl.ac.uk)
Group Manager, IT Services Mrs J Cropper MSc DipLib (020 7679 7373; e-mail: j.cropper@ucl.ac.uk)
Group Manager, Reader Services V Matthews BSc(Econ) MA MA PhD MCLIP (020 7679 2607; e-mail: v.matthews@ucl.ac.uk)
Group Manager, Bibliographic Services Ms D Mercer MSc DipLib (020 7679 2625; e-mail: d.mercer@ucl.ac.uk)

Sectional libraries

- Institute of Archaeology Library, University College London, 31-34 Gordon Square, London WC1H 0PY
  ☎020 7679 4788
  e-mail: library@ucl.ac.uk
  Librarian i/c R T Kirby MA
- Boldero Library, University College London, Middlesex Hospital, Mortimer Street, London W1P 7PN
  ☎020 7679 9454
  e-mail: bolderolib@ucl.ac.uk
  Librarian i/c Mrs P A Campbell BA DipInfSci
- Clinical Sciences (Cruciform) Library, University College London, Cruciform Building, Gower Street, London WC1E 6AU
  ☎020 7679 6079
  e-mail: clinscilib@ucl.ac.uk
  Librarian i/c Ms K Cheney
- Environmental Studies Library, University College London, Faculty of the Built Environment, Wates House, 22 Gordon Street, London WC1H 0QB
  ☎020 7679 4900
  e-mail: library@ucl.ac.uk
  Librarian i/c S Page BA(Hons) MSc

- Institute of Laryngology and Otology Library, University College London, Royal National Throat, Nose and Ear Hospital, Gray's Inn Road, London WC1X 8EE
  ☎020 7915 1445
  e-mail: iollib@ucl.ac.uk
  Librarian i/c A Stagg BA
- Institute of Neurology, University College London, Rockefeller Medical Library, The National Hospital, Queen Square, London WC1N 3BG
  ☎020 7829 8709
  Fax 020 7278 5069
  e-mail: library@ion.ucl.ac.uk
  Librarian Mrs L J Shepherd BA (e-mail: shepherd@ion.ucl.ac.uk)
- Institute of Orthopaedics Library, University College London, Royal National Orthopaedic Hospital, Brockley Hill, Stanmore, Middlesex HA7 4LP
  ☎020 8954 2300
  Fax 020 8954 1213
  Librarian i/c B Adams BA MSc
- Royal National Institute for Deaf People Library, University College London, Royal National Throat, Nose and Ear Hospital, Gray's Inn Road, London WC1X 8EE
  ☎020 7915 1553
  Fax 020 7915 1443
  Librarian i/c Ms M Plackett
- Human Communication Science Library, University College London, Chandler House, 2 Wakefield Street, London WC1N 1PF
  ☎020 7679 4210
  Fax 020 7713 0861
  e-mail: hcs.library@ucl.ac.uk
  Librarian i/c Ms S Russell
- Institute of Child Health Library, University College London, 30 Guilford Street, London WC1N 1EE
  ☎020 7242 9789 ext 2424
  Fax 020 7831 0488
  e-mail: library@ich.ucl.ac.uk
  Librarian i/c J Clarke
- Medical Library, Royal Free and University College Medical School, University College London, Royal Free Hospital, Rowland Hill Street, London NW3 2PF
  ☎020 7794 0500 ext 3202
  Fax 020 7794 3534
  e-mail: library@rfc.ucl.ac.uk
  Librarian Ms B Anagnostelis BSc(Hons) MSc DipLib (e-mail: b.anagnostelis@ucl.ac.uk)
- Library, School of Slavonic and East European Studies, University College London, 2nd Floor, Senate House North Wing, Malet Street, London WC1E 7HU
  ☎020 7862 8525
  e-mail: ssees-library@ssees.ac.uk
  url: http://www.ssees.ac.uk/libarch.htm
  Librarian and Director of Information Services Ms L Pitman BA DipLib
- Information Centre, Eastman Dental Institute for Oral Health Care Sciences, University College London, 256 Grays Inn Road, London WC1X 8LD

☎020 7915 1045/1262
Fax 020 7915 1147
e-mail: ic@eastman.ucl.ac.uk
Librarian H Lodge BLib MSc MCLIP (e-mail: h.lodge@eastman.ucl.ac.uk)

- Institute of Ophthalmology Library, University College London, 11-43 Bath Street, London EC1V 9EL
  ☎020 7608 6814 (tel/fax)
  e-mail: ophthlib@ucl.ac.uk
  Librarian Ms D Heatlie

Warburg Institute

Library, Warburg Institute, School of Advanced Study, Woburn Square, London WC1H 0AB
☎020 7862 8935 (reading room)
Fax 020 7862 8939
e-mail: warblib@sas.ac.uk
url: http://www.sas.ac.uk/warburg/
telnet (for library): library.sas.ac.uk
Librarian W F Ryan MA DPhil FSA FBA

LOUGHBOROUGH UNIVERSITY

Pilkington Library, Loughborough University, Loughborough, Leics LE11 3TU
☎(01509) 222360 (enquiries), (01509) 222341 (administration)
Fax (01509) 223993
e-mail: library@lboro.ac.uk
url: http://info@lboro.ac.uk/library/index/html
University Librarian Mrs M D Morley BA DipLib MCLIP

UNIVERSITY OF LUTON

Learning Resources Centre, University of Luton, Park Square, Luton, Beds LU1 3JU
☎(01582) 743262 (library), (01582) 489312 (administration)
Fax (01582) 489325
e-mail: lynda.boston@luton.ac.uk (administration)
url: http://www.luton.ac.uk/studentresources/lrc.shtml
Director of Learning Resources T Stone MA MCLIP

Site libraries

- Putteridge Bury Resource Centre, University of Luton, Hitchin Road, Luton, Beds LU2 8LE
  ☎(01582) 489079
  Fax (01582) 482689
  Academic Liaison Librarian (Luton Business School) Mrs A Stewart MCLIP (e-mail: audrey.stewart@luton.ac.uk)
- Healthcare Library, University of Luton, School of Community and Mental Health, Britannia Road, Bedford MK40 2NU
  ☎(01234) 792215
  Health Sites Service Manager Ms D Boden (e-mail: debbi.boden@luton.ac.uk)

- Healthcare Library, School of Acute Care/Midwifery, University of Luton, Luton and Dunstable Hospital, Lewsey Road, Luton, Beds LU4 0DT
  ☎(01582) 497296
  Health Sites Service Manager Ms D Boden (e-mail: debbi.boden@luton.ac.uk)
- Healthcare Library, University of Luton, Lovelock-Jones Nurse Education Centre, Barracks Road, High Wycombe, Bucks HP11 1QN
  ☎(01494) 425137
  Health Studies Librarian Ms D Boden (e-mail: debbi.boden@luton.ac.uk)
- Healthcare Library, University of Luton, Nuffield Research Centre, Stoke Mandeville Hospital, Mandeville Road, Aylesbury, Bucks HP21 8AL
  ☎(01296) 315900
  Health Studies Librarian Ms D Boden (e-mail: debbi.boden@luton.ac.uk)

MANCHESTER BUSINESS SCHOOL

Library and Information Service, Manchester Business School, Booth Street West, Manchester M15 6PB
☎0161 275 6507 (enquiries), 0161 275 6500 (administration)
Fax 0161 275 6505
url: http://www.mbs.ac.uk/lis
Librarian and Information Services Manager Miss K Kirby MA MCLIP PGCE (e-mail: kkirby@man.mbs.ac.uk)

MANCHESTER METROPOLITAN UNIVERSITY

Library, Manchester Metropolitan University, All Saints, Manchester M15 6BH
☎0161 247 3096
Fax 0161 247 6349
url: http://www.mmu.ac.uk/services/library/lib2.htm
Chief Librarian Professor C G S Harris BA MA MLS BPhil PhD FCLIP FRSA (0161 247 6100; e-mail: c.harris@mmu.ac.uk)
Deputy Librarian Mrs G R Barry BA MSc MCLIP (Head of Reader Services) (0161 247 6101, e-mail: g.r.barry@mmu.ac.uk)
Faculty Librarian (Crewe & Alsager) Dr M Robinson BA DipLib (0161 247 5138; e-mail: m.g.robinson@mmu.ac.uk)

Site libraries

- Alsager Library, Manchester Metropolitan University, Hassall Road, Alsager, Stoke-on-Trent, Staffs ST7 2HL
  ☎0161 247 5356
  Site Manager Ms M Pickstone BSc DipLib MCLIP (0161 247 5355; e-mail: m.pickstone@mmu.ac.uk)
- Aytoun Library, Manchester Metropolitan University, Aytoun Street, Manchester M1 3GH
  ☎0161 247 3093
  Site Librarian Mrs K Morrison BA MCLIP (0161 247 3091; e-mail: k.morrison@mmu.ac.uk)
- Crewe Library, Manchester Metropolitan University, Crewe Green Road, Crewe, Cheshire CW1 1DU

☎0161 247 5002
Site Manager Mrs F Hughes BA MLib MCLIP (0161 247 5012; e-mail: f.hughes@mmu.ac.uk)

- Didsbury Library, Manchester Metropolitan University, 799 Wilmslow Road, Manchester M20 8RR
☎0161 247 6126
Site Librarian Ms J Evans BA Mlib (0161 247 6120; e-mail: j.e.h.evans@mmu.ac.uk)
- Elizabeth Gaskell Library, Manchester Metropolitan University, Hathersage Road, Manchester M13 0JA
☎0161 247 6134
Site Librarian Ms A Mackenzie BA MCLIP (0161 247 6561; e-mail: a.mackenzie@mmu.ac.uk)
- Hollings Library, Manchester Metropolitan University, Old Hall Lane, Manchester M14 6HR
☎0161 247 6119
Site Librarian Ms D Massam BA MCLIP (0161 247 6118; e-mail: d.massam@mmu.ac.uk)

UNIVERSITY OF MANCHESTER

The John Rylands University Library of Manchester, University of Manchester, Main Library, Oxford Road, Manchester M13 9PP
☎0161 275 3738 (enquiries), 0161 275 3760 (administration)
Fax 0161 273 7488
url: http://rylibweb.man.ac.uk/
Director and University Librarian W G Simpson BA MA MCLIP FRSA

Books and Special Collections Library, John Rylands University Library, University of Manchester, 150 Deansgate, Manchester M3 3EH
☎0161 834 5343/6765
Fax 0161 834 5574
Librarian W G Simpson BA MA MCLIP FRSA

See also UMIST

MIDDLESEX UNIVERSITY

Library Services, Middlesex University, Level 5 Bounds Green Road, London N11 2NQ
☎020 8411 5234
Fax 020 8411 5163
url: http://www.mdx.ac.uk/ilrs/lib/libinfo.htm
Head of ILRS and University Librarian W A J Marsterson MA MCLIP (020 8411 5234; e-mail: w.marsterson@mdx.ac.uk)
Assistant Head of ILRS Ms J Cattermole BA MCLIP (020 8411 6947; e-mail: j.cattermole@mdx.ac.uk)

Bibliographical Services, Middlesex University, Bounds Green Road, London N11 2NQ
☎020 8411 5254 (direct)
e-mail: libbg1@mdx.ac.uk
Bibliographical Services Librarian Mrs E M Barton BSc MCLIP

Campus libraries

- Library, Middlesex University at Bounds Green, Middlesex University, Bounds Green Road, London N11 2NQ
  ☎020 8411 5240 (direct)
  e-mail: libbg1@mdx.ac.uk
  Campus Librarian Ms S Fellows BA MCLIP
- Library, Middlesex University at Cat Hill, Middlesex University, Barnet, Herts EN4 8HT
  ☎020 8411 5042 (direct)
  e-mail: libch1@mdx.ac.uk
  Campus Librarian Vacant
- Library, Middlesex University at Enfield, Middlesex University, Queensway, Enfield, Middlesex EN3 4SF
  ☎020 8411 5334 (direct)
  e-mail: liben1@mdx.ac.uk
  Campus Librarian Ms K McGowan MA MCLIP
- Library, Middlesex University at Hendon, Middlesex University, The Burroughs, London NW4 4BT
  ☎020 8411 5852 (direct)
  e-mail: libhe1@mdx.ac.uk
  Campus Librarian Ms H Cummings BSc
- Library, Middlesex University at Quicksilver Place, Middlesex University, Western Road, London N22 6XH
  ☎020 8411 5000 ext 2139
  e-mail: libqp1@mdx.ac.uk
  Assistant Librarian Ms M Brownlie BA
- Library, Middlesex University at Tottenham, Middlesex University, White Hart Lane, London N17 8HR
  ☎020 8411 5165
  e-mail: libtm1@mdx.ac.uk
  Campus Librarian Vacant
- Library, Middlesex University at Trent Park, Middlesex University, Bramley Road, London N14 4XS
  ☎020 8411 5646 (direct)
  e-mail: libtp1@mdx.ac.uk
  Campus Librarian Ms R Sinden-Evans BA MA BMus MMus MCLIP
- Health Campus Library, Middlesex University, Chase Farm Education Centre, Chase Farm Hospital, The Ridgeway, Enfield, Middlesex EN2 8JL
  ☎020 8366 9112
  e-mail: libcf1@mdx.ac.uk
  Campus Librarian Ms S Hill BA DMS MCLIP
- Health Campus Library, Middlesex University, Royal Free Education Centre, Royal Free Hospital, Pond Street, London NW3 2XA
  ☎020 7830 2788
  e-mail: librf1@mdx.ac.uk
  Site Librarian Ms C May BA
- Library, Middlesex University, London College of Dance, 10 Linden Road, Bedford MK40 2DA

☎(01234) 213331
Librarian i/c Ms D Bennett BA MCLIP

(The Health Campus libraries are also served by multidisciplinary libraries at: David Ferriman Library, North Middlesex Hospital, Sterling Way, London N18 1QX (020 8887 2223; e-mail: libnm1@mdx.ac.uk, libnm2@mdx.ac.uk) and The Archway Healthcare Library, Holborn Union Building, The Archway Campus, Highgate Hill, London N19 3UA (020 7288 3567; e-mail: libwh1@mdx.ac.uk, libwh2@mdx.ac.uk)

NAPIER UNIVERSITY

Main learning centre

Sighthill Learning Centre, Napier University, Sighthill Court, Edinburgh EH11 4BN
☎0131 455 3426 (enquiries)
Fax 0131 455 3428
url: http://www.napier.ac.uk/
Director of Learning Information Services C Pinder BA MLib DipLib MCLIP (0131 455 3301)
Head of Customer Services and Deputy Director M Lobban MA DipLib DipEdTech MCLIP (0131 455 3508)
Head of Information Services M Jones BA DipLib MCLIP (0131 455 2693)
Head of Resource Management and Development G S Forbes BA MA MBA MCLIP (0131 455 3558)
External Support Adviser J White MA MBA DipLib MCLIP (0131 455 2580)
Research and Projects Manager G Dunsire BSc MCLIP (0131 455 3427)
Research Support Adviser Dr D Cumming BSc DipLib MLib PhD FGS MCLIP (0131 455 2367; fax 0131 455 2358)

Campus learning centres

- Sighthill Learning Centre, Napier University, Sighthill, Edinburgh EH11 4BN
  ☎0131 455 3426
  Fax 0131 455 3428
  Librarian
- Canaan Lane Learning Centre, Napier University, 74 Canaan Lane, Edinburgh EH10 4TB
  ☎0131 536 5616
  Fax 0131 536 5608
  Librarian
- Comely Bank Learning Centre, Napier University, 13 Crewe Road South, Edinburgh EH4 2LD
  ☎0131 343 7919
  Fax 0131 343 7958
  Librarian
- Craighouse Learning Centre, Napier University, Craighouse Road, Edinburgh EH10 5LG
  ☎0131 455 6020
  Fax 0131 455 6022
  Librarian
- Livingston Learning Centre, Napier University, Education Centre, St John's Hospital, Howden Road West, Livingston EH54 6PP

☎(01506) 422831
Fax (01506) 422833
Librarian

- Melrose Learning Centre, Napier University, Education Centre, Borders General Hospital, Melrose TD6 9BD
  ☎(01896) 661632
  Fax (01896) 823869
  Librarian
- Merchiston Learning Centre, Napier University, 10 Colinton Road, Edinburgh EH10 5DT
  ☎0131 455 2582
  Fax 0131 455 2377
  Librarian

UNIVERSITY OF NEWCASTLE UPON TYNE

Robinson Library, University of Newcastle upon Tyne, Newcastle upon Tyne NE2 4HQ
☎0191 222 7662 (enquiries), 0191 222 7674 (administration)
Fax 0191 222 6235
e-mail: library@newcastle.ac.uk
url: http://www.ncl.ac.uk/library/
Librarian T W Graham MA PhD DipLib MCLIP

Divisional libraries

- The Walton Library (Medical and Dental), University of Newcastle upon Tyne, The Medical School, Framlington Place, Newcastle upon Tyne NE2 4HH
  ☎0191 222 7550
  Librarian Mrs H MacFarlane BA DipLib MCLIP
- Law Library, University of Newcastle upon Tyne, School of Law, 22-24 Windsor Terrace, Newcastle upon Tyne NE1 7RU
  ☎0191 222 7944
  Librarian Mrs L Kelly BA MCLIP

NEWMAN COLLEGE OF HIGHER EDUCATION

Library, Newman College of Higher Education, Genners Lane, Bartley Green, Birmingham B32 3NT
☎0121 476 1181 ext 2208
e-mail: library@newman.ac.uk
url: http://www.newman.ac.uk/nw3/library
Director of Library and Learning Support Mrs J C Bell BEd PGDipLIS MCLIP (ext 2327; e-mail: j.c.bell@newman.ac.uk)
Senior Assistant Librarian Miss A Huggan BA MA

NORTH EAST WALES INSTITUTE OF HIGHER EDUCATION

Information and Student Services, North East Wales Institute of Higher Education, Plas Coch, Mold Road, Wrexham LL11 2AW

☎(01978) 293250
Fax (01978) 293254
url: http;//www.newi.ac.uk
User Services Manager P Jeorrett BA MCLIP (e-mail: p.jeorrett@newi.ac.uk)

UNIVERSITY OF NORTH LONDON

The University of North London and London Guildhall University are merging on 1 August 2002, and will be known as London Metropolitan University from that date. The University of North London buildings will become part of the London North Campus of London Metropolitan University and London Guildhall buildings will become part of the London City Campus. All telephone and e-mail addresses will continue to operate for the next year. The new main phone number for the University is 020 7432 0000.

Learning Centre, University of North London, 236-250 Holloway Road, London N7 6PP
☎020 7753 5170 (enquiries)
Fax 020 7753 7037
url: http://www.unl.ac.uk/library/
Director of Information Systems and Services R Williams BA MCLIP DipLib GradIPM (e-mail: r.williams@unl.ac.uk)
Library Services Manager Ms J Howell BSc(SocSci)Hons DipLib (e-mail: j.howell@unl.ac.uk)

Section libraries

- Academic Information Services Team, University of North London, 236-250 Holloway Road, London N7 6PP
  ☎020 7973 4888
  Fax 020 7753 7037
  Team Manager Ms S Davy BA MCLIP (e-mail: s.davy@unl.ac.uk)
- Circulation and Customer Services Team, University of North London, 236-250 Holloway Road, London N7 6PP
  ☎020 7753 3369
  Fax 020 7753 7037
- Learning Materials Team, University of North London, 236-250 Holloway Road, London N7 6PP
  ☎020 7753 3132
  Fax 020 7753 7037
- Ladbroke House Team, University of North London, Ladbroke House, 62-66 Highbury Grove, London N5 2AD
  ☎020 7753 5149
  Fax 020 7753 5100
  Team Manager Ms A Aungle BA MCLIP DipLib (e-mail: a.aungle@unl.ac.uk)
- European Documentation Centre, University of North London, 236-250 Holloway Road, London N7 6PP
  ☎020 7753 5142
  Fax 020 7753 7037
  Subject Librarian Ms J Bacchus BA(Hons) DipLib MCLIP (e-mail: j.bacchus@unl.ac.uk)

- Trades Union Congress Library Collections, University of North London, 236-250 Holloway Road, London N7 6PP
  ☎020 7753 3184
  Fax 020 7753 3191
  Librarian Ms C Coates MA MCLIP (e-mail: c.coates@unl.ac.uk)

UNIVERSITY COLLEGE NORTHAMPTON

Park Campus Library, University College Northampton, Boughton Green Road, Northampton NN2 7AL
☎(01604) 735500 ext 2477 (enquiries), ext 2046 (administration)
Fax (01604) 718819
url: http://www.northampton.ac.uk
Chief Librarian Ms H J Johnson BA MA MCLIP (ext 2045; e-mail: hilary.johnson@northampton.ac.uk)
Deputy Librarian A Martin BSc MA MCLIP (ext 2047; e-mail: andrew.martin@northampton.ac.uk)

Avenue Campus Library, Maidwell Building, St George's Avenue, Northampton NN2 6JD
☎01604) 735500 ext 3900
Fax (01604) 719618
Other details: as above

NORTHERN SCHOOL OF CONTEMPORARY DANCE

Library, Northern School of Contemporary Dance, 98 Chapeltown Road, Leeds LS7 4BH
☎0113 219 3020
Fax 0113 219 3030
url: http://www.nscd.ac.uk
Librarian Miss S King BA(Hons) (e-mail: samk@nscd.ac.uk)
Assistant Librarian Miss H Cox BA(Hons) (e-mail: hesterc@nscd.ac.uk)

NORTHUMBRIA UNIVERSITY
(formerly University of Northumbria at Newcastle)

Learning Resources Department, Northumbria University, City Campus Library, Ellison Place, Newcastle upon Tyne NE1 8ST
☎0191 227 4125 (enquiries), 0191 227 4143 (administration)
Fax 0191 227 4563
Director of Learning Resources Prof J Core

Site libraries

- Coach Lane Learning Resource Centre, Northumbria University, Coach Lane, Newcastle upon Tyne NE7 7XA
  ☎0191 215 6540
  Fax 0191 215 6560
- Carlisle Library, Northumbria University, Milbourne Street, Carlisle, Cumbria CA2 5UZ

☎01228 404660
Fax 01228 404669

- Longhirst Campus Library, Northumbria University, Longhirst Hall, Longhirst, Morpeth, Northumberland NE61 3LL
☎(01670) 795050
Fax (01670) 795052

NORWICH SCHOOL OF ART AND DESIGN

Library, Norwich School of Art and Design, St George Street, Norwich NR3 1BB
☎(01603) 610561
Fax (01603) 615728
url: http://www.nsad.ac.uk
Librarian T Giles BA (e-mail: tim.g@nsad.ac.uk)
Assistant Librarians Ms K Guiver MA MCLIP (e-mail: kitty.g@nsad.ac.uk), Ms J McLachlan BA(Hons) DipLIS (e-mail: jan.mc@nsad.ac.uk)

NOTTINGHAM TRENT UNIVERSITY

The Boots Library, Library and Information Services, Nottingham Trent University, Goldsmith Street, Nottingham NG1 5LS
☎0115 848 2175 (enquiries), 0115 848 6446 (administration)
Fax 0115 848 2286
url: http://www.ntu.ac.uk
Director of Library and Information Services Ms E Lines BSc MCLIP (e-mail: liz.lines@ntu.ac.uk)

Site libraries

- Clifton Campus Library, Nottingham Trent University, Clifton Lane, Nottingham NG11 8NS
☎0115 848 3570/3246
Fax 0115 848 6304
Information Manager Mrs C Coates BA MCLIP (e-mail: celia.coates@ntu.ac.uk)
- Brackenhurst Campus Library, Nottingham Trent University, Southwell, Notts NG25 0QF
☎(01636) 817049
Information Specialist Ms B Gibbs (e-mail: beth.gibbs@ntu.ac.uk)

UNIVERSITY OF NOTTINGHAM

Hallward Library, Information Services Directorate, University of Nottingham, University Park, Nottingham NG7 2RD
url: http://www.nottingham.ac.uk/is
Director of Information Services Ms K Stanton (0115 951 3502; e-mail: karen.stanton@nottingham.ac.uk)
Assistant Director, Customer Services S Smith (0115 951 3896; e-mail: stan.smith@nottingham.ac.uk)
Assistant Director, Research and Learning Resources S Pinfield MA MA MCLIP (0115 951 5109; e-mail: stephen.pinfield@nottingham.ac.uk)

Assistant Director, IT Systems Ms J Graves (0115 951 3352; e-mail: joyce.graves@nottingham.ac.uk)
Assistant Director, Planning and Quality Ms P Manning (0115 849 3251; e-mail: paula.manning@nottingham.ac.uk)

Library sites

- Hallward Library (Arts, Law, Social Sciences), University of Nottingham, University Park, Nottingham NG7 2RD
  ☎0115 951 4557
  Fax 0115 951 4558
- Hallward Library (Department of Manuscripts and Special Collections), University of Nottingham, University Park, Nottingham NG7 2RD
  ☎0115 951 4565
  Fax 0115 951 4558
  Keeper D B Johnston BA PhD DipLib (0115 951 4563)
- George Green Library of Science and Engineering, University of Nottingham, University Park, Nottingham NG7 2RD
  ☎0115 951 4570
  Fax 0115 951 4578
- Greenfield Medical Library, University of Nottingham, Queen's Medical Centre, Nottingham NG7 2UH
  ☎0115 970 9435
  Fax 0115 970 9449
- James Cameron-Gifford Library of Agricultural and Food Sciences, University of Nottingham, Sutton Bonington Campus, Sutton Bonington, nr Loughborough, Leics LE12 5RD
  ☎0115 951 6390
  Fax 0115 951 6389
- Djanogly LRC (Education, Business, Computer Science), University of Nottingham, Jubilee Campus, Wollaton Road, Nottingham NG8 1FF
  ☎0115 846 6700
  Fax 0115 846 6705
- School of Nursing Library (Derby), University of Nottingham, Derby Centre, Derbyshire Royal Infirmary, London Road, Derby DE1 2QY
  Librarian C James (01332 347141, ext 2561)
- School of Nursing Library (Mansfield), University of Nottingham, Mansfield Education Centre, Dukeries Centre, Kings Mill Hospital, Mansfield Road, Sutton-in-Ashfield, Nottinghamshire NG17 4JL
  Librarian S Carlile (01623 465634)
- Shakespeare Street Learning Resource Centre, University of Nottingham, Adult Education Centre, 14-22 Shakespeare Street, Nottingham NG1 4FQ
  Manager R Bell (0115 951 6510)

OPEN UNIVERSITY

Library, Open University, Walton Hall, Milton Keynes MK7 6AA
☎(01908) 653138
Fax (01908) 653571

e-mail: oulibrary@open.ac.uk
url: http://www.open.ac.uk/library
Director of Library Services Mrs N Whitsed MSc FCLIP (01908 653254; e-mail: n.whitsed@open.ac.uk)
Acting Assistant Director of Library Services Ms A Davies BSc MSc (01908 652057; e-mail: ann.davies@open.ac.uk)
Collections and Facilities Manager R Stubbs BA DMS (01908 653252; e-mail: g.r.stubbs@open.ac.uk)
Senior Librarian Ms E Simpson BA (01908 655703; e-mail: e.simpson@open.ac.uk)
Information Manager Ms L Wilks BA MA MCLIP (01908 653530; e-mail: l.j.wilks@open.ac.uk)
Library Manager, Building Project Ms M Hunt (01908 652672; e-mail: m.e.hunt@open.ac.uk)
Manager, Interactive Open Learning Centre and Media Archive Ms E Mallett (01908 659283; e-mail: e.a.mallett@open.ac.uk)

OXFORD BROOKES UNIVERSITY

Library, Oxford Brookes University, Gipsy Lane Campus, Headington, Oxford OX3 0BP
☎(01865) 483156 (enquiries), (01865) 483130 (administration)
Fax (01865) 483998
e-mail: library@brookes.ac.uk
url: http://www.brookes.ac.uk/services/library
Director of Learning Resources and University Librarian Dr H M Workman PhD MCLIP
Head of Academic Library Services Ms J Haines BLib MA DipM MCLIP
Head of Administration A Robbins BA MSc MCLIP

Site libraries

- Wheatley Library, Oxford Brookes University, Wheatley Campus, Wheatley, Oxford OX9 1HX
  ☎(01865) 485869
  Fax (01865) 485750
  Head of Learning Resources: Harcourt Hill and Wheatley Ms C M Jeffery BSc DipLib DMS MCLIP
- Harcourt Hill Library, Oxford Brookes University, Harcourt Hill Campus, Oxford OX2 9AT
  ☎(01865) 488222
  Fax (01865) 488224
  Head of Learning Resources: Harcourt Hill and Wheatley Ms C M Jeffery BSc DipLib DMS MCLIP

UNIVERSITY OF OXFORD

Bodleian Library, University of Oxford, Broad Street, Oxford OX1 3BG
☎(01865) 277000 (enquiries), (01865) 277170 (administration)
Fax (01865) 277182
e-mail: enquiries@bodley.ox.ac.uk

url: http://www.bodley.ox.ac.uk/
Director of University Library Services and Bodley's Librarian R P Carr BA MA HonDLitt FRSA
Deputy to the Director of University Library Services and to Bodley's Librarian Vacant

Libraries which are part of the Bodleian Library

- Bodleian Law Library, University of Oxford, St Cross Building, Manor Road, Oxford OX1 3UR
  ☎(01865) 271463
  Fax (01865) 271475
  e-mail: law.library@bodley.ox.ac.uk
  Librarian Miss B M Tearle LLB MCLIP
- Hooke Library, University of Oxford, Parks Road, Oxford OX1 3QP
  ☎(01865) 272812
  e-mail: hooke.library@bodley.ox.ac.uk
  Hooke Librarian Ms J K L Ralph MSc MCLIP
- Indian Institute Library, University of Oxford, Bodleian Library, Broad Street, Oxford OX1 3BG
  ☎(01865) 277082
  Fax (01865) 277182
  e-mail: indian.institute@bodley.ox.ac.uk
  Librarian Dr G A Evison MA DPhil MPhil
- Bodleian Japanese Library at the Nissan Institute, University of Oxford, 27 Winchester Road, Oxford OX2 6NA
  ☎(01865) 284506
  Fax (01865) 284500
  e-mail: japanese@bodley.ox.ac.uk
  Librarian Mrs I K Tytler MA
- Oriental Institute Library, University of Oxford, Pusey Lane, Oxford OX1 2LE
  ☎(01865) 278202
  Fax (01865) 278190
  e-mail: library@orinst.ox.ac.uk
  Librarian i/c M J Minty MA MCLIP
- Institute for Chinese Studies Library, University of Oxford, Walton Street, Oxford OX1 2HG
  ☎(01865) 280430
  Fax (01865) 280431
  e-mail: chinese.studies.library@bodley.ox.ac.uk
  Librarian i/c Minh Chung MA
- Philosophy Library, University of Oxford, 10 Merton Street, Oxford OX1 4JJ
  ☎(01865) 276927
  Fax (01865) 276932
  e-mail: philosophy.library@bodley.ox.ac.uk
  Librarian Dr H A Wait MA DPhil
- Radcliffe Science Library, University of Oxford, Parks Road, Oxford OX1 3QP
  ☎(01865) 272800

Fax (01865) 272821
e-mail: rsl.enquiries@bodley.ox.ac.uk
Keeper of Scientific Books Dr J M P Palmer PhD FCLIP MIIS

- Bodleian Library of Commonwealth and African Studies at Rhodes House, University of Oxford, South Parks Road, Oxford OX1 3RG
☎(01865) 270909
Fax (01865) 270912
e-mail: rhodes.house.library@bodley.ox.ac.uk
Librarian J R Pinfold MA
- Vere Harmsworth Library at the Rothermere American Institute, University of Oxford, South Parks Road, Oxford OX1 3TG
☎(01865) 282700
Fax (01865) 282709
e-mail: rhodes.house.library@bodley.ox.ac.uk
Librarian J R Pinfold MA

UNIVERSITY OF OXFORD

(College, Institute and Departmental)

All Souls College

Codrington Library, All Souls College, Oxford OX1 4AL
☎(01865) 279318
Fax (01865) 279299
e-mail: codrington.library@all-souls.ox.ac.uk
url: http://www.all-souls.ox.ac.uk
Librarian in Charge Dr N Aubertin-Potter BA PhD MCLIP

Balliol College

Library, Balliol College, Oxford OX1 3BJ
☎(01865) 277709
Fax (01865) 277803
e-mail: library@balliol.oxford.ac.uk
url: http://www.balliol.ox.ac.uk/library/library.html
Librarian Dr P A Bulloch MCLIP FSA
Assistant Librarian A Tadiello BA

Brasenose College

Library, Brasenose College, Oxford OX1 4AJ
☎(01865) 277827
Fax (01865) 277831
e-mail: library@bnc.ox.ac.uk
url: http://www.bnc.ox.ac.uk
Fellow Librarian Dr E H Bispham
College Librarian Mrs S Glen FCSD DipLib MCLIP
Assistant Librarian Ms L Kay

Campion Hall
Library, Campion Hall, Brewer Street, Oxford OX1 1QS
☎(01865) 286104
Librarian Dr N Tanner BTh MA DPhil FRHistSoc
Assistant Librarian L Weeks MA

Christ Church
Library, Christ Church, Oxford OX1 1DP
☎(01865) 276169
e-mail: library@christ-church.ox.ac.uk
url: http://www.chch.ox.ac.uk/library/
Assistant Librarians Mrs J E McMullin MA MCLIP, M E Phillips MA MA MCLIP

Corpus Christi College
Library, Corpus Christi College, Merton Street, Oxford OX1 4JF
☎(01865) 276744
Fax (01865) 276767
e-mail: library.staff@ccc.ox.ac.uk
url: http://www.ccc.ox.ac.uk/library/library.htm
Librarian i/c Miss J R Snelling MA MCLIP (e-mail: joanna.snelling@ccc.ox.ac.uk)
Senior Library Assistant Mrs G Beadnell MA BA (e-mail: gail.beadnell@ccc.ox.ac.uk)

Department of Educational Studies
Library, Department of Educational Studies, 15 Norham Gardens, Oxford OX2 6PY
☎(01865) 274028 (library)
Fax (01865) 274027 (department)
url: http://www.edstud.ox.ac.uk/library/webpage_main.htm
Librarian Ms J Reading MA MCLIP
Assistant Librarian Miss V Murray MA

Economics Library
Economics Library, Manor Road Building, Manor Road, Oxford
OX1 3UL
☎(01865) 271071 (Librarian), (01865) 271093 (library)
Fax (01865) 271072
url: http://www.ssl.ox.ac.uk
Social Studies Librarian Ms M Robb BS MA MLS MCLIP

Exeter College
Library, Exeter College, Turl Street, Oxford OX1 3DP
☎(01865) 279600 (switchboard), (01865) 279657 (direct)
Fax (01865) 279645
e-mail: library@exeter.ox.ac.uk
Fellow Librarian Dr J R Maddicott DPhil FBA
Sub-Librarian Ms J Chadwick

Faculty of Music
Faculty of Music Library, St Aldate's, Oxford OX1 1DB
☎(01865) 276146 (librarian), (01865) 276148 (enquiries)
Fax (01865) 286260
url: http://www.music.ox.ac.uk/library/
Librarian D J Wagstaff MMus MCLIP (e-mail: john.wagstaff@music.ox.ac.uk)

Green College
Library, Green College (at the Radcliffe Observatory), Woodstock Road, Oxford OX2 6HG
☎(01865) 274788 (library), (01865) 274770 (lodge)
Fax (01865) 274796
Assistant Librarian Ms G C Edwards BSc (e-mail: gill.edwards@green.ox.ac.uk)

Harris Manchester College
Library, Harris Manchester College, Mansfield Road, Oxford OX1 3TD
☎(01865) 271016 (enquiries), (01865) 281472 (administration)
Fax (01865) 271012
e-mail: librarian@hmc.ox.ac.uk
Librarian Ms S Killoran BA PGDipLib MCLIP

Hertford College
Library, Hertford College, Catte Street, Oxford OX1 3BW
☎(01865) 279409
Fax (01865) 279466
Fellow Librarian Dr S R West FBA
Librarian Mrs S Griffin BA DipLib (e-mail: susan.griffin@hertford.ox.ac.uk)

International Development Centre
Library, International Development Centre, Queen Elizabeth House, 21 St Giles, Oxford OX1 3LA
☎(01865) 273590
Fax (01865) 273607
e-mail: library@qeh.ox.ac.uk
url: http://www.qeh.ox.ac.uk/library/
Librarian and Information Services Manager Mrs S Allcock BSc
Deputy Librarian Ms G Short BEd

Jesus College
Library, Jesus College, Oxford OX1 3DW
☎(01865) 279704
Fax (01865) 279687 (attn. Librarian)
e-mail: library@jesus.ox.ac.uk
Fellow Librarian T J Horder MA PhD
College Librarian Miss S A Cobbold MA DipLib
Archivist Dr B Allen (01865 279761)
(The Fellows' Library is available to bona fide scholars only by prior appointment with the College Librarian)

Keble College
Library, Keble College, Oxford OX1 3PG
☎(01865) 272797
e-mail: library@keb.ox.ac.uk
Librarian Mrs M A Sarosi BA HDipLib

Lady Margaret Hall
Library, Lady Margaret Hall, Norham Gardens, Oxford OX2 6QA
☎(01865) 274361
Fax (01865) 270708
Librarian Miss R Staples BA (e-mail: roberta.staples@lmh.ox.ac.uk)
Archivist Mrs J Courtenay BA
(The library is for the use of members of college only, though bona fide researchers may be allowed access to books by arrangement with the Librarian)

Linacre College
Library, Linacre College, St Cross Road, Oxford OX1 3JA
☎(01865) 271661
Fax (01865) 271668
e-mail: library@linacre.ox.ac.uk
Fellow Librarian Ms M Robb BS MLS MCLIP
Assistant Librarian Miss L Trevelyan (e-mail: louise.trevelyan@linacre.ox.ac.uk)

Lincoln College
Library, Lincoln College, Turl Street, Oxford OX1 3DR
☎(01865) 279831
e-mail: library@lincoln.ox.ac.uk
Librarian Mrs F Piddock BA DipLib

Magdalen College
Library, Magdalen College, Oxford OX1 4AU
☎(01865) 276045 (enquiries)
Fax (01865) 276057
e-mail: magdlib@ermine.ox.ac.uk
Fellow Librarian Dr C Y Ferdinand BA MA MA MA DPhil
Assistant Librarian Ms K S Speirs BA BA MSt MLIS

Mansfield College
Library, Mansfield College, Mansfield Road, Oxford OX1 3TF
☎(01865) 270975
Fax (01865) 270970
Fellow Librarian Professor M S Freeden DPhil (01865 270977)
Librarian Ms A Jenner (e-mail: alma.jenner@mansfield.ox.ac.uk)

Merton College
Library, Merton College, Oxford OX1 4JD
☎(01865) 276380

Fax (01865) 276361
e-mail: library@admin.merton.ox.ac.uk
url: http://www.merton.ox.ac.uk/college/library.html
Librarian Dr J C Walworth BA MA PhD
Assistant Librarian Ms C Ross BA DipLib MCLIP

New College

Library, New College, Oxford OX1 3BN
((01865) 279580 (enquiries & administration)
Fax (01865) 279590
Librarian Mrs N van Loo MA BA MCLIP (e-mail: naomi.vanloo@new.ox.ac.uk)

Nuffield College

Library, Nuffield College, New Road, Oxford OX1 1NF
☎(01865) 278550
Fax (01865) 278621
url: http://www.nuff.ox.ac.uk/library
Librarian E Martin DipLib MA MCLIP (e-mail: librarian@nuf.ox.ac.uk)

Oriel College

Library, Oriel College, Oxford OX1 4EW
☎(01865) 276558
e-mail: library@oriel.ox.ac.uk
Librarian Ms M Szurko BA MRef DipLib MCLIP

Pembroke College

McGowin Library, Pembroke College, Oxford OX1 1DW
☎(01865) 276409
Fax (01865) 276418
e-mail: library@pembroke.oxford.ac.uk
url: http://www.pmb.ox.ac.uk/library/library.html
Fellow Librarian Dr C Melchert BA MA PhD
Librarian Miss E J Pike MA(Oxon) MSc

Plant Sciences Library and Oxford Forest Information Service

Plant Sciences Library and Oxford Forest Information Service, South Parks Road, Oxford OX1 3RB
☎(01865) 275082
Fax (01865) 275095
e-mail: enquiries@plantlib.ox.ac.uk
url: http://www.plantlib.ox.ac.uk
Librarian R A Mills MA MCLIP

Politics, International Relations and Sociology Library

Politics, International Relations and Sociology Library, Politics/IR Department, George Street, Oxford OX1 2RL
☎(01865) 278710

Fax (01865) 278711
e-mail: library@socstud.ox.ac.uk
url: http://www.ssl.ox.ac.uk
Social Studies Librarian Ms M Robb BS MA MLS MCLIP (e-mail: margaret.robb@socstud.ox.ac.uk)

Queen's College

Library, Queen's College, Oxford OX1 4AW
☎(01865) 279130
Fax (01865) 790819
e-mail: library@queens.ox.ac.uk
Librarian Ms A Saville MA MCLIP (01865 279213)
Assistant Librarian (Administration) Ms T M Shaw
Assistant Librarian (Cataloguing & Cataloguer of College Paintings) Mrs V Vernier
Fellow Librarian Dr W J Blair

Refugee Studies Centre

Library, Refugee Studies Centre, Queen Elizabeth House, 21 St Giles, Oxford OX1 3LA
☎(01865) 270298
Fax (01865) 270721
e-mail: rsclib@qeh.ox.ac.uk
url: http://www.bodley.ox.ac.uk/rsc/
Librarian Ms S Rhodes BA DipLib MA
Assistant Librarian Ms J Soedring BSc(Hons)

Regent's Park College

Library, Regent's Park College, Pusey Street, Oxford OX1 2LB
((01865) 288120; (01865) 288142 (Angus Library direct line)
Fax (01865) 288121
url: http://www.rpc.ox.ac.uk/rpc/
Librarian Mrs S J Mills MA MCLIP (e-mail: sue.mills@regents-park.oxford.ac.uk)
Archivist Mrs J D Thorp BA (e-mail: jennifer.thorpe@regents-park.oxford.ac.uk)
(General College Library open to members of College only. The Angus Library, a research library for Baptist history, incorporating the former libraries of the Baptist Union of Great Britain and the Baptist Historical Society, and the archives of the Baptist Missionary Society on deposit, available by appointment to bona fide researchers.)

Sackler Library

Sackler Library, Oxford OX1 2LG
☎(01865) 278092
Fax (01865) 278098
url: http://www.saclib.ox.ac.uk
Librarian J Legg MA (e-mail: james.legg@saclib.ox.ac.uk)
(Access to the Library is limited to members of Oxford University and holders of Bodleian Library reader's tickets)

St Anne's College
Library, St Anne's College, Woodstock Road, Oxford OX2 6HS
☎(01865) 274810
Fax (01865) 274899
url: http://www.stannes.ox.ac.uk/college/services/library.htm
Librarian Dr D F Smith MA DPhil MCLIP (e-mail: david.smith@st-annes.ox.ac.uk)

St Antony's College
Library, St Antony's College, Oxford OX2 6JF
☎(01865) 274480
Fax (01865) 310518
Librarian R Campbell

St Benet's Hall
Library, St Benet's Hall, 38 St Giles, Oxford OX1 3LN
☎(01865) 280556 (Tel/Fax)
e-mail: henry.wansbrough@st-benets.ox.ac.uk
url: http://www.st-benets.ox.ac.uk
The Master

St Catherine's College
Library, St Catherine's College, Manor Road, Oxford OX1 3UJ
☎(01865) 271707
e-mail: library:ox.ac.uk
Librarian Dr A G Rosser MA PhD
Assistant Librarian Mrs S Collins

St Cross College
Library, St Cross College, St Giles, Oxford OX1 3LZ
☎(01865) 278481
e-mail: librarian@stx.ox.ac.uk
url: http://www.stx.ox.ac.uk
Librarian Mrs S L Allcock BSc

St Edmund Hall
Library, St Edmund Hall, University of Oxford, Oxford OX1 4AR
☎(01865) 279000
Fax (01865) 279062
e-mail: library@seh.ox.ac.uk
url: http://www.she.ox.ac.uk/index.cfm?do=library
Librarian Ms D Eaton BA MA
(The Library is for the use of members of St Edmund Hall only. Housed in 12th century church of historical interest. Visitors welcome but only by prior application to the Librarian; groups shown round only during vacations.)

St Hilda's College
Library, St Hilda's College, Oxford OX4 1DY

☎(01865) 276848/276849 (general enquiries)
Librarian Miss M Croghan MA MCLIP (e-mail: maria.croghan@st-hildas.ox.ac.uk)

St Hugh's College
Library, St Hugh's College, St Margaret's Road, Oxford OX2 6LE
☎(01865) 274900 (enquiries), (01865) 274938 (administration)
Fax (01865) 274912
e-mail: library@st-hughs.ox.ac.uk
url: http://www.st-hughs.ox.ac.uk
Librarian Miss D C Quare BA MLitt MCLIP

St John's College
Library, St John's College, Oxford OX1 3JP
☎(01865) 277300 (main lodge), (01865) 277330/1 (direct to library)
Fax (01865) 277435 (College office), (01865) 277421 (main lodge)
e-mail: library@fyfield.sjc.ox.ac.uk
Fellow Librarian Dr P M S Hacker MA DPhil
Librarian Mrs C E Hilliard MA MLIS
Library Administrator Mrs R Ogden BA DipLib

St Peter's College
Library, St Peter's College, New Inn Hall Street, Oxford OX1 2DL
☎(01865) 278882
Fax (01865) 278855
Librarian Mr A Ricketts MA(Oxon) DipLib(Wales) (e-mail: alistair.ricketts@st-peters.ox.ac.uk)

Somerville College
Library, Somerville College, Oxford OX2 6HD
☎(01865) 270694
Fax (01865) 270620
Librarian Miss P Adams BLitt MA DipLib (01865 270694; e-mail: pauline.adams@somerville.ox.ac.uk)
Assistant Librarian Miss S Purver MA DipLIS (01865 270694; e-mail: susan.purver@somerville.ox.ac.uk)

Taylor Institution
Library, Taylor Institution, St Giles, Oxford OX1 3NA
☎(01865) 278154 (office), 278158/278161 (main desk)
Fax (01865) 278165
e-mail: enquiries@taylib.ox.ac.uk
url: http://www.taylib.ox.ac.uk
Librarian Ms E A Chapman BA MA DipLib FCLIP

Templeton College
Information Centre, Templeton College, Kennington, Oxford OX1 5NY
☎(01865) 422564

Fax (01865) 422501
e-mail: infocent@templeton.oxford.ac.uk
Information Centre Team Leader Ms M Walker
(Restricted access: enquiries to Information Centre Manager)

Trinity College
Library, Trinity College, Oxford OX1 3BH
☎(01865) 279863 (enquiries & administration)
Fax (01865) 279911
Librarian Mrs J Martin MA (e-mail: jan.martin@trinity.ox.ac.uk)

University College
Library, University College, Oxford OX1 4BH
☎(01865) 276621
Fax (01865) 276987
e-mail: library@university-college.ox.ac.uk
url: http://www.lib.ox.ac.uk/guides/colleges/uni.htm
Fellow Librarian Dr T W Child MA BPhil DPhil(Oxon)
Librarian Miss C M Ritchie MA(Aber) MA(Lond) MCLIP

Wadham College
Library, Wadham College, Oxford OX1 3PN
☎(01865) 277900
Fax (01865) 277937
Librarian Ms S Bailey BA MA DipLib (e-mail: sandra.bailey@wadh.ox.ac.uk)

Wolfson College
The Library, Wolfson College, Oxford OX2 6UD
☎(01865) 274076
e-mail: library@wolfson.ox.ac.uk
url: http://www.wolfson.ox.ac.uk/library/
Fellow Librarian Dr S R J Woodell
Librarian Ms F E Wilkes BA MA DipLib MCLIP
(Open to members of College and Common Room only)

Worcester College
Library, Worcester College, Oxford OX1 2HB
☎(01865) 278354
Fax (01865) 278387
url: http://www.lib.ox.ac.uk/libraries/guides/WOR.html
Librarian Dr J Parker MA DPhil

UNIVERSITY OF PAISLEY

Library, University of Paisley, Paisley PA1 2BE
☎0141 848 3758 (enquiries), 0141 848 3751 (administration)
Fax 0141 887 0812
e-mail: library@paisley.ac.uk

url: http://www.library.paisley.ac.uk/libhome.htm
Librarian S James BA FCLIP FRSA (e-mail: stuart.james@paisley.ac.uk)

Site libraries

- Ayr Campus Library, University of Paisley, Beech Grove, Ayr KA8 0SR
  ☎(01292) 886000
  Fax (01292) 886006
  Librarian Ms T Gilbert BA DipLib (e-mail: teresa.gilbert@paisley.ac.uk)
- Library, University of Paisley, Royal Alexandra Hospital, Corsebar Road, Paisley PA2 9BN
  ☎0141 580 4757
  Fax 0141 887 4962
  Librarian Ms R Robinson BA DipLib MCLIP (e-mail: ruth.robinson@paisley.ac.uk)

UNIVERSITY OF PLYMOUTH

Library, University of Plymouth, Drake Circus, Plymouth, Devon PL4 8AA
☎(01752) 232323 (enquiries); (01752) 232352 (administration)
Fax (01752) 232340
url: http://www.plym.ac.uk
Director of Information and Learning Services R H Sharpe BSc MSc DMS (e-mail: rhsharpe@plymouth.ac.uk)
Head of Customer Services Ms P Holland BA DipLib MCLIP (e-mail: pholland@plymouth.ac.uk)
Head of Learning and Research Support Ms J Gosling BSc DipLib MCLIP (e-mail: jgosling@plymouth.ac.uk)

Campus libraries

- Library, University of Plymouth, Seale Hayne Campus, Newton Abbot, Devon TQ12 6NQ
  ☎(01626) 325828
  Fax (01626) 325836
  Campus Coordinator Mrs A Blackman BA MCLIP (e-mail: ablackman@plymouth.ac.uk)
- Library, University of Plymouth, Earl Richards Road North, Exeter, Devon EX2 6AS
  ☎(01392) 475049
  Fax (01392) 475053
  Campus Coordinator Mrs J Cartwright BA MCLIP (e-mail: jcartwright@plymouth.ac.uk)
- Library, University of Plymouth, Douglas Avenue, Exmouth, Devon EX8 2AT
  ☎(01395) 255332
  Fax (01395) 255337
  Campus Coordinator Ms R Smith BA(Hons) DLIS MCLIP (e-mail: rsmith@plymouth.ac.uk)

UNIVERSITY OF PORTSMOUTH

Frewen Library, University of Portsmouth, Cambridge Road, Portsmouth, Hants PO1 2ST

☎023 9284 3228/9 (enquiries), 023 9284 3222 (administration)
Fax 023 9284 3233
e-mail: library@port.ac.uk
url: http://www.libr.port.ac.uk
University Librarian I Bonar BSc MCLIP

QUEEN MARGARET UNIVERSITY COLLEGE

Library, Queen Margaret University College, Clerwood Terrace, Edinburgh EH12 8TS
☎0131 317 3300
Fax 0131 339 7057
e-mail: Library_Enquiries@qmuc.ac.uk
url: http://www.qmuc.ac.uk/lb
Librarian Mrs P Aitken BA AALIA (e-mail: paitken@qmuc.ac.uk)

Leith Campus Library

Library, Queen Margaret University College, Leith Campus, Duke Street, Edinburgh EH6 8HF
☎0131 317 3308
Fax 0131 317 3308
Librarian Miss V Cormie MSc MCLIP

QUEEN'S UNIVERSITY OF BELFAST

University Library, Queen's University of Belfast, Belfast BT7 1LS
☎028 9027 5020
Fax 028 9032 3072
url: http://www.qub.ac.uk/lib/
Director of Information Services N J Russell BA MPhil MCLIP (e-mail: n.russell@qub.ac.uk)

Site libraries

- Agriculture Library, Agriculture and Food Science Centre, Queen's University of Belfast, Newforge Lane, Belfast BT9 5PX
  ☎028 9025 5226
  Fax 028 9025 5400
  Agriculture Librarian K Latimer MA DipLibStud MCLIP (e-mail: k.latimer@qub.ac.uk)
- Medical Library, Institute of Clinical Science, Queen's University of Belfast, Grosvenor Road, Belfast BT12 6BJ
  ☎028 9026 3154
  Fax 028 9024 7068
  Medical Librarian G Creighton BA DipLibStud (e-mail: g.creighton@qub.ac.uk)
- Science Library, Queen's University of Belfast, Chlorine Gardens, Belfast BT9 5EQ
  ☎028 9033 5441
  Fax 028 9038 2636
  Science Librarian Ms S Landy BA DipLibStud (e-mail: s.landy@qub.ac.uk)
- Main Library, Queen's University of Belfast, Belfast BT7 1LS
  ☎028 9033 5023

Fax 028 9032 3340
Assistant Director (User Services) J McCurry BA DipLibStud (e-mail: j.mccurry@qub.ac.uk)

RAVENSBOURNE COLLEGE OF DESIGN AND COMMUNICATION

Library, Ravensbourne College of Design and Communication, Walden Road, Chislehurst, Kent BR7 5SN
☎020 8289 4900 ext 8117
Fax 020 8325 8320
Head of Library and Information Services Ms S Hocking BA MCLIP MA(Ed) (020 8289 4919; e-mail: s.hocking@rave.ac.uk)
Media Librarian P Rogers (e-mail: p.rogers@rave.ac.uk)
Information Services Officer Ms C Kennedy (e-mail: c.kennedy@rave.ac.uk)
Library Services Officer Ms R Todd BA MA (e-mail: r.todd@rave.ac.uk)

THE UNIVERSITY OF READING

Reading University Library, The University of Reading, Whiteknights, PO Box 223, Reading, Berks RG6 6AE
☎0118 931 8770 (enquiries), 0118 931 8773 (administration)
Fax 0118 931 6636
e-mail: library@reading.ac.uk
url: http://www.library.rdg.ac.uk
University Librarian Mrs J H Munro BSc MSc MBA MCLIP (0118 931 8774; e-mail: j.h.munro@reading.ac.uk)
Head of Collections Vacant
Head of Systems Miss C A Ayres BSc DipInfSc MCLIP (0118 931 8781; e-mail: c.a.ayres@reading.ac.uk)
Support Services Manager I J P Burn BA (0118 931 8775; e-mail: i.j.burn@reading.ac.uk)

Site libraries

- Bulmershe Library, The University of Reading, Bulmershe Court, Woodlands Avenue, Earley, Reading, Berks RG6 1HY
  ☎0118 931 8652
  Fax 0118 931 8651
  Institute of Education Librarian G Connell MA MSc MCLIP (0118 987 5123 ext 4820; e-mail: g.connell@reading.ac.uk)
- Music Library, The University of Reading, 35 Upper Redlands Road, Reading, Berks RG1 5JE
  ☎0118 931 8413
  Fax 0118 931 8412
  Music Liaison Librarian C B Cipkin BA MA ARCO MCLIP (0118 931 8413; e-mail: c.b.cipkin@reading.ac.uk)

COLLEGE OF RIPON AND YORK ST JOHN see YORK ST JOHN COLLEGE

THE ROBERT GORDON UNIVERSITY

The Georgina Scott Sutherland Library, The Robert Gordon University, Garthdee Road, Aberdeen AB10 7QE
☎(01224) 263451
Fax (01224) 263455
e-mail: library@rgu.ac.uk
url: http://www.rgu.ac.uk/library
Chief Librarian Mrs E M Dunphy MA MCLIP (e-mail: e.dunphy@rgu.ac.uk)
Depute Librarian Ms D M Devine MA MCLIP (e-mail: d.devine@rgu.ac.uk)
Senior Librarian Dr S Copeland MA MPhil PhD MCLIP (e-mail: s.copeland@rgu.ac.uk)
Senior Librarian Ms J Brown MA MCLIP (e-mail: j.brown@rgu.ac.uk)

Site library

St Andrew Street Library, The Robert Gordon University, St Andrew Street, Aberdeen AB25 1HG
☎(01224) 262888
Fax (01224) 262889
e-mail: library@rgu.ac.uk
url: http://www.rgu.ac.uk/library/
Site Librarian K Fraser BA DMS MCLIP (e-mail: k.fraser@rgu.ac.uk)

ROEHAMPTON UNIVERSITY OF SURREY
(formerly University of Surrey Roehampton)

Roehampton Lane Learning Resources Centre, Roehampton University of Surrey, Digby Stuart College, Roehampton Lane, London SW15 5SZ
☎020 8392 3700 (enquiries), 020 8392 3053 (administration)
Fax 020 8392 3259
e-mail: edesk@roehampton.ac.uk
url: http://www.roehampton.ac.uk/support/infoserv/index.asp
Director of Information Services Ms S Clegg BA MBA MCLIP (020 8392 3051; e-mail: s.clegg@roehampton.ac.uk)
Assistant Director P Scarsbrook BA MA (020 8392 3052; e-mail: p.scarsbrook@roehampton.ac.uk)
Assistant Director J Hill MSc (020 8392 3446; e-mail: j.hill@roehampton.ac.uk)
LRC Site Manager Vacant

Whitelands Learning Resources Centre, Roehampton University of Surrey, West Hill, London SW15 3SN
☎020 8392 3554
Fax 020 8392 3559
LRC Site Manager Vacant

ROSE BRUFORD COLLEGE

Library, Rose Bruford College, Lamorbey Park, Sidcup, Kent DA15 9DF
☎020 8308 2626 (enquiries), 020 8300 3024 (administration)
Fax 020 8308 0542
url: http://www.bruford.ac.uk
College Librarian J Collis BA MCLIP ARCM (e-mail: john@bruford.ac.uk)
Assistant Librarian Ms E Skedgell BA

ROYAL ACADEMY OF MUSIC

Library, Royal Academy of Music, Marylebone Road, London NW1 5HT
☎020 7873 7323 (enquiries & administration)
Fax 020 7873 7322
e-mail: library@ram.ac.uk
url: http://www.ram.ac.uk
Librarian Ms K Adamson BA MA DipLib

ROYAL AGRICULTURAL COLLEGE

Library, Royal Agricultural College, Stroud Road, Cirencester, Gloucestershire GL7 6JS
☎(01285) 655214 ext 2274
Fax (01285) 889844
e-mail: library@royagcol.ac.uk
Head of Library Services Ms S Howie BA MPhil DipLib MCLIP (01285 655214 ext 2276)

ROYAL COLLEGE OF ART

College Library, Royal College of Art, Kensington Gore, London SW7 2EU
☎020 7590 4224 (enquiries)
Fax 020 7590 4500
e-mail: info@rca.ac.uk
url: http://www.rca.ac.uk
Head of Information and Learning Services P Hassell MCLIP (e-mail: peter.hassell@rca.ac.uk)
Library Manager Ms P Rae (e-mail: pauline.rae@rca.ac.uk)

ROYAL COLLEGE OF NURSING OF THE UNITED KINGDOM

Library, Royal College of Nursing of the United Kingdom, 20 Cavendish Square, London W1G 0RN
☎020 7647 3610/3613
Fax 020 7647 3420
e-mail: rcn.library@rcn.org.uk
url: http://www.rcn.org.uk
Head of Library and Information Services J Lord BA(Hons) DipLib MCLIP
(Access for non-members is by appointment)

ROYAL COLLEGE OF MUSIC

Library, Royal College of Music, Prince Consort Road, London SW7 2BS
☎020 7591 4325
Fax 020 7589 7740
url: http://www.rcm.ac.uk
Chief Librarian Ms P Thompson BA (020 7591 4323; e-mail: pthompson@rcm.ac.uk)
Reference Librarian Dr P Horton (020 7591 4324; e-mail: phorton@rcm.ac.uk)

ROYAL NORTHERN COLLEGE OF MUSIC

Library, Royal Northern College of Music, 124 Oxford Road, Manchester M13 9RD
☎0161 907 5243
Fax 0161 273 7611
e-mail: library@rncm.ac.uk
url: http://www.library.rncm.ac.uk
Librarian Miss A E Smart BA MA MCLIP
Senior Assistant Librarian G Thomason MusB MusM ARCM LTCL DipLib

ROYAL SCOTTISH ACADEMY OF MUSIC AND DRAMA

Library, Royal Scottish Academy of Music and Drama, 100 Renfrew Street, Glasgow G2 3DB
☎0141 270 8268
Fax 0141 270 8353
e-mail: library@rsamd.ac.uk
url: http://www.rsamd.ac.uk
Head of Information Services G Hunt MA

RUSKIN COLLEGE

College Library, Ruskin College, Walton Street, Oxford OX1 2HE
☎(01865) 554331
Fax (01865) 554372
e-mail: library@ruskin.ac.uk
Librarian D Horsfield MA
(Admission by appointment only)

UNIVERSITY OF ST ANDREWS

University Library, University of St Andrews, North Street, St Andrews, Fife KY16 9TR
☎(01334) 462281 (enquiries & administration), (01334) 462280 (management)
Fax (01334) 462282
e-mail: library@st-and.ac.uk
url: http://www-library.st-and.ac.uk
Librarian Mr N F Dumbleton MA MA

COLLEGE OF ST MARK AND ST JOHN

Library, College of St Mark and St John, Derriford Road, Plymouth, Devon PL6 8BH
☎(01752) 636845 (enquiries), (01752) 636700 ext 4206 (administration)
Fax (01752) 636712
Director of Information Services F A Clements FCLIP (01752 636700 ext 4215; e-mail: fclements@marjon.ac.uk)
Librarian Mrs A Bidgood MCLIP (ext 4200; e-mail: abidgood@marjon.ac.uk)

ST MARTIN'S COLLEGE

Harold Bridges Library, St Martin's Services Ltd, St Martin's College (Lancaster), Bowerham Road, Lancaster, Lancashire LA1 3JD
☎(01524) 384243
Fax (01524) 384588
e-mail: library@ucsm.ac.uk
url: http://www.ucsm.ac.uk/users/library/
College Librarian D Brown BA MA MCLIP (01524 384238; e-mail: d.brown:@ucsm.ac.uk)

Site libraries

- Library, St Martin's Services Ltd, St Martin's College, St Martin's College (Ambleside), Rydal Road, Ambleside, Cumbria LA22 9BB
  ☎(01539) 305274 (tel/fax)
  e-mail: amb.library@ucsm.ac.uk
  Site Librarian Ms L Bruce BA DipLib MCLIP (01539 305244; e-mail: l.bruce@ucsm.ac.uk)
- Library, St Martin's Services Ltd, St Martin's College, St Martin's College (Carlisle), Fusehill Street, Carlisle, Cumbria CA1 2HG
  ☎(01228) 616218
  Fax (01228) 616263
  e-mail: car.library@ucsm.ac.uk
  Senior Information Officer Ms S Green BA MCLIP (01228 616219; e-mail: s.h.green@ucsm.ac.uk)

ST MARY'S COLLEGE, STRAWBERRY HILL

Learning Resources Centre, St Mary's College, Strawberry Hill, Waldegrave Road, Strawberry Hill, Twickenham, Middlesex TW1 4SX
☎020 8240 4097
Fax 020 8240 4270
e-mail: enquiry@smuc.ac.uk
url: http://www.smuc.ac.uk
Director of Information Services and Systems Ms M Lanigan BSc(Hons) DipLib (e-mail: laniganm@smuc.ac.uk)
LRC Systems Co-ordinator Ms C O'Sullivan BA MCLIP (e-mail: osullivc@smuc.ac.uk)
Assistant Director: Operations Mrs N Prieg (020 8240 4295; e-mail: priegn@smuc.ac.uk)

UNIVERSITY OF SALFORD

Information Services, University of Salford, Clifford Whitworth Building, Salford, Lancs M5 4WT
☎0161 295 5028
Fax 0161 295 5666
e-mail: advisor@salford.ac.uk
url: http://www.salford.ac.uk
Director of Information Services A M Lewis
Deputy Director Mrs M Duncan (0161 295 5180)

Campus libraries

- Academic Information Services, University of Salford, Clifford Whitworth Building, Salford, Lancs M5 4WT
  ☎0161 295 5848
  Fax 0161 295 5888
  Campus Manager Mrs J Berry (0161 295 5037)
- Academic Information Services, University of Salford, Allerton Campus, Frederick Road, Salford, Lancs M6 6PU
  ☎0161 295 2448
  Fax 0161 295 2437
  Campus Managers Mrs L Leader, Mrs J Wilson (0161 295 2440)
- Academic Information Service, University of Salford, Adelphi Campus, Peru Street, Salford, Lancs M3 6EQ
  ☎0161 295 6185
  Fax 0161 295 6189
  Campus Manager Ms G Barlow (0161 295 6187)
- Academic Information Services, University of Salford, Eccles Campus, Peel House, Albert Street, Eccles, Lancs M30 0NJ
  ☎0161 295 2747
  Fax 0161 295 2796
  Campus Managers Mrs L Leader, Mrs J Wilson (0161 295 2440)
- Academic Information Services, University of Salford, Irwell Valley Campus, Blandford Road, Salford, Lancs M6 6BD
  ☎0161 295 2633
  Fax 0161 295 2631
  Campus Manager Ms G Barlow (0161 295 6186)

SCOTTISH AGRICULTURAL COLLEGE

Library and Information Centre, Scottish Agricultural College, Edinburgh Campus, West Mains Road, Edinburgh EH9 3JG
☎0131 535 4117 (enquiries), 0131 535 4116 (administration)
Fax 0131 535 4246
url: http://www.sac.ac.uk/library/external/default.htm
Senior Librarian Mrs M Mullay MA MCLIP (e-mail: m.mullay@ed.sac.ac.uk)

Campus libraries

- Library, Scottish Agricultural College, Auchincruive Campus, Auchincruive, Ayr KA6 5HW
  ☎(01292) 525208
  Fax (01292) 525211
  Senior Librarian Ms E P Muir MA PGDipLib MCLIP (e-mail: e.muir@au.sac.ac.uk)
- SAC Library, Scottish Agricultural College, Ferguson Building, Craibstone Estate, Aberdeen AB21 9YA
  ☎(01224) 272600
  Fax (01224) 491989
  url: http://www.abdn.ac.uk/
  Librarian E Buchan BA(Hons) (e-mail: e.buchan@ab.sac.ac.uk)

SHEFFIELD HALLAM UNIVERSITY

Learning Centre, Sheffield Hallam University, City Campus, Sheffield S1 1WB
☎0114 225 2103
Fax 0114 225 3859
e-mail: learning.centre@shu.ac.uk
url: http://students.shu.ac.uk/lc/
Director, Learning Centre, and University Librarian G Bulpitt MA MCLIP CertEd

Campus learning centres

- Learning Centre, Sheffield Hallam University, City Campus, Sheffield S1 1WB
  ☎0114 225 2109
  Fax 0114 225 3859
  Head of Academic Services and Development Ms B M Fisher MLib MCLIP
  Head of Technical Services and Development E Oyston BA MSc MCLIP
- Learning Centre, Sheffield Hallam University, Collegiate Crescent Campus, Sheffield S10 2BP
  ☎0114 225 2474
  Fax 0114 225 2476
  Information Specialist Ms K Moore BA DipLib MCLIP
- Learning Centre, Sheffield Hallam University, Psalter Lane Campus, Sheffield S11 8UZ
  ☎0114 225 2721
  Fax 0114 225 2717
  Information Specialist Ms C Abson BA MA MCLIP

THE UNIVERSITY OF SHEFFIELD

Main Library, The University of Sheffield, Western Bank, Sheffield S10 2TN
☎0114 222 7200 (general enquiries); 0114 222 7224 (library administration)
Fax 0114 222 7290
e-mail: library@sheffield.ac.uk
url: http://www.shef.ac.uk/~lib/
Director of Library Services and University Librarian Vacant
Deputy Director M J Lewis MA DipLib MCLIP (0114 222 7225; e-mail: m.j.lewis@sheffield.ac.uk)
Assistant Director (Division of Collections and Information Services) D E Jones BA(Econ) MA MCLIP (0114 222 7226; e-mail: d.e.jones@sheffield.ac.uk)

Assistant Director (Division of User Services and Systems) Mrs K O'Donovan BA MCLIP (0114 222 7227; e-mail: kath.odonovan@sheffield.ac.uk)

Major libraries

- St George's Library (Engineering & Management), The University of Sheffield, Mappin Street, Sheffield S1 4DT
  ☎0114 222 7300
  Fax 0114 279 6406
  e-mail: sgl@sheffield.ac.uk
  Assistant Director/St George's Librarian P H Stubley BSc DipLib (0114 222 7327; e-mail: p.stubley@sheffield.ac.uk)
- Health Sciences Library, The University of Sheffield, Royal Hallamshire Hospital, Sheffield S10 2JF
  ☎0114 271 2030
  Fax 0114 278 0923
  e-mail: hsl.rhh@sheffield.ac.uk
  Assistant Director/Health Sciences Librarian J van Loo BA DMS DipLib MCLIP (0114 271 3025; e-mail: j.vanloo@sheffield.ac.uk)

SOUTH BANK UNIVERSITY

Perry Library, South Bank University, 250 Southwark Bridge Road, London SE1 6NJ
☎020 7815 6607 (enquiries), 020 7815 6602 (administration)
Fax 020 7815 6699
url: http://www.sbu.ac.uk/lis
Head of Learning and Information Services J Akeroyd MPhil BSc MCLIP DipLibInfSc (e-mail: akeroyJ@sbu.ac.uk)
Deputy Head C Muller BA MCLIP (e-mail: mullerc@sbu.ac.uk)

Learning Resources Centre, 105-108 Borough Road, London SE1 0AA
☎020 7815 6670

Site libraries

- Faculty of the Built Environment Library, South Bank University, Wandsworth Road, London SW8 2JZ
  ☎020 7815 8320
  Learning Resources Manager P Noble MCLIP (e-mail: noblep@sbu.ac.uk)
- Library, Redwood College, South Bank University, Harold Wood Hospital, Gubbins Lane, Romford, Essex RM3 0BE
  ☎020 7815 5982
  Learning Resources Manager M Lawson
- Library, South Bank University, Whipps Cross Education Centre, Whipps Cross Hospital, Leytonstone, London E11 1NR
  ☎020 7815 4747
  Learning Resources Manager Ms D Watmough

SOUTHAMPTON INSTITUTE

Mountbatten Library, Southampton Institute, Southampton SO14 0RJ
☎023 8031 9681 (enquiries), 023 8031 9248 (administration)
Fax 023 8031 9672
url: http://www.solent.ac.uk/library/
Head of Library J Moore BA MCLIP (e-mail: john.moore@solent.ac.uk)
Information Resources Manager R Burrell MSc(Econ) MCLIP (023 8031 9342; e-mail: robert.burrell@solent.ac.uk)
Learning Centres Manager M Walton (023 8031 9803; e-mail: martin.walton@solent.ac.uk)

Site library

Warsash Library, Southampton Institute, Newtown Road, Warsash, Southampton SO31 9ZL
☎(01489) 556269
Site Librarian Mrs H Dixon BA DipLib

UNIVERSITY OF SOUTHAMPTON

Hartley Library, University of Southampton, Highfield, Southampton SO17 1BJ
☎023 8059 2180 (enquiries), 023 8059 2677 (administration)
Fax 023 8059 5451
e-mail: library@soton.ac.uk
url: http://www.library.soton.ac.uk/
University Librarian M L Brown MA PhD DipLib MCLIP (023 8059 2677; e-mail: mlb@soton.ac.uk)
Deputy Librarian R L Wake MA MA MCLIP (023 8059 2371; e-mail: rlw1@soton.ac.uk)
Head of Archives and Special Collections C M Woolgar BA PhD DipArchAdmin FRHistS (023 8059 2721; e-mail: cmw@soton.ac.uk)

Site libraries

- Biomedical Sciences Library, University of Southampton, Bassett Crescent East, Southampton SO16 7PX
  ☎023 8059 4215
  Fax 023 8059 3251
  e-mail: b.s.library@soton.ac.uk
  url: http://www.soton.ac.uk/~library/biomedical
  Site Librarian Miss A M Norman BA DipLib MCLIP
- Health Services Library, University of Southampton, Mailpoint 883, Southampton General Hospital, Southampton SO16 6YD
  ☎023 8079 6541
  Fax 023 8079 8939
  e-mail: hslib@soton.ac.uk
  url: http://www.soton.ac.uk/~library/health
  Head of Health Care Services Division Ms C A Fowler MA BSc(Hons) MCLIP
- National Oceanographic Library, University of Southampton, Southampton Oceanography Centre, Waterfront Campus, European Way, Southampton SO14 3ZH

☎023 8059 6111 (marine information and advisory service), 023 8059 6116 (general)
Fax 023 8059 6115
e-mail: mias@soc.soton.ac.uk (marine inf/adv serv); nol@soc.soton.ac.uk (general)
url: http://www.soc.soton/lib
Head of Information Services Mrs P Simpson BA MCLIP (e-mail: pauline.simpson@soc.soton.ac.uk)

- New College Library, University of Southampton, The Avenue, Southampton SO17 1BG
  ☎023 8021 6220
  Fax 023 8023 0944
  url: http://www.soton.ac.uk/~library/new
  Head of Library and Information Services Mrs E Upson BA MCLIP (e-mail: eu@soton.ac.uk)
- Winchester School of Art Library, University of Southampton, West Side, Park Avenue, Winchester, Hants SO23 8DL
  ☎023 8059 6986
  url: http://www.soton.ac.uk/~library/wsa
  Head of Library and Information Services Ms L A Newington BA(Hons) (e-mail: L.A.newington@soton.ac.uk)

SPURGEON'S COLLEGE

Library, Spurgeon's College, 189 South Norwood Hill, London SE25 6DJ
☎020 8653 0850
Fax 020 8771 0959
e-mail: library@spurgeons.ac.uk
Librarian Mrs J C Powles BA MCLIP (e-mail: j.powles@spurgeons.ac.uk)

STAFFORDSHIRE UNIVERSITY

Library and Learning Resources Services, Staffordshire University, PO Box 664, College Road, Stoke-on-Trent, Staffs ST4 2XS
☎(01782) 294443
Fax (01782) 295799
e-mail: library@staffs.ac.uk
url: http://www.staffs.ac.uk
Director of Library and Learning Resources Service Ms E A Hart BA DipLib FCLIP

Site libraries

- Thompson Library, Staffordshire University, PO Box 664, College Road, Stoke-on-Trent, Staffs ST4 2XS
  ☎(01782) 295770
  Fax (01782) 295799
  Site Operations Manager Mrs J Broad
- Law Library, Staffordshire University, Leek Road, Stoke-on-Trent, Staffs ST4 2DF
  ☎(01782) 294307
  Fax (01782) 294306
  Site Operations Manager Ms N Adams
- Nelson Library, Staffordshire University, PO Box 368, Beaconside, Stafford ST18 0YU

☎(01785) 353236
Fax (01785) 251058
Site Operations Manager Mrs G Edwards

- Health Library, Staffordshire University, School of Health, Royal Shrewsbury Hospital (North), Mytton Oak Road, Shrewsbury SY3 8XQ
  ☎(01743) 261440
  Fax (01743) 261061
  Subject and Learning Support Librarian S Kennedy

UNIVERSITY OF STIRLING

University Library, University of Stirling, Stirling FK9 4LA
☎(01786) 467235 (enquiries), (01786) 467227 (administration)
Fax (01786) 466866
e-mail: library@stirling.ac.uk
url: http://www.stir.ac.uk/infoserv/library/
Director of Information Services P Kemp MA PhD

Campus library

Highland Health Sciences Library, University of Stirling, Highland Campus, Inverness IV2 3UJ
☎(01463) 705269
Librarian Mrs A Gillespie BA DipLibStud MCLIP

UNIVERSITY OF STRATHCLYDE

Andersonian Library, University of Strathclyde, Curran Building, 101 St James' Road, Glasgow G4 0NS
☎0141 548 3701 (enquiries), ext 4621 (administration)
Fax 0141 552 3304
e-mail: library@strath.ac.uk
url: http://www.lib.strath.ac.ukj/home
Librarian and Director of Information Strategy D Law MA DipLib FCLIP FKC FRSE (0141 548 4619; e-mail: d.law@strath.ac.uk)

Constituent libraries

- Law Library, University of Strathclyde, Stenhouse Building, 173 Cathedral Street, Glasgow G4 0RQ
  ☎0141 552 3701 ext 3293
  Librarian
- Jordanhill Library, University of Strathclyde, 76 Southbrae Drive, Glasgow G13 1PP
  ☎0141 950 3000
  Fax 0141 950 3150
  e-mail: jordanhill.library@strath.ac.uk
  Librarian

UNIVERSITY OF SUNDERLAND

Information Services, University of Sunderland, Chester Road, Sunderland SR1 3SD

☎0191 515 2900 (enquiries)
Fax 0191 515 2904
Director of Information Services A McDonald BSc FCLIP (0191 515 2905; e-mail: andrew.mcdonald@sunderland.ac.uk)

Site libraries

- Ashburne Library, University of Sunderland, Tyne and Wear SR2 7EG
  ☎0191 515 2119
  Fax 0191 515 3166
  Site Librarian Ms J Dodshon BA(Hons) DipLib (0191 515 2120; e-mail: jan.dodshon@sunderland.ac.uk)
- Hutton Library, University of Sunderland, Chester Road, Sunderland SR1 3SD
  ☎0191 515 2644
  Fax 0191 515 2422
  Site Librarian Mrs E Wilkinson BSc MSc (0191 515 2637; e-mail: eileen.wilkinson@sunderland.ac.uk)
- St Peter's Library, University of Sunderland, Prospect Building, St Peter's Riverside Campus, St Peter's Way, Sunderland SR6 0DD
  ☎0191 515 3059
  Fax 0191 515 3061
  Site Librarian Mrs E Astandoust BA MCLIP (e-mail: elizabeth.astandoust@sunderland.ac.uk)
- The Murray Library, University of Sunderland, Chester Road, Sunderland SR1 3SD
  ☎0191 515 2900
  Fax 0191 515 2904
  Site Librarian Ms J Archer BA (0191 515 3272; e-mail: julie.archer@sunderland.ac.uk)

SURREY INSTITUTE OF ART AND DESIGN, UNIVERSITY COLLEGE

Library, Surrey Institute of Art and Design, University College, Falkner Road, The Hart, Farnham, Surrey GU9 7DS
☎(01252) 892709
Fax (01252) 892725
Institute Librarian Ms R Lynch BA(Hons) MALib MCLIP
Deputy Librarian Ms G Wilkey BA(Hons) DipLib MCLIP

Site library

Library, Surrey Institute of Art and Design, University College, Epsom Campus, Ashley Road, Epsom, Surrey KT18 5BE
☎(01372) 202458
Fax (01372) 747050
Site Librarian Ms J Seabourne BA(Hons) DipLib MCLIP

UNIVERSITY OF SURREY

University Library, University of Surrey, George Edwards Building, Guildford, Surrey GU2 7XH

☎(01483) 683325 (enquiries), (01483) 689232 (administration)
Fax (01483) 689500
e-mail: library-enquiries@surrey.ac.uk
url: http://www.surrey.ac.uk/Library
Director of Information Services and Librarian T J A Crawshaw BEng DLIS
Head of Library Services R B Hall BA MA MCLIP
Head of Learning Technology Services C C Ring BSc PGCE MBA

UNIVERSITY OF SURREY ROEHAMPTON see ROEHAMPTON UNIVERSITY OF SURREY

UNIVERSITY OF SUSSEX

University Library, University of Sussex, Falmer, Brighton, Sussex BN1 9QL
☎(01273) 678163 (enquiries), (01273) 678158 (administration)
Fax (01273) 678441
e-mail: library@sussex.ac.uk
url: http://www.sussex.ac.uk/library/
University Librarian Mrs D Shorley BA MCLIP

British Library for Development Studies, Institute of Development Studies, University of Sussex, Falmer, Brighton, Sussex BN1 9RE
☎(01273) 678263 (enquiries), 606261 (administration)
Fax (01273) 621202
e-mail: blds@ids.ac.uk
url: http://www.ids.ac.uk/blds/
Librarian M G Bloom BA DipLib

Library, SPRU – Science and Technology Policy Research, University of Sussex, Mantell Building, Falmer, Brighton, Sussex BN1 9RF
☎(01273) 678178 (enquiries), (01273) 678066 (administration)
Fax (01273) 685865
e-mail: spru_library@sussex.ac.uk
url: http://www.sussex.ac.uk/spru/
url for catalogue: http://sprulib.central.sussex.ac.uk/
Librarian Ms B Merchant BSc MCLIP (e-mail: b.a.merchant@sussex.ac.uk)
Information Officer Ms M Winder BA MSc MCLIP (e-mail: m.e.winder@sussex.ac.uk)

SWANSEA INSTITUTE OF HIGHER EDUCATION

Townhill Road, Townhill Library, Swansea Institute of Higher Education, Swansea SA2 0UT
☎(01792) 481000 ext 2293
Fax (01792) 298017
e-mail: library2@sihe.ac.uk
url: http://www.sihe.ac.uk
Head of Library and Learning Support Services A Lamb BA MCLIP GradCertEd
(e-mail: tony.lamb@sihe.ac.uk)

Site libraries

- Owen Library, Swansea Institute of Higher Education, Mount Pleasant, Swansea SA1 6ED
  ☎(01792) 481000 ext 4221
- Thompson Library, Swansea Institute of Higher Education, Mount Pleasant, Swansea SA1 6ED
  ☎(01792) 481000 ext 4141
  Site Librarian Ms A Harvey LLB (e-mail: anne.harvey@sihe.ac.uk)

UNIVERSITY OF TEESSIDE

Library and Information Services, Learning Resource Centre, University of Teesside, Middlesbrough TS1 3BA
☎(01642) 342100 (enquiries), (01642) 342103 (administration)
Fax (01642) 342190
url: http://www.tees.ac.uk/lis/
Director of Library & Information Services I C Butchart MSc BA PGCE MCLIP (e-mail: ian.butchart@tees.ac.uk)

THAMES VALLEY UNIVERSITY

Learning Resources Service, Thames Valley University, St Mary's Road, Ealing, London W5 5RF
☎020 8231 2248 (enquiries), 020 8231 2246 (administration)
Fax 020 8231 2631
e-mail: lrs@tvu.ac.uk
url: http://www.tvu.ac.uk/
Head of Learning Resources J Wolstenholme BA(Hons) MSc(Ed) (020 8231 2678; fax 020 8231 2631; e-mail: john.wolstenholme@tvu.ac.uk)

Learning resource centres

- St Mary's Road LRC, Thames Valley University, Ealing, London W5 5RF
  ☎020 8231 2248
  Fax 020 8231 2565
  LRC Manager D McGrath BA MA MPhil MCLIP (e-mail: david.mcgrath@tvu.ac.uk)
- Westel House Health Sciences LRC, Thames Valley University, Westel House, 32 Uxbridge Road, Ealing, London W5 2BS
  ☎020 8280 5043
  Fax 020 8280 5045
  LRC Manager B Evans PGDip (e-mail: brent.evans@tvu.ac.uk)
- Paul Hamlyn LRC, Thames Valley University, Wellington Street, Slough, Berks SL1 1YG
  ☎(01753) 697536
  Fax (01753) 697538
  LRC Manager S Whitby (e-mail: simon.whitby@tvu.ac.uk)
- Royal Berkshire Hospital LRC, Thames Valley University, Royal Berkshire Hospital, London Road, Reading, Berks RG1 5AN
  ☎0118 987 7661
  Fax 0118 986 8675
  LRC Coordinator F Oliver-Tasker (e-mail: felix.oliver-tasker@tvu.ac.uk)

- Wexham Park LRC, Thames Valley University, Wolfson Institute of Health Sciences, Wexham Park Hospital, Slough, Berks SL2 4HL
  ☎(01753) 634343
  Fax (01753) 634344
  LRC Manager S Whitby (e-mail: simon.whitby@tvu.ac.uk)

TRINITY AND ALL SAINTS COLLEGE

Library, Trinity and All Saints College, Brownberrie Lane, Horsforth, Leeds LS18 5HD
☎0113 283 7244
Fax 0113 283 7200
url: http://www.tasc.ac.uk/iss/lib/index.htm
Director of Information Support Services E Brush BA (e-mail: e_brush@tasc.ac.uk)
Librarian Ms E Murphy BSocSci MA MCLIP (e-mail: e.murphy@tasc.ac.uk)

TRINITY COLLEGE CARMARTHEN

Library, Trinity College Carmarthen, College Road, Carmarthen, Carmarthenshire SA31 3EP
☎(01267) 676780
Fax (01267) 676766
e-mail: library@trinity-cm.ac.uk
url: http://www.trinity-cm.ac.uk/english/library/
Learning and Information Resources Manager Ms E Le Bourdon BA DipLib

UNIVERSITY OF ULSTER

Library, University of Ulster, Shore Road, Jordanstown, Newtownabbey, Co Antrim, N Ireland BT37 0QB
☎028 9036 6370
Fax 028 9036 6849
Assistant Director, Library Mrs E Urquhart MA DipLibInfoStud (028 9036 6370; e-mail: ee.urquhart@ulster.ac.uk)

Campus libraries

- Library, Faculty of Art and Design, University of Ulster at Belfast, York Street, Belfast, N Ireland BT15 1ED
  ☎028 9026 7269
  Fax 028 9026 7278
  Belfast Campus Contact Mrs M Khorshidian BA DipLIS MCLIP (e-mail: m.khorshidian@ulster.ac.uk)
- Library, University of Ulster at Coleraine, Cromore Road, Co Londonderry, N Ireland BT52 1SA
  ☎028 7032 4364
  Fax 028 7032 4928
  Coleraine Campus Contact D McClure BA(Hons) DipEd DLS (e-mail: dj.mcclure@ulster.ac.uk)
- Library, University of Ulster at Jordanstown, Shore Road, Jordanstown, Newtownabbey, Co Antrim, N Ireland BT37 0QB

☎028 9036 6929
Fax 028 9036 6849
Jordanstown Campus Contact Mrs M McCullough BA DipLibStud (e-mail: m.mccullough@ulster.ac.uk)

- Library, University of Ulster at Magee, Northland Road, Londonderry, N Ireland BT48 7JL
  ☎028 7137 5386
  Fax 028 7137 5626
  Magee Campus Contact Miss S McMullan BA LibStud (e-mail: sa.mcmullan@ulster.ac.uk)

UMIST

Library and Information Service, UMIST, PO Box 88, Manchester M60 1QD
☎0161 200 4924 (enquiries), 0161 200 4921 (Librarian's secretary)
Fax 0161 200 4941
url: http://www.umist.ac.uk/library
University Librarian M P Day BSc MSc (e-mail: m.day@umist.ac.uk)

UNIVERSITY OF WALES ABERYSTWYTH

Hugh Owen Library, University of Wales Aberystwyth, Penglais, Aberystwyth, Dyfed SY23 3DZ
☎(01970) 622399 (enquiries), (01970) 622391 (administration)
Fax (01970) 622404
e-mail: library@aber.ac.uk
url: http://www.inf.aber.ac.uk
Director of Information Services M Hopkins BA PhD MCLIP

Site/departmental libraries

- Education Library, University of Wales Aberystwyth, Old College, King Street, Aberystwyth, Dyfed SY23 2AX
  ☎(01970) 622130
  Fax (01970) 622122
  Librarian i/c E P Davies BA DipLib
- Thomas Parry Library, University of Wales Aberystwyth, Llanbadarn Fawr, Aberystwyth, Dyfed SY23 3AS
  ☎(01970) 622412 (enquiries), (01970) 622417 (administration)
  Fax (01970) 622190
  e-mail: parrylib@aber.ac.uk
  Librarian i/c A J Clark BSocSci DipLib MCLIP
- Law Library, University of Wales Aberystwyth, The Hugh Owen Building, Penglais, Aberystwyth, Dyfed SY23 3DZ
  ☎(01970) 622401
  e-mail: as Hugh Owen Library
  Librarian i/c Mrs L Stevenson LLB DipLib MCLIP
- Physical Sciences Library (Mathematics, Computer Sciences and Physics), University of Wales Aberystwyth, Penglais, Aberystwyth, Dyfed SY23 3BZ

☎(01970) 622407
e-mail: as Hugh Owen Library
Librarian i/c Mrs T Meredith

UNIVERSITY OF WALES BANGOR

Main Library, University of Wales Bangor, College Road, Bangor, Gwynedd LL57 2DG
☎(01248) 382981 (enquiries), (01248) 383772 (Secretary)
Fax (01248) 382979
e-mail: library@bangor.ac.uk; ill@bangor.ac.uk (interlibrary loans)
url: http://www.library.bangor.ac.uk
Head of Library Services N S Soane MA DipLib (e-mail: n.s.soane@bangor.ac.uk)

Site libraries

- Science Library, University of Wales Bangor, Deiniol Building, Deiniol Road, Bangor, Gwynedd LL57 2UN
  ☎(01248) 382984/382802
  Fax (01248) 383826
  e-mail: iss061@bangor.ac.uk
  Librarian S Harling BA MA
- Normal Site Library, University of Wales Bangor, Holyhead Road, Bangor, Gwynedd LL57 2PX
  ☎(01248) 383087
  Fax (01248) 383976
  e-mail: iss186@bangor.ac.uk
  Librarian Ms B W Jones
- Ocean Sciences Library, University of Wales Bangor, Menai Bridge, Anglesey LL59 5EY
  ☎(01248) 382967
  Fax (01248) 382615
  e-mail: iss064@bangor.ac.uk
  Librarian P Rolfe BA MA
- Health Studies Library, University of Wales Bangor, Archimedes Centre, Technology Park, Wrexham LL13 7YP
  ☎(01978) 316368/9/70
  Fax (01978) 311154
  e-mail: iss059@bangor.ac.uk
  Librarian Mrs G Haylock BA DipLib
- Health Studies Library, University of Wales Bangor, Fron Heulog, Holyhead Road, Bangor, Gwynedd LL57 2EF
  ☎(01248) 383173
  e-mail: iss070@bangor.ac.uk
  Librarian Vacant

UNIVERSITY OF WALES COLLEGE OF MEDICINE

Sir Herbert Duthie Library, Division of Information Services, University of Wales College of Medicine, Heath Park, Cardiff CF14 4XN
☎029 2074 2875 (enquiries), 029 2074 2874 (administration)

Fax 029 2074 3651
e-mail: duthielib@cf.ac.uk
url: http://www.uwcm.ac.uk/support/information_services/libraries
Director of Library Services S J Pritchard BA MCLIP
Acting Deputy Director of Library Services Dr A L Weightman BSc MA PhD

Site libraries

- Brian Cooke Dental Library, University of Wales College of Medicine, Heath Park, Cardiff CF14 4XY
  ☎029 2074 2523
  Fax 029 2074 3834
  e-mail: dentlib@cf.ac.uk
  Librarian Miss J Stevens BA MCLIP
- Sir Herbert Duthie Medical Library, Division of Information Services, University of Wales College of Medicine, Heath Park, Cardiff CF14 4XN
  ☎029 2074 2875/3121
  Fax 029 2074 3651
  e-mail: duthielib@cf.ac.uk
  Librarian Mrs E M Kelly MA
- Cochrane Library, University of Wales College of Medicine, Llandough Hospital, Penarth, South Glamorgan CF64 2XX
  ☎029 2071 1711
  e-mail: cochranelib@cf.ac.uk
  Librarian Ms R Soper BA DipLib MCLIP
- Cancer Research Wales Library, University of Wales College of Medicine, Velindre Hospital, Whitchurch, Cardiff CF14 7XL
  ☎029 2061 5888
  e-mail: vhvlib@cf.ac.uk
  Librarian Mrs B M Coles BSc MSc MCLIP
- Library, School of Nursing and Healthcare Studies, University of Wales College of Medicine, Ty Dewi Sant, Heath Park, Cardiff CF14 4XN
  ☎029 2074 2387
  Fax 029 2074 7763
  e-mail: healthlib@cf.ac.uk
  Librarian Ms M Gorman BA DipLib
- Library, School of Nursing Studies, University of Wales College of Medicine, Grounds of St Cadoc's Hospital, Caerleon, Newport NP6 1XR
  ☎(01633) 430346 ext 222
  Fax (01633) 430717
  e-mail: caerleonlib@cf.ac.uk
  Librarian Ms M Gorman BA DipLib
- Library, Postgraduate Medical Centre, University of Wales College of Medicine, Whitchurch Hospital, Whitchurch, Cardiff CF14 7XB
  ☎029 2069 3919 ext 6382
  Fax 020 2052 0170
  e-mail: whitlib@cf.ac.uk
  Librarian Vacant

UNIVERSITY OF WALES COLLEGE, NEWPORT

Library and Learning Resources, University of Wales College, Newport, Caerleon Campus, PO Box 179, Newport, South Wales NP18 3YG
☎(01633) 432652
Fax (01633) 432920
e-mail: llr@newport.ac.uk
url: http://www.library.newport.ac.uk
Head of Library and Learning Resources Mrs J Peters BA MLS MCLIP (e-mail: janet.peters@newport.ac.uk)

Campus libraries

- Caerleon Campus, University of Wales College, Newport, PO Box 179, Newport, South Wales NP18 3YG
  ☎(01633) 432294
  Deputy Head of Library and Learning Resources Mrs L May BA DipLib MCLIP PGCE(FE) (e-mail: lesley.may@newport.ac.uk)
- Allt-yr-yn Campus, University of Wales College, Newport, PO Box 180, Newport, South Wales NP20 5XR
  ☎(01633) 432310
  Campus Librarian Ms D Leatherdale MBA MCLIP (e-mail: dawne.leatherdale@newport.ac.uk)

UNIVERSITY OF WALES INSTITUTE, CARDIFF

Library Division, University of Wales Institute, Cardiff, Llandaff Campus, Western Avenue, Cardiff CF5 2YB
☎029 2041 6240
Fax 029 2041 6908
url: http://www.uwic.ac.uk
Head of Library Division P Riley BA(Hons) (029 2041 6240; e-mail: priley@uwic.ac.uk)

UNIVERSITY OF WALES LAMPETER

The Library, University of Wales Lampeter, Lampeter, Ceredigion SA48 7ED
☎(01570) 424772 (enquiries/Librarian)
Fax (01570) 423875
e-mail: library@lamp.ac.uk
url: http://www.lamp.ac.uk/library
Systems Librarian Ms M Perrett MA DipLib (e-mail: m.perrett@lamp.ac.uk)
Library Administrator Ms J Bracher (e-mail: j.bracher@lamp.ac.uk)

UNIVERSITY OF WALES SWANSEA

Library and Information Centre, University of Wales Swansea, Singleton Park, Swansea SA2 8PP
☎(01792) 295697 (enquiries), (01792) 295175 (administration)
Fax (01792) 295851
e-mail: library@swansea.ac.uk

url: http://www.swan.ac.uk/lis/index.htm
Director of Library and Information Services C West MA BA MCLIP

Branch libraries

- Natural Sciences Library, University of Wales Swansea, Singleton Park, Swansea SA2 8PP
  ☎(01792) 295024
  e-mail: nslmail@swansea.ac.uk
  Science and Engineering Librarian A B Montgomery BSc DipLib MCLIP
- Education Library, University of Wales Swansea, Hendrefoelan House, Gower Road, Swansea SA2 7NB
  ☎(01792) 518659
  e-mail: edmail@swansea.ac.uk
  Branch Librarian Ms M M Rogerson BA DipLib PGCE(FE)
- South Wales Miners' Library, University of Wales Swansea, Hendrefoelan House, Gower Road, Swansea SA2 7NB
  ☎(01792) 518603
  e-mail: miners@swansea.ac.uk
  Branch Librarian Ms S F Williams BSc MCLIP
- Nursing Library, University of Wales Swansea, Morriston Hospital, Morriston, Swansea SA6 6NL
  ☎(01792) 703767
  e-mail: s.m.storey@swansea.ac.uk
  Health Science Librarian Ms R Davies BLib PGCE

UNIVERSITY OF WARWICK

Library, University of Warwick, Gibbet Hill Road, Coventry, Warwickshire CV4 7AL
☎024 7652 3033
Fax 024 7652 4211
e-mail: library@warwick.ac.uk
url: http://www.library.warwick.ac.uk
Chief Librarian J A Henshall MA PhD
Deputy Librarian C Fyfe BA MA MBA

WELSH COLLEGE OF MUSIC AND DRAMA

Library, Welsh College of Music and Drama, Castle Grounds, Cathays Park, Cardiff CF10 3ER
☎029 2034 2854
Fax 029 2039 1304
url: http://www.library.wcmd.ac.uk
Librarian Ms J Agus BA BMus MCLIP (029 2039 1330; e-mail: agusjm@wcmd.ac.uk)

UNIVERSITY OF THE WEST OF ENGLAND, BRISTOL

Library Services, University of the West of England, Bristol, Frenchay Campus, Coldharbour Lane, Bristol BS16 1QY

☎0117 344 2279 (enquiries), 0117 344 2404 (administration)
Fax 0117 344 2407
url: http://www.uwe.ac.uk/library
Head of Library Services Ms A Taylor BA DipLib MCLIP (e-mail: ali.taylor@uwe.ac.uk)

UNIVERSITY OF WESTMINSTER

Information Systems and Library Services, University of Westminster, 115 New Cavendish Street, London W1W 6UW
☎020 7911 5095
Fax 020 7911 5093
url: http://www.wmin.ac.uk/isls/
Director of Information Systems and Library Services (ISLS) Ms S Enright BA DipLib MCLIP (e-mail: s.enright@wmin.ac.uk)

Campus libraries

- Cavendish Campus Library, University of Westminster, 115 New Cavendish Street, London W1W 6UW
  ☎020 7911 5000 ext 3613
  Fax 020 7911 5871
  Library Manager Ms A Sainsbury BA MCLIP (e-mail: a.sainsbury@wmin.ac.uk)
- Harrow LRC, Harrow Campus, University of Westminster, Watford Road, Northwick Park, Harrow, Middlesex HA1 3TP
  ☎020 7911 5000 ext 4664
  Fax 020 7911 5952
  Library Manager Ms C Symes BA MCLIP (e-mail: c.symes@wmin.ac.uk)
- Marylebone Campus Library, University of Westminster, 35 Marylebone Road, London NW1 5LS
  ☎020 7911 5000 ext 3212
  Fax 020 7911 5058
  Library Manager Ms J Harrington BA MLib MCLIP (e-mail: j.harrington@wmin.ac.uk)
- Regent Campus Library, University of Westminster, 4-12 Little Titchfield Street, London W1W 7UW
  ☎020 7911 5000 ext 2537
  Fax 020 7911 5846
  Library Manager Ms E Salter BA DipLib MLib (e-mail: e.salter@wmin.ac.uk)
- University Archives, University of Westminster, Regent Campus, 4-12 Little Titchfield Street, London W1W 7UW
  ☎020 7911 5000 ext 2524
  Fax 020 7911 5846
  Archivist Ms B Weeden MA MSc DipArchAdmin (e-mail: b.c.weeden@wmin.ac.uk)

WIMBLEDON SCHOOL OF ART

Library, Wimbledon School of Art, Merton Hall Road, London SW19 3QA
☎020 8408 5027 (enquiries)
Fax 020 8408 5050
Head of Learning Resources P Jennett MA MCLIP (e-mail: p.jennett@wimbledon.ac.uk)

Librarian Miss P Harrison BA(Hons) MCLIP DipHA (e-mail: p.harrison@wimbledon.ac.uk)
Assistant Librarian P Crollie BA(Hons) (e-mail: p.crollie@wimbledon.ac.uk)

UNIVERSITY OF WOLVERHAMPTON

Harrison Learning Centre, University of Wolverhampton, St Peter's Square, Wolverhampton, West Midlands WV1 1RH
☎(01902) 322300 (enquiries), (01902) 322302 (administration)
Fax (01902) 322668
e-mail: lib@wlv.ac.uk
Director of Learning Centres Ms M Heaney BA DipLib MCLIP FRSA
Assistant Director of Learning Centres (Resources) Ms F Mill MA DipLib
Assistant Director of Learning Centres (Operations) C Evans MCLIP MLS

Site libraries

- Compton Learning Centre, University of Wolverhampton, Compton Road West, Wolverhampton, West Midlands WV3 9DX
  ☎(01902) 323642
  Fax (01902) 323702
  Learning Centre Manager Mrs L Thomas MCLIP
- Harrison Learning Centre, University of Wolverhampton, St Peter's Square, Wolverhampton, West Midlands WV1 1RH
  ☎(01902) 322300
  Fax (01902) 322194
  Learning Centre Manager Mrs I Ordidge BSc PGDipLib
- Telford Learning Centre, University of Wolverhampton, Old Shifnal Road, Priorslee, Telford, Shropshire TF2 9NT
  ☎(01902) 323983
  Fax (01902) 323985
  Learning Centre Manager D W Clare BA MCLIP
- Walsall Learning Centre, University of Wolverhampton, Gorway, Walsall, West Midlands WS1 3BD
  ☎(01902) 323275
  Fax (01902) 323079
  Learning Centre Manager Mrs G Hughes BLib MCLIP

Nursing and Midwifery site libraries

Learning Centre Manager (Nursing and Midwifery) Mrs P Collins BA(Hons)

- Burton Learning Centre, University of Wolverhampton, Burton Nurse Education Centre, Belvedere Road, Burton upon Trent, Staffs DE13 0RB
  ☎(01283) 566333 ext 2217/2237
  Fax (01283) 515978
  Site Librarian Ms E Watson BA(Hons) PGDipLib MCLIP
- Manor Learning Centre, University of Wolverhampton, Education and Training Centre, Manor Hospital, Moat Road, Walsall, West Midlands WS2 9PS
  ☎(01922) 721172 ext 7181
  Fax (01922) 649008
  Acting Site Librarian Vacant

- New Cross Learning Centre, University of Wolverhampton, Education Centre, New Cross Hospital, Wolverhampton, West Midlands WV10 0QP
  ☎(01902) 644805
  Fax (01902) 306072
  Resource Librarian Ms K Ewart
- Russells Hall Learning Centre, University of Wolverhampton, Esk House, Russells Hall Hospital, Dudley, West Midlands DY1 2HQ
  ☎(01384) 456111 ext 2594
  Fax (01384) 237543
  Site Librarian Mrs G Williamson BA(Hons) MCLIP

UNIVERSITY COLLEGE WORCESTER

Peirson Library, University College Worcester, Henwick Grove, Worcester WR2 6AJ
☎(01905) 855414
Fax (01905) 855132
Head of Library Services Ms A Hannaford BA(Hons) DipLib (e-mail: a.hannaford@worc.ac.uk)
Customer Services Manager Mrs G Walford (e-mail: g.walford@worc.ac.uk)

WRITTLE COLLEGE

Library, Writtle College, Chelmsford, Essex CM1 3RR
☎(01245) 424245
Fax (01245) 420456
e-mail: library@writtle.ac.uk
Head of Learning Information Services Mrs R M Hewings BSc(Econ) DMS DipLib MCLIP (ext 26009; e-mail: rmh@writtle.ac.uk)
Subject Librarian (Science) Ms J Lamb BA(Hons) DipLib MCLIP (ext 26008; e-mail: jl@writtle.ac.uk)
Subject Librarian (Horticulture) Mrs C Gosden BSc(Hons) MSc (ext 26008; e-mail: cg@writtle.ac.uk)
Subject Librarian (Business and Leisure Management) Mrs J V Scully BA MCLIP (ext 26008; e-mail: jvs@writtle.ac.uk)

UNIVERSITY OF YORK

J B Morrell Library, University of York, Heslington, York YO10 5DD
☎(01904) 433865 (enquiries), (01904) 433863 (administration)
Fax (01904) 433866
url: http://www.york.ac.uk/services/library/
University Librarian Ms A E M Heaps BA MA DipLib (e-mail: aemh1@york.ac.uk)

Branch/department libraries

- King's Manor Library, University of York, The King's Manor, York YO1 7EP
  ☎(01904) 433969
  Fax (01904) 433949
  Librarian Ms P A Haywood BA MA (e-mail: ph16@york.ac.uk)

- Library and Information Service, University of York, The Strayside Education Centre, Harrogate District Hospital, Lancaster Park Road, Harrogate HG2 7SX
  ☎(01423) 553104
  e-mail: hslibhg@york.ac.uk
  Manager of Library and Information Service Mrs G Jarrett BA (e-mail: gj7@york.ac.uk)

YORK ST JOHN COLLEGE
(formerly College of Ripon and York St John)

Library, York St John College, Lord Mayor's Walk, York YO31 7EX
☎(01904) 716700
Fax (01904) 612512
e-mail: library@yorksj.ac.uk
url: http://www.yorksj.ac.uk/library
College Librarian A Chalcraft BA MA MCLIP (01904 716701; e-mail: a.chalcraft@yorksj.ac.uk)
Principal Assistant Librarian (IT) Ms H Westmancoat BA MCLIP (e-mail: h.westmancoat@yorksj.ac.uk)
Senior Assistant Librarians Ms J Munks BA MCLIP (e-mail: j.munks@yorksj.ac.uk); J Hagart BA MCLIP (e-mail: j.hagart@yorksj.ac.uk); B Jones BA (e-mail: b.jones@yorksj.ac.uk); Ms F Ware BA MCLIP (e-mail: f.ware@yorksj.ac.uk)

Selected Government, National and Special Libraries in the United Kingdom

ADVISORY, CONCILIATION AND ARBITRATION SERVICE (ACAS)

Information Centre, Advisory, Conciliation and Arbitration Service (ACAS), Brandon House, 180 Borough High Street, London SE1 1LW
☎020 7210 3911 (enquiries)
Fax 020 7210 3615
e-mail: rwilsher@acas.org.uk
url: http://www.acas.org.uk
Acting Information Centre Manager R Wilsher MA DipLib (020 7210 3917)

ADVOCATES LIBRARY

Advocates Library, Parliament House, Edinburgh EH1 1RF
☎0131 260 5683 (enquiries), 0131 260 5637 (Librarian)
Fax 0131 260 5663 (9am–5pm weekdays)
Librarian Ms A Longson BSc DipLib (e-mail: andrea.longson@advocates.org.uk)
Open to members only. Non-members may access stock at the National Library of Scotland.

ALDERSHOT MILITARY MUSEUM

Military Museum and Archive, Aldershot Military Museum, Evelyn Woods Road, Queens Avenue, Aldershot, Hants GU11 2LG
☎(01252) 314598
Fax (01252) 342942
url: http://www.hants.gov.uk/museum/aldershot
Curator I Maine BA MA
(Accessible to enquirers by appointment)

AMBLESIDE'S ARMITT MUSEUM AND LIBRARY
(formerly The Armitt Trust)

Ambleside's Armitt Museum and Library, Rydal Road, Ambleside, Cumbria LA22 9BL
☎(015394) 31212
Fax (015394) 31313
e-mail: mail@armitttrust.fsbusiness.co.uk
url: http://www.armitt.com
Curator Ms M Kelly BA

AMBLESS CARES LIBRARY

Ambless Cares Library, Shalom House, Lower Celtic Park, Enniskillen, Co Fermanagh, N Ireland BT74 6HP
☎028 6632 0320
Fax 028 6632 0320
Librarian J Wood

AMERICAN MUSEUM LIBRARY

American Museum Library, Claverton Manor, Bath BA2 7BD
☎(01225) 460503
Fax (01225) 469160
e-mail: amibbath@aol.com
url: http://www.americanmuseum.org
Librarian Mrs A Armitage BA

THE ARMITT TRUST see AMBLESIDE'S ARMITT MUSEUM AND LIBRARY

ASSOCIATION OF COMMONWEALTH UNIVERSITIES

Reference Library, Association of Commonwealth Universities, John Foster House, 36 Gordon Square, London WC1H 0PF
☎020 7380 6700
Fax 020 7387 2655
e-mail: info@acu.ac.uk
url: http://www.acu.ac.uk
Librarian N Mulhern

THE BABRAHAM INSTITUTE

Library, The Babraham Institute, Babraham, Cambridge CB2 4AT
☎(01223) 496214 (enquiries)
Fax (01223) 496020
e-mail: babraham.library@bbsrc.ac.uk
Librarian Miss J R Maddock BA DipLib MCLIP (01223 496235; e-mail: jennifer.maddock@bbsrc.ac.uk)

BANK OF ENGLAND

Information Centre, Bank of England, Threadneedle Street, London EC2R 8AH
☎020 7601 4715 (enquiries), 020 7601 4668 (administration)
Fax 020 7601 4356
e-mail: informationcentre@bankofengland.co.uk
Information Centre Manager Ms P A Hope BA MA MSc DipLib MCLIP

BG GROUP PLC

Information Centre, BG Group plc, Building A2, 100 Thames Valley Park Drive, Reading, Berkshire RG6 1PT
☎0118 929 2496 (enquiries and administration)
Fax 0118 929 2482
Information Analysts P Cronin (0118 929 2496), D Freemantle (0118 929 2497)

BIRMINGHAM AND MIDLAND INSTITUTE

Library, Birmingham and Midland Institute, 9 Margaret Street, Birmingham B3 3BS
☎0121 236 3591
Fax 0121 212 4577
Librarian Mrs S Utley BA
(Private members' library)

BISHOPSGATE INSTITUTE

Reference Library, Bishopsgate Institute, 230 Bishopsgate, London EC2M 4QH
☎020 7247 6198
Fax 020 7247 6318
e-mail: library@bishopsgate.org.uk
Chief Librarian Ms A Mackay MA MCLIP

BOOKTRUST

Children's Reference Library, Booktrust, Book House, 45 East Hill, London SW18 2QZ
☎020 8516 2977
Fax 020 8516 2978
e-mail: ed@booktrust.org.uk
url: http://www.booktrust.org.uk; http://www.booktrusted.com
Children's Librarian E Zaghini MCLIP

BRITANNIA ROYAL NAVAL COLLEGE

College Library, Britannia Royal Naval College, Dartmouth, Devon TQ6 0HJ
☎(01803) 677279
Fax (01803) 677015
Librarian R J Kennell MCLIP (e-mail: r.kennell@brnc.ac.uk)
Assistant Librarian R Wardle BA(Hons) DipLib MCLIP
(Prior appointment necessary)

BRITISH ANTARCTIC SURVEY

Library, British Antarctic Survey, High Cross, Madingley Road, Cambridge CB3 0ET
☎(01223) 221617
Fax (01223) 362616
url: http://www.antarctica.ac.uk
Librarian Ms C Phillips MA MCLIP (e-mail: cmp@bas.ac.uk)

BRITISH BROADCASTING CORPORATION

BBC Information and Archives, British Broadcasting Corporation, B259 Television Centre, Wood Lane, London W12 7RJ
☎020 7765 0720 (Customer service desk)
Head of Information and Archives P Fiander MSc

Research Centre, British Broadcasting Corporation, Room L928, Centre Block, BBC Bush House, PO Box 76, The Strand, London WC2B 4PH
e-mail: commercial.unit@bbc.co.uk
Business Development Manager, Information and Archives G Strickland (020 7557 2452)
Further sites at:
Research Centre: B209 Television Centre, Wood Lane, London W12 7RJ
Research Centre: G067 Broadcasting House, Portland Place, London W1A 1AA

BRITISH COUNCIL

Information Services Management, British Council, Bridgewater House, 58 Whitworth Street, Manchester M1 6BB
☎0161 957 7755 (enquiries), 0161 957 7170 (administration)
Fax 0161 957 7762 (enquiries), 0161 957 7168 (administration)
e-mail: firstname.surname@britishcouncil.org
Director Ms G Kempster OBE MLIS BA(Hons) MCLIP (e-mail: grace.kempster@britishcouncil.org)
Deputy Director D Skinner (e-mail: david.skinner@britishcouncil.org)
Deputy Director Ms J Ugonna (e-mail: judy.ugonna@britishcouncil.org)
Regional Information Coordinators
Middle East and North African Libraries N Lack (e-mail: nick.lack@britishcouncil.org)
East and Central African Libraries Ms J Brittain (e-mail: julie.brittain@britishcouncil.org)
South Asia Libraries Ms F Tait (e-mail: frances.tait@britishcouncil.org)
West African Libraries Ms K Sanders (e-mail: karrine.sanders@britishcouncil.org)
European Libraries (New Products and Services) Ms A Hartley (e-mail: annette.hartley@britishcouncil.org)
European Libraries (Change Management) W Harper (e-mail: wayne.harper:britishcouncil.org)
East Asia and Americas R Drury (e-mail: russell.drury@britishcouncil.org), Ms K Johnson (e-mail: kathryn.johnson@britishcouncil.org)
Southern African Libraries Ms S Metcalfe (e-mail: sarah.metcalfe@britishcouncil.org)

British Council enquiries (e-mail: general.enquiries@britishcouncil.org)
(For details of British Council information services in 110 countries see url: http://www.britishcouncil.org)

Education Information Service (London), British Council, 10 Spring Gardens, London SW1A 2BN
☎020 7389 4383
e-mail: education.enquiries@britishcouncil.org
Librarians Ms E Fryd, Ms J Aafjes-Sinnadurai (job-share)

BRITISH DENTAL ASSOCIATION

BDA Information Centre, British Dental Association, 64 Wimpole Street, London W1G 8YS
☎020 7563 4545
Fax 020 7935 6492

e-mail: infocentre@bda-dentistry.org.uk
url: http://www.bda-dentistry.org.uk
Librarian R Farbey BA DipLib MCLIP

BRITISH FILM INSTITUTE

BFI National Library, British Film Institute, 21 Stephen Street, London W1T 1LN
☎020 7255 1444 (enquiries), ext 2264 (administration)
Fax 020 7436 2338
e-mail: library@bfi.org.uk
url: http://www.bfi.org.uk/nationallibrary/
Head of Library and Education R Templeton BA DipLib MCLIP FRSA
Deputy Head (User Services) D Sharp BA MCLIP
Deputy Head (Technical Services) S Pearson BA MLS CertEd MCLIP
(Incorporates Independent Television Commission Library collections)

BRITISH GEOLOGICAL SURVEY

Library and Information Services, British Geological Survey, Kingsley Dunham Centre, Keyworth, Nottingham NG12 5GG
☎0115 936 3205 (enquiries), 0115 936 3472 (Chief Librarian)
Fax 0115 936 3015
e-mail: libuser@bgs.ac.uk
Chief Librarian G McKenna MA MCLIP (e-mail: g.mckenna@bgs.ac.uk)

Branch libraries

- Library, British Geological Survey, Scottish Regional Office, Murchison House, West Mains Road, Edinburgh EH9 3LA
  ☎0131 667 1000, 0131 650 0322 (direct dial)
  Fax 0131 668 2683
  e-mail: librarymh@bgs.ac.uk
  Site Librarian R P McIntosh BSc DipLib
- London Information Office, British Geological Survey, Natural History Museum, Exhibition Road, South Kensington, London SW7 2DE
  ☎020 7589 4090
  Fax 020 7584 8270
  e-mail: bgslondon@bgs.ac.uk
  Officer-in-Charge Miss S J Brackell (e-mail: s.brackell@bgs.ac.uk)

BRITISH HOROLOGICAL INSTITUTE

Library, British Horological Institute, Upton Hall, Upton, Newark, Notts NG23 5TE
☎(01636) 813795
Fax (01636) 812258
e-mail: clocks@bhi.co.uk
url: http://www.bhi.co.uk
Librarian Viscount A Midleton FBHI

BRITISH LIBRARY

Board Headquarters, British Library, 96 Euston Road, London NW1 2DB
☎020 7412 7332 (general and visitor enquiries), 020 7412 7000 (switchboard)
url: http://www.bl.uk
Chairman Lord Eatwell
Chief Executive Mrs L Brindley
Enquiry points
The following are based at 96 Euston Road, London NW1 2DB. Admission to the Library's London reading rooms is by pass only. Most of the Library's catalogues are available on its website, http://www.bl.uk. For general enquiries about the collections, reader services and advance reservations, tel 020 7412 7676, e-mail: reader-services-enquiries@bl.uk.

Other useful numbers/e-mail addresses
Reader Admissions (advice on who may use the Library and how to apply for a reader's pass)
☎020 7412 7677, e-mail: Reader-Admissions@bl.uk
Visitor Services (for general enquiries and details of exhibitions, events)
☎020 7412 7332, e-mail: Visitor-Services@bl.uk)

Northern Site, British Library, Boston Spa, Wetherby, Yorkshire LS23 7BQ
☎(01937) 546060
e-mail: dsc-cusomter-services@bl.uk
Director of Finance and Corporate Resources I Millar
Director of Operations and Services Ms N Ceeney
Director of Scholarship and Collections Dr C Field
Director of Strategic Marketing and Communications Ms J Finney

St Pancras Reading Rooms

- Librarianship and Information Sciences Service (LIS)
  ☎020 7412 7676, e-mail: LIS@bl.uk
- Maps
  ☎020 7412 7702, e-mail: maps@bl.uk
- Music Collections
  ☎020 7412 7772, e-mail: music-collections@bl.uk
- National Sound Archive
  ☎020 7412 7440, e-mail: nsa@bl.uk
- Asia/Pacific and African Collections (formerly Oriental and India Office Collections)
  ☎020 7412 7873, e-mail: oioc-enquiries@bl.uk
- Philatelic
  ☎020 7412 7635, e-mail: philatelic@bl.uk
- Rare Book Collections
  ☎020 7412 7676, e-mail: rare-books@bl.uk
- Science, Technology and Business
  ☎020 7412 7288/7494/7496, e-mail: scitech@bl.uk
- Western Manuscripts
  ☎020 7412 7513, e-mail: mss@bl.uk

Other Reading Rooms

- Newspaper Library, Colindale Avenue, London NW9 5HE
  ☎020 7412 7353/7356
  e-mail: newspaper@bl.uk
- Boston Spa, Wetherby, Yorkshire LS23 7BQ
  ☎ (01937) 546070
  (For material in the collection of the Document Supply Centre)

BRITISH MEDICAL ASSOCIATION

Library, British Medical Association, BMA House, Tavistock Square, London WC1H 9JP
☎020 7383 6060
Fax 020 7383 2544
e-mail: bma-library@bma.org.uk
url: http://www.bma.org.uk
Librarian T McSeán FCLIP
Deputy Librarian Ms J E Smith BA(Hons)

BRITISH MUSEUM

Anthropology Library, British Museum, Department of Ethnography (formerly Museum of Mankind), 6 Burlington Gardens, London W1S 3EX
☎020 7323 8031
Fax 020 7323 8013 (British Museum)
Librarian i/c Ms S Mackie BA DipEd DipLib MCLIP (020 7323; e-mail: smackie@thebritishmuseum.ac.uk)
(Although the Dept of Ethnography (Museum of Mankind) has closed to the public in order to prepare for its move back to the main British Museum site, the library will remain open until nearer the move. Open to Fellows of the Royal Anthropological Institute; also to researchers and other readers by appointment.)

Paul Hamlyn Library, British Museum, Great Russell Street, London WC1B 3DG
☎020 7323 8000
e-mail: readingroom@thebritishmuseum.ac.uk
url: http://www.thebritishmuseum.ac.uk
The Fleming Librarian Ms P Smith (020 323 8907; e-mail: psmith@thebritishmuseum.ac.uk)
(The Paul Hamlyn Library is an open access public reference library. It contains over 13,000 books and 20 current journals on subjects relating to the Museum's collections, e.g. ancient history, archaeology, art history, museology. The Library is freely open to the public without any membership or prior appointment.)

BRITISH NATIONAL SPACE CENTRE

Information Unit, British National Space Centre, 151 Buckingham Palace Road, London SW1W 9SS
☎020 7215 0901 (enquiries)
Fax 020 7215 0936
e-mail: bnscinfo@dti.gsi.gov.uk

url: http://www.bnsc.gov.uk
Librarian S Grayson

BRITISH PSYCHOLOGICAL SOCIETY

c/o Psychology Library, British Psychological Society, University of London Library, Senate House, Malet Street, London WC1E 7HU
☎020 7862 8451/8461
Fax 020 7862 8480
e-mail: ull@ull.ac.uk
url: http://www.ull.ac.uk
Psychology Librarian, University of London Library Mrs S E Tarrant BA MCLIP
(The BPS collection of periodicals is held at the Psychology Library and amalgamated with the University of London Library collection of psychology periodicals. For details of services etc see under University of London Library.)

BRITISH STANDARDS INSTITUTION

Library, British Standards Institution, 389 Chiswick High Road, London W4 4AL
☎020 8996 7004
Fax 020 8996 7005
e-mail: library@bsi-global.com
url: http://www.bsi-global.com
Library Manager Ms M Yates BSc DipLib (020 8996 7041)
(The Library may be used for reference free of charge by members and students. For non-members there is a charge)

BRITISH UNIVERSITIES FILM & VIDEO COUNCIL

Information Service, British Universities Film & Video Council, 77 Wells Street, London W1T 3QJ
☎020 7393 1500
Fax 020 7393 1555
e-mail: ask@bufvc.ac.uk
url: http://www.bufvc.ac.uk
Head of Information L McKernan BA

BROMLEY HOUSE LIBRARY
(formerly Nottingham Subscription Library)

Bromley House Library, Bromley House, Angel Row, Nottingham NG1 6HL
☎0115 947 3134
Librarian Mrs J V Wilson BA MCLIP
(Subscription library available to the public for reference purposes only, by prior appointment)

BTG INTERNATIONAL LTD

BTG International Ltd, 10 Fleet Place, London EC4M 7SB
☎020 7575 0000

Fax 020 7575 0010
url: http://www.btgplc.com
Knowledge Manager Miss A Newman BA MSc (020 7575 1549; e-mail: anna.newman@btgplc.com)
Knowledge Administrator Ms L Clarke BA (020 7575 1550; e-mail: louise.clarke@btgplc.com)
Knowledge Researcher Ms S Geist BA MA (020 7575 1548; e-mail: samantha.geist@btgplc.com)

CANCER RESEARCH UK
(formerly Imperial Cancer Research Fund)

Library and Information Services, Cancer Research UK, 44 Lincoln's Inn Fields, London WC2A 3PX
☎020 7269 3206 (enquiries), 020 7269 3290 (administration)
Fax 020 7269 3084
e-mail: lib.info@cancer.org.uk
url: http://www.science.cancerresearchuk.org/; http://www.cancerresearch.uk/org/
Head of Library & Information Services Ms J Chester BA MCLIP

CANTERBURY CATHEDRAL

Cathedral Library, Canterbury Cathedral, The Precincts, Canterbury, Kent CT1 2EH
☎(01227) 865287
e-mail: library@canterbury-cathedral.org
url: http://www.canterbury-cathedral.org/library.html
Cathedral Librarian K M C O'Sullivan BA MA MSc(Econ) MCLIP

CCLRC (COUNCIL FOR THE CENTRAL LABORATORY OF THE RESEARCH COUNCILS)

Chadwick Library, CCLRC (Council for the Central Laboratory of the Research Councils), Daresbury Laboratory, Daresbury, Warrington, Cheshire WA4 4AD
☎(01925) 603397 (enquiries)
Fax (01925) 603779
e-mail: library@dl.ac.uk
url: http://www.cclrc.ac.uk/Activity/ACTIVITY=LIS
Librarian Mrs D Franks BSc MCLIP (01925 603189)

Library, CCLRC (Council for the Central Laboratory of the Research Councils), Rutherford Appleton Laboratory, Chilton, Didcot, Oxon OX11 0QX
☎(01235) 445384 (general enquiries)
Fax (01235) 446403
e-mail: library@rl.ac.uk
url: http://www.cclrc.ac.uk/Activity/ACTIVITY=LIS
Senior Librarian Mrs S Lockley BSc MSc(Econ) MCLIP (01235 446668)

CENTRAL POLICE TRAINING AND DEVELOPMENT AUTHORITY (formerly National Police Training)

National Police Library, Central Police Training and Development Authority, Centrex Bramshill, Bramshill, Hook, Hants RG27 0JW
☎(01256) 602650 (enquiries), (01256) 602100 (main switchboard)
Fax (01256) 602285
e-mail: library@bramshill.ac.uk
url: http://www.centrex.police.uk
Chief Librarian Mrs S E King MCLIP

CENTRE FOR ECOLOGY AND HYDROLOGY

Library Service, Centre for Ecology and Hydrology, CEH Edinburgh, Bush Estate, Penicuik, Midlothian EH26 0QB
☎0131 445 4343
Fax 0131 445 3943
url: http://library.ceh.ac.uk
Head of Library Services Miss S Scobie MA DipLib (e-mail: ssco@ceh.ac.uk)

Research station libraries

- Library, Centre for Ecology and Hydrology, Banchory Research Station, Hill of Brathens, Glassel, Banchory, Kincardineshire AB31 4BY
  ☎(01330) 826300
  Fax (01330) 823303
  Librarian Ms F Robertson (e-mail: fmr@ceh.ac.uk)
- Library, Centre for Ecology and Hydrology, Bangor Research Station, University of Wales, Deiniol Road, Bangor, Gwynedd LL57 2UP
  ☎(01248) 370045
  Fax (01248) 355365
  Librarian J Cooper (e-mail: jrco@ceh.ac.uk)
- Library, Centre for Ecology and Hydrology, Winfrith Technology Centre, Winfrith Newburgh, Dorchester, Dorset DT2 8ZD
  ☎(01305) 213550
  Fax (01305) 213600
  Librarian S Smith (e-mail: ssmi@ceh.ac.uk)
- Library, Centre for Ecology and Hydrology, Merlewood Research Station, Grange-over-Sands, Cumbria LA11 6JU
  ☎(01539) 532264
  Fax (01539) 534705
  Librarian C Cook (e-mail: ccc@ceh.ac.uk)
- Library, Centre for Ecology and Hydrology, Monks Wood Research Station, Abbots Ripton, Huntingdon, Cambridgeshire PE17 2LS
  ☎(01487) 773381
  Fax (01487) 773467
  Librarian P Moorhouse (e-mail: pmo@ceh.ac.uk)
- Library, Centre for Ecology and Hydrology, Mansfield Road, Oxford OX1 3SR
  ☎(01865) 281630

Fax (01865) 281696
Librarian C Wilson (e-mail: cjw@ceh.ac.uk)

- National Hydrosciences Library, Centre for Ecology and Hydrology, Wallingford Research Station, Maclean Building, Crowmarsh Gifford, Wallingford, Oxon OX10 8BB
☎(01491) 838800
Fax (01491) 692424
Librarian S Wharton (e-mail: sbw@ceh.ac.uk)
- Library, Centre for Ecology and Hydrology, Windermere, The Ferry House, Far Sawry, Ambleside, Cumbria LA22 0LP
☎(01539) 442468
Fax (01539) 446914
Librarian I McCulloch (e-mail: idm@ceh.ac.uk)

CENTRE FOR INFORMATION ON LANGUAGE TEACHING AND RESEARCH (CILT)

CILT Resources Library, Centre for Information on Language Teaching and Research (CILT), 20 Bedfordbury, London WC2N 4LB
☎020 7379 5110
Fax 020 7379 5082
e-mail: library@cilt.org.uk
url: http://www.cilt.org.uk; http://www.cilf.org.uk/libcat (library catalogue)
Librarian J E Hawkins BA

CENTRE FOR POLICY ON AGEING

Library, Centre for Policy on Ageing, 19–23 Ironmonger Row, London EC1V 3QP
☎020 7553 6500
Fax 020 7553 6501
e-mail: ageinfo@cpa.org.uk
url: http://www.cpa.org.uk
Deputy Director and Head of Information Ms G Crosby BA MCLIP (e-mail: gcrosby@cpa.org.uk)
Librarian Ms R Hayes BA
Assistant Librarian Ms K Jones BA MCLIP
Information Officer M Webber BA MSc

CHARTERED INSTITUTE OF MANAGEMENT ACCOUNTANTS (CIMA)

Technical Advisory Service, Chartered Institute of Management Accountants (CIMA), 26 Chapter Street, London SW1P 4NP
☎020 8849 2259
Fax 020 8849 2464
e-mail: Tas@cimaglobal.com
url: http://www.cimaglobal.com
Information Manager Mrs D Metcalf BSc(Hons)

CHARTERED INSTITUTE OF PERSONNEL AND DEVELOPMENT

Library and Information Services, Chartered Institute of Personnel and Development, CIPD House, Camp Road, London SW19 4UX
☎020 8263 3355 (enquiries), 020 8263 3410 (administration)
Fax 020 8263 3400
e-mail: lis@cipd.co.uk
url: http://www.cipd.co.uk
Head of Library and Information Services Ms B Salmon

CHARTERED INSURANCE INSTITUTE

Library, Chartered Insurance Institute, 20 Aldermanbury, London EC2V 7HY
☎020 7417 4415/4416
Fax 020 7972 0110
e-mail: library@cii.co.uk
url: http://www.ciilo.org
Librarian R L Cunnew BA FCLIP

CHARTERED MANAGEMENT INSTITUTE
(formerly Institute of Management)

Management Information Centre, Chartered Management Institute, Management House, Cottingham Road, Corby, Northants NN17 1TT
☎(01536) 204222, (01536) 207400 (enquiries)
Fax (01536) 401013
e-mail: mic.enquiries@managers.org.uk
url: http://www.managers.org.uk
Head of Information Services R Norton BA FCLIP
(Information services, principally to Institute members)

CHETHAM'S LIBRARY

Chetham's Library, Long Millgate, Manchester M3 1SB
☎0161 834 7961
Fax 0161 839 5797
e-mail: librarian@chethams.org.uk
url: http://www.chethams.org.uk
Chetham's Librarian M R Powell BD PhD

CHILD ACCIDENT PREVENTION TRUST

Resource Centre, Child Accident Prevention Trust, 4th Floor, Clerk's Court, 18-20 Farringdon Lane, London EC1R 3HA
☎020 7608 3828
Fax 020 7608 3674
e-mail: info@capt.org.uk
url: http://www.capt.org.uk
Information Manager Ms C Stark

CILIP: THE CHARTERED INSTITUTE OF LIBRARY AND INFORMATION PROFESSIONALS

(formerly The Library Association)

Information Services, CILIP: the Chartered Institute of Library and Information Professionals, 7 Ridgmount Street, London WC1E 7AE
☎020 7255 0500
Textphone 020 7255 0505
Fax 020 7255 0501
e-mail: info@cilip.org.uk
url: http://www.cilip.org.uk
Information Manager, Information Centre Ms C Nolan BA MA MCLIP

CIVIC TRUST

Library, Civic Trust, 17 Carlton House Terrace, London SW1Y 5AW
☎020 7930 0914
Fax 020 7321 0180
e-mail: pride@civictrust.org.uk
url: http://www.civictrust.org.uk
Policy Officer Vacant

CIVIL AVIATION AUTHORITY

Library and Information Centre, Civil Aviation Authority, Aviation House, South Area, Gatwick Airport South, West Sussex RH6 0YR
☎(01293) 573725
Fax (01293) 573181
e-mail: library-general-enquiries@srg.caa.co.uk
url: http://www.caa.co.uk
Manager S R Moore BA MCLIP (e-mail: stephen.moore@srg.caa.co.uk)

COLLEGE OF OCCUPATIONAL THERAPISTS

Library, College of Occupational Therapists, 106-114 Borough High Street, Southwark, London SE1 1LB
☎020 7450 2316 (direct line)
Fax 020 7450 2364
e-mail: library@cot.co.uk
url: http://www.cot.org.uk
Librarian Ms A Mason

COMMISSION FOR RACIAL EQUALITY

CRE Library, Commission for Racial Equality, Elliott House, 10-12 Allington Street, London SW1E 5EH
☎020 7932 5296/5274
url: http://www.cre.gov.uk
Librarian P J A Pinto BA DipLib MCLIP

COMMISSION OF THE EUROPEAN COMMUNITIES

Press and Information Office, Commission of the European Communities, 8 Storey's Gate, London SW1P 3AT
☎020 7973 1992
Fax 020 7973 1900/1910
BT Gold DGX004
Librarian Mrs M M Brenchley
(Enquiries may only be referred to this library via a recognized EPIC (European Public Information Centre, formerly known as PiR). For details of your nearest centre please contact your local library or check on http://www.europe.org.uk)

COMMON SERVICES AGENCY

Information and Statistics Division, Common Services Agency, NHS in Scotland, Trinity Park House, South Trinity Road, Edinburgh EH5 3SQ
☎0131 551 8775
Fax 0131 551 8495
Health Information Scientist A H Jamieson MA DipLib MCLIP (e-mail: alan.jamieson@isd.csa.scot.nhs.uk)

COMMONWEALTH INSTITUTE

Commonwealth Resource Centre, Commonwealth Institute, Kensington High Street, London W8 6NQ
☎020 7603 4535 ext 210
Fax 020 7603 2807
e-mail: crc@commonwealth.org.uk
url: http://www.commonwealth.org.uk/
Head of Library Services Ms M Bastiampillai BA MA MCLIP

COMMONWEALTH SECRETARIAT

Library, Commonwealth Secretariat, Marlborough House, Pall Mall, London SW1Y 5HX
☎020 7747 6164/6165/6166/6167
Fax 020 7747 6168
e-mail: library@commonwealth.int
url: http://www.thecommonwealth.org
Librarian D Blake BA DipLib MSc MCLIP (e-mail: d.blake@commonwealth.int)
Deputy Librarian and Archivist J Gilbert BA MAS MSc (e-mail: j.gilbert@commonwealth.int)

COMPETITION COMMISSION

Information Centre, Competition Commission, Room 567, 48 Carey Street, London WC2A 2JT
☎020 7271 0243
Fax 020 7271 0367

e-mail: info@competition-commission.gsi.gov.uk
url: http://www.competition-commission.org.uk
Information Centre Manager Miss L J Fisher MA MCLIP
Press and Publicity Officer F Royle
(Open to government libraries by appointment. Not open to the public, but deals with public telephone and written enquiries.)

CONFEDERATION OF BRITISH INDUSTRY

Information Centre, Confederation of British Industry, Centre Point, 103 New Oxford Street, London WC1A 1DU
☎020 7395 8019
Fax 020 7240 0988
url: http://www.cbi.org.uk
Information Centre Manager Ms E Hollingsworth BA(Hons) (e-mail: emma.hollingsworth@cbi.org.uk)

CONSERVATIVE RESEARCH DEPARTMENT

Library, Conservative Research Department, Conservative Central Office, 32 Smith Square, London SW1P 3HH
☎020 7222 9000 (main)
Fax 020 7984 8273
e-mail: library@conservatives.com
url: http://www.conservatives.com
Head of Library S Westlake MA(Oxon) MSc MPhil
(Not open to the public)

CORUS RESEARCH, DEVELOPMENT AND TECHNOLOGY

Information and Library Services, Corus Research, Development and Technology, Swinden Technology Centre, Moorgate, Rotherham, South Yorkshire S60 3AR
☎(01709) 820166
Fax (01709) 825464
e-mail: stc.library@corusgroup.com
Information Officer M L Nott

COUNTRYSIDE AGENCY

Library, Countryside Agency, John Dower House, Crescent Place, Cheltenham, Gloucestershire GL50 3RA
☎(01242) 533311
Fax (01242) 584270
url: http://www.countryside.gov.uk
Librarian Ms J Bacon MSc MCLIP
(The Countryside Agency was formed on 1 April 1999 when the Countryside Commission merged with the national, advisory and countrywide functions of the Rural Development Commission.)

COUNTRYSIDE COUNCIL FOR WALES (CYNGOR CEFN GWLAD CYMRU)

Library, Countryside Council for Wales (Cyngor Cefn Gwlad Cymru), Plas Penrhos, Ffordd Penrhos, Bangor, Gwynedd LL57 2LQ
☎(01248) 385522
Fax (01248) 385510
e-mail: library@ccw.gov.uk
url: http://www.ccw.gov.uk
Librarian Ms D Lloyd BA MCLIP

CPRE (COUNCIL FOR THE PROTECTION OF RURAL ENGLAND)

Library and Information Unit, CPRE (Council for the Protection of Rural England), 128 Southwark Street, London SE1 0SW
☎020 7976 6433
Fax 020 7976 6373
e-mail: info@cpre.org.uk
url: http://www.cpre.org.uk
Head of Library and Information Ms H Morris BA MCLIP
Library and Information Officer Mrs E Lipworth BA HDE HDLIS
Library and Information Assistant O Hilliam BA

COURT SERVICE see LORD CHANCELLOR'S DEPARTMENT

CROWN PROSECUTION SERVICE

Library Information Services, Crown Prosecution Service, 50 Ludgate Hill, London EC4M 7EX
☎020 7796 8320/8364
e-mail: library@cps.gov.uk
url: http://www.cps.gov.uk
CPS Librarian R Brall

DEFENCE EVALUATION AND RESEARCH AGENCY see QINETIQ

DEPARTMENT FOR CULTURE, MEDIA AND SPORT

Information Centre, Department for Culture, Media and Sport, 2-4 Cockspur Street, London SW1Y 5DH

☎020 7211 6200 (enquiries), 020 7211 6041 (administration)
Fax 020 7211 6032
e-mail: enquiries@culture.gov.uk
url: http://www.culture.gov.uk
Manager Ms F Montgomery BEd DipLib MCLIP

DEPARTMENT FOR EDUCATION AND SKILLS (DFES)

Library and Information Services Team (LIST), Department for Education and Skills (DfES), LG, Sanctuary Buildings, London SW1P 3BT
☎020 7925 5040 (enquiries); 0870 000 2288 (Public Enquiry Unit)
Fax 020 7925 5085
e-mail: enquiries.library@dfes.gsi.gov.uk
url: http://www.dfes.gov.uk
Chief Librarian Vacant
Deputy Chief Librarian Ms J Reid BA MA MA(InfSc) MCLIP (0114 259 3339; e-mail: julia.reid@dfes.gsi.gov.uk)
Systems Librarian P Collins BA(Hons) MCLIP (020 7925 5451; e-mail: paula.collins@dfes.gsi.gov.uk)
Information Services Librarian (London) J Denmead BA MA (020 7925 5798; e-mail: james.denmead@dfes.gsi.gov.uk)

Site library

Library and Information Services Team (LIST), Department for Education and Skills (DfES), Room E307, Moorfoot, Sheffield S1 4PQ
☎020 7925 5040 (enquiries); 0870 000 2288 (Public Enquiry Unit)
Fax 020 7925 5085
e-mail: enquiries.library@dfes.gsi.gov.uk
Information Services Librarian (Sheffield) Miss H L Challinor BA(Hons) (0114 259 4450; e-mail: helen.challinor@dfes.gsi.gov.uk)

DEPARTMENT FOR ENVIRONMENT, FOOD AND RURAL AFFAIRS (DEFRA)

Whitehall Place Library, Department for Environment, Food and Rural Affairs (DEFRA), Room 15, (West Block), Whitehall Place, London SW1A 2HH
☎020 7270 8000
Fax 020 7270 8419
e-mail: wpw.library@defra.gsi.gov.uk
url: http://www.defra.gov.uk
Librarian Mrs J Carpenter BA DipLib DipBIT MCLIP
(General collection on temperate agriculture. Visitors must give 24 hours' notice.)

Nobel House Library, Department for Environment, Food and Rural Affairs (DEFRA), Room 320, Nobel House, 17 Smith Square, London SW1P 3JR
☎020 7238 6575

Fax 020 7238 6609
e-mail: nobel.library@defra.gsi.gov.uk
url: http://www.defra.gov.uk
Librarian C van Dort BSc(Hons) MSc MCLIP
(Specializes in food and environmental issues. Visitors must give 24 hours' notice.)

DEFRA Helpline
☎08459 33 55 77 (09.00–17.00 Mon-Fri)
e-mail: helpline@defra.gsi.gov.uk
All calls charged at local call rate
(Provides an enquiry service to the general public who need access to information or specialist contacts relating to the work of DEFRA)

DEPARTMENT FOR INTERNATIONAL DEVELOPMENT

Information Services, Department for International Development, Abercrombie House, Eaglesham Road, East Kilbride, Glasgow G75 8EA
☎0845 300 4100 (public enquiries), (01355) 843880 (library enquiries)
Fax (01355) 843632
e-mail: enquiry@dfid.gov.uk
url: http://www.dfid.gov.uk
eLibrary Manager Ms S A Skelton

DEPARTMENT FOR REGIONAL DEVELOPMENT

Library, Department for Regional Development, Room G-40, Clarence Court, 10-18 Adelaide Street, Belfast BT2 8GB
☎028 9054 1045/6
Fax 028 9054 1081
Librarian Ms F Sawey BA MCLIP (e-mail: fiona.sawey@drdni.gov.uk)

DEPARTMENT FOR WORK AND PENSIONS (DWP)

Information Services, Department for Work and Pensions (DWP), Room 114, The Adelphi, 1-11 John Adam Street, London WC2N 6HT
☎020 7712 2500
Fax 020 7962 8491
e-mail: library@dwp.gsi.gov.uk
url: http://www.dwp.gov.uk
Head of Information Services G Monk BA(Hons)Lib MCLIP
Information Services Team Manager Ms M Harris
Information Services Manager Ms A Tailby BA(Hons)
Acquisitions Librarian P Warnock
Cataloguer Ms H Cahill
Industrial Injuries Advisory Council Research Librarian Ms A Lannon BA(Hons) MA DipLib MCLIP
Agencies Librarian Ms S Mitchell BSc(Hons) PGDip

Information Services (BFI) A Fernando
Intranet Content Team
Manager Ms J Lewis
Librarians C Sheppard BSc(Hons) MSc, D Taylor
Assistant Librarians B Anderson BA(Hons) MSc(Econ), Ms A Kemp BA(Hons) MSc MCLIP

Solicitors Library, Department for Work and Pensions (DWP), 4th Floor, New Court, Carey Street, London WC2A 2LS
☎020 7412 1333
Fax 020 7412 1332
Legal Librarian Ms E Murray BA(Hons) DipLib
Assistant Librarian Vacant

Public Enquiry Office, Room 113, The Adelphi, 1-11 John Adam Street, London WC2N 6HT
☎020 7712 2171
Public Enquiry Office Manager A Ramzan

DEPARTMENT FOR TRANSPORT see OFFICE OF THE DEPUTY PRIME MINISTER AND DEPARTMENT OF TRANSPORT

DEPARTMENT OF EDUCATION

Library, Department of Education, Rathgael House, 43 Balloo Road, Bangor, Co Down, Northern Ireland BT19 7PR
☎028 9127 9345
Fax 028 9127 9100
e-mail: deni@nics.gov.uk
Librarian Miss A McNamara

DEPARTMENT OF HEALTH

Library, Department of Health, Skipton House, 80 London Road, London SE1 6LH
☎020 7972 (+ extension), 020 7210 4580 (public enquiries)
Fax 020 7972 1609
url: http://www.doh/gov.uk
Head, Library and Information Services Mrs P L Bower BA(Hons) DipLib MCLIP (ext 5927)
Senior Librarians J Scott Cree MA MCLIP (Customer Services – London, ext 5928); Miss K Hanson BA (Customer Services – Leeds, 0113 254 5071)

Libraries

- Library, Department of Health, Skipton House, 80 London Road, Elephant and Castle, London SE1 6LH
  ☎020 7972 6541 (enquiries)
  Fax 020 7972 5976
  Librarian Ms L Vickers BA

- Library, Department of Health, Quarry House, Quarry Hill, Leeds LS2 7UE
  ☎0113 254 5080/81
  Fax 0113 254 5084
  Librarian Miss J Goodfellow MA(Hons) MA MCLIP

Agency libraries

- Medical Devices Agency Library, Department of Health, Room 1001, Hannibal House, Elephant and Castle, London SE1 6TQ
  ☎020 7972 8075
  Fax 020 7972 8079
  e-mail: library@medical-devices.gov.uk
  url: http://www.medical-devices.gov.uk
  Librarian Mrs K L Morgan BSc(Hons) MSc MCLIP
- Medicines Control Agency Information Centre, Department of Health, Market Towers, 1 Nine Elms Lane, London SW8 5NQ
  ☎020 7273 0344
  Fax 020 7273 0353
  Head of Information Resources Mrs D Leakey
- NHS Estates Library, Department of Health, 1 Trevelyan Square, Boar Lane, Leeds LS1 6AE
  ☎0113 254 7070
  Fax 0113 254 7167
  e-mail: nhs.estates@doh.gov.uk
  url: http://www.nhsestates.gov.uk
  Librarian Ms M Lum BA

DEPARTMENT OF TRADE AND INDUSTRY

Department of Trade and Industry, 1 Victoria Street, London SW1H 0ET
url: http://www.dti.gov.uk
Minicom 020 7215 6740
Assistant Director, Information Management and Process Engineering
Mrs M A Bridge OBE MA MCLIP (020 7215 6542)
Head of Information and Library Services Miss A Cotterill BLib(Hons) MA MCLIP (020 7215 5755; fax 020 7215 5713)
Assistant Head of Information and Library Services M Byng BA(Hons) DipLib MA MCLIP, Miss R Zolynski BA(Hons) DipLib MCLIP (020 7215 6697 or 6007; fax 020 7215 5713) (job-share)

Information and Library Services, Department of Trade and Industry, 1 Victoria Street, London SW1H 0ET
☎020 7215 5006 (enquiries)
Fax 020 7215 5665
Information Services Manager Ms D Rowland BLib(Hons) MSc MCLIP (020 7215 6896)
(Limited public access by appointment only)

Legal Library and Information Centre, Department of Trade and Industry, 10 Victoria Street, London SW1H 0NN

☎020 7215 3054
Fax 020 7215 3535
Librarian N A Hasker LLB MCLIP
(Open to Departmental Staff only)

ELECTRICITY ASSOCIATION

Business Information Centre, Electricity Association, 30 Millbank, London SW1P 4RD
☎020 7963 5789
Fax 020 7963 5870
e-mail: enquiries@electricity.org.uk
url: http://www.electricity.org.uk
Manager, Business Information Centre Mrs M Deighton BSc MLS

ENGLISH FOLK DANCE AND SONG SOCIETY

Vaughan Williams Memorial Library, English Folk Dance and Song Society, Cecil Sharp House, 2 Regent's Park Road, London NW1 7AY
☎020 7485 2206 exts18/19
Fax 020 7284 0523
e-mail: library@efdss.org
url: http://www.efdss.org
Librarian M H Taylor BA(Lib) MCLIP OBE
Assistant Librarian Ms E Bradtke, Ms P Webb
Indexer T Black

ENGLISH HERITAGE

Library, English Heritage, Room B1, Fortress House, 23 Savile Row, London W1S 2ET
☎020 7973 3031 (general enquiries)
Fax 020 7973 3001
e-mail: library@english-heritage.org.uk
url: http://www.english-heritage.org.uk
Librarian Ms C Phillpotts BA MA MCLIP (020 7973 3029; e-mail: catherine.phillpotts@english-heritage.org.uk)
Assistant Librarian Ms S England BA MA (e-mail: sally.england@english-heritage.org.uk)
(Prior appointment necessary)

Library, English Heritage, National Monuments Record Centre, Kemble Drive, Swindon, Wilts SN2 2GZ
☎(01793) 414600
Fax (01793) 414606
e-mail: info@rchme.co.uk
url: http://www.english-heritage.org.uk
Librarian F Gilmour (01793) 414632
Communications Assistant J Satchwell

London Search Room and Library, English Heritage, National Monuments Record, 55 Blandford Street, London W1H 3AF

☎020 7208 8200
Fax 020 7224 5333
e-mail: london@rchme.co.uk
Librarian
(For architectural information on Greater London)

ENGLISH NATURE (NATURE CONSERVANCY COUNCIL FOR ENGLAND)

The Library, Information Delivery Team, English Nature (Nature Conservancy Council for England), Northminster House, Peterborough PE1 1UA
☎(01733) 455094 (library enquiry desk), (01733) 455100 (general nature conservation enquiry service)
Fax (01733) 568834 (library), (01733) 455103 (general enquiry service)
e-mail: enquiries@english-nature.org.uk
url: http://www.english-nature.org.uk
Team Manager J Budd
Librarian/Records Manager Ms I Chivers BA(Hons) DipLib MCLIP
Enquiry Service Manager G R Seamons BSc DipLib

ENGLISH-SPEAKING UNION

Page Memorial Library, English-Speaking Union, Dartmouth House, 37 Charles Street, London W1J 5ED
☎020 7529 1587
Fax 020 7495 6108
e-mail: library@esu.org.uk
url: http//www.esu.org
Librarian/Information Officer Ms A K Wathern BA(Hons) DipLib

EQUAL OPPORTUNITIES COMMISSION

Information Centre, Equal Opportunities Commission, Arndale House, Arndale Centre, Manchester M4 3EQ
☎0161 838 8324
Fax 0161 838 8303
url: http://www.eoc.org.uk
Librarian Ms J Foster BA MCLIP (e-mail: julie.foster@eoc.org.uk)

FOOD STANDARDS AGENCY

The FSA Library (The Dr Elsie Widdowson Library), Food Standards Agency, Aviation House, 125 Kingsway, London WC2B 6NH
☎020 7276 8181/2
Fax 020 7276 8069
e-mail: FSALibrary&info@foodstandards.gsi.gov.uk
url: http://www.food.gov.uk
Head of Library and Information Service Mrs R A Lister BA(Hons) PGCertHSM MCLIP (e-mail: rita.lister@foodstandards.gsi.gov.uk)

FOREIGN AND COMMONWEALTH OFFICE

Main Library, Foreign and Commonwealth Office, King Charles Street, London SW1A 2AH
☎020 7270 3925 (enquiries)
Fax 020 7270 3270
Librarian S Latham BA MA MPhil MSc MCLIP

Departmental library
Legal Library, Foreign and Commonwealth Office, Room K168, King Charles Street, London SW1A 2AH
☎020 7270 3050 (enquiries); 020 7270 3082 (administration)
Fax 020 7270 4259
Legal Librarian Mrs S Halls BA MCLIP

FORESTRY COMMISSION

Library, Forestry Commission, Forest Research Station, Alice Holt Lodge, Wrecclesham, Farnham, Surrey GU10 4LH
☎(01420) 22255. (01420) 526216 (direct line)
Fax (01420) 23653
e-mail: library@forestry.gsi.gov.uk
url: http://www.forestry.gov.uk
Librarian Miss C A Oldham BA MA DipLib MCLIP (e-mail: catherine.oldham@forestry.gsi.gov.uk)

FRANCIS SKARYNA BELARUSIAN LIBRARY AND MUSEUM

Francis Skaryna Belarusian Library and Museum, 37 Holden Road, London N12 8HS
☎020 8445 5358
Fax 020 8445 5358
url: http://www.skaryna.clara.co.uk/skaryna/
Librarian Mgr A Nadson

FRESHWATER BIOLOGICAL ASSOCIATION

Library, Freshwater Biological Association, Ferry House, Far Sawrey, Ambleside, Cumbria LA22 0LP
☎(01539) 442468
Fax (01539) 446914
e-mail: ifelibrary@ceh.ac.uk
url: http://www.fba.org.uk
Librarian I McCulloch BA(Hons) DipLIS MCLIP (e-mail: idm@ceh.ac.uk)
Assistant Librarian Ms D A McAlpine BA(Hons) DipLIS (e-mail: dam@ceh.ac.uk)

GEOLOGICAL SOCIETY OF LONDON

Library, Geological Society of London, Burlington House, Piccadilly, London W1J 0BG
☎020 7734 5673

Fax 020 7439 3470
e-mail: library@geolsoc.org.uk
url: http://www.geolsoc.org.uk
Librarian Miss S Meredith

GERMAN HISTORICAL INSTITUTE LONDON

Library, German Historical Institute London, 17 Bloomsbury Square, London WC1A 2NJ
☎020 7309 2019/2022 (enquiries), 020 7309 2020 (administration)
Fax 020 7404 5573
e-mail: library-ghil@ghil.co.uk
url: http://www.ghil@ghil.uk
Librarians Ms A-M Klauk, Mr C Schönberger

GOETHE-INSTITUT LONDON

Library, Goethe-Institut London, 50 Princes Gate, Exhibition Road, London SW7 2PH
☎020 7596 4040 (brief enquiries), 020 7596 4044 (information service)
Fax 020 7594 0230
e-mail: library@london.goethe.org
url: http://www.goethe.de/gr/lon/enibib.htm
Head Librarian Ms G Buck DiplBibl (e-mail: buck@london.goethe.org)

GREATER LONDON AUTHORITY

Research Library, Greater London Authority, City Hall, The Queen's Walk, London SE1 2AA
☎020 7983 4000 (GLA switchboard), 020 7983 4455 (library enquiries)
Fax 020 7983 4674
e-mail: rlinfo@london.gov.uk
url: http://www.london.gov.uk
Head of Research Library Ms A Davies BA(Hons) MCLIP
(The Research Library was formerly part of the London Research Centre)

GUILDFORD INSTITUTE

Library, Guildford Institute, University of Surrey, Ward Street, Guildford, Surrey GU1 4LH
☎(01483) 562142
Fax (01483) 451034
Librarian Mrs E C Miles BA AMA (e-mail: c.miles@surrey.ac.uk)

HEALTH AND SAFETY EXECUTIVE

Information Services, Health and Safety Executive, Magdalen House, Trinity Road, Bootle, Merseyside L20 3QZ
☎0151 951 4382
Fax 0151 951 3674
url: http://www.hse.gov.uk
Head of Information Services Ms S Brown (e-mail: sandie.brown@hse.gsi.gov.uk)

Information centres

- Information Services, Health and Safety Executive, Magdalen House, Trinity Road, Bootle, Merseyside L20 3QZ
  ☎0151 951 4382
  Fax 0151 951 3674
  Site Manager Ms S Cornmell
- Information Centre, Health and Safety Executive, Rose Court, 2 Southwark Bridge Road, London SE1 9HS
  ☎020 7717 6104
  Fax 020 7717 6134
  Site Manager D Taft
- Information Centre, Health and Safety Executive, Broad Lane, Sheffield S3 7HQ
  ☎0114 289 2330
  Fax 0114 289 2333
  Site Manager Mrs L Parker
- Information Centre, Nuclear Safety Division, Health and Safety Executive, St Peter's House, Balliol Road, Bootle, Merseyside L20 3LZ
  ☎0151 951 4042
  Fax 0151 951 4004
  Site Manager Mrs K McNichol MA MCLIP

(General requests for information on health and safety at work should be referred to the HSE Infoline on 0870 154 5500. Written enquiries to HSE Information Services, Caerphilly Business Park, Caerphilly CF83 3GG, e-mail: hseinformationservices@natbrit.com; fax 029 2085 9260)

HEALTH DEVELOPMENT AGENCY

Health Development Agency, Holborn Gate, 330 High Holborn, London WC1V 7BA
☎020 7061 3160
Fax 020 7061 3393
e-mail: enquiry@hda-online.org.uk
url: http://www.had-online.org.uk
Head of Research and Information A Morgan

HEALTH EDUCATION BOARD FOR SCOTLAND

Health Promotion Library Scotland, Health Education Board for Scotland, The Priory, Canaan Lane, Edinburgh EH10 4SG
☎0845 912 5442 (enquiries - Scotland only), 0131 536 5582 (administration), textphone 0131 536 5593
Fax 0131 536 5502
e-mail: library.enquiries@hebs.scot.nhs.uk
url: http://www.hebs.com/library
Librarian Ms M Forrest MA(Hons) MSc DipLib FCLIP FSA(Scot)
Assistant Librarian Ms C McGlew MA(Hons) MSc

HEALTH MANAGEMENT LIBRARY

Health Management Library, Scottish Health Service Centre, Crewe Road South, Edinburgh EH4 2LF
☎0131 623 2535
Fax 0131 315 2369
e-mail: library@shsc.csa.scot.nhs.uk
url: http://www.show.scot.nhs.uk/shsc/
Library Services Manager Ms G Hewitt BA MCLIP
Assistant Librarian Mrs A Bogle MA DipLib MCLIP

HIGH COMMISSION OF INDIA

Library, High Commission of India, India House, Aldwych, London WC2B 4NA
☎020 7836 8484 ext 115
Fax 020 7836 2632
Librarian W S Mour
Hon Librarian Miss M S Travis
(Staff library only)

HIGHGATE LITERARY AND SCIENTIFIC INSTITUTION

Library, Highgate Literary and Scientific Institution, 11 South Grove, Highgate, London N6 6BS
☎020 8340 3343
Fax 020 8340 5632
e-mail: admin@hlsi.demon.co.uk
Librarian R Walker BA
(Public access allowed for reference)

HIGHWAYS AGENCY

Library and Information Centre, Ground Floor, Romney House, Marsham Street, London SW1
☎020 7921 4614
Fax 020 7921 4005
url: http://www.highways.gov.uk
Librarian/Information Manager Ms P Lewis MCLIP
(Note: access by appointment only and loans via the British Library)

HISPANIC AND LUSO-BRAZILIAN COUNCIL

Canning House Library, Hispanic and Luso-Brazilian Council, 2 Belgrave Square, London SW1X 8PJ
☎020 7235 2303
Fax 020 7235 3587
e-mail: enquiries.library@canninghouse.com
url: http://www.canninghouse.com

Librarian Ms C Suárez BA MA
Assistant Librarian Ms J Hickton BA MCLIP

HISTORICAL MANUSCRIPTS COMMISSION

National Register of Archives and Manorial Documents Register, Historical Manuscripts Commission, Quality House, Quality Court, Chancery Lane, London WC2A 1HP
☎020 7242 1198
Fax 020 7831 3550
e-mail: nra@hmc.gov.uk
url: http://www.hmc.gov.uk
Secretary Dr C J Kitching BA PhD FSA
Senior Curatorial Officer L A Ritchie MA

HM CUSTOMS AND EXCISE

Library Service, HM Customs and Excise, 4th Floor West, Ralli Quays, 3 Stanley Street, Salford M60 9LA
☎0161 827 0447/0454
Fax 0161 827 0491
Head of Service Ms L Bankes BA(Hons) MCLIP (0161 827 0465)

Branch/department library

Library Service, HM Customs and Excise, 2nd Floor, New Kings Beam House, 22 Upper Ground, London SE1 9PJ
☎020 7865 5668/9
Fax 020 7865 5720
e-mail: LibraryEnquiries{NKBH}@hmce.gsi.gov.uk
Librarian C Leppington BA(Hons) MA MCLIP (020 7865 5671)

HM TREASURY AND CABINET OFFICE

Library and Information Service, HM Treasury, Information Gateway Team, 1 Horse Guards Road, London SW1A 2HQ
☎020 7270 5290 (enquiries)
Fax 020 7270 5681
e-mail: library@hm-treasury.gov.uk
url: http://www.hm-treasury.gov.uk/
Chief Librarian Miss J E Clayton BA MCLIP

HMS SULTAN

Library, HMS Sultan, Military Road, Gosport, Hants PO12 3BY
☎023 9254 2678
Fax 023 9254 2555
e-mail: sultanlibrary@gtnet.gov.uk
Librarian J R C Quibell BA MCLIP
(Visits by arrangement)

HOME OFFICE

Information Services Unit, Home Office, Communication Directorate, 50 Queen Anne's Gate, London SW1H 9AT
☎020 7273 3398 (enquiries)
Fax 020 7273 3957
e-mail: library@homeoffice.gsi.gov.uk
url: http://www.homeoffice.gov.uk
Senior Librarian Ms K George BA PGDipLib
Library Manager Ms H Lee

Site library

Prison Service Headquarters Library, Home Office, Room 224, Abell House, John Islip Street, London SW1P 4LH
☎020 7217 5548/5253
Fax 020 7217 5209
Librarian M Gilbert BA MCLIP

HORTICULTURE RESEARCH INTERNATIONAL

Library, Horticulture Research International, East Malling, West Malling, Kent ME19 6BJ
☎(01732) 843833
Fax (01732) 849067
url: http://www.hri.ac.uk
Librarian Ms Sarah M Loat BA MCLIP (e-mail: sarah.loat@hri.ac.uk)

HOUSE OF COMMONS

Department of the Library, House of Commons, London SW1A 0AA
☎020 7219 4272
Fax 020 7219 5839
e-mail: hcinfo@parliament.uk
url: http://www.parliament.uk
Librarian of the House of Commons Miss P J Baines MA BLitt
(There are specialist sections which deal with enquiries from Members of Parliament only. Outside enquirers should approach the Department's public interface, the House of Commons Information Office (address as above) 020 7219 4272 (5 lines))
Head of Information Office B Morgan

HOUSE OF LORDS

Library, House of Lords, London SW1A 0PW
☎020 7219 5242 (enquiries), 020 7219 3240 (administration)
Fax 020 7219 6396
e-mail: hllibrary@parliament.uk
Librarian D L Jones MA FSA MCLIP

HULTON/ARCHIVE

Hulton/Archive, Unique House, 21-31 Woodfield Road, London W9 2BA

☎020 7266 2662 (Sales), 020 7579 5777 (Research)
Fax 020 7266 3154
e-mail: hultonsales@getty-images.com
url: http://www.hultonarchive.com
Research Manager Ms C Theakstone
Curator Ms S McDonald
(Hulton/Archive is part of Getty Images)

IGER (INSTITUTE OF GRASSLAND AND ENVIRONMENTAL RESEARCH)

Stapledon Library and Information Service, IGER (Institute of Grassland and Environmental Research), Plas Gogerddan, Aberystwyth SY23 3EB
☎(01970) 823053 (library desk)
Fax (01970) 828357
e-mail: igerlib.igerlib-wpbs@bbsrc.ac.uk
url: http://www.iger.bbsrc.ac.uk/igerweb/
Institute Librarian S Smith BSc DipLib MCLIP
Collections Librarian P R Drew BLib MPhil

IMPERIAL CANCER RESEARCH FUND see CANCER RESEARCH UK

IMPERIAL WAR MUSEUM

Department of Printed Books, Imperial War Museum, Lambeth Road, London SE1 6HZ
☎020 7416 5342
Fax 020 7416 5246
e-mail: books@iwm.org.uk
url: http://www.iwm.org.uk
Keeper of Printed Books R Golland BA DipLib MCLIP
Head of Public Services C J V Hunt BA MCLIP (020 7416 5341)
Head of Acquisitions, Cataloguing and Computing Ms M Wilkinson BA MCLIP (020 7416 5348)
(Coverage of conflicts since 1914 involving Great Britain and Commonwealth countries – military, civilian and social historical aspects). Services: Reading Room (appointment required) Mon–Sat 10-5; telephone enquiry service Mon–Fri.

INDEPENDENT TELEVISION COMMISSION see BRITISH FILM INSTITUTE

INLAND REVENUE

Library, Inland Revenue, Room 28, Somerset House, Strand, London WC2R 1LB
☎020 7438 6648
Fax 020 7438 7562

Librarian P Woods MA DipLib MCLIP
Library Manager F Higginson
(By appointment only)

INSTITUT FRANÇAIS D'ÉCOSSE

Library, Institut français d'Écosse, 13 Randolph Crescent, Edinburgh EH3 7TT
☎0131 225 5366
Fax 0131 220 0648
e-mail: library@ifecosse.org.uk
url: http://www.ifecosse.org.uk
Librarian Ms A-M Usher

INSTITUT FRANÇAIS DU ROYAUME-UNI

La Médiathèque, Institut français du Royaume-Uni, 17 Queensberry Place, London SW7 2DT
☎020 7838 2144 (enquiries)
Fax 020 7838 2145
e-mail: library@ambafrance.org.uk
url: http://www.institut-francais.org.uk
Head Librarian Mme J Palot

Children's Library, Institut français du Royaume-Uni, 32 Harrington Road, London SW7 3HD
☎020 7838 2157
Librarian Mme J Gerlier

INSTITUTE OF ACTUARIES

Library, Institute of Actuaries, Napier House, 4 Worcester Street, Oxford OX1 2AW
☎(01865) 268206/7
Fax (01865) 268211
e-mail: libraries@actuaries.org.uk
url: http://www.actuaries.org.uk
Librarian Ms S Grover MA MCLIP
Deputy Librarian Ms F J McNeil BA MCLIP

INSTITUTE OF ARABLE CROPS RESEARCH – ROTHAMSTED LIBRARY

Institute of Arable Crops Research – Rothamsted Library, Rothamsted Experimental Station, Harpenden, Herts AL5 2JQ
☎(01582) 763133
Fax (01582) 760981
url: http://www.res.bbsrc.ac.uk/library/tlibindex.html
Librarian Mrs S E Allsopp BA MCLIP DipLib (e-mail: liz.allsopp@bbsrc.ac.uk)

INSTITUTE OF CHARTERED ACCOUNTANTS IN ENGLAND AND WALES

Library and Information Service, Institute of Chartered Accountants in England and Wales, Chartered Accountants' Hall, PO Box 433, Moorgate Place, London EC2P 2BJ
☎020 7920 8620
Fax 020 7920 8621
e-mail: library@icaew.co.uk
url: http://www.icaew.co.uk/library
Head of Library and Information Service Ms S P Moore BA(Hons)Lib MCLIP
Deputy Head of LIS Ms A Dennis BA(Hons) DipLib MCLIP
Customer Services Manager N Williams BA(Hons)Lib MCLIP
(The Library is for members of the ICAEW and ICAEW registered students.)

INSTITUTE OF CHARTERED SECRETARIES AND ADMINISTRATORS

Information Centre, Institute of Chartered Secretaries and Administrators, 16 Park Crescent, London W1B 1AH
☎020 7580 4741*
Fax 020 7612 7034
e-mail: informationcentre@icsa.co.uk
url: http://www.icsa.org.uk
Information Centre Manager A Tillbrook
(*Enquiries should be sent by letter, fax or e-mail)

INSTITUTE OF CONTEMPORARY HISTORY AND WIENER LIBRARY

Institute of Contemporary History and Wiener Library, 4 Devonshire Street, London W1W 5BH
☎020 7636 7247
Fax 020 7436 6428
e-mail: library@wienerlibrary.co.uk
url: http://www.wienerlibrary.co.uk
Librarian Ms G Müller-Oelrichs
Director B Barkow
Education Officer Ms K Klinger

INSTITUTE OF DIRECTORS

Business Library, Institute of Directors, 116 Pall Mall, London SW1Y 5ED
☎020 7451 3100
Fax 020 7321 0145
e-mail: businessinfo@iod.co.uk
url: http://www.iod.com
Head of Information and Advisory Services Ms A Burmajster MA MCLIP

INSTITUTE OF FINANCIAL SERVICES (*IFS*)

Library and Information Service, Institute of Financial Services (IFS), 90 Bishopsgate, London EC2N 4DQ
☎020 7444 7100 (general enquiries), 020 444 7123 (business research and information service)
Fax 020 7444 7109
e-mail: library@ifslearning.com
url: http://www.ifslearning.com (Institute); http://www.ifsis.org.uk (Information Service)
Manager, Information Service Miss S Vázquez BA(Hons) (020 7444 7125; e-mail: svazquez@ifslearning.com)

THE INSTITUTE OF LOGISTICS AND TRANSPORT

Logistics and Transport Centre, The Institute of Logistics and Transport, PO Box 5787, Corby, Northants NN17 4XQ
☎(01536) 740112 or 740139 (library), (01536) 740100 (reception)
Fax (01536) 740102 (FAO Librarian)
url: http://www.iolt.org.uk
Librarian P Huggins MA (e-mail: phuggins@iolt.org.uk)
Library Assistant Ms L Mayhew BA(Hons) (e-mail: lmayhew@iolt.org.uk)
(Access: free to Institute members and full-time students; a charge is made for non-member usage. London reading room open to members only – for details contact the Librarian)

INSTITUTE OF MANAGEMENT see CHARTERED MANAGEMENT INSTITUTE

THE INSTITUTE OF MATERIALS

Institute of Materials, The, 1 Carlton House Terrace, London SW1Y 5DB
☎020 7451 7360 (enquiries), 020 7451 7300 (switchboard)
Fax 020 7839 1702/020 7451 7406
url: http://www.materials.org.uk
Information Officer Ms H Kaune BA(Hons) DipLib (e-mail: Hilda_Kaune@materials.org.uk)

INSTITUTE OF OCCUPATIONAL MEDICINE

Library, Institute of Occupational Medicine, Roxburgh Place, Edinburgh EH8 9SU
☎0131 667 5131
Fax 0131 667 0136
e-mail: iom@iomhq.org.uk
Scientific Information Officer K Dixon MA(Hons) MA MCLIP

INSTITUTE OF PETROLEUM

Library and Information Service, Institute of Petroleum, 61 New Cavendish Street, London W1G 7AR

☎020 7467 7113/4/5 (enquiries), 020 7467 7111 (administration)
Fax 020 7255 1472
e-mail: lis@petroleum.co.uk
url: http://www.petroleum.co.uk
Head of Library and Information Service Mrs C M Cosgrove BSc(Hons) BA MCLIP FInstPet
Senior Information Officer C L Baker BA(Hons) MInstPet
Information Officer Miss S K Ball BA(Hons)

INSTITUTE OF PSYCHO-ANALYSIS

Library, Institute of Psycho-Analysis, 112a Shirland Road, Maida Vale, London W9 2EQ
☎020 7563 5008
Fax 020 7563 5001
e-mail: ipa_library@compuserve.com
url: http://www.psychoanalysis.org.uk
Library Executive Officer Ms A Chandler

INSTITUTION OF CHEMICAL ENGINEERS

Library and Information Services, Institution of Chemical Engineers, Davis Building, 165-189 Railway Terrace, Rugby, Warwicks CV21 3HQ
☎(01788) 578214
Fax (01788) 560833
url: http://www.icheme.org
Information Officer Miss T Farthing BA(Hons) (e-mail: library@icheme.org.uk)

INSTITUTION OF CIVIL ENGINEERS

Library, Institution of Civil Engineers, Great George Street, Westminster, London SW1P 3AA
☎020 7222 7722
Fax 020 7976 7610
e-mail: library@ice.org.uk
url: http://www.ice.org.uk
Librarian M M Chrimes BA MLS MCLIP

INSTITUTION OF ELECTRICAL ENGINEERS

Library, Institution of Electrical Engineers, Savoy Place, London WC2R 0BL
☎020 7344 5461 (enquiries & administration), 020 7344 5451 (management)
Fax 020 7497 3557
e-mail: libdesk@iee.org.uk
url: http://www.iee.org/library
Head of Library Services J Coupland BA MCLIP (020 7344 5451; e-mail: jcoupland@iee.org.uk)
Deputy Librarian Ms H Sparks BA MCLIP (020 7344 5705; e-mail: hsparks@iee.org.uk)
(Also includes the British Computer Society Library and Institution of Manufacturing Engineers Library)

INSTITUTION OF MECHANICAL ENGINEERS

Information and Library Service, Institution of Mechanical Engineers, 1 Birdcage Walk, London SW1H 9JJ
☎020 7973 1267/1274
Fax 020 7222 8762
e-mail: ils@imeche.org.uk
url: http://www.imeche.org.uk/library
Senior Librarian and Archivist K Moore MA
Information Officers Ms A Spiers BA MSc, Ms S Vinsen MA, Ms F Whittaker
Librarian M Claxton BSc

INSTITUTION OF MINING AND METALLURGY

Library, Institution of Mining and Metallurgy, 77 Hallam Street, London W1W 5BS
☎020 7580 3802
Fax 020 7436 5388
e-mail: lis@imm.org.uk
url: http://www.imm.org.uk
Head, Library and Information Services M McGarr BSc

THE INSTITUTION OF OCCUPATIONAL SAFETY AND HEALTH

Technical Enquiry and Information Service, The Institution of Occupational Safety and Health, The Grange, Highfield Drive, Wigston, Leicestershire LE18 1NN
☎0116 257 3199
Fax 0116 257 3107
e-mail: techinfo@iosh.co.uk
url: http://www.iosh.co.uk
Information Officers Mrs M Griggs, Miss K Mistry, Miss A Wells (e-mail: margaret.griggs@iosh.co.uk; kalpna.mistry@iosh.co.uk; anne.wells@iosh.co.uk)

INSTITUTO CERVANTES

Library, Instituto Cervantes, 102 Eaton Square, London SW1W 9AN
☎020 7201 0757
Fax 020 7235 0329
e-mail: biblon@cervantes.es
url: http://www.cervantes.es
Chief Librarian Ms C Alvarez

Site libraries

- Library, Instituto Cervantes, 58 Northumberland Road, Ballsbridge, Dublin 4, Republic of Ireland
  ☎(00 353 1) 668 2024
  Fax (00 353 1) 668 8416
  e-mail: cendub@cervantes.es
  Chief Librarian S Diaz-Jove

- Library, Instituto Cervantes, 326-330 (Unit 8), Deansgate, Campfield Avenue Arcade, Manchester M3 4FN
  ☎0161 661 4200
  Fax 0161 661 4203
  e-mail: cenman@cervantes.es
  Librarian J M Fernandez

INTERNATIONAL INSTITUTE FOR STRATEGIC STUDIES (IISS)

Library, International Institute for Strategic Studies (IISS), Arundel House, 13-15 Arundel Street, London WC2R 3DX
☎020 7395 9122 (library enquiries) or 020 7379 7676
Fax 020 7836 3108
e-mail: library@iiss.org
url: http://www.iiss.org
Chief Librarian Ms E Peacock BA(Hons)
Deputy Librarian Ms E Sullivan BA(Hons) MSc
Assistant Librarian Ms S Delfolie BA(Hons)

INTERNATIONAL LABOUR OFFICE

Library, International Labour Office, Millbank Tower, 21-24 Millbank, London SW1P 4QP
☎020 7828 6401
Fax 020 7233 5925
e-mail: ipu@ilo-london.org.uk
url: http://www.ilo.org/london
Head, Publications/Information Unit N Evans
(Library available by appointment, 10.00–16.30 Mon–Fri. Closed 1–2 for lunch)

INTERNATIONAL MARITIME ORGANIZATION

Library, International Maritime Organization, 4 Albert Embankment, London SE1 7SR
☎020 7735 7611
Fax 020 7587 3236
url: http://www.imo.org
Librarian Ms M Harvey (e-mail: mharvey@imo.org)

ISLE OF MAN FAMILY HISTORY SOCIETY

Library, Isle of Man Family History Society, Above Shoprite, 13 Michael Street, Peel, Isle of Man IM5 1HB
☎(01624) 843105
Librarian Ms D Quayle
(Open Tuesdays, Wednesdays and Saturday afternoons)

ISLE OF MAN GOVERNMENT

Tynwald Library, Isle of Man Government, Legislative Buildings, Isle of Man Government Office, Buck's Road, Douglas, Isle of Man IM1 3PW

☎(01624) 685520
Fax (01624) 685522
e-mail: library@tynwald.org.im
Librarian G C Haywood MCLIP
Deputy Librarian Miss S Gooding BA(Hons) PGDip (e-mail: S.Gooding@Tynwald.org.im)

ITALIAN INSTITUTE

Library, Italian Institute, 39 Belgrave Square, London SW1X 8NX
☎020 7235 1461 (switchboard), 020 7235 1461 ext 203/204 (library), 020 7396 4425 (library direct line)
Fax 020 7235 4618
e-mail: library@italcultur.org.uk
url: http://www.italcultur.org.uk
Acting Librarian Mrs M Reidy

JERWOOD LIBRARY OF THE PERFORMING ARTS

Jerwood Library of the Performing Arts, Trinity College of Music, King Charles Court, Old Royal Naval College, Greenwich, London SE10 9JF
☎020 8305 3950
Fax 020 8305 3999
e-mail: library@tcm.ac.uk
url: http://www.tcm.ac.uk
Chief Librarian Dr R Williamson PhD MA BMus
(Houses the Mander and Mitchenson Theatre Collection)

JOINT SERVICES COMMAND AND STAFF COLLEGE

Library, Joint Services Command and Staff College, Faringdon Road, Watchfield, Swindon, Wilts SN6 8TS
☎(01793) 788236
Fax (01793) 788281
e-mail: library@jscsc.org
Librarian C M Hobson MCLIP MBE

THE KENNEL CLUB

The Kennel Club Library, The Kennel Club, 1-5 Clarges Street, London W1J 8AB
☎020 7518 1009
Fax 020 7518 1045
e-mail: library@the-kennel-club.org.uk
url: http://www.the-kennel-club.org.uk/library/library.htm
Library and Collections Manager Miss S Tyrrell BA
(Open Mondays to Fridays, 9.30 am–4.30 pm by appointment)

KING'S FUND

Information and Library Service, King's Fund, 11-13 Cavendish Square, London W1G 0AN
☎020 7307 2568/9 (enquiries)
Fax 020 7307 2805
e-mail: library@kingsfund.org.uk
url: http://www.kingsfund.org.uk/library
Information and Library Service Manager Ms L Cawthra MA DipLib MCLIP

LABOUR PARTY

Labour Party, 16-18 Old Queen Street, London SW1H 9HP
☎020 7802 1000
Fax 020 7802 1111
e-mail: info@new.labour.org.uk
url: http://www.labour.org.uk

Additional site
Communications and Information Unit, Labour Party, Labour North, 131 Bedford Street, North Shields, Tyne and Wear NE29 6LA
☎0191 296 6012
Fax 0191 238 0136
e-mail: info@new.labour.org.uk
url: http://www.labour.org.uk
Communications/Information Supervisor Ms Z Edmonds

LAMBETH PALACE LIBRARY

Lambeth Palace Library, London SE1 7JU
☎020 7898 1400
Fax 020 7928 7932
url: http://www.lambethpalacelibrary.org
Librarian and Archivist R J Palmer PhD MCLIP

LAW COMMISSION

Library, Law Commission, Conquest House, 37/38 John Street, Theobalds Road, London WC1N 2BQ
☎020 7453 1241 (enquiries), 020 7453 1242 (administration)
Fax 020 7453 1297
e-mail: library@lawcommission.gsi.gov.uk
url: http://www.lawcom.gov.uk
Librarian K Tree BA

LAW SOCIETY

Library, Law Society, Law Society's Hall, 113 Chancery Lane, London WC2A 1PL
☎0870 606 2511 (enquiries), 020 7320 5699 (administration)
Fax 020 7831 1687
e-mail: lib-enq@lawsociety.org.uk

url: http://www.library.lawsociety.org.uk
Librarian and Head of Information Services C J Holland BA MCLIP

THE LIBRARY AND MUSEUM OF FREEMASONRY

The Library and Museum of Freemasonry, Freemasons' Hall, Great Queen Street, London WC2B 5AZ
☎020 7395 9257
Fax 020 7404 7418
Director Ms D Clements
Librarian Ms R Coombes
Curator M Dennis

THE LIBRARY ASSOCIATION see CILIP

LIBRARY FOR IRANIAN STUDIES

Library for Iranian Studies, The Woodlands Hall, Crown Street, London W3 8SA
☎020 8993 6384
Fax 020 8752 1300
Librarian Dr M Ajoudani

THE LINEN HALL LIBRARY

The Linen Hall Library, 17 Donegall Square North, Belfast BT1 5GB
☎028 9032 1707
Fax 028 9043 8586
e-mail: info@linenhall.com
url: http://www.linenhall.com
Librarian J C Gray BA DLIS

LINNEAN SOCIETY OF LONDON

Library, Linnean Society of London, Burlington House, Piccadilly, London W1J 0BF
☎020 7434 4479
Fax 020 7287 9364
e-mail: gina@linnean.org
url: http://www.linnean.org
Librarian G Douglas BSc FLS

LITERARY AND PHILOSOPHICAL SOCIETY OF NEWCASTLE UPON TYNE

Library, Literary and Philosophical Society of Newcastle upon Tyne, 23 Westgate Road, Newcastle upon Tyne NE1 1SE
☎0191 232 0192
Fax 0191 261 4494
e-mail: library@litandphil.org.uk
Librarian Ms K Easson

LONDON CHAMBER OF COMMERCE AND INDUSTRY

Information Centre, London Chamber of Commerce and Industry, 33 Queen Street, London EC4R 1AP
☎020 7248 4444 (members), 0906 476 1234 (premium line for non-members)
Fax 020 7203 1863
e-mail: info@londonchamber.co.uk
Head of Information Ms M Ewins

LONDON LIBRARY

London Library, 14 St James's Square, London SW1Y 4LG
☎020 7930 7705
Fax 020 7766 4766
e-mail: membership@londonlibrary.co.uk
url: http://www.londonlibrary.co.uk
Librarian Miss I T P A Lynn BA MLitt MCLIP

LONDON METROPOLITAN ARCHIVES

Library, London Metropolitan Archives, 40 Northampton Road, London EC1R 0HB
☎020 7332 3820; Minicom: 020 7278 8703
Fax 020 7833 9136
e-mail: ask.lma@corpoflondon.gov.uk
url: http://www.cityoflondon.gov.uk/lma
Senior Librarian Ms M Miller BA(Hons) DipLib MCLIP

LONDON'S TRANSPORT MUSEUM

Reference Library, London's Transport Museum, 39 Wellington Street, Covent Garden, London WC2E 7BB
☎020 7379 6344 ext 2253
Fax 020 7565 7252
e-mail: library@ltmuseum.co.uk
url: http://www.ltmuseum.co.uk
Library and Information Services Manager Ms C Warhurst BA MCLIP
Librarian Ms J Grant BA(Hons) DipIM MCLIP
(Readers by appointment Wednesday and Thursdays only)

LORD CHANCELLOR'S DEPARTMENT

HQ Library, Lord Chancellor's Department, Southside, 105 Victoria Street, London SW1E 6QT
☎020 7210 1979/1980
Fax 020 7210 1981
url: http://www.lcd.library@courtservice.gsi.gov.uk
Librarian Miss C Younger BLib MCLIP

MANX NATIONAL HERITAGE

Library, Manx National Heritage, Manx Museum, Douglas, Isle of Man IM1 3LY
☎(01624) 648000
Fax (01624) 648001
e-mail: library@mnh.gov.im
url: http://www.gov.im/mnh
Librarian A G Franklin MA MCLIP (e-mail: Alan.Franklin@mnh.gov.im)
Librarian/Archivist R M C Sims BA DAA DPESS RMSA
Assistant Archivist Ms W Thirkettle BA DipAS

MARINE BIOLOGICAL ASSOCIATION
(formerly Plymouth Marine Laboratory)

National Marine Biological Library, Marine Biological Association, Citadel Hill, Plymouth, Devon PL1 2PB
☎(01752) 633266
Fax (01752) 633102
e-mail: nmbl@pml.ac.uk
http://www.pml.ac.uk/nmbl/
Head of Library and Information Services Miss L Noble BSc MCLIP (01752 633270; e-mail: lno@pml.ac.uk)

MARX MEMORIAL LIBRARY

Marx Memorial Library, 37A Clerkenwell Green, London EC1R 0DU
☎020 7253 1485
Fax 020 7251 6039
e-mail: marx.library@britishlibrary.net
url: http://www.marxmemoriallibrary.sageweb.co.uk
Librarian Ms T Collins BA MSc

MARYLEBONE CRICKET CLUB

Library, Marylebone Cricket Club, Lord's Ground, St John's Wood, London NW8 8QN
☎020 7289 1611
Fax 020 7432 1062
Curator, Librarian and Archivist S E A Green MA DipArchAdmin
Assistant Curator Ms G Williams BA MPhil

MET OFFICE (formerly the Meteorological Office)

National Meteorological Library and Archives, Met Office, London Road, Bracknell, Berks RG12 2SZ
☎(01344) 854841 (enquiries)
Fax (01344) 854840
e-mail: metlib@metoffice.com
url: (Library) http://www.meto.gov.uk/sec1/sec1pg7.html; (Met Office) http://www.meto.gov.uk/home.html

Manager Ms J Claiden BA MCLIP
(Open to the public)

THE METEOROLOGICAL OFFICE see MET OFFICE

MINISTRY OF DEFENCE

MOD Information and Library Services, Ministry of Defence, Whitehall Library, 3-5 Great Scotland Yard, London SW1A 2HW
☎020 7218 4445 (general enquiries), 020 7218 4184 (administration)
Fax 020 7218 5413
e-mail: info-libsucsad@defence.mod.uk
Chief Librarian P Ryan BA MBA MCLIP

Site library

Library, Ministry of Defence, Kentigern House, 65 Brown Street, Glasgow G2 8EX
☎0141 224 2500
Fax 0141 224 2257
e-mail: library@khinf.demon.co.uk
Librarian Ms M J Gair BA(Hons) DipLib MCLIP

MORRAB LIBRARY

Morrab Library, Morrab Gardens, Penzance, Cornwall TR18 4DA
☎(01736) 364474
url: http://www.morrablibrary.co.uk
Librarian Mrs A Read
(Available on payment of an annual subscription or a daily fee)

MUSEUM OF LONDON

Library, Museum of London, London Wall, London EC2Y 5HN
☎020 7600 3699
Fax 020 7600 1058
e-mail: info@museumoflondon.org.uk
url: http://www.museumoflondon.org.uk
Library Officer Ms S Brooks MA MCLIP
(Readers by appointment only)

MUSEUM OF WELSH LIFE (AMGUEDDFA WERIN CYMRU)

Library, Museum of Welsh Life (Amgueddfa Werin Cymru), St Fagans, Cardiff CF5 6XB
☎029 2057 3446
Fax 029 2057 3490
Librarian N L Walker MA DipLib MCLIP (e-mail: Nic.Walker@nmgw.ac.uk)

NATIONAL ARMY MUSEUM

Library, National Army Museum, Royal Hospital Road, London SW3 4HT
☎020 7730 0717 ext 2222 (enquiries), ext 2215 (administration)
Fax 020 7823 6573
e-mail: info@national-army-museum.ac.uk
url: http://www.national-army-museum.ac.uk
Head of Department of Printed Books M B Ball MA AMA
Head of Archives, Photographs, Film and Sound A W Massie MA DPhil
Head of Fine and Decorative Art Miss J M Spencer-Smith MA AMA

NATIONAL ART LIBRARY

National Art Library, Victoria and Albert Museum, South Kensington, London SW7 2RL
☎020 7942 2400 (enquiries)
Fax 020 7924 2394
e-mail: nal-enquiries@vam.ac.uk
url: http://www.nal.vam.ac.uk/
Chief Librarian Ms S Lambert
Deputy Keeper J Meriton

Site library

Archive of Art and Design, National Art Library, Museum Archives, 23 Blythe Road, West Kensington, London W14 0QF
☎020 7603 1514
Fax 020 7602 6907
e-mail: archive@vam.ac.uk
Head of Archives Ms S Kelly
Archivist G Baxter

NATIONAL ASSEMBLY FOR WALES

Library, National Assembly for Wales, Cathays Park, Cardiff CF10 3NQ
☎029 2092 5449/3683
Fax 029 2082 5508
e-mail: AssemblyLibraryCathaysPark@wales.gsi.gov.uk
url: http://www.wales.gov.uk
Senior Librarian Vacant

NATIONAL CHILDREN'S BUREAU

Library and Information Service, National Children's Bureau, 8 Wakley Street, London EC1V 7QE
☎020 7843 6008 (enquiry line)
Fax 020 7843 6007
e-mail: library@ncb.org.uk
url: http://www.ncb.org.uk
Head of Library & Information Ms N Hilliard BA MCLIP

THE NATIONAL GALLERY

Libraries and Archive, The National Gallery, Trafalgar Square, London WC2N 5DN
☎020 7747 2830
Fax 020 7747 2892
Head of Libraries and Archive Ms E Hector MA MCLIP (e-mail: elspeth.hector@ng-london.org.uk)
Archivist Ms I Hunter MA (e-mail: isobel.hunter@ng-london.org.uk)
(Readers by appointment only)

NATIONAL HERITAGE LIBRARY

National Heritage Library, 313-315 Caledonian Road, London N1 1DR
☎020 7609 9639
Founder Director M McNiel
(A comprehensive reference collection covering every aspect of the landscape and culture of the British Isles: open by appointment only)

NATIONAL INSTITUTE FOR MEDICAL RESEARCH (MEDICAL RESEARCH COUNCIL)

Library, National Institute for Medical Research (Medical Research Council), The Ridgeway, Mill Hill, London NW7 1AA
☎020 8913 8630
Fax 020 8913 8534
e-mail: library@nimr.mrc.ac.uk
url: http://www.nimr.mrc.ac.uk/library
Librarian F Norman BSc DipLib MCLIP

NATIONAL INSTITUTE OF ADULT CONTINUING EDUCATION (NIACE)

Library, National Institute of Adult Continuing Education (NIACE), 21 De Montfort Street, Leicester LE1 7GE
☎0116 204 4200
Fax 0116 204 4253
e-mail: information@niace.org.uk
url: http://www.niace.org.uk
Librarian Ms H C Biggs BA MCLIP

NATIONAL INSTITUTE OF ECONOMIC AND SOCIAL RESEARCH

Library, National Institute of Economic and Social Research, 2 Dean Trench Street, Smith Square, London SW1P 3HE
☎020 7654 7665
Fax 020 7654 1900

e-mail: library@niesr.ac.uk
Librarian Ms P Oliver BA MCLIP (020 7654 1907; e-mail: poliver@niesr.ac.uk)

NATIONAL LIBRARY FOR THE BLIND

National Library for the Blind, Far Cromwell Road, Bredbury, Stockport, Cheshire SK6 2SG
☎0161 355 2000
Fax 0161 355 2098
e-mail: enquiries@nlbuk.org.uk
Minicom: 0161 355 2043
url: http://www.nlbuk.org
Chief Executive Ms H Brazier MA MCLIP (0161 355 2004)

NATIONAL LIBRARY OF SCOTLAND

National Library of Scotland, George IV Bridge, Edinburgh EH1 1EW
☎0131 226 4531
Fax 0131 622 4803
e-mail: enquiries@nls.uk
url: http://www.nls.uk
Librarian I D McGowan BA

Branch/regional libraries

- Inter-Library Services, National Library of Scotland, 33 Salisbury Place, Edinburgh EH9 1SL
  ☎0131 466 3815
  Fax 0131 466 3814
  e-mail: ils@nls.uk
- Map Library, National Library of Scotland, 33 Salisbury Place, Edinburgh EH9 1SL
  ☎0131 466 3813
  Fax 0131 466 3812
  e-mail: maps@nls.uk

NATIONAL LIBRARY OF WALES: LLYFRGELL GENEDLAETHOL CYMRU

National Library of Wales: Llyfrgell Genedlaethol Cymru, Aberystwyth, Ceredigion SY23 3BU
☎(01970) 632800
Fax (01970) 615709
e-mail: holi@llgc.org.uk
url: http://www.llgc.org.uk
Librarian A M W Green MA DipLib MCLIP

NATIONAL MARITIME MUSEUM

Caird Library, National Maritime Museum, Greenwich, London SE10 9NF
☎020 8312 6673/6529
Fax 020 8312 6632
e-mail: library@nmm.ac.uk; manuscripts@nmm.ac.uk

url: http://www.nmm.ac.uk
Head of Library and Manuscripts Ms J Davies BSc DipLib
Information Services Manager Ms J Buddle BA MA
Manuscripts Manager Mrs D Knott BA DipArch

NATIONAL MUSEUMS & GALLERIES OF WALES

Library, National Museums & Galleries of Wales, Cathays Park, Cardiff CF10 3NP
☎029 2057 3202
Fax 029 2057 3216
Librarian J R Kenyon BA MCLIP FSA FRHistS FSA(Scot)

NATIONAL MUSEUMS OF SCOTLAND

Library, National Museums of Scotland, Chambers Street, Edinburgh EH1 1JF
☎0131 247 4137 (enquiries), 0131 247 4153 (administration)
Fax 0131 247 4311
e-mail: library@nms.ac.uk
url: http://www.nms.ac.uk
Head of Library Ms E Rowan MSc
Depute Librarians A Martin MA DipLib, Ms C Whittaker MA
(Amalgamated collections of Royal Museum of Scotland and the former Museum of Antiquities libraries now based on the Chambers Street site)

Branch library
Library, National Museums of Scotland, National War Museum of Scotland, The Castle, Edinburgh EH1 2NG
☎0131 225 7534 ext 204
Curatorial Assistant Mrs E Philip

NATIONAL PHYSICAL LABORATORY

Main Library, National Physical Laboratory, Queen's Road, Teddington, Middlesex TW11 0LW
☎020 8943 6809
Fax 020 8943 6458
e-mail: library@npl.co.uk
url: http://www.npl.co.uk
Librarian Ms B M Sanger MCLIP

NATIONAL POLICE TRAINING see CENTRAL POLICE TRAINING AND DEVELOPMENT AUTHORITY

NATIONAL PORTRAIT GALLERY

Heinz Archive and Library, National Portrait Gallery, 2 St Martin's Place, London WC2H 0HE
☎020 7306 0055 ext 257
Fax 020 7306 0056

url: http://www.npg.org.uk
Head of Archive and Library R K Francis BSc(Hons) MA MCLIP
Librarian Ms A Leak BA(Hons) MA
(Readers by appointment only)

NATIONAL RAILWAY MUSEUM

Library and Archive, National Railway Museum, Leeman Road, York YO26 4XJ
☎(01904) 621261 (switchboard); (01904) 686235 (for appointments)
Fax (01904) 611112
e-mail: nrm.library@nmsi.ac.uk
url: http://www.nmsi.ac.uk/nrm
Librarian C P Atkins BSc (01904 686208; e-mail: p.atkins@nmsi.ac.uk)
Archivist R D Taylor (01904 686289; e-mail: r.taylor@nmsi.ac.uk)
(Open Mon–Fri 10.00–17.00 by prior appointment)

NATIONAL UNION OF TEACHERS

Library and Information Unit, National Union of Teachers, Hamilton House, Mabledon Place, London WC1H 9BD
☎020 7380 4713
Fax 020 7387 8458
url: http://www.teachers.org.uk
Information Officer Ms J Friedlander BA MCLIP (e-mail: j.friedlander@nut.org.uk)

NATIONAL YOUTH AGENCY

Information Centre, National Youth Agency, 17-23 Albion Street, Leicester LE1 6GD
☎0116 285 3700 (enquiries & administration)
Fax 0116 285 3775
e-mail: nya@nya.org.uk
url: http://www.nya.org.uk
Library Officer Ms J Poultney BA (e-mail: jop@nya.org.uk)
(Information collection on young people, the youth service and youth affairs. Provides a postal loan and enquiry answering service. Personal visitors welcome, by appointment)

NATURAL HISTORY MUSEUM

Library, Natural History Museum, Cromwell Road, London SW7 5BD
☎020 7942 5460 (general enquiries)
Fax 020 7942 5559
e-mail: library@nhm.ac.uk
url: http://www.nhm.ac.uk
Head of Information and Library Systems G Higley BSc
(The Library is divided into four specialist sections at South Kensington: General & Zoology (020 7942 5460); Botany (020 7942 5685); Entomology (020 7942 5751) and Earth Sciences (020 7942 5476). There is an out-station library: The Library, The Walter Rothschild Museum, Akeman Street, Tring, Herts HP23 6AP (020 7942 6159), which contains the collection of works on ornithology.)

NORTHERN IRELAND ASSEMBLY

Library, Northern Ireland Assembly, Parliament Buildings, Stormont, Belfast BT4 3XX
☎028 9052 1250
Fax 028 9052 1715/1922
e-mail: issuedesk.library@niassembly.gov.uk
Reader Services Librarian G D Woodman BA DipLib MCLIP (028 9052 1256; e-mail: george.woodman@niassembly.gov.uk)

NOTTINGHAM SUBSCRIPTION LIBRARY see BROMLEY HOUSE LIBRARY

OCCUPATIONAL PENSIONS REGULATORY AUTHORITY (OPRA)

Library, Occupational Pensions Regulatory Authority (Opra), Invicta House, Trafalgar Place, Brighton, East Sussex BN1 4DW
☎(01273) 627686
Fax (01273) 627760
url: http://www.opra.gov.uk
Information Officer Mrs J Godfrey BA(Hons) MCLIP BIALL (e-mail: jan.godfrey@opra.gov.uk)
(The Library is not open to the public.)

OFFICE FOR NATIONAL STATISTICS

National Statistics Information and Library Service, Office for National Statistics, 1 Drummond Gate, London SW1V 2QQ
☎020 7533 6262 (visits), 0845 601 3034 (enquiries)
Fax (01633) 652747
e-mail: info@statistics.gov.uk
url: http://library.ons.gov.uk
Chief Librarian J Birch BLib MCLIP (020 7533 6250; e-mail: john.birch@ons.gov.uk)
London Site Librarian A Cliftlands BA (020 7533 6257; e-mail: alan.cliftlands@ons.gov.uk)
(This library is open to the public. Includes most major government statistical series.)

Site libraries

- National Statistics Information and Library Service, Office for National Statistics, Room 1.001, Government Buildings, Cardiff Road, Newport, South Wales NP9 1XG
  ☎0845 601 3034 (enquiries), (01633) 812399 (administration)
  Fax (01633) 652747
  Librarian I W Bushnell BA MCLIP (01633 813033; e-mail: ian.bushnell@ons.gov.uk)
  (Library open to the public. Specializes in micro-economic data.)
- National Statistics Information and Library Service, Office for National Statistics, Segensworth Road, Titchfield, Fareham, Hants PO15 5PR
  ☎(01329) 813606

Fax (01329) 813406
url: http://library.ons.gov.uk
Librarian W Anderson BA MCLIP
(This library is not open to the public.)

OFFICE OF FAIR TRADING

Library and Information Centre, Office of Fair Trading, LC/7 Fleetbank House, 2-6 Salisbury Square, London EC4Y 8JX
☎020 7211 8938/9
Fax 020 7211 8940
For general OFT enquiries 0845 722 44 99; e-mail: enquiries@oft.gsi.gov.uk
OFT Publications orderline 0870 606 0321
url: http://www.oft.gov.uk
Librarian M Shrive BA(Hons) MCLIP

OFFICE OF THE DEPUTY PRIME MINISTER AND DEPARTMENT OF TRANSPORT (ODPM-DFT)

Information Sources and Services, Office of the Deputy Prime Minister and Department of Transport (ODPM-DFT), 2/H24 Ashdown House, 123 Victoria Street, London SW1E 6DE
☎020 7944 3333 (public information); 020 7944 3000 (switchboard)
Fax 020 7944 6098
url: http://www.odpm.gov.uk (ODPM); http://www.dft.gov.uk (DFT)
Information Sources and Services Branch Head Ms S Westcott MA DipLib MCLIP (020 7944 5830)

Library and information centres

- Ashdown House Information Centre, Office of the Deputy Prime Minister and Department of Transport (ODPM-DFT), 2/H24 Ashdown House, 123 Victoria Street, London SW1E 6DE
  ☎020 7944 3039 (for external enquiries)
  Fax 020 7944 6098
- Eland House Information Centre, Office of the Deputy Prime Minister and Department of Transport (ODPM-DFT), 1/F9 Eland House, London SW1E 5DU
  ☎020 7944 3199
  Fax 020 7944 3189
  Librarian
- Great Minster House Information Centre, Office of the Deputy Prime Minister and Department of Transport (ODPM-DFT), 1/10 Great Minster House, London SW1P 4DR
  ☎020 7944 2002
  Fax 020 7944 4716

OFFICE OF THE PARLIAMENTARY AND HEALTH SERVICE OMBUDSMAN (Office of the Parliamentary Commissioner for Administration and Health Service Commissioners)

Library and Information Service, Office of the Parliamentary and Health Service Ombudsman (Office of the Parliamentary Commissioner for Administration and Health Service Commissioners), 15th Floor, Millbank Tower, Millbank, London SW1P 4QP
☎020 7217 4104/4102
Fax 020 7217 4295
e-mail: library@ombudsman.gsi.gov.uk
url: http://www.ombudsman.org.uk
Information Manager Ms S Burge BA FCLIP

OFFICE OF THE RAIL REGULATOR

Office of the Rail Regulator, 1 Waterhouse Square, 138-142 Holborn, London EC1N 2TQ
☎020 7282 2001
Fax 020 7282 2045
e-mail: rail.library@orr.gsi.gov.uk
url: http://www.rail-reg.gov.uk
Librarian Ms S MacSwan BA MSc

OFGEM (OFFICE OF GAS AND ELECTRICITY MARKETS)

Research and Information Centre, OFGEM (Office of Gas and Electricity Markets), 9 Millbank, London SW1P 3GE
☎020 7901 7003/7004
Fax 020 7901 7378
e-mail: library@ofgem.gov.uk
url: http://www.ofgem.gov.uk
Librarian Ms B M Scott MSc MCLIP
Assistant Librarian K Smith
(Open 2pm–4.30pm Monday to Friday. By appointment only: 24 hours notice required.)

OFTEL (OFFICE OF TELECOMMUNICATIONS)

Research and Intelligence Unit, OFTEL (Office of Telecommunications), 50 Ludgate Hill, London EC4M 7JJ
☎020 7634 8761
Fax 020 7634 8946
e-mail: infocent@oftel.gov.uk
url: http://www.oftel.gov.uk
Head of Research and Intelligence Unit Ms A Cameron BA(Hons) (020 7634 8958)

OFWAT (OFFICE OF WATER SERVICES)

Library and Information Services, OFWAT (Office of Water Services), Centre City Tower, 7 Hill Street, Birmingham B5 4UA
☎0121 625 1361 (general enquiries)
Fax 0121 625 1362
e-mail: enquiries@ofwat.gsi.gov.uk
url: http://www.ofwat.gov.uk
Librarian and Information Services Manager Miss J W Fisher BSc MCLIP (0121 625 1361)

THE OMNIBUS SOCIETY

The John F. Parke Memorial Library, The Omnibus Society, Museum of Iron, Coalbrookdale, Ironbridge, Shropshire
Librarian A Mills (01922 631867 (tel/fax); e-mail: alanavrilmills@hotmail.com)
(Manned by volunteers, the Library is currently open to casual callers on the 1st, 3rd and 5th Wednesdays of the month (09.30–16.30), although other weekday appointments can be made by prior arrangement.)

ORDNANCE SURVEY

Library and Information Centre, Ordnance Survey, Room C128, Romsey Road, Southampton SO16 4GU
☎023 8079 2334
Fax 023 8079 2879
e-mail: scaine@ordsvy.gov.uk
url: http://www.ordnancesurvey.co.uk
Librarian Ms S Caine BSc MCLIP

PARTNERSHIP HOUSE MISSION STUDIES LIBRARY

Partnership House Mission Studies Library, 157 Waterloo Road, London SE1 8XA
☎020 7803 3215
Fax 020 7928 3627
e-mail: phmslib@freenet.co.uk
url: http://phmsl.soutron.com
Principal Librarian C E Rowe BA MA MCLIP

PIRA INTERNATIONAL

Information Services, PIRA International, Randalls Road, Leatherhead, Surrey KT22 7RU
☎(01372) 802050 (enquiries); 802061 (photocopy requests)
Fax (01372) 802239
e-mail: docdel@pira.co.uk
url: http://www.piranet.com
Business Manager Ms D Deavin

PLUNKETT FOUNDATION

Library, Plunkett Foundation, 23 Hanborough Business Park, Long Hanborough, Oxon OX29 8SG
☎(01993) 883636
Fax (01993) 883576
e-mail: info@plunkett.co.uk
url: http://www.plunkett.co.uk
Information Services Manager Ms K Targett BA(Hons)
(Focus on history and practice of cooperatives and rural enterprise)

PLYMOUTH MARINE LABORATORY see MARINE BIOLOGICAL ASSOCIATION

PLYMOUTH PROPRIETARY LIBRARY

Plymouth Proprietary Library, Alton Terrace, 111 North Hill, Plymouth, Devon PL4 8JY
☎(01752) 660515
Librarian J R Smith

POETRY LIBRARY

Poetry Library, Royal Festival Hall, London SE1 8XX
☎020 7921 0943/0664
Fax 020 7921 0939
e-mail: info@poetrylibrary.org.uk
url: http://www.poetrylibrary.org.uk
Librarian Ms M Enright BA DipLib
(Opening hours 11am-8pm 6 days a week; closed on Mondays)

POLISH LIBRARY

Polish Library, 238-246 King Street, London W6 0RF
☎020 8741 0474
Fax 020 8741 7724
e-mail: bibliotekapolska@posklibrary.fsnet.co.uk
Librarian Mrs J Szmidt MA

THE PORTICO LIBRARY AND GALLERY

The Portico Library and Gallery, 57 Mosley Street, Manchester M2 3HY
☎0161 236 6785
Fax 0161 236 6785
url: http://www.theportico.org.uk
Librarian Miss E Marigliano BA(Hons) (e-mail: librarian@theportico.org.uk)
(Tours by arrangement. Nineteenth-century stock available for scholarly research. Gallery open to the public.)

PROUDMAN OCEANOGRAPHIC LABORATORY

Library, Proudman Oceanographic Laboratory, Bidston Observatory, Bidston Hill, Prenton, Wirral CH43 7RA
☎0151 653 1581
Fax 0151 653 6269
url: http://www.pol.ac.uk
Librarian Ms J Martin BA MSc MCLIP (e-mail: jul@pol.ac.uk)
Assistant Librarian Ms N McShane BA

PUBLIC HEALTH LABORATORY SERVICE

Central Library, Public Health Laboratory Service, Central Public Health Laboratory, 61 Colindale Avenue, London NW9 5HT
☎020 8200 4400 ext 4616 (enquiries), ext 4617 (Chief Librarian)
Fax 020 8200 7875
url: http://www.phls.co.uk
Chief Librarian Miss M A Clennett BA MCLIP (e-mail: mclennett@phls.nhs.uk)
Deputy Librarian D J Keech MSc DipLib MCLIP (e-mail: dkeech@phls.nhs.uk)

PUBLIC RECORD OFFICE

Resource Centre and Library, Public Record Office, Kew, Richmond, Surrey TW9 4DU
☎020 8876 3444 ext 2458 (general library enquiries)
Fax 020 8878 8905
e-mail: enquiry@pro.gov.uk
url: http://www.pro.gov.uk
Librarian Ms H Pye-Smith MA (020 8392 5278; e-mail: library@pro.gov.uk)

QINETIQ (formerly Defence Evaluation and Research Agency)

Information Centre, Qinetiq, Winfrith Technology Centre, Building A22, Dorchester, Dorset DT2 8XJ
☎(01305) 212447
Fax (01305) 212444
Information Specialist D W Low (e-mail: dwlow@qinetiq.com)

RADIOCOMMUNICATIONS AGENCY

Information and Library Service, Radiocommunications Agency, 9th Floor, Wyndham House, 189 Marsh Wall, London E14 9SX
☎020 7211 0502/0505
Fax 020 7211 0507
e-mail: library@ra.gsi.gov.uk
url: http://www.radio.gov.uk
Information and Publicity Manager Ms J Fraser
Librarian Ms J Cann BSc DipLib MCLIP

RELIGIOUS SOCIETY OF FRIENDS IN BRITAIN (QUAKERS)

Library, Religious Society of Friends in Britain (Quakers), Friends House, 173-177 Euston Road, London NW1 2BJ
☎020 7663 1135
Fax 020 7663 1001
e-mail: library@quaker.org.uk
url: http://www.quaker.org.uk/library.html
Librarian Ms H L Rowland BA MCLIP

THE RESEARCH COUNCILS

Joint Information and Library Service, Research Councils, The, Polaris House, North Star Avenue, Swindon, Wiltshire SN2 1SZ
☎(01793) 442103 (enquiries)
Fax (01793) 442042
e-mail: jils@pparc.ac.uk or library@pparc.ac.uk
url: http://www.pparc.ac.uk/jils/
Senior Librarian Ms I Howard BA MCLIP (01793 442008; e-mail: howardi@pparc.ac.uk)

Library serves the following research councils based at this site:
Biotechnology and Biological Sciences Research Council (BBSRC)
(01793 413200; fax 01793 413201)
Engineering and Physical Sciences Research Council (EPSRC)
(01793 444000; fax 01793 444010)
Natural Environment Research Council (NERC)
(01793 411500; fax 01793 411501
Particle Physics and Astronomy Research Council (PPARC)
(01793 442000; fax 01793 442002)
Economic and Social Sciences Research Council (ESRC) (01793 413000; fax 01793 413001)
(some enquiries answered on behalf of ESRC)

ROYAL ACADEMY OF ARTS

Library, Royal Academy of Arts, Burlington House, Piccadilly, London W1J 0BD
☎020 7300 5737 (enquiries), 020 7300 5740 (administration)
Fax 020 7300 5765
e-mail: library@royalacademy.org.uk
url: http://www.royal.academy.org.uk
Head of Library Services A M Waterton
Schools Librarian Ms L Weston

ROYAL AERONAUTICAL SOCIETY

Library, Royal Aeronautical Society, 4 Hamilton Place, London W1J 7BQ
☎020 7670 4362 (enquiries)
Fax 020 7670 4359
url: http://www.aerosociety.com
Librarian B L Riddle (e-mail: brian.riddle@raes.org.uk)

ROYAL AIR FORCE COLLEGE

Library, Royal Air Force College, Cranwell, Sleaford, Lincs NG34 8HB
☎(01400) 261201 ext 6329
Fax (01400) 261201 ext 6266
e-mail: college.library@dial.pipex.com
College Librarian & Archivist Ms M Guy BA(Hons) DipLib MCLIP

ROYAL AIR FORCE MUSEUM

Department of Research and Information Services, Royal Air Force Museum, Hendon, London NW9 5LL
☎020 8205 2266
Fax 020 8200 1751
e-mail: info@rafmuseum.com
url: http://www.rafmuseum.com
Senior Keeper P J V Elliott MA BSc MCLIP
(Prior appointment necessary)

ROYAL ASTRONOMICAL SOCIETY

Library, Royal Astronomical Society, Burlington House, Piccadilly, London W1J 0BQ
☎020 7734 3307/4582
Fax 020 7494 0166
e-mail: info@ras.org.uk
url: http://www.ras.org.uk
Librarian P D Hingley BA MCLIP RD (e-mail: pdh@ras.org.uk)
Assistant Librarian Miss M I Chibnall BA MCLIP (e-mail: mic@ras.org.uk)
(Extensive archive and rare book collection covering astronomy and geophysics. Enquiries in writing or by e-mail preferred, access by appointment)

ROYAL BOTANIC GARDEN, EDINBURGH

Library, Royal Botanic Garden, Edinburgh, 20A Inverleith Row, Edinburgh EH3 5LR
☎0131 248 2853 (enquiries), 0131 248 2850 (administration)
Fax 0131 248 2901
e-mail: library@rbge.org.uk
url: http://www.rbge.org.uk
Head of Library Mrs H J Hutcheon BSc MCLIP

ROYAL BOTANIC GARDENS, KEW

Library & Archives, Royal Botanic Gardens, Kew, Richmond, Surrey TW9 3AE
☎020 8332 5414
Fax 020 8332 5430
e-mail: library@rbgkew.org.uk
url: http://www.rbgkew.org.uk/collections
Head of Library & Archives J Flanagan MCLIP
Archivist Ms K Manners MA MArAd
Illustrations Curator Miss M Ward

ROYAL COLLEGE OF PHYSICIANS AND SURGEONS OF GLASGOW

Library, Royal College of Physicians and Surgeons of Glasgow, 232-242 St Vincent Street, Glasgow G2 5RJ
☎0141 227 3204 (enquiries), 0141 221 6072 (administration)
Fax 0141 221 1804
url: http://www.rcpsglasg.ac.uk
Librarian J Beaton MA(Hons) DipLib MCLIP FSA(Scot) (e-mail: james.beaton@rcpsglasg.ac.uk)
Archivist Mrs C Parry BA(Hons) DAA FETC (e-mail: carol.parry@rcpsglasg.ac.uk)
Assistant Librarian Mrs V McClure MA(Hons) MSc

ROYAL COLLEGE OF PHYSICIANS OF EDINBURGH

Library, Royal College of Physicians of Edinburgh, 9 Queen Street, Edinburgh EH2 1JQ
☎0131 225 7324
Fax 0131 220 3939
e-mail: library@rcpe.ac.uk
url: http://www.rcpe.ac.uk
Librarian I A Milne MLib MCLIP

ROYAL COLLEGE OF PHYSICIANS OF LONDON

Library, Royal College of Physicians of London, 11 St Andrews Place, Regent's Park, London NW1 4LE
☎020 7935 1174 ext 312/3
Fax 020 7486 3729
Minicom 020 7486 5687
e-mail: info@rcplondon.ac.uk
url: http://www.rcplondon.ac.uk
Manager, Library and Information Service Ms C Moss-Gibbons BLib(Hons) PGCE

ROYAL COLLEGE OF PSYCHIATRISTS

Library and Information Service, Royal College of Psychiatrists, 17 Belgrave Square, London SW1X 8PG
☎020 7235 2351 ext 138/152
Fax 020 7259 6303
e-mail: infoservices@rcpsych.ac.uk
url: http://www.rcpsych.ac.uk
Librarian Ms M Davis
Honorary Librarian Dr D Tate

ROYAL COLLEGE OF SURGEONS OF ENGLAND

Libary and Lumley Study Centre, Royal College of Surgeons of England, 35-43 Lincoln's Inn Fields, London WC2A 3PE
☎020 7869 6555/6556 (enquiries), 020 7405 3474 (College switchboard)

Fax 020 7405 4438
e-mail: library@rcseng.ac.uk
url: http://www.rcseng.ac.uk
Librarian Mrs T Knight MA MA DipLib MCLIP

ROYAL COLLEGE OF VETERINARY SURGEONS

RCVS Library and Information Service, Royal College of Veterinary Surgeons, Belgravia House, 62-64 Horseferry Road, London SW1P 2AF
☎020 7222 2021
Fax 020 7222 2004
e-mail: library@rcvs.org.uk
url: http://www.rcvs.org.uk
Head of Library and Information Services T Roper BA DipLib MCLIP (e-mail: t.roper@rcvs.org.uk)
Reader Services Librarian Ms J Harris BA MCLIP (e-mail: j.harris@rcvs.org.uk)
Systems Librarian Ms V Carbines BA (e-mail: v.carbines@rcvs.org.uk)
Senior Library Assistant Mrs P Greening (e-mail: p.greening@rcvs.org.uk)
Library Assistant Mrs A Marsh (e-mail: a.marsh@rcvs.org.uk)

ROYAL COMMISSION ON THE ANCIENT AND HISTORICAL MONUMENTS OF WALES

National Monuments Record of Wales, Royal Commission on the Ancient and Historical Monuments of Wales, Crown Building, Plas Crug, Aberystwyth, Ceredigion SY23 1NJ
☎(01970) 621200
Fax (01970) 627701
e-mail: nmr.wales@rcahmw.org.uk
url: http://www.rcahmw.org.uk
Secretary P R White BA FSA
Librarian Ms P Moore BA MCLIP

ROYAL ENGINEERS LIBRARY

Royal Engineers Library, Brompton Barracks, Chatham, Kent ME4 4UX
☎(01634) 822416
Fax (01634) 822419
Assistant Librarian Mrs M Magnuson

ROYAL ENTOMOLOGICAL SOCIETY

Library, Royal Entomological Society, 41 Queen's Gate, London SW7 5HR
☎020 7584 8361
Fax 020 7581 8505
e-mail: lib@royensoc.co.uk
url: http://www.royensoc.co.uk
Librarian Ms B I Pedersen BA(Hons) MCLIP

ROYAL GEOGRAPHICAL SOCIETY (with the Institute of British Geographers)

Library, Royal Geographical Society (with the Institute of British Geographers), Kensington Gore, London SW7 2AR
☎020 7591 3040
Fax 020 7591 3001
e-mail: library@rgs.org
url: http://www.rgs.org
Librarian E Rae BA(Hons) MA DipLIS
Deputy Librarian Miss J C Turner BA(Hons)
Library Assistant Miss Miss J Carrington BA(Hons)
(The library will be closed until Autumn 2003)

ROYAL HORTICULTURAL SOCIETY

The Lindley Library, Royal Horticultural Society, 80 Vincent Square, London SW1P 2PE
☎020 7821 3050
Fax 020 7828 3022
e-mail: library.london@rhs.org.uk
url: http://www.rhs.org.uk/libraries/libraries_london.asp
Librarian and Archivist Dr B Elliott BA MA PhD

ROYAL INSTITUTE OF BRITISH ARCHITECTS

British Architectural Library, Royal Institute of British Architects, 66 Portland Place, London W1B 1AD
☎020 7307 3707 (24-hr recorded information service); 020 7580 5533 (switchboard)
Fax 020 7631 1802
Public information line (calls 50p per min): (0906) 302 0400
e-mail: info@inst.riba.org
url: http://www.architecture.com
Director Ms R H Kamen BA MAMat MLS FCLIP FRSA

Branch library

British Architectural Library Drawings Collection, Royal Institute of British Architects, 21 Portman Square, London W1H 9HF
☎020 7580 5533
Fax 020 7486 3797
Assistant Director, Special Collections and Curator, Drawings Collection C Hind MA DipLib MCLIP

ROYAL INSTITUTE OF INTERNATIONAL AFFAIRS

Library, Royal Institute of International Affairs, Chatham House, 10 St James's Square, London SW1Y 4LE
☎020 7957 5723 (enquiries)
Fax 020 7957 5710
e-mail: libenquire@riia.org

url: http://www.riia.org
Librarian Mrs C Hume BA DipLib MSc MCLIP (020 7957 5720; e-mail: chume@riia.org)
Deputy Librarian Mrs M Bone BSc (020 7314 2775; e-mail: mbone@riia.org)

ROYAL INSTITUTE OF NAVIGATION

Library, Royal Institute of Navigation, 1 Kensington Gore, London SW7 2AT
☎020 7591 3130
Fax 020 7591 3131
e-mail: info@rin.org.uk
url: http://www.rin.org.uk
Librarian
(The library stocks 2000 titles on land, sea and air navigation. It is free to members and open to the public on an appointment-only basis)

ROYAL INSTITUTION OF GREAT BRITAIN

Library, Royal Institution of Great Britain, 21 Albemarle Street, London W1S 4BS
☎020 7670 2939
Fax 020 7629 3569
e-mail: ril@ri.ac.uk
Keeper of Collections Dr F James (020 7670 2924; e-mail: fjames@ri.ac.uk)

ROYAL INSTITUTION OF NAVAL ARCHITECTS

Library, Royal Institution of Naval Architects, 10 Upper Belgrave Street, London SW1X 8BQ
☎020 7235 4622
Fax 020 7259 5912
e-mail: hq@rina.org.uk
url: http://www.rina.org.uk
Technical Information Officer J Date MEng

ROYAL MILITARY ACADEMY SANDHURST

Central Library, Royal Military Academy Sandhurst, Camberley, Surrey GU15 4PQ
☎(01276) 412367
Fax (01276) 412538
Senior Librarian A A Orgill MA DipLib MCLIP (e-mail: aaorgill@aol.com)

ROYAL NATIONAL INSTITUTE FOR DEAF PEOPLE

RNID Library, Royal National Institute for Deaf People, Institute of Laryngology and Otology, 330-332 Gray's Inn Road, London WC1X 8EE
☎020 7915 1553 (Voice and Minicom; enquiries & administration)
Fax 020 7915 1443
e-mail: rnidlib@ucl.ac.uk
url: http://www.ucl.ac.uk/Library/RNID
Librarian Ms M Plackett MCLIP

ROYAL NATIONAL INSTITUTE FOR THE BLIND

Research Library, Royal National Institute for the Blind, 105 Judd Street, London WC1H 9NE
☎020 7391 2052
Fax 020 7388 0891
e-mail: library@rnib.org.uk
url: http://www.rnib.org.uk/library
Research Library Manager J B Roland BA DipLib MCLIP
Librarian Ms E Bell MA MA

RNIB Braille Library; RNIB Cassette Library; RNIB Talking Books Library
Contact 0845 702 3153

Library Services, Royal National Institute for the Blind, PO Box 173, Peterborough PE2 6WS
☎(01733) 375333
Fax (01733) 371555
e-mail: libraryinfo@rnib.org.uk
Library Services Manager J Crampton MCLIP

ROYAL PHARMACEUTICAL SOCIETY OF GREAT BRITAIN

Library, Royal Pharmaceutical Society of Great Britain, 1 Lambeth High Street, London SE1 7JN
☎020 7735 9141 (switchboard); 020 7572 2300 (direct)
Fax 020 7572 2499
e-mail: library@rpsgb.org.uk
url: http://www.rpsgb.org.uk
Head of Information Centre R T Allcorn BSc MCLIP
Librarian R Morrison BLib
Assistant Librarian Miss A S Walker BA(Hons) MCLIP

ROYAL PHOTOGRAPHIC SOCIETY

RPS Collection, Royal Photographic Society, Insight: Collections and Research Centre, National Museum of Photography, Film & Television, Bradford BD1 1MQ
☎(01274) 202030 (switchboard)
Fax (01274) 723155
url: http://www.nmpft.org.uk
Curator Vacant
Librarian Vacant
(The collection is moving to the new address above during 2002/3. Please see website for progress. Prior appointment essential for members and non-members)

ROYAL SOCIETY

Library, Royal Society, 6–9 Carlton House Terrace, London SW1Y 5AG
☎020 7451 2606
Fax 020 7930 2170

e-mail: library@royalsoc.ac.uk
url: http://www.royalsoc.ac.uk
Head of Library and Information Services Ms K Peters MCLIP

ROYAL SOCIETY FOR THE PREVENTION OF ACCIDENTS

Information Centre, Royal Society for the Prevention of Accidents, Edgbaston Park, 353 Bristol Road, Birmingham B5 7ST
☎0121 248 2063/6
Fax 0121 248 2081
e-mail: infocentre@rospa.org.uk
url: http://www.rospa.org.uk
Information Services Manager Ms P Siddall BSc MSc MCLIP (0121 248 2065; e-mail: psiddall@rospa.org.uk)
Senior Information Officer (Statistics) Ms D Hooper BA(Hons) (0121 248 2064; e-mail: d.hooper@rospa.org.uk)
Information Officer Mrs L Lawson BSocSc MA (0121 248 2063; e-mail: llawson@rospa.org.uk)

ROYAL SOCIETY OF CHEMISTRY

Library and Information Centre, Royal Society of Chemistry, Burlington House, Piccadilly, London W1J 0BA
☎020 7437 8656; 020 7440 3373 (direct)
Fax 020 7287 9798
e-mail: library@rsc.org
url: http://www.rsc.org/library
Librarian N Lees MSc MCLIP

ROYAL SOCIETY OF MEDICINE

Library, Royal Society of Medicine, 1 Wimpole Street, London W1G 0AE
☎020 7290 2940 (enquiries), 020 7290 2931 (administration)
Fax 020 7290 2939 (requests), 020 7290 2976 (administration)
e-mail: library@rsm.ac.uk
url: http://www.rsm.ac.uk
Director of Information Services I R Snowley BA MBA MCLIP FRSA

ROYAL STATISTICAL SOCIETY

Royal Statistical Society, 12 Errol Street, London EC1Y 8LX
☎020 7638 8998
Fax 020 7256 7598
e-mail: rss@rss.org.uk
url: http://www.rss.org.uk
Society Archivist Ms J Foster (e-mail: j.foster@rss.org.uk)
(Yule and Newmarch Collections; pre-1800 books and Society archives. Viewing by appointment only)

Historical Collection housed at the Albert Sloman Library, University of Essex, Wivenhoe Park, Colchester CO4 3SQ
☎ (01206) 873172/181
Sub-Librarian N Cochrane (e-mail: nigelc@essex.ac.uk)
Assistant Librarian A Macmillen (e-mail: amacmi@essex.ac.uk)

ROYAL TOWN PLANNING INSTITUTE

Library, Royal Town Planning Institute, 41 Botolph Lane, London EC3R 8DL
☎020 7929 9494 (switchboard); 020 7929 9452 (direct)
Fax 020 7929 9490
e-mail: library@rtpi.org.uk
url: http://www.rtpi.org.uk
Librarian Ms P Dobby BA MCLIP

RSA

Library, RSA, 8 John Adam Street, London WC2N 6EZ
☎020 7451 6874 (Library), 020 7451 6845 (Archive)
Fax 020 7839 5805
e-mail: library@rsa.org.uk; archive@rsa.org.uk
url: http://www.theRSA.org.uk
Library Service Co-ordinator Mrs J Cranage
Archivist C Denvir
(Access by appointment)

ST DEINIOL'S RESIDENTIAL LIBRARY

St Deiniol's Residential Library, Hawarden, Deeside, Flintshire CH5 3DF
☎(01244) 532350
Fax (01244) 520643
e-mail: deiniol.visitors@btinternet.com
url: http://www.st-deiniols.org
Warden Rev. P B Francis MTheol
Librarian: Miss P J Williams BA DipLib
(This is a residential library specializing in theology, history and Victorian studies. The collection of over 250,000 volumes includes W E Gladstone's personal library. Modern residential accommodation is available at modest charges. Day readers welcome. Testimonial required)

SCIENCE FICTION FOUNDATION COLLECTION

Science Fiction Foundation Collection, University of Liverpool Library, PO Box 123, Liverpool L69 3DA
☎0151 794 2696 (library)
Fax 0151 794 2681
url: http://sca.lib.liv.ac.uk/collections/index.html
Librarian/Administrator A Sawyer MPhil MCLIP (0151 794 3142; e-mail: asawyer@liverpool.ac.uk)

SCIENCE MUSEUM LIBRARY

Science Museum Library, Imperial College Road, London SW7 5NH
☎020 7942 4242
Fax 020 7942 4243
e-mail: smlinfo@nmsi.ac.uk
url: http://www.nmsi.ac.uk/library/
Head of Library Ms P Dingley BA MCLIP (020 7942 4240)
(A national library for the history and public understanding of science and technology. Open free to the public. Enquiries accepted in person, by letter or by telephone. Some services are run jointly with Imperial College, Central Libraries.)

SCOTTISH ASSOCIATION FOR MARINE SCIENCE

Library, Scottish Association for Marine Science, Dunstaffnage Marine Laboratory, Dunbeg, Oban, Argyll PA37 1QA
☎(01631) 559000
Fax (01631) 559001
url: http://www:sams.ac.uk
Librarian Ms E Walton MA MCLIP (e-mail: ew@dml.ac.uk)

SCOTTISH BOOK TRUST

Children's Reference Library, Scottish Book Trust, 137 Dundee Street, Edinburgh EH11 1BG
☎0131 229 3663
Fax 0131 228 4293
e-mail: info@scottishbooktrust.com
url: http://www.scottishbooktrust.com
Library Contact Ms A Liddle

SCOTTISH CONSERVATION BUREAU

Resource Centre, Scottish Conservation Bureau, Room G20, Longmore House, Salisbury Place, Edinburgh EH9 1SH
☎0131 668 8642
Fax 0131 668 8669
Research Officer Ms D Mattison MA (e-mail: denise.mattison@scotland.gov.uk)

SCOTTISH ENTERPRISE

The Knowledge Exchange, Scottish Enterprise, 150 Broomielaw, Glasgow G2 8LU
☎0141 248 2700 (main), 0141 228 2268 (direct line)
Fax 0141 228 2818
url: http://www.Scottish-enterprise.com
Manager Ms G Rogers MA DipLib (e-mail: gail.rogers@scotent.co.uk)

SCOTTISH EXECUTIVE

Library and Information Services Centre, Scottish Executive, K Spur, Saughton House, Broomhouse Drive, Edinburgh EH11 3XD

☎0131 244 4565
Fax 0131 244 4545
e-mail: library@scotland.gsi.gov.uk
Head of Library and Information Services Ms J Mackenzie BA MA MCLIP

SCOTTISH NATURAL HERITAGE

Library Services, Scottish Natural Heritage, 2 Anderson Place, Edinburgh EH6 5NP
☎0131 446 2479 (enquiries), 0131 446 2478 (library management)
Fax 0131 446 2405
e-mail: library@snh.gov.uk
Library Manager Ms A Coupe MCLIP (e-mail: alwyn.coupe@snh.gov.uk)

SCOTTISH PARLIAMENT

Scottish Parliament Information Centre (SPICe), Scottish Parliament, George IV Bridge, Edinburgh EH99 1SP
☎0131 348 5000
Fax 0131 348 5378
e-mail: spice@scottish.parliament.uk
url: http://www.scottish.parliament.uk
Head of Research and Information Group Ms J Seaton FCLIP

SIGNET LIBRARY

Signet Library, Parliament Square, Edinburgh EH1 1RF
☎0131 225 4923
Fax 0131 220 4016
e-mail: library@wssociety.co.uk
url: http://www.signetlibrary.co.uk
Librarian Ms A R Walker BA MCLIP

SOCIÉTÉ JERSIAISE

Lord Coutanche Library, Société Jersiaise, 7 Pier Road, St Helier, Jersey, Channel Islands JE2 4XW
☎(01534) 730538 (enquiries), (01534) 633392 (administration)
Fax (01534) 888262
e-mail: library@societe-jersiaise.org
url: http://www.societe-jersiaise.org
Librarian Ms A M Max BA DipLib MCLIP

SOCIETY FOR COOPERATION IN RUSSIAN AND SOVIET STUDIES

Library, Society for Cooperation in Russian and Soviet Studies, 320 Brixton Road, London SW9 6AB
☎020 7274 2282
Fax 020 7274 3230

e-mail: ruslibrary@scrss.co.uk
url: http://www.scrss.co.uk
Librarian/Information Officer Ms J Rosen BA(Hons) DipLib

SOCIETY OF ANTIQUARIES OF LONDON

Library, Society of Antiquaries of London, Burlington House, Piccadilly, London W1J 0BE
☎020 7479 7084
Fax 020 7287 6967
e-mail: library@sal.org.uk
url: http://www.sal.org.uk
Librarian E B Nurse MA FSA MCLIP

SOCIETY OF GENEALOGISTS

Library, Society of Genealogists, 14 Charterhouse Buildings, Goswell Road, London EC1M 7BA
☎020 7250 0291
Fax 020 7250 1800
e-mail: library@sog.org.uk
url: http://www.sog.org.uk
Librarian Ms S Gibbons BA MCLIP

STRATEGIC RAIL AUTHORITY

The Secretariat, Strategic Rail Authority, 55 Victoria Street, London SW1H 0EU
☎020 7654 6000
Fax 020 7654 6010
Head of Secretariat J Watson

SUPREME COURT LIBRARY

Supreme Court Library, Royal Courts of Justice, Queens Building, Strand, London WC2A 2LL
☎020 7947 6587 (enquiries), 020 7947 7198 (administration)
Fax 020 7947 6661
Supreme Court Librarian Ms J M Robertson BA MCLIP

TATE BRITAIN (formerly the Tate Library)

The Hyman Kreitman Research Centre for the Tate Library and Archive, Tate Britain, Millbank, London SW1P 4RG
☎020 7887 8838
Fax 020 7887 3952
e-mail: research.centre@tate.org.uk
url: http://www.tate.org.uk/research
Head of Library and Archive Ms B Houghton DipAD
Librarian Ms M Duff BA DipEd DipNZLS
Archivist Vacant

Head of Readers' Services Ms E Foden-Lenahan BA MA
(Readers by appointment only)

THE TATE LIBRARY see TATE BRITAIN

TAVISTOCK AND PORTMAN NHS TRUST

Tavistock and Portman Library, Tavistock and Portman NHS Trust, 120 Belsize Lane, London NW3 5BA
☎020 7447 3776 (direct line)
Fax 020 7447 3734
e-mail: library@tavi-port.org
Librarian Ms A Douglas MCLIP BSc MA

THE THEATRE MUSEUM

The Theatre Museum Research Department, The Theatre Museum, 1E Tavistock Street, London WC2E 7PR
☎020 7943 4700
Fax 020 7943 4777
url: http://www.theatremuseum.org
Head of Information Services and Collections Management Ms C Hudson BA MCLIP

TPS CONSULT LTD

The Information Centre, TPS Consult Ltd, Centre Tower, Whitgift Centre, Croydon, Surrey CR9 0AU
☎020 8256 4110
Fax 0870 128 4894
url: http://www.tpsconsult.co.uk
Information Centre Manager G Ziynettin (e-mail: ziynettin.gursel@tpsconsult.co.uk)

TRADE PARTNERS UK

Information Centre, Trade Partners UK, Kingsgate House, 66-74 Victoria Street, London SW1E 6SW
☎020 7215 5444/5
Fax 020 7215 4231
e-mail: 'E-mail us your question' on url: http://www.tradepartners.gov.uk
Acting Senior Manager, Information Centre and Enquiries Ms A Hughes BA(Hons) MLIS
Manager, Information Centre Ms C Johnson BA(Hons) MA MA
Manager, Enquiries, Trade Partners UK Ms C Llewellyn BA(Hons)

TRADES UNION CONGRESS

TUC Library Collections, Trades Union Congress, University of North London Learning Centre, 236-250 Holloway Road, London N7 6PP
☎020 7753 3184

Fax 020 7753 3191
e-mail: tuclib@unl.ac.uk
url: http://www.unl.ac.uk/library/tuc/
Librarian Ms C Coates MA MCLIP (e-mail: c.coates@unl.ac.uk)
The University of North London and London Guildhall University are merging on 1 August 2002, and will be known as London Metropolitan University from that date. The University of North London buildings will become part of the London North Campus of London Metropolitan University and London Guildhall buildings will become part of the London City Campus. All telephone and e-mail addresses above will continue to operate for the next year. The new main phone number for the University is 020 7432 0000.

UNITED NATIONS INFORMATION CENTRE

Library, United Nations Information Centre, Millbank Tower (21st Floor), 21-24 Millbank, London SW1P 4QH
☎020 7630 1981
Fax 020 7976 6478
e-mail: info@uniclondon.org
url: http://www.unitednations.org.uk
Librarian Ms K Davies (020 7630 2716; e-mail: k.davies@uniclondon.org)

UNITED STATES EMBASSY

Information Resource Center, United States Embassy, American Embassy, 24 Grosvenor Square, London W1A 2AE
☎020 7894 0925 (10am–12 noon, enquiries), 020 7499 9000 ext 2643 (administration)
Fax 020 7629 8288
e-mail: reflond@pd.state.gov
url: http://www.usembassy.org.uk
Director Ms K Bateman MA DipLib

VETERINARY LABORATORIES AGENCY

Library, Veterinary Laboratories Agency, New Haw, Addlestone, Surrey KT15 3NB
☎(01932) 357314 (enquiries), (01932) 357603 (administration)
Fax (01932) 357608
e-mail: enquiries@vla.defra.gsi.gov.uk
Senior Librarian Mrs H Hulse BA(Hons)
Deputy Librarian Miss M French BA(Hons) PGDip

WELLCOME LIBRARY FOR THE HISTORY AND UNDERSTANDING OF MEDICINE

Wellcome Library for the History and Understanding of Medicine, 183 Euston Road, London NW1 2BE
url: http://www.wellcome.ac.uk/library; http://library.wellcome.ac.uk (online catalogue)
Librarian D Pearson BA MA DipLib MCLIP
Head of Public Services Ms W Fish BA DipLib

History of Medicine
☎020 7611 8582 (enquiries)
Fax 020 7611 8369
e-mail: library@wellcome.ac.uk
Information Service – Current biomedical topics
☎020 7611 8722 (enquiries)
Fax 020 7611 8726
e-mail: infoserv@wellcome.ac.uk
Medical Photographic Library
☎020 7611 8348
Fax 020 7611 8577
e-mail: photolib@wellcome.ac.uk
Medical Film and Audio Collections
☎020 7611 8596/7
Fax 020 7611 8765
e-mail: mfac@wellcome.ac.uk

WESTMINSTER ABBEY

Muniment Room and Library, Westminster Abbey, London SW1P 3PA
☎020 7222 5152 ext 4830
Fax 020 7654 4827
e-mail: library@westminster-abbey.org
url: http://www.westminster-abbey.org
Librarian Dr T A Trowles DPhil

WILLIAM SALT LIBRARY

William Salt Library, 19 Eastgate Street, Stafford ST16 2LZ
☎(01785) 278372
Fax (01785) 278414
e-mail: william.salt.library@staffordshire.gov.uk
url: http://www.staffordshire.gov.uk/archives/salt.htm
Librarian Mrs T Randall BA DAS

DR WILLIAMS'S LIBRARY

Dr Williams's Library, 14 Gordon Square, London WC1H 0AR
☎020 7387 3727
e-mail: enquiries@dwlib.co.uk
Director of Dr Williams's Trust and Library D L Wykes BSc PhD FRHistSc
(The Congregational Library at 15 Gordon Square is administered by Dr Williams's Library, to whom any application should be made. Other details are the same)

THE WOMEN'S LIBRARY

The Women's Library, London Guildhall University, Old Castle Street, London E1 7NT
☎020 7320 2222
Fax 020 7320 2333

e-mail: enquirydesk@thewomenslibrary.ac.uk
url: http://www.thewomenslibrary.ac.uk
Head of Library Services Ms W Thomas

WORKING CLASS MOVEMENT LIBRARY

Working Class Movement Library, Jubilee House, 51 The Crescent, Salford M5 4WX
☎0161 736 3601
Fax 0161 737 4115
e-mail: enquiries@wcml.org.uk
url: http://www.wcml.org.uk
Librarian/Keeper A Kahan BA MCLIP
Library Assistant P Ward

YORK MINSTER

Library, York Minster, Dean's Park, York YO1 7JQ
☎(01904) 625308
Fax (01904) 611119
Librarian Mrs D M Mortimer MA MCLIP
Archivist Ms E Pridmore UDipArchAdmin

ZOOLOGICAL SOCIETY OF LONDON

Library, Zoological Society of London, Regent's Park, London NW1 4RY
☎020 7449 6293
Fax 020 7586 5743
e-mail: library@zsl.org
url: http://www.zsl.org
Librarian Ms A Sylph MSc MCLIP

Libraries in Academic, National and Special Libraries in the Republic of Ireland

ARCHBISHOP MARSH'S LIBRARY

Archbishop Marsh's Library, St Patrick's Close, Dublin 8, Republic of Ireland
☎(00 353 1) 454 3511 (enquiries & administration)
Fax (00 353 1) 454 3511
url: http://www.marshlibrary.ie
Keeper Dr M McCarthy MA LLD (e-mail: keeper@marshlibrary.ie)
(Archbishop Marsh's Library includes a book conservation bindery and a print, drawing, water-colour, map and flat paper conservation service in the Delmas Conservation Bindery (00 353 1 454 4609))

CENTRAL CATHOLIC LIBRARY

Central Catholic Library, 74 Merrion Square, Dublin 2, Republic of Ireland
☎(00 353 1) 676 1264 (enquiries & administration)
Fax (00 353 1) 678 7618
Librarian Ms T Whitington MA DLIS

CHESTER BEATTY LIBRARY

Chester Beatty Library, The Clocktower Building, Dublin Castle, Dublin 2, Republic of Ireland
☎(00 353 1) 407 0750
Fax (00 353 1) 407 0760
e-mail: info@cbl.ie
url: http://www.cbl.ie
Director and Librarian Dr M Ryan (e-mail: mryan@cbl.ie)
Reference Librarian C Ward BA DLIS (e-mail: cward@cbl.ie)

AN CHOMHAIRLE LEABHARLANNA (LIBRARY COUNCIL)

Research Library, An Chomhairle Leabharlanna (Library Council), 53-54 Upper Mount Street, Dublin 2, Republic of Ireland
☎(00 353 1) 678 4900
Fax (00 353 1) 676 6721
e-mail: info@librarycouncil.ie
url: http://www.librarycouncil.ie
Research & Information Officer A Bevan MLib MCLIP (00 353 1 678 4905; Fax: 00 353 1 676 6721; e-mail: abevan@librarycouncil.ie)

DUBLIN CITY UNIVERSITY

Library, Dublin City University, Dublin 9, Republic of Ireland
☎(00 353 1) 700 5418 (enquiries); (00 353 1) 700 5212 (administration)
Fax (00 353 1) 700 5010
url: http://www.dcu.ie/~library/
Director of Library Services P Sheehan (e-mail: paul.sheehan@dcu.ie)

DUBLIN INSTITUTE OF TECHNOLOGY

Central Services Unit, Dublin Institute of Technology, Rathmines Road, Dublin 6, Republic of Ireland
☎(00 353 1) 402 7800 (enquiries), 7801 (administration)
Fax (00 353 1) 402 7802
e-mail: csu.library@dit.ie
url: http://www.dit.ie/library
Head of Library Services W Price BA FCLIP (00 353 1 402 7803; e-mail: warwick.price@dit.ie)
Senior Librarian, Collection Development Ms A McSweeney BA DLIS MLIS (00 353 1 402 7804; e-mail: ann.mcsweeney@dit.ie)
Senior Librarian, Systems Development Ms U Gavin BA DLIS MLIS (00 353 1 402 7805; e-mail: ursula.gavin@dit.ie)
Faculty Librarian Ms Y Desmond BA DLIS (00 353 1 402 7807; e-mail: yvonne.desmond@dit.ie)

Library, Dublin Institute of Technology, Aungier Street, Dublin 2, Republic of Ireland
☎(00 353 1) 402 3068/9
Fax (00 353 1) 402 3289
e-mail: ast.library@dit.ie
Faculty Librarian Ms A Ambrose BA DLIS (00 353 1 402 3067; e-mail: anne.ambrose@dit.ie)

Library, Dublin Institute of Technology, Bolton Street, Dublin 1, Republic of Ireland
☎(00 353 1) 402 3681
Fax (00 353 1) 402 3995
e-mail: bst.library@dit.ie
Faculty Librarian P Cahalane BA DipLib (00 353 1 402 3682; e-mail: peter.cahalane@dit.ie)

Library, Dublin Institute of Technology, Cathal Brugha Street, Dublin 1, Republic of Ireland
☎(00 353 1) 402 4423/4 (enquiries & administration)
Fax (00 353 1) 402 4499
e-mail: cbs.library@dit.ie
Faculty Librarian B Gillespie BA DipLib (00 353 1 402 4361; e-mail: brian.gillespie@dit.ie)

Library, Dublin Institute of Technology, Kevin Street, Dublin 8, Republic of Ireland
☎(00 353 1) 402 4894 (general enquiries)
Fax (00 353 1) 402 4651
e-mail: kst.library@dit.ie
Faculty Librarian Ms M H Davis BSc(Hons) MLIS MCLIP (00 353 1 402 4631; e-mail: mary.davis@dit.ie)

Library, Dublin Institute of Technology, Learning and Teaching Centre, 14 Upper Mount Street, Dublin 2, Republic of Ireland
☎(00 353 1) 402 7889

Fax (00 353 1) 676 7243
e-mail: ltc.library@dit.ie
Librarian Ms D Mitchell BA(Hons)

Library, Dublin Institute of Technology, 40-45 Mountjoy Square, Dublin 1, Republic of Ireland
☎(00 353 1) 402 4108
Fax (00 353 1) 402 4290
e-mail: mjs.library@dit.ie
Faculty Librarian Ms A Wrigley BA DLIS (00 353 1 402 4128; e-mail: ann.wrigley@dit.ie)

Library, Dublin Institute of Technology, Rathmines House, 143-149 Lower Rathmines Road, Dublin 6, Republic of Ireland
☎(00 353 1) 402 3461
Fax (00 353 1) 402 3499
e-mail: rmh.library@dit.ie
Faculty Librarian Ms A Wrigley BA DLIS (00 353 1 402 4128; e-mail: ann.wrigley@dit.ie)
Librarian Ms A O'Brien BA DLIS (00 353 1 402 3462; e-mail: aoife.obrien@dit.ie)

ECONOMIC AND SOCIAL RESEARCH INSTITUTE

Library, Economic and Social Research Institute, 4 Burlington Road, Dublin 4, Republic of Ireland
☎(00 353 1) 667 1525
Fax (00 353 1) 668 6231
url: http://www.esri.ie
Senior Librarian Ms S Burns BSocSc (e-mail: sarah.burns@esri.ie)
Assistant Librarian K Dillon BA DipLIS (e-mail: kevin.dillon@esri.ie)

ENTERPRISE IRELAND

Client Information Services, Enterprise Ireland, Glasnevin, Dublin 9, Republic of Ireland
☎(00 353 1) 808 2325
Fax (00 353 1) 837 8854
e-mail: infocentre@enterprise-ireland.com
Head of Department C Fahy
Librarian in charge Ms M Glennon (00 353 1 808 2389)

NATIONAL ARCHIVES

National Archives, Bishop Street, Dublin 8, Republic of Ireland
☎(00 353 1) 407 2300
Fax (00 353 1) 407 2333
e-mail: mail@nationalarchives.ie
url: http://www.nationalarchives.ie
Director Dr D Craig
(Formed by the amalgamation of the Public Record Office of Ireland and the State Paper Office.)

NATIONAL GALLERY OF IRELAND

Library, National Gallery of Ireland, Merrion Square West, Dublin 2, Republic of Ireland
☎(00 353 1) 661 5133; ext 3543 (Librarian); ext 3546 (Library)
Fax (00 353 1) 661 5372
e-mail: info@ngi.ie
url: http://www.nationalgallery.ie
Librarian Ms A Lydon MA DLIS
(Opening hours 10–5 Mon–Fri.)

NATIONAL LIBRARY OF IRELAND

National Library of Ireland, Kildare Street, Dublin 2 Republic of Ireland
☎(00 353 1) 603 0200
Fax (00 353 1) 676 6690
e-mail: info@nli.ie
url: http://www.nli.ie
Director B O'Donoghue
Keeper (Collections) D Ó Luanaigh MA BComm DipArchStud
Keeper (Systems) B McKenna BA
Keeper (Genealogical Office) F Gillespie MA DipArchStud
Keeper (Manuscripts) N Kissane MA PhD HDipEd
Keeper (Administration) A Ó hAonghusa BSc MPA

Photographic Collection
National Photographic Archive, Meeting House Square, Temple Bar, Dublin 2, Republic of Ireland
☎(00 353 1) 603 0200
Fax (00 353 1) 677 7451
e-mail: photoarchive@nli.ie
url: http://www.nli.ie
Curator Ms G MacLochlainn BA DipLIS

NATIONAL UNIVERSITY OF IRELAND, GALWAY

James Hardiman Library, National University of Ireland, Galway, University Road, Galway, Republic of Ireland
☎(00 353 91) 524411 ext 2540 (enquiries); (00 353 91) 524809 (administration)
Fax (00 353 91) 522394; (00 353 91) 750528 (interlibrary loans)
e-mail: library@nuigalway.ie
Chief Librarian Ms M Reddan DipLib DipSyAn FLAI MCLIP (00 353 91 524809; e-mail: marie.reddan@nuigalway.ie)
Deputy Librarian J Cox MA DipLib (ext 3712; e-mail: john.cox@nuigalway.ie)
Sub-Librarians:
Systems Administrator P Corrigan BA DipLIS (ext 2497; e-mail: peter.corrigan@nuigalway.ie)
Reader Services Ms A Mitchell BA HDipEd DipLIS (ext 2738; e-mail: ann.mitchell@nuigalway.ie)
Bibliographic Services S Scanlon BSc DLIS (ext 3338; e-mail:

seamus.scanlon@nuigalway.ie)
Information Services N McSweeney BA HDipinEd DipLib

Branch libraries

- Medical Library, National University of Ireland, Galway, Clinical Sciences Institute, University Road, Galway, Republic of Ireland
  ☎(00 353 91) 524411 ext 2791
  Fax (00 353 91) 750517
  Medical Librarian T Collins BSc HDipEd DipLib DipSyAn FCLIP (ext 2791; e-mail: tim.collins@nuigalway.ie)
- Nursing Library, National University of Ireland, Galway, University College Hospital, University Road, Galway Republic of Ireland
  ☎(00 353 91) 524222 ext 4361
  Fax (00 353 91) 527214
  Nursing Librarian Ms M Ó hAodha BA DipLIS (ext 4361; e-mail: maire.ohaodha@nuigalway.ie)

NATIONAL UNIVERSITY OF IRELAND, MAYNOOTH

The Library, National University of Ireland, Maynooth, Co Kildare, Republic of Ireland
☎(00 353 1) 708 3884
Fax (00 353 1) 628 6008
e-mail: library.information@may.ie
url: http://www.may.ie/library
Librarian Miss A Neligan BA HDipEd MCLIP ALAI
Deputy Librarian Ms H Fallon MA DLIS
Sub-Librarian Ms V Seymour BA(Mod) MCLIP

OIREACHTAS LIBRARY

Oireachtas Library, Leinster House, Kildare Street, Dublin 2, Republic of Ireland
☎(00 353 1) 618 3451
Fax (00 353 1) 618 4109
e-mail: lib@oireachtas.ie
url: http://www.oireachtas.ie
Chief Librarian Ms M Corcoran

REPRESENTATIVE CHURCH BODY

Library, Representative Church Body, Braemor Park, Churchtown, Dublin 14, Republic of Ireland
☎(00 353 1) 492 3979
Fax (00 353 1) 492 4770
e-mail: library@ireland.anglican.org
url: http://www.ireland.anglican.org/
Librarian & Archivist Dr R Refaussé BA PhD

ROYAL COLLEGE OF SURGEONS IN IRELAND

The Mercer Library, Royal College of Surgeons in Ireland, Mercer Street Lower, Dublin 2, Republic of Ireland
☎(00 353 1) 402 2407 (enquiries); 402 2411 (administration)
Fax (00 353 1) 402 2457
e-mail: library@rcsi.ie
url: http://www.rcsi.ie/library
Librarian Miss B M Doran BA MBA DipLibr ALAI (e-mail: bdoran@rcsi.ie)

Branch library

RCSI Library, Royal College of Surgeons in Ireland, Beaumont Hospital, Beaumont Road, Dublin 9, Republic of Ireland
☎(00 353 1) 809 2531
Fax (00 353 1) 836 7396
e-mail: bhlibrary@rcsi.ie
Librarian J Molloy (e-mail: jmolloy@rcsi.ie)

ROYAL DUBLIN SOCIETY

Library, Royal Dublin Society, Ballsbridge, Dublin 4, Republic of Ireland
☎(00 353 1) 668 0866 ext 256; (00 353 1) 240 7288 (direct line)
Fax (00 353 1) 660 4014
Librarian Ms M Kelleher BA(Hons) DipLibInfS (00 353 1 668 0866 ext 288; e-mail: mary.kelleher@rds.ie)
Assistant Librarian G Whelan (e-mail: ger.whelan@rds.ie)

ROYAL IRISH ACADEMY

Library, Royal Irish Academy, 19 Dawson Street, Dublin 2, Republic of Ireland
☎(00 353 1) 676 2570/676 4222
Fax (00 353 1) 676 2346
e-mail: library@ria.ie
url: http://www.ria.ie
Librarian Mrs S O'Rafferty BA HDipEd DLIS (e-mail: s.orafferty@ria.ie)
Deputy Librarian Ms B Cunningham MA DipLib (e-mail: b.cunningham@ria.ie)

TEAGASC

Library, TEAGASC, 19 Sandymount Avenue, Dublin 4, Republic of Ireland
☎(00 353 1) 637 6000
Fax (00 353 1) 668 8023
e-mail: library@hq.teagasc.ie
Librarian Ms D Brennan BA DipLIS

Research libraries

- Library, TEAGASC, Moorepark Research Centre, Fermoy, Co Cork, Republic of Ireland
  ☎(00 353 25) 42222
  Fax (00 353 25) 42340

Librarian Ms S Keating (e-mail: skeating@moorepark.teagasc.ie)

- Library, TEAGASC, National Food Centre, Dunsinea, Castleknock, Dublin 15, Republic of Ireland
  ☎(00 353 1) 805 9500
  Fax (00 353 1) 805 9550
  e-mail: xxx@nfc.teagasc.ie
  Librarian P Letellier
- Library, TEAGASC, Johnstown Castle Research Centre, Wexford, Republic of Ireland
  ☎(00 353 53) 42888
  Fax (00 353 53) 42004
  Librarian Ms S Lacey (e-mail: slacey@johnstown.teagasc.ie)
- Library, TEAGASC, Oak Park Research Centre, Carlow, Republic of Ireland
  ☎(00 353 503) 70200
  Fax (00 353 503) 42423
  Librarian Ms M Collins (e-mail: mcollins@oakpark.teagasc.ie)
- Library, TEAGASC, Grange Research Centre, Dunsany, Co Meath, Republic of Ireland
  ☎(00 353 46) 25214
  Fax (00 353 46) 26154
  Librarian Ms A Gilsenan (e-mail: agilsenan@grange.teagasc.ie)
- Library, TEAGASC, Kinsealy Research Centre, Malahide Road, Dublin 17, Republic of Ireland
  ☎(00 353 1) 846 0644
  Fax (00 353 1) 846 0524
  e-mail: xxx@kinsealy.teagasc.ie

TRINITY COLLEGE DUBLIN

Library, Trinity College Dublin, College Street, Dublin 2, Republic of Ireland
☎(00 353 1) 608 1127 (general enquiries); (00 353 1) 608 1661 (Librarian's office)
Fax (00 353 1) 608 3774
e-mail: library@tcd.ie
url: http://www.tcd.ie/library/
Librarian and College Archivist Vacant
Deputy Librarian D R H Adams BA DipLib (e-mail: radams@tcd.ie)

Departmental libraries

- Medical Library, Trinity College Dublin, St James's Hospital, James's Street, Dublin 8, Republic of Ireland
  ☎(00 353 1) 453 3922
  Fax (00 353 1) 453 6087
  Site Librarian Ms T Pope BA DipLib (e-mail: thelma.pope@tcd.ie)
- Occupational Therapy Library, Trinity College Dublin, School of Occupational Therapy, Rochestown Avenue, Dun Laoghaire, Co Dublin, Republic of Ireland
  ☎(00 353 1) 284 9687 (afternoons only in term time)
  Fax (00 353 1) 285 5531
  Site Librarian Vacant
- Science and Engineering Library, Trinity College Dublin, College Street, Dublin 2, Republic of Ireland

☎(00 353 1) 608 1805
Fax (00 353 1) 671 9003
Site Librarian Ms A Healy BA MLIS (e-mail: arlene.healy@tcd.ie)

UNIVERSITY COLLEGE CORK

The Boole Library, University College Cork, Cork, Republic of Ireland
☎(00 353 21) 490 2281/2851
Fax (00 353 21) 490 3119
e-mail: library@ucc.ie
Librarian A Fitzgerald BA MPhil DLIS

Branch/department library

Medical Library, University College Cork, Cork University Hospital, Wilton, Cork City, Republic of Ireland
☎(00 353 21) 490 2976/490 1298
Fax (00 353 21) 434 5826
Assistant Librarian Ms R Bultimer BA HDE DCS DLIS (e-mail: r.bultimer@ucc.ie)

UNIVERSITY COLLEGE DUBLIN

Library, University College Dublin, Belfield, Dublin 4, Republic of Ireland
☎(00 353 1) 716 7583 (enquiries); (00 353 1) 716 7694 (administration)
Fax (00 353 1) 283 7667
e-mail: library@ucd.ie
url: http://www.ucd.ie/~library/
Chief Librarian S Phillips BA MCLIP ALAI (e-mail: sean.phillips@ucd.ie)
Deputy Librarian Miss P Corrigan BA DipLib ALAI (e-mail: pauline.corrigan@ucd.ie)

Site libraries

- Architecture Library, University College Dublin, Richview, Clonskeagh, Dublin 14, Republic of Ireland
  ☎(00 353 1) 716 2741
  Fax (00 353 1) 283 0329
  Librarian i/c Ms J Barrett BMus DipLib (e-mail: julia.barrett@ucd.ie)
- Medical Library, University College Dublin, Earlsfort Terrace, Dublin 2, Republic of Ireland
  ☎(00 353 1) 716 7471
  Fax (00 353 1) 475 4568
  Librarian i/c Miss S Murphy BA DipLib (e-mail: sheila.murphy@ucd.ie)
- Veterinary Library, University College Dublin, Belfield, Dublin 4, Republic of Ireland
  ☎(00 353 1) 668 7988
  Fax (00 353 1) 668 9732
  Librarian i/c Ms R Warner MA DLIS ALAI (e-mail: rosemary.warner@ucd.ie)
- Library and Business Information Centre, University College Dublin, Michael Smurfit Graduate School of Business, Blackrock, Co Dublin, Republic of Ireland
  ☎(00 353 1) 716 8920
  Fax (00 353 1) 283 1991
  Librarian i/c Mr J Steele BA DipLib MLIS FLAI (e-mail: john.steele@ucd.ie)

UNIVERSITY OF LIMERICK

Library and Information Services, University of Limerick, Limerick, Republic of Ireland
☎(00 353 61) 202166 (enquiries); 202156 (administration)
Fax (00 353 61) 213090
url: http://www.ul.ie
Director, Library and Information Services J M Lancaster MPhil MCLIP

Schools and Departments of Information and Library Studies

ABERDEEN

School of Information and Media, The Robert Gordon University, Garthdee Road, Aberdeen AB10 7QE
☎(01224) 263900 (administration & enquiries)
Fax (01224) 263939/263553
e-mail: sim@rgu.ac.uk
url: http://www.rgu.ac.uk/schools/~sim/sim.htm
Head of School Ian M Johnson BA FCLIP MIMgt (e-mail: i.m.johnson@rgu.ac.uk)
Associate Head of School R Newton MA PgDip PhD MCLIP (e-mail: r.newton@rgu.ac.uk)

ABERYSTWYTH

Department of Information and Library Studies, University of Wales Aberystwyth, Llanbadarn Fawr, Aberystwyth, Ceredigion SY23 3AS
☎(01970) 622155
Fax (01970) 622190
e-mail: dils@aber.ac.uk
url: http://www.dil.aber.ac.uk/index.htm
Head of Department Gwilym Huws BA MCLIP

BIRMINGHAM

School of Information Studies, University of Central England in Birmingham, Franchise Street, Perry Barr, Birmingham B42 2SU
☎0121 331 5625 (enquiries & administration)
Fax 0121 331 5675
e-mail: sis@uce.ac.uk
url: http://www.cie.uce.ac.uk
Head of School William Foster BSc DipLib MCLIP (e-mail: william.foster@uce.ac.uk)
Faculty Director of Research Dr Graham Matthews BA DipLib MCLIP (e-mail: graham.matthews@uce.ac.uk)

BRIGHTON

The School of Computing, Mathematical and Information Sciences, University of Brighton, Watts Building, Lewes Road, Moulsecoomb, Brighton, Sussex BN2 4GJ
☎(01273) 643500
Fax (01273) 642405
url: http://www.bton.ac.uk/structure.sim.html
Head of School Dr John Taylor
Head of Research Prof Peter G B Enser BA(Econ) MTech PhD MBCS HonFCLIP (e-mail: p.g.b.enser@bton.ac.uk)

BRISTOL

Graduate School of Education, University of Bristol, 8–10 Berkeley Square, Clifton, Bristol BS8 1HH
☎0117 928 7147

Fax 0117 925 4975
url: http://www.bristol.ac.uk/education/ilm
Course Contact for MSc in Information and Library Management Mrs Cathy Badley (0117 928 7147; e-mail: cathy.badley@bristol.ac.uk)

DUBLIN

Department of Library and Information Studies, University College Dublin, Belfield, Dublin 4, Republic of Ireland
☎(00 353 1) 716 7055 (administration); (00 353 1) 716 7080 (voice mail)
Fax (00 353 1) 716 1161
e-mail: DepLIS@ucd.ie
url: http://www.ucd.ie/~lis
Head of Department Prof Mary Burke BSc MSc PhD (e-mail: mary.burke@ucd.ie)

EDINBURGH

Faculty of Arts, Department of Information Management, Queen Margaret University College, Clerwood Terrace, Edinburgh EH12 8TS
☎0131 317 3502
Fax 0131 316 4165
url: http://www.qmuc.ac.uk/lm
Head of Department James E Herring MA MA(Lib) MCLIP (0131 317 3508; e-mail: j.herring@qmc.ac.uk)

GLASGOW

Department of Computer and Information Sciences, Graduate School of Informatics, Strathclyde University, Livingstone Tower, 26 Richmond Street, Glasgow G1 1XH
☎0141 548 3700
Fax 0141 553 1393
e-mail: secretary@dis.strath.ac.uk
url: http://www.cis.strath.ac.uk/
Head of Department Prof A D McGettrick BSc PhD CEng FIEE FBCS FRSE

LEEDS

School of Information Management, Leeds Metropolitan University, Priestley Hall, Beckett Park, Leeds LS6 3QS
☎0113 283 2600 ext 7421 (course enquiries); ext 3242 (school office)
Fax 0113 283 7599
url: http://www.lmu.ac.uk/ies
Head of School John Blake BSc MSc CSTAT MBCS (e-mail: j.blake@lmu.ac.uk)

LIVERPOOL

Centre for Information and Library Management, School of Business Information, Liverpool John Moores University, The John Foster Building, 98 Mount Pleasant, Liverpool L3 5UZ
☎0151 231 2121 (switchboard), 0151 231 3596 (Centre)
Fax 0151 707 0423

e-mail: k.russell@livjm.ac.uk
url: http://www.cwis.livjm.ac.uk/bus/cilm
Librarian Ms J Farrow MA BA MCLIP (0151 231 3596; e mail: a.j.farrow@livjm.ac.uk)

LONDON

City University

Department of Information Science, City University, Northampton Square, London EC1V 0HB
☎020 7040 8381
Fax 020 7040 8584
e-mail: dis@city.ac.uk
url: http://www.soi.city.ac.uk
Head of Department Dr David A R Nicholas MPhil PhD MCLIP (020 7477 8381; e-mail: nicky@soi.city.ac.uk)
Course Director, Information Science and Technology Dr Penny Yates-Mercer BSc MSc PhD FCLIP MInstAM (020 7477 8382; e-mail: paym@soi.city.ac.uk)
Course Director, Information Science Dr Ian Rowlands BSc MSc MCLIP (020 7477 8382; e-mail: ir@soi.city.ac.uk)

Thames Valley University

Faculty of Professional Studies, Thames Valley University, St Mary's Road, Ealing, London W5 5RF
☎020 8579 5000 (switchboard); 020 8231 2314 (faculty)
Fax 020 8231 2553
url: http://www.tvu.ac.uk
Programme Leaders, Information Management (Librarianship and Business) Dr Tony Olden MA, Dr Stephen Roberts MSc (e-mail: tony.olden@tvu.ac.uk; stephen.roberts@tvu.ac.uk)

University College London

School of Library, Archive and Information Studies, University College London, Gower Street, London WC1E 6BT
☎020 7679 7204
Fax 020 7383 0557
e-mail: slais-enquiries@ucl.ac.uk
url: http://www.ucl.ac.uk/SLAIS/
Director of School Prof Susan Hockey MA (020 7679 2477; e-mail: s.hockey@ucl.ac.uk)

University of North London

School of Law, Governance and Information Management, University of North London, Ladbroke House, 62-66 Highbury Grove, London N5 2AD
☎020 7753 5032 (enquiries & administration)
Fax 020 7753 5763
e-mail: l.waller@unl.ac.uk; p.collis@unl.ac.uk (for MA course enquiries)
url: http://www.unl.ac.uk
Acting Head of School Dr Dr Aidan Rose
Senior Lecturer (with responsibility for placements, professional liaison and international links in Information Management) Anthony Beard BA CertEd DipLib MCLIP

The University of North London and London Guildhall University are merging on 1 August 2002, and will be known as London Metropolitan University from that date. The University of North London buildings will become part of the London North Campus of London Metropolitan University and London Guildhall buildings will become part of the London City Campus. All telephone and e-mail addresses will continue to operate for the next year. The new main phone number for the University is 020 7432 0000.

LOUGHBOROUGH

Department of Information Science, Loughborough University, Ashby Road, Loughborough, Leics LE11 3TU
☎(01509) 223052
Fax (01509) 223053
e-mail: dis@lboro.ac.uk
url: http://www.lboro.ac.uk/departments/dis/
Head of Department Prof Ron Summers BSc MSc PhD MInstMC CEng SMIEEE (e-mail: r.summers@lboro.ac.uk)
Director of LISU (Library & Information Statistics Unit) Dr J Eric Davies MA FCLIP MIMgt FInstAM FRSA (01509 223071; fax 01509 223072; e-mail: j.e.davies@lboro.ac.uk)
Project Co-Director (Learning and Teaching Support Network Centre, Information Science Component) Prof John Feather

MANCHESTER

Department of Information and Communications, Manchester Metropolitan University, Geoffrey Manton Building, Rosamond Street West, off Oxford Road, Manchester M15 6LL
☎0161 247 6144
Fax 0161 247 6351
e-mail: infcomms-hums@mmu.ac.uk
url: http://www.mmu.ac.uk/h-ss/dic/
Head of Department R J Hartley BSc MLib FCLIP
Professor of Information Management and Director of the Centre for Research in Library and Information Management (CERLIM) Prof Peter Brophy JP BSc FCLIP FRSA

NEWCASTLE UPON TYNE

Division of Information and Communication Studies, School of Informatics, Northumbria University, Lipman Building, Sandyford Road, Newcastle upon Tyne NE1 8ST
☎0191 227 4917
Fax 0191 227 3671
e-mail: il.admin@northumbria.ac.uk
url: http://ics.unn.ac.uk
Dean of School Ms G Lovegrove
Head of Subject Division Ms S McTavish BA PGCE MCLIP

SHEFFIELD

Department of Information Studies, University of Sheffield, Western Bank, Sheffield S10 2TN
☎0114 222 2630 (dept/administration)
Fax 0114 278 0300
e-mail: dis@sheffield.ac.uk
url: http://www.shef.ac.uk/~is
Head of School Prof Peter Willett MA MSc PhD DSc FCLIP (0114 222 2633; e-mail: p.willett@sheffield.ac.uk)

Key Library Agencies and other Relevant Organizations

Note: Organizations are listed using their full names. If searching for an organization by its acronym, please use the general index.

AFRICAN CARIBBEAN LIBRARY ASSOCIATION (ACLA)

52 Burgundy House, 9 Bedale Road, Enfield, London EN2 0NZ
☎020 8345 7209
e-mail: acla_uk@yahoo.co.uk
url: http://www.la-hq.org.uk/groups/acla/acla.html
Acting Chair Ms Doreen Dankyi
Secretary Ms Ann Thompson (e-mail: libraryannie@yahoo.co.uk)
Founded in 1981 by Ann Thompson, ACLA is an independent fully constituted organization committed to the full implementation of race equality principles and policies throughout librarianship. It welcomes as members any library or information workers of African or Caribbean origin. It is a member of the Diversity Council of CILIP.

ART LIBRARIES SOCIETY OF THE UK AND IRELAND (ARLIS)

18 College Road, Bromsgrove, Worcs B60 2NE
☎(01527) 579298 (tel/fax)
e-mail: sfrench@arlis.demon.co.uk
url: http://arlis.org.uk
Chair Ms Margaret Young (e-mail: margaret.young@edinburgh.gov.uk)
The Society aims to promote all aspects of the librarianship of the visual arts, including architecture and design.

ASIAN LIBRARIANS AND ADVISERS GROUP (ALAG)

c/o K K Dutt, Library Support Centre, Ealing Council Sports Ground, Horsenden Lane South, Greenford, Middlesex UB6 8AP
☎020 8810 7650
Fax 020 8810 7651
Secretary K K Dutt (e-mail: kdutt@ealing.gov.uk)
ALAG's mission is to promote Asian languages, history, culture and heritage through library and information services to Asians in particular and the population at large.

ASLIB, THE ASSOCIATION FOR INFORMATION MANAGEMENT

Temple Chambers, 3-7 Temple Avenue, London EC4Y 0HP
☎020 7583 8900
Fax 020 7583 8401
e-mail: aslib@aslib.com
url: http://www.aslib.com
Chief Executive Officer Roger Bowes

Aslib is a corporate membership organization promoting best practice in resource management and lobbying on all aspects of management of and legislation concerning information at all levels.

ASSOCIATION OF INFORMATION OFFICERS IN THE PHARMACEUTICAL INDUSTRY (AIOPI)

PO Box 297, Slough PDO, SL1 7XT
url: http://www.aiopi.org.uk
President Ms Christine Cameron MSc MCLIP
AIOPI provides a forum for the exchange of experience and the advancement of all aspects of medical, scientific, technical and business information relating to the pharmaceutical industry.

ASSOCIATION OF SENIOR CHILDREN'S AND EDUCATION LIBRARIANS (ASCEL)

c/o Susan McCulloch, Libraries and Heritage HQ, County Hall East, Bythesea Road, Trowbridge, Wilts BA14 8BS
☎(01225) 713742
Fax (01225) 350029
url: http://www.ascel.org.uk
Secretary Ms Susan McCulloch (e-mail: susanmcculloch@wiltshire.gov.uk)
Chair 2002/3 Jeremy Saunders, Head of Service, Education Library Resource Centre, Reading, Berkshire
ASCEL's mission is to provide a proactive forum in order to stimulate development and respond to initiatives so that all children and young people are offered high quality library services through public libraries and education services, working actively with all governmental, professional and other relevant organizations and individuals.

ASSOCIATION OF UK MEDIA LIBRARIANS (AUKML)

c/o Sara Margetts, PO Box 14254, London SE1 9WL
url: http://www.aukml.org.uk
Chair Ian Watson (e-mail: ian.watson@smg.plc.uk)
Membership contact: Ms Sara Margetts (e-mail: sara.margetts@FT.com)
The AUKML is the organization for print and broadcast news librarians, news researchers and information workers in the media industry.

BOOK INDUSTRY COMMUNICATION (BIC)

39/41 North Road, London N7 9DP
☎020 7607 0021
Fax 020 7607 0415
url: http://www.bic.org.uk
Managing Agent Brian Green (e-mail: brian@bic.org.uk)

Chairman Roger Woodham
Book Industry Communication was set up and sponsored by the Publishers Association, The Library Association and the British Library to develop and promote standards for electronic communication and supply chain efficiency in the book and serials industries.

BOOKTRUST

Book House, 45 East Hill, London SW18 2QZ
☎020 8516 2977
Fax 020 8516 2978
url: http://www.booktrust.org.uk; http://www.booktrusted.com
Executive Director Chris Meade
Booktrust is the national charity for books and reading in the UK. It aims to bring books and people together in a variety of ways through its work helping readers of all ages to discover books.

BRITISH AND IRISH ASSOCIATION OF LAW LIBRARIANS (BIALL)

26 Myton Crescent, Warwick CV34 6QA
☎(01926) 491717 (tel/fax)
url: http://www.biall.org.uk
BIALL Administrator Ms Susan Frost (e-mail: susanfrost@compuserve.com)
Chair Ms Valerie Stevenson
BIALL was formed in 1969 with the objectives of pursuing policies to bring benefits to its members, enhancing the status of the legal information profession and promoting better administration and exploitation of law libraries and legal information units nationwide.

BRITISH ASSOCIATION FOR INFORMATION AND LIBRARY EDUCATION AND RESEARCH (BAILER)

c/o Linda Ashcroft, Liverpool Business School, Liverpool John Moores University, 98 Mount Pleasant, Liverpool L3 5UZ
☎0151 231 3425
Fax 0151 707 0423
url: http://www.bailer.ac.uk
Chair Ms Linda Ashcroft (e-mail: l.s.ashcroft@livjm.ac.uk)
BAILER includes all teaching and research staff in the 18 Information and Library Schools in the UK and Ireland and aims to reflect and help focus the evolution of the field of information and library studies through the development and encouragement of members. It acts as a forum within the UK for matters relating to information and library studies education and research, and maintains contact with organizations outside the UK concerned with education for information work.

BRITISH ASSOCIATION OF PICTURE LIBRARIES AND AGENCIES (BAPLA)

18 Vine Hill, London EC1R 5DZ
☎020 7713 1780
Fax 020 7713 1211
e-mail: enquiries@bapla.org.uk
url: http://www.bapla.org
Chief Executive Officer Ms Linda Royles
BAPLA represents over 400 member picture libraries and agencies, which collectively manage in excess of 350 million images. All members sign a code of conduct. The website provides details about BAPLA services and benefits to picture researchers, to photographers and of membership. The site also has a useful search engine facility.

BRITISH COMPUTER SOCIETY – INFORMATION RETRIEVAL SPECIALIST GROUP (BCS IRSG)

c/o Jane Reid, Dept of Computer Science, Queen Mary, University of London, Mile End Road, London E1 4NS
☎020 7882 5236
Fax 020 8980 6533
url: http://irsg.eu.org
Secretary Ms Jane Reid (e-mail: jane@dcs.qmul.ac.uk)
Chair Ayse S Goker-Arslan
The BCS IRSG provides a forum for academic and industrial researchers and practitioners to discuss core issues involved in the representation, management, searching, retrieval and presentation of multimedia electronic information.

BUBL INFORMATION SERVICE

c/o Dennis Nicholson, Andersonian Library, Strathclyde University, 101 St James Road, Glasgow G4 0NS
☎0141 548 4752
Fax 0141 548 2102
e-mail: bubl@bubl.ac.uk
url: http://www.bubl.ac.uk
Director Dennis Nicholson
Information Officer Andrew Williamson
BUBL is an internet-based information service covering all subject areas, which also offers a specialist service to librarians and information professionals.

CENTRE FOR RESEARCH IN LIBRARY AND INFORMATION MANAGEMENT (CERLIM)

Department of Information and Communications, Manchester Metropolitan University, Geoffrey Manton Building, Rosamond Street West, Manchester M15 6LL
☎0161 247 6142

Fax 0161 247 6979
e-mail: cerlim@mmu.ac.uk
url: http://www.mmu.ac.uk/h-ss/cerlim
Director Prof P Brophy BSc HonFCLIP FCLIP FRSA
CERLIM undertakes research and consultancy in the library and information management field.

THE CHARTERED INSTITUTE OF LIBRARY AND INFORMATION PROFESSIONALS (CILIP) (formerly The Library Association and the Institute of Information Scientists)

7 Ridgmount Street, London WC1E 7AE
☎020 7255 0500
Textphone 020 7255 0505
Fax 020 7255 0501
e-mail: info@cilip.org.uk
url: http://www.cilip.org.uk
Chief Executive Bob McKee PhD MCLIP FRSA
CILIP (the Chartered Institute of Library and Information Professionals) is the leading professional body for librarians and information managers in the UK, with members in all sectors, including business and industry, further and higher education, schools, local and central government departments and agencies, the health service, the voluntary sector and national and public libraries. CILIP is committed to enabling its members to achieve and maintain the highest professional standards, and encouraging them in the delivery and promotion of high quality library and information services responsive to the needs of users.

THE CHARTERED INSTITUTE OF LIBRARY AND INFORMATION PROFESSIONALS IN IRELAND (CILIP IN IRELAND)

(formerly Library Association Northern Ireland Branch (LANI))

c/o Madeleine Coyle, NWIFHE LLRC, North West Institute, Strand Road, Londonderry BT48 7AL
☎028 7127 6127
Fax 028 7126 7054
Chief Officer Ms Madeleine E M Coyle (e-mail: memc@nwifhe.ac.uk)
The function of CILIP in Ireland is to represent the interests of library staff across the sectors. It supports staff by providing access to expert advice on qualifications and continuing professional development. It identifies issues of concern to the profession, and where necessary provides intervention in the form of both advice and advocacy. CILIP in Ireland works with relevant bodies such as LISC (NI) and the relevant departments of the Northern Ireland Assembly.

CILIP staff are currently working with members in Northern Ireland and the Republic of Ireland to determine the Branch structure that best meets the needs of members and of other interested parties in Ireland.

THE CHARTERED INSTITUTE OF LIBRARY AND INFORMATION PROFESSIONALS IN SCOTLAND (CILIPS) (formerly The Scottish Library Association)

Scottish Centre for Library and Information Services, First Floor, Brandon Gate, Leechlee Road, Hamilton, South Lanarkshire ML3 6AU
☎(01698) 458888
Fax (01698) 458899/428159
e-mail: cilips@slainte.org.uk
url: http://www.slainte.org.
Director Robert Craig OBE BA MA MCLIP (retiring end December 2002)
Assistant Director Ms Rhona Arthur BA FCLIP
CILIPS is the professional body for librarians and information personnel, and represents personal members from all sectors – public, school, FE/HE libraries, and libraries/information services from both the voluntary and private sectors.

THE CHARTERED INSTITUTE OF LIBRARY AND INFORMATION PROFESSIONALS WALES (CILIP WALES)/SEFYDLIAD SIARTREDIG LLYFRGELLWYR A GWEITHWYR GWYBODAETH CYMRU (CILIP CYMRU) (formerly the Welsh Library Association)

Department of Information and Library Studies, Llanbadarn Fawr, Aberystwyth SY23 3AS
☎(01970) 622174
Fax (01970) 622190
e-mail: hle@aber.ac.uk
url: http://www.dils.aber.ac.uk/holi/
President A M W Green MA MCLIP
CILIP Wales promotes the professional development of individual members; seeks to influence the development of policies on the provision of information and library services at a local and national level; provides and disseminates information about/promoting library and information services in Wales.

AN CHOMHAIRLE LEABHARLANNA (THE LIBRARY COUNCIL)

53-54 Upper Mount Street, Dublin 2, Republic of Ireland
☎(00 353 1) 676 1167/676 1963/678 4900
Fax (00 353 1) 676 6721
e-mail: info@librarycouncil.ie
url: http://www.librarycouncil.ie
Director Ms Norma McDermott
An Chomhairle Leabharlanna/The Library Council is the statutory agency that advises the Minister for the Environment and Local Government and public library authorities in Ireland on public library development. An Chomhairle also promotes policies, strategies

and activities that foster co-operation and partnership between library and information services and other relevant agencies in Ireland, with the United Kingdom, and within Europe.

CIRCLE OF OFFICERS OF NATIONAL AND REGIONAL LIBRARY SYSTEMS (CONARLS)

c/o Kate Holliday, Library HQ, Yorkshire Libraries and Information, Balne Lane, Wakefield WF2 0DQ
☎(01924) 302214
Fax (01924) 302245
url: http://thenortheast.com/conarls
Officer c/o Ms Kate Holliday (e-mail: kholliday@wakefield.gov.uk)
CONARLS's mission is to support, encourage and assist the development of the interlibrary lending network and all forms of interlibrary co-operation within the UK and the Republic of Ireland, and to facilitate international library co-operation wherever practical.

CITY INFORMATION GROUP (CIG)

PO Box 13297, London SW19 8GH
☎020 8543 7339
Fax 020 8543 7639
e-mail: admin@cityinfogroup.co.uk
url: http://www.cityinfogroup.co.uk
Chair 2001/2 Ms Sue Mucenieks
The City Information Group (CiG) is a membership organization which was established in 1989. The aims of the Group are to stimulate the exchange of knowledge, experience and ideas between specialists in the financial and business information sector. The Management Committee organizes monthly evening seminars on information related topics, and a variety of social events, based in London.

CONSORTIUM OF UNIVERSITY LIBRARIES (CURL)

c/o Dr Marie-Pierre Détraz, Room 1211, 12th Floor, Muirhead Tower, University of Birmingham, Edgbaston, Birmingham B15 2TT
☎0121 415 8106
Fax 0121 415 8109
url: http://www.curl.ac.uk
Executive Secretary Dr Marie-Pierre Détraz
CURL's mission is to promote, maintain and improve library resources for research, learning and teaching in research-led universities.

CONSORTIUM OF WELSH LIBRARY AND INFORMATION SERVICES (CWLIS)

c/o Rhidian Griffiths, National Library of Wales, Aberystwyth, Ceredigion SY23 3BU

☎(01970) 632807
Fax (01970) 632882
e-mail: wrg@llgc.org.uk
url: http://www.dils.aber.ac.uk/holi/
Secretary Dr Rhidian Griffiths
CWLIS's mission is to facilitate development, instigate research, respond to reports and initiatives, and to lobby on behalf of the library and information sector in Wales.

CONSTRUCTION INDUSTRY INFORMATION GROUP (CIIG)

c/o The Building Centre, 26 Store Street, London WC1E 7BT
url: http://www.ciig.org.uk
Chair Malcolm Weston (e-mail: malcolm_k_weston@urscorp.com
CIIG is an organization for professionals concerned with the provision, dissemination and use of information in the construction industry.

CONVENTION OF SCOTTISH LOCAL AUTHORITIES (COSLA)

Rosebery House, 9 Haymarket Terrace, Edinburgh EH12 5XZ
☎0131 474 9200
Fax 0131 474 9292
e-mail: enquiries@cosla.gov.uk
url: http://www.cosla.gov.uk
Chief Executive Rory Mair
Policy Officer Ms Sylvia Murray (e-mail: sylvia@cosla.gov.uk)
COSLA is the representative voice of Scotland's unitary local authorities. Its main objectives are to promote the interests of its member councils and of local government; to liaise with the Scottish Parliament, Scottish Executive, UK Government, European institutions and appropriate partner organizations on issues of mutual interest; and to provide support for member councils in strengthening local democracy and raising awareness of and support for local government.

COUNCIL FOR LEARNING RESOURCES IN COLLEGES (COLRIC)

122 Preston New Road, Blackburn, Lancashire BB2 6BU
☎(01254) 662923
Fax (01254) 610979
e-mail: colric@colric.org.uk
url: http://www.colric.org.uk
Executive Director Jeff Cooper MA FCLIP
CoLRiC is an independent organization dedicated to enhancing and maintaining the quality of learning resources services in further education colleges throughout the United Kingdom and Ireland.

COUNCIL OF ACADEMIC AND PROFESSIONAL PUBLISHERS (CAPP)

The Publishers Association, 29B Montague Street, London WC1B 5BH
☎020 7691 9191
Fax 020 7691 9199
e-mail: mail@publishers.org.uk
url: http://www.publishers.org.uk
Director Graham Taylor
CAPP is a trade association for academic and professional publishers.

DEPARTMENT FOR CULTURE, MEDIA AND SPORT (MUSEUMS, LIBRARIES AND ARCHIVES DIVISION) (DCMS)

1st Floor, 2-4 Cockspur Street, London SW1Y 5DH
☎020 7211 6131
Fax 020 7211 6130
e-mail: libraries@culture.gov.uk
url: http://www.culture.gov.uk
Head of Museums, Libraries and Archives Division Ms Janet Evans
The Department for Culture, Media and Sport is the government department with overall policy responsibility for the public library sector in the UK.

DEPARTMENT OF CULTURE, ARTS AND LEISURE, NORTHERN IRELAND EXECUTIVE (DCAL)

Interpoint, 20-24 York Street, Belfast BT15 1AQ
☎028 9025 8911
Fax 028 9025 8883
e-mail: dcalni@nics.gov.uk
url: http://www.dcalni.gov.uk
Director of Culture and Recreation Division Nigel Carson (e-mail: nigel.carson.gov.uk)
DCAL is responsible for the central administration of arts and culture, museums, libraries, sport and leisure visitor amenities, inland waterways and inland fisheries. It also has responsibility for Ordnance Survey, the Public Record Office, language policy, matters relating to National Lottery distribution, Millennium events and the Northern Ireland Events Company.

EAST MIDLANDS MUSEUMS, LIBRARIES AND ARCHIVES COUNCIL (EMMLAC)

56 King Street, Leicester LE1 6RL
☎0116 285 1350
Fax 0116 285 1351
Chief Executive Dr Tim Hobbs PhD DipLib MCLIP

EMMLAC's mission is to provide strategic leadership for museums, archives and libraries in the East Midlands so that they provide a better service to the public. It's aim, working in partnership with the region's domain-specific bodies, is to ensure that the region's museums, libraries and archives play a full role in the social, educational, cultural and economic life of the region.

EAST MIDLANDS REGIONAL LIBRARY SYSTEM (EMRLS)

c/o Lynn Hodgkins, Alfreton Library, Severn Square, Alfreton, Derbyshire DE55 7BQ
☎(01773) 835064
Fax (01773) 521020
e-mail: emrls@derbyshire.gov.uk
Regional Librarian Ms Lynn Hodgkins BA MCLIP
Chair David Lathrope BSc DMS MCLIP
The East Midlands Regional Library System is the strategic body for libraries across all sectors in the East Midlands. Funded entirely from membership subscriptions, its members include all the public and university libraries together with many of the further education and special libraries in the region. Associate membership is available to libraries and information services from outside the East Midlands. The Regional Library System continues to encourage and support regional co-operation and partnership working related to resource sharing.

EMRLS is actively working to deliver a number of key tasks arising from its strategy 'Sharing the Future' and is developing a close working relationship with the Regional Agency EMMLAC (East Midlands, Museums, Libraries and Archives Council) and other regional bodies.

EAST OF ENGLAND LIBRARY AND INFORMATION SERVICES DEVELOPMENT AGENCY (ELISA)

c/o Janet Bayliss, County Library, Northgate Street, Ipswich, Suffolk IP1 3DE
☎(01473) 583719
Fax (01473) 583700
url: http://www.elisa.org.uk
Regional Librarian Mrs J Bayliss (e-mail: janet.bayliss@libher.suffolkcc.gov.uk)
ELISA's mission is to develop a regional information and library service to support the regional cultural and economic strategies in the East of England.

EDUCATIONAL PUBLISHERS COUNCIL (EPC)

The Publishers Association, 29B Montague Street, London WC1B 5BH
☎020 7691 9191
Fax 020 7691 9199
e-mail: mail@publishers.org.uk
url: http://www.publishers.org.uk
Director Graham Taylor
EPC is a trade association for school publishers.

INSTITUTE OF INFORMATION SCIENTISTS see THE CHARTERED INSTITUTE OF LIBRARY AND INFORMATION PROFESSIONALS (CILIP)

INTER-LIBRARY SERVICES – NATIONAL LIBRARY OF SCOTLAND (NLS-ILS)

Causewayside Building, 33 Salisbury Place, Edinburgh EH9 1SL
☎0131 466 3815 (direct), 0131 226 4531 ext 3329 (switchboard)
Fax 0131 466 3814
e-mail: ils@nls.uk
url: http://www.nls.uk or http://www.nls.uk/professional/interlibraryservices/index.html
Head of Inter-Library Services Miss Patricia M A McKenzie BA MCLIP
The Inter-Library Services (ILS) Division of the National Library of Scotland operates as the Scottish centre for interlibrary loans and represents Scotland in the interlending community. It provides bibliographic verification and location search services, is responsible for the Scottish Union Catalogue and is, therefore, heavily involved with the UnityWeb database. Additionally, ILS has its own collection of c.140,000 titles which are available via interlibrary loan to libraries anywhere in the world. Electronic or postal document delivery is also available.

JANET USER GROUP FOR LIBRARIES (JUGL)

c/o Evelyn Simpson, Open University Library, Walton Hall, Milton Keynes MK17 6AA
☎(01908) 655703
Fax (01908) 659005
url: http://bubl.ac.uk/org/jugl/
Chair Ms Evelyn Simpson
Treasurer Ms J Haines, Oxford Brooks University
JUGL provides a forum for discussion on the use of networks for libraries in higher and further education. It also plays an important role in raising awareness of new developments and issues and aims to represent the views of the professions to the JANET User Group, the JISC and other relevant organizations and committees.

JOINT INFORMATION SYSTEMS COMMITTEE (JISC)

Northavon House, Coldharbour Lane, Bristol BS16 1QD
☎0117 931 7256
Fax 0117 931 7255
e-mail: k.gardener@jisc.ac.uk
url: http://www.jisc.ac.uk
Secretary Dr Malcolm Read
The Joint Information Systems Committee (JISC) promotes the innovative application and use of information systems and information technology in higher and further education across the UK.

LAUNCHPAD see THE READING AGENCY

LIBRARIES NORTH WEST (LNW)

(formerly North Western Regional Library System (NWRLS)

Chester College, Parkgate Road, Chester CH1 4BJ
☎(01244) 220362 (direct line)
Fax 0161 236 3813
e-mail: nwrls@nwrls.org.uk
url: http://www.nwrls.org.uk
Director Ms C Connor BA PgDipLIS MCLIP MILT (e-mail: c.connor@chester.ac.uk)
Company Secretary Ms Deborah Ryan BA MCLIP
The purpose of LNW is to bring together all sectors within the library and information domain in the North West; to provide a strategic lead for the domain through the formulation of plans, policies, representations and expressions of view; and to support effective service provision, including interlending, through co-operation.

THE LIBRARIES PARTNERSHIP – WEST MIDLANDS (TLP-WM)

3rd Floor, Central Library, Birmingham B3 3HQ
☎0121 303 2613
Fax 0121 464 1609
e-mail: tlpwm@dial.pipex.com
url: http://www.tlp-wm.org.uk
Acting Director L Saunders BA(Hons) DipLib MCLIP
TLP-WM is a regional agency for all kinds of libraries in the West Midlands, providing strategic representation, development support and operational services.

LIBRARY AND INFORMATION RESEARCH GROUP (LIRG)

c/o Biddy Fisher, Academic Services and Development, Sheffield Hallam University, Howard Street, Sheffield S1 1WB
☎0114 225 2104
Fax 0114 225 3859
url: http://www.cilip.org.uk/groups/lirg/index.htm
Chair Biddy Fisher (e-mail: b.m.fisher@shu.ac.uk)
LIRG promotes the value of information research and links research with practice; the Group was formed to bring together those interested in library and information research.

LIBRARY AND INFORMATION SERVICES COUNCIL (LISC(NI))

PO Box 1231, Belfast BT8 6AL
☎028 9070 5441

Fax 028 9040 1180
url: http://www.liscni.co.uk
Executive Officer Ms Mairead Gilheany (e-mail: mairead@liscni.freeserve.co.uk)
LISC(NI)'s mission is to enhance the standard of library and information services by providing advice to the Department of Culture, Arts and Leisure (NI) and other government departments, providing a voice for the sector and acting as a catalyst for progress and development in all areas of provision.

LIBRARY AND INFORMATION SERVICES COUNCIL (WALES)

Culture and the Welsh Language Division, Welsh Assembly Government, Cathays Park, Cardiff CF10 3NQ
☎029 2082 5440
Fax 029 2082 6112
Secretary Ms Penny Hall (e-mail: penny.hall@wales.gsi.gov.uk)
The purpose of LISC (Wales) is to advise the Minister for Culture, Sport and the Welsh Language on matters concerning library and information services, including the development of national policies and the promotion of co-operation between services.

LIBRARY AND INFORMATION STATISTICS UNIT (LISU)

Loughborough University, Loughborough, Leics LE11 3TU
☎(01509) 223071
Fax (01509) 223072
e-mail: lisu@lboro.ac.uk
url: http://www.lboro.ac.uk/departments/dis/lisu/lisuhp.html
Director Dr J Eric Davies MA PhD FCLIP MIMgt FInstAM FRSA
LISU is a national research and information centre focusing on the analysis, interpretation, development and dissemination of statistics performance assessment measures and related management data to contribute to good management practice in the information economy and cultural services.

THE LIBRARY ASSOCIATION see CHARTERED INSTITUTE OF LIBRARY AND INFORMATION PROFESSIONALS (CILIP)

LIBRARY ASSOCIATION NORTHERN IRELAND BRANCH (LANI) see CHARTERED INSTITUTE OF LIBRARY AND INFORMATION PROFESSIONALS IN IRELAND

LIBRARY ASSOCIATION OF IRELAND (CUMANN LEABHARLANN NA HÉIREANN)

53-54 Upper Mount Street, Dublin 2, Republic of Ireland
☎086 607 0462
e-mail: lai@eircom.net
url: http://www.libraryassociation.ie
President Ms Marjory Sliney MSocSc MCLIP ALAI (e-mail: msliney@eircom.net; pres@libraryassociation.ie)
Administration Secretary Vacant
The Library Association of Ireland is the professional body in Ireland for those engaged in librarianship and information management. It encourages professional training for library staff and acts as an educational and examining body whose fellowship diploma is a recognized qualification in librarianship.

THE LIBRARY CAMPAIGN

22 Upper Woburn Place, London WC1H 0TB
☎0127 388 7321 (tel/fax)
e-mail: librarycam@aol.com
url: http://www.librarycampaign.co.uk
Director Ms Jill Wight
The Library Campaign is the only UK organization representing and co-ordinating friends and user groups of publicly-funded libraries.

LIBRARY INFORMATION TECHNOLOGY CENTRE (LITC)

Department of Information Science, City University, Northampton Square, London EC1V 0HB
☎020 7040 8381
Fax 020 7040 8584
e-mail: litc@soi.city.ac.uk
url: http://www.soi.city.ac.uk/litc
Centre Manager Andrew Cox
LITC's objectives are to maintain current awareness in information technology, to disseminate knowledge, to develop and maintain a centre of excellence, to facilitate the exchange of information and ideas and to provide clients with expertise within this specialized field.

LOCAL GOVERNMENT ASSOCIATION (LGA)

Local Government House, Smith Square, London SW1P 3HZ
☎020 7664 3000
Fax 020 7664 3030 (switchboard); 020 7664 3131 (information helpline)
url: http://www.lga.gov.uk

The LGA's mission is to promote better local government. It works with and for its member authorities to realize a shared vision of local government that enables local people to shape a distinctive and better future for their locality and its communities.

LONDON LIBRARIES DEVELOPMENT AGENCY (LLDA)

35 St Martin's Street, London WC2H 7HP
☎020 7641 5266 (tel/fax)
url: http://www.llda.org.uk
Director David Murray (e-mail: david.murray@llda.org.uk)
Personal Assistant Jenny Warner (e-mail: jenny.warner@llda.org.uk)
The LLDA has been created to develop and realise a co-ordinated strategic vision for all library and information services across London.

MUSEUMS ASSOCIATION (MA)

24 Calvin Street, London E1 6NW
☎020 7608 2933
Fax 020 7250 1929
e-mail: info@museumsassociation.org
url: http://www.museumsassociation.org
Director Mark Taylor
The Museums Association is the professional membership body for anyone involved in museums, galleries and related organizations.

NATIONAL ACQUISITIONS GROUP (NAG)

Lime House, Poolside, Madeley, Crewe, Cheshire CW3 9DX
☎(01782) 750462 (tel/fax)
e-mail: nag@psilink.co.uk
url: http://www.nag.org.uk/new/index.html
Administrator Ms Carmel Martin BA, Ms Diane Roberts BA
Chair David Fisher
NAG's mission is to recruit and unite members in common discussion of acquisitions policies and practices, and to promote knowledge and understanding of technological developments in publishing, bookselling and library and information work, and their use in acquisitions.

NATIONAL FORUM FOR INFORMATION PLANNING (NFIP)

c/o SINTO (the Sheffield Information Organization) Learning Centre, Sheffield Hallam University, Collegiate Crescent, Sheffield S10 2BP
☎0114 225 5739/40
Fax 0114 225 2476
e-mail: sinto@shu.ac.uk
url: http://www.bl.uk/concord/linc/nfip.html
Chair Carl Clayton BA MCLIP DMS

The National Forum for Information Planning (NFIP) is a forum for organizations involved in the practical implementation of information planning in the United Kingdom and Republic of Ireland.

NATIONAL LITERACY TRUST

Swire House, 59 Buckingham Gate, London SW1E 6AJ
☎020 7828 2435
Fax 020 7931 9986
e-mail: contact@literacytrust.org.uk
url: http://www.literacytrust.org.uk; http://www.rif.org.uk
Director Neil McClelland
The National Literacy Trust aims to make an independent, strategic contribution to the creation of a society in which all enjoy the skills, confidence and pleasures of literacy to support their educational, economical, social and cultural goals. The Trust incorporates Reading Is Fundamental, UK and runs the National Reading Campaign.

NORTH EAST MUSEUMS, LIBRARIES AND ARCHIVES COUNCIL (NEMLAC)

House of Recovery, Bath Lane, Newcastle upon Tyne NE4 5SQ
☎0191 222 1661
Fax 0191 261 4725
e-mail: nemlac@nemlac.co.uk
url: http://www.nemlac.co.uk
Chief Executive Ms Sue Underwood MA FMA
The North East Museums, Libraries and Archives Council (NEMLAC) is the regional development agency for museums, libraries and archives in North East England. NEMLAC will facilitate the sector's development across the region through strategic leadership, advocacy, advice, exemplar projects and service delivery.

PUBLIC LENDING RIGHT (PLR)

PLR Office, Richard House, Sorbonne Close, Stockton-on-Tees TS17 6DA
☎(01642) 604699
Fax (01642) 615641
e-mail: registrar@plr.uk.com
url: http://www.plr.uk.com
Registrar Dr Jim Parker
PLR is a statutory scheme which makes payments to authors for the free lending of their books by public libraries in the UK.

THE READING AGENCY
(replaces the bodies formerly known as Launchpad, The Reading Partnership and Well Worth Reading)

PO Box 96, St Albans, Herts AL1 3WP
url: www.readingagency.org.uk

Development Director Ms Miranda McKearney
Head of Resources Penny Shapland (e-mail: penny.shapland@readingagency.org.uk)
The Reading Agency is a library development agency working in new ways with both adult and young people's librarians to inspire a reading nation.

READING IS FUNDAMENTAL, UK

Swire House, 59 Buckingham Gate, London SW1E 6AJ
☎020 7828 2435
Fax 020 7931 9986
e-mail: rif@literacytrust.org.uk
Director Lis Coulthard
Reading Is Fundamental, UK, is a national initiative that motivates children and young people aged 0 to 19 to read. Working with volunteers, we deliver literacy projects that promote the fun of reading, the importance of book choice and the benefits to families of having books in the home.

RECORDS MANAGEMENT SOCIETY OF GREAT BRITAIN (RMS)

Woodside, Coleheath Bottom, Speen, Princes Risborough, Bucks HP27 0SZ
☎(01494) 488599
Fax (01494) 488590
e-mail: info@rms-gb.org.uk
url: http://www.rms-gb.org.uk
Administration Secretary Jude Awdry
Chair Ms Ceri Hughes
Records management is the system(s) by which an organization seeks to control the creation, distribution, filing, retrieval, storage and disposal of those records, regardless of media, which are created or received by that organization in the course of its business. Membership is open to all regardless of status, from students to corporate entities.

REGIONAL DEVELOPMENT OFFICER (FOR LIBRARIES IN ENGLAND)

c/o 15 Stagborouough Way, Stourport-on-Severn, Worcestershire DY13 8SS
☎(01299) 827757
e-mail: rdo@stagborough15.freeserve.co.uk
Regional Officer (for Libraries in England) Geoff Warren BA MCLIP
The Regional Development Officer (for Libraries in England) is a post and project jointly funded by the British Library, CILIP and Resource.

RESOURCE: THE COUNCIL FOR MUSEUMS, ARCHIVES AND LIBRARIES

16 Queen Anne's Gate, London SW1H 9AA
☎020 7273 1444

Fax 020 7273 1404
e-mail: info@resource.gov.uk
url: http://www.resource.gov.uk
Chief Executive Anna Southall
Media & Events Manager Ms Emma Wright (e-mail: emma.wright@resource.gov.uk)
Resource: The Council for Museums, Archives and Libraries, is a strategic agency working with and on behalf of museums, archives and libraries. It replaced the Museums and Galleries Commission and the Library and Information Commission in April 2000. Resource has three main objectives: to provide strategy, advocacy and advice. The organization undertakes work in all three of these areas to improve the context in which museums, archives and libraries operate and to improve services for users and potential users.

THE SCHOOL LIBRARY ASSOCIATION (SLA)

Unit 2, Lotmead Business Village, Lotmead Farm, Wanborough, Swindon SN4 0UY
☎(01793) 791787
Fax (01793) 791786
e-mail: info@SLA.org.uk
url: http://www.SLA.org.uk
Chief Executive Ms Kathy Lemaire BA DipLib MCLIP
The SLA believes that every child/learner is entitled to effective school library provision. It is committed to supporting everyone involved in school libraries, promoting high-quality learning and development opportunities for all, and provides advice, training, publications and a quarterly journal, The School Librarian.

SCOTTISH BOOK TRUST

137 Dundee Street, Edinburgh EH11 1BG
☎0131 229 3663
Fax 0131 228 4293
e-mail: info@scottishbooktrust.com
url: http://www.scottishbooktrust.com
Chairman Rt Rev Richard Holloway
Scottish Book Trust (SCO27669) promotes reading literacy and reading confidence through outreach, publications and information provision. SBT operates the Writers in Scotland Scheme.

SCOTTISH EXECUTIVE EDUCATION DEPARTMENT

Victoria Quay, Edinburgh EH6 6QQ
☎0131 244 0346
Fax 0131 244 0353
Head of Museums and Libraries Branch Gavin Barrie
The Scottish Executive Education Department is responsible for sponsorship of the National Library of Scotland and development of policy on and administration of libraries in Scotland.

SCOTTISH LIBRARY AND INFORMATION COUNCIL (SLIC)

1st Floor, Building C, Brandon Gate, Brandon Street, Hamilton, South Lanarkshire ML3 6AB
☎(01698) 458888
Fax (01698) 458899
e-mail: slic@slainte.org.uk
url: http://www.slainte.org.uk
Director Robert Craig OBE BA MA MCLIP (retiring end December 2002)
Assistant Director Ms Elaine Fulton BA MCLIP (e-mail: e.fulton@slainte.org.uk)
SLIC is an independent body that promotes the development of library and information services in Scotland. It advises Scottish Ministers, the Scottish Parliament and the Executive on library and information matters, provides support to library and information services and facilitates the co-ordination of services.

SCOTTISH LIBRARY ASSOCIATION see THE CHARTERED INSTITUTE OF LIBRARY AND INFORMATION PROFESSIONALS IN SCOTLAND (CILIPS)

SHARE THE VISION (STV)

c/o National Library for the Blind, Far Cromwell Road, Bredbury, Stockport, Cheshire SK6 2SG
☎0161 355 2079
Fax 0161 355 2098
e-mail: sharethevision@nlbuk.org
url: http://www.nlbuk.org/bpm
Executive Director David Owen OBE BA DipLib MCLIP
Established in 1989, STV is a partnership of the main voluntary sector and publicly-funded library bodies which aims to enhance lis for visually impaired people via greater co-operation and co-ordination of service delivery and campaigning services.

SHEFFIELD INFORMATION ORGANIZATION (SINTO)

Learning Centre, Sheffield Hallam University, Collegiate Crescent, Sheffield S10 2BP
☎0114 225 5739/40
Fax 0114 225 2476
e-mail: sinto@shu.ac.uk
url: http://www.shu.ac.uk/sinto
Director Carl Clayton BA MCLIP DMS
SINTO's mission is to promote library and information services in South Yorkshire and North Derbyshire through co-operation and partnership.

SOCIETY OF ARCHIVISTS

40 Northampton Road, London EC1R 0HB

☎020 7278 8630
Fax 020 7278 2107
e-mail: societyofarchivists@archives.org.uk
url: http://www.archives.org.uk
Executive Secretary Patrick Cleary
The principal aims of the Society are achieved both through the work of the Society's Council and its various committees, groups and regions, and by its position as spokesman for the profession, submitting evidence and comment on matters of professional concern to any official body which seeks advice or whose activities affect archives.

SOCIETY OF CHIEF LIBRARIANS (SCL)

c/o Catherine Blanshard, The Town Hall, The Headrow, Leeds LS1 3AD
☎0113 247 8330
Fax 0113 247 8331
Hon Secretary Ms Catherine Blanshard (e-mail: catherine.blanshard@leeds.gov.uk)
President Martin Molloy
The mission of SCL is to advance the interests and influences of libraries by representing the views and interests of Chief Librarians in England and Wales.

SOCIETY OF COLLEGE, NATIONAL AND UNIVERSITY LIBRARIES (SCONUL)

102 Euston Street, London NW1 2HA
☎020 7387 0317
Fax 020 7383 3197
url: http://www.sconul.ac.uk
Secretary A J C Bainton
SCONUL works to improve the quality and extend the influence of UK higher education libraries, of Irish university libraries, and of the national libraries of the UK and Ireland. Through its expert groups, SCONUL seeks to develop and promote policy at a national and international level. SCONUL's advisory groups also disseminate good practice and shared knowledge to strengthen the roles of senior library management.

SOUTH EAST MUSEUM, LIBRARY AND ARCHIVE COUNCIL (SEMLAC)

15 City Business Centre, Hyde Street, Winchester, Hants SO23 7TA
☎(01962) 858844
Fax (01962) 878439
e-mail: info@semlac.org.uk
url: http://www.semlac.org.uk
Chief Executive Helen Jackson
SEMLAC is the regional development agency for museum, library and archive activity in the South East of England.

SOUTH WESTERN REGIONAL LIBRARY SYSTEM (SWRLS)

c/o Bridget Powell, Central Library, College Green, Bristol BS1 5TL
☎0117 927 3962
Fax 0117 923 0216
e-mail: swrls@swrls.org.uk
url: http://www.swrls.org.uk
Librarian i/c Ms Bridget Powell
SWRLS is a co-operative of member libraries set up to promote co-operation and facilitate interlending.

SPRIG – PROMOTING INFORMATION IN LEISURE, TOURISM AND SPORT

Sport England, Yorkshire Region, 4th Floor Minerva House, East Parade, Leeds LS1 5TS
☎0113 205 3319
Fax 0113 242 2189
url: http://www.sprig.org.uk
Publicity Officer Daniel Park (e-mail: daniel.park@sprig.org.uk)
Chair Martin Scarrott
SPRIG promotes information sources in leisure, tourism, sport, recreation and hospitality management. It aims to: act as a special interest group for information managers; disseminate information to users; lobby information providers – such as government organizations – for better provision; and improve awareness of information sources to those outside the library and information profession.

THEATRE INFORMATION GROUP (TIG)

c/o Claire Hudson, Theatre Museum, 1E Tavistock Street, London WC2E 7PR
☎020 7943 4720
Secretary John Collis (e-mail: john@bruford.ac.uk)
The Theatre Information Group is a support organization for libraries, archives, museums and other bodies dealing with performing arts information and collections.

UK LIBRARIES PLUS

c/o Central School of Speech and Drama, Embassy Theatre, Eton Avenue, London NW3 3HY
☎020 7559 3995
Fax 020 7722 4132
url: http://www.uklibrariesplus.ac.uk
Convenor J Adam Edwards BA MSc MCLIP (e-mail: a.edwards@cssd.ac.uk)
UK Libraries Plus is a reciprocal access and borrowing scheme linking over 100 UK higher education libraries. Borrowing membership is open to all part-time, distance learning and full-time placement students and offers reference access to all other users of the member libraries.

THE UK NATIONAL COMMISSION FOR UNESCO

Secretariat, 10 Spring Gardens, London SW1A 2BN
☎020 7389 4687
Fax 020 7389 4468
url: http://www.unesco.org.uk
Information Manager Ms Penny Alsac (e-mail: penny.alsac@britishcouncil.org)
UNESCO stands for 'the United Nations Organization for Education, Science and Culture' – this also includes Communication and Information. The National Commission works with civil society throughout the UK to support UNESCO's aims and enhance participation in UNESCO's programmes. The National Commission has a small resource of UNESCO publications which, although not public access, supports its public enquiry service.

UK OFFICE FOR LIBRARY AND INFORMATION NETWORKING (UKOLN)

The Library, University of Bath, Bath BA2 7AY
☎(01225) 386250
Fax (01225) 386838
e-mail: ukoln@ukoln.ac.uk
url: http://www.ukoln.ac.uk
Director Dr Elizabeth Lyon
UKOLN is a national focus of expertise in digital information management. It provides policy, research and awareness services to the UK library, information and cultural heritage communities.

UK SERIALS GROUP (UKSG)

Hilltop, Heath End, Newbury, Berks RG20 0AP
☎(01635) 254292
Fax (01635) 253826
e-mail: uksg.admin@dial.pipex.com
url: http://www.uksg.org
Chair Ms C Fyfe
Business Manager Ms Alison Whitehorn
The UKSG exists to encourage the exchange and promotion of ideas on printed and electronic serials and the process of scholarly communication.The organization aims to increase professional awareness, to stimulate research and to provide a training and education programme, bringing together all parties in the serials information chain.

WELL WORTH READING see THE READING AGENCY

WELSH LIBRARY ASSOCIATION see THE CHARTERED INSTITUTE OF LIBRARY AND INFORMATION PROFESSIONALS WALES (CILIP WALES)

YORKSHIRE LIBRARIES AND INFORMATION (YLI)

Library HQ, Balne Lane, Wakefield WF2 0DQ
☎(01924) 302210
Fax (01924) 302245
url: http://www.yli.org.uk
Manager Ms Kate Holliday (e-mail: kholliday@wakefield.gov.uk)
YLI is the regional library system for Yorkshire and Humber.

The Regions of England

Public library authorities are arranged within the nine Government regions in England. (Upper Norwood Joint Library is included. This is not a public library authority but a service jointly managed by the London Boroughs of Croydon and Lambeth. However it has a separate entry). Full entries for these public library authorities will be found in the English sections of both the Public Libraries and Children's, Youth and Schools Library Services categories.

East

Bedfordshire
Cambridgeshire
Essex
Hertfordshire
Luton
Norfolk
Peterborough
Southend on Sea
Suffolk
Thurrock

East Midlands

Derby
Derbyshire
Leicester
Leicestershire
Lincolnshire
Northamptonshire
Nottingham
Nottinghamshire
Rutland

London

Barking and Dagenham
Barnet
Bexley
Brent
Bromley
Camden
City of London
Croydon
Ealing
Enfield
Greenwich
Hackney
Hammersmith and Fulham
Haringey
Harrow
Havering
Hillingdon
Hounslow
Islington
Kensington and Chelsea
Kingston upon Thames
Lambeth
Lewisham
Merton
Newham
Redbridge
Richmond upon Thames
Southwark
Sutton
Tower Hamlets
Upper Norwood Joint Library
Waltham Forest
Wandsworth
Westminster

North East

Darlington
Durham
Gateshead
Hartlepool
Middlesbrough
Newcastle upon Tyne
North Tyneside
Northumberland
Redcar and Cleveland
South Tyneside
Stockton-on-Tees
Sunderland

North West and Merseyside

Blackburn with Darwen
Blackpool
Bolton
Bury
Cheshire
Cumbria
Halton
Knowsley
Lancashire
Liverpool
Manchester

Oldham
Rochdale
St Helens
Salford
Sefton
Stockport
Tameside
Trafford
Warrington
Wigan
Wirral

South East

Bracknell Forest
Brighton and Hove
Buckinghamshire
East Sussex
Hampshire
Isle of Wight
Kent
Medway
Milton Keynes
Oxfordshire
Portsmouth
Reading
Slough
Southampton
Surrey
West Berkshire
West Sussex
Windsor and Maidenhead
Wokingham

South West

Bath and North East Somerset
Bournemouth
Bristol
Cornwall
Devon
Dorset
Gloucestershire
North Somerset
Plymouth
Poole
Somerset
South Gloucestershire
Swindon
Torbay
Wiltshire

West Midlands

Birmingham
Coventry
Dudley
Herefordshire
Sandwell
Shropshire
Solihull
Staffordshire
Stoke-on-Trent
Telford and Wrekin
Walsall
Warwickshire
Wolverhampton
Worcestershire

Yorkshire and The Humber

Barnsley
Bradford
Calderdale
Doncaster
East Riding of Yorkshire
Kingston upon Hull
Kirklees
Leeds
North East Lincolnshire
North Lincolnshire
North Yorkshire
Rotherham
Sheffield
Wakefield
York

Name index

All page numbers from 3 to 186 refer to public libraries or public library authorities; page numbers from 253 to 433 refer to academic institutions and special libraries. Pages 445 to 467 refer to key library agencies. Numbers in italic relate to the Children's, Youth and Schools Library Services sections (pages 189–249)

Subject Index

The following is an index of known specialist libraries, but does not reflect specialist collections in general libraries. Please refer to the name index for page numbers, or consult the main sequence.

Law

Mathematics

Media

Medicine and Dentistry

Music and the Performing Arts

Pharmacy

Philosophy

Politics and International Relations

Psychology and Psychiatry